The SAGE Handbook of
Learning

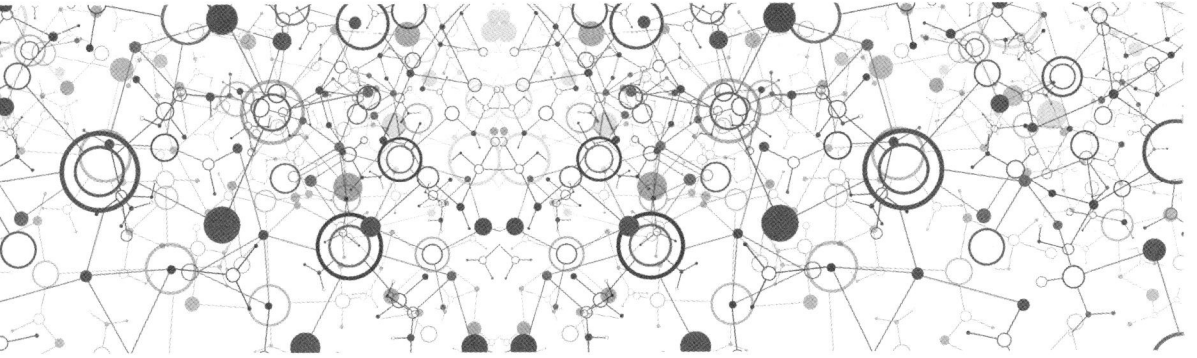

The SAGE Handbook of
Learning

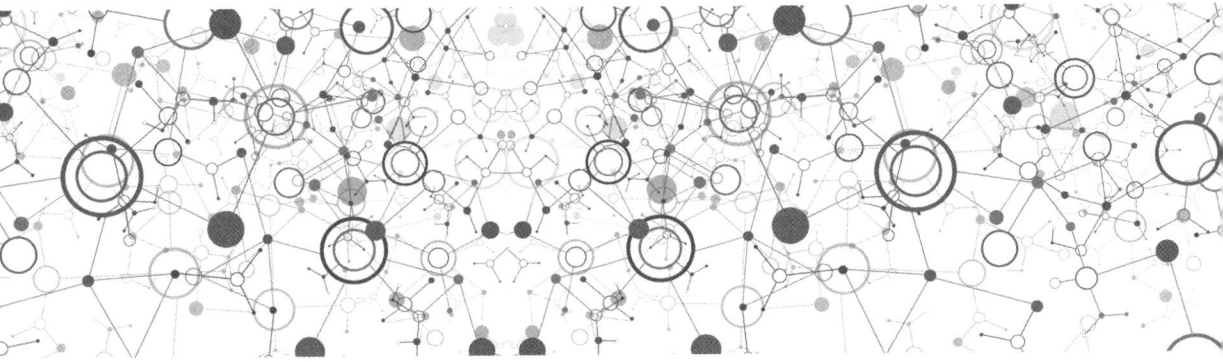

Edited by
David Scott and
Eleanore Hargreaves

⑤SAGE reference

Los Angeles | London | New Delhi
Singapore | Washington DC

Los Angeles | London | New Delhi
Singapore | Washington DC

SAGE Publications Ltd
1 Oliver's Yard
55 City Road
London EC1Y 1SP

SAGE Publications Inc.
2455 Teller Road
Thousand Oaks, California 91320

SAGE Publications India Pvt Ltd
B 1/I 1 Mohan Cooperative Industrial Area
Mathura Road
New Delhi 110 044

SAGE Publications Asia-Pacific Pte Ltd
3 Church Street
#10-04 Samsung Hub
Singapore 049483

Editor: Marianne Lagrange
Editorial assistant: Matthew Oldfield
Production editor: Shikha Jain
Copyeditor: Rosemary Campbell
Proofreader: Jill Birch
Marketing manager: Lucia Sweet
Cover design: Wendy Scott
Typeset by: Cenveo Publisher Services
Printed in Great Britain by Henry Ling
Limited, at the Dorset Press,
Dorchester, DT1 1HD

MIX
Paper from
responsible sources
FSC www.fsc.org FSC™ C013985

At SAGE we take sustainability seriously.
Most of our products are printed in the UK
using FSC papers and boards. When we
print overseas we ensure sustainable
papers are used as measured by the
Egmont grading system. We undertake an
annual audit to monitor our sustainability.

Library of Congress Control Number: 2014958314

British Library Cataloguing in Publication data

A catalogue record for this book is available from the British Library

ISBN 978-1-4462-8756-9

Contents

PART II   ELEMENTS OF LEARNING

PART III   CURRICULUM, PEDAGOGY AND ASSESSMENT

PART IV   THE LEARNER

List of Figures and Tables

FIGURES

TABLES

Notes on the Editors and Contributors

THE EDITORS

Eleanore Hargreaves is Senior Lecturer in Learning and Teaching at the UCL Institute of Education, London, UK. She leads the Effective Learning and Teaching MA and has carried out extensive research and consultancy about Assessment for Learning and feedback. She is also engaged in research and development programmes relating to learning and teacher development overseas, including in Egypt, Palestine, Lebanon and Pakistan.

David Scott is Professor of Curriculum, Pedagogy and Assessment at the UCL Institute of Education, London, UK. Recent research projects include: *Teacher Cadre Management in Indian Schools*; *Teaching and Learning in Higher Education*; *Assessment for Learning in Hong Kong Schools*; *Curriculum Structures 14–18 in Nayarit State, Mexico*; *National Curriculum Standards and Structures in Mexico*; and *India Capacity Building to the Elementary Education Programme*. He has been Editor of *The Curriculum Journal* 1995–2001; Visiting Professor – Lincolnshire and Humberside University 2000–2001; UCL Institute of Education 2000–2005 and University of Cyprus 2000–2005; and is Series Editor for *International Perspectives on the Curriculum*. His most recent books are: *New Perspectives on Curriculum, Pedagogy and Assessment*; (Springer, 2014, with R. Mota) *Educating for Innovation: A Guide to Independent Learning in Brazil and England*; (Elsevier, 2014, with C. Posner, C. Martin, E. Guzman and O. Alvarez) *Interventions in Education Systems: Reform Processes and Capacity Development*; (Continuum, 2011, with R. Usher) *Researching Education*; *Education, Epistemology and Critical Realism* (Routledge, 2010) and *Critical Essays on Major Curriculum Theorists* (Routledge, 2008).

THE CONTRIBUTORS

Alyson Adams, PhD is a Clinical Associate Professor in the School of Teaching and Learning at the University of Florida. Her research interests focus on teacher learning, professional development and teacher leadership. Dr Adams specializes in designing and delivering job-embedded graduate programmes for practicing educators at the masters, specialist and doctoral levels, through online, blended and face-to-face delivery. She is also affiliated with the Lastinger Center for Learning, an endowed centre at UF specializing in improving teacher quality in high poverty schools through whole-school reform efforts centred on learning within communities.

David Aldridge is Principal Lecturer in Philosophy of Education at Oxford Brookes University. He is Programme Lead for Professional Education, with responsibility for Secondary Initial Teacher Education, PGCE (Post-Compulsory), MA Programmes in Education, the Postgraduate Certificate in Teaching in Higher Education and the Educational Doctorate (EdD). He has published on a wide range of issues in Philosophy of Education, drawing on both analytical and continental perspectives, and he has a particular interest in hermeneutics and phenomenology.

Jeff Bezemer is Reader in Learning and Communication at the UCL Institute of Education, London, UK. He is interested in ethnographic approaches to the study of meaning making in classrooms and (clinical) work places, and in theories and methodologies in multimodality.

Deborah L. Butler is Professor in Educational and Counselling Psychology, and Special Education at the University of British Columbia in Vancouver, British Columbia, Canada. Across a 10-year period (2003–2012), she served as Director for the Centre of Cross-Faculty Inquiry, Associate Dean for Graduate Programs and Research, Associate Dean for Strategic Development and Senior Associate Dean for the Faculty of Education. She is current Past-President of the Canadian Association for Educational Psychology (2014–16). Supported by multiple, sequential grants from Canada's Social Sciences and Humanities Research Council, her research has advanced understanding about strategic, self-regulated engagement in learning and practice, professional development processes, knowledge mobilization, inclusive and special education, and case study research methodology.

Seth Chaiklin is a Researcher at University College UCC in Copenhagen, Denmark. He has worked within the cultural-historical tradition for over thirty years, with a special focus on subject-matter teaching and learning. He also investigates the concept of practice through a combination of theoretical and analytical studies, including preschool and nursing. These investigations are motivated in part by studies about the relationship between educational research and educational practice, using theoretical concepts from the cultural-historical tradition. This has led to an idea of practice-developing research as a way to integrate these theoretical concerns in a practical form.

David R. Cole is Associate Professor in Education at the University of Western Sydney, Australia and Honorary Professor at UTS. He has published nine academic books and numerous journal articles, book chapters and conference presentations (100+). He has been involved with 10 major educational research projects across Australia and internationally, and is an expert in mixed-methods design and execution, and the application of the philosophy of Gilles Deleuze and Félix Guattari to education. David's latest monograph is called *Capitalised Education: An Immanent Material Account of Kate Middleton* (Zero Books, 2014).

Bill Cope is Professor in the Department of Educational Policy Studies at the University of Illinois. He is Principal Investigator in a series of major projects funded by the Institute of Educational Sciences in the US Department of Education and the Bill and Melinda Gates Foundation researching and developing multimodal writing and assessment spaces. From 2010 to 2013 he was Chair of the Journals Publication Committee of the American Educational Research Association. Recent books include: *The Future of the Academic Journal* (edited with

Angus Phillips; Elsevier, 2009/2nd edition 2014); and *Towards a Semantic Web: Connecting Knowledge in Academic Research* (with Mary Kalantzis and Liam Magee; Elsevier, 2010).

Barbara Crossouard is a Senior Lecturer in Education and a member of the Centre for International Education at the University of Sussex, UK. Her research interests include citizenship, gender and education, and exploring their intersection through post-structural theories of identity. The data for her sections of the chapter published here derive from a project led by Professor Máiréad Dunne. Her support and those of fellow researchers Dr Naureen Durrani and Dr Kathleen Fincham are gratefully acknowledged, as are the contributions of the project participants.

Harry Daniels is Professor of Education at the University of Oxford and Fellow of Green Templeton College. He holds chairs in Moscow, Osaka and Brisbane. He has produced a series of books on the implications of the writings of Vygotsky. He was introduced to the Russian tradition in psychology when he was a student of Basil Bernstein at the Institute of Education in London. Much of his empirical work has involved investigations of institutional effects on learning. His current major project is an AHRC-sponsored examination of the influence that the design of spaces in schools exerts on children and teachers.

Richard Edwards is Professor of Education at the University of Stirling, UK. He has researched and written extensively on social theory and lifelong learning, in particular drawing upon writings associated with aspects of postmodernist, post-structuralist and actor-network theory. His recent books include, with Tara Fenwick, *Actor-network Theory and Education* (Routledge, 2010) and, with Tara Fenwick and Peter Sawchuk, *Emerging Approaches to Eductional Research: Tracing the Sociomaterial* (Routledge, 2011). He is currently researching learning in the context of citizen science projects.

Carol Evans is a Professor of Higher Education at the University of Southampton, UK; a Principal Fellow of the Higher Education Academy, UK; National Teaching Fellow and Secretary for the Committee of the Association of National Teaching Fellows. She is President of the Education, Learning, Styles, Individual Differences Network (ELSIN), and Associate Editor of the *British Journal of Educational Psychology*. She is also a Visiting Fellow at the UCL Institute of Education, London, UK. Recent work includes: 'Making sense of assessment feedback in higher education', published in *Review of Educational Research* (2013) (available at: http://rer.sagepub.com/cgi/reprint/83/1/70?ijkey=x/CimNd6vjZWI&keytype=ref&siteid=sprer); *Understanding Pedagogy: Developing a Critical Approach to Teaching and Learning* (Routledge , 2015 with M. Waring); 'Cognitive style as environmentally sensitive individual differences in cognition: a modern synthesis and applications in education, business and management', *Psychological Science in the Public Interest*, 15(1): 3–33, with M. Kozhevnikov and S. Kosslyn (2014) (available at: http://psi.sagepub.com/content/15/1/3.full.pdf+html).

Tara Fenwick is a Professor of Education at the University of Stirling, and Director of ProPEL, an international network for research in Professional Practice, Education and Learning. Her own research examines the workplace learning and education of diverse professionals with a particular interest in materiality of practice and knowledges. Her recent books include *Reconceptualising Professional Learning: Sociomaterial Knowledge, Practice and Responsibilities* (with M. Nerland; Routledge, 2014); *Materialities, Textures, Pedagogies* (with P. Landri; Routledge, 2014); and *Governing Knowledge* (with J. Ozga and E Mangez; Routledge, 2013).

Carla M. Firetto is currently a postdoctoral research fellow on an Institute of Education Sciences (IES) funded grant in the Department of Educational Psychology, Counseling, and Special Education at The Pennsylvania State University. She is currently studying the role of text-based discussions, particularly *Quality Talk*, in promoting students' high-level comprehension of text in language arts classrooms.

Clive Harber is Emeritus Professor of International Education at the University of Birmingham and Honorary Professor at the University of South Africa in Pretoria. From 1995 to 1999 he was Head of the School of Education at the then University of Natal, now KwaZulu Natal and from 2003 to 2006 he was Head of the School of Education at the University of Birmingham. He has a long-standing interest in education and democracy – and its opposites – and a particular interest in the relationships between schooling and violence. He has carried out research, and published widely, on these themes in an international context.

Knud Illeris is a retired Professor of Lifelong Learning at the Danish University of Education. He is internationally acknowledged as an innovative contributor to learning theory and adult education. In 2005 he became an Honorary Adjunct Professor of Teachers College, Columbia University, New York, and in 2006 he was inducted into The International Hall of Fame of Adult and Continuing Education. He is the author of numerous books, including *How We Learn: Learning and Non-Learning in School and Beyond* (Routledge, 2007), which provides a comprehensive understanding of human learning and non-learning.

Carolyn Jackson is Professor of Gender and Education at Lancaster University and Co-Director of the Centre for Social Justice and Wellbeing in Education. She has researched and published on numerous gender and education issues including: fear; constructions and performances of 'laddish' masculinities and femininities in schools and higher education; and single-sex and mixed-sex learning environments. Her books include *Lads and Ladettes in School: Gender and a Fear of Failure* and *Girls and Education 3–16* (co-edited with Carrie Paechter and Emma Renold, Open University Press, 2006).

Mary Kalantzis is Dean of the College of Education at the University of Illinois, Urbana-Champaign. She was formerly Dean of the Faculty of Education, Language and Community Services at RMIT University in Melbourne, Australia, and President of the Australian Council of Deans of Education. With Bill Cope, she is co-author of *New Learning: Elements of a Science of Education* (Cambridge University Press, 2008/2nd edition 2012) and *Literacies* (Cambridge University Press, 2012), and co-editor of *Ubiquitous Learning* (University of Illinois Press, 2009).

Gunther Kress is Professor of Semiotics and Education at the UCL Institute of Education, London, UK. He is interested in communication and meaning (-making) in contemporary environments. His broad aims are to continue developing a social semiotic theory of multimodal communication; and, within that, to develop an apt theory of learning and apt means for the 'recognition' and 'valuation of learning'.

Martin Lawn is an Emeritus Professor, University of Edinburgh, an Honorary Senior Research Fellow, University of Oxford and a Visiting Professor in CELE, University of Turku. He researches European education policy and the history of the educational sciences across Europe. Recent books include: *The Rise of Data in Education Systems: Collection, Visualisation and Use* (Symposium Books, 2014); and *Europeanizing Education: Governing a New Policy Space* (with Sotiria Grek; Symposium Books, 2012).

Valerie A. Long is a graduate student in The College of Education at The Pennsylvania State University. She holds a Master's Degree in Psychological Foundations of Reading from New York University. Valerie has over fifteen years of experience working in public and private schools as a Supervisor of Curriculum and Instruction, Reading Specialist and classroom teacher. She has also offered dozens of Professional Development workshops for teachers and taught graduate and undergraduate courses in Literacy Instruction, English Literature and Writing.

Rosario Sergio Maniscalco obtained his PhD in educational sciences at the University of Turku, Finland. He studied the European education policy and its intertwinement with globalization and the knowledge economy. His research interests include adult education, citizenship education and the EU's Lisbon Strategy.

Bethan Marshall is a Senior Lecturer at King's College London and specializes in issues relating to the teaching of English and assessment, on both of which she has written extensively including *English Teachers: The Unofficial Guide* (Routledge, 2000) and *Testing English: Formative and Summative Approaches to English Assessment* (Continuum Publishing Corporation, 2011). She was a co-author of *Assessment for Learning: Putting it into Practice* (Open University Press, 2003) and *Improving Learning How to Learn: Classrooms, Schools and Networks* (Routledge, 2007).

Alex Moore is an Emeritus Professor at the UCL Institute of Education, London, UK. A former schoolteacher and teacher educator, his published works include *Teaching and Learning: Pedagogy, Curriculum and Culture* (Routledge, 2012), *Understanding the School Curriculum: Theory, Politics and Principles* (Routledge, 2014), and the edited volume *Schooling, Society and Curriculum* (Routledge, 2006). An internationally acknowledged expert in the field of Curriculum Studies, he has presented numerous papers, seminars and keynote speeches in England and around the world, including in China, Australia and the USA. He is currently interested in applying psychosocial approaches to understandings of public education policy and practice, drawing in particular on the 'schizoanalysis' approach of Deleuze and Guattari. His new book, *Love and Fear in the Classroom*, is due to be published in 2016.

Aki Murata is an Assistant Professor of elementary mathematics education and teacher education at University of California, Berkeley, in the United States. Her research focuses on developing a better understanding of how mathematics is taught and learned in elementary classrooms, to ultimately help improve classroom practice. Her work helps unpack and explain the complex interactive processes between teaching and learning, using teaching supports as windows of investigation. Dr Murata also uses lesson study as a research context to examine interactions, how teachers learn in collaboration, and how lesson study supports instructional improvement.

P. Karen Murphy is the Harry and Marion Eberly Fellow and Professor of Education at The Pennsylvania State University where she holds a joint appointment in the Educational Psychology programme and the Children, Youth, and Families Consortium. She is currently serving as Vice-President of Division C of the American Educational Research Association. Her current research, funded by IES and NSF, focuses on the role of classroom discussion on students' high-level comprehension (see www.qualitytalk.psu.edu). Dr Murphy is a Fellow of the American Psychological Association (APA) and American Educational Research Association (AERA), and she received the Richard E. Snow Early Career Achievement award from the APA. She currently serves on numerous editorial boards.

Iskra Nunez is an Assistant Professor with a joint appointment between the Department of Mathematics and the Department of Curriculum and Instruction at The University of Texas-Pan American. Her most recent publications include: 'Qué aporta el realismo crítico a la investigación en matemática educativa?' in Y. Morales and A. Ramirez (eds), *Memorias I CEMACYC* (CEMACYC, 2013, pp. 1–15); 'Transcending the dualisms of activity theory', *Journal of Critical Realism*, 12(2): 141–65 (2013); and her book, *Critical Realist Activity Theory: An Engagement with Critical Realism and Cultural-Historical Activity Theory* (Routledge, 2014).

Deborah Osberg is Senior Lecturer in Education at the University of Exeter, UK where she is also Director of Professional Doctoral Studies for the Graduate School of Education. She has an interdisciplinary research background spanning an initial career in evolutionary ecology followed by subsequent work in educational theory. Her current research draws on insights from 'biological philosophy', complexity theories, emergentism and post-structural perspectives to rethink various philosophically intractable problems of power in educational contexts. From 2007 to 2010, she was Editor-in-chief of the journal *Complicity: An International Journal of Complexity and Education* and her recent edited book, with Gert Biesta, *Complexity Theory and the Politics of Education* (Sense Publishers, 2010) makes an important contribution towards putting the question of power and politics more explicitly on the agenda of work on complexity and education.

John Pryor is Professor of Education and Social Research at the University of Sussex, where he is also Director of the ESRC Doctoral Training Centre in the Social Sciences. He began his career as teacher in primary and secondary schools with a particular interest in development education. Following a doctorate on gender and group work in education, John took up a post as research fellow and subsequently lecturer at Sussex. His research interests centre on aspects of social identity and equity in education including formative assessment and pedagogy, international and intercultural study and research training and the doctorate in the social sciences. John has directed research projects in both the UK and sub-Saharan Africa, mostly of a broadly micro-sociological nature, including collaborative ethnography and action research.

Diane Reay is a Professor of Education in the Faculty of Education, University of Cambridge with particular interests in social justice issues in education, Pierre Bourdieu's social theory, and cultural analyses of social class. She has researched extensively in the areas of social class, gender and ethnicity across primary, secondary and post-compulsory stages of education. Recent funded research projects include primary–secondary school transfer, choice of higher education, pupil consultation and voice, working-class students in higher education, and the white middle classes and comprehensive schooling. Her most recent book (with Gill Crozier and David James) is *White Middle Class Identities and Urban Schooling* (Palgrave Press, 2011).

Alina Reznitskaya received her doctoral degree in Educational Psychology from the University of Illinois at Urbana-Champaign and did her post-doctoral research at Yale University. Currently, Alina is a Professor at Montclair State University in New Jersey, USA. She teaches courses in educational psychology, quantitative research and educational measurement. Alina's research interests include investigating the role social interaction plays in the development of argument literacy, designing measures of argumentation, and examining professional development programmes that help teachers evaluate and improve their language use in a classroom.

Tone Saevi is an Associate Professor in Education at NLA University College, School of Education, Norway, and Editor-in Chief of the open access journal *Phenomenology & Practice*. She is the author of a number of articles and authored books, among them, 'Phenomenology in educational research' (*Oxford Bibliographies in Education*, 2014), 'Between being and knowing: addressing the fundamental hesitation in hermeneutic phenomenological writing' (*Indo-Pacific Journal of Phenomenology*, 2013) and 'Lived relationality as fulcrum for pedagogical-ethical practice' (*Studies in Philosophy and Education*, 2011).

Anna Sfard is a Professor of Mathematics Education at the University of Haifa and a Visiting Professor in the UCL Institute of Education, London, UK. Her research focuses on relations between thinking and interpersonal communication, and, more specifically, on the development and role of mathematical discourses in individual lives and in the course of history. She is an author and editor of several books, including *Thinking as Communicating* (Cambridge University Press), and the recipient of the 2007 Freudenthal Award.

Lisa Smulyan is Henry C. and Charlotte Turner Professor of Educational Studies and Chair of the Department at Swarthmore College, Swarthmore, Pennsylvania. She teaches courses in educational foundations, adolescence, gender and education and comparative education. Her teaching, scholarship and administrative work focus on how historical, social and cultural contexts influence teachers, teaching and learning. Her publications include articles on teacher education and the liberal arts and the personal and professional development of women teachers and doctors, as well as books, including *Balancing Acts: Women Principals at Work*.

Paul Standish is Professor and Head of the Centre for Philosophy at the UCL Institute of Education, London, UK. His work spans the range of philosophy of education. He is interested particularly in tensions between analytical and continental philosophical traditions and the creative possibilities that arise from them. His most recent books are *Stanley Cavell and the Education of Grownups* (Fordham University Press, 2012) and *Education and the Kyoto School of Philosophy: Pedagogy for Human Transformation* (Springer, 2012), both co-edited with Naoko Saito, *The Philosophy of Nurse Education* (Palgrave Macmillan, 2007), co-edited with John Drummond, and *The Therapy of Education: Philosophy, Happiness, and Personal Growth* (Palgrave Macmillan, 2006), co-authored with Paul Smeyers and Richard Smith. He is Associate Editor and was Editor (2001–2011) of the *Journal of Philosophy of Education*.

Vicki A. Vescio, PhD is a Clinical Assistant Professor in the School of Teaching and Learning at the University of Florida. Her current research interests are related to pre-service teachers' professional development, in-service teachers' job-embedded professional development, teacher education programme development, and issues of equity in education. Dr Vescio specializes in working with pre-service and in-service teachers in high poverty elementary schools as well as teaching masters, specialist and doctoral level courses in traditional and online teacher education programmes.

Chris Watkins is an Emeritus Reader in Education at the UCL Institute of Education, London, UK and an independent project leader with schools. In 1999 he founded the MA in Effective Learning and since then has been involved with a range of schools and local authorities. His publications include: *Learning, Performance and Improvement* (International Network for School Improvement, 2010); (with E. Carnell and C. Lodge) *Effective Learning in Classrooms* (Paul Chapman and Sage, 2007); *Classrooms as Learning Communities: What's In It for Schools?* (Routledge, 2005); *Learning and Leading* (National College for School Leadership, 2004); *Learning: A Sense-maker's Guide* (Association of Teachers and Lecturers, 2003).

Rebecca Webb is a newly appointed Lecturer in International Teacher Education and a member of the Centre for Teaching and Learning Research in the Department of Education at the University of Sussex. Her substantive research interests include 'rights' and ideas of citizenship in schooling contexts; and ethnographic and post-structural research methodologies. The data for this research are taken from her recently submitted doctoral thesis: 'Doing the *rights* thing: an ethnography of a discourse of rights in a primary school in England'.

Ian Wilkinson is a Professor in the School of Teaching and Learning at The Ohio State University in Ohio, USA. Originally from Australia, Ian has lectured and conducted research in Australia, New Zealand and the United States. He also served as Co-Editor of *Reading Research Quarterly* from 2006 to 2012. Ian has a background in educational psychology with special interests in cognition, instruction and research methodology, especially as they relate to the study of literacy. His research focuses on school and classroom contexts for literacy learning and the cognitive consequences for students.

Emma Williams is Assistant Professor in the Department of Education Studies, University of Warwick. She was previously Philosopher-in-Residence at Rugby School, where she taught Philosophy across the curriculum and helped develop interdisciplinary courses for the new A Level Qualification: The Extended Project. She has a background in Philosophy, particularly Post-Kantian European Philosophy, and the Philosophy of Education. Her work explores the themes of language, rationality and subjectivity within the context of education. Her recent publications include *The Ways We Think: from the straits of reason to the possibilities of thought* (Wiley, 2012).

An Introduction and a Theory of Learning

David Scott and Eleanore Hargreaves

INTRODUCTIONS AND THEORISATIONS

An introduction to a book is always problematic, and this is because it is difficult to be precise about its function. Should it be a critique, a summation, a framing, a landscaping or a cynosure? All of these have different purposes. A prolegomenic introduction, with due acknowledgement to Immanual Kant (1997 [1783]), is a formal exposition of the concept or concepts to be discussed in the main body of the text (in Kant's case, the *Critique of Pure Reason* (2007 [1781]), and this has a critical component as to how this concept has been treated in the past. A summary suggests a synthesis of a number of different views of the subject matter of the book, without taking or advocating a preferred position. If this introduction were to serve exclusively as a framing device, then it would seek to position the body of work in its epistemic, social, spatial and temporal locales, to, in effect, historicise it. An introduction, however, can have more modest

aspirations, so that all it seeks to do is point to what there is in the main body of the work, and signpost where it can be found. Finally, an introduction may seek to make, or at least begin the process of making, sense of the central concept, drawing boundaries round the concept (it doesn't matter whether these are natural or manufactured, or even whether this distinction is credible), delineating between what it is and what it is not, and framing the concept, in this case learning, so that it can be used, modified, understood, genealogised and related to other concepts and ideas.

A history, exposition, delineation or explanation of an idea is always a contested activity. Whether we adopt a conventional view of narration or chronicling with its trans-historical subject and immersion in originary knowledge modes, or we seek to genealogise such a narrative or chronicle by subverting the naturalness of the categories and delineations in common-sense discourses (after all everyone knows what learning is), we still have to confront our own position as historian, genealogist, expositor, academic or critic. In other words we still have to take account of the originary status of our viewpoint about knowledge, our epistemic position.

Our role here then, will be to uncover, or begin the process of deciphering, the rules (overt or hidden) that constitute particular framings of learning, without at the same time becoming embroiled in logocentric discourses that are underpinned by originary knowledge structures. To do otherwise would be to fall into the trap of what Foucault (1980) suggests is the 'illusion of formalisation', in which the chronicler seeks to explain types of knowledge in terms of a formal logic that transcends those knowledge constructions: a logocentric viewpoint. Foucault also urges us to avoid the illusion of doxa where appearances in relation to power are treated as opportunities to unmask them and replace them with more truthful versions of reality.

REPRESENTATION AND EMERGENCE

A learning environment (or temporal and spatial locale for learning) has a number of constituents or elements. Two of these stand out. The first is the mode of representation of the entity that concerns us, and the second is the notion of change or how one situation emerges from another, both in relation to the individual and society. The first of these then is the representational principle. Something in nature, which we are pointing at, is convened as already known before it is represented in some medium or another. Heidegger (2002: 59), for example, suggested in relation to physics, that:

> When, therefore, physics assumes an explicitly 'mathematical' form, what this means is the following: that through and for it, in an emphatic way, something is specified in advance as that which is already known.

These characteristics and constituents are not given in nature and then represented in an unmediated form in our descriptions of them. The essence of the object, in this case,

learning, cannot be read off from what exists in nature. There is a social dimension to knowledge-construction, but this does not eliminate the possibility of reference to a world that is separate from the way it is being described. Conceptual framings and sets of descriptors are constrained and enabled by the world or reality at the particular moment in time in which they are being used, and in turn, the constitution of the world is influenced by the types of knowledge that are being developed. Our conceptual frameworks, perspectives on the world, and descriptive languages, interpenetrate what we are calling reality to such an extent that it is impossible to conceive of a pre-schematised world (cf. Putnam, 2004). Thus representation, especially in its most fundamental sense, as in correspondent theories of truth, should always be understood as fallible, and even as potentially distorting.

This is the first point and it refers to the problem of representational knowledge. The second point when we are referring to learning essences is the issue of emergence. There are two forms that it can take. The first is ontological and the second is temporal. In the first case, emergence refers to the powers held by a person in their life-world. At the ontological level, reality is stratified and the properties of objects, including people, are emergent. This stratified reality includes level distinctions, which refer to the actual, the empirical and the real; and divisions in the intransitive world between, for example, the atomic, the molecular, the biological, the social and so forth (Bhaskar, 1989). The actual refers to things and events in their concrete historical contexts, only some of which will ever be known or experienced by human beings. The empirical is related to the actual, consisting of those phenomena that are experienced by people in the world. The actual and the empirical are both real, and consequently, are a part of the third domain. But the domain of the real also includes the structures of objects, for example, the relations between their constituent parts and the emergent properties to which their structuring gives rise. Since these powers of structures, when exercised, may bring about certain effects, we can describe them as generative mechanisms.

In the second case, emergence is temporal. Social objects are structured in various ways, and because of this, they possess powers (cf. Brown et al., 2002). The powers of these structures (or mechanisms) are of three types. Powers can be possessed, exercised or actualised. Objects possess powers even if they are not triggered by external circumstances and combinations of other powers, and therefore they lie dormant. On the other hand, powers that have been exercised have been triggered and are now having an effect in an open system. Such powers are interacting with other powers of other mechanisms within their sphere of influence. Finally, powers that have been actualised are causally efficacious within the open system they are operating in, but in this case they have not been suppressed or counteracted. Embodied, institutional or discursive structures can be possessed and not exercised or actualised, possessed and exercised, or possessed and actualised. As a result, a causal model based on constant conjunctions is rejected and replaced by a generative-productive one, and objects and relations between objects have emergent properties, including discursive objects operating in the epistemological domain.

Consequently, if we are to describe the structures of a learning environment, we have to understand them as traces from the past, configurations in the present and projections into the future. In developing a theory of learning, we need to understand how the activity to which it refers is constituted. There are three alternatives, though they are not mutually exclusive. The first of these suggests that within the form of words we employ it is possible to establish reference points, so that the words themselves and the relations between these words refer to a learning process that de facto happened, but the one does not correspond to, or is not isomorphic with, the other. The second alternative is to suggest that the form of words we employ cannot represent the particularity, concreteness and materiality of an experience of learning; but, given that

we are now operating in a different medium, can provide a general account of a particular learning experience, which in turn can provide us with some understanding of the object, even if this is not definitive. However, this does not indicate or point to the existence of a causal relationship. There is a third possibility which is that the form of words which collectively constitute a theory of learning can also cause something to happen at the ontological level; this is the performative function of discourse. Learning, whether as a mental construct or material reality, is causally efficacious, that is, it potentially, but not necessarily, has the power to change what exists outwith it.

DELINEATIONS, BOUNDARIES, CLASSIFICATIONS

Learning is conditioned by an arrangement of resources, including spatial and temporal elements. These arrangements are embodied, discursive, institutional, systemic or agential, and this has implications for the types of learning that can take place. Each learning episode has socio-historical roots. What is learnt in the first place is formed in society and outside the individual. It is shaped by the life that the person is leading. It is thus both externally and internally mediated, and the form taken is determined by whether the process is cognitive, affective, meta-cognitive, conative or expressive. Thus, learning has an internalisation element where what is formally external to the learner is interiorized by the learner and a performative element where what is formally internal to the learner is exteriorized by the learner in the world. Within this framework, behaviourists, complexity theorists, cultural-historical activity theorists, social constructivists, symbol-processing theorists, socio-cultural theorists of learning, actor network theorists and critical realists conceptualise the various elements of learning and the relations between them in different ways.

Wenger (2008), for example, and particularly in relation to classifications of the concept, distinguishes between psychological and social theories of learning. In the first category he places behaviourist theories focusing on behaviour modification, cognitivist theories focusing on internal cognitive structures, constructivist theories focusing on building mental structures whilst interacting with an environment, and social interaction theories that focus on interactive processes but understand them from a primarily psychological perspective. In the second category there are a series of social theories of learning. These include activity theories such as cultural-historical activity frameworks, socialisation theories such as community of learning theories (cf. Wenger, 1998), and organisational theories that concern themselves both with the ways individuals learn in organisational contexts and with the ways in which organisations can be said to learn as organisations.

A theory of learning pivots on the idea that there is an entity called, for the sake of convenience, a human, and that this entity has a relationship (both inward and outward) with an environment (for some, this entails a post-humanising and materialising process – cf. Edwards, this volume). A further complication is that any description of this process and set of relations further entails another and different set of actions and relations. In mapping or characterising the field, here we are concerned with epistemic differences between the range of theories presented, though these differences also focus, as I have already indicated, on the probative force and attached value we give to these relations and entities. Four examples of learning theory are examined here, behaviourist, phenomenological, constructivist and materialist, and these are differentiated by their epistemic relations.

BEHAVIOURISM

Behaviourism is a philosophical theory and has been used specifically within the discipline of education to provide an explanation for the play of social and educational objects in history. It makes three interrelated claims. The first of these is that if we are trying to understand the psychology of a human being, we shouldn't be concerned with what is in their mind but with how they behave. The second claim is that behaviours can be fully and comprehensively explained without recourse to any form of mental construct or event. The source of these behaviours is the environment and not the mind of the individual. And the third claim which behaviourists are likely to make and which follows from the first two claims is that if mental terms are used as descriptors then they should be replaced by behavioural terms or, at least, those mental constructs should be translated into behavioural descriptors. These three claims provide the foundations for three behaviourist sub-theories: a methodological theory of behaviourism, a psychological theory of behaviourism, and an analytical theory of behaviourism.

Methodological behaviourism has its origins in the sociological theory of positivism and the philosophical theory of empiricism, which can be understood as having the following characteristics: determinacy (there is a singular truth which can be known); rationality (there are no contradictory explanations); impersonality (the more objective and the less subjective the better); verificationism (the meaning of statements about human behaviours and their origins are understood in terms of observational or experimental data); and prediction (explanations of human behaviours are knowledge claims formulated as generalisations from which predictions can be made, and events and phenomena controlled). John Watson (1930: 11), one of the originators of behaviourism, in this vein wrote as follows in relation to the purposes of investigating human behaviour: 'to predict, given the stimulus, what reaction will take place; or, given the reaction, state what the situation or stimulus is that has caused the reaction'. Psychological behaviourism has its roots in British empiricism and in particular in the associational theory of David Hume. Observed or experimentally-induced associations allow the investigator to uncover causal structures on the basis of processes of spatio-temporal contiguity, succession and constant conjunction. Learning is therefore understood as associational without recourse to mental states or events, with an emphasis on the reinforcement histories of subjects. For psychological behaviourists any reference to experiences (especially if couched in the language of mental states or events) should be replaced by observations of events in the environment; and references to thoughts, ideas, or schemata should be replaced by references to overt observable behaviours and responses to stimuli. Analytical behaviourism, whilst sharing many of the elements of methodological and psychological behaviourism, in addition, has the advantage that it avoids what has come to be known as substance dualism; that is, the belief that mental states take place in, and should be treated as separate from, non-physical mental substances, and yet are causally efficacious, especially with regards to events in the material world.

Behaviourism as a theory of learning then suffers from a number of misconceptions. Because of its strictures against immaterial mental substances, agents endowed with the capacity to operate outside of embodied, socially-derived or genetic causal impulses, reasons being conceived as causes of human behaviour, intentionality as a central element in any theory of human behaviour, and the internal conversation in learning (cf. Archer, 2007), behaviourism is now rarely thought of as a coherent or convincing theory of learning. A number of problems with it have been identified, and perhaps the most important of these is the claim that a theory of human learning is not sufficient unless reference is made to non-behavioural mental states, whether this is cognitive, representational or interpretive. In particular, this refers to the way an individual represents the world in relation to how they have done so in the past, and how this is conditioned by institutional, systemic, embodied and discursive structures; stories, narratives, arguments and chronologies; and structures of agency. For example, Michael Bratman (1999: 124) refers to the 'subjective normative authority for the agent'. This narrative agential structure impacts on intentionality, and in particular on what constitutes a good reason for an agent to act; what, in short, gives that agent the subjective normative authority for their planned and intentional activity. A second reason for rejecting behaviourism is the existence of internal or inner processing activities. We feel, intuit, experience, and are aware of, our own inner mental states in the learning process. To reduce these phenomenal qualities to behaviours or dispositions to behave is to ignore the immediacy and instantaneous nature of those processes which condition learning. Finally, it is suggested that reducing learning to individual reinforcement histories is to develop an impoverished or incomplete theory, and consequently marginalise pre-existing structures, developed schemata, complex inner lives, prior representations, and structural enablements and constraints, which allow learning to take place.

PHENOMENOLOGY

In contrast to behaviourist perspectives on learning are phenomenological approaches. Phenomenology is a meta-philosophy that focuses on the three key aspects of learning, the relationship of the individual to and with the world involving a process of change, the subsequent conception and activation of being in the world, and how our descriptions, words, schema, theories can provide us with some purchase on that world. The focus is on the givens of immediate experience and this is an attempt to capture that experience as it is lived, both by the individual themselves and the external observer. This knowledge-making activity is directed in the first instance to the things in themselves that are the objects of consciousness, and that try to find 'a first opening' (Merleau-Ponty, 1962 [1945]) on the world, free of those presuppositions that we bring to any learning setting. This entails a learning methodology which foregrounds subjective experiences and understands them in their own terms, both linguistically and conceptually, whilst at the same time treating these two modes separately. This presupposes that the experience of others is accessible to us, even if with the greatest of difficulty. And this points to the break with behaviourism that phenomenologists generated. Whereas behaviourists were concerned above all with the behaviour of individuals and eschewed the inner workings of the mind, phenomenologists understand behaviour and consciousness as essential to any theory of learning. They are different aspects of the same phenomena; the world as it is lived by the individual and as it is known by that individual and others.

A variety of key terms are used by phenomenological meta-theorists. The first of these is a bracketing or suspending of our everyday understandings, beliefs and habitual modes of thought. This involves the bracketing out of our facticity (a belief in the factual characteristics of objects) and transferring our focus to our experience. This complements the epoché where we learn (through a process of change) to see (because this is more truthful) only what is given directly in consciousness. The phenomenological reduction then is this attempt to suspend self and other viewpoints and preconceived perspectives on the world.

A number of distinct phenomenological learning approaches have been developed: individualist, situated structural descriptive, dialogical and hermeneutic. The first of these, the individualist strand, comprises a process of introspection, where the learner assumes an external viewpoint towards him- or herself and tries to understand their experiences from this external perspective. The second of these is a situated structural descriptive or empirical approach to learning. Here the learner looks for commonalities in the many appearances of the phenomenon, which is the object of the investigation. Beliefs are understood in most circumstances as causes of behaviours. Dialogical phenomenology is a pedagogic approach, which prioritises personal and structural change delivered through bracketing and the epoché. Hermeneutic phenomenology is concerned with understanding texts, and, in the first instance, the learner seeks to understand

and acknowledge the implicit assumptions they make in relation to the text and their bracketing out of these presumptions (cf. Aldridge and Saevi in this volume).

CONSTRUCTIVIST THEORIES OF LEARNING

In contrast to phenomenological perspectives, Jerome Bruner (1996) distinguishes between symbol-processing views of learning, which he rejects, and socio-cultural or constructivist views of learning. Typically he avoids taking up a position in which these two theories of learning are seen as polar opposites, so that if one position is advocated, any reference to the other is excluded. However, he does want to draw clear lines and boundaries between them. The first of these theories, the computational or symbol-processing view, conceptualises learning as a three-fold process of sorting, storing and retrieving coded information which has been received from an external source, and this mirrors the way a computer processes data. The mind is a tabula rasa, and learning comes from experience and perception. Information or data is inputted into the mind, and this consists of pre-digested facts about the world, which represent in a clear and unambiguous way how the world works. The theory of mind that this represents conceptualises each act of learning in input and output terms, and this assimilative process means that, as a result of the learning process, adjustments are made to the store of facts and theories that the person already holds, in the light of new information that the learner receives. This is a mechanistic process, and the notion of interpretation is subsequently reduced to the assimilation of new information and the reformulation of the mind-set of the learner. Learning is understood as a passive reflection of the world, with particular learning episodes being understood as more or less efficiently realised.

Symbol processing approaches have their origins in the philosophical theory of empiricism, proponents of which understand the world as given and then received by individual minds. This theoretical framework separates out language from reality, mind from body and the individual from society (cf. Bredo, 1999). The first of these, the language-reality split suggests that facts can be collected about the world, which are atheoretic and separate from the belief systems of the collector. These facts are understood as true statements about the world. Furthermore, the theory of learning which emanates from this points to the need to discover what they are, and then develop appropriate models to explain them. The claim being made here is that language is a transparent medium and has the capacity to faithfully represent what is external to it. There is, however, a more appropriate solution to the problem of the relationship between mind and reality and this is that representations of reality are not given in a prior sense because of the nature of reality, or because the mind is constructed in a certain way, but as a result of individual human beings actively constructing and reconstructing that reality in conjunction with other human beings – some contemporary, some long since dead. This brings to the fore the dispute between constructivists and situated cognitivists, in that the former suggest that this active process of learning occurs in the mind, while the latter locate the process of categorising, classifying and framing the world in society and not in individual minds.

Symbol-processing approaches to cognition also suggest a further dualism, between mind and body. This separation of mind and body locates learning and cognition in the mind, as it passively receives from the bodily senses information that it then processes. The mind is conceived of as separate from the material body and from the environment in which the body is located. Learning is understood as a passive process of acquiring information from the environment. Socio-cultural theorists take issue with the supposed passivity of the process, and want to build into it active and transformatory elements. There is a third dualism that critics of symbol-processing approaches have suggested is problematic. This is the

separation of the individual from society. If a learner is given a task to complete, they have to figure out for themselves what the problem is and how it can be solved. The task is framed by a set of social assumptions made by the teacher. The problem with the symbol-processing view is that an assumption is made that the task, and the way it can be solved, are understood in the same way by both learner and teacher. However, this is an assumption which shouldn't be made, and one of the consequences of making it is that the learner who then fails to solve the problem is considered to be inadequate in some specified way, rather than someone who has reconfigured or interpreted the problem in a way which is incongruent with that of the teacher or observer. The individual/civic distinction which is central to a symbol-processing view of cognition separates out individual mental operations from the construction of knowledge by communities of people and this leaves it incomplete as a theory of learning.

Winogrand and Flores (1986: 73) suggest that the symbol-processing approach has the following characteristics:

> At its simplest, the rationalistic (i.e. symbol-processing) view accepts the existence of an objective reality made up of things bearing properties and entering into relations. A cognitive being 'gathers information' about these things and builds up a 'mental model', which will be in some respects correct (a faithful representation of reality) and in other respects incorrect. Knowledge is a store-house of representations, which can be called upon for use in reasoning and which can be translated into language. Thinking is a process of manipulating representations.

This symbol-processing or computational view of learning can be compared with learning theories which foreground cultural aspects, situated or embedded in society. Situated-cognition or socio-cultural theories of learning view the person and the environment as mutually constructed and mutually constructing. As a result they stress active, transformative and relational dimensions to learning; indeed they understand learning as contextualised.

A particular iteration of social-cultural or constructivist theory is cultural-historical activity theory. That we now have a three-generation model of cultural-historical activity theory is part of its formation as an established theory. This and each generation of activity theory can be understood in two distinct ways. The first is in terms of its historical trajectory, so we can understand Lev Vygotsky's (1978) theory of mediation as a reaction against what it emerged from, i.e. it sought to replace the stimulus–response model of the behaviourists because it became apparent that there were aporias, gaps, contradictions and muddles in the theory itself (the theory in short was inadequate); or it can be understood as an attempt to frame the concept as a universalising category. Both of these versions have meta-theoretical and thus universalising elements, in so far as the first requires a theory of history and the second requires a theory of social psychology. However, these universalising elements are framed in different ways.

The story then, replete with simplifications, is that the first generation of Cultural-Historical Activity Theory was inspired by Vygotsky, and as its centrepiece it had the well-known triangular model of subject, object and mediating artefact. When people engage in a learning activity (and in a sense this constitutes the principal activity of consciousness) they do so by interacting with the material world around them (though here the material world is embodied, structured and discursive). What they are doing is entering into a social practice, which is mediated by artefacts. This needs to be qualified in two ways: firstly, there cannot be an unmediated practice, so, for example, a discursive practice cannot be atheoretic; and secondly, as a consequence, we cannot have direct access to the practice itself; indeed, it is difficult to understand the idea of a practice which is separate from the way it is mediated for us. For Vygotsky, our contacts with people or the environment are mediated by artefacts, such as: physical tools, technologies, spatial and temporal properties of objects in the environment, language, number, picture, discourse structures, a division of labour, social norms, cognitive or affective schema, desires, wants or

fears (cf. Fenwick et al., 2011). This in turn led Vygotsky to a preoccupation with the notion of meaning and thus to the development of a notion of semiotic mediation and in particular to a rejection of the behaviourist paradigm, which posited a passive object-to-subject relationship (cf. Daniels and Chaiklin in this volume).

Learning can be seen as adaptive rather than transformative, and Vygotsky's work has always been associated with the latter rather the former. However, the notions of adaptation and transformation are complex. The idea of adaptation would suggest that the learning conforms to those sets of behaviours, norms and strategies which constitute the social world, and which are external to the learner. The learner enters into a state of equilibrium, so that what is inside the mind of the learner (this changes) is now synchronised with what is outside the mind of the learner (which hasn't undergone any change at all). On the other hand, a transformative approach would suggest that both the mind of the learner and the object in the environment have changed. What this implies is not that one theory is misguided and should be replaced by another – a better account of a practice – but that we need to build into our theory the possibility that some learning is adaptive and some is transformatory.

Four issues are of concern here. The first relates to whether meaning resides in the object itself or is created in conjunction with or through the interaction between subject and object. The second relates to the idealist tendencies in Vygotsky's thought (cf. Bakhurst, 2009). The third issue is that all these mediating devices are expected to work in the same way, even though they have different grammars and constitutions. And what follows from this, specifically in relation to learning, is that it is hard to believe that every interaction has an equal possibility of influencing and thus changing the zeitgeist or at least the learning environment. For Vygotsky the focus of his analysis was tool mediation and the activity system where these mediations occurred, rather than the individual per se. However, we are suggesting here that this activity can be transformational both for the system (or learning environment) and for the individual, but not in every circumstance.

The second generation of cultural historical activity theory (cf. Engeström, 2001) is usually though not necessarily associated with the development of the original theory by Alexei Leontiev, and in particular, his elaboration of the concept of activity, so that a distinction is now drawn between an action and an activity. An action is said to be motivated by the intentionality of the person: the person has an object or objective in mind; an activity is understood as undertaken by a community and thus has some of the characteristics of that community, i.e. a division of labour, various means of production and so forth. Leontiev (1978: 10) explains his notion of activity in the following way:

> In all its varied forms, the activity of the human individual is a system set within a system of social relations. ... Human activity is not a relation between a person and a society that confronts him. ... a person does not simply find external conditions to which he must adapt his activity, but, rather, these very social conditions bear within themselves the motives and goals of his activity, its means and modes.

This still leaves many unanswered questions about both the mind–world relation and the way both of these and the relationship between them is transformed.

Five principles underpin the third iteration of cultural-historical activity theory, and in its articulation we can discern its Marxist and Vygotskyian origins (Engeström, 2001: 136). The first principle is that the activity system is central to the process of learning; that activity system being collective, artefact-mediated, object-orientated and networked with other activity systems. This constitutes the primary focus of analysis. The second principle emphasises the way the activity system is stratified, historicised (traces of other human activity are present), and multiply-layered. The third principle is that activity systems are in a state of constant flux and thus are transformed as they are shaped. The fourth principle is that a notion of contradiction is central to the transformation of the activity system. These contradictions are both internal and external to the activity system being examined, and, as Engeström (2001: 173) reminds us:

> [they are] not the same as problems or conflicts. Contradictions are historically accumulating structural tensions within and between activity systems. ... Activities are open systems. When an activity system adopts a new element from the outside ... it often leads to an aggravated secondary contradiction where some old element ... collides with the new one. Such contradictions generate disturbances and conflicts, but also innovative attempts to change the activity.

Finally, the fifth principle suggests that activity systems move through long cycles of change, as the internal and external contradictions lead to and indeed cause individual and collective changes. This is what Engeström refers to as 'expansive transformation', and a full cycle 'is the distance between the present day everyday actions of ... individuals and the historically new form of the societal activity that can be collectively generated as a solution to the double bind potential embedded in ... everyday actions' (Engeström, 1987: 174).

An influential learning theory derived from, and with clear connections to, first generation socio-cultural activity theory is social constructivism. This is both a theory of mind as well as a theory of learning; so that learning is constructed in relation to and as a necessary element of the theory of mind that underpins it. In opposition to a belief in a mind-independent reality, strong social constructivists avoid epistemically-based commitments, and locate truth-forming mechanisms, justificationary rationales, and the means for determining that one type of knowledge is superior to another, in specific discursive formations, which have no external referents. What is being suggested here is that any truth claim comes from and indeed comes about as a result of agreements reached in society by influential and important individuals and groups of these individuals located in history; that is, what determines the validity of any argument about knowledge is power arrangements in society. And what this means is that different knowledge claims where one claim is considered to be more true, more adequate or more reliable than another are not acceptable, nor are knowledge claims which are underpinned by metaphysics, rationality, logic, essentialism (in particular, an essential human nature) or even intuition (direct non-discursive access to the real – a Platonic position). Knowledge is developed through contestations and struggles in the past and in the present about the means for distinguishing true from false statements, and thus knowledge and those apparatus and technologies which act to legitimise it come about through the contingencies of history.

Social constructivists hold to a belief that representations of both physical and social objects are social constructs. So, for example, if an investigation is being undertaken into the issue of gender in educational settings, then a moderate social constructivist (in so far as they subscribe to some but not all of the ascribed characteristics of the belief system) would argue that it is only social actors' representations or conceptions of gender which are socially constructed. On the other hand, a strong social constructivist would assert that both the representations made by individuals and the referents of those representations, the actual entities to which these representations refer, are socially constructed. A moderate social constructivist would accept that reality (at the ontological level) can exert an influence on the way it is represented (at the epistemological level), though this is not isomorphic with, or a mirror image of, what it is meant to represent. A strong social constructivist would argue, in contrast, that what it is that is being represented is either fictitious or fabricated, and thus has no reality outside of, and external to, how it is represented. Some strong social constructivists go so far as to extend this extreme form of idealism to the physical world and the project of science (cf. Barnes et al., 1996).

Social realists argue for a position that separates out the nature of reality from its being socially constructed. In other words, an object can be a social construction, or at least has been constructed in the past, and yet still be real, in that it exists as a social object regardless of whether a knower is engaged in the act of knowing it. Objects and relations between objects change their form. An example of this change process at the epistemological level is the invention (in so far as the set of concepts and relations between them is new) of the notion of probability (cf. Hacking, 1990, 2000) in the nineteenth century, and this changed the way social objects could be conceived and ultimately arranged. Change then can occur in four ways: contingent ontological, planned ontological, epistemically-driven ontological, and, in the transitive realm of knowledge, epistemological (cf. Scott, 2010). With regards to the example above, the invention of probability, two phases of change can be identified. The first is where knowledge is created and thus operates at the epistemological level – the new arrangement of knowledge. The second is where this knowledge has real effects at the ontological level, so that new arrangements, new formations, new assemblages come into being. This last is an example of epistemically-driven ontological change. The dilemma is that the social world, in contrast to the physical world, is always in a state of transition and flux, so that it is hard to argue that there are invariant laws by which the world works, at all times and in all places, except in a basic logical and rational sense.

Ian Hacking (2000: 20) has written extensively on the case for something to be thought of as socially constructed. He suggests that two conditions have to be met. The first of these is that '[i]n the present state of affairs, X is taken for granted; X appears to be inevitable' (2000: 20). However, the second is a necessary part of the equation: 'X need *not* have existed, or need *not* be at all as it is. X, or X as it is at present, is *not* determined by the nature of things; it is *not* inevitable' (2000: 20). Further to this, he suggests that the following claims are implied by the use of the term: 'X is quite bad as it is' (2000: 20); and '[w]e would be much better off if X were done away with, or at least radically transformed' (2000: 20). The point is that if these embodied, institutional and discursive structures could be shown to be merely social constructions and thus arbitrary, then in principle they could be changed or amended. The problem then is that any replacements are also likely to be arbitrary, given that their justification is of the same type and has the same status.

Constructivism is a theory of knowledge, and it is also a theory of learning. In support of this, Ernst von Glasersfeld (1988: 83) has argued that knowledge is not and cannot be passively received but involves an active process that is coordinated by the learner, the cognising subject. This cognition is adaptive to the experiential world, and is a qualitatively different activity from discovering 'an objective ontological reality' (von Glasersfeld, 1988: 83). A distinction needs to be drawn between activities which generate understanding and those which lead to a repetition of behaviours. Thus, in contrast to behaviourism, we find out what is going on by inferring from the mind of the active subject rather than focusing on induced behaviours in the world. And, this has pedagogical implications. Von Glasersfeld (1988: 83) suggests that:

> The teacher [should] try to maintain the view that students are attempting to make sense in their experiential world. Hence he or she will be interested in students' 'errors' and, indeed, in every instance where students deviate from the teacher's expected path because it is these deviations that throw light on how the students, at that point in their development, are organizing their experiential world.

POST-HUMAN, ACTOR-NETWORK AND COMPLEXITY THEORIES OF LEARNING

What distinguishes a complexity theory of learning from conventional theories is the different foci of researchers and investigators, so that it is now the flows and relations between objects rather than the objects themselves which solicit our attention (cf. Davis and Sumara, 2006). Complexity theorists generally subscribe to a version of emergence, which we described at the beginning of this chapter as temporal emergence; society is characterised by notions of continuous emanation, flux and change, which though non-predictive, can be adequately captured in language. Objects in the world cannot be characterised by their essential qualities, but only through their interactions with other objects. Complexity resides in all these various interactions which produce new objects (characterised as different forms of structure), and results in a bewildering array of arrangements of material and human objects; and because they are difficult to characterise they rarely allow definitive accounts of what is going on to be produced. It is the complexity of these object-interactions and their subsequent and temporary coalescences that makes it difficult to provide complete descriptions of them. The epistemic level is unsynchronised with the ontological level because we have not developed sufficiently our instruments and conceptual schema for capturing something which is both ever-changing and has too many elements to it, i.e. it is too complex. However, this doesn't categorically rule out the possibility of providing more complete descriptions of events, structures, mechanisms and their relations in the world, and this suggests a notion of human fallibility which means that our actions (which correspond to learning episodes) are corrigible. The twin elements of complexity and temporal emergence (where systemic formations are understood as not incommensurable) cannot preclude correct descriptions being made of activities in the world, only that these elements can create considerable difficulties. This is further compounded by how emergence operates epistemically.

Many of these theorists go further than this (for example, Osberg and Biesta, 2007), and hold to a version of emergence in which there is a radical incommensurability between different formations over time (whether material, embodied or discursive). Furthermore, it is impossible to predict what inter-connections, new formations and iterations of the object-system will be realised because the principles of the new mechanism are not given in the current arrangements. In other words, the relations between objects and the objects themselves, which make up activity systems, are not patterned in any meaningful sense; there is a radical incommensurability between these different iterations. What this also suggests is that any attempt to describe even the basic outline of the system and the way it works is incompatible with this idea of radical incommensurability. For example, the autopoetic principle (Maturana and Varela, 1987) cannot coexist with radical incommensurability and chaos theory. In a similar way, localism, historicity, holism, organisational necessity, complex causality, logical circularity, non-linear dynamics and uncertainty, positive feedback, self-organisation and inter-connected diversity, are all principles which pertain to and indeed define complex systems (Alhadeff-Jones, 2008); but which act to order our understanding of these complex systems and thus in part contradict the more important principles of radical incommensurability and chaos.

We are able to focus on the formations, but not on the way they were formed. This operates at the ontological level. In other words, though one formation, it is acknowledged, has emerged from a concatenation of others (prior to it in time), this process cannot be codified or captured symbolically (using words, numbers or pictures) except by using words such as chance, non-linearity, or non-predictability. However, each of these as we have already acknowledged is contested conceptually. Because something is non-predictable at the time it operates does not mean that it cannot be described after it has happened; a post-hoc theorisation of the object or arrangement. Non-linearity implies that the sequence of events we are concerned with here has not followed the accepted pattern, whether this has been deduced from previous occurrences or from logical and normative investigations, i.e. what should happen if X is transformed into Y, if certain logical canons are adhered to. Chance by virtue of what it is precludes an explanation of it. We might want to say here that it just happened (cf. Osberg in this volume).

Actor Network Theorists argue for a symmetricality of human and non-human elements, which means that at the level of analysis they should be treated in the same way. This has the effect of marginalising the hermeneutic dimension of learning, and fits better a structuralist and materialist ontology. The intention is to understand history not as the outcomes of originary actions by individuals or collectivities of individuals, but as sets of material objects (human and non-human) coalescing and working together. It is the networks, confluences, collective action sets which produce the conditions of action. Fenwick and Edwards (2010: 9) suggest that:

> Actor Network Theory's (ANT) unique contribution is first, to focus on the individual nodes holding these networks together, examining how these connections came about and what sustains them. These include negotiations, forces, resistances and exclusions, which are at play in these micro-interactions that eventually forge links. Second ... Actor Network Theory (ANT) accepts nothing as given, including 'humanity', 'the social', 'subjectivity', 'mind', 'the local', 'structures' and other categories common in educational analyses. What we usually take to be unitary objects with properties are understood as assemblages, built of heterogeneous human and non-human things, connected and mobilized to act together through a great deal of ongoing work.

What follows here is that the contents of these networks and the inevitability of flux and change as essential elements are likely to mean that our descriptions of them are incomplete and fragmentary. However, what applies to the networks and assemblages themselves and to the relations between them, also applies to the meta-theory itself. Thus we should understand notions of symmetry, translation, problematisation, interessement, immutable mobility, delegation, multiple-perspectivism and actor-networking as incomplete and undeveloped as we try to plot what is happening and what has happened.

Translation is the process by which entities come together to form networks, assemblages and the like. Fenwick et al. (2011: 98) explain that an entity 'is a loose way to refer to various things that can be entanglings of human and non-human, including different kinds of material things and immaterial (conceptual, moral, virtual) things and actions, that are not pre-given, essentialised and defined'. The problem of symmetricality is foregrounded here, as this does not allow different entities and therefore different networks to potentially have different effects because they have different grammars and different capacities to influence the internal and external relations of a network or assemblage. By forgoing boundary and capacity analysis, the investigator is left bereft of explanatory tools.

Actor network theorising cannot then, amount to an argument in favour of social patterning or systemic predictability. Actor network theorists have argued against treating those traditional educational constructs and forms, such as curriculum, learning, leadership, management, standards, etc., as stable, expressing their opposition to the conventional understandings of these terms by pointing to the emergent and unstable ontology of material, discursive and human objects, and the need to move away from prioritising intentionality and therefore human agency over other objects in the world. Determinism would imply in its strongest form that our thoughts, feelings and subsequent behaviours do not deviate from the impulsions laid down in our genetic make-up or in customised knowledge within our bodies or in the social arrangements (i.e. embodied, discursive, agential, institutional and systemic) that constitute our lives. However, if we want to build in a notion of agency, then we have to believe that our cognitive and volitional capacities can operate without recourse to, and outside of, those causal impulses that come from these determining impulses. Furthermore, if we hold to a belief that our cognitive and volitional capacities are inextricably tied to our genetically-determined, embodied or socially-determined impulses, then it follows that our capacity to determine whether or not we are being deceived, i.e. our capacity to tell the truth or not about our fundamental belief in determinism, is thoroughly compromised. Agency therefore involves a set of activities

which are not caused or influenced by those impulses that emanate from our genetic, embodied or social beings; that is, they do not involve an affirmation or a negation of them or even a reaction against them.

By disprivileging the agential and giving it equal status to other objects, action network theorists are making a point about what happens in the world. They are implicitly if not explicitly arguing not just that as theorists they should foreground something other than human agency, i.e. the relations between different networks of human and non-human material objects, but that this gives us a better purchase on the world than theories which privilege an essentialised version of the human being and their relations.

All discussions of a person over time require some understanding of change; that is, the notion of change is built into the conception of human being that we are operating with. There is also the problem of persistence. If there was no cohering element between time moments, so that every moment entailed a change of person, we would not have a sense of personhood, which therefore has to include a notion of persistence over time, and, in addition, has a notion of emergence. And this is emergence understood in its two modes: as a temporal phenomenon and as a response to the stratified nature of reality.

This sense of agency, structured in different spatial and temporal ways, allows and conditions the various acts of learning. Charles Taylor (1989: 12) writes about this sense of agency and its differential structuring in the following way:

So autonomy has a central place in our understanding of respect. So much is generally agreed. Beyond this lie various rich pictures of human nature and our predicament, which offer reasons for this demand. These include, for instance, a notion of ourselves as disengaged subjects, breaking free from a comfortable but illusory sense of immersion in nature, and objectifying the world around us; or the Kantian picture of ourselves as pure rational agents; or the romantic picture …, where we understand ourselves in terms of organic metaphors and a concept of self-expression. As is well known the partisans of these different views are in sharp conflict with each other.

A theory of learning pivots on the idea that there is an entity called for the sake of convenience a human and that this entity has a relationship (both inward and outward) with an environment. Four theories, which give different emphases to these elements have been examined here: behaviourist, phenomenological, constructivist and materialist. In characterising the field, we have been concerned with epistemic differences between the principal theories of learning, and therefore inevitably these differences also focus on the strength, probative force and attached value we give to those relations and entities. This is the way the field is constructed. And this has implications for all the other issues discussed in this book: formative and summative modes of assessment, pedagogy and curriculum.

REFERENCES

Alhadeff-Jones, M. (2008) 'Three generations of complexity theories: nuances and ambiguities', *Educational Philosophy and Theory*, 40, 1: 66–82.

Archer, M. (2007) *Making our Way through the World*, Cambridge: Cambridge University Press.

Bakhurst, D. (2009) 'Reflections on activity theory', *Education Review*, 61, 2: 197–210.

Barnes, B., Bloor, D. and Henry, J. (1996) 'Scientific knowledge: a sociological analysis', *Education Research*, 31: 445–57.

Bhaskar, R. (1989) *Reclaiming Reality*, London: Verso.

Bratman, M.E. (1999) *Faces of Intention*, Cambridge: Cambridge University Press.

Bredo, E. (1999) 'Reconstructing educational psychology', in P. Murphy (ed.) *Learners, Learning and Assessment*, London: Sage Publications, pp. 23–45.

Brown, A., Fleetwood, S. and Roberts, J. (2002) *Critical Realism and Marxism*, London and New York: Routledge.

Bruner, J. (1996) *The Culture of Education*, Cambridge, MA: Harvard University Press.

Davis, B. and Sumara, D.J. (2006) *Complexity and Education: Inquiries into Learning, Teaching and Research*, Mahwah, NJ: Lawrence Erlbaum.

Engeström, Y. (1987) *Learning by Expanding: An Activity-Theoretical Approach to Developmental Research*, Helsinki: Orienta-Konsultit.

Engeström, Y. (2001) 'Expansive learning at work: toward an activity theoretical reconceptualization', *Journal of Education and Work*, 14, 1: 133–56.

Fenwick, T. and Edwards, R. (2010) *Actor-Network Theory in Education*, London and New York: Routledge.

Fenwick, T., Edwards, R. and Sawchuk, P. (2011) *Emerging Approaches to Educational Research*, London and New York: Routledge.

Foucault, M. (1980) *Power/Knowledge*, Brighton: Harvester Press.

Hacking, I. (1990) *The Taming of Chance*, Cambridge, MA: Harvard University Press.

Hacking, I. (2000) *The Social Construction of What?* Cambridge, MA: Harvard University Press.

Heidegger, M. (2002) *The Essence of Human Freedom: An Introduction to Philosophy*, Ted Sadler (trans.), London and New York: Continuum.

Kant, I. (1977 [1783]) *Prolegomena to any Future Metaphysics That Will Be Able to Come Forward to Science*, London: Hackett Publishing Company.

Kant, I. (2007 [1781]) *Critique of Pure Reason* (Penguin Modern Classics), London: Penguin.

Leontiev, A. (1978) *Activity, Consciousness and Personality*, Englewood Cliffs, NJ: Prentice Hall.

Maturana, H. and Varela, F. (1987) *The Tree of Knowledge: The Biological Roots of Human Understanding*, Boston, MA: Shambhala.

Merleau-Ponty, M. (1962) [1945] *Phenomenology of Perception*, Colin Smith (trans.), New York: Humanities Press and London: Routledge.

Osberg, D. and Biesta, G. (2007) 'Beyond presence: epistemological and pedagogical implications of strong emergence', *Interchange*, 38, 1: 31–51.

Putnam, H. (2004) *The Collapse of the Fact/Value Dichotomy and Other Essays*, Cambridge, MA: Harvard University Press.

Scott, D. (2010) *Education, Epistemology and Critical Realism*, London and New York: Routledge.

Taylor, C. (1989) *Sources of the Self: The Making of the Modern Identity*, Cambridge, MA: Harvard University Press.

von Glasersfeld, E. (1988) 'The reluctance to change a way of thinking', *The Irish Journal of Psychology*, 9, 1: 83–90.

Vygotsky, L. (1978) *Mind in Society: The Development of Higher Psychological Processes*, M. Cole, V. John-Steirner and S. Scribner (eds), Cambridge, MA: Harvard University Press.

Watson, J.B. (1930) *Behaviourism*, New York: W.W. Norton and Company Inc.

Wenger, E. (1998) *Communities of Practice: Learning, Meaning, and Identity*, Cambridge, MA: Harvard University Press.

Wenger, E. (2008) 'A Social Theory of Learning', in K. Illeris (ed.) *Contemporary Theories of Learning … in their own words*, London and New York: Routledge.

Winogrand, T. and Flores, F. (1986) *Understanding Computers and Cognition*, Reading, MA: Addison-Wesley.

Theories of Learning

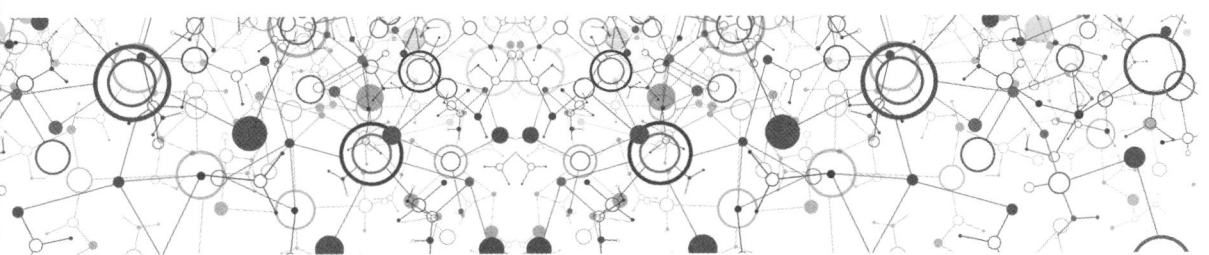

Introduction (Part I)

David Scott and Eleanore Hargreaves

This book is divided into four parts: *Theories of Learning*; *Elements of Learning*; *Curriculum, Pedagogy and Assessment*; and *The Learner*. The theories, frameworks, schema and perspectives discussed in this first part are central to learning and indeed always refer to something. This form of words avoids the problem of representation, and, indeed, though rarely acknowledged, this is the most pressing issue faced by theorists and framers of learning. As we suggested in the 'Introduction' (Scott and Hargreaves, Chapter 1 in this volume) it is possible to organise theories of learning into four categories: behaviourist, phenomenological, constructivist (cf. Chaiklin and Daniels in this volume) and materialist (cf. Fenwick, Edwards and Osberg in this volume), and to distinguish between them in terms of this referential relationship.

Epistemology has traditionally been concerned with what distinguishes different knowledge claims; specifically between legitimate knowledge *and* opinion and belief. We want to suggest that theorising, and in

particular, theorising learning, is a contested activity and this is in part because it is epistemically framed. There are four possible types: positivist/empiricist, interpretivist, critical and postmodernist. When in the nineteenth century the social sciences were beginning to be developed, they did so under the shadow of the physical sciences. Therefore as immature sciences they sought to mirror the procedures and approaches adopted by the natural sciences (or at least by an etiolated version of scientific methodology which rarely equated with how scientists actually behaved).

Such positivist/empiricist approaches can be characterised in the following way. There is a real world out there and a correct way of describing it. This allows us to think that theorising is simply a matter of following the right methods or procedures. What follows from this is that the knowledge produced from this algorithmic process is always considered to be superior to common-sense understandings of the world, by virtue of its systematicity and rigour. Science works by accumulating knowledge, that is, it builds incrementally on previous knowledge. However, it is hard to argue that the social sciences have developed a body of knowledge which presents unequivocal truths about its subject matter. Furthermore, twentieth- and twenty-first-century philosophy has generally accepted that any observations we make about the world, including those which are central to the research process and can be construed as 'facts', are always conditioned by prior understandings we have of the world. There are no theory-free facts, and this puts at risk the distinction made by positivists/empiricists between observation and theory.

The positivist/empiricist method equates legitimacy with science (although this is very much an idealised view of scientific activity) and is characterised as a set of general methodological rules. A clear distinction is made between knowers *and* people and objects in the world. Facts can be identified, free of the values and personal concerns of the observer. Thus, any assertions or statements we make about the world are about observable measurable phenomena, and this implies that two theorists if they apply the correct method would come to the same conclusions. It is the correct application of the method that guarantees certainty and trust in the theories we produce. Although all these assumptions are significant in their own right, they give the impression that positivism and empiricism are simply highly idealised abstruse doctrines; however, such theories have important social consequences and speak as authorities in the world about social and physical matters.

As we have suggested above, this view of theory-development has been disputed by interpretivists, critical theorists and postmodernists, who in their turn have been criticised for not providing a way of developing their theories which fulfils the Enlightenment desire for universal knowledge that is shorn of superstition, personal preference and special pleading. Interpretivists, critical theorists and postmodernists thus sought to provide an alternative to a view of theory-building

which prioritised reduction to a set of variables, a separation between the knower and what they sought to know, a means for predicting and controlling the future, and a set of perfectly-integrated descriptions of the world with a view of the social actor as mechanistic and determined. Interpretivist approaches provide one possible alternative. Interpretivists focus on the meanings that social actors construct about their lives and in relation to the world, and argue that human beings negotiate this meaning in their social practices. Human action then cannot be separated from meaning-making, with our experiences organised through pre-formulated interpretive frames. We belong to traditions of thought, and the task of the theorist is to make sense of these interpretations, even though such interpretive activity is mediated by the theorist's own interpretive frame of reference. This is a practical matter for each individual, though of course they cannot make meanings on their own, since all meaning-making is located within culturally and historically located communities of practice. The field of study is therefore the meaningful actions of social actors and the social construction of reality; and one of the consequences is that the social sciences are now thought of as distinct from the natural sciences.

Learning is therefore understood as a practice in the world, primed for investigation, but resistant to algorithmic and mechanistic methods for describing it used in the natural sciences. Critical theorists and critical realists take the interpretivist critique of positivism/empiricism one stage further. In the search for a disinterested universal knowledge, they look for a solution either in communicative competence or in the stratified nature of reality itself (cf. Nunez in this volume). We will focus here on the former, and in particular Habermas's (1987) argument that any claim to theoretical credibility must be able to make the following assertions: this work is intelligible and hence meaningful in the light of the structuring principles of the discourse community it is positioned within; what is being asserted propositionally is true;

what is being explained can be justified; and the person who is making these claims is sincere about what they are asserting. These four conditions if they are fulfilled allow a theorist to say something meaningful about learning. The aim above all for a critical theorist is to develop knowledge that is potentially transformative or emancipatory: to detect and unmask those practices in the world that limit human freedom. Its purposes are therefore the direct replacement of one set of values (unjust, muddled and discriminatory) with another (rational, just and emancipatory).

The fourth framework is a postmodernist one, and again it should be noted that it was developed in reaction to positivist and empiricist epistemic frameworks, and in particular to all those epistemologies which posit a real world separate from the activities of the knower. As Lather (2007) suggests, any work or theory should give a voice to those social actors that have been traditionally marginalised (an explicit emancipatory purpose), and in the process undermine and subvert the agendas held by those with more power in the world than others; surface for public discussion those textual devices (both spoken and written) used in conventional theory-development, and suggest ways of countering these powerful knowledge constructions; question how theorists construct their texts and organise their sets of meaning in the world; and re-introduce the theorist into the research text by locating them within those frameworks which act to construct them as theorists and as human beings (cf. Cole in this volume).

All these frameworks cannot be equally correct, and this explains why theorists produce conflicting and contradictory results about important educational and learning matters. However, the situation is more serious than this, since even though theorists may subscribe to the same epistemology, they may still disagree with one another, even if they are focusing on the same set of social problems. The dispute might be about correct and incorrect uses of the method, different views and interpretations of the epistemological tradition to which they claim to belong, or using different interpretive frameworks in relation to the data-set which has been collected. This has been called the crisis of representation, and it is hard to imagine how one can escape from it, since the alternative is to revert back to a pre-Enlightenment time of knowledge being privileged because of who could command the most attention.

However, theorising is too important to simply ignore the problems of representation that we have alluded to above. Indeed, we need to understand how our theories are constructed and how power is ever present in their construction. This is because theory-development is conducted with and through other people (some of them more powerful than others), and the theorist is always in the business of collecting accounts by social actors of their lifeworlds and activities in the world. These accounts are always self-serving, and what we mean by this is not that they are wrong per se, but that they are living documents that enable them to go on in life. They are thus always conditional, and this works in four ways: social actors are unaware of some of the conditions for their actions (every action has a set of conditions underpinning it, for example a speech act requires a language, vocabulary and grammar); they are unlikely to be able to predict all the consequences of their actions, so there are going to be unintended consequences; social actors may not be aware of much of their own knowledge and expertise, in other words, much of their knowledge is tacit, and thus they cannot, except with the greatest of difficulty, surface it in their accounts of their lives; and equally they may be motivated by unconscious forces and impulsions which they find great difficulty in articulating (cf. Sfard in this volume).

In this Part of the book, Deborah Osberg writes on complexity theory and emergentism; Harry Daniels on learning, culture and social interaction; Emma Williams and Paul Standish on learning and philosophy; Iskra Nunez on transcending the dualisms of activity theory from a critical realist perspective; David Cole on Deleuze and learning; Tara Fenwick on socio-materiality and learning; Seth Chaiklin on cultural-historical perspectives on learning; Richard Edwards on post-human and responsible experimentation in learning; David Aldridge on phenomenology and learning; and, finally, Anna Sfard on learning, commognition and mathematics.

REFERENCES

Habermas, J. (1987) *Knowledge and Human Interests*, Cambridge: Polity Press.

Lather, P. (2007) 'Validity, qualitative', *The Blackwell Encyclopaedia of Sociology*, George Ritzer (ed.), Oxford: Blackwell Publisher, pp. 5161–5.

3

Learning, Complexity and Emergent (Irreversible) Change

Deborah Osberg

PART 1: BERGSON'S FOLD

Introduction

In this chapter I attempt to map the influence of the 'field' of complexity theory on the 'field' of learning theory' in a way that adds something new to the field of 'complexity and education' research. However, the task of bringing together the notion of complexity *in general* and the notion of learning *in general* is one that is somewhat challenging as both notions are somewhat 'baggy': that is, they only very loosely 'fit' the ideas that they characterise. This is well known in the case of learning which Illeris broadly defines as 'any process that in living organisms leads to permanent capacity change and which is not solely due to biological maturation or ageing' (Illeris, 2007: 3). This broad definition calls upon a notoriously complex and diverse array of ideas and renders the problem of learning (what it is *as a phenomenon*) particularly intractable. Complexity too, however, is a 'loose-fitting' notion for it points to a science that is unified only by the notion of 'emergent' or 'irreversible' change, this being a notion that can be used to describe almost anything. Indeed emergence can be considered to apply *not only* to physical phenomena such as hurricanes, ecosystems, consciousness, traffic congestion and rock concerts (Corning, 2002) *but also* to a wide range of human interactions that are underpinned by power, agency and language (Osberg, 2008b; Osberg and Biesta, 2010a). Bearing in mind there are already many well developed scientific and philosophical languages for describing and understanding these phenomena, one question arising from the apparently universal applicability of emergence is whether it is capable of adding anything fundamentally new to already well established philosophical and scientific understandings of the phenomena concerned. In other words, if not simply to *colonise* existing theorisations of learning, then what is the point of mapping, in a single chapter, the way in which complexity theory relates to learning theory?

A further problem with the task of mapping the influence of the 'field' of complexity theory on the 'field' of learning theory is that 'complexity science' or 'complexity theory' and its unifying idea of emergence is not a unified field or theory in the usual sense of the word. Rather, it is a science/theory that is based on two incommensurable theories (which will be discussed later in the chapter) concerning the appearance of 'irreversible' or 'progressive' change. Despite the 'ubiquitous' or 'universal' nature of emergence there is, in other words, no straightforward way to map the influence of the 'field' of complexity theory on the 'field' of learning theory. In what follows in this chapter, I have therefore attempted to foreground the hybridity of what might be called 'complexity-compatible' thought; this being a collection of ideas 'enfolded' together around the question about irreversible change: a collection of ideas which can be richly brought to bear on the immeasurably complex field (and problem) of the irreversible phenomenon of human learning

In this approach the work of Henri Bergson (1859–1941) appears as central to the entire 'project' of understanding the way in which emergence can elucidate theories of learning *if learning is a process of irreversible change*. Bergson's ideas about irreversible change are used because they not only substantially *predate* complexity science but, in many respects, have been influential in the *development* of complexity science, and also in the development of a number of philosophies that developed independently of complexity science, but which have used certain concepts that are compatible with insights developed within complexity science. I argue that since this 'complexity compatibility' can be traced to Bergson's questioning of the notion of irreversible change, any understanding of the use of complexity, in learning theory, incorporates a much larger field than simply 'complexity science'. One might refer to this larger field as 'Bergson's fold', for this concept *not only* facilitates the idea of multiple perspectives held together (in their difference) in a kind of 'fold' (enclosure) through their multifarious

relationships with Bergson's question about irreversible change, *but also* presents these different perspectives as simultaneously inside and outside of this 'fold' like the surfaces of a Möbius strip, which is 'folded' to form a loop in which there is no separation (or discontinuity) between its 'interior' and 'exterior' surfaces.

This 'Bergsonian' theorisation of the relationship between 'complexity theory' and 'learning theory' thus avoids the charge that complexity can be indiscriminately used to 'colonise' existing theories of learning. It does so by foregrounding the inextricable relationships that exist between a number of pre-existing theories which explore the question of irreversible change in the context of human learning. Moreover, the foregrounding of this relationship (a foregrounding made possible by the notion of emergence) allows for a more integrated approach to our understandings of the notion of learning, this being an integration that opens the potential for even deeper analyses of the richly complex phenomenon of learning.

Bergson's Metaphysics of Change

In Euro-American historical contexts, an explicit focus on the notion of irreversible change is not endemic to complexity theory. It can be traced to ancient Greek thinking dating back to the seventh century BC. Heraclitus' poetical fragments suggest pre-Socratic Greek thought engaged with the metaphysical idea that *contention* (ἡ ἔρις) rather than *stability* could be the basis of reality 'itself' (Robinson, 1987). That is, the ultimate source of all being is instability and change. In later fragments of Greek thought, however, Heraclitus' early metaphysics appears to have been obliterated. Instead we find Parmenides' 'iron clad' idea that all that is possible in reality is 'being' or 'not being'. With this idea in place, the notion of change as the *ultimate source* of all being was logically impossible, as 'being' could not arise from 'not being' (i.e. you cannot get something from nothing). Parmenides considered change, therefore, as merely appearance, an effect of being, whilst reality itself (that which was metaphysically prior to change) was considered to be 'a single continuous changeless and motionless plenum' (Gallop, 1991: 5). Interestingly, in the history of Western philosophy ever since Parmenides, metaphysics is said to have been concerned largely with substance rather than with change (see Seibt, 2012). While there may have been some variations and 'softenings' of this, for example, in Aristotle, Leibniz, Hegel, Fichte, Schelling, and others (Seibt, 2012), the tendency towards substance has largely prevailed and it would appear that it was only with Bergson's thinking at the turn of the twentieth century (that is, prior to Hubble's presentation of the Big Bang theory in 1930, which arguably presented for the first time the idea that something can arise from nothing), that a fully-fledged metaphysics of change (the idea that something can arise from nothing) could again present itself as a viable possibility, at least in the West.

At a time when the dominant trends in Western science were (i) towards separating processes that characterised the living world from those that characterised inert matter, and (ii) towards understanding the processes that characterised the living world as basically reducible to those that characterised inert matter (the former being merely a 'strange variant' of the latter), Bergson presented a theory of change which, by his own account, aimed towards 'preparing the way for a reconciliation between the inert and the living' (1911: 186). Although his philosophy has often been discredited as a form of 'vitalism', mainly due to his use of the term *élan vital* (Durie, 2006), his ideas present a substantial break from earlier vitalisms (see Bennett (2010), for a history of vitalism), for Bergson's *élan vital* did not refer to a discrete and 'actualised' entity (for example a 'life force' that could perhaps be implanted in dead or inert things to give them life) but to a 'tendency' or 'potentiality' that can

never be fully actualised, and which, moreover, is itself continuously subject to other 'tendencies' in an ongoing and vital movement ('flux') of 'creative evolution'. In other words, for Bergson *élan vital* is not substance but dynamic movement, and this movement is metaphysically prior to substance. Indeed, Bergson went so far as to claim that 'movement is reality itself' (1946: 169).

To achieve this metaphysics, Bergson put forward a theory of change that emphasised 'the *continual* elaboration of the *absolutely* new' (Bergson, 1911: 11, my emphasis). That is, he presented change as fundamentally irreversible: open-ended, and hence continually 'on the move' towards the unforeseeable (rather than always returning to stability). Moreover, he argued that such change cannot be understood through a mechanistic logic, in which 'the whole of the real is resolvable into elements' (1911: 354) and in which the passage of the real (from past to present, to future) is understood in 'cinematographical terms' (1911: 272–347), as a series of 'snapshots, as it were, of the passing reality' (1911: 332), strung together in time, with a predictable cause-and-effect relationship between each discrete 'snapshot' and the next. Instead, he presented change through the notion of 'duration', which he interpreted as representing the 'totality' of the past, the present and future, inseparably enfolded together as a 'flux' of *movement* (1911: 186) rather than enfolded in a Parmenidian 'totality' of *stability*. For Bergson, as Juarrero and Rubino explain:

> [duration is the] continuous progress of the past, which gnaws into the future and swells as it advances, … it represents the emergence of the new and unforeseeable, even in principle because in living things the past overflows into their present and future states. (2010: 12)

Most importantly, at least from the perspective of the argument put forward in this chapter, Bergson's challenge to the primacy of mechanistic or 'cinematographic' conceptualisations of change was influential in the formalisation of the concept of emergence.

Bergson and the Possibility for a Comprehensive Theory of Emergence

While the concept of emergence was not new at the time of Bergson's writing – the notion having been used by Aristotle, Galen, Hegel, Kant, Mill (1843), Lewes (1875) and Drummond (1894) (see Reid, 2007: 30; also Seibt, 2012) – O'Connor and Wong (2012) suggest that it was only through the work of the late nineteenth- and early twentieth-century thinkers of the so-called 'British emergentist movement',[1] which came into being contemporaneously with Bergson's thinking, that a comprehensive theory of emergence could be developed. Being contemporaneous with Bergson's thought, the philosophy of British Emergentism was similarly taking place at a time when the dominant trend in science and philosophy was to separate the vital processes that characterised the living world from those that characterised the inertial or inorganic realm. Like Bergson, however, (some) members of this movement – Broad, in particular – were interested not only in *the fact* that there were differences between the processes characterising the stable/inertial and dynamic/vital realms, *but also in the question of whether one kind of process could ultimately be explained in terms of the other.* For example Broad comments:

> The question: Is chemical behaviour ultimately different from dynamical behaviour? seems just as reasonable as the question: Is vital behaviour ultimately different from non-vital behaviour? And we are much more likely to answer the latter question rightly if we see it in relation to similar questions which might be raised about other apparent differences of kind in the material realm. (1925: 44)

Indeed, it could be argued that the emergence of a comprehensive theory of emergence was simply not possible prior to Bergson's questioning of the idea that the logic of mechanism is not the only logic possible. Together with Bergson, Broad was clearly engaged with metaphysical concerns,[2] that is, with the question of whether the ultimate source of all reality is change or stability, and, together with Bergson, denied the metaphysical prioritisation of mechanism.

Emergent properties, for Broad, *are metaphysically irreducible* (1925: 80). Unsurprisingly, perhaps, British Emergentism is reported to have reached its zenith (O'Connor and Wong, 2012) with the publication of Broad's *The Mind and Its Place in Nature* (1925) shortly after Alexander's *Space, Time and Deity* (1920) and Morgan's *Emergent Evolution* published in 1923, which covered similar themes to those covered by Bergson in 1911. By this stage, emergentist thinking rested on the core idea that:

> as systems acquire increasingly higher degrees of organisational complexity they begin to exhibit novel properties that in some sense transcend the properties of their constituent parts, and behave in ways that cannot be predicted on the basis of the laws governing simpler systems. (Kim, 1999: 3)

PART 2: FOLLOWING BERGSON

Breaking with Bergson (1)

Following its heyday in the 1920s the emergentist movement entered a period of quiescence which Kim (1999) describes as resulting from its controversial nature within the mainstream scientific thinking of the time. This controversy, according to Kim, was largely due to its 'dubious' connections with vitalism (that is, Bergson's metaphysics, which had been criticised not only from scientific perspectives but also from multiple philosophical perspectives and treated as incoherent and inaccurate). Interestingly, in many accounts that describe British Emergentism as a precursor to complexity science, the 'dubious' influence of Bergson's metaphysics is conveniently omitted (see, e.g., Corning, 2002), as dominant thinking in science – even complexity science – still holds fast to an idea, contra-Bergson, that could perhaps be termed 'a metaphysics of reductionism': an ontology/metaphysics in which the object is prioritised over the process.

Nevertheless, despite the quiescence of the emergentist movement following the 1920s, the formalisation of the idea of emergence in the early twentieth century – made possible by Bergson's questioning of the universality of mechanistic change – unquestionably fuelled what various scholars have described as an unprecedented period of growth in philosophical schools of thought such as phenomenology (see Smith, 2013) and pragmatism (see Hookway, 2013) that were explicitly focused on the emergent phenomena of 'lived experience' that could not easily be understood through mainstream, mechanistic scientific framings. Such phenomena included human consciousness, identity, intentionality, volition, agency, autonomy, meaning, perception, thought, imagination, emotion, desire, communication, awareness, and so on. The idea of emergence within these discourses was liberally used in articulating the primarily 'transcendent' nature of the objects of study. That is, it proved useful in articulating the internal coherence of stable new 'states' that came into existence as a result of emergent processes. Bergson's philosophy, however, was not easily able to accommodate such ideas owing to his emphasis on the irreducible difference (contention and instability rather than internal coherence) within all being. Hence, although some (e.g. James, Mead, Whitehead and others) openly acknowledged the importance of Bergson's metaphysics in their 'process-based' thinking, few working with 'emergentist' notions adopted Bergson's metaphysical assumptions and indeed many actively spurned them (Kelly, 2010), turning rather to Hegel's 'protostructuralism' (Taylor, 2003: 61) as a theoretical underpinning for the emergent phenomena they studied (Guerlac, 2006). Suffice to say, despite Bergson's important conceptual groundwork regarding the formalisation of the concept of emergence (that is, his questioning of the metaphysical universality of mechanical or 'cinematographical' logic) his metaphysics largely fell into obscurity and even disrepute (Guerlac, 2006), just a few decades after it was initially hailed as full of promise. Moreover, aside from its

use in discourses that understood it primarily in terms of a transcendent process that produced coherent (internally stable) new states, the concept of emergence remained relatively obscure until the second half of the twentieth century, when developments in both science and philosophy gave it new life.

Returning to Bergson (1)

With Bergson's metaphysics of change having faded into obscurity by the middle of the twentieth century (Guerlac, 2006) and the concept of emergence for the most part being interpreted only in an 'object-based' transcendent sense within abstruse philosophical discourse, the current popularity of the concept of emergence might never have taken place except for two independent developments in the second half of the twentieth century that rejuvenated interest in Bergson's metaphysics. One was initiated within the realm of philosophy, representing Bergson's metaphysics, in the 1960s, as a challenge to Hegelian inspired structuralist and phenomenological lines of thought, the proponents of which had largely spurned Bergson's metaphysics (in which change originates *in irreducible difference* rather than with internal coherence). The other took place in the physical sciences, presenting itself, in the 1970s, as a renewed challenge to the prioritisation of mechanism in scientific understandings of irreversible change. It is in this latter development that 'complexity science' as a recognisable field of enquiry begins to emerge. In both developments the renewed interest in Bergson's metaphysics is linked to the idea that emergent matter is continuously engaged in a movement of internal differentiation. In keeping with the historical trajectory I have developed so far, I shall deal with the philosophical movement first, as it has its origins in phenomenology, which pre-dates the emergence of complexity science and which has already been touched on in the previous section.

In what has been described as a move that initiated 'a Bergsonian renaissance' (Durie,

2006: 64) in philosophy, Deleuze (1966, 1986) has explicitly drawn attention to the *foundational* importance of difference and instability in Bergson's notion of duration. He achieved this by emphasising the fact that Bergson understood duration as 'multiplicity' and understood multiplicity in two senses,[3] *quantitative*, which refers to a multiplicity of discrete entities (the many) and *qualitative*, which refers to a multiplicity of difference (see Douglass, 1992). Furthermore, Deleuze points out that it was only the latter that had a place in Bergson's theory of duration. Bergson's *élan vital* – which is not substance but movement or 'flux' – is qualitative or continuous multiplicity. In this regard, it is inherently unstable: it does not ever 'settle' on a unitary or coherent new quality (identity), however temporarily, but only 'exists' as the continuous (and open-ended) multiplication of difference and instability, an instability which, nevertheless 'holds together' *as difference* rather than as unity and coherence. Difference, in this sense is not separative (it does not define separate identities) but creative: *it holds reality together*, albeit only as unformed and unstructured potential, and in this sense *brings being into being*. Thus difference is 'immanent' to Bergson's *élan vital*, and *élan vital* is an instability that can be defined neither from its inside nor its outside but only through its irreversible movement. While Bergson held that 'movement is reality itself' (1946: 169, my emphasis), Deleuze might argue that this insight also suggests that *difference* is reality itself. In developing this line of Bergson's thinking, in his own philosophy of immanence, Deleuze (1966) and Deleuze and Guatari (1994) have been able to challenge phenomenological perspectives in which difference is 'always exterior to itself' (Deleuze, 1999: 58). This move is said to have resulted in an explosive proliferation of work, in both philosophy and the social sciences, in which the differentiating properties of emergent matter are foregrounded. Furthermore, as Douglass (1992) has argued, Deleuze's reading of Bergson has made it possible to conceive of Bergson's metaphysics

as a precursor to an array of philosophical traditions that may be defined as broadly 'post-structural' (abstruse as this label may be) even while the 'post-structuralisms' in question may have emerged independently of Deleuze's re-reading of Bergson. While these various discourses may disagree on certain important points, they all develop critiques of the self-sufficiency and internal coherence of the emergent structures that structuralism posits, and hence have much in common with Bergson's metaphysics of movement and instability. Although work which explicitly foregrounds a concern with the differentiating properties of matter (philosophies of difference) has been developed under various philosophical guises, some of this work has been brought together in edited collections under the umbrella of 'new materialisms' (see, e.g., Coole and Frost, 2010; Dolphijn and van der Tuin, 2012).

Within the sciences an explosion of interest in the notion of emergence took place following the discovery, in the 1970s, of the idea of 'self-organisation' which describes a form of irreversible change in which the micro-level elements of a system spontaneously co-ordinate their behaviour (self-organise) to produce unpredictable macro-level properties that in some sense 'transcend' the properties of their constituent parts. The development of this idea, which enables an explanation of emergence that is recognisably 'scientific', allowed science to make a U-turn with respect to its relationship with the notion of emergence: not only did it allow the insights of the British Emergentist movement to (at last) be incorporated into mainstream science, but did so in a way that allowed science to present emergence as ubiquitous in reality. In particular, work emerging from the Santa Fe Institute, which is primarily concerned with the scientific investigation of emergent phenomena, routinely describes emergence in terms similar to the following:

> Emergence is what 'self-organising' processes produce. Emergence is the reason why there are hurricanes, and ecosystems, and complex organisms like humankind, not to mention traffic congestion

and rock concerts. Indeed, the term is positively awe-inspiring. (Corning, 2002: 18)

Although the notion of self-organisation has multiple origins, it could be argued that it was Ilya Prigogine's Bergsonian interpretation of this concept that 'catalysed' it into a recognisable area of scientific study (Jantsch, 1980: 13), which later became more commonly known as 'complexity science' or 'complexity theory'. Prigogine's work on irreversible thermodynamic change in conditions far-from-equilibrium (1980, 1988, 1997),[4] can be said to have catalysed the materialisation of this field because he showed not only that the concept of self-organisation in conditions far-from-equilibrium had very broad applicability (that is, it could be understood to underpin almost all of reality rather than only a few processes peculiar to a tiny branch of theoretical physics), but (again) brought into question the scientific obsession with mechanistic change and for the first time did so from a position within science rather than within philosophy. He thus introduced an argument – or point of contention/instability – about irreversible change[5] around which an entire field of study could materialise (self-organise). At stake in this argument (or field of study) is the place of mechanism in theorisations of irreversible change (emergence) underpinned by 'self-organising' principles. On the one hand, mainstream scientific perspectives have held fast to the idea that mechanistic logic is sufficient to fully explain self-organisation, while, on the other hand, Prigogine's perspective shows that mechanistic logic is insufficient for describing such processes. The point is, it is the *irreconcilable difference* between these two perspectives that arguably brought 'complexity science' into being, as a distinct field of study. The term 'weak emergence' has become popular for describing the mechanistic (mainstream scientific) interpretation of self-organised change, while the term 'strong emergence' is used to describe the non-mechanistic (Prigoginean) interpretation of self-organised change (see Chalmers, 2006), which resonates with many post-structural philosophical perspectives, including those of theorists as different as Deleuze and Derrida (Guerlac, 2006).

In his more philosophical works (with Isabelle Stengers), Prigogine made frequent reference to the importance of Bergson's metaphysics to his own theorisation of irreversible change which he understood to be objective, material and creative (Prigogine and Stengers, 1984), and in his Nobel Prize acceptance speech made several remarks in which he explicitly acknowledged the formative impact of Bergson's ideas on his thinking:

> Since my adolescence, I have read many philosophical texts, and I still remember the spell *'L'évolution créatrice'* cast on me. More specifically, I felt that some essential message was embedded, still to be made explicit, in Bergson's remark: 'The more deeply we study the nature of time, the better we understand that duration means invention, creation of forms, continuous elaboration of the absolutely new.' … my interest was the study of irreversible phenomena … From the very start, I always attributed to these processes a constructive role, in opposition to the standard approach, which only saw in these phenomena degradation and loss of useful work. Was it the influence of Bergson's *'L'évolution créatrice'* …? (Prigogine, 1977)

Suffice to say that, for Prigogine, it is the process of self-organisation that produces an irreversible 'arrow of time', which in his interpretation is a kind of *material historicity* that inhabits all (strongly) emergent phenomena. To fully appreciate the importance of Prigogine's theorisation of irreversible (emergent) change it is helpful to first engage with the notion of material historicity itself. Such engagement enables an appreciation of the difference between Prigogine's scientific theorisation of irreversible change (strong emergence) as opposed to mainstream scientific theorisations of such change (weak emergence).

The notion of material historicity relates to the fact that emergent processes are 'irreversible' because their history of change operates as a material structural element that acts together with the system's other material structural elements to play a part in determining the system's future. Hence the system's history can be understood to have been 'written into' or 'embodied' in the system's physical structure (see Holland, 1998; Prigogine and Stengers, 1984). In *non-emergent* systems (e.g. a clock, or a rock) this is not the case; while their history describes their change trajectory, it does not function as a material element in their change trajectory. The difference between Prigogine's scientific theorisation of irreversible change (material historicity), as opposed to mainstream scientific theorisations of such change, is particularly clear when accounts of self-organisation provided by mainstream complexity theorists, such as John Holland (1998), are compared with those provided by Prigogine.

With Holland (1998), the 'historicity' of emergent systems is fully explained by the non-linearity of the deterministic rules governing a closed system's change processes. Such rules produce self-generated feedback within the system, which in turn generates an interlocking and irreversible hierarchy of change, which causes the properties that emerge in prior levels to constrain the properties capable of emerging in subsequent levels. Thus any emergent features of the system are generated in a fully determined series or 'trajectory', which, provided the initial conditions remain the same, can be replicated with absolute precision time and again. Although the future of these emergent systems cannot be predicted in advance, this unpredictability arises simply as a result of the computational impossibility of prediction[6] rather than as a result of any indeterminism within the emergent mechanism. Importantly, while this form of material historicity produces matter that is constantly 'evolving' this matter is also fully autonomous and self-contained. That is, its internal state can be defined (and can differentiate itself) *only in relation to that which is external to, and separate from it*. It is, in other words, not capable of internal differentiation, or the production of difference within itself. Moreover, it cannot differentiate itself (in relation to what it is not) as a singularly unique entity because its 'evolution' can be precisely replicated simply by replicating its initial conditions.

With Prigogine (1980) the situation is markedly different. In Prigogine's analysis the irreversibility or material historicity of the self-organising system is the product of both deterministic and indeterministic factors. While the deterministic elements of Prigogine's theorisation of self-organisation are fairly routine (the non-linear, lower-level rules of the system determine the organisational possibilities of the emergent or 'higher level') he insists that these rules do not determine what actually emerges at the higher level because there are always more possibilities for self-organisation than can be realised in actuality. This idea stems from Prigogine's understanding of nonequilibrium thermodynamic systems, which he describes as becoming increasingly 'destabilised' as they are pushed further away from equilibrium (for example by applying heat). The destabilisation takes the form of an 'oscillation' (an internally differentiated state) around the system's stable state and as the system is pushed even further from equilibrium, this oscillation increases to the extent that the system is in danger of collapsing unless it lowers its energy by choosing *one* of the symmetrically equivalent possibilities produced by the oscillation (differentiated state). In choosing only *one* potential way forward, a substantial portion of the system's potential is lost forever (it is 'dissipated' as heat).

Prigogine refers to the critical moment at which this choice is made as 'symmetry breaking'. He argues, furthermore, that the choice taken by the system at this critical moment *is purely a matter of chance* (if the experiment is repeated, the system may choose a different alternative within its own internally differentiated state. Importantly, since a nonequilibrium system will be faced with many such critical moments as it evolves further away from equilibrium, the introduction of chance at each critical moment means the 'material historicity' of the system will not only be unpredictable in practice (as it is with weakly emergent systems) but also unpredictable in principle. Furthermore, the introduction of chance at each bifurcation means the 'material historicity' of the system will also be unrepeatable. Under nonequilibrium conditions, therefore, a system is capable of: (a) internally differentiating itself; (b) becoming different from itself as it selects one of the differentiated alternatives on offer; and (c) becoming a singular and unique (id)entity, *qualitatively and unpredictably different from all others, as well as qualitatively and unpredictably different from previous iterations of 'itself'*. Indeed, one could say nonequilibrium systems are engaged in a continual process of differentiation or 'becoming qualitatively different'. In this regard, 'strong emergence' can be said to be aligned with a Bergsonian metaphysics of difference/change and hence also with a number of post-structural perspectives; and 'weak emergence' can be aligned with phenomenological and structuralist perspectives in which emergent change is understood as productive of coherence and self-containment, producing matter that can be understood as different only in relation to that which it is not (there is no internal difference within such matter).

PART 3: THE ENFOLDING OF 'COMPLEXITY-COMPATIBLE' LEARNING THEORIES

Breaking with Bergson (2)

Prigogine's insights have been slow in appearing in education. An initial spurt of interest took place in the 1980s, soon after the publication in 1984 of Prigogine and Stenger's massively popular book, *Order Out of Chaos*. This body of work was inspired largely by Prigogine's notion of self-organising 'dissipative structures' (see, e.g., Small, 1983; Sawada and Caley, 1985; Doll, 1986; Fisher, 1986), which, as Doll remarked, seemed to hold the promise of a new paradigm for education; one which would make possible 'a transformative not a measured curriculum' (Doll, 1986: 16). However, despite this promising start for complexity-inspired theorising

about learning (and teaching), this was not immediately followed up with work drawing on Prigogine's specifically Bergsonian understanding of irreversible change. As equally plausible but fully mechanistic understandings of self-organisation were in existence at the time Prigogine put forward his contentious interpretation of irreversible change – for example Maturana and Varela's theory of 'autopoeisis' (1987) – which could account for the unpredictability of learning outcomes without overturning entrenched understandings of determinism, it was initially non-Prigoginean understandings of irreversible change (weak emergence) that gained popularity in complexity-inspired research relating to education and learning, at least in English-speaking nations.[7]

One line of thinking following this path that has proved quite popular amongst educational researchers drawing on insights from complexity theory to understand processes of learning, is 'enactivism'. This perspective is strongly hybrid in nature, having historical links with phenomenology (Merleau-Ponty, 1962) and drawing also on insights from systems theory and ecology (Bateson, 1972; Capra, 1996), as well as biology and cognitive science (Maturana and Varela, 1987; Varela et al., 1991), especially through Maturana and Varela's idea of 'autopoeisis' (1987) which develops the idea that the living organism is a 'self-producing' entity which distinguishes itself as an operationally and organisationally closed 'unity' within its 'environment'.

Underpinning the enactivist perspective is the idea that the living entity or 'organism' can, on the one hand, be considered as a self-organising 'unity' in its own right (organising its own organisation) and, on the other hand, as a 'lower-level' element or 'part' of a 'higher-level' self-organising unity (which in turn forms part of an even higher level unity, and so on, in a nested series, see Davis (2008)). Understood in this way, it is not possible to understand the organism's 'self-production' as independent of the larger system to which it belongs. Rather the living organism, in its environment, must be understood to be inseparably interlocked in an ongoing sequence of co-specified, deterministic change. Maturana and Varela (1987) refer to this sequence of mutual co-specification as 'structural coupling' and argue that in living organisms structural coupling sequences are 'cognitive' in the sense that they constitute an embodied history that has meaning to the organism because it enables it to retain its organisational closure (as a unity) despite externally specified change.

Importantly, by presenting cognition in living organisms as the embodied history of the reciprocal co-specification of the organism and its environment, enactivism is able to present 'knowing' as involving multiple threads of lived experience across both space and time and hence is able to present 'knowers' as co-emerging *with* the 'knowable'. However, as Sumara and Davis (1997) have argued, the idea of 'knowers' as co-emerging *with* the 'knowable' does not imply simply that the learning of learners can only be adequately understood *within* the learning context. It implies, rather, that the learning of learners can only be adequately understood as *part* of the learning context. That is:

> As the learner learns, the context changes, simply because one of its components changes. Conversely, as the context changes, so does the very identity of the learner … Both the cognising agent and everything that it is connected to are in constant flux, each adapting to the other in the same way that the environment evolves simultaneously with the species that inhabit it. (Sumara and Davis, 1997: 414)

For enactivists, therefore, individual learners are always interconnected and mutually specifying subsystems (unities) in a nested series of increasingly complex subsystems (unities) 'such as a classroom, a school, a neighbourhood, a culture, humanity, the biosphere' (Sumara and Davis, 1997: 416). In this regard, enactivist perspectives – which share with mainstream constructivism the idea of an active biological base for cognition – have claimed to be able to 'extend' mainstream constructivist theories of learning (see Begg, 2001; Proulx, 2008) by understanding the individual and the collective (or learner and

environment) as enfolded in, and unfolding from each other. This, so it is argued, challenges mainstream constructivism's insistence on the separation of the learner from his or her environment, this being a separation that reifies the idea of rational control and mastery, which is considered to support Eurocentric and 'masculinist' views of knowledge (see, e.g., Fenwick, 2000, 2001; Begg, 2001).

It could also be argued, however, that while enactivist perspectives understand 'knower' and 'knowable' as co-emerging in a reciprocal relation of engaged participation, this does not *completely* overcome the 'mastery' discourse so prevalent in mainstream constructivist theories of learning. This is because, with the enactivist perspective, an organism's 'learning' (the process by which it extends and transforms itself) must still be understood as a product of its attempts to maintain its organisational unity (and hence its survival *as* a unity) in the face of (or despite) externally specified change. In other words learning, for enactivists, is still about 'taking control' of – or *mastering* – the externally specified changes presented by the environment. That said the enactivist perspective on mastery is somewhat different from that of mainstream constructivist perspectives. With mainstream constructivist perspectives, knowledge/mastery is understood to be initially in deficit, with learning being necessary to correct this deficit. Thus the continuous 'improvement' of knowledge/mastery is considered as the primary goal to be achieved by the learner and this goal is understood to be achievable primarily through the active adoption, replication or linear extension of knowledge deemed more powerful (in terms of mastery) than the learner's own current knowledge. This understanding of knowledge and learning leaves little room for learning to proceed in unexpected and novel directions.

With the enactivist perspective, in contrast, mastery is not considered as something to be *acquired through learning,* but rather as something that *learning merely maintains. That is enactivism considers mastery to be always already present in living organisms, which could not survive without already being 'in control' of their environment.* With this perspective, learning and change are understood to emerge as the unintended by-products of living beings' tendency towards maintaining their operational stability and structural closure (mastery) within a radically contingent present. Because any apparent change (or 'growth') of knowledge in such a process is an unintended by-product (of the organisms' efforts to remain stable amidst change), this opens the possibility for knowledge and learning to proceed in unexpected and even novel directions. Enactivist perspectives are therefore more sensitive (and open) to novelty and unpredictability in learning than is possible with mainstream constructivist perspectives, and in this regard are able to bring into view approaches to learning that are more open to the appearance of radical innovation within the 'learning relation'.

Influential as enactivist insights may be in learning theory (linking as they do with so many other perspectives and schools of thought that have themselves influenced learning theory), it is nevertheless important to remember that the enactivist perspective suggests that living beings exhibit a 'natural' tendency towards stability, with change and innovation being secondary. To recap on arguments made earlier in this chapter, this is precisely the view that Bergson's philosophy challenged. For Bergson, it is movement (internal differentiation) not stability (internal coherence) that has metaphysical priority. Bergson's alternative metaphysics suggests that the framing of all learning as a survivalist mechanism is not the only option available for theorising learning. It is in this regard that insights from strong emergence – that is, perspectives on irreversible change that are compatible with a Bergsonian understanding of irreversible change – present themselves as offering an alternative way forward.

Returning to Bergson (2)

Although a Bergsonian-inspired perspective on irreversible change was slow to 'catch on'

within educational thinking and learning – aside from a brief appearance in the 1920s, during Bergson's heyday, when his ideas were connected, amongst numerous other developments, to the 'progressive' educational movement more usually attributed to Dewey (see Wheeler, 1922) – a significant body of work which develops what could be termed a 'strong emergence' perspective on learning began to appear following the turn of the twenty-first century. Within this body of work there appear to be three main lines of thought: Deweyan, Deleuzian and Derridean which I shall deal with separately although they are interlinked in various ways, with each other as well in the way they approach Prigoginean readings of emergence.

Again, relying on the historical trajectory I have developed so far, I shall deal with the Deweyan perspective first, as Dewey's ideas about education and learning emerged prior to Prigogine's work and contemporaneously with Bergson's oeuvre, and, although widely misunderstood in Dewey's own lifetime (Garrison et al., 2012), have since experienced something of a revival, being better understood (a) as a critique of the Cartesian mind/body (or learner/world) split that characterises contemporary mainstream constructivist perspectives and (b) as developments in complexity science, and particularly Prigoginean readings of 'emergence' (Osberg and Biesta, 2007) facilitate a more nuanced understanding of his central ideas (Semetsky, 2008). In short, whilst contemporary mainstream constructivist understandings have aligned themselves with scientific empiricism, Dewey's 'constructivism' can now be understood to have certain commonalities with post-structural perspectives that are aligned with Bergson's perspective on change. Dewey's thinking cannot, however, be positioned as a 'precursor' to post-structural ideas in the same way as Bergson's work can be because Dewey, like the phenomenologists, understood the emergent *products* of engaged (inter)action as unitary, rather than divided within themselves, and understood the process of learning to be fundamentally underpinned by the tendency towards survival (and hence the maintenance of stability) rather than fundamentally underpinned by change and instability. Nevertheless, Dewey's perspectives can be roughly grouped with other 'Bergsonian' perspectives on irreversible change because of the nature of his understanding of emergence (Dewey, 1896) which is compatible with a Prigoginean line of thought, in that for Dewey, like Prigogine, what emerges in the future is *in principle* indeterminate (rather than being indeterminate only in practice). While Doll (1986), Semetsky (2008), Osberg, Biesta and Cilliers (2008) and a few others have made explicit links from Dewey to (Prigoginean) complexity theories, such links are largely implicit in much of the contemporary work that revisits Deweyan perspectives on education (see, e.g., Biesta and Burbules, 2003; Biesta, 2009; Garrison et al., 2012).

For Dewey, as with the enactivists (and the phenomenological perspectives the enactivists draw upon), 'living' is the continual interaction between individuals and their environment, with individuals *actively* bringing about their own change relative to the environmental constraints with which they engage. However, Dewey takes this one step further by arguing that the continual interaction between individuals and their environment entails a form of action in which there is 'experimental tentative exploration of *possible* lines of action' (Biesta, 2009: 64, my emphasis), rather than only responses that are fully determined by the system's structure. It is this insight, in particular, that links Dewey's perspective with the notion of strong emergence. The very possibility of experimentation, so it could be argued, implies the presence of predetermined *but alternative* ways forward, which in turn implies that the organism must make a choice regarding its potential actions. Furthermore, some of the potential actions that the organism will need to choose between may be equally acceptable in terms of the organism's survival. In this regard Dewey begins to develop what Biesta (2009) describes as '*a theory of experimental learning*' (p. 64, original emphasis), in which the learner's agency is orientated

not simply towards mastery or survival *in the present*, but to resolving an instability or uncertainty regarding an action that *might* be taken *in the future*. To place this more firmly in the context of a Prigoginean understanding of emergence, it is worth stressing that for Dewey, the 'meaning' of the present, from the perspective of the cognising agent, is never fully specified. This is because the action contemplated, but not yet taken in the face of several equally possible experimental 'solutions', will acquire the *full* extent of its meaning *only after the action has been taken and the consequences felt*. This introduces into the embodied history of the cognising agent a series of critical points at which uncertainty with regard to future actions is unavoidable. As the choices taken at such points are not fully determined by past experiences (embodied cognition), the future trajectory of the cognising agent is in principle *indeterminate and unrepeatable* as the consequences of the agent's indeterminate choices are written into its embodied history. This opens the possibility for meaning to function *not only* as a historical determinant of future actions (embodied cognition), *but also* as an active force that continuously regenerates meanings. As Semetsky comments, quoting both Dewey and Garrison:

> 'deliberation has the power of genesis' (Garrison, 1997, p. 121). It results in a modification, as Dewey says, of the whole objective order and involves dissolution of old objects together with creative and unpredictable 'suddenness of emergence' (Dewey, 1934/1980, p. 75) of new *objects*, among which the self, as emerging *subject*, is just one. (Semetsky, 2008: 87, emphasis original)

Nevertheless, despite all this, Dewey's understanding of learning remains connected with 'survivalist' interpretations of 'progress', and hence must ultimately be understood in teleological terms as specified by a world that already exists. For this reason, while a Deweyan line of thinking can be said to resonate with some post-structural perspectives (see Garrison et al., 2012) that are compatible with (some) complexity theories, it cannot fully espouse a post-structural mode of thought. Furthermore, since Dewey's perspective on education and learning also does not easily fit within the 'enactivist' line of thought, the Deweyan revival is seldom associated with *any* complexity-compatible understandings of learning (either of the Prigoginean or non-Prigoginean variety). Despite its many overlaps with other complexity-compatible perspectives, the Deweyan perspective largely falls between the gaps.

By far the bulk of educational and learning theory that draws on a Bersonian perspective on irreversible change is positioned within a post-structural framing that is distinctly Deleuzean in nature. As with the Deweyan perspective, much of this work makes only indirect reference to complexity theories or complexity science (see Gough, 2011: vii–xiii). Although references to the notion of 'complexity' and 'emergence' may in some works be frequent (see, e.g., Cole, 2011; Holdsworth, 2013) – which helps signpost links to complexity theory – much of this alignment is veiled and indeed some authors specifically try to bracket out (particular) understandings of complexity (see, e.g., Fenwick and Edwards, 2010: 2), either because of its apparent universalising tendency or because of a disagreement with (one of) its metaphysical arguments. While the growing body of Deleuzian thought in the context of educational practice is tremendously diverse (and hence will not be discussed here), much of this work nevertheless focuses primarily on the Bergsonian theme of the uncontrollable, and yet profoundly 'life-generating' nature of irreversible 'becoming'. Within this framing, education and learning are conceptualised as 'becoming' and the pedagogical task as a 'plurivocal' endeavour, in which 'explanation' is replaced with 'presentation of ideas' as the pedagogue works to 'intensify connections in actuality while seeking to release new potentiality' (Semetsky and Masny, 2013: 16). While this perspective is usually defined primarily in terms of the Deleuzian concept of 'immanent difference' (or internal differentiation) and contrasted with post-structuralisms which

focus primarily on the 'transcendent' nature of change (for example in Derridean thought which emphasises the irreducible movement of change), some theorists working within this perspective hold that '[a] genuine education is … characterised by *a transcendental movement* as much as by *being immanent* to experiences and events' (Semetsky and Masny, 2013: 16, my emphasis).

In contrast to Deweyan and Deleuzian perspectives, the Derridean line of 'complexity-compatible' thinking in relation to education and learning positions itself directly and primarily within complexity theory by drawing explicitly on Prigoginean concepts (see Osberg, 2005, 2008a, 2010; Osberg and Biesta, 2007, 2008, 2010b), while only secondarily linking to a 'Derridean' line of post-structural theory (rather than secondarily linking to a 'Deleuzean' line). This perspective explicitly foregrounds the 'transcendent' directionality of the radical incommensurability between different formations over time (whether material, embodied or discursive) through highlighting the indeterminism that Prigogine's notion of bifurcation introduces into the irreversible change trajectory. For authors working within this line of thought, the moment in which choice is undetermined – the moment of 'free play'– is the moment in which agency becomes possible. That is, *agency lies outside of any determined scheme*. Since the 'decisions' made in such moments are not predetermined, it can be argued that they are not constrained by the notion of 'survival' which brings the full weight of necessity to bear on the individual at any given time. These 'decisions', rather, are superfluous to and *in excess of necessity*: they are truly free and as such they make possible the 'unthinkable' (that which cannot be thought possible within the constraints of the present: they exceed/transcend these constraints). With respect to learning theory, such perspectives have nothing to say regarding the important and irreversible transformations that take place as survivalist responses to changing environmental constraints. While survival is clearly a *crucially important* aspect of learning, which no living organism can do without, the main point being made by this perspective is that *'survival' is not all there is to learning*. Learning is also about the free play of ideas. This refers not simply to the (Deweyan) experimental rehearsal of ideas in mind, which will ultimately (even if only in retrospect) determine the one 'best' or 'most correct' way forward, but to an experimental attitude in which multiple possibilities present themselves *as equal possibilities* with no predetermined 'best' solution (even in retrospect). In the presence of such possibility, the future is radically open-ended, filled with creative and as yet unimagined potential. While the realisation of particular futures can always be traced *in retrospect* to deterministic causes, what is always (necessarily) left out of such tracings are the innumerable *undetermined* (because equally possible/desirable) choices that were made in the process: the choices where agency becomes possible. This perspective therefore offers a 'surplus' understanding of learning, an understanding in which the truly creative – that which serves no immediate determinable function connected to survival, but for which a new function will ultimately be found – can have a place in our understandings of what it means to be human.

CONCLUSION

In this chapter I have tried to make the point that in as much as 'complexity-compatible' perspectives on learning can be traced to a divided Bergsonian origin, the perspectives themselves are not 'pure' but have 'hybridised' with other perspectives on learning, and it is this hybridisation that gives them their 'vigour' or meaning in contemporary theorising about learning. For example, if one divides 'complexity-compatible' perspectives into 'non-Prigoginean' and 'Prigoginean' perspectives, one finds, on the one hand, a hybridised collection of perspectives that call themselves 'enactivist', drawing their meaning from non-Prigoginean, 'weak' emergence

perspectives as well as phenomenology, systems theory and biological and cognitive science, and generating 'constructivist' theories of learning that in some ways challenge mainstream constructivist theories of learning. On the other hand, the 'Prigoginean' branch of theorising is a hybridised collection of perspectives that might be termed 'post-structural' owing to their compatibility with the notion of 'strong' emergence which resonates with philosophies of action, difference and change and which present a challenge to theorisations of learning that are broadly 'survivalist' in their orientation. Hence 'complexity-compatible' perspectives are themselves divided along the lines of incompatibility that Bergson's metaphysics made possible as well as being internally hybridised. Furthermore, this division into just two incompatible and internally hybridised camps, is itself divided from itself. Deweyan perspectives, for example, share some important features with enactivist and phenomenological perspectives (aligning with an 'anti-Bergsonian' perspective), yet in other respects are incompatible with these perspectives, belonging (and yet not quite belonging because of other incompatibilities that Bergson's thinking made possible) with 'post-structural' perspectives. Even within seemingly clear-cut 'divisions' there is contention and division. Within the post-structural camp, an incompatibility manifests in the form of the idea of immanence (Deleuzian) versus transcendence (Derridean), which some have nevertheless managed to 'reconcile'.

In describing these various incompatibilities within 'complexity-compatible' perspectives, the purpose of the chapter has been to make clear that in referring to a 'complex' approach to learning, one is referring *not* to a set of ideas that have been 'unified' by complexity theory, and which can, as some fear, be indiscriminately used to 'colonise' existing theorisations of learning, but to an ongoing and continuously hybridising movement that engages with a metaphysical argument that has – and will continue to have – profound significance for the way in which we come to structure not only our thinking, being and doing (and hence our learning) but also our ongoing learning about learning.

complexity-based philosophy, which, according to Montuori (2008: xxviii) uses insights from both deterministic and nondeterministic perspectives on self-organisation to present a way of approaching the organisation of our thinking, and thinking about organisation.

NOTES

1   The movement included thinkers such as Mill (1843), Lewes (1875), Broad (1925), Morgan (1912, 1923), Alexander and others. Morgan and Alexander explicitly claimed Bergson as a forebear of their emergentism.
2   O'Connor and Wong (2012) argue that while Broad and Mill prioritised movement, Alexander took the opposite view, and held that while certain qualities that emerged were novel, they were still underpinned by fundamentally deterministic properties.
3   Deleuze (1986: 13) reports that Bergson got the idea of two forms of multiplicity from Reimann who was working in the field of physics and mathematics and Reimann's idea was also (separately) developed in Husserl's *Formal and Transcendental Logic*.
4   Prigogine named the systems he studied 'dissipative structures' because they efficiently dissipate the heat generated to sustain them and hence are not stable equilibrial entities but can be said to exist only in conditions 'far-from-equilibrium'. Prigogine's work explains how these nonequilibrium structures are limited by the amount of heat they are able to disperse yet are capable of evolving to levels of order that require more energy to sustain them than the levels of order they replace. The way in which this movement is accomplished – through the process of 'self-organisation' – allows the structure to dissipate more of its energy and maintain its integrity.
5   See Pomian (1990), for a collection of perspectives on what has been termed the 'determinism row' in relation to Prigogine's interpretation of irreversible change.
6   It is the non-linear or 'web-like' nature of the system's interactions which prevents computational predictability by ensuring that no one element in the system has a discrete effect on any other element and by producing feedback loops in which responses can be unpredictably magnified or cancel each other out. Furthermore, the hierarchically interlocked (nested) structure of the system's emergent trajectory prevents predictability because much of the information needed for computational predictability is not materially available (it lies in the system's historical trajectory, rather than in its material parts and rules of interaction).
7   In non-English speaking nations, some complexity inspired work in education has drawn on Morin's

REFERENCES

Alexander, S. (1920). *Space, Time and Deity: The Gifford Lectures at Glasgow 1916–1918 (in two volumes)*. New York: The Humanities Press.

Bateson, G. (1972). *Steps to an Ecology of Mind: Collected Essays in Anthropology, Psychiatry, Evolution, and Epistemology*. Chicago: University of Chicago Press.

Begg, A. (2001). 'Why more than constructivism is needed', in S. Gunn and A. Begg (eds), *Mind, Body and Society*. Department of Mathematics and Statistics, The University of Melbourne.

Bennett, J. (2010). *Vibrant Matter: A Political Ecology of Things*. Durham: Duke University Press.

Bergson, H. (1911). *Creative Evolution*, trans. A. Mitchell. New York: Henry Holt and Company.

Bergson, H. (1946). *The Creative Mind: An Introduction to Metaphysics*, trans. M.L. Andison. New York: Wisdom Library.

Biesta, G.J.J. (2009). 'Pragmatism's contribution to understanding learning in context', in R. Edwards, G. Biesta and M. Thorpe (eds), *Rethinking Contexts for Learning and Teaching: Communities, Activities and Networks*. Abingdon: Routledge. pp. 61–75.

Biesta, G.J.J. and Burbules, N. (2003). *Pragmatism and Educational Research*. Lanham, MD: Rowman and Littlefield.

Broad, C.D. (1925). *The Mind and Its Place in Nature*. New York: Routledge.

Capra, F. (1996). *The Web of Life: A New Scientific Understanding of Living Systems*. New York: Anchor Books.

Chalmers, D. (2006). 'Strong and weak emergence', in P. Davies and P. Clayton (eds), *The Re-Emergence of Emergence*. Abingdon: Oxford University Press. pp. 244–256.

Cole, D.R. (2011). *Educational Life Forms: Deleuzian Teaching and Learning Practice*. Rotterdam: Sense Publishers.

Coole, D. and Frost, S. (2010). *New Materialisms: Ontology, Agency, and Politics*. Durham, NC: Duke University Press.

Corning, P.A. (2002). 'The Re-emergence of "emergence": a venerable concept in search of a theory', *Complexity* 7(6): 18–30.

Davis, B. (2008). 'Complexity and education: vital simultaneities', *Educational Philosophy and Theory* 40(1): 46–61.

Deleuze, G. (1966). *Bergsonism*, trans. Hugh Tomlinson and Barbara Habberjam. New York: Zone.

Deleuze, G. (1986). *Foucault*, trans. Sean Hand. London: Althone.

Deleuze, G. (1999). 'Bergson's conception of difference', in J. Mullarkey (ed.), *The New Bergson*. Manchester: Manchester University Press. pp. 42–66.

Deleuze, G. and Guattari, F. (1994). *What is Philosophy*, trans. G. Burchell and H. Tomlinson. London and New York: Verso.

Dewey, J. (1896). 'The reflex arc concept in psychology', *Psychological Review* 3: 357–370.

Dewey, J. (1934/1980). *Art as Experience*. New York: Perigee Books.

Doll, W.E. Jr (1986). 'Prigogine: a new sense of order, a new curriculum', *Theory into Practice* 25(1): 10–16.

Dolphijn, R. and van der Tuin, I. (2012). *New Materialism: Interviews & Cartographies*. Ann Arbor, MI: Open Humanities Press.

Douglass, P. (1992). 'Deleuze's Bergson: Bergson Redux', in F. Burwick and P. Douglass (eds), *The Crisis in Modernism: Bergson and the Vitalist Controversy*. Cambridge: Cambridge University Press. pp. 368–388.

Drummond, H. (1894). *The Ascent of Man*. London: Hodder and Stoughton.

Durie, R. (2006). 'Bergson, Henri (1859–1941)', in J. Protevi (ed.), *A Dictionary of Continental Philosophy*. New Haven: Yale University Press. pp. 62–64.

Fenwick, T. (2000). 'Expanding conceptions of experiential learning: a review of the five contemporary perspectives on cognition', *Adult Education Quarterly* 50: 243–272.

Fenwick, T. (2001). *Experiential Learning: A Theoretical Critique from Five Perspectives*. ERIC Clearninghouse on Adult, Career, and Vocational Education (Information Series Number 385), Ohio State University, Columbus.

Fenwick, T. and Edwards, R. (2010). *Actor Network Theory in Education*. Abingdon: Routledge.

Fisher, R.M. (1986). 'Dissipative structures theory: a "new alchemy" in the transformation of education', *Educational Researcher* 15(3): 24–25.

Gallop, D. (1991). *Parmenides (of Elea): Fragments. A Text and Translation with an Introduction*. Toronto: University of Toronto Press.

Garrison, J. (1997). *Dewey and Eros: Wisdom and desire in the art of teaching*. New York and London: Teachers College Press.

Garrison, J., Neubert, S. and Reich, K. (2012). *John Dewey's Philosophy of Education: An Introduction and Recontextualization for Our Times*. New York: Palgrave Macmillan.

Gough, N. (2011). 'Escaping the Program: A Foreword', in D.R. Cole, *Educational Life Forms: Deleuzian Teaching and Learning Practice*. Rotterdam: Sense Publishers.

Guerlac, S. (2006). *Thinking in Time: An Introduction to Henri Bergson*. New York: Cornell University Press.

Hall, W.P. (2006). 'Emergence and growth of knowledge and diversity in hierarchically complex living systems', http://ssrn.com/abstract=1758090 or http://dx.doi.org/10.2139/ssrn.1758090 (last accessed 20/10/2014).

Holdsworth, D. (2013). 'Philosophical problematization and mathematical solution: learning science with Gilles Deleuze', in I. Semetsky and D. Masny (eds), *Deleuze and Education*. Edinburgh: Edinburgh University Press. pp. 137–154.

Holland, J. (1998). *Emergence: From Chaos to Order*. New York: Oxford University Press Inc.

Hookway, C. (2013). 'Pragmatism', in E.N. Zalta (ed.), *The Stanford Encyclopedia of Philosophy*, http://plato.stanford.edu/archives/win2013/entries/pragmatism/ (last accessed 20/10/2014).

Illeris, K. (2007). *How We Learn: Learning and Non-learning in Schools and Beyond*. London and New York: Routledge.

Jantsch, E. (1980). *The Self-Organizing Universe: Scientific and Human Implications of the Emerging Paradigm of Evolution*. Oxford: Pergamon Press.

Juarrero, A. and Rubino, C.A. (2010). *Emergence, Complexity, and Self-Organization: Precursors and Prototypes*. Litchfield Park, AZ: ISCE Publishing.

Kelly, M.R. (2010). 'Introduction: Bergson's phenomenological reception: the spirit of a dialogue of self-resistance', in M.R. Kelly (ed.), *Bergson and Phenomenology*. Basingstoke: Palgrave Macmillan. pp. 1–21.

Kim, J. (1999). 'Making sense of emergence', *Philosophical Studies* 95: 3–36.

Lewes, G.H. (1875). *Problems of Life and Mind*. London: Kegan Paul, Trench, Turbner and Co.

Maturana, H.R. and Varela, F.J. (1987). *The Tree of Knowledge: The Biological Roots of Human Understanding*. Boston: Shambhala Publications.

Merleau-Ponty, M. (1962). *Phenomenology of Perception*, trans. C. Smith. London: Routledge and Kegan Paul Ltd.

Mill, J.S. (1843). *System of Logic*. London: Longmans, Green, Reader, and Dyer.

Montuori, A. (2008). 'Foreword: Edgar Morin's path of complexity', trans. R. Postel and S.M. Kelly, in E. Morin, *On Complexity*. Cresskill, NJ: Hampton Press Inc. pp. i–xliv.

Morgan, C.L. (1912). *Instinct and Experience*. London: Methuen.

Morgan, C.L. (1923). *Emergent Evolution*. London: Williams and Norgate.

O'Connor, T. and Wong, H.-Y. (2012) 'Emergent properties', in E.N. Zalta (ed.), *The Stanford Encyclopedia of Philosophy*, http://plato.stanford.edu/archives/spr2012/entries/properties-emergent/ (last accessed 20/10/2014).

Osberg, D. (2005). 'Redescribing education in complex terms', *Complicity: An International Journal of Complexity and Education* 2(1): 81–83.

Osberg, D. (2008a). 'The logic of emergence: an alternative conceptual space for theorising critical education', *Journal of the Canadian Association for Curriculum Studies* 6(1): 133–161.

Osberg, D. (2008b) 'The politics in complexity', *Journal of the Canadian Association for Curriculum Studies* 6(1): iii–xiv.

Osberg, D. (2010). 'Taking care of the future? The complex responsibility of education and politics', in D. Osberg and G. Biesta (eds), *Complexity Theory and the Politics of Education*. Rotterdam: Sense Publishers. pp. 157–170.

Osberg, D. and Biesta, G. (2007). 'Beyond presence: epistemological and pedagogical implications of "strong" emergence', *Interchange* 38(1): 31–51.

Osberg, D. and Biesta, G. (2008). 'The emergent curriculum: navigating a complex course between unguided learning and planned enculturation', *Journal of Curriculum Studies* 40(3): 313–328.

Osberg, D. and Biesta, G. (eds) (2010a). *Complexity Theory and the Politics of Education*. Rotterdam: Sense Publishers.

Osberg, D. and Biesta, G. (2010b). 'The end/s of education: complexity and the conundrum of the inclusive educational curriculum', *International Journal of Inclusive Education*, 14(6): 593–607

Osberg, D., Biesta, G. and Cilliers, P. (2008). 'From representation to emergence: complexity's challenge to the epistemology of schooling'. *Educational Philosophy and Theory* 40(1): 213–227.

Pomian, K. (ed.) (1990). *La querelle du déterminisme. Philosophie de la science aujourd'hui*. Paris: Gallimard/Le Débat.

Prigogine, I. (1977). 'Biographical' in Nobel Media AB 2014, http://www.nobelprize.org/nobel_prizes/chemistry/laureates/1977/prigogine-bio.html (last accessed 20/10/2014).

Prigogine, I. (1980). *From Being to Becoming*. New York: Freeman.

Prigogine, I. (1988). 'Origins of Complexity', in A.C. Fabian (ed.), *Origins: The Darwin College Lectures*. Cambridge: Cambridge University Press. pp. 69–88.

Prigogine, I. (1997). *The End of Certainty: Time, Chaos, and the New Laws of Nature*. London: The Free Press.

Prigogine, I. and Stengers, I. (1984). *Order Out of Chaos: Man's New Dialogue with Nature*. London: Bantam Books.

Proulx, J. (2008). 'Some differences between Maturana and Varela's theory of cognition and constructivism', *Complicity: An International Journal of Complexity and Education* 5(1): 11–26.

Reid, R.G.B. (2007). *Biological Emergences: Evolution by Natural Experiment*. Cambridge, MA: MIT Press.

Robinson, T.M. (1987). *Heraclitus (of Ephesus): Fragments. A Text and Translation with a Commentary*. Toronto: University of Toronto Press.

Sawada, D. and Caley, M. (1985). 'Dissipative structures: new metaphors for becoming in education', *Educational Researcher* 14(3): 13–19.

Seibt, J. (2012). 'Process philosophy', in E.N. Zalta (ed.), *The Stanford Encyclopedia of Philosophy*, http://plato.stanford.edu/archives/fall2013/entries/process-philosophy/ (last accessed 20/10/2014).

Semetsky, I. (2008). 'Re-reading Dewey through the lens of complexity science, or: on the creative logic of education', in M. Mason (ed.), *Complexity Theory and the Philosophy of Education*. Hoboken, NJ: Wiley-Blackwell. pp. 79–90.

Semetsky, I. and Masny, D. (2013). 'Introduction: unfolding Deluze', in I. Semetsky and D. Masny (eds), *Deleuze and Education*. Edinburgh: Edinburgh University Press. pp. 1–18.

Small, M.G. (1983). 'Emergent man: new areas for education – the evolutionary approach', in G.E. Lasker (ed.), *The Relation Between Major World Problems and Systems Learning, Proceedings of the 27th Annual Conference of The Society for General Systems Research, May 23–27, 1983*. Seaside, CA: Intersystems Publications. pp. 97–105.

Smith, D.W. (2013). 'Phenomenology', in E.N. Zalta (ed.), *The Stanford Encyclopedia of Philosophy*, http://plato.stanford.edu/archives/win2013/entries/phenomenology/ (last accessed 20/10/2014).

Sumara, D. and Davis, B. (1997). 'Enactivist theory and community learning: towards a complexified understanding of action research', *Educational Action Research* 5(3): 403–422.

Taylor, N.C. (2003). *The Moment of Complexity: Emerging Network Culture*. Chicago: University of Chicago Press.

Varela, F., Thompson, E. and Rosch, E. (1991). *The Embodied Mind: Cognitive Science and Human Experience*. Cambridge, MA: MIT Press.

Wheeler, O.A. (1922). *Bergson and Education*. Manchester: Manchester University Press.

4

Learning in Relation to Culture and Social Interaction

Harry Daniels

INTRODUCTION

This chapter is concerned with the ways in which the cultures of institutions and the patterns of social interaction within them exert a formative effect on the 'what' and 'how' of learning. This is part of a more general argument to which I subscribe. This is that we need a social science that articulates the formative effects of a much broader conception of the 'social' than that which inheres in much of the slew of research which emanates from the writings of Vygotsky and his colleagues. The boundaries which shape researchers' horizons often serve to severely constrain the research imagination. Sociologists have sought to theorise relationships between forms of social relation in institutional settings and forms of talk. Sociocultural psychologists have done much to understand the relationship between thinking and speech in a range of social settings with relatively little analysis and description of the institutional arrangements that are in place in those settings. At present there is a weak connection between these theoretical traditions.

An important point of departure is with the understanding of learning itself. The Russian word, used by Vygotsky and his colleagues, *obuchenie* is often translated as *instruction*. The cultural baggage of a transmission-based pedagogy is easily associated with *obuchenie* in its guise as *instruction*. Davydov's (1995) translator suggests that teaching or teaching-learning is more appropriate as the translation of *obuchenie* in that it refers to all the actions of the teacher in engendering cognitive development and growth. In the plethora of approaches to the analysis of teaching and learning, whether they be situated or distributed, or espousing an internalisation, participation or transformational model, there have been relatively few attempts to forge the elusive connection between macrostructures of power and control and micro processes of the formation of pedagogic consciousness (see Daniels, 2001 and 2008, for details). There also appears to be an assumption in many accounts of learning that it may be described and analysed as a homogeneous phenomenon. In his original formulation of expansive learning, Engeström (1987) draws on Bateson's (1972) formulation of levels of learning. Down (2004) provides a summary of Bateson's levels as shown in Table 4.1.

Engeström draws attention to Learning III. He argues that this form of learning involves the reformulation of problems and the creation of new tools for engaging with these problems. This ongoing production of new problem-solving tools enables subjects to transform the entire activity system, and potentially create, or transform and expand, the objects of the activity (Engeström, 1987: 158–9).

Expansive learning involves the creation of new knowledge and new practices for a newly emerging activity; that is, learning embedded in and constitutive of qualitative transformation of the entire activity system. Such a transformation may be triggered by the introduction of a new technology or set of regulations, but it is not reducible to it. All three types of learning may take place within expansive learning, but these gain a different meaning, motive and perspective as parts of the expansive process. A full cycle of expansive transformation may be understood as a collective journey through the zone of proximal development of the activity (Engeström, 1999a).

Whatever the type or form of learning that is taking place there is a need to understand its emergence in relation to the circumstances in which it is taking place. My argument is that the way forward is to be found in an exploration of the dialectical relation between theoretical and empirical work which draws on the strengths of the legacies of sociological and psychological sources to provide a theoretical model which is capable of descriptions at levels of delicacy which may be tailored to the needs of specific research questions. The development of the theoretical model along with the language of description it generates will hopefully open the way for new avenues of research in which different pedagogic practices are designed and evaluated in such a way that the explicit and tacit features of processes of the mutual shaping of person and context may be examined (e.g. Daniels, 2010). This will enable significant contributions to be made to the possibilities for studying fields or networks of interconnected practice (such as those of the home, school and community) with their partially shared and often contested objects. Alongside this enhancement of the 'outward' reach of the theory must be increased capacity and agility in tackling 'inward' issues of subjectivity, personal sense, emotion, identity and moral commitment. In the past these two directions have tended to remain the incompatible research objects of different disciplines with an emphasis on collective activity systems, organisations and history on the one hand and subjects, actions and situations on the other hand (Engeström and Sannino, 2010).

Here I will consider the institutional level of social formation. I will outline an approach to the study of learning which examines the way in which societal needs and priorities and/or curriculum formations are recontextualised within institutions such as schools or universities. This approach seeks to understand, analyse and describe the structural relations of power and control within institutions and deploy a language of description to the discursive formations to which the structural formations give rise. I argue that the practices of interaction which particular institutions seek to maintain differentially deflect and direct

Table 4.1 Bateson's levels of learning

	Description	Example
Level I	Conditioning through the acquisition of responses deemed correct within a given context.	Learning the correct answers and behaviours in a classroom.
Level II	Acquisition of the deep-seated rules and patterns of behaviour characteristic to the context itself.	Learning the 'hidden' curriculum of what it means to be a student.
Level III	Radical questioning of the sense and meaning of the context and the construction of a wider alternative context.	Learning leading to change in organisational practices.

From Down (2004)

the attention, gaze and patterns of interaction of socially positioned participants.

INSTITUTIONS AND THE SOCIAL FORMATION OF MIND

The way in which the social relations of institutions are regulated has cognitive and affective consequences for those who live and work inside them. The current state of the art in the social sciences struggles to provide a theoretical connection between specific forms, or modalities, of institutional regulation and consciousness. Attempts which have been made to do so tend not to be capable of generating analyses and descriptions of institutional formations that are predictive of consequences for individuals. At the same time social policy tends not to engage with the personal consequences of different forms of institutional regulation. I will discuss an approach to making connections between the principles of regulation in institutions, discursive practices and the shaping of consciousness. This approach is based on the work of the British sociologist, Basil Bernstein, and the Russian social theorist, Lev Vygotsky.

From a sociological point of view Bernstein (1996: 93) outlined the challenge as follows:

> The substantive issue of … [this] theory is to explicate the process whereby a given distribution of power and principles of control are translated into specialised principles of communication differentially, and often unequally, distributed to social groups/classes. And how such a differential/ unequal distribution of forms of communication, initially (but not necessarily terminally) shapes the formation of consciousness of members of these groups/classes in such a way as to relay both opposition and change.

The following assertion from Vygotsky (1981: 163) recasts the issue in more psychological terms but with the same underlying intent and commitment:

> Any function in the child's cultural [i.e. higher] development appears twice, or on two planes. First it appears on the social plane, and then on the psychological plane. First it appears between people as an inter-psychological category, and then within the child as an intra-psychological category.

I argue that, taken together, the Vygotskian and Bernsteinian social theory has the potential to make a significant contribution to the development of a theory of the social formation of mind in specific pedagogic modalities.

A sociological focus on the rules which shape the social formation of discursive practice may be brought to bear on those aspects of psychology which argue that cultural artefacts, such as pedagogic discourse, both explicitly and implicitly, mediate human thought and action. Sociocultural theorists argue that individual agency has been significantly under acknowledged in Bernstein's sociology of pedagogy (e.g. Werstch, 1998a). Vygotsky's work provides a compatible account that places an emphasis on individual agency through its attention to the notion of mediation. Sociologists complain that post-Vygotskian psychology is particularly weak in addressing relations between local, interactional contexts of 'activity' and 'mediation', where meaning is produced and wider structures of the division of labour and institutional organisation act to specify social positions and their differentiated orientation to activities and cultural artefacts (e.g. Fitz, 2007).

VYGOTSKY'S SOCIOGENETIC APPROACH

Vygotsky provided a rich and tantalising set of suggestions that have been taken up and transformed by social theorists as they attempt to construct accounts of the formation of mind which to varying degrees acknowledge social, cultural and historical influences. There is also no doubt that Vygotsky straddled a number of disciplinary boundaries. Davydov (1995: 15) went as far to suggest that he was involved in 'a creative reworking of the theory of behaviourism, gestalt psychology, functional and descriptive psychology, genetic psychology, the French school of sociology, and Freudianism'.

Recent developments in post-Vygotskian theory have witnessed considerable advances in the understanding of the ways in which human action shapes and is shaped by the contexts in which it takes place. They have given rise to a significant amount of empirical research within and across a wide range of fields in which social science methodologies and methods are applied in the development of research-based knowledge in policy making and practice in academic, commercial and industrial settings. His is not a legacy of determinism and denial of agency, rather he provides a theoretical framework which rests on the concept of mediation. These developments have explored different aspects of Vygotsky's legacy at different moments.

It is clear that many disciplines contributed to the formation of Vygotsky's ideas. For example, Van der Veer (1996) argues that Humboldt with reference to linguistic mediation and Marx with reference to tool-use and social and cultural progress influenced Vygotsky's concept of culture. He suggested that the limitations in this aspect of Vygotsky's work are with respect to non-linguistically mediated aspects of culture and the difficulty in explaining innovation by individuals. Vygotsky's writing on the way in which psychological tools and signs act in the mediation of social factors does not engage with a theoretical account of the appropriation and/or production of psychological tools within specific forms of activity within or across institutions. Just as the development of Vygotsky's work fails to provide an adequate account of social praxis, so much sociological theory is unable to provide descriptions of micro-level processes, except by projecting macro-level concepts on to the micro level unmediated by intervening concepts through which the micro can be both uniquely described and related to the macro level.

BERNSTEIN'S SOCIOLOGY OF PEDAGOGY

Amongst sociologists of cultural transmission, Bernstein (2000) provides the sociology of this social experience which is most compatible with, but absent from, Vygotskian psychology. His theoretical contribution was directed towards the question as to how institutional relations of power and control translate into principles of communication and how these differentially regulate forms of consciousness. It was through Luria's attempts to disseminate his former colleague's work that Bernstein first became acquainted with Vygotsky's writing.

> I first came across Vygotsky in the late 1950s through a translation by Luria of a section of Thought and Speech published in *Psychiatry* 2 1939. It is difficult to convey the sense of excitement, of thrill, of revelation this paper aroused: literally a new universe opened. (Bernstein, 1993, xxiii)

This paper along with a seminal series of lectures given by Luria at the Tavistock Institute in London sparked an intense interest in the Russian Cultural Historical tradition and went on to exert a profound influence on post-war developments in English in education, the introduction of education for young people with severe and profound learning difficulties, and theories and practices designed to facilitate development and learning in socially disadvantaged groups in the United Kingdom. In November 1964 Bernstein wrote a letter to Vygotsky's widow outlining her late husband's influence on his developing thesis.

> As you may know, many of us working in the area of speech (from the perspective of psychology as well as from the perspective of sociology) think that we owe a debt to the Russian school, especially to works based on Vygotsky's tradition. I should say that in many respects, many of us are still trying to comprehend what he said. (Bernstein, 1964b: 1)

In a commentary on the 1971 publication of *The Psychology of Art* V.V. Ivanov (1971: 269) identifies Bernstein's influence on the dissemination of Vygotsky's ideas in the west, despite somewhat inaccurate claims about publication and disciplinary identity.

It was Vygotsky's (1978) non-dualist cultural historical conception of mind claims that 'intermental' (social) experience shapes 'intramental' (psychological) development that continued to influence Bernstein's thinking. This was understood as a mediated process in which culturally produced artefacts (such as forms of talk, representations in the form of ideas and beliefs, signs and symbols) shape and are shaped by human engagement with the world (e.g. Vygotsky, 1987; Daniels, 2008).

Durkheim influenced both Vygotsky and Bernstein. On the one hand Durkheim's notion of collective representation allowed for the social interpretation of human cognition, on the other it failed to resolve the issue of how the collective representation is interpreted by the individual. This is the domain so appropriately filled by the later writings of Vygotsky.

Although Vygotsky discussed the general importance of language and schooling for psychological functioning, he failed to provide an analytical framework to analyse and describe the real social systems in which these activities occur. The analysis of the structure and function of semiotic psychological tools in specific activity contexts is not explored. The challenge is to address the demands created by this absence.

Bernstein outlined a model for understanding the construction of pedagogic discourse. In this context pedagogic discourse is a source of psychological tools or cultural artefacts.

> The basic idea was to view this (pedagogic) discourse as arising out of the action of a group of specialised agents operating in [a] specialised setting in terms of the interests, often competing interests, of this setting. (Bernstein, 1996: 116)

In Engeström's (1996) work within activity theory, which to some considerable extent has a Vygotskian root, the production of the outcome of activity is discussed but not the production and structure of cultural artefacts such as discourse. The production of discourse is

not analysed in terms of the context of its production, that is, the rules, community and division of labour which regulate the activity in which subjects are positioned. It is therefore important that the discourse is seen within the culture and structures of schooling where differences in pedagogic practices, in the structuring of interactions and relationships, and the generation of different criteria of competence, will shape the ways in which children are perceived and actions are argued and justified. This is the agenda which Hasan (2005) has pursued in an approach that draws on Halliday, Vygotsky and Bernstein.

The application of Vygotsky by many social scientists (e.g. linguists, psychologists and sociologists) has been limited to relatively small-scale interactional contexts, often within schooling or some form of educational setting. The descriptions and the form of analysis are in some sense specific to these contexts.

In his work on schooling, Bernstein (2000) argues that pedagogic discourse is constructed by a recontextualising principle which selectively appropriates, relocates, refocuses and relates other discourses to constitute its own order. He argues that in order to understand pedagogic discourse as a social and historical construction attention must be directed to the regulation of its structure, the social relations of its production and the various modes of its recontextualising as a practice. For him symbolic 'tools' are never neutral; intrinsic to their construction are social classifications, stratifications, distributions and modes of recontextualising.

The language that Bernstein (2000) has developed allows researchers to take measures of institutional modality; that is, to describe and position the discursive, organisational and interactional practice of the institution. His model is one that is designed to relate macro-institutional forms to micro-interactional levels and the underlying rules of communicative competence. He focuses on two levels: a structural level and an interactional level. The structural level is analysed in terms of the social division of labour it creates (e.g. the degree of specialisation, and thus strength of boundary between professional groupings) and the interactional with the form of social relation it creates (e.g. the degree of control that a manager may exert over a team member's work plan). The social division is analysed in terms of the strength of the boundary of its divisions; that is, with respect to the degree of specialisation (e.g. how strong the boundary is between professions such as teaching and social work or one school curriculum subject and another). Bernstein (1996) refined the discussion of his distinction between instructional and regulative discourse. The former refers to the transmission of skills and their relation to each other, and the latter refers to the principles of social order, relation and identity. Regulative discourse communicates the school's (or any institution's) public moral practice, values, beliefs and attitudes, principles of conduct, character and manner. Pedagogic discourse is modelled as one discourse created by the embedding of instructional and regulative discourse. Bernstein provides an account of cultural transmission which is avowedly sociological in its conception. In turn the psychological account that has developed in the wake of Vygotsky's writing offers a model of aspects of the social formation of mind which is underdeveloped in Bernstein's work.

MEDIATION

Discourse may mediate human action in different ways. There is visible (Bernstein, 2000) or explicit (Wertsch, 2007) mediation in which the deliberate incorporation of signs into human action is seen as a means of reorganising that action. This contrasts with invisible or implicit mediation that involves signs, especially natural language, whose primary function is *in* communications which are part of a pre-existing, independent stream of communicative action that becomes integrated with other forms of goal-directed behaviour (Wertsch, 2007). Invisible semiotic mediation occurs in discourse embedded

in everyday ordinary activities of a social subject's life.

As Hasan (2001: 8) argues, Bernstein further nuances this claim:

> What Bernstein referred to as the 'invisible' component of communication (see Bernstein 1990: 17, Figure 3.1 and discussion): the code theory relates this component to the subject's social positioning. If we grant that 'ideology is constituted through and in such positioning' (Bernstein 1990: 13), then we grant that subjects' stance to their universe is being invoked: different orders of relevance inhere in different experiences of positioning and being positioned. This is where the nature of what one wants to say, not its absolute specifics, may be traced. Of course, linguists are right that speakers can say what they want to say, but an important question is: what is the range of meanings they freely and voluntarily mean, and why do they prioritize those meanings when the possibilities of making meanings from the point of view of the system of language are infinite? Why do they want to say what they do say? The regularities in discourse have roots that run much deeper than linguistics has cared to fathom.

This argument is strengthened through its reference to a theoretical account which provides greater descriptive and analytical purchase on the principles of regulation of the social figured world, the possibilities for social position and the voice of participants.

These challenges of studying implicit or invisible mediation have been approached from a variety of theoretical perspectives. Holland et al. (1998) have studied the development of identities and agency specific to historically situated, socially enacted, culturally constructed worlds in a way that may contribute to the development of an understanding of the situatedness of the development of social capital. This approach to a theory of identity in practice is grounded in the notion of a figured world in which positions are taken up constructed and resisted. The Bakhtinian concept of the 'space of authoring' is deployed to capture an understanding of the mutual shaping of figured worlds and identities in social practice. They refer to Bourdieu (1977) in their attempt to show how social position becomes disposition. Holland et al. (1998) argue that when a social position is taken up it gives rise to a positional identity. This positional identity leads to the shaping and formation of dispositions and what Bourdieu refers to as 'habitus'. Bernstein is critical of habitus, arguing that the internal structure of a particular habitus, the mode of its specific acquisition, which gives it its specificity, is not described. For him habitus is known by its output not its input (Bernstein, 2000).

Wertsch (1998a) turned to Bakhtin's theory of speech genres rather than habitus. A similar conceptual problem emerges with this body of work. Whilst Bakhtin's views concerning speech genres are 'rhetorically attractive and impressive',

> the approach lacks … both a developed conceptual syntax and an adequate language of description. Terms and units at both these levels in Bakhtin's writings require clarification; further, the principles that underlie the calibration of the elements of context with the generic shape of the text are underdeveloped, as is the general schema for the description of contexts for interaction. (Hasan, 2005: 126)

Bernstein acknowledges the importance of Foucault's analysis of power, knowledge and discourse as he attempts to theorise the discursive positioning of the subject. He complains that it lacks a theory of transmission, its agencies and its social base.

IDENTITY AND AGENCY

Hasan brings Bernstein's concept of social positioning to the fore in her discussion of social identity. Bernstein (1990: 13) used this concept to refer to the establishing of a specific relation to other subjects and to the creating of specific relationships within subjects. He forged a link between social positioning and psychological attributes. This is the process through which Bernstein talks of the shaping of the possibilities for consciousness. The dialectical relation between discourse and subject makes it possible to think of pedagogic discourse as a semiotic means that regulates or traces the generation of subjects'

positions in discourse. We can understand the potency of pedagogic discourse in selectively producing subjects and their identities in a temporal and spatial dimension (Diaz, 2001: 106–8). As Hasan (2005) argues, within the Bernsteinian thesis there exists an ineluctable relation between one's social positioning, one's mental dispositions and one's relation to the distribution of labour in society. Here the emphasis on discourse is theorised not only in terms of the shaping of cognitive functions but also, as it were invisibly, in its influence on 'dispositions, identities and practices' (Bernstein, 1990: 33).

Within Engeström's approach to Cultural Historical Activity Theory the subject is often discussed in terms of individuals, groups or perspectives/views. I would argue that the way in which subjects are positioned with respect to one another within an activity carries with it implications for engagement with tools and objects. It may also carry implications for the ways in which rules, the community and the division of labour regulate the actions, including learning, of individuals and groups.

Holland et al. (1998) have studied the development of identities and agency specific to historically situated, socially enacted, culturally constructed worlds. They draw on Bakhtin (1978, 1986) and Vygotsky to develop a theory of identity as constantly forming and in which the person is understood as a composite of many, often contradictory, self understandings and identities which are distributed across the material and social environment and are rarely durable (Holland et al., 1998: 8). Holland et al. draw on Leont'ev in the development of the concept of socially organized and reproduced *figured worlds* which shape and are shaped by participants and in which social position establishes possibilities for engagement. They also argue that figured worlds:

> distribute 'us' not only by relating actors to landscapes of action (as personae) and spreading our senses of self across many different fields of activity, but also by giving the landscape human voice and tone. … Cultural worlds are populated by familiar social types and even identifiable persons, not simply differentiated by some abstract division of

labour. The identities we gain within figured worlds are thus specifically historical developments, grown *through continued participation in the positions defined by the social organization of those worlds' activity.* (Holland et al., 1998: 41, my italics)

This approach to a theory of identity in practice is grounded in the notion of a figured world in which positions are taken up constructed and resisted. They argue for the development of social position into a positional identity into disposition and the formation of what Bourdieu refers to as 'habitus'. It is here that I feel that this argument could be strengthened through reference to a theoretical account which provides greater descriptive and analytical purchase on the principles of regulation of the social figured world, the possibilities for social position and the voice of participants.

Engeström (1999b), who has tended to concentrate on the structural aspects of CHAT, offers the suggestion that the division of labour in an activity creates different positions for the participants and that the participants carry their own diverse histories with them into the activity. This echoes the earlier assertion from Leont'ev:

> Activity is the minimal meaningful context for understanding individual actions. ... In all its varied forms, the activity of the human individual is a system set within a system of social relations. ... The activity of individual people *thus depends on their social position*, the conditions that fall to their lot, and an accumulation of idiosyncratic, individual factors. Human activity is not a relation between a person and a society that confronts him ... in a society a person does not simply find external conditions to which he must adapt his activity, but, rather, these very social conditions bear within themselves the motives and goals of his activity, its means and modes. (Leont'ev, 1978: 10, my italics)

In activity the possibilities for the use of artefacts depend on the social position occupied by an individual. Sociologists and sociolinguists have produced empirical verification of this suggestion (e.g. Hasan and Cloran, 1990; Bernstein, 2000; Hasan, 2001). My suggestion is that the notion of 'subject' within activity theory requires expansion and clarification.

In many studies the term 'subject perspective' is used which arguably infers subject position but does little to illuminate the formative processes that gave rise to this perspective.

Holland et al. (1998: 41) also argue that multiple identities are developed within figured worlds and that these are 'historical developments, grown through continued participation in the positions defined by the social organization of those worlds' activity'. This body of work represents a significant development in our understanding of the concept of the 'subject' in activity theory.

CONCLUSION

The language that Bernstein has developed allows researchers to develop measures of school modality. That is, to describe and position the discursive, organisational and interactional practice of the institution. He also noted the need for the extension of this work in his discussion of the importance of Vygotsky's work for research in education.

> His theoretical perspective also makes demands for a new methodology, for the development of languages of description which will facilitate a *multi-level* understanding of pedagogic discourse, the varieties of its practice and contexts of its realization and production. (Bernstein, 1993: xxiii)

This approach to modelling the structural relations of power and control in institutional settings, taken together with a theory of cultural-historical artefacts that invisibly or implicitly mediate the relations of participants in practices, forms a powerful alliance. It carries with it the possibility of rethinking notions of agency and reconceptualising subject position in terms of the relations between possibilities afforded within the division of labour and the rules that constrain possibility and direct and deflect the attention of participants.

It accounts for the ways in which the practices of a community, such as school and the family, are structured by their institutional context and that social structures impact on the interactions between the participants and the cultural tools. Thus, it is not just a matter of the structuring of interactions between the participants and other cultural tools; rather it is that the institutional structures themselves are cultural products that serve as mediators in their own right. In this sense, they are the 'message', that is a fundamental factor of education. As Hasan (2001) argues, when we talk, we enter the flow of communication in a stream of both history and the future. There is therefore a need to analyse and codify the mediational structures as they deflect and direct the attention of participants and as they are shaped through interactions which they also shape. In this sense, combining the intellectual legacies of Bernstein and Vygotsky permits the development of cultural historical analysis of the invisible or implicit mediational properties of institutional structures which themselves are transformed through the actions of those whose interactions are influenced by them. This move would serve to both expand the gaze of post Vygotskian theory and at the same time bring sociologies of cultural transmission into a framework in which institutional structures are analysed as historical products which themselves are subject to dynamic transformation and change as people act within and on them.

REFERENCES

Bakhtin, M.M. (1978) 'The Problem of the Text', *Soviet Studies in Literature*, 14(1): 3–33.

Bakhtin, M.M. (1986) *Speech Genres and Other Late Essays*, translated by Vern W. McGee, edited by Caryl Emerson and Michael Holquist, University of Texas Press Slavic Series 8. Austin: University of Texas Press.

Bateson, G. (1972) *Steps to an Ecology of Mind*. Chicago: University of Chicago.

Bernstein, B. (1964b) Letter to Vygotsky's Widow, Mimeo.

Bernstein, B. (1990) *The Structuring of Pedagogic Discourse: Class, Codes and Control*, Volume 4. London: Routledge.

Bernstein, B. (1993) 'Foreword', in H. Daniels (ed.), *Charting the Agenda: Educational Activity after Vygotsky*. London: Routledge.

Bernstein, B. (1996) *Pedagogy Symbolic Control and Identity: Theory, Research, Criticism*. London: Falmer Press.

Bernstein, B. (2000) *Pedagogy, Symbolic Control and Identity: Theory, Research, Critique* (revised edition). Lanham, Maryland: Rowman & Littlefield Publishers.

Bourdieu, P. (1977) *Outline of a theory of practice*. Cambridge: Cambridge University Press.

Daniels, H. (2001) *Vygotsky and Pedagogy*. London: Routledge.

Daniels, H. (2008) *Vygotsky and Research*. London: Routledge.

Daniels, H. (2010) 'The Mutual Shaping of Human Action and Institutional Settings: A Study of the Transformation of Children's Services and Professional Work', *The British Journal of Sociology of Education*, 31(4): 377–93.

Davydov, V.V. (1995) 'The Influence of L.S. Vygotsky on Education Theory, Research, and Practice', *Educational Researcher*, 24(3): 12–21.

Diaz, M. (2001) 'The Importance of Basil Bernstein', in *A Tribute to Basil Bernstein 1924–2000*, edited by S. Power, P. Aggleton, J. Brannen, A. Brown, L. Chisholm and J. Mace. Institute of Education, University of London, pp. 106–8.

Down (2004) Bateson's Levels of Learning. http://www.cade-aced.ca/icdepapers/down.htm (Accessed 15 May 2015).

Engeström, Y. (1987) *Learning by Expanding*. Helsinki: Orienta-Konsultit Oy.

Engeström, Y. (1996) 'Development as breaking away and opening up: A challenge to Vygotsky and Piaget'. *Swiss Journal of Psychology*, 55: 126–132.

Engeström, Y. (1999a) 'Activity Theory and Individual and Social Transformation', in Y. Engeström, R. Miettinen and R.-L. Punamäki (eds), *Perspectives on Activity Theory*. Cambridge: Cambridge University Press, pp. 19–38.

Engeström, Y. (1999b) 'Innovative Learning in Work Teams: Analyzing the Cycles of Knowledge Creation in Practice', in Y. Engeström, R. Miettinen and R.-L. Punamäki (eds.), *Perspectives on Activity Theory*. Cambridge: Cambridge University Press, pp. 377–404.

Engeström, Y. and Sannino, A. (2010) 'Studies of Expansive Learning: Foundations, Findings and Future Challenges', *Educational Research Review*, doi: 10.1016/j.edurev.2009.12.002.

Fitz, J. (2007) 'Review Essay: Knowledge, Power and Educational Reform, Applying the Sociology of Basil Bernstein', *British Journal of Sociology of Education*, 28(2): 273–9.

Hasan, R (2001) 'Understanding talk: directions from Bernstein's sociology', *International Journal of Social Research Methodology*, 4(1): 5–9.

Hasan, R. (2005) 'Semiotic Mediation, Language and Society: Three Exotripic Theories – Vygotsky, Halliday and Bernstein', in J. Webster (ed.), *Language, Society and Consciousness: Ruqaiya Hasan*. London: Equinox.

Hasan, R. and Cloran, C. (1990) 'A Sociolinguistic Study of Everyday Talk Between Mothers and Children', in M.A.K. Halliday, J. Gibbons and H. Nicholas (eds), *Learning, Keeping and Using Language*, Volume 1. Amsterdam: John Benjamins.

Holland, D., Lachiotte, L., Skinner, D. and Cain, C. (1998) *Identity and Agency in Cultural Worlds*. Cambridge, MA: Harvard University Press.

Ivanov, V.V. (1971) 'Commentary', in L.S. Vygotsky, *The Psychology of Art*. Cambridge MA: MIT Press, pp. 265–95.

Leont'ev, A.N. (1978) *Activity, Consciousness and Personality*. Englewood Cliffs: Prentice Hall.

Roth, W.M. (2007) 'Heeding the Unit of Analysis', *Mind, Culture and Activity*, 14(3): 143–9.

Van der Veer, R. (1996) 'The Concept of Culture in Vygotsky's Thinking', *Culture and Philosophy*, 2(3): 247–63.

Vygotsky, L.S. (1978) *Mind in Society: The Development of Higher Psychological Processes*, edited and translated by M. Cole, V. John-Steiner, S. Scribner and E. Souberman. Harvard: Harvard University Press.

Vygotsky, L.S. (1981) 'The Genesis of Higher Mental Functions', in *The Concept of Activity in Soviet Psychology*, edited by James Wertsch. Armonk: M.E. Sharpe.

Vygotsky, L.S. (1987) *The Collected Works of L.S. Vygotsky, Volume 1: Problems of General Psychology*, including the volume *Thinking and Speech*, edited by R.W. Rieber and A.S. Carton and translated by N. Minick. New York: Plenum Press.

Wertsch, J.V. (1998a) 'Review of Basil Bernstein, Pedagogy, Symbolic Control and Identity: Theory, Research, Critique', *Language in Society*, 27(2): 257–9.

Wertsch, J.V. (1998b) *Mind as Action*. New York: Oxford University Press.

Wertsch, J.V. (2007) 'Mediation', in H. Daniels, M. Cole and J.V. Wertsch (eds), *The Cambridge Companion to Vygotsky*. New York: Cambridge University Press.

5

Learning and Philosophy

Emma Williams and Paul Standish

LEARNING AND KNOWLEDGE

Learning is a complex process, which embodies a range of characteristics, configurations and conditions. Perhaps at the most basic level, however, learning can be seen as a process of gaining and developing knowledge. Such a conception is underwritten by familiar definitions of learning; hence the *Oxford Dictionaries Online* depicts learning as 'the acquisition of knowledge or skills through study, experience, or being taught'. As a concept, then, learning is internally related to knowledge.[1] Indeed, it would be difficult to think about learning and the practices of learning without also making reference to *what is (to be) learned* – and typically what we are aiming at in such considerations is some form of knowledge. We say 'some form' here so as to draw attention to the fact that there are, of course, many different types of knowledge that can be gained through learning, and this is something that philosophers, throughout the history of the Western tradition, have helped to draw out.

Philosophers typically divide knowledge into three categories, defined as 'knowing-that', 'knowing-how' and 'knowing-by-acquaintance'. There is significant controversy surrounding these notions and their inter-relations, and we return to some of these below. A typical reading of these categories, however, is that philosophers are hereby drawing a distinction between knowledge that is propositional (the kind of knowledge we have when we know *that* something is the case), knowledge that is practical (when we know *how* to do something), and what is sometimes referred to as knowledge with a direct object (when we know something or someone directly or through immediate experience). Fleshing out the distinctions a bit further, we might say that we are in the realm of knowing-that when we are talking about facts and theories; hence the student in the history classroom who is told, 'the battle of Waterloo was fought on the 18th of June, 1815', and the student in the science classroom who is instructed, 'the chemical structure of water molecules is H_2O', can be said to be acquiring propositional knowledge. In contrast to this, we are in the sphere of knowing-how when we are talking about skills and techniques; hence the student in the music class who is able to play the violin, or the student of languages who knows how to speak French can be said to have gained practical knowledge. To know by acquaintance, meanwhile (so the usual story goes), is not a matter of acquiring facts or skills in some practice, but is rather a matter of having *familiarity* with something or someone, gained through a direct experience of that thing or person. Hence through listening to compositions by Debussy we come in this sense to know his music, and likewise by meeting and conversing with someone, we come to know them as a friend, a colleague, and so forth.

Many familiar debates within education, particularly those pertaining to curriculum and pedagogical matters, draw upon these philosophical conceptions of knowledge. One example of this was when the New Labour government introduced a skills-based discourse into the UK National Curriculum through notions such as 'ICT-skills', 'thinking-skills' and 'personal and learning-skills'. Such a move brought with it much discussion of the importance of practical knowledge within education. Of course, in recent years, David Cameron's Conservative Government has gone the other way and has aimed to turn the focus of education back onto the pupil's acquisition of 'hard' facts and theories; thus foregrounding *propositional* knowledge as the key aim of education. Beyond this, changing conceptions of teacher education in many countries have typically been towards a skills-based approach, while in practical fields such as nursing and physiotherapy there has been an oscillation of emphasis between knowing-how and knowing-that. In the sphere of educational theory, the distinction between propositional and practical knowledge has come under extensive scrutiny in recent years. A particularly vigorous debate has emerged over the extent to which knowing-how to do something might also require the mastery of certain (theoretical) rules or procedures: is knowing-how a subspecies of knowing-that, or is such a view merely

intellectualism, the privileging of theory over practice?[2] Beyond this, serious questions have been raised over the understanding of practical knowledge that currently predominates in vocational education, wherein the acquisition of skills seems to be reductively conceived in terms of the mastery of manual or coordinative short-term tasks.[3]

It is not our intention in the present paper to address such debates. What we are interested in examining, rather, is the sphere of knowledge that seems to have been left out of consideration while such debates have continued. For comparatively little attention appears to have been given by either policy makers or educational theorists to knowledge-by-acquaintance. In philosophy, this sphere of knowledge became familiar in the works of Bertrand Russell in the early twentieth century, but fell out of favour for a number of reasons such as the fall of epistemological foundationalism (the view that knowledge was a system that needed to be constructed upon unshakable first principles) and an increased scepticism in regarding the idea that something can be simply 'given' to the mind. We do not aim to reject such criticisms or re-invoke the tenets of Russell's acquaintance theory here. Rather, what we want to explore is the possibility of offering an alternative way of developing the notion of knowing-by-acquaintance; one that is both richer and more robust than that proposed by Russell. Furthermore, we want to consider how this alternative conception of knowledge itself gives rise to a renewed account of what it is to learn. For, as we shall come to see, conceptions of knowledge necessarily give rise to particular understandings of the *ways* knowledge is gained. Through offering an enriched conception of knowledge in this chapter, then, we also hope to open up the richness of learning.

LEARNING AND PHILOSOPHY

Before moving on, let us take a moment to say something more general about the kinds of purchase philosophy can have on the topic of learning. For, in so far as questions about the nature of the human mind, knowledge and understanding are key topics within the discipline of philosophy, it is clear that much could be said about learning from a philosophical perspective. In fact, from its earliest beginnings philosophy has always been in part a philosophy of education, concerned not only with the nature of knowledge but with how we come to know, not only with the nature of the good life but with how we might learn to live better. The tensions between different conceptions of knowledge and learning that have so much shaped the development of modern schooling derive from divergences within philosophy itself. The thought that learners are empty vessels waiting to be filled is a popular expression of epistemological empiricism, a crude caricature of Locke's *tabula rasa*. The rise of child-centred education manifestly owes much to Rousseau's thought-experiment in *Emile*, as well as to Dewey's more realistic reflections on democracy and education. And the arguments for a liberal education that arose, partly in resistance to such trends, acknowledge lines of influence leading back through Michael Oakeshott and J.H. Newman to the *artes liberales* and Plato himself. Advocates for liberal education, such as Israel Scheffler, R.S. Peters, Paul Hirst and Robert Dearden were continually exercised by curricular questions concerning the value of what was to be learned and the bearing this had on the young person's developing mind, while the idea of *Bildung*, with its Humboldtian roots, oriented a particularly rich and in some ways parallel line of thought within the German tradition.

Philosophy of mind has long wrestled with the problem of how the deliverances of the senses are to be related to the spontaneous powers of the mind. When treated well, such explorations are not severed from the broader social and political context, such that problems of learning and education are inseparable, as Plato and Confucius saw, from the question of the *polis* – that is, the kind of society we seek to create or sustain. The legacy of logical positivism's one-tracked 'verificationist' response

to this in the first half of the 20th century continues to have deleterious effects in our lives and social world, while the linguistic turn in philosophy, which occurred around the same time and in which Wittgenstein and Heidegger were key figures, harbours insights that are only gradually being realized. Furthermore, the topic of learning has itself occupied the attention of philosophers of education within a number of different traditions, and the concept has been investigated in a number of different ways. For example, some theorists have worked to explore the significance of a key philosopher or philosophical concept for contemporary understandings of learning in education (Cole (present volume); Britton, 1987); while others have investigated key philosophical accounts of the mind in ways that can inform theories and practices of learning (Backhurst, 2011; Bonnett, 1994; Derry, 2013; Dunne, 1993; Winch, 1998). Moreover, philosophers of education have made important contributions to a number of vexed questions about learning that have come to the fore in recent years, such as the way neuroscientific insights on brain development are employed in education (Davies, 2004; Howard-Jones, 2014; Standish, 2013) and the way ICT and 'Technology Enhanced Learning' works to transform learning and conceptions of knowledge (Burbules and Callister, 2000; Standish, 1999; Sternberg, 2005). As many of these philosophical approaches show, perhaps one of the main contributions philosophy can make to discussions about learning comes through the careful analysis of certain *presuppositions* (concerning knowledge, the human mind, the human being) that stand behind many accounts of learning and underpin educational initiatives. In the present chapter we seek, in a similar vein, to demonstrate that certain presuppositions about knowledge are informing approaches to learning in education today, and argue that a re-thinking of this conceptual field can, in fact, open up a much richer conception of knowledge, which has significant implications for learning.

Such thoughts, no doubt, may at this stage sound rather oblique. To help us to get to a place from which we might better approach them, let us first sketch out a more familiar picture. More specifically, let us begin with propositional and practical knowledge as they are currently conceived within education, and the corresponding image of learning they produce.

THE PROPOSITIONAL AND THE PRACTICAL

Knowledge-that has always been an integral part of schooling, but it has become big business today. E.D. Hirsch has provided the kind of simplistic, conservative account of education that is so ready for adoption by politicians, manifested in the UK recently with Michael Gove's 'back to basics' approach to schooling, which prioritises learning content and 'hard facts'.[4] Hirsch argues that children need both to acquire a body of 'core knowledge' that includes certain facts, concepts, sayings and literary works, and to 'learn these facts in a highly organised, structured way' (Abrams, 2012). The reference to a structured approach is worth highlighting here. Indeed, Hirsch's works emphasise a foundational approach to learning, wherein the pupil starts with basic facts and then builds up to more complex ones, over a thematic treatment of ideas. Furthermore, these facts need to be fully *assimilated* by the pupil for such a construction to take place; one should not build on shaky foundations. Hence the core material that is to be studied in education (the facts, concepts, sayings, and so forth) will need to be grasped and got to grips with, even involving perhaps its being systematically learned by rote.

Alongside the focus on knowing-that, and despite the party rhetoric that has emerged in recent years, knowing-how also continues to be a key focus in education in the UK today. One area in which this can be seen is in the 'skills-talk' that is now applied to a wealth of educational matters, including the domain of thinking itself. Indeed, much of the literature defending the conception

of 'thinking skills' construes this explicitly as a form of knowing-how or, as it is sometimes termed, 'procedural knowledge'.[5] In so doing, proponents equate thinking skills acquisition with the learning of certain techniques, schemas and rule-governed ways of thinking. Furthermore, and as the influential McGuinness Report emphasises, the know-how involved in thinking skills should be something that is maximally transferable; it must be capable of being utilised 'beyond the context' in which the initial acquisition occurs (1999: 1). Through this, knowing-how comes to be portrayed as a domain of knowledge that is largely divorced from specific subject matter, and what is seen as being essential in the learning of procedural knowledge is that we master a technique that can be invariably applied and repeated in a number of different contexts.

A similar conception of knowing-how is put to work within certain traditions of the psychology of learning. A current buzz-word in this field is 'metacognition' or the notion of 'learning how to learn'. The main idea at play here is that part of being an effective learner involves recognising and perfecting the methods or strategies *through which* one learns. Learning *how* to learn is thus, as the phrase itself suggests, a matter of practical knowledge; what we are learning is not some particular content or fact, but rather techniques that will better enable us to learn some particular content or fact. In addition to this, and not wholly distinct from it, the notion of 'reflective practice' has also come in recent years to be big business for the psychology of learning. In its original form, developed by Donald Schön, reflection was viewed as a form of thinking that would enable practitioners to draw out and become aware of the implicit knowledge they had accumulated from their own experience.[6] Yet this rich conception of reflection seems to have been somewhat lost in the anaemic versions that are now *de rigueur* (particularly, it is worth noting, in teacher education).

For the conceptual framework employed here is the somewhat reductive schema that, through becoming adept at reflecting on one's progress, one's abilities, one's self in general (via the mastery of some technique), there will be an increase in effectiveness in one's performance and output. Further examples of such schematic approaches to knowing-how can be found in the multifarious 'models for learning' that are frequently invoked in education and training today. One such example is David Kolb's 'learning cycle', in which learning is seen to require a logical four-stage sequence (crudely: initial experience-reflection-analysis-application); a method that can be applied to suit a particular person's 'learning style' and hence provides an instrumental blueprint for learning. It is perhaps worth highlighting how, in all of these notions (metacognition, reflective learning, learning models), knowing-how is construed as a handmaiden to knowing-that in so far as it is seen as a means through which knowledge pertaining to the propositional sphere might be acquired. This hierarchy attests to a continued valuation of the propositional over the practical. And it is also worth noting here that a number of scholars have taken issue with the apparent hollowing out of knowing-how that has occurred as a result, suggesting as they have that we are still far from doing justice to the full dimensions of practical knowledge within our lives (see, for example, Dunne, 1993; Smith, 2014).[7]

REPRESENTING LEARNING

What image of learning is produced by this conception of knowledge? To answer this question, it will be necessary to analyse the assumptions that appear to stand behind its construal of knowledge and learning and make it possible. In the present context, it will not be possible to give an exhaustive analysis of these; indeed the background story may be, and has been, cast in many ways, as our remarks about Wittgenstein and Heidegger have suggested (see also, for example, Cavell, 1979; Rorty, 1979; Taylor, 1997). Rather, what we will aim to do here is bring out the

way these conceptions of propositional and practical knowledge are based on a particular understanding of both what it is to know and the human being as knower.

To develop this point, let us firstly point to the way that, in this account of knowing-that, knowledge (and by implication the ways of coming to know, or learning) is understood in terms of conceptual determination. On this reckoning, I can appropriately be described as knowing x when I grasp it, have a grip on it, and when I fully understand and comprehend it. Moreover, and somewhat as a result of this, learning and the ways of *coming to know* get tied to mastery (or, perhaps better, a particular conception of mastery). Thus I can be taken to have learned or gained knowledge of a particular mathematical theorem, for example, when it presents no problem to me, when I have conquered it and hence can make it work and put it to use with relative ease and efficiency.

Yet it is not only in the field of propositional knowledge that such an understanding comes through. For similar thematics are invoked within the above accounts of knowing-how. As we have seen, through notions such as 'thinking skills', 'metacognition' and 'reflective learning', acquiring practical knowledge comes to be construed in the quasi-technical sense of becoming proficient in the practice and application of skills, procedures or techniques. Yet, taken in this way, the gaining of know-how comes to be understood in quite similar terms to the acquisition of knowledge-that; although in the practical sphere, to be sure, the focus is not so much on the mastery of *propositions* as on becoming adept in the application of certain *procedures or methods*. Furthermore, it can be seen that the techniques we must master in the sphere of knowing-how are themselves portrayed as means through which we might better come to determine and manipulate data; hence the stress on maximal transferability that informs much 'skills-talk', and the concerns that are raised about the way knowing-how has been transformed into little more than a handmaiden to knowing-that. Two things are to be noticed here. One is to do with the questionable firmness of the distinction between knowing-how and knowing-that, which appears to be continually upheld in education today. The other, more pressing one, in our view, has to do with the way both are theorised in a manner that puts unwarranted emphasis on determination. In short, within these two types of knowledge, a shared stress on mastery is at play, and one that works to mutually reinforce a particular conception of knowledge and learning.

We might push this analysis further and say that, in philosophical terms, the conceptions of knowing-how and knowing-that that we have articulated here, and the corresponding image of learning they foster, can be read as operating squarely within the framework of *representationalism*. More particularly, we might say that such conceptions take their cue from the particular image of both human thinking and the human being *who* thinks that is afforded by such a tradition. For representationalism takes human thought as primarily a cognitive and intellectual process, as the forming of determinate, abstracted conceptualisations of the world. Correspondingly, it portrays the human being as the disengaged 'subject' who stands over and against an inert and passive world of objects, which are there to be treated and manipulated according to our own projects and goals. Yet if we understand knowledge in terms of conceptual determination, and take the learning of such determinations to be a matter of mastery and conquest, we are surely not too far away from such a model. Indeed, for the predominant portrayal of knowledge to make sense, and for its corresponding picture of learning to be possible, we must surely assume the representationalist vision – or, indeed, forget that such a vision *is* a vision, and assume it is *the* account of our relation to the world.

KNOWING-BY-ACQUAINTANCE: THREE EXAMPLES

How might we get a richer account of learning than that which is produced from knowing-how and knowing-that, and their associated representative conceptions of human thought? As we have stated, we propose that taking seriously the notion of knowledge-by-acquaintance might bring a different understanding of knowledge into view and, through this, a different approach to learning. Notably, we do not aim to offer a comprehensive account of knowing-by-acquaintance here.[8] Rather we will draw upon three illustrations, two taken from philosophical accounts that develop this thematic and the other from our own experience as teachers, in order to indicate the range of considerations that might be opened through the notion of knowledge-by-acquaintance.[9]

Our first example comes from Heidegger's account of the cabinet-maker's apprentice, developed in his lecture series *What is Called Thinking?* The apprentice, Heidegger states, is one who seeks to learn to build cabinets; yet in order to do this he will not simply need to gain 'facility in the use of tools', nor will he just need to gain knowledge about the forms of cabinets and their structure (2004 [1954]: 14). These are skills that, in the language of traditional philosophy, might well be *necessary* to becoming a cabinet-maker's apprentice, but they are not *sufficient*. What is missing from this skill-based picture, then? Heidegger states that the apprentice will also need to learn something that is not a matter of skill alone, but is more a matter of 'relatedness' to wood itself (2004 [1954]: 14). This is, more specifically, a matter of learning structures of receptiveness and responsiveness to the different kinds of woods, their material and their shapes. Now, this notion of relatedness or receptivity need not be understood in any *romanticised* or *idealised* kind of way. Rather, we can see that it is simply a matter of learning, for example, what kinds of wood will work well for a TV cabinet, or what kinds of wood will work well for a kitchen cabinet, and so on. And we might say, more broadly, that such an approach would also be relevant to wider questions in, for example, industrial design where the development of new, synthetic materials offers scope to the designer in unprecedented ways. Furthermore, it would be relevant to the usage and production of new technology, of the kind exploited for example in desk-top publishing or 3D printing. Importantly, however, the kind of learning that takes place here is something that is learned *by way of the material itself.* Put another way, the material *lends itself* to use in particular ways, and we thus learn what works well by being *attentive* to the way the material shows itself. The way of learning structures of receptiveness, then, is not through skills or knowledge acquisition alone. It is a learning that takes place through an experience with the material itself.

Now, defenders of the conceptions of knowing-how and knowing-that might here object that this kind of learning could equally be achieved by sitting in a classroom and being taught about different types of wood by a teacher. Perhaps, indeed, we could devise a chart comprising 'yes/no' information for uses of wood that would do just as well. For example we could have a chart such as shown in Table 5.1.

What such a model of teaching lacks, of course, is the actual experience of the wood itself. But why is this so important? We have already intimated the answer above; for it is by way of the experience of the wood itself that such knowledge comes to be possible for us in the first place. By teaching cabinet making in the chart-inspired way, then, we in effect sever the apprentice from the actual conditions of possibility of such knowledge about the wood in the first place. We sever their learning from the way the wood lends itself to us, shows itself up in a certain way, namely as 'too hard' or 'too soft' for a particular purpose. Moreover, we also work to elevate abstracted knowledge about the wood to a central position in our relationship with the wood. The role of the wood itself completely slips out of the picture. Cabinet making appears, then, as a process that is completely within our control. On Heidegger's picture, by contrast, we acknowledge and are open to the way our knowledge about wood is something that arises by way of the wood itself. We thus recognise a co-dependency and conditionality between our knowledge and learning, and the wood itself (see Bonnett, 1994; Standish, 1999; Williams, 2013).

Of course, this recognition is not something that is confined to the activities of cabinet making or apprenticeships alone. We might say indeed that such relatedness to the objects of study is something that is a key part of learning in a number of different contexts. Before moving on to develop this point, let us draw upon another way of developing the thematic of knowledge-by-acquaintance. Stanley Cavell (1969) has explored the ways in which the challenges posed by modernist experiments in the arts – his example is post-war music – divided audiences, between traditionalist, knee-jerk rejection, on the one hand, and fashion-following, earnest endorsement, on the other. Both responses were ideological in a way that risked denying the space of judgement in the face of the kinds of challenges these experiments in the arts posed. Such aesthetic judgement does not depend upon recourse to theory (inherited or avant-garde), but upon what Cavell calls 'knowledge in feeling'. Such knowledge is not simply a matter of having a grip on some fact or theory about an artwork or mastering some procedure for judging it. Rather, knowing-by-feeling is a matter of seeing meaning in what is presented. An experience of art, we might say, *calls for* a response; it puts me into a place in which I am opened to the questions: What does this mean? And how can this be meant? The response that is needed to such a call involves offering my voice, my judgement,

Table 5.1 The concept of wood

Type of wood	Can be used for TV cabinet?	Can be used for kitchen cabinet?	Can be used for bookshelf?
Oak	Yes	Yes	Yes
Pine	No	Yes	No
Mahogany	Yes	Yes	Yes

which will itself depend upon how I see it and feel it. And it is important that this is not a merely 'subjective' matter. Ultimately, as Cavell shows, such judgements are crucial for our moral and political lives together.

In this way, we see that through his account of knowing-by-feeling Cavell sensitises us to a different relation, a different understanding of knowledge, which itself requires new description of what it is to know. For knowledge-by-feeling is a type of knowledge that resists conceptual clarification in the form of the articulation of propositions or facts. It is also quite unlike competence in a certain method or procedure (as may be the practice of the art critic, for example). Knowing-by-feeling is rather a matter of exercising a certain kind of judgement in response to something that exceeds our conceptual grasp.

Our third illustration of knowledge-by-acquaintance comes from the teaching experience of one of the authors of the present chapter, Emma, and is written from a personal perspective.

> I had been invited by a colleague in the Foreign Languages Department to join one of her lessons, in which they had been reading Albert Camus' play, *Les Justes*, which is based on the true story of a group of Russian socialist revolutionaries who plan and execute the assassination of the Grand Duke Sergei Alexandrovich. In the course of studying this text a number of themes for discussion had emerged within the class. Knowing my background in philosophy, my colleague invited me along to stimulate further discussion of some of the themes. The brief was quite open: the teacher simply wanted her students to have the chance to re-engage with some of the interesting themes that had arisen in the course of the lessons.
>
> I hence decided to structure the lesson loosely around a number of themes that I had found prevalent within the text, offering a hand-out of five key quotes from the play as illustrative examples. I stated at the outset that the themes I had picked out were likely to have been largely informed by my prior knowledge of Camus as a philosopher. I thus invited the pupils to challenge my interpretations. We read and re-read the passages I had selected, opening up new meanings and significances. One pupil, for example, drew the class's attention to the epigraph at the outset of the play, which had interestingly not been included in my English translation. It was a quotation from Romeo

> and Juliet, Act IV Scene 5: 'O love! O life! Not life but love in death'. Does this mean the play, which is often cast as having a political message, could be re-read as a love story? And what kind of 'love' is being invoked? We also pondered the differences between reading text in the English translation I had provided and the original French version the students had studied. One student felt that it seemed like a different play to her when she read it in English; this provoked discussion about whether one language can ever do justice to another, or whether there is a sense in which something is lost in translation. These difficulties and experiences of translation were highly pertinent to the learning that took place. Through our discussions the students were brought to realise the incommensurability and the unavoidability of judgement that is at stake when reading and interpreting a play. I do not think we got past the first two quotes I had selected in the forty-minute lesson.
>
> This lesson did not end with a sense of self-satisfied contentment, as though we had got to the bottom of *Les Justes* and worked it all out. Rather we left realising the openness and richness of the text and the possibilities of interpretation that had emerged from our engagement with just a few sections of it. And I was struck at the end of this class by just how different such a lesson had been from my usual experience of teaching existentialism within the A Level Philosophy course. Here, Sartre's philosophy is introduced as a version of 'Libertarianism', and is pitted against the 'other views' on the Free Will–Determinism debate, cast as 'Determinism' and 'Compatibilism'. Given the demands of the A level course (Free Will and Determinism is only one module out of four required to be studied in the first year), it is impossible to spend more than two forty-minute lessons discussing existentialism. The result is that there is no room for thinking about and responding to existentialism as there was in the above-cited Camus lesson. In fact, what my students (and we might recall here that these are philosophy students) often end up with is a sense that they know all there is to know about Sartre's philosophy, simply because they can cite his argument in nugget form, and are able to roll out stock 'criticisms' of it (which often largely comprise those listed in mark-schemes for previous exam questions). Of course, this is not my students' fault. It is a result of an exam system that is driven by quantitative assessment, by the tick-box culture that prevails over education as a whole.

Rather than provide the space for open and rigorous thinking of the kind we have articulated in this chapter and would contend is in operation in the above-cited example of the

Camus class, the A Level Philosophy lesson on Sartre seems to enforce learning by means of closed regurgitation.

LEARNING AS RECEPTIVITY

These illustrations demonstrate something of the range of considerations that might be opened by the notion of knowing-by-acquaintance we intend here. For what is common in each case is a mode of *receptivity* to what is being studied. Heidegger's cabinet-maker is receptive to the wood she works with, feeling resistances in the grain of wood and releasing its possibilities. In Cavell's account of aesthetic judgement, we give ourselves to, are taken in by, the subject matter – we *see* or *hear* it – and through this are open to its challenges and questions. Finally the Language lesson was led by the text and practices of translation, rather than by an imposed structure of facts or interpretations that needed to be delivered.

What might learning look like, through this conception? As has already been indicated, learning should not here be conceived as an attempt to grasp and appropriate what is to be known, whether this is understood in terms of herding some fact into a pre-defined conceptual pen or mastering some preordained methodology or procedure. The account of learning opened here is not an attempt at domination. Neither should it be understood as a process that aims at reaching some firm and final conclusion (for example, assimilation of new material into a body of knowledge, or proficiency in some procedure or technique). Such a conception leads to the hubristic belief that one has exhausted a topic, and learned 'all there is to know'. Of course, there may well be instances where this kind of approach to learning is appropriate. Indeed, there are bits of received information, certain propositions and certain techniques that it is useful and interesting for us to learn. Yet as the above illustrations have served to show, not all knowledge is knowledge of facts or propositions, and hence not all learning is a

matter of consumption. Indeed, this is precisely why we feel dissatisfied by the crafts-person who learns about her material solely by means of a chart; by the overly theoretical or traditional judgement of artwork; and by the specification-led interpretation of literature. And it is why we should also feel a deficiency in the scientist, the engineer, or the designer who has technical know-how up to a point but who lacks imagination. Something essential is lost when we subsume all knowing and learning under the same blueprint.

Ignoring this variety in knowing and coming to know leads to a kind of 'knowingness' that arrests the possibility of receptive thought itself. For if we are too ready to corral new thoughts and experiences into an already-worked-out conceptual framework, we will not be open to the objects of our understanding and hence, ironically, may allow them to slip away and evade us. This point should not be misread as a sceptical comment about whether there can be knowledge or about whether we do know what we think we know. Rather, the point we are making here is that certain kinds of knowledge are not to be approached with a grasping hand: for if we grip and clutch them too tightly, we crush them under our grasp. A similar point is expressed by Emerson (1844: 36), who saw the 'evanescence and lubricity of all objects, which lets them slip through our fingers then when we clutch hardest' to be 'the most unhandsome part of our condition'. And it is from a similar perspective that Heidegger speaks of thinking in terms of a 'handicraft'; thus foregrounding the receptive, open gesture, rather than the grasping hand that encloses and clutches.

Such an open, receptive conception of learning also points us towards the *transformative* dimensions of learning, which similarly appear to be blocked by the assumption that learning is simply the acquisition of bodies of information or skills and abilities. Notably, the notion of transformation we are opened to here is radically unlike progression through a series of linear steps, which is often the tacit or explicit assumption about learning that is adopted in developmental accounts. Furthermore learning, following this more receptive approach, cannot easily be captured by means of a self-conscious, meta-cognitive process such as Kolb's 'learning cycle'. Following the preceding discussion, we might in fact re-open a notion of absorption in learning or getting lost in learning. This would not be understood in a sentimentalised way but rather in more Deleuzian terms as the sensuous nature of thought; felt in the complex puzzle of a detective story or the problem in mathematics, or in coming to a new understanding or interpretation of an idea, or in seeing an art-work from a different angle. It would not be inappropriate to see this more or less physiological disturbance or excitation in terms of *eros*.

By way of concluding this chapter, it is perhaps worth pointing out how much this conception of learning will also work to disturb many typical distinctions that appear to underpin conceptions of knowledge and learning at work in educational policy, practice and theory. Indeed, the range of considerations that can be brought into the notion of knowing-by-acquaintance we have sought to illustrate here serves to highlight that knowledge and, by implication, the ways we learn are much richer and, indeed, much messier than is often recognised. Hence knowing-by-acquaintance cannot be seen as merely one further category of knowledge to be added to the already-accepted taxonomy of knowing-how and knowing-that. Indeed, we should rather see that knowing-how, knowing-that and knowing-by-acquaintance are forms of knowledge that cannot be held in distinction from each other; for they overlap and interconnect with each other in multiple ways. Such interconnection has already been recognised by philosophers who challenge the standard propositional/procedural divide. By exploring the conception of knowing-by-acquaintance here, we open up the variety of learning and the multi-dimensional processes that are involved when we learn. Of course, we would not want to deny that some learning might solely be about assimilating a certain proposition, and some learning might be a matter of learning a process or mastering a

method that can be invariably applied across a number of different contexts. But most learning is not and could not be like this. To fail to recognise this is to reduce the learning experience to an artificial, inorganic process. It is to fail to do justice to the richer and more familiar ways in which we learn.

NOTES

1 Of course, not all accounts of learning foreground knowledge, and such a definition may thus appear reductive. For example, Dewey defined learning in terms of an adaptation of behaviour, hence drawing out the more practical, pragmatic dimensions of learning. And on a more everyday level, we speak of the learning of animals, which invokes a more engaged conception of learning than the definition in terms of knowledge is apt to suggest. We do not reject such conceptions of learning in this chapter. Rather we take our cue from the connection between knowledge and learning so as to demonstrate the way that, through this relation itself, a rich conception of learning may be opened.

2 Stanley and Williamson (2001) argue that knowing-how is a subspecies of knowing-that.

3 For more discussion on this see, for example, Lum, 2003; Winch, 2008; Hager and Halliday (2006).

4 See for example the BBC article 'Cultural literacy: Michael Gove's school of hard facts' (Abrams, 2012).

5 See for example the 2004 National Curriculum (QCA, 2004: 23).

6 Of course, Dewey also saw reflection as a key part of learning, in so far as reflection itself expressed a sense of perplexity or hesitation and was thus a means through which further inquiry and problem resolution could be brought about.

7 Aristotle's account of *phronesis* is an important reference point for a number of recent attempts to re-investigate the notion of practical knowledge. Perhaps one of the key differences between Aristotle's account of practical reasoning and contemporary invocations of 'know-how' is the role Aristotle accords to judgement (for more discussion see Dunne, 1993; Smith, 2014).

8 Further aspects of this notion are discussed in Standish (2012; 2013).

9 Although here we focus on Heidegger and Cavell, this thematic can be perceived in a number of other thinkers such as Merleau-Ponty's (1945: 4) account of the sense of self that has 'already sided with the world … is already open to certain of its aspects, and synchronised with them'.

REFERENCES

Abrams, F. (2012). 'Cultural literacy: Michael Gove's school of hard facts', October 25. Retrieved May 10, 2014 from BBC News: http://www.bbc.co.uk/news/education-20041597

Backhurst, D. (2011). *The Formation of Reason*. Oxford: Wiley-Blackwell.

Bonnett, M. (1994). *Children's Thinking*. London: Cassell.

Britton, J. (1987). 'Vygotsky's contribution to pedagogical theory', *English in Education*, 21(3): 22–26.

Burbules, N. and Callister, T., Jr (2000). *Watch IT: The Promises and Risks of Information Technologies for Education*. Boulder, CO: Westview Press.

Cavell, S. (1969) Music Discomposed, in: *Must We Mean What We Say?* Cambridge: Cambridge University Press.

Cavell, S. (1979). *The Claim of Reason*. New York: Oxford University Press.

Davies, A.J. (2004). 'The credentials of brain-based learning', *Journal of Philosophy of Education*, 38(1): 21–36.

Derry, J. (2013). *Vygotsky: Philosophy and Education*. Oxford: Wiley-Blackwell.

Dunne, J. (1993). *Back to the Rough Ground: Practical Judgment and the Lure of Technique*. USA: Notre Dame Press.

Emerson, R. (1844) Experience Essays, Second Series, London: John Chapman.

Hager, P. and Halliday, J.S. (2006). *Recovering Informal Learning: Wisdom, Judgement and Community*. Dordrecht, Netherlands: Springer.

Heidegger, M. (2004 [1954]). *What is Called Thinking?* New York: Harper and Row.

Howard-Jones, P. (2014) *Neuroscience and Education*. Bristol: University of Bristol.

Lum, G. (2003). 'Towards a richer conception of vocational preparation', *Journal of Philosophy of Education*, 37(1): 1–15.

McGuinness, C. (1999). *From Thinking Skills to Thinking Classrooms*. Belfast: Gueen's University.

Merleau-Ponty, M. (1945). *Phenomenologie de la Perception*. Paris: Gallimard.

Oxford Dictionaries Online (2014). *Learning*. Retrieved 15 May 2014 from Oxford Dictionaries: http://www.oxforddictionaries.com/definition/english/learning

Qualification and Curriculum Authority (2004) *The National Curriculum*. London: QCA.

Rorty, R. (1979) *Philosophy and the Mirror of Nature*. Princeton, NJ: Princeton University Press.

Smith, R. (2014). 'Judgement calls: the ethics of educational deliberation', *Kultura Pedagogiczna*, 1: 101–114.

Standish, P. (1999). 'Only connect: computer literacy from Heidegger to cyberfeminism', *Educational Theory*, 49(3): 417–435.

Standish, P. (2012). '"THIS is produced by a brain-process!" Wittgenstein, transparency and psychology today', *Journal of Philosophy of Education*, 46(1): 60–72.

Standish, P. (2013). 'The vocabulary of acts: neuroscience, phenomenology, and the mirror neuron', in P. Smeyers and M. Depaepe (eds), *Educational Research: The Attraction of Psychology*, Vol. 6. Dordrecht, Netherlands: Springer, pp. 105–118.

Stanley, J. and Williamson, T. (2001). ' Knowing how', *Journal of Philosophy*, 98(8): 411–444.

Taylor, C. (1997). 'Overcoming epistemology', in C. Taylor, *Philosophical Arguments*. Cambridge, MA: Harvard University Press, pp. 1–19.

Williams, E. (2013). '"Ahead of all beaten tracks": Heidegger, Ryle and the ways of thinking', *Journal of Philosophy of Education*, 47(1): 53–70.

Winch, C. (1998) *The Philosophy of Human Learning*. London: Routledge.

6

A Dialogical Relationship with Cultural-Historical Activity Theory: A Realist Perspective

Iskra Nunez

INTRODUCTION

Imagine a dialogue of two persons in which the statements of the second speaker are omitted, but in such a way that the general sense is not all violated. The second speaker is present invisibly, his words are not there, but deep traces left by these words have a determining effect on the present and visible worlds of the first speaker. We sense that this is a conversation, although only one person is speaking, and it is a conversation of the most intense kind, for each present uttered word responds and reacts with its every fiber to the invisible speaker, points to something outside itself, beyond its own limits, to the unspoken words of another person.

Bakhtin, *Problems of Dostoevsky's Poetics*

In treatises on learning, the theses of Cultural-Historical Activity Theory (CHAT) and Critical Realism have received exceptional attention in recent years. Each of these theses makes a contribution to the conception of learning that stems from its particular notion of the dialectic, which, while inspired by the philosophies of Hegel and Marx, is different

and original in its own right. A Cultural-Historical Activity Theoretical understanding of dialectics informs a conception of learning that follows the logic of expansion; that is, expansion as 'a social and practical process, having to do with collectives of people reconstructing their material practice' (Engeström, 1987: 242). A Critical Realist understanding of dialectics informs a conception of learning that follows a logic of freedom; that is, freedom as 'a two-way process. Freedom is as much a condition of truth as vice versa, and in the learning process, which is the dialectic of theory and practice, each mutually informs the other' (Bhaskar, 2008b: 292). These two distinct albeit related dialectical concepts on learning form an initial motivation for initiating this dialogical relationship with Cultural-Historical Activity Theory on the basis of Critical Realism.

This chapter thus endeavours to make a contribution to the conception of learning through a dialogue with Cultural-Historical Activity Theory and Critical Realism. This combination of lenses has been employed in a wide variety of research studies, ranging from the need to theorize 'the relationship between the individual and society, rather than reducing one to the other' (Wheelahan, 2007: 195), and the practical resolution of contradictions in 'the introduction and expansion of sustainable agricultural practices in southern Africa' (Mukute and Lotz-Sisitka, 2012: 342), to new formulations of the dynamics of learning as 'a passage through the dialectic' (Nunez, 2014: xvii). The objective of this chapter is not to combine Cultural-Historical Activity Theory and Critical Realism, but to show how followers of the activity-theoretical school may benefit from engaging in dialogue with critical realists to, firstly, conceptualize the nature of reality, secondly, formulate a deeper understanding of the basic concept of contradiction, and, thirdly, transcend macro and micro dualisms of social theory and thus of those dualisms found in Cultural-Historical Activity Theory.

A DIALOGUE WITH CULTURAL-HISTORICAL ACTIVITY THEORY AND CRITICAL REALISM

Since its introduction in the late 1980s, there has been an exponential 'interest shown in Cultural-Historical Activity Theory over the past three decades' (Roth and Lee, 2007: 188). This interest reveals the range of applications of Cultural-Historical Activity Theory, from interventionist research encompassing the efforts of universities and schools 'in designing change in education' (Engeström et al., 2014: 129), to literature reviews on learning from 'contradictions as sources of change' (Nunez, 2009: 7), to empirical studies to resolve, for example, 'the dichotomy of individual and collective planes of activity' (Stetsenko, 2012: 70).

The activity-theoretical approach, originally formulated by Yrjö Engeström, set out to critique one-dimensional learning theories with a new theory of *expansive learning*.

The essence of [expansive] learning activity is production of objectively, societally new activity structures (including new objects, instruments, etc.) out of actions manifesting the inner contradiction of the preceding form of the activity in question ... [Expansive learning] is mastery of expansion from actions to a new activity. (Engeström, 1987: 125)

The Engeströmian system of activity-theoretical thought may be outlined as follows.

- Thesis (1): Cultural-Historical Activity Theory maintains the analytic primacy of collective over individual levels of labour with the *activity system*, an enhanced unit of analysis, depicted by a triangular array of six interconnected relations between the categories of subject, object, tools, division of labour, rules and community.
- Thesis (2): This collective activity system conveys its *multi-voicedness* in a pluralistic way to account for multiple perspectives.
- Thesis (3): The management of the *historicity* of the activity system aims to include the often-neglected cycles of historical development, without reducing the system's evolution to its biography.
- Thesis (4): The concept of *contradiction* puts forward the insufficient driver of transformation and development in the activity system. Methodologically, it differentiates between four types of contradiction: inner or primary contradictions, those that are internal to the activity system under investigation precisely because they may occur *within* each of the components that constitute it; secondary contradictions, which may occur between the six components; tertiary contradictions, which may occur between the objects of activity of two or more systems; and quaternary contradictions, which may occur between the main activity system under investigation and other surrounding analytic systems.
- Thesis (5): The possibility of learning collectively as a 'full cycle of expansive transformation' (Engeström, 2001: 137).

With the above five theses, this Engeströmian system offers a new epistemological approach focused on understanding and resolving 'the inner contradictions of capitalist production and organization of work' (Engeström, 2011: 75). In particular, the idea that 'transcending the dualism between thought and activity, theory and practice, facts and values has much in common with the theoretical aims of activity theory' (Engeström and Miettinen, 1999: 5). This theoretical objective in transcending dualisms may be understood as a reaction to the status quo in social theory and philosophy since these disciplines appear to be 'riven by dichotomies, ultimately reflecting social splits and contradictions, which are debilitating for social science and emancipation alike' (Hartwig, 2007b: 92). It is crucial to understand the philosophical predecessors of Cultural-Historical Activity Theory to gain insight into the possible causes of the dualisms referred to above.

CHAT'S PHILOSOPHICAL PREDECESSORS AND THE NEED TO THEORIZE REALITY

The activity-theoretical approach is rooted in a threefold legacy 'in classical German philosophy (from Kant to Hegel), in the writings of Marx and Engels and in the Soviet Russian cultural-historical psychology of Vygotsky, Leont'ev, and Luria' (Engeström, 1999: 20). Elsewhere, I have argued that in this legacy, starting with Kant, there is an omission of a critique of Hume and Humean classical empiricism (Nunez, 2013). The problem with this omission is that Cultural-Historical Activity Theorists may be prone to follow a Kantian philosophy of transcendental idealism. In other words, Kant's error was to inherit an implicit ontology, and thus accept a Humean theory of causal laws, including its dualistic implications, which functions as

a philosophical Trojan horse leading directly to sceptical despair. [This is because] Hume was fully aware of the sceptical implication of this theory [i.e. a theory of causal laws] ... Hume adopted the view that the immediate objects of the mind are always 'perceptions' because he thought it correct, and in spite of the fact that it leads to scepticism about the external world. Satisfied that the battle to establish absolutely reliable links between thought and reality had been fought and lost, [in his theory of causal laws] Hume made no attempt to explain how our impression of sensations are

linked to their entirely 'unknown causes'. (Norton, 2005: 399)

This Humean-Kantian issue is not the only problem in discussing the philosophical predecessors of Cultural-Historical Activity Theory. In the passage from German idealism to materialism, the notion of activity (or *Tätigkeit* in German) underwent a conceptual transformation, 'especially [since] in Marxist-Leninist theory, the meaning of "activity" was inflected towards a notion of "labour" and the material conditions of human productivity' (Hardcastle, 2009: 184). This shift brought with it other problems in translating psychological and philosophical concepts from German and Russian, to English (see e.g. Davydov, 1999; Engeström, 1999).

In the passage from Vygotsky and Leont'ev to other major influences on Soviet thought, we see the emergence of other Cultural-Historical Activity Theory problems. For example, in the emergence of the dualism of individual and collective levels of activity, which began to be theorized via the notion of a 'division of labour [and a methodological distinction] achieved by individual participation in the collective labour activity [i.e. the individual participation in groups or the individual participation of groups]' (Leont'ev, 1978: 408). Such a problem was justified 'in light of rhetorical goals of activity theorists at the early stages in developing this approach ... perhaps linked to the one-sided version of a communitarian ideology that prevailed in the Soviet Union' (Stetsenko, 2012: 80). Turning such communitarian ideology upside down perhaps leads to the hedonistic ideology prevailing in our Western democracies and rationalized by the logic of neo-liberal capitalism.

Other problems deal with the concept of contradiction. In Cultural-Historical Activity Theory, '[c]ontradictions are the necessary but insufficient engine of expansive learning' (Engeström, 2011: 78). This conception of contradiction derives its meaning from Ilyenkov's understanding of dialectics as described in what follows.

Objective reality always develops through the origin within it of a concrete contradiction that finds its resolution in the generation of a new, higher and more complex form of development; the contradiction is unresolvable. When expressed in thought it naturally appears as a contradiction in the determinations of the concept that reflects the initial stage of development ... A contradiction of that type in determinations is not resolved by way of refining the concept that reflects the given form of development, but by further *investigating reality*, by discovering another, new, higher form of development in which the initial contradiction finds its *real, actual, empirically* established resolution. (Ilyenkov, 1977: my emphasis)

In other words, contradiction is not conceptualized as an obstacle or impasse to development; rather, the resolutions of contradictions are seen as development's driving force in the world. With its dual legacy in Marx-Illyenkov, this notion forms part of the foundational principles of Cultural-Historical Activity Theory's 'analysis of the contradictory motives of human activities and human psyche in capitalist society' (Engeström and Miettinen, 1999: 5). A problem here is that most 'people who talk about contradictions have a wrong concept of contradiction' (Bhaskar and Hartwig, 2010: 21).

There are at least three main problems with this Marxian-Ilyenkovian understanding of contradictions, however. First, the notion of contradiction, in the Ilyenkovian sense, tends to be criticized because although it 'may reflect some deep contradiction in our thinking ... [it] can scarcely be said to reflect a contradiction in reality itself' (Bakhurst, 1991: 170). The immediate need is thus to *question the nature of reality*, including its constitution and structure. Second, the Marxian notion of contradiction tends to be criticized for being philosophically underdeveloped because in 'the overwhelming majority of cases, Marxists have not even suspected that there are *two* types of opposition [i.e. the Kantian *Realrepugnanz* and dialectical contradiction], and that they are radically different' (Colletti, 1975: 9). Third, a resolution to a contradiction or problem cannot occur in a manner that is internal to the activity

system alone; that is, employing the same thinking that created it. This is because '[f]or Marx the solution to an internal contradiction of the structures of the relations of production is not created solely by the internal development of this contradiction. The greater part of the conditions of this solution is outside the contradiction, and *irreducible* to its content' (Godelier, 1967: 108, my emphasis).

To deepen Cultural-Historical Activity Theory's concept of contradiction, Critical Realism provides a reading of Marx's analysis of contradiction that refines the basic concept in such a way as to differentiate five species of contradiction: (1) *logical inconsistencies*, referring to intra-discursive logical/theoretical anomalies (e.g. the logical contradiction A = Not A); (2) *non-dialectical oppositions*, referring to extra-discursive opponents (e.g. the Kantian *Realrepugnanz* or the conceptually mediated forces of supply and demand); (3) *structural* or *synchronic contradiction*, referring to a social form in particular (e.g. use-value versus exchange-value); (4) *geo-historically specific dialectical contradictions*, referring to crises that require a course of development and transformation that such contradictions enable to manifest (e.g. between the relations and forces of production); and (5) a *generative separation*, referring to a split (e.g. the alienation of the workers/producers from the materials/means of their production) (Bhaskar, 2008b: 64–5). Thus, we see that the need for philosophical under-labouring for Cultural-Historical Activity Theory is at least threefold: to theorize the nature of reality, including its constitution and structure; to deepen our understanding of the basic concept of contradiction; and to resolve various dualisms in social thought.

PHILOSOPHICAL UNDER-LABOURING FOR CULTURAL-HISTORICAL ACTIVITY THEORY

The use of Critical Realism as an under-labourer for Cultural-Historical Activity Theory may provide a new theory of reality, deepen its basic conception of contradiction, and resolve its dualisms. But what does under-labouring mean? It denotes, after the British empiricist John Locke, the purpose of philosophy for critical realists. Unlike empiricism, however, philosophical under-labouring 'entails clarifying and explicating what it is the sciences do and how they do it, as well as, on occasion, criticizing existing scientific practices for failing to meet the standards of scientificity they set for themselves' (Sprinker, 1992: 123).

In particular, the focal premise of this section is that Basic Critical Realism may under-labour for Cultural-Historical Activity Theory. Three main groups of theory constitute Basic Critical Realism. The first group is Transcendental Realism, which is a philosophy of science. The second group is Critical Naturalism, which is a philosophy of social science. The third group is the theory of Explanatory Critique, which is a philosophical theory of value. The formula BASIC CRITICAL REALISM = TRANSCENDENTAL REALISM + CRITICAL NATURALISM + EXPLANATORY CRITIQUE conveys these foundations. Here we outline Transcendental Realism as a philosophy of science capable of providing Cultural-Historical Activity Theory with a non-empiricist, non-Humean ontology, which shows how Critical Naturalism is capable of resolving prevailing dualisms in social thought and in Cultural-Historical Activity Theory.

This philosophy of science, as understood in Transcendental Realism, has long been preoccupied with theorizing 'ontology, not epistemology' (Sayer, 2000: 78). On the one hand, ontology is the branch of philosophical inquiry most generally concerned with the study of being. In other words, the realm of ontology focuses on 'the nature, constitution, and structure of reality. It is broader in scope than science, e.g. physics and even cosmology [since] it investigates questions science does not address but the answers to which it presupposes' (Butchvarov, 2005a: 563). On the other hand, epistemology is the branch of philosophical inquiry centrally concerned with the study of knowledge. In other words, the realm of epistemology includes the models and various other means by which to acquire knowledge about being and thus focuses on 'the scope and limits of human knowledge' (Norris, 2007: 335). The issues generated by either a gap or a conflation between these two distinct branches of philosophical inquiry, that is, the branch of knowledge created by human beings (epistemology) and the other independent of them (ontology), have accounted historically for the different types of naïve realist, non-realist and anti-realist views of the world.

EXEMPLIFYING NAÏVE REALIST, NON-REALIST AND ANTI-REALIST THESES

In the widest possible sense, a realist view of reality starts from the following triad of theses.

(a) [T]here are real objects (usually the view is concerned with spatio-temporal objects), (b) they exist independently of our experience or our knowledge of them, and (c) they have properties and enter into relations independently of the concepts with which we understand them or of the language with which we describe them. (Butchvarov, 2005b: 562)

Gravity and peer pressure are examples of such real objects in the natural sciences and in the social sciences, respectively. A double problem for realism is that it tends to be 'dismissed as obvious, and replaced by a non-realist account which is supposedly less "naïve"' (Collier, 1994: 3). Because 'Cultural-Historical Activity Theorists are generally naïve realists' (Blunden, 2009: 5), the exemplification of realist, non-realist, and anti-realist perceptions concerns them. To illustrate, let us consider the following example of global warming.

Non-realists err in presupposing that global warming is merely an idea that is causally generated by human beings' imagination, much like unicorns. Anti-realists err in presupposing that global warming is a mere concept that is created by our discourses without an account for the causal mechanisms that generate it. Naïve realists err in presupposing that the winning argument about global warming, the effects of which are no less real for having been discovered, depends on the techniques and interventions of human beings to account for it. For realists, global warming is a real object, which means that there are mechanisms (actualized or not) that determine its structure and causes, and thus how it works; these causal mechanisms are the internal workings, the enduring powers of this real object that exist quite independently of our daily experience or our (practical or theoretical) knowledge of them; and these causal mechanisms have properties and enter into a flux of relations at various levels of reality independently of the concepts and discourses with which we generally describe this phenomenon.

What is missing in our conception of learning about, for example, global warming but also learning in general, is a theory of realism capable of a scientifically informed non-reductionist vision of the world. Concurring with this view, 'activity theory (also taken up by many followers of this school) needs to be resolved to move to new levels of a consequentially materialist and non-reductionist theory' (Stetsenko, 2012: 80). Hence, the theory of realism that this chapter argues for as appropriate to the activity-theoretical approach is Critical Realism. In what follows, I provide a brief introduction to its foundational principles.

A BRIEF INTRODUCTION TO TRANSCENDENTAL REALISM

In the mid-1970s, Roy Bhaskar published *A Realist Theory of Science* to theorize ontology through a problematization of the assumptions about the nature of the world required for science to occur. In it, he put forward the foundations of Critical Realism, the above-mentioned Transcendental Realism, with a double argument; namely,

the separation of ontology from epistemology and the inclusion of epistemology as part of ontology (Bhaskar, 2008a: 11–14).

In Transcendental Realism, the Bhaskarian system also included ideas with which to theorize a structured and differentiated world into three nested domains, $d_{empirical} < d_{actual} < d_{real}$, i.e. the x < y formula means that x is argued to be contained in the larger realm of y. The domain of the empirical ($d_{empirical}$) is argued to be constituted by our experiences. The actual is argued to be constituted by events and experiences. The real is argued to be constituted by causal mechanisms that tend to be out-of-phase with both events and also experiences in open conditions (Bhaskar, 2008a: 35–47).

To see parallels between Cultural-Historical Activity Theory and this view of reality, it is crucial to refer the reader to Ilyenkov's understanding of dialectics 'in which the initial contradiction finds its *real, actual, empirically* established resolution' (Ilyenkov, 1977: my emphasis). This quotation suggests that Bhaskar drew upon such Ilyenkovian ideas to conceptualize $d_{empirical} < d_{actual} < d_{real}$ as the structured and differentiated nature of reality. A problem with Ilyenkov's under-development of the *real, actual, empirically* established domains of reality results in a failure to observe the gaps between these domains in open systems. Any closure between them, that is when $d_{empirical} = d_{actual} = d_{real}$, is argued to be possible only under experimental conditions in the laboratory.

Furthermore, the failure to observe the gap between the realm of ontology and the realm of epistemology (epistemology = ontology) is argued to result in the *epistemic fallacy*, 'the analysis or definition of statements about being in terms of statements about our knowledge of being' (Bhaskar, 2008b: 397); the failure to observe the gap between ontology and language in the most general sense (discourse = ontology) is argued to result in the *linguistic fallacy*, 'the analysis of being as our discourse about being' (Bhaskar, 2008b: 192); and the failure to observe the gap between the domains of the actual and the real ($d_{actual} = d_{real}$) is argued to result in *actualism*, 'the view that causal laws are constant conjunctions of events which overlooks that invariances are normally experimentally produced results under artificially closed conditions and that closures are the exceptions outside the laboratory' (Hartwig, 2007a: 15).

SUMMARY OF SECTION

To sum up this section, the activity-theoretical approach has long been preoccupied with theorizing epistemology primarily, not ontology. Cultural-Historical Activity Theory's philosophical predecessors, in the legacy that begins with Kant, followed by Hegel, Marx and the Soviet school of thought, provide the ideas for its quintuple set of foundations in (1) an *activity system* that puts primacy on collective labour, (2) a *multi-voiced* awareness of different perspectives, (3) a Marxian-Ilyenkov concept of *contradiction* that includes (4) the idea of *historicity* to avoid reductionist views, and learning as (5) an *expansive transformation*. It is in these philosophical precursors that there is the starting point of (a) an empiricist, implicit Humean, ontology; (b) elements in the philosophical under-development of basic concepts, such as in the nature of reality and in the concept of contradiction; and (c) the seeds of various dualisms. We have seen that Basic Critical Realism = Transcendental Realism + Critical Naturalism + Explanatory Critique, and this may be important particularly for activity theorists as it provides the following conceptual arsenal.

- Thesis (1): The ontology/epistemology gap and the all-encompassing notion of ontology (epistemology < ontology).
- Thesis (2): The epistemic fallacy (epistemology = ontology).
- Thesis (3): The linguistic fallacy (discourse = ontology).
- Thesis (4): A model of a stratified and differentiated reality ($d_{empirical} < d_{actual} < d_{real}$).

- Thesis (5): The fallacy of actualism ($d_{actual} = d_{real}$).
- Thesis (6): The difference between open and experimentally closed systems.
- Thesis (7): Ontologically developed concepts of eight species of contradictions.

To continue with a critical realist and Cultural-Historical Activity Theory dialogue, it is necessary to outline Critical Naturalism as a philosophy of science and explain how it might be capable of resolving prevailing dualisms in social thought and in Cultural-Historical Activity Theory.

OUTLINING DUALISMS IN SOCIAL THEORY → RESOLUTIONS VIA CRITICAL NATURALISM

What is wrong with dualisms? Whereas a non-pejorative understanding of 'duality encompasses a valid categorical distinction, *dualism* [or dichotomy] embodies a false one on the categorical error of fission or split' (Hartwig, 2007c: 150). With the goal of transcending dualisms, Bhaskar published *The Possibility of Naturalism* in the late 1970s. This publication provided the thesis of Critical Naturalism (see Bhaskar, 2005). In particular, Critical Naturalism explained that the philosophy of social science, and to an extent substantive social theory, is characterized by the following set of micro and macro dichotomies, and provided for their resolution through their corresponding concepts (denoted below by → and outlined in Hartwig (2007b: 92)).

Macro dualisms are:

1 Collectivism (holism) versus individualism → a resolution via Social Relationism.
2 Reification versus voluntarism (structure versus agency) → a resolution via a Transformational Model of Social Activity (TMSA).
3 Naturalism versus anti-naturalism (positivism versus hermeneutics or nature versus society) → a resolution via Critical Naturalism (non-positivist).

Micro dualisms are:

a   Body versus mind (together with reductionism) → a resolution via Synchronic Emergent Powers Materialism.
b   Causes versus reasons → a resolution via reasons being, when acted upon, causes.
c   Facts versus values → a resolution via Explanatory Critique.

By outlining Engeström's (1999: 21–3) six dichotomies of Cultural-Historical Activity Theory, we see that these fall into the micro and macro dualisms of social theory, and we identify them below, with comments in brackets.

1   Psychic process versus object-related activity [i.e. the dualisms of body versus mind (together with reductionism) → Critical Naturalist resolution via Synchronic Emergent Powers Materialism; and causes versus reasons → a Critical Naturalist resolution via reasons being, when acted upon, causes].
2   Goal-directed action versus object-related activity [i.e. the dualisms of body versus mind (together with reductionism) → a Critical Naturalist resolution via Synchronic Emergent Powers Materialism; and causes versus reasons → a resolution via reasons being, when acted upon, causes].
3   Instrumental tool-mediated production versus expressive sign-mediated communication [i.e. the discursive fallacy → a resolution via a commitment to minding the gap between ontology and discourse, addressed in Section – A brief introduction to transcendental realism].
4   Relativism versus historicism [i.e. the dualism of facts versus values → a resolution via an Explanatory Critique].
5   Internalization versus creation and externalization [i.e. the dualisms of reification versus voluntarism (structure versus agency) → a Critical Naturalist resolution via a Transformational Model of Social Activity; and collectivism versus individualism → a Critical Naturalist resolution via Social Relationism].
6   The principle of explanation versus the object of study [i.e. the epistemic and discursive fallacies → resolutions via a commitment to minding the gaps between ontology and epistemology and ontology and discourse, addressed in Section – A brief introduction to transcendental realism].

In addition, it is worth outlining Davydov's (1999: 39–49) eight unsolved complications for Cultural-Historical Activity Theory to illustrate the much-needed philosophical under-labouring performed by Critical Naturalism. These are the problems of:

1   Understanding transformation [i.e. the limits of dialectics → a resolution via a critical realist understanding of dialectics of change as freedom in absenting absences in the ontology of transformation].
2   Collective and individual activity [i.e. the dualism of collectivism versus individualism → a Critical Naturalist resolution via Social Relationism].
3   Structure and components of activity [i.e. the dualism of reification versus voluntarism (structure versus agency) → a Critical Naturalist resolution via a Transformational Model of Social Activity].
4   Different kinds of activity [i.e. the dualisms of reification versus voluntarism (structure versus agency) → a Critical Naturalist resolution via a Transformational Model of Social Activity; and collectivism versus individualism → a Critical Naturalist resolution via Social Relationism].
5   Understanding communication [i.e. the discursive fallacy → a resolution via a commitment to minding the gap between ontology and discourse, addressed in Section – A brief introduction to transcendental realism].
6   Connections to other theories [i.e. the epistemic fallacy → the trinity of interdisciplinary research beginning with a commitment to minding the gap between ontology and epistemology, addressed in Section – A brief introduction to transcendental realism].
7   The biological and the social [i.e. the dualism of body versus mind (together with reductionism) → a Critical Naturalist resolution via Synchronic Emergent Powers Materialism].
8   Organizing interdisciplinarity [i.e. the epistemic fallacy → the trinity of interdisciplinary research beginning with a commitment to minding the gap between ontology and epistemology, addressed in Section – A brief introduction to transcendental realism].

There is more than can be said here about a complete resolution of all the micro and macro dualisms (for a more complete analysis, see Nunez (2013)). Instead, we focus our attention on the third and fourth dualisms referred to above and their resolution via the key ideas of the Transformational Model of Social Activity and Social Relationism.

TMSA AS A RESOLUTION OF THE DICHOTOMY OF STRUCTURE VERSUS AGENCY

The dualism between structure and agency refers to the problem of voluntarism versus reification. Where voluntarism goes wrong is in presupposing that social structures – relatively autonomous objects such as social institutions, culture, language, and so on – are simply the product of agency reflected in the production of individuals' wishes and desires. Where reification goes wrong is in presupposing that social structures exist independently of agency and the efficacy of individual's actions to impact relatively the conditions and organization of social structures.

Both Cultural-Historical Activity Theory and Critical Realism agree on the double-feedback effect between structure and agency, as shown below.

> [I]nternalization is related to reproduction of culture, [and] externalization is the creation of new artefacts that makes possible its transformation. These two processes are interpretably intertwined. Roy Bhaskar, elaborating on the notion of emancipatory social activity [TMSA], comes to essentially the same conclusion. (Engeström and Miettinen, 1999: 10)

Cultural-Historical Activity Theory's internalization-externalization resolution, however, does not take into account, firstly, the temporal element in which structure precedes agency, and, secondly, the fact that actions of agents still serve to reproduce the social structure (of activity), albeit unwillingly. For example, a couple might get married for reasons other than to reproduce the social structure of marriage.

In contrast, Critical Naturalism resolves the structure/agency dualism with the

Transformational Model of Social Activity concept, which features two levels: first, the level at which the agent is producing or a achieving a certain result, and second, the level of the social structure, which, in their substantive activity, agents reproduce or transform. The Transformational Model of Social Activity emphasizes that

> people do not create society. For it always pre-exists them and is a necessary condition for their activity. Rather, society must be regarded as an ensemble of structures, and practices and conventions, which individuals produce or transform, but which would not exist unless they did so. Society does not exist independently of human activity (the error of reification). But it is not the product of it (the error of voluntarism). (Bhaskar, 2005: 36)

SOCIAL RELATIONISM AS A RESOLUTION OF THE DICHOTOMY OF COLLECTIVISM (OR HOLISM) VERSUS INDIVIDUALISM

The dualism of individualism and collectivism (or holism) refers to the problem of methodologically identifying the proper unit of analysis for the social sciences. Where individualism goes wrong is in, firstly, reducing the notion of society to individuals and, secondly, reducing all phenomena to behaviour or events without relations and without social structures. Where collectivism goes wrong is in confusing the unit of analysis of the social sciences, i.e. its subject matter, with the study of either the analysis of behaviour in groups or the analysis of the behaviour of groups.

While Cultural-Historical Activity Theory's resolution of the collectivism/individualism dichotomy is epistemological, a Critical Realist critique is ontological. On the one hand, Cultural-Historical Activity Theory employs the activity system, intended 'to enable an examination of systems of activity at the macro-level of *the collective* and the community *in preference* to a micro-level concentration on *the individual actor*' (Daniels, 2004: 123, my emphasis). Although this resolution emphasizes the relations between its six components (subject, object, tools, division of labour, rules and community), it tends to encourage a view that often misconstrues the nature of the macro-level of society as the object/motive of individual activity in groups or the object/motive of individual activity of groups (the error of collectivism). By contrast, Critical Naturalism builds upon the nature of society, theorized with the Transformational Model of Social Activity model, to propose a relational conception of society, or Social Relationism.

[Social relations] exist only in virtue of material things, possessing no material substance of their own (i.e. they are 'VIRTUAL' or 'ideal') and so are in principle imperceptible (non-empirical), hence can only be ascribed as real causally, by their effects on material things. Or their material presence consists only in their effect on material things. (Hartwig, 2007d: 410)

This idea emphasizes the point that we are dealing with relations, such as the relations between husband and wife, worker and employer, student and teacher, and so on, at a number of different, irreducible ontological levels.

SUMMARY OF CHAPTER

This chapter has allowed us to see the limits of dialectics inspired by the philosophies of Hegel and Marx, as interpreted by Cultural-Historical Activity Theory and critiqued by Critical Realism, which are nevertheless still important for a more complete explanation of the concept of learning through firstly, a realist ontology, secondly, a deepening of the basic concept of contradiction, and thirdly, a resolution of dualisms in social thought. The significance of this dialogical interaction with Cultural-Historical Activity Theory and Critical Realism has allowed us to open up a space for critique, especially in the introduction of this ontologically grounded theory of activity.

REFERENCES

Bakhtin, M. M. (1984) *Problems of Dostoevsky's Poetics*. Edited and translated by Caryl Emerson, Minneapolis: University of Minnesota Press.

Bakhurst, D. (1991) *Consciousness and Revolution in Soviet Philosophy: From the Bolsheviks to Evald Ilyenkov*, Cambridge: Cambridge University Press.

Bhaskar, R. (2005) *The Possibility of Naturalism: A Philosophical Critique of the Contemporary Human Sciences*, London: Taylor and Francis (1st edition, 1979).

Bhaskar, R. (2008a) *A Realist Theory of Science*, London: Taylor and Francis (1st edition, 1975).

Bhaskar, R. (2008b) *Dialectic: The Pulse of Freedom*, London: Taylor and Francis (1st edition, 1993).

Bhaskar, R. and Hartwig, M. (2010) *The Formation of Critical Realism: A Personal Perspective*, London: Routledge.

Blunden, A. (2009) 'An interdisciplinary concept of activity', *Critical Practice Studies*, 11(1): 1–26.

Butchvarov, P. (2005a) 'Metaphysics', in R. Audi (ed.), *The Cambridge Dictionary of Philosophy*, Cambridge: Cambridge University Press, pp. 563–6 (1st edition, 1995).

Butchvarov, P. (2005b) 'Metaphysics Realism', in R. Audi (ed.), *The Cambridge Dictionary of Philosophy*, Cambridge: Cambridge University Press, pp. 562–3 (1st edition, 1995.)

Colletti, L. (1975) 'Marxism and the dialectic', *New Left Review*, 93(4): 3–29.

Collier, A. (1994) *Critical Realism: An Introduction to Roy Bhaskar's Philosophy*, London: Verso.

Daniels, H. (2004) 'Activity theory, discourse and Bernstein', *Educational Review*, 56(2): 121–32.

Davydov, V. V. (1999) 'The content and unsolved problems of activity theory', in Y. Engeström, R. Miettinen, and R. L. Punamäki-Gitai (eds), *Perspectives on Activity Theory*, Cambridge: Cambridge University Press, pp. 39–52.

Engeström, Y. (1987) 'Learning by expanding: an activity-theoretical approach to developmental research', PhD dissertation, Orienta-Konsultit Oy, Helsinki.

Engeström, Y. (1999) 'Activity theory and individual and social transformation', in Y. Engeström, R. Miettinen, and R. L. Punamäki-Gitai (eds), *Perspectives on Activity Theory*, Cambridge: Cambridge University Press, pp. 19–38.

Engeström, Y. (2001) 'Expansive learning at work: toward an activity theoretical reconceptualization', *Journal of Education and Work*, 14(1): 133–56.

Engeström, Y. (2011) 'Activity theory and learning at work', in M. Malloch, L. Cairns, K. Evans and B. N. O'Connor (eds), *The SAGE Handbook of Workplace Learning*, Thousand Oaks, CA: SAGE, pp. 86–104.

Engeström, Y. and Miettinen, R. (1999) 'Activity theory: a well-kept secret', in Y. Engeström, R. Miettinen, and R. L. Punamäki-Gitai (eds), *Perspectives on Activity Theory*, Cambridge: Cambridge University Press, pp. 1–15.

Engeström, R., Batane, T., Hakkarainen, K., Newnham, D. S., Nleya, P., Senteni, A. and Sinko, M. (2014) 'Reflections on change labouratory: toward a dynamic interplay of global and local forces in designing change in education', *Mind, Culture, and Activity*, 21(2): 129–47.

Godelier, M. (1967) 'System, structure and contradiction in capital', *Socialist Register*, 4(4): 91–119.

Hardcastle, J. (2009) 'Vygotsky's Enlightenment precursors', *Educational Review*, 61(2): 181–95.

Hartwig, M. (2007a) 'Actualism', in M. Hartwig (ed.), *Dictionary of Critical Realism*, London: Routledge, pp. 14–16.

Hartwig, M. (2007b) 'Critical naturalism', in M. Hartwig (ed.), *Dictionary of Critical Realism*, London: Routledge, pp. 91–6.

Hartwig, M. (2007c) 'Duality and dualism', in M. Hartwig (ed.), *Dictionary of Critical Realism*, London: Routledge, pp. 149–50.

Hartwig, M. (2007d) 'Relationality', in M. Hartwig (ed.), *Dictionary of Critical Realism*, London: Routledge, pp. 410–11.

Ilyenkov, E. (1977) *Dialectical Logic*, translated by H. Campbell Creighton, Moscow: Progress Publishers (http://www.marxists.org/archive/ilyenkov/works/essays/essay10.htm).

Leont'ev, A. N. (1978) *Activity, Consciousness, and Personality*, Englewood Cliffs, NJ: Prentice-Hall (1st edition, 1975).

Mukute, M. and Lotz-Sisitka, H. (2012) 'Working with Cultural-Historical Activity Theory and critical realism to investigate and expand farmer learning in Southern Africa', *Mind, Culture, and Activity*, 19(4): 342–67.

Norris, C. (2007) 'Ontology', in M. Hartwig (ed.), *Dictionary of Critical Realism*, London: Routledge, pp. 334–8.

Norton, D. F. (2005) 'David Hume', in R. Audi (ed.), *The Cambridge Dictionary of Philosophy*, Cambridge: Cambridge University Press, pp. 398–403.

Nunez, I. (2009) 'Contradictions as sources of change: a literature review on activity theory and the utilisation of the activity system in mathematics education', *Educate*, 9(3): 7–20.

Nunez, I. (2013) 'Transcending the dualisms of activity theory', *Journal of Critical Realism*, 12(2): 141–65.

Nunez, I. (2014) *Critical Realist Activity Theory: An Engagement with Critical Realism and Cultural-Historical Activity Theory*, London: Routledge.

Roth, W. M. and Lee, Y. J. (2007) '"Vygotsky's neglected legacy": Cultural-Historical Activity Theory', *Review of Educational Research*, 77(2): 186–232.

Sayer, A. (2000) *Realism and Social Science*, London: SAGE.

Sprinker, M. (1992) 'The royal road: Marxism and the philosophy of science', *New Left Review*, 1(191): 122–44.

Stetsenko, A. (2012) 'Activity as object-related: resolving the dichotomy of individual and collective planes of activity', *Mind, Culture, and Activity*, 12(1): 70–88.

Wheelahan, L. (2007) 'Blending activity theory and critical realism to theorise the relationship between the individual and society and the implications for pedagogy', *Studies in the Education of Adults*, 39(2): 183–96.

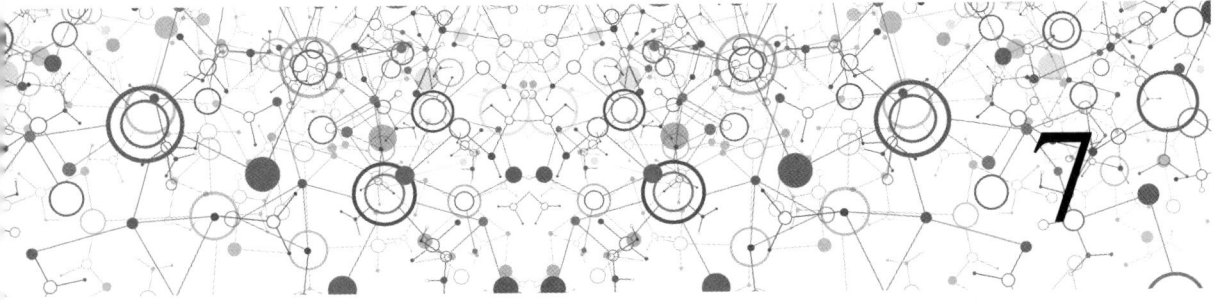

7

Deleuze and Learning

David R. Cole

INTRODUCTION

This chapter will examine the philosophical and intellectual oeuvre of the French philosopher, Gilles Deleuze. The work that this chapter attempts to do is to give access to the learning theory of Deleuze without overly simplifying or unnecessarily reducing the complexity of his ideas. Gilles Deleuze (1925–1995) was a philosopher who worked for the majority of his life as an intellectual and university academic. He was propelled into the public eye in 1972, after the success of his first collaborative work with Félix Guattari, called *Anti-Oedipus*. Deleuze did not write a book on learning, or specifically on education as such, so we must piece together his ideas on learning from comments interspersed from within his oeuvre. Despite this apparent lack of direct information and analysis of learning, Deleuze's ideas have recently begun to gain traction in many educational and creative circles (see Cole, 2011a). Perhaps this is because Deleuze

provides what he described as 'a conceptual toolbox' (Deleuze, 1980: 17), which can be readily applied to other areas such as education in terms of a philosophical framing and theoretical base that resists dogmatism and encourages the novel and imaginative (re) creation of theory and practice. In this chapter, I will argue that this conceptual toolbox does not represent a *free-for-all* in terms of an *anything-goes* learning and educational theory, but, on the contrary, the Deleuzian toolbox is in many ways deliberately hard to accept and necessarily challenging to put into action.

Deleuze's most direct statements with respect to learning come in his book on *Difference and Repetition*. In it, he says: '… "learning" always takes place in and through the unconscious, thereby establishing the bond of a profound complicity between nature and mind' (Deleuze, 1994: 165). This is the last sentence of a paragraph on problematic ideas, and an explanation of how we learn to swim with respect to the idea of the sea. Deleuze's argument is that we learn to swim in the sea not by opposing the sea in dialectical fashion nor by deconstructing it, still less by imposing a person's will upon the waves in a mythological, Cnut style. According to Deleuze, we learn through an apprenticeship with signs, education is 'amorous yet fatal' (Deleuze, 1994: 23), in the case of swimming in the sea, the swimmer is able to cope with the waves and the currents of the seas, not by copying or repeating their existence and forms, or through any processes of familiarisation or thoughts about being a 'natural sea swimmer', but by becoming attuned over time to the way in which one has to swim in the seas in order to survive and stay afloat. Deleuze (1994: 23) states that we learn from teachers who say 'do with me' and not from teachers who say 'do as I do'; in other words, learning is a necessarily complex and relational process (including elements of non-relation), which makes questioning of accepted knowledge an imperative and working together communally around knowledge problems essential. Inna Semetsky (2009) has suggested that Deleuze's approach to learning solves Plato's paradox in *Meno* about learning in that the production of new knowledge according to Socrates is merely the function of memory or recollection. Plato surmised that all knowledge is locked in the unconscious, so that we don't learn at all, but recollect what we already know through the recognition of truths through argumentation and Socratic dialogue. Deleuze (1994) turns this formulation around in *Difference and Repetition*, in that the unconscious is no longer a passive receiver of knowledge and the memory the active disseminator of knowledge. Contrariwise, the unconscious does profoundly synthetic and positive, i.e. paradoxically conscious, work according to Deleuze, through the clashing of affect and the playing with chaotic material processes through, for example, creative experimentation. The unconscious is in the Deleuzian frame a creative and vital cauldron of new thought. However, to get to this new vision of the unconscious as the place that learning fundamentally happens, one has to first attend to issues concerning philosophy and the image of thought that it has projected over time.

PHILOSOPHY AND LEARNING

Deleuze executed a number of philosophical studies during his career, specifically focusing on the philosophies of David Hume, Friedrich Nietzsche, Henri Bergson, Benedictus de Spinoza, Immanuel Kant, Michel Foucault and Gottfried Leibniz. However, these books do not constitute a history of philosophy as such, nor do they provide straightforward commentaries on the philosophy of these named thinkers. Rather, one could argue that Deleuze executed these studies to come up with new thought, in order to question the classical or accepted image of thought, and to ultimately produce a philosophical system that promotes learning through the unconscious and nature, and questions knowledge as given. One could argue that every philosophy produces an image of thought, even Deleuze's project to come up with a new image of thought and to return the thought of the philosophers to learning. Deleuze's project is to enable an image of thought that may be infinitely divisible or possible to be differentiated *in-itself*, until thought and learning themselves become apparent to the thinker and learner. In terms of western metaphysics, one could argue that the dominant and most far reaching 'image of thought' comes from Plato in terms of what constitutes metaphysics. Deleuze (1994) could be positioned as one of many thinkers who have tried to overcome Plato's image of thought, yet the approach that he takes in *Difference and Repetition* is distinguished from many others in that the eight postulates that he proposes in order to question the dogmatic image of thought suggest an ultimate escape route from representation as the basis for metaphysics in general into learning *per se*, and not only with reference to Plato.

The eight postulates from *Difference and Repetition* (see below) constitute a framing of the dogmatic image of thought that specifically attempts to dismantle the manner in which thought has been created and recreated more recently through thinkers such as Kant and Heidegger. According to Deleuze, Kant and Heidegger create dogmatic images of thought because their systems for thought must be understood before any new thought can happen. The eight postulates signify a means to fully examine such images of thoughts, and to allow for unthoughts, non-thoughts and, importantly given the context of this chapter, learning through the unconscious and nature to make its way into a *new arena for thought*. One could argue that everything that Deleuze writes after the 'Image of Thought' section of *Difference and Repetition* during his career relates to these postulates in some way, and is an attempt to create thought without an image that makes philosophy more democratic and fully open to novel reinterpretation. One could argue that this proposition is perhaps most fully realised in the rhizomatics of *1000 Plateaus*, because the 'rhizomic text' and multiple conceptual elements of *1000 Plateaus* attempt to fully engage with the notion of immanence, including how immanence relates to time, power and the fluctuations present in everyday life (see, for example, Cole, 2013). Immanence is for Deleuze the great levelling concept, which makes new thought accessible beyond a philosophical specialism, seen, for example, in Kant or Heidegger, and learning in the moment becomes apparent. The eight Deleuzian postulates, that a new image of thought and any consequent learning from Deleuze rest upon, are:

THE EIGHT POSTULATES: from *Difference and Repetition* (Deleuze, 1994: 167)

1 The Postulate of the Principle, or the *Cogitatio Natural Universalis*: the good will of the thinker and the good nature of thought.
2 The Postulate of the Ideal, or Common Sense: common sense as the *concordia facultatum* and good sense as the distribution that guarantees this accord.
3 The Postulate of the Model, or of Recognition: recognition presupposes the harmonious exercise of our faculties on an object that is supposedly *identical* for each of these faculties, and the consequent possibility of *error* in the distribution when one faculty confuses one of its objects with a different object of another faculty.
4 The Postulate of the Element, or Representation: difference is subordinated to the complementary dimensions of the *same* and the *similar*, the *analogous* and the *opposed*.
5 The Postulate of the Negative, or of Error: error expresses everything that can go *wrong* in thought, but only as a product of *external* mechanisms.
6 The Postulate of the Logical Function, or the Proposition: designation or denotation [theory of reference] is taken to be the locus of truth, sense being no more than a neutralised double or the infinite doubling of the proposition.
7 The Postulate of the Modality, or Solutions: problems are materially traced from propositions, or are formally defined by the possibility of them being solved.
8 The Postulate of the End or the Result, or the Postulate of Knowledge: the subordination of learning to knowledge, and of culture [or *paideia*] to method.

These eight postulates from *Difference and Repetition* work on the level of problematising and questioning the image of thought. The first two postulates refer to the ways in which philosophers have made implicit agreements between themselves about what thought is and what thought should be. These agreements might jeopardise learning according to Deleuze. Likewise, postulates three and four refer to the ways in which philosophical systems have produced models and represented the image of thought as the 'self-same'. The philosophical systems of Kant and Heidegger are good examples of these types of thinking models or modes of representation that require thinking through their tenets before any new thought or learning can happen. Postulate five is a reference to the Hegelian system of thought that prioritises negation in thought to create difference (see Somers-Hall, 2012), therefore making learning dependent on the negation of, for example, the thought of nature and the unconscious, which is exactly what Deleuze wants learning to connect with. Postulates six and seven refer to propositional logic and how the definition of the image of thought in these terms can produce thought that excludes problems that do not fit with the strictures of propositional logic, i.e. irrational and illogical thought. Learning itself would also be trammelled along the lines of propositional logic according to these postulates. Postulate eight refers to the ways in which knowledge can dominate learning and create methods that intercede and take away from the force of culture. Deleuze wants to return thought to learning and culture, and not to a set of pre-defined methods or sets of instructions that can take away from the impact and veracity of new thought.

One needs to systematically go through the postulates from *Difference and Repetition* to arrive at the last postulate, number eight, that directly relates to learning, and is the starting point for a new metaphysics of learning from Deleuze that disavows representation in thought, i.e. gets back to learning *qua* learning and not the thought of learning. Deleuze (1994: 167) in *Difference and Repetition* immediately qualifies and questions the eight postulates and says that they function best in silence. How can we make sense of the notion that the thought that escapes the dogmatic image of thought through the eight postulates returns us to a state of learning, and hence helps to reverse the traditionally philosophical or classical 'image of thought' and its accompanying dogmas, and is born 'in thought' (Deleuze, 1994: 167)? In terms of philosophical analysis, the genesis of 'the image of thought' and the consequent critique of the image of thought through the eight postulates comes from Deleuze's earlier (1983) book, *Nietzsche and Philosophy*.

Here, Deleuze begins his eventual yet sustained move away from the tenets of representative thought, and looks to understand how Nietzschean forces may power thought, such as the contrast between reactive (moral) forces and life affirming forces. One could

argue that according to Nietzsche, paramount amongst the forces of reaction and affirmation is the force of now, which congeals everyday forces from a contemporary perspective that may work to corrupt and subjugate the mobility of thought. In Nietzschean terms, the power of the philosopher is derived from the ability to think (and learn) outside of the prejudices, clichés and banalities contained in the social forces of the contemporary situation. This is why Nietzsche refined his writing technique to such an extent in order to come up with a new form of aphoristic writing that attempted to pierce the bubble of contemporary values and thought, and that could execute a powerful critique on the image of thought connected to 'now' and to reconnect thinking with learning. In consequence, Nietzsche teaches us to be wary of contemporary fashion and to exercise our critical and affective energies when approaching thought, which might turn out to be merely reactive or responding to moral, narrow-minded, reproductive or power-based dictates. This is one of the reasons why Deleuze qualifies his eight postulates with silence and with their birth 'in thought', which means they are precisely designed to escape the clamour of the contemporary moment, and in order to connect to learning, the unconscious and to nature. The concern to make Deleuze's postulates receptive to and part of an exploration of the unconscious predominantly comes from his examination of the formulation of the drives for thinking in Nietzsche and in the writing processes of Proust in *Proust and Signs*.

In *Proust and Signs* the section on 'the image of thought' concerns the ways in which the thinking of the philosopher can miss out on specific types of knowledge, aesthetic sensitivities, the learning that comes from the heart, and the thought processes contained in Proust's writing style. Proust's *In Search of Lost Time* sets up a wholly different image of thought to the philosophical image of thought, and it is through understanding the processes contained in the writing of this book that one is able to go beyond the rational, historic and communal assumptions of the philosophers as listed by the eight postulates. Deleuze's argument in *Proust and Signs* is that the writing of Proust adds to the endeavours and insights of the philosophers, and that Proust is himself philosophical, precisely because he out-manoeuvres what Plato calls, 'simultaneously contrary perceptions' (Deleuze, 2000: 101). In other words, Proust has the ability to write around such perceptions, and to make art of them, or to touch upon 'sensations common to 2 places, to 2 moments' (2000: 101). Proust is a Deleuzian exemplar of a writer who is able to deal with involuntary signs in a creative way and in a manner which forces us to think and learn.

Parallel to Nietzsche, who is a thinker out of time (as exemplified by Zarathustra), Proust is a thinker of time. Proust creates an image of thought that does not represent the tropes of our time, but gets inside the mechanisms of time to encounter fleeting affects, an apprenticeship in signs and the delayed action in thought and learning. In Proust's writing, obvious and scenic or exterior imagery is substituted for the time dimension to produce what Deleuze and Guattari (1988: 380) describe in *A Thousand Plateaus* in a parallel manner, and with reference to nomadism, as: '(a)ll of thought is a becoming, a double becoming, rather than the attribute of a Subject and the representation of a Whole'. For Deleuze, Proust and Nietzsche allow for and give mobility to thought through their art and hence show us what the image of thought is through learning, the unconscious and nature. As has been noted above, and in contrast to, for example, Kant and Heidegger, whose intellectual comprehension requires steadfast study of the structural aspects of *their* thought before new thought can happen, i.e. with respect to Being, the faculties of thought and the possibility of experience, according to the approach of Deleuze, Proust and Nietzsche have injected freedom into the construction of thought and into the consequent image of thought with respect to how new thought and learning happens.

However, if we accept Deleuze's notion of thinking and learning and how it proceeds empirically, we must be able to configure these processes in the world in some way. This point comes about not because Deleuze's transcendental empiricism as he names this approach in *Difference and Repetition* requires any extra-sensory or universal validity; but because the ways in which we can make sense of the eight postulates, learning and the image of thought that they refer to must relate in some way to practice. This is because it is in practice that the Deleuzian postulates can reach their tipping points and any breakthrough in the image of thought towards learning can be realised; i.e. immanently, and in tandem with a concern for power. However, to get to this juncture in 'learning practice' (see Cole and Hager, 2010), one must first pass through Deleuze's two most powerful and well-known collaborations with the French anti-psychiatrist, Félix Guattari, called *Anti-Oedipus* and *A Thousand Plateaus*.

SCHIZOPHRENIA, CAPITALISM AND LEARNING

Gilles Deleuze is perhaps best known for his dual writing projects with the French theorist and activist, Félix Guattari, which resulted in two extraordinary books that focused on the relationships between schizophrenia and capitalism. These works are almost impossible to summarise and deserve multiple readings before one comes close to understanding their range and importance. However, for the purposes of this chapter, I will attempt to make a connection between the theme of this writing, i.e. Deleuze's notion of learning and the multifarious aspects of Deleuze and Guattari's writings on capitalism and schizophrenia. Firstly, a coherent line of argumentation appears if we follow the 'image of thought' discussion that was raised by Deleuze in *Nietzsche and Philosophy*, *Proust and Signs* and in *Difference and Repetition* and applied to the *Capitalism and Schizophrenia* texts. The basic argument taken from Deleuze's early texts with respect to learning and in relation to the 'image of thought', is that if one questions the image of thought as it has appeared in philosophical texts such as those of Kant and Heidegger, Hegel or Schopenhauer, one is able to come closer to thought *qua* learning as a form of transcendental empiricism (Deleuze, 1994).

Learning can henceforth be achieved because one is able to effectively critique the 'difference as difference' of these texts and the repetitions in thought set up by the philosophers as dogma. In consequence, one is able to make wider and more profound connections through thought, i.e. via the unconscious and with nature. The wider connections, that Deleuze and Guattari are interested in *Anti-Oedipus* and *1000 Plateaus*, concern capitalism and schizophrenia, which are taken as two poles in the contemporary, fluctuating situation. The point of analysis here is not that we are all becoming more schizophrenic due to capitalism or that schizophrenia is directly caused by capitalism. The analysis that is given by Deleuze and Guattari (1984) subtends towards the processes invoked by capitalism that can have long-term psychoanalytic effects which could be bracketed and organised through the rubric of schizophrenia.

Deleuze changes the name of his philosophical approach in *Difference and Repetition*, which he termed as 'transcendental empiricism', to 'transcendental materialism' in *Anti-Oedipus*. However, the transcendental aspect of the approach advocated by Deleuze in both texts is not transcendent, i.e. leading to a type of exploration of the conditions for experience or of 'I', and as we find, for example, in Kant. Rather, the transcendental in *Difference and Repetition* refers to the difference and repetition of empirical events and thought embodied as partial objects and through learning. In *Anti-Oedipus*, the transcendental refers to the material flow of things that pass through the (de)centred subject in a parallel manner to Whitehead's (1929) panpsychism, which lends mind to objects in the world through process.

In the case of *Anti-Oedipus* and *A Thousand Plateaus*, a dizzying array of conceptual and intellectual units, methods and ideas are invented and made apparent that link schizophrenia with capitalism such as: (re-) and (de-)territorialisation, coding, decoding and over-coding, rhizomatics, desire and desiring-machines, assemblage, the Body-without-Organs or BwO, the war machine, abstract machines, the plane of immanence and schizoanalysis. Rather than trying to futilely and half-heartedly explain this rich array of theoretical constructions from the two capitalism and schizophrenia volumes, I will relate these ideas to learning in order to discern the manner in which we learn in the current social and psychological situation according to the approach that can be gleaned from Deleuze and Guattari's two most famous books.

Deleuze and Guattari's aim in their *Capitalism and Schizophrenia* books is to understand the underlying psychic, cognitive and affective processes that pass through us and to an extent determine and play with our beings and becomings as we live through the dictates of capitalist social life. For example, Deleuze and Guattari (1984: 190) take the fact of debt and how the reality of debt has expanded and broadened beyond the confines of straightforward, flesh-to-debt relationships that one finds, for example, in pre-modern societies that literally mark the body of the debtors. Today, the reality of debt is pan-global and complex as the lines of credit have been extended from small communities of inter-dependents and the overlords of their land and territory. The identifiable overlord figure has been replaced by a mixture of banking systems, mortgage-credit-finance packages, as were exposed during the 2008 global financial crisis, state systems and their taxation, bond and monetary systems, interest rates, student loans, corporate finance systems and consumer debt arrangements.

In sum, the relationship between learning and debt has complexified, as the notion of debt itself has gone from a recognisable bodily practice of power exemplified by marking and scarring, to an omnipresent form of financial control and submission. In many countries, debt now accompanies most college- or university-level study and learning, and reaches down into the education system as a whole through private education. Unless one is literally able to pay the study fees upfront (i.e. one comes from a privileged, previously capitalised position), one is caught in the web of debt over time, as soon as one goes to university and starts to study and learn. Of course, this new global reality of unrestrained and global finance capitalism has consequences for what one learns and how one learns, as the debt incessantly mounts up and repayments incur interest. Under these conditions, one inevitably plays it safe and chooses a subject to study that should lead to a high-earning career, which will facilitate the repayment of the debt as quickly as possible. Moreover, these conditions of debt have effects on the body and mind as well as practical lifestyle and career choices.

Deleuze and Guattari's (1984, 1988) complex interlinked arguments about capitalism and schizophrenia importantly include the incursion of machines into the frame about what it is like to live, think and learn in the contemporary capitalist situation. Machines are not a metaphor for the way we think and learn under the present conditions, but machines termed as 'the machinic' are a literal means to grasp the effects on desire that being in debt for the whole of your life can have, as can be expressed through the conjunction 'desiring-machines'. Importantly, the insertion of the machine is not a categorical or projective stance taken by Deleuze and Guattari (1984, 1988) to replace the human self with something less comforting, but opens up, for example, a passage to understand how debt can disturb the way one learns and thinks. As one goes ever further into debt – which is ironically often framed by metaphors of freedom and self-reliance – the necessity to make up the time of repayment becomes an imperative. A type of restlessness and agitation overwhelms the agent as

the reality of the financial interest rates and the timeframe of debt looms, and this psychic disturbance may be interpreted through forms of mental disease such as depression, neurosis, psychosis or schizophrenia. The agent ultimately incorporates debt into themselves as a dead part of his or her being. One could say that debt is a machinic form of non-becoming that doesn't change other than as a number or percentage, and is an anathema to the chaos of the natural world, or the creativity of the unconscious imagination – furthermore, debt importantly affects the desire of the agent. The desires of the agent becomes embroiled by debt as 'machinic-desire', and as a form of the death-drive or as constant repetitions of financial repayments that (re) figure life as a tunnel with financial salvation at the end of that tunnel, and the only possible light coming from inheritance or from receiving some great windfall from an unexpected source.

Clearly, under these conditions, one does not learn in the way that Deleuze states in *Difference and Repetition*, i.e. in contact with nature and through the creativity of the unconscious. On the contrary, one could argue that the way one learns under capitalism is funnelled through debt repayment and having the means to make these instalments. However, Deleuze and Guattari (1984, 1988) do not give a simple, moralistic interpretation of the capitalised situation, and attribute all evil or wrongdoing to the beneficiaries and elites of capitalism. Rather, they offer a sophisticated analysis of how the present situation has been arrived at, and how we can diagnose and explore the symptoms of what capitalism can do to us. Deleuze and Guattari (1984, 1988) show that the question of the precise effects of capitalism on the contemporary psyche is a complicated and convoluted one, that it is based in non-linear history and in developments in the ways in which we socialise and produce collectives, and, furthermore, these processes have developed significantly since the time of their two major publications. It is clear that children now learn through online environments and social media such as Facebook as well as at school or in informal face-to face situations (see Cole and Pullen, 2010).

The online environments are often fully connected to commercial interests, and this pressure to accept commercial dictates as norms has therefore intensified since the specific time of Deleuze and Guattari's *opus maxima* during the 1970s. One can read Deleuze and Guattari's work on capitalism and schizophrenia as a sophisticated extension of Guy Debord's (1994) analysis of the *Society of the Spectacle* in that: '[i]n societies where modern conditions of production prevail, all of life presents itself as an immense accumulation of spectacles. Everything that was directly lived has moved away into a representation' (Debord, 1994: 3). In Deleuze and Guattari (1984), the representation of life and learning is enacted by the three synthesises of capitalism (connective-disjunctive-conjunctive), and these cannot be directly opposed, but only followed as flows and diverted through intense thought and a new mode of learning if we take Deleuze at his word.

IMPLICATIONS OF 'DELEUZIAN LEARNING' FOR EDUCATIONAL PRACTICE

The most direct question with respect to the perspective that one may derive from Deleuze and that pertains to learning is: What is the point of articulating the Deleuzian perspective on learning? In an attempt to answer this question, I will list the possible ways in which Deleuze's philosophy may be taken up by educational practitioners and researchers:

1   The eight postulates as listed above in the philosophy and learning section of this chapter can be used for what could be termed Deleuzian critical-thinking-practice. This practice involves examining texts and the representation of thought, e.g. cinema, in order to understand the image of thought on offer and the assumptions and dogmas inherent in those thoughts.

2   The application of 'Deleuzian learning' to literacy learning opens up the field away from border control work around illiteracy and (re)introduces other multiple literacies that could be overlooked in the everyday life of the classroom (see Masny and Cole, 2009).

3   The nature of schools as sedentary markers in society, and therefore schooling as such, and the conditioning processes in schooling, e.g. institutionalisation, are put under pressure due to the application of Deleuzian learning as a practice.

4   The value of the end processes of learning such as final examinations is seriously questioned according to the Deleuzian approach to learning. Deleuze and Guattari would applaud formative types of assessment as well as quality feedback and the playing with the authority of having the 'right' answer or even reframing the question. Of paramount importance to Deleuzian learning is the process of thinking as has been described above.

5   Deleuzian learning puts emphasis on experimentation, role playing and the questioning of global power games. At the heart of this practice would be an affinity with environmental concerns and the nonhuman world and the subversion of commercial culture as a banal imposition on what one learns. For example, many 'innovations' in educational practice are merely attempts by educational software designers to sell their new products.

6   The unconscious is not an inaccessible other, but at the centre of Deleuzian learning. This means that exercises designed to stimulate the unconscious are important markers with respect to what one should do as an educator influenced by Deleuze. For example, one should be able to act spontaneously and in the moment following unexpected cracks in the set curriculum according to Deleuze.

7   Deleuzian learning indicates a move away from right-wing, market-based influences in education, often described under the rubric of 'neoliberalism'. This point of Deleuzian learning is not to head for a utopic, anarchic, communist or agrarian state, but to create a space wherein other forms of socialisation may become apparent in the future through education.

8   Educational policy and curriculum design may be complexified and made more responsive to context and change if the principles of Deleuzian learning were applied.

Lastly, Deleuzian learning rests on affect, and the ways in which affect circulates in life. Hence, affect needs to be recognised as a major component in all educational contexts (see Cole, 2011b).

CONCLUSION

If one compares Deleuze's ideas on learning with, for example, John Hattie's (2009) recent book called *Visible Learning*, one could state that many of Deleuze's thoughts on learning describe a form of 'invisible learning'. Deleuze designates pre-personal, fluctuating grounds for learning that can seem to be worlds apart from the systematic analysis of the factors and strategies for improving the efficiency of learning environments as analysed statistically by Hattie (2009). However, if one digs deeper into the two approaches to learning represented by Deleuze and Hattie, one can realise that the two positions are not so far apart. Deleuze is not averse to scientific and mathematical explanation of phenomena; in fact he deploys such means frequently in his writing with respect to, for example, 'singularities' and 'the virtual'.

The difference in the two approaches to learning is that Hattie (2009) stops at the 'effect size' of every strategy or factor in learning from the more than 800 meta-analyses that he appropriates, which enables him to be able to produce a ranking of the effects sizes. In contrast, Deleuze has analysed philosophy, literature, cinema, capitalism, science and history to come up with his notion of learning. Certainly, one could argue that Deleuze's notion of learning requires evidence-based studies of the type that Hattie (2009) has used in his ranking of the effects sizes of factors and strategies to enhance learning. I believe that this is a task for future educators and future education researchers that have been influenced by the work of Deleuze to attend to, as they work together to make changes in mainstream educational provision. Deleuze's philosophical and intellectual approach to learning has the capacity to radically alter the course of educational practice beyond the short term, and to make a difference in terms of the measurable 'effect sizes' as calculated by Hattie (2009) in the close analysis of educational provision.

REFERENCES

Cole, D. (2011a) *Educational Life-forms: Deleuzian Teaching and Learning Practice*, Rotterdam: Sense Publishers.

Cole, D. (2011b) 'The actions of affect in Deleuze – others using language and the language that we make ...', *Educational Philosophy and Theory*, 43(6): 549–61.

Cole, D. (2013) *Traffic-jams: Analysing Everyday Life through the Immanent Materialism of Deleuze and Guattari*, New York: Punctum Books.

Cole, D. and Hager, P. (2010) 'Learning-practice: the ghosts in the education machine', *Education Inquiry*, 1(1): 21–40.

Cole, D. and Pullen, D. (eds) (2010) *Multiliteracies in Motion: Current Theory and Practice*, London and New York: Routledge.

Debord, G. (1994) *The Society of the Spectacle*, translated by D. Nicholson-Smith, New York: Zone Books.

Deleuze, G. (1980) 'A Thousand Plateaus' [newspaper article], *Libération*, 23 October, p. 17.

Deleuze, G. (1983) *Nietzsche and Philosophy*, translated by H. Tomlinson, London: The Athlone Press.

Deleuze, G. (1994) *Difference and Repetition*, translated by P. Patton, New York: Columbia University Press.

Deleuze, G. (2000) *Proust and Signs*, translated by R. Howard, London: The Athlone Press.

Deleuze, G. and Guattari, F. (1984) *Anti-Oedipus: Capitalism and Schizophrenia*, translated by R. Hurley, M. Steem and H.R. Lane, London: The Athlone Press.

Deleuze, G. and Guattari, F. (1988) *A Thousand Plateaus: Capitalism and Schizophrenia II*, translated by B. Massumi, London: The Athlone Press.

Hattie, J. (2009) *Visible Learning: A Synthesis of over 800 Meta-Analyses Relating to Achievement*, London and New York: Routledge.

Masny, D. and Cole, D. (2009) *Multiple Literacies Theory: A Deleuzian Perspective*, Rotterdam: Sense Publishers.

Semetsky, I. (2009) 'Deleuze as a Philosopher of Education: Affective Knowledge/Effective Learning', *The European Legacy: Toward New Paradigms*, 14(4): 443–56. DOI: 10.1080/10848770902999534.

Somers-Hall, H. (2012) *Hegel, Deleuze and the Critique of Representation: Dialectics of Negation and Difference*, Albany: SUNY Press.

Whitehead, A. (1929) *Process and Reality: An Essay in Cosmology*, Gifford Lectures Delivered in the University of Edinburgh During the Session 1927–1928, Cambridge, UK: Cambridge University Press.

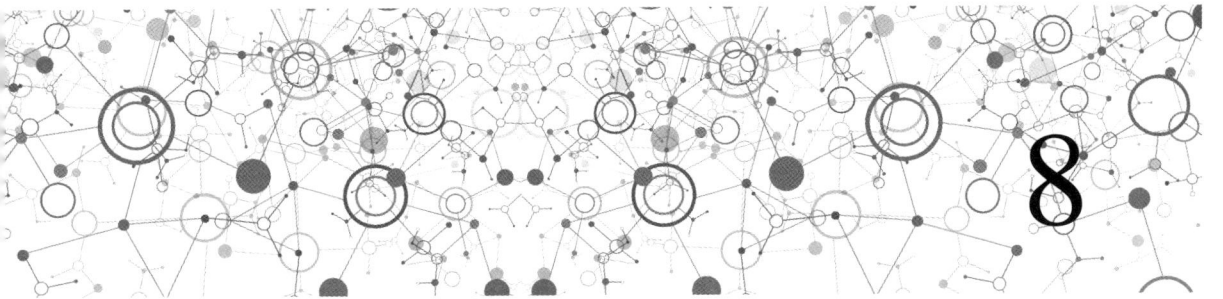

Sociomateriality and Learning: A Critical Approach

Tara Fenwick

INTRODUCTION

As many have argued throughout this volume, context is critical: learning cannot be considered effectively if the sole focus is upon individual cognitive processing. The content and process of learning change dramatically as it pulses through particular situations and discourses, the tools available, technologies, social relations and environmental dynamics. Conventional metaphors of knowledge 'acquisition' and transfer are being replaced with understandings of 'participation' and active collective engagement in particular contexts. Thus we have seen a vast swarming of interest in examining learning in 'communities of practice', experiential or informal learning, and notions of 'expansive' affordances for learning in situated environments. These sociocultural orientations have eschewed representationalist conceptions of knowledge that continue to dominate educational curricula. They explore ways that learning and knowing emerge in action, including the ongoing action that brings forth the objects and identities constituting our worlds. These views also have been important for interrupting fixed notions of knowledge as powerful packages of ideas developed by some and ingested by others; the others are assumed to be individual learning minds who can be tested for attaining acceptable levels of both ingestion and subjectivisation.

Yet notions of participation take us only so far. The community of practice approach has been critiqued not only for its conservatism, managerialism and limited analysis of power relations in learning situations, but also for its romantic notions of 'community', and its vague analyses of practice and participation (Hughes, Jewson and Unwin, 2007). Context may be critical, but to treat context as an abstract container is to miss the turmoil of relationships among these myriad non-human as well as human elements that shape, moment to moment, particular dynamics of context.

Materials – things that matter – are often missing from accounts of learning and practice. Materials tend to be ignored as part of the backdrop for human action, dismissed in a preoccupation with consciousness and cognition, or relegated to brute tools subordinated to human intention and design. This treatment still tends to privilege the intentional human subject, which is assumed to be different or separate from the material; the material is the non-human. In educational research therefore, Sørensen argued in 2009 that there was a 'blindness toward the question of how educational practice is affected by materials' (p. 2), a consequence of which was a general tendency to grossly underestimate materials as mere instruments to advance educational performance.

Today, however, it is fair to acknowledge a growing educational interest in understanding everyday material and social inter-relations: why *matter* matters, and how to unpick the abstractions that can blind us to the microdynamics that influence everyday practices. This interest moves beyond the nineteenth-century materialism of Marx or Nietzsche, informed by Newtonian mechanics, to materialist understandings enlivened by twentieth-century insights of new physics and fractal geometry, dark matter and multiple causality, biotechnical innovations, the frighteningly rapid proliferation of powerful software, and new materialist studies of power circulating through discursive practices. Researchers have pressed for much more recognition of the ways that materials *actively* configure practice and knowing. Educators working from sociomaterial approaches are encouraging learners to attend to these quotidian material details that stitch together their practice, knowledge and environments – not just to *attune* very closely to the connections, but also to *tinker* and improvise, to interrupt, and to seize emerging possibilities.

What socio-material approaches offer to educational research are resources to systematically consider both the patterns as well as the unpredictability that makes educational activity possible. They promote methods by which to recognise and trace the multifarious struggles, negotiations and accommodations whose effects constitute the 'things' in education: students, teachers, learning activities and spaces, knowledge representations such as texts, pedagogy, curriculum content, and so forth. Rather than take such concepts as foundational categories, or objects with properties, they become explored as themselves effects of heterogeneous relations. Finally, sociomaterial perspectives offer important approaches for understanding the power relations and politics that constitute learning: not just analytic tools for picking apart the ways powerful webs become assembled as knowledge, but also pointing to affirmative ways to intervene, disturb or amplify these webs. These ideas are particularly useful for reconsidering what it means to promote 'critical learning', which arguably is a central concern for educators at all levels.

The remaining discussion is divided into four main sections. The first offers some examples from current educational research. These are diverse, but help to illustrate the questions and understandings that are emerging through sociomaterial approaches. The second overviews certain theoretical understandings that are associated with the different perspectives that can be roughly grouped into the category 'sociomaterial'. The third examines questions of politics and critique in terms of insights from different sociomaterial sensibilities. The fourth returns to issues of learning, suggesting implications for educators who might be interested in adopting a critical sociomaterial approach in developing learning. The overall sociomaterial argument is about shifting from a subject-centred view of learning that insists upon the overriding importance of the personal and the social, to accepting a more-than-human world (see Richard Edwards, this volume) and what it means for education.

HOW MATTER *MATTERS* IN LEARNING AND EDUCATION

Practices of knowing are specific material engagements that participate in (re)configuring the world. (Barad, 2007: 91)

Materials – objects, bodies, technologies and settings – permit some actions, and prevent others. They convey particular knowledges, and can become powerful. Think of how everyday things such as doors, seat belts, keys and car parks are indeed political locations where values and interests are negotiated and ultimately inscribed into the very materiality of the things themselves – thereby rendering these values and interests more or less permanent. Waltz (2006) is one who argues strongly for attention to things in educational research. He claims that material non-human things too often are analytically subsumed by human intention, design and drive and treated merely as representatives of human ends. As tools, the role of non-human things is typically limited to extension, transportation, distribution and prevention. Overall, this subjugation of things to humans obscures their own particular contributions and hides the qualities of the entities themselves. One example Waltz (2006: 56) offers is the school playground, where equipment combines with children's behaviours to produce particular activities, speech, social groupings and exclusions, injuries, even gender identities. The point is here that material things are performative. They act, together with other types of things and forces, to exclude, invite and regulate particular forms of participation. What then is produced can appear to be 'gender identity' or 'expertise' or 'knowledge' or a social 'structure' such as racism. A focus on things therefore helps us to untangle the heterogeneous relationships holding together these larger categories, tracing their durabilities as well as their weaknesses.

The aim here is not simply to identify the things involved in learning, but to make visible and analyse the particular relations among them. The focus is on relational materiality, or patterns of materiality infused with affect, power relations and cognition. This is quite different to conceiving a material world as inherently separate from a human world of consciousness and interpretation, and then reinstating links between them. In explaining this critical notion of material relations in terms of human learning, Hultman and Lenz Taguchi (2010: 536) put it this way:

> We can never reflect upon something on our own; to reflect means to inter-connect with something. This corresponds to Latour's concept of infra-reflection that takes into account that reflection is always done in the midst of a complex network and thus immanent to a wide variety of forces and never the product of an isolated individual that reflects upon something from an external point of view (see Latour, 1988). Thinking is not something that is grounded on a decision or a rational cataloguing of different external objects: rather, it is an event that happens to us – it 'hits us' or 'invades us'.

Sørensen (2009), in fact, argues that even to speak of 'relations' is to reify a sense of well-defined entities that become linked. In her own research on the materiality of learning, Sørensen traces the patterns that emerge in education to produce different learning practices. Things matter, not as discrete and reified objects with properties, but as effects of dynamic materializing processes that cause them to emerge and act in indeterminate entanglements of local everyday practice. For example, she examines the children's learning activities at a blackboard, then in a classroom project to build a bed loft, and finally in an online virtual environment. Each material pattern produces different forms of knowledge (representational, communal, and what she calls 'liquid'), and different performances of human presence. Her conclusions are that:

> Liquid knowledge is inseparable from learning. Representational knowledge can be stagnant. It is not dependent on learning taking place, and it is indifferent to whether or not learning takes place. Communal knowledge can endure without learning, but, when learning happens, the communal knowledge is affected. The ongoing mutation that characterizes liquid knowledge is the epitome of learning. (Sørensen, 2009: 131)

Sociomaterial studies also have brought new insights to issues of intercultural learning and inclusive education. Verran, for example, has been illuminating cross-cultural implications of materiality and learning. One of her most influential studies (Verran, 2001) examined how Nigerian Yoruba children learned science concepts in schools that employed British curricula dictating abstract Western notions about what numbers represent and how they can be manipulated (e.g. measuring volume, quantities and distance and calculating changes in matter). But Yoruba scientific understandings are ontologically very different: they begin with particular sorts of matter and then generate units appropriate to quantify that matter in the here-and-now. What surprised Verran was finding that Yoruba children not only learned to inhabit these two profoundly different accounts of what was real, but that the children also could move across both sociomaterial worlds working-thinking with the same objects: choosing one reality or the other, or juggling both simultaneously. Verran (2007: 34–5) characterised this as 'learning to manage knowing along with doubt; weaning oneself from certainty that is allowed by working within just one metaphysical frame'. For her, it showed that children can learn to interrupt the very structures of knowledge, to recognise multiple ways of enacting reality, and even to intervene among these different realities.

These are just a few examples of the alternative understandings of learning that can be yielded through sociomaterial analysis, when educators permit themselves to explore the radical suggestion that 'entities lie suspended between enactments of their possibilities' (Verran, 2007: 38). But let us pause to examine more closely the theoretical bases being employed in these 'sociomaterial' approaches to educational research.

WHAT ARE SOCIOMATERIAL PERSPECTIVES?

A range of theoretical 'families' emerging in educational research can be described as sociomaterial, from actor-network theory (and 'after-ANT') or 'new materialisms' to complexity theory, to name only a few.[1]

These families each have very different theoretical and ontological roots, and have developed particular traditions in their different scholarly fields such as philosophy, political science, science and technology studies, human geography, theoretical physics and organisation studies. This chapter can only provide a very brief introduction to certain shared commitments and approaches across these theories. One danger of this tactic, of course, is its potential to suggest that these theoretical families are more or less the same, as though there were a single 'sociomaterial' theory to apply to learning. There is not, and social science researchers drawing from these perspectives are usually very careful to situate their particular analysis in terms of one particular set of ideas and writers. Another danger in presenting the similarities is that useful theoretical details and debates will necessarily be obscured, oversimplified, or omitted. However, for newcomers to this whole area, the aim here is to point to the range of contributions and questions for educators that are opened in different regions of this rich new theoretical landscape. A secondary aim is to avoid promoting any one theory in particular as the only or the 'best' sociomaterial approach. Hopefully, interested educators will pursue in greater depth the studies suggested by the references provided.

SHARED COMMITMENTS

What all of these perspectives tend to share, first, is a *focus on materials* as dynamic, and enmeshed with human activity in everyday practices. This is what Orlikowski (2010) describes as the constitutive entanglement of the social and material. 'Material' refers to all the everyday stuff of our lives that is both organic and inorganic, technological and natural: flesh and blood, forms and checklists, electronic records and databases, furniture and passcodes, snowstorms and dead cell zones, and so forth. 'Social' refers to symbols and meanings, desires and fears, and cultural discourses. Both material and social forces are mutually implicated in bringing forth everyday activities. This is an understanding of relationships that pushes beyond assumptions that objects and subjects *interact*, as though they are separate entities that develop connections. Instead, sociomaterial accounts examine what the physicist Barad (2007) describes as *intra*-actions of heterogeneous elements of nature, technologies, humanity and materials of all kinds. These elements and forces penetrate one another – they act together – to bring forth what appear to be actors, objects and phenomena of everyday life.

This is a second shared understanding: that all materials or, more accurately, all sociomaterial objects, are in fact *heterogeneous assemblages*. They are gatherings of *heterogeneous* natural, technical and cognitive elements. All objects and material settings embed a history of these gatherings in the negotiation of their design and accumulated uses, whether lecture halls, presentation software, testing instruments, essays, pedagogical protocols, etc. In examining particular educational practices, researchers ask how and why particular elements became assembled, why some elements become included and others excluded, and, most important, how elements change as they come together, as they *intra*-act.

Third, most sociomaterial perspectives – in different ways – accept the fundamental *uncertainty* of everyday life, as well as of the knowledge, tools, environments and identities that are continually produced in it. Unpredictable novel possibilities and patterns are always *emerging*. This may be a familiar notion, but sociomaterial theories offer specific analytic tools that can examine much more precisely just how these new webs or assemblages are emerging – why they come together to produce and mobilise particular effects, and when they do not. These are processes that complexity theory explains in terms of 'strong emergence' (see Deborah Osberg, this volume), actor-network theorists

call 'translation', and Deleuzian new materialists call 'becoming'. The focus is on the relations between things; how things influence and alter one another in ways that are continuously opening as well as foreclosing new possibilities.

Fourth, a sociomaterial perspective tends to views all things – human, and non-human, hybrids and parts, knowledge and systems – as *effects* of connections and activity. Everything is *performed* into existence in webs of relations. Materials are enacted, not inert; they are matter and they matter. They *act*, together with other types of things and forces, to exclude, invite, and regulate activity. This is not arguing that objects have agency: an essay does not write itself. But its particular production is an agentic assemblage of assignment protocols and literary traditions, books and other content sources (entailing all the materialities of library line-ups, slow internet browsers, fortuitous tweets, etc.), post-it notes and piles of paper and iPads, the particular affordances and directives of word processing software – all working in and through human bodies and consciousness. Any educational practice is a collective sociomaterial enactment, not a question solely of one individual's skills or agency.

'Agency' is a problematic term for some sociomaterial researchers. Some refuse to use it altogether with its associations of human individuals' intention, initiative and exercises of power. The categories of 'structure' and 'agency' have long histories and deeply embedded assumptions: using these categories in analysis as though they are inherently valid or real begs many questions for sociomaterial researchers about the predetermined relations that are set in motion. Others like Orlikowski (2010) write about agency as relational and distributed capacity. Bennet (2010), a political philosopher, argues that agency is possible only through assemblages whereby human desire and interests are infused in things like ageing transmission wires, understaffed power plants, buildings with increased demand for electricity, energy trading corporations, deregulation policies, and a brush fire – to cite her example of the massive 2003 New York City blackout. The important issues are not *where* agency is located or *what* kind of agency is human or non-human, but rather the profound uncertainty about the nature of action, and controversies about how agency is distributed. Holifield (2009) points out that sociomaterial analyses register a range of competing accounts of agency, seeking to understand not what agency *is* but how certain accounts of it become stabilised. When agency is recognised as a distributed effect produced in material webs of human and non-human assemblages, Bennett suggests that a more responsible, ecological politics is possible. For education, this touches a core purpose for learning, which will be discussed further in the third section of this chapter.

DIFFERENT INTERESTS, DIFFERENT APPROACHES

For those who are interested in more in-depth exploration, a primer to these sociomaterial perspectives is available elsewhere (Fenwick, Edwards and Sawchuk, 2011). Those that appear most frequently in contemporary research of educational practice and learning include actor-network theory and 'after-ANT' approaches, complexity theory, new geographies, 'new materialisms', practice theory and activity theory. ANT emerges from poststructural orientations, and is more a diffuse cloud of sensibilities than a theory given its many internal contestations among key writers such as Latour (2005) and Mol (2002). Many terms in the literature such as 'relational materiality', 'material semiotics', STS (science and technology studies), and 'sociotechnical' studies share core commitments with ANT. Its lasting influences are a networked view of reality, and a radical treatment of human and non-human elements as equal contributors to the 'networks' that continually assemble and reassemble to generate particular activities, objects and knowledge. A lengthy discussion of ANT and 'after-ANT' studies in education is available (Fenwick and Edwards, 2010).

Complexity theory is quite different in orientation, another range of competing approaches emerging not from sociology but chiefly from evolutionary biology and physics (as well as cybernetics and general systems theories). Complexity theorists Barad (2007), Osberg (2008), and Davis and Sumara (2006) have become particularly influential in educational studies, suggesting that we examine dynamics of 'emergence', diffraction, and connectivity in practices of knowing.

Turning to new human and cultural geographies, these theories examine the material spaces and places of educational practice to show how they help produce the social, but are also produced by human activity and meaning. In education research, geographers such as Doreen Massey, Thrift and Lefebvre are widely influential in sociomaterial analyses (e.g. see Gulson and Symes, 2007).

Another branch of studies that is gaining much traction in education is calling itself the 'new materialisms' (Coole and Frost, 2010; Dolphijn and van der Tuin, 2012). These often work from ideas of philosopher Gilles Deleuze such as immanence, creativity and assemblage to examine how particular social and material forces bring forth very different ways of being.

Cultural-historical activity theory or CHAT is becoming widely taken up in education research (see Harry Daniels, this volume), and is thoroughly developed methodologically. However, some would argue that CHAT does not really belong with 'sociomaterial' studies, given its fundamentally different material analysis rooted in a structural Marxist explanation of the relations of capitalist production and the internal contradictions of activity systems. And, while CHAT emphasises the importance of material artefacts that mediate human activity systems, these are secondary to its central concern for *human* activity: divisions of labour, cultural rules and languages, and social purposes.

Finally, it is important to mention the growing educational interest in 'practice theory', working from conceptions of 'knowing-in-practice' as enactments performed through assemblages that are more-than-human (Gherardi and Strati, 2012; Hager, Lee and Reich, 2012).

Obviously this chapter cannot provide adequate explanation of these and other sociomaterial orientations. Also omitted here are discussions of all these theories' limitations. Critique and rejoinders abound, as one would expect in any vibrant and maturing field, and these critiques may be found elsewhere (Fenwick et al., 2011). Yet they share assumptions that are growing in influence on educational research: that educational processes are more-than-human, and that to understand activity and learning we need to move beyond preoccupations with human meanings and human agency.

CONSIDERING POLITICS AND CRITIQUE IN SOCIOMATERIALITY

Criticality is a key concern both for educational curricula and for research. A broadly shared aim is to stimulate critical learning that will recognise and interrupt patterns that control and limit: particularly when these assemblages produce injustice and inequities. Despite what is sometimes alleged, many researchers in this diffuse realm of 'sociomaterial' explorations offer critiques of existing exercises of power and advance fundamental commitments to social change through equity and justice. What they tend to resist are forms of critique as the imposition of normative categories and ideologies on phenomena without sufficient attention being given to their specificities and contemporary material dynamics.

One example is Latour (2005), largely associated with actor-network theory. He asks how, among these effects, do some practices and objects become stabilised and entrenched as powerful assemblages (such

as standardised tests) while others go unnoticed? Latour delineates matters of fact from matters of concern. Matters of fact are all those things that are assumed to be decided, certain and settled. Like a car that we drive without really knowing how it works, these things are 'black boxes' that are used in practice without critical questioning about how and why they were constructed. Black boxes can be 'facts' but also practices, policies, texts and tools in everyday work. Matters of concern are issues, controversies, uncertainties. But as Latour (2005) contends, most things accepted as settled facts of practice are really matters of concern whose debates have been foreclosed or obscured.

Critical learning is often described in terms of developing a standpoint or emancipating ourselves from something. For Latour, the danger of such enactments is that they can result in too hasty closures, turning matters of concern into matters of fact and creating hegemonic social explanations that reproduce inequalities. He argues that traditions of critical thinking promulgated by education and academia work from a logic of taking apart, separating and unveiling – using categories that reify their own explanations. He urges educators to resist available explanatory categories and examine more closely the controversies and uncertainties about how resources and agency are distributed, the kinds of agencies that are enacted in different sociomaterial formations, and the ways that actors contextualise one another. His approach registers a range of competing accounts of agency and of flows of power, particularly in the production of inequities and how different actors are rendered more active or more passive through sociomaterial relations. Most importantly, Latour's 'anti-critical' critical attention is on the mechanisms of these relations that act to stabilise and 'black-box' particular categories, hierarchies and practices. The effort of analysis, for Latour, should be 'to highlight the stabilizing mechanisms so that the premature transformation of matters of concern into matters of fact is counteracted' (Latour, 2005: 261).

In a similar line of argument, Braidotti (2013) is an enthusiastic exhorter of an affirmative posthuman politics. She suggests that teachers embrace a transversal and relational materialist conception that expands the limitations of idealist, universalist humanism. Working from Deleuze's conceptions of becoming-other, Braidotti advocates a movement of becoming more-than-human. This movement is grounded in lived experience, examining the concrete, complex materiality of bodies as part of relations of power. However, it ultimately seeks to extend justice to humans and non-humans, and to understand how to share complex environments sustainably. Both Braidotti and Latour urge engagement with the natural environment as integral, rather than other, to being human. Without the non-human, the materiality of the human may come not to matter at all in the many senses of the term.

A similar impetus informs Bennett's argument (2010). Like many sociomaterial writers, she examines the 'vitality of materiality', drawing from Deleuzian concepts of vital energies coursing through matter. This notion of vitalism, combined with new understandings of ontological emergence signalled by complexity theories, offers an affirmative politics. For Bennett, notions of generative materiality are critical for a politics of ecology that moves beyond blame and self-interest. The aim is towards learning how to construct sustainable alternative futures, and extending what Braidotti terms present 'horizons of hope' (Braidotti, 2011). Braidotti eschews traditions of criticality that focus primarily on what the analyst identifies as the problem – negative critique. She argues instead for a 'critical creativity' that 'entails the creation of sustainable alternatives geared to the construction of social horizons of hope, while at the same time doing critical theory, which implies resistance to the present' (Braidotti, 2011: 267). As with Latour, the politics and critical learning involved here embraces more than the human.

Our continuing categories of critique, such as those driving educational notions of critical learning, emanate from what Law (2011) calls a 'quadruple lock' of interlocking institutions and technologies, metaphysics, particular descriptions and the things being described. The hope for progressive change, he suggests, is radically different forms of knowing and versions of the world that could go along with that knowing: 'different normativities, politics and ethics co-exist and intersect with one another too; ... if we can make parts of these explicit then they become debatable and contestable' (Law, 2011: 10–11). To disregard or minimise the centrality of materials in enacting networks that exert powerful forces, combine and translate people and things into these networks, and configure these forces to exclude or include, is to overlook important levers for change as well as reproduction and the fact that changes will not come from human intentions and actions alone.

Persistent deep social inequalities, and other failures of justice and fairness evident in globally rampant dehumanizing biotechnological and biopolitical practices, are precisely what these writers claim are driving their efforts to seek sharper, more nuanced analytic tools. Barad (2007) is concerned about analyses that reduce every aspect of human life to an effect of social structure. She experiments with alternate analytic tools such as diffraction, intra-activity, and tracing the effects of material-discursive apparatuses. Her aim is to enable some appreciation of the extent to which social structures are themselves perpetuated through material practices, and material inequalities produced through situated everyday practices. This lies at the heart of much sociomaterial work, which itself remains an open controversy and matter of concern. The politics may be incomplete, but it is passionate and very much focused on a worldly progressive agenda – not simply one which is human.

RECONSIDERING LEARNING: A CRITICAL SOCIOMATERIAL APPROACH

To reiterate the central idea underpinning this chapter, learning and knowing in sociomaterial perspectives are enactments, not simply mental activity or received knowledge. Mind, after all, is a dynamic of continuous neurological connections with the myriad matter of environments. Sociomaterial perspectives join those which focus not on the individual *learning subject* but on the larger *sociomaterial collective*.

When we accept a view of the world full of agency, *doing* things, learning shifts from a sole emphasis on preparing for this world by acquiring knowledge representations, to participating wisely in situ. Learning issues become more interested in ways to attune to minor fluctuations and surprises, or to track one's own and other's effects on the emerging sociomaterial situation, and how to improvise alternative actions. In critical terms, the aim is learning how to interrupt matters that seem settled and masquerade as fact, and how to hold open the controversies for matters of concern. This suggests a turn from learning as preparation and acquisition of competency to learning as attunement, response and even interruption.

Educators as well as students can look more closely at what material elements most influence their learning and teaching processes, how materials limit or enhance possibilities for learning, why particular educational or learning practices become stabilised and powerful and when these black boxes create problems. This is not about stuffing more activities into crowded curricula, but about opening out ways of engaging students. For example, they might be encouraged to understand 'learning' in terms of recognising their sociomaterial entanglements:

- attending to minor, even mundane, fluctuations and uncanny slips;
- attuning to emerging ideas and action possibilities – the intra-actions of ongoing mattering processes;
- noticing one's own and others' effects on what is emerging;
- tinkering amidst uncertainty; and
- interrupting black boxes of practice to hold open their controversies and disturbances.

Orlikowski (2010) emphasises that we need to challenge the existence of independent objects with given properties and boundaries, and focus instead on situated, relational practices that enact entangled and contingent identities and effects. Curricula might cultivate students' awareness of how their everyday performances, too, are provoked through dynamic and always-shifting sociomaterial configurations, and how multiple agencies act on these configurations. Coole and Frost (2010) suggest practices of 'critical materialism', which presents a useful provocation to educators. These practices would integrate politically engaged critical social theory with an analysis of actual conditions of material existence and their inherent inequality, combined with ongoing invention of new concepts/frames to understand the complexities of global capitalism and its diverse, localised effects on everyday lives. Barad (in Dolphijn and van der Tuin 2012: 113) argues for developing new mapping practices, 'genealogies of the material-discursive apparatuses of production which take account of the intra-active topological dynamics that reconfigure the spacetime manifold'.

As can be expected, sociomaterial analysts emphasise different positions about the political role of materials in constituting particular forms of everyday life and learning, and they promote diverse strategies for critical engagement. However, all share a commitment to restoring a focus on material bodies, substances, settings and devices to show how these both configure flows of power and mediate forms of political engagement. Second, all advance a commitment to social change through equity and justice. What they tend to resist are normative categories and ideologies imposed to formulate critique of particular phenomena without sufficient attention to their continually emerging material dynamics. As Law (2011) points out, many critiques of sociomaterial approaches emanate from their threat to deep metaphysical assumptions embedded in Western or Northern common sense. These assumptions are unused to being treated as 'effects' rather than as de facto canons defining the objects, problems and procedures that perpetuate the very problems they purport to solve. To incorporate a critical sociomaterial approach into education is to disturb, not just particular prevailing models of practice and assumptions about learning, but central foundations and investments. Sociomaterial perspectives offer a way to trace the capillaries of human/non-human relationships that bring forth particular realities in practice and learning, while highlighting the opportunities and entry points for change. With such a perspective, educators are encouraged to appreciate fully the violence of their material engagements as well as the unknown radical future possibilities that are available at every encounter.

NOTE

1 Readers familiar with Heidegger's important conception of Dasein (being-in-the-world), where objects can become ready-to-hand in ways that dissolve the illusion of boundaries between materials and humans, will no doubt see the influences of these ideas in many sociomaterial accounts. Similarly influential have been Bourdieu's theory of practice, as well as major feminist and post-structuralist developments in the later twentieth century, including Derrida's challenges to logo-centrism and the dichotomous categories structuring Western reality, Judith Butler's elaborations of embodiment and performativity, Donna Haraway and Rosi Braidotti's developments of Deleuzian thought, and many others (see Coole and Frost (2010) for an overview).

REFERENCES

Barad, K. (2007) *Meeting the Universe Halfway*, Durham, NC: Duke University Press.

Dolphijn, R. and van der Tuin, I. (2012) 'Matter feels, converses, suffers, desires, yearns and remembers: interview with Karen Barad', in R. Dolphijn and I. van der Tuin (eds), *New Materialism: Interviews and Cartographies*, University of Michigan: Open Humanities Press.

Bennett, J. (2010) *Vibrant Matter: A Political Ecology of Things*, Durham, NC: Duke University Press.

Braidotti, R. (2011) *Powers of Affirmation in Nomadic Theory: The Portable Rosi Braidotti*, New York: Columbia University Press.

Braidotti, R. (2013) *The Posthuman*, Cambridge: Polity Press.

Coole, D. and Frost, D. (2010) 'Introducing the new materialisms', in D. Coole and S. Frost (eds), *New Materialisms: Ontology, Agency, and Politics*, Durham: Duke University Press.

Davis, B. and Sumara, D.J. (2006) *Complexity and Education: Inquiries into Learning, Teaching and Research*, Mahwah, NJ: Erlbaum.

Fenwick, T. and Edwards, R. (2010) *Actor-Network Theory in Educational Research*, London: Routledge.

Fenwick, T., Edwards, R. and Sawchuk, P. (2011) *Emerging Approaches to Educational Research: Tracing the Socio-material*, London: Routledge.

Gherardi, S. and Strati, A. (2012) *Learning and Knowing in Practice-Based Studies*, Cheltenham: Edward Elgar.

Gulson, K. and Symes, C. (eds) (2007) *Spatial Theories of Education: Policy and Geography Matters*, Routledge: New York.

Hager, P., Lee, A. and Reich, A. (2012) *Practice, Learning and Change*, Netherlands: Springer.

Holifield, R. (2009) 'Actor-network theory as a critical approach to environmental justice: a case against synthesis with urban political ecology', *Antipode*, 41(4): 637–58.

Hughes, J., Jewson, N. and Unwin, L. (eds) (2007) *Communities of Practice: Critical Perspectives*, London: Routledge.

Hultman, K. and Lenz Taguchi, H. (2010) 'Challenging anthropocentric bias in analyzing visual data: A relational materialist methodological approach to educational research', *International Journal of Qualitative Studies in Education*, 23(5): 525–42.

Latour, B. (1988) *The Pasteurization of France*, Cambridge, MA: Harvard University Press.

Latour, B. (2005) *Reassembling the Social*, Oxford: Oxford University Press.

Law, J. (2011) 'Knowledge places, or putting STS in its place', ESRC Centre for Research on Socio-Cultural Change, The Open University.

Mol, A.-M. (2002) *The Body Multiple*, Durham: Duke University Press.

Orlikowski, W.J. (2010) 'The sociomateriality of organizational life', *Cambridge Journal of Economics*, 34: 125–41.

Osberg, D. (2008) 'The logic of emergence: An alternative conceptual space for theorizing critical education', *Journal of the Canadian Association for Curriculum Studies*, 6(1): 133–61.

Sørensen, E. (2009) *The Materiality of Learning: Technology and Knowledge in Educational Practice*, Cambridge and New York: Cambridge University Press.

Verran, H (2001) *Science and an African Logic*, Chicago, IL: The University of Chicago Press.

Verran, H. (2007) 'Metaphysics and learning', *Learning Inquiry*, 1(1): 31–9.

Waltz, S.B. (2006) 'Nonhumans unbound: Actor-network theory and the reconsideration of "things" in educational foundations', *Journal of Educational Foundations*, 20(3/4): 51–68.

The Concept of *Learning* in a Cultural-Historical Perspective

Seth Chaiklin

INTRODUCTION

In the early twenty-first century, the name *Vygotsky* and the term *zone of proximal development* (ZPD) have become common-place (or at least widely recognised) among educational researchers and in a broad range of other academic and professional disciplines. A main research focus for Vygotsky was the development of higher psychological functions (e.g. Vygotsky, 1997b [1931]), which suggests that his theoretical approach might offer a perspective for analysing the psychological process of learning. Subsequent theoretical developments in the decades after Vygotsky's death in 1934, such as the concept of motive (e.g. Leontiev, 1978 [1975]; El'konin, 1999 [1971]) and developmental teaching (e.g. Davydov, 2008 [1986]), have built substantially on and moved far beyond Vygotsky's general theoretical insights, to provide a theoretical and practical foundation for concrete applications such as school teaching or professional education. The aim of this chapter is to present an overview of

these initial and subsequent developments as a way of understanding how learning is addressed in the cultural-historical tradition.

LOCATING THE THEORETICAL PERSPECTIVE

To locate the focus and content of the analysis, clarifications need to be made about (a) the meaning of the term *learning*, (b) the referent of the term *cultural-historical*, and (c) the role of the concept of *learning* in cultural-historical theory.

Meaning of learning

Learning is a familiar everyday term, which is used in a multiplicity of ways in different scientific and professional vernaculars. In most of this chapter, *learning* is used to refer to a psychological event: a relatively permanent change in the way in which action is achieved, as a result of prior experience. This stipulative definition is meant to cover or include the wide variety of situations commonly referred to as *learning*. Change in performance is commonly used as an indicator of a change in the way in which an action is achieved. Many different forms of performance change are interpreted as indicators of learning. Simple examples, which serve to highlight these different forms, include memory operations (e.g. being able to repeat specific assertions such as the names of capital cities for different countries), particular motor sequences (e.g. walking to school), operational procedures (e.g. adding numbers or balancing chemical equations), constructive actions (e.g. writing, interpretive arguments, calculation), and so forth. More complicated performance changes are also implied by this definition, for example, choosing an appropriate method to investigate a research question.

An explanation of learning must account for the origin of the psychological change in the way in which action is achieved. This change is the *mechanism* that underlies instances of learning and observed performance changes. When one wants to give a more precise, theoretical account of the change, then ontological assumptions are needed, which has implications for the dynamic account of the changes. The main task of this chapter is to give a general account for these changes, using ontological and dynamic assumptions from cultural-historical theory.

Meaning of cultural-historical

In this chapter, the term *cultural-historical* is used as a kind of 'umbrella' to cover a historical complex of related ideas found among Vygotsky, Luria, Leontiev, Gal'perin, Davydov, El'konin and so forth (cf. Chaiklin, 2001a). It is possible to discuss whether it is misleading to collect the ideas developed by these individual researchers under the designation *cultural-historical* (see Keiler, 2012, for an interesting historical analysis of the origin of the term, including the fact that Vygotsky did not use the term to describe

his own theoretical work), or whether one should use a more restricted definition. For example, Yasnitsky, van der Veer and Ferrari (2014) focus primarily on ideas developed by Vygotsky and Luria, without paying much attention to subsequent developments in the theory of activity.

The broad designation 'cultural-historical' provides a simple way to signify the 'community of researchers', which was located initially in the 1930s in a few research institutions in Moscow, Leningrad and Kharkov, whose researchers had regular exchanges and interactions with each other (cf. Yasnitsky, 2011), and the subsequent generations educated within this community. Even if there were specific differences and divergences among these individual researchers, with no standard or common view among them, there is still a commonality in the kinds of problems being addressed, for example, the structure and genesis of psychological action, the kinds of conceptual perspectives employed in pursuing these problems, for example, the genesis of psychological capabilities through engagement in socially and societally organised interactions, and the kinds of theoretical concepts being developed through investigations of the development of psychological systems, for example, a genetic, historical approach, where Vygotsky's formulations were an important orienting point.

Role of learning *in cultural-historical theory*

In classical texts of cultural-historical theory, the term *learning* is barely mentioned. It appears only rarely in the six volumes in the English translation of Vygotsky's *Collected Works*, where it is used mostly in an everyday sense to refer to the acquisition of a particular capability, for example, learning language or learning to write. The term *learning* barely appears in Leontiev's (1978 [1975]) integrative work *Activity, Consciousness, and Personality*, and only a few times in the collection of articles published in *Problems of the Development of the Mind* (1981 [1959]).

Several reasons can explain this. In part, other theoretical or technical terms are used to refer to situations that are covered by the learning definition. For example, Vygotsky and Leontiev (in translation) sometimes use 'assimilate' (though not in the technical sense found in Piaget) or 'master'. Leontiev sometimes uses 'interiorization' or 'appropriation'. (For additional examples of the use of these terms, see Menchinskaya, 1968 [1967]: 184.) But this discrepancy cannot be explained solely by terminological differences. Vygotsky's main research objective was directed to a different issue than what is normally implied by the definition of learning given here. His main focus was to account for the psychological development of whole persons, where a particular focus was on the development of psychological functions as the key underpinning for development and behaviour, including learning. In the theoretical structure he developed, the different examples of learning named above are understood as examples of, to use his terminology, 'higher or complex forms of behaviour', where specific examples can be explained, at least in their broad outline, within the general theoretical perspective that Vygotsky developed in relation to psychological functions. *Learning* (in general) as described here has a secondary role in the theoretical system, primarily for its consequences for psychological development.

Although Vygotsky did not focus on learning, his theoretical analysis of the formation of psychological functions provides a simple and direct way to answer the question about central ontological and dynamic aspects involved in learning. In its most abstract form, a large number of learning events can be understood or explained as a matter of 'controlling one's own actions'. The focus on action reflects an ontological conception in cultural-historical theory. The creation of this control is what enables change in action (see the definition of learning above). Dynamic principles must explain how this control is formed. To understand the profound implications of this apparently trivial answer (as well as some of its boundaries), it is necessary to consider some basic points about Vygotsky's theory of cultural development.

THEORY OF CULTURAL DEVELOPMENT

Human action is underpinned by a range of general psychological capabilities such as perception, attention, memory, thinking, speech, writing, use of number, which Vygotsky designated as functions. At birth, a child has some of these functions (e.g. perception, attention, memory), but lacks others (e.g. speech, intentional use of number). For all these psychological functions, a child usually comes to develop capabilities that exceed the capabilities of the newborn infant. A central research objective for Vygotsky was to explain or understand the appearance or development (i.e. ontogenesis) of these psychological functions.

Vygotsky acknowledged 'natural' psychological functions, i.e. organic processes (biological, zoological, physiological), which often mature after birth, but reflect characteristics of the human species in general, formed through biological evolution, and independent of human traditions of action. However, he argued that human individuals develop another set of psychological capabilities, which cannot be understood as mere extensions of or creations through natural functions, and more importantly, these cultural forms enable qualitatively new possibilities of action. A key aim was to introduce, explore and defend a view that these 'cultural' (sometimes called 'higher') psychological functions are ontologically and conceptually distinct from and in contrast to natural psychological functions.

In Vygotsky's usage, 'cultural' refers to any humanly created capabilities, such as speech, logical memory or arithmetic, that are assumed to arise through social interaction in societal practices. The term is used in contrast to innate or organic, where cultural is meant to emphasise the generic human origin of these capabilities. This usage contrasts with a common colloquial meaning of 'cultural' that refers to substantive variations in forms of human action. The term 'higher' is meant to indicate that something beyond the natural function was formed. At best, it is a mildly normative judgement in relation to natural functions, but it is not used hierarchically among different cultural functions.

Restating the same points in the argument, but now using Vygotsky's terminology, there are two 'lines of development' in human behaviour. One reflects biological evolution 'from protozoa to man' (Vygotsky, 1997b [1931]: 15) and is called the 'natural line of development'. According to this argument, through biological evolution (e.g. the development of brain structures), humans are now born with a variety of psychological capabilities that do not depend on culturally-developed practices. The other line of development, historical or cultural development, 'begins where the line of biological evolution ends' (1997b [1931]: 16) and corresponds to 'the whole historical path of humanity from the primordial half-animal humanity to our contemporary culture' (1997b [1931]: 16). These two lines of development 'must differ from each other since each process is part of more general processes – history and evolution', where the cultural line is 'a process of [psychological][1] development *sui generis*, a process of a special type' (1997b [1931]: 16).

A central interest for Vygotsky was to understand how 'cultural' forms of these functions developed, where the assumption is that these forms develop through participation in interactions that involve certain demands or requirements. Note that cultural development involves both internal functions (i.e. cultural forms of memory, attention, thinking), as well as external functions such as speech, writing, arithmetic and drawing (Vygotsky, 1997b [1931]: 14, 228–9), where 'cultural development' refers both individually to different functions and collectively to the overall effect of functional development.

Holistic approach (personality)

For strategic reasons, Vygotsky studied individual functions separately, but his theoretical intention was always oriented to a unified perspective. His basic approach, reflecting a monist ontology (cf. Luria, 2002 [1925]: 32), was to consider the whole person, which was designated by the concept of personality. The use of the term *personality* in psychology (in general) was still novel in 1931 when Vygotsky used this term (see Danziger, 1997: 124–8), so he makes clear that his intended meaning stands in contrast to a focus on individual traits or unique qualities of individuals. Rather the term is meant to be a 'social concept' which 'encompasses what is supernatural and historical in humanity. It is not innate, but arises as a result of cultural development because "personality" is a historical concept' (Vygotsky, 1997b [1931]: 242). (The terms *supernatural* and *historical* are used in opposition to *natural*.)

This focus on personality can be seen clearly both in the beginning and the end of the *History of the Formation of the Higher [Psychological] Functions*. In the second sentence of this book-length manuscript, Vygotsky (1997b [1931]: 1) notes the 'enormous importance of studying the processes in the development of higher [psychological] functions for proper understanding and logical elucidation of all aspects of the child's personality', where the 'history of the cultural development of the child brings us to the history of the development of the personality' (1997b [1931]: 26). The concluding chapter is an 'attempt to present a plan or picture of the whole cultural development of the child' (1997b [1931]: 241), where this synthesis starts by characterising 'the process of cultural development ... as development of the personality and world view of the child' (1997b [1931]: 242). The relation between personality and psychological functions will be discussed after the idea of 'higher psychological function' is explained.

Meaning of higher psychological function

A definite meaning of function is difficult to find in Vygotsky's texts (as is an indication of possible inspirational sources from particular psychological research traditions). The definitional problem can be understood partially from Vygotsky's (1997b [1931]: 1) explanation that 'the very concept of development of higher [psychological] functions as applied to child psychology … remains vague and obscure … inadequately distinguished from other close and related concepts'. Although Vygotsky then goes on to assert the need for explaining the basic concepts, I have not been able to find a comprehensive discussion of key concepts, or a systematic enumeration of higher psychological functions in this or other texts (Chaiklin, 2003a). Nonetheless, it is possible to reconstruct a plausible interpretation by considering how the concept is used in Vygotsky's texts.

As a way to understand the key general features of higher psychological functions, let us consider the following (simplified) situation that involves the psychological function of memory, which is then generalised to highlight critical features. Imagine a situation where you are given a set of ten drawings (of everyday objects) and then asked to memorise a list of ten words. Most likely, you have also already imagined that you will try to form some meaningful connection between each word and each picture as a way to improve the likelihood that you will be able to recall these words. This rudimentary example contains all the main features in a psychological function. First, the memory operation has depended on other psychological functions (e.g. thinking and/or imagination) to create the connections. Second, the memory operation has used an auxiliary support (i.e. the pictures). Third, small children do not 'naturally' use pictures as an auxiliary in this way (according to Vygotsky's empirical investigations), but have, most likely, acquired this technique, which was historically developed through instruction, or invented in response to the demands of various tasks in everyday

interaction. Fourth, the ability to control this operation is an example of self-mastery of behaviour. These four features – interfunctional organisation, use of auxiliaries, historically formed and acquired through social interaction, and self-mastery – are essential characteristics of all higher psychological functions. In this particular example, the demand was to use a relation between pictures and words, but if a person has developed 'memory' as a higher psychological function, then it will be possible, in other situations, through mastery of one's actions in relation to memory, to use other auxiliaries to support a memory process. This higher psychological function of memory is not innate to a person. While the function may involve the use of natural memory, the higher psychological function of memory (sometimes called *logical* memory) transcends the natural function through self-mastery of one's own action including other psychological functions and the use of auxiliaries (see Vygotsky, 1997b [1931]: 62–3). This mastery is not a matter of will or intention, but of controlling one's own actions in relation to stimuli (1997b [1931]: 86–7).

Relation between functions, behaviour, and personality

As noted above, Vygotsky often studied individual functions for strategic reasons, but the intention was always to consider them in an integrated systemic way (e.g. 1997a [1930]: 91–2; Vygotsky, 1997b [1931]: 242–3). That is, interfunctional relationships are critical for understanding behaviour, rather than assuming that behaviour (or action) can be reduced to a single function (see also Leontiev and Luria, 2005 [1937]: 35). The distinction between a psychological function and complex (or higher) forms of behaviour (or action) can be difficult to grasp, because functions are always manifest in behaviour. Functions are formed through processes of psychological development, i.e. originating in social interactions and over a period of time (of the order of years), ending with self-mastery of the function. Complex forms of behaviour are enabled by these psychological functions.

Similarly, a potential ambiguity arises because external cultural means such as 'cultural arithmetic' and 'writing' necessarily involve behaviour, and sometimes Vygotsky refers to them as 'behaviour', but it is usually clear that the focus of his arguments are on the qualitative change in action enabled by these external means, rather than a particular behavioural instance (e.g., Vygotsky, 1997b [1931]: 87, 94). Vygotsky's research was focused on explaining the origins of psychological capabilities that underlie observed behaviour. This focus on the structure and formation of psychological functions arose because of an interest in their implications for understanding human development, rather than an interest in studying specific examples of action (e.g. learning particular content). This focus on the developmental significance of functions (as opposed to behaviour) is important for understanding the theoretical significance of Vygotsky's zone of proximal development concept, discussed below.

Justification for this distinction between function and behaviour will not be provided here, but by way of illustration it is worth noting that Vygotsky identifies three basic concepts in his research: 'the concept of higher [psychological] function, the concept of cultural development of behavior, and the concept of mastery of behavior by internal processes' (1997b [1931]: 7), and highlights the dialectical relation between function and behaviour: '(f)rom the perspective that interests us, this means that the development of higher [psychological] functions comprises one of the most important aspects of cultural development of behavior' (1997b [1931]: 18).

Functions, behaviour and personality are considered in a unified way, where personality is manifest in the development of psychological functions, and functions are always developed through meaningful, whole action. For example:

The essence of cultural development … consists of man mastering processes of his own behavior, but an indispensable prerequisite for mastery is the formation of personality and for this reason, development of one function or another is always a derivative of development of the personality as a whole and is determined by it. (Vygotsky, 1997b [1931]: 242–3)

A simple implication of this unified view is the need to consider that functions develop in relation to the demands of meaningful tasks in human practices, rather than viewing functions operating independently from practical situations. Leontiev (1978 [1975]) continued to develop a personality concept as a social and historical concept, but now in terms of motive hierarchy rather than psychological functions (cf. Chaiklin, 2001a).

Formation of higher psychological functions

The basic question addressed in this section is how higher psychological functions are formed (i.e. to give an account of self-mastery of action). Cultural development refers to a psychological transformation where a child gains control of a psychological function that has originally been developed in a human culture. This general analysis of psychological functions applies both to functions that have 'natural' counterparts and to functions that have developed through human history (Vygotsky, 1987 [1934]: 229).

In all cases, functions are bootstrapped, in the sense that they are created (over time) by a person's actions in meaningful situations, where existing psychological functions are used as a foundation for action. Externalisation (i.e. action in relation to the demands of the task) is an important and necessary part of the process of learning to control one's actions, in part because of mistakes that are made, as well as forming actions that are appropriate to the demands of the situation (cf. Leontiev, 1981 [1959]: 313–14). For example, as part of developing control over one's attention or mastering cultural arithmetic, it is necessary to attempt to produce controlled actions. What were once external actions become transformed through self-mastery as an internal form of the function, which having been established, can serve as a prerequisite or precondition for meaningful action.

A CULTURAL-HISTORICAL PERSPECTIVE ON LEARNING

To this point, Vygotsky's theory of the development of psychological functions has been in focus. The main theoretical interest is the development of the whole person, where psychological functions develop through participation in meaningful practices. Accordingly, the idea of 'learning' (as defined here) has not been an important part of the classical theoretical tradition, though there was an interest in the role of instruction in relation to development (which again underlines the point that Vygotsky focused on development). Although learning (as defined here) is not a central focus in Vygotsky's theory, it is still possible to use his theoretical concepts to construct a dynamic explanation of learning.

To make clear what an account of learning must explain, it is necessary to highlight several analytic qualities of the definition used here (see Figure 9.1). The definition is fairly standard, specific and comprehensive, best characterised as an event, rather than a process, product, or as content. Its universality is achieved in part because it is abstract (i.e. it does not consider the content involved). These analytic implications apply to any theoretical account of learning (as defined here), not just a cultural-historical theory. The fifth feature in Figure 9.1 highlights the focus on a structural change. The cultural-historical ontology (and dynamics) appear in response to this point.

Change of action

Although the definition of learning is abstract, the cultural-historical ontological account of the formation of mechanism is not. In cultural-historical theory, 'action' is a key ontological entity. The event of learning involves forming a change in action. Changes in action are taken as indicators of learning,

---

1. **Standard Definition**
   Similar to those commonly given in introductory psychology textbooks, except for the critical difference which focuses on 'change in mechanism'[2].

2. **Relatively Definite Event**
   Stipulates empirical conditions (i.e. observation of a change in performance from one moment to another) that allow one to identify or classify situations as potentially indicative of learning, together with an assumption that the mechanism behind the observed change was formed from experience.

3. **Tautologous**
   In this sense can be considered as universal.

4. **Abstract (even if it is definite)**
   It does not refer to particular content in the change.

5. **Ontological Implications**
   It focuses on a change in a psychological structure as the underlying cause of the observed performance change.

Figure 9.1 Five key features of the learning definition

where the explanatory problem is to account for the origins of these changes.

Many different kinds of mechanisms can be formed – not a single principle

A large class of learning events can be explained in general as involving mastery of one's own actions. A key idea in cultural-historical theory is to conceptualise the formation of action as grounded in existing higher psychological functions (e.g. speech, concepts, memory), where new actions appear as a result of a person being able to use their psychological functions to control their own action. This acquisition of control is the 'change in mechanism' that enables a change in performance.

Within this class, there are many kinds of processes by which changes in action can be achieved. The example given previously about memory is one illustration of how different psychological mechanisms can lead to a change in action (with the same task). This control depends in part on controlling both internal and external psychological functions. From this point of view, the ability to recall the names of capital cities, or calculate the volume of a cube, or interpret the meaning of a poem, depend on a person being able to generate appropriate actions. Such performances involve the use of several psychological functions, including memory, writing, thinking and so forth.

It is relevant to note that when one speaks about 'learning' in most vernaculars, then higher psychological functions (in Vygotsky's sense) are already taken for granted. That is, analyses of learning presuppose that a person has already mastered basic psychological and cultural functions such as memory, imagination, attention, thinking, speech, writing, number and so forth. Vygotsky's focus on the development of higher psychological functions can be understood as trying to explain the origins of psychological capabilities that were preconditions for learning (as typically discussed in different research traditions),

but less on the process of learning particular content.

The general principle of 'control of own action' cannot be used to explain all kinds of learning, i.e. there can be other mechanisms. For example, in some situations, laws of conditioning, rather than self-control, may explain the origin of the mechanism that underlies change in performance. Consistent with Vygotsky's (1997b [1931]: 8) critique of the idea of seeking a single universal principle for explaining psychological phenomena, these conditioning cases are understood as having an ontologically different origin.

New ways to form mechanisms

Learning (as defined here) is understood as an historical phenomenon. As human culture develops, new possibilities for forming and controlling actions can arise. Similarly, as individuals develop new psychological functions or relations among existing functions change, then a person has new ways to gain control over their own actions, which are manifest in changed performance. This critical point is a consequence of understanding the cultural development of psychological capabilities (for learning) as historically formed. The term *historical* is used in contrast to *natural* to emphasise that capabilities are developed through action over time.

Learning is social

Note that Vygotsky (1997b [1931]: 106) equates the word *social* with *cultural*. Thus, to say that 'learning is social' is to indicate that the sources of learning content are found in human history, and not necessarily through social interaction. As individuals develop psychological functions, or learning activity (see below), then it becomes possible for individuals to acquire historically-accumulated knowledge, which is social in Vygotsky's usage, even if the control of action was not achieved through interpersonal (social) interaction.

A comment on internalisation

In the English language reception of Vygotsky's ideas (particularly in the last two decades of the twentieth century) the idea of *internalisation* was introduced, and debated. In the English translation of Vygotsky's *Collected Works*, the term *internalised* or *internalisation* appears only a few times, usually when discussing Janet or Busemann, and the idea of an external function becoming an internal function. In Leontiev's main works, comparable terms *interiorise* and *interiorisation* appear a few times in *Problems of the Development of the Mind*, when he refers to Vygotsky, but this is now generalised to the idea of the interiorisation of action or the structure of activity, rather than psychological functions. The term barely appears in his final main work, *Activity, Consciousness, and Personality.* In other words, these terms do not have a central significance in cultural-historical theory. The terms simply provide a way to refer to the structural transformation in which individuals, through mastery of mediating means, are able to control actions that were originally distributed across persons (cf. Gal'perin, 1967 [1966]).

For example, it is possible to 'internalise' a wristwatch if a person is able to use the watch as part of controlling their actions, for example, to leave a party to catch the last bus home. The internalised action still involves extra-corporal aspects, i.e. the watch is an auxiliary stimulus used to control action, but the critical issue here is that the individual has been able to master self-control of their actions in using the watch. The idea of 'internalised' is a way to refer to the transformation of self-control, rather than a particular bodily location for this control. If internalisation is interpreted biologically, then it is likely to generate images that confuse rather than illuminate cultural-historical theory.

A COMMENT ABOUT ZPD

The concept, *zone of proximal development*, as developed by Vygotsky, describes a structural relation used in conceptualising human development. The concept has been widely misinterpreted (and misunderstood) as being part of a learning process or as an individual learner characteristic. Unfortunately, these misunderstandings are well established in both scientific and popular usage. The distortions introduced by these misunderstandings obscure Vygotsky's important use of the concept to form a hypothesis about the relation between instruction and psychological development.

Vygotsky conceptualises development as organised in age periods, where each period is historically formed and characterised as a configuration of psychological functions. The *zone* for the next development refers to the functions that a child must acquire to move from one age period to another. Part of the conceptual force of the idea can be understood by considering that the individual acquisition of a new higher psychological function enables qualitatively new possibilities for action (e.g. speech, writing, conceptual thinking) for the person. Vygotsky's basic point was that instruction should be focused on developing functions that are important for the next development, for example, '[w]e have given the child a penny's worth of instruction and the consequence has been a dollar's worth of development' (Vygotsky, 1987 [1934]: 198). Chaiklin (2003b) provides a detailed reconstruction of Vygotsky's concept, underpinned by an examination of the available texts.

LEARNING ACTIVITY

School-based instruction is a significant societal practice where the achievement of learning is central. Vygotsky's studies of everyday and academic concepts, by his own analysis, were not an adequate theoretical basis for designing school instruction. Vygotsky's (1987 [1934]: 239) analysis was focused on general features of concept learning rather than particular content, even though he recognised 'the mutually conditioned nature, the organic integration, and the internal unity of content and form in the development of thinking' (1987 [1934]: 132); in other words, that thinking and knowledge must be analysed in relation to content. Furthermore, he did not 'address the internal connections in the system' of concepts, which is 'a fundamental issue concerning the development of the concept system' (1987 [1934]: 240). Subsequent developments in the cultural-historical tradition have addressed these shortcomings in a substantial way.

During the period from 1932 to 1934, Vygotsky travelled regularly to Leningrad to give lectures and supervise research at the Herzen Pedagogical Institute. Daniil El'konin was a research assistant with Vygotsky during this period. In the late 1950s El'konin started to work directly with the consequences of Vygotsky's theoretical ideas (e.g. El'konin, 1961). The approach was designated 'developmental teaching-learning',[3] to reflect and engage with Vygotsky's idea that instruction should lead development (i.e. to provide challenges that support the development of new psychological functions). His collaborator from the beginning was Vasili Davydov, who continued to work with these ideas after El'konin's death in 1983, until his own death in 1998.

The developmental teaching-learning approach is focused on content (Davydov, 1988 [1986]: 19), where 'psychology and didactics can now no longer speak of "knowledge" in general' (Davydov, 1990 [1972]: 341). 'The term "knowledge" is an abbreviated way of designating abstraction, generalization, and concept in their combination' (1990 [1972]: 300). In addition to a unity between form and content, there is also a unity between knowledge and action (Davydov, 1988 [1986]: 21). That is, knowledge is expressed through action, where learning can now be understood as developing control over one's own action in relation to subject matter content.

Davydov (1990 [1972]) introduced an important, empirically-grounded analytic distinction between empirical forms of knowledge, those based on observation that categorised external properties of objects, and theoretical forms of knowledge, i.e. an understanding of the significant internal relations that generate or underlie an empirical object. (See Davydov (1990 [1972]: 300–1) for a summary of the main differences.) As a simple illustration, empirical knowledge would describe the distribution of plant species in a land area, while theoretical knowledge would appeal to an internal principle such as the interaction between plant needs and environmental conditions, to understand this distribution.

Furthermore, he introduced the idea of *learning activity* to refer to a historically developed form for persons 'to master knowledge and skills that are in some way linked with the theoretical thought of their times' (Davydov, 1988 [1986]: 8). In acquiring learning activity (as a general form), a person has a new general tool for approaching the acquisition of action (i.e. theoretical knowledge) in relation to content areas. The acquisition of principles proceeds through content-based abstractions and generalisations, where instruction aims to create conditions to support pupils in developing these generalisations. This insight requires that teachers are able to analyse the conceptual structure of subject matter content (e.g. germ cells and other substantive generalisations), which in turn have implications for how teaching is organised. Controlling the conceptual structure is critical for subject-matter learning; this illustrates the importance of content as part of a (cultural-historical) analysis of learning.

Although not discussed in terms of a psychological function, learning activity can be understood in the same spirit as Vygotsky's external cultural development that extends a person's possibilities for developing new actions, and probably a function in the zone for development to the next age period. Note that the word *learning* has a different meaning in this expression, namely to describe the function of the activity, i.e. ways of engaging with substantive content in order to achieve the event of learning, as initially defined here. Researchers who have drawn directly from and/or worked with Davydov include Aidarova (1982); Hedegaard (2008), Hedegaard and

Chaiklin (2005); Lompscher and Giest (2006); Markova (1979 [1974]); Repkin (2003); and Zuckerman (2011 [2010]).

ADDITIONAL RELEVANT ISSUES

Several researchers who were connected with Vygotsky and/or Leontiev also developed life-long research programmes that are relevant to the topic of learning. Gal'perin focused on the formation of mental action, developing a theoretical account of stages by which the control of action could be formed (e.g. Gal'perin, 1992). Talyzina (1981 [1975]) has been centrally involved in the development of this approach. Menchinskaya focused on the characteristics of how children engaged with learning concepts in different school subjects (see Iakimanskaia, 1996).

The present chapter has focused on change in action in relation to learning, but there are other kinds of psychological change over time, such as motives, intentions, emotions, interpretations or conceptions, that could also be included as examples or kinds of learning phenomena. The cultural-historical tradition provides theoretical resources to address these kinds of developments (sometimes called personality development), where an interest in affective and emotional aspects was present in Vygotsky's initial work. Research groups associated respectively with Menchinskaya and Bozhovich (e.g. 2004 [1979]) have made relevant, extensive empirical investigations into these kinds of questions in relation to school children.

IMPLICATIONS

This chapter has highlighted some central ontological assumptions that underpin a cultural-historical perspective on learning. It introduced the idea of acquiring control of one's own actions as a general way of analysing a large class of phenomena that are identified

as learning. This way of conceptualising learning shifts attention to a learner's 'production' and how to help persons develop mastery of their actions, rather than focus on 'input' and 'proper delivery method'. To use this theoretical account of learning, it is critical to take into account the structure of the content and the meaning of learning to control that content in relation to societal practice.

For researchers who want to pursue this line of thinking further, there are at least three productive lines of investigation that are under-explored. These are: (a) analysis of motives; (b) the demands of content; and (c) the development of psychological functions. In the first case, with regards to motives, learning is developed in relation to participation in meaningful action. The study of motive in concrete practices is relevant for understanding the kinds of actions that an individual is trying to control (see Hedegaard, Edwards and Fleer, 2012). In the second case, the work of Davydov and those who have followed have appreciated the need to understand the conceptual logic of subject matter as a part of creating conditions to support individuals to acquire control of appropriate content-based generalisations. Many kinds of content remain to be analysed from this perspective. In the third case, the idea of psychological functions and their relation to qualitative changes in action have not been a part of the contemporary understanding of Vygotsky's theory. What other cultural functions remain to be identified, and their development studied?

NOTES

1   The word *psychological* is a better translation than *mental* in all quotes from Vygotsky (1997b [1931]).
2   The focus on change in the source (or mechanism) of action and the distinction between learning (as change in mechanism) and performance (as an indicator) of learning are important. These ideas are discussed by Domjan (2015: 14–15) in relation to animal learning, where his analysis of a range of factors (e.g. fatigue, maturation, motivation and working conditions) that might prevent observations in performance seem applicable to humans as well.

In the present discussion, the general idea is modified to consider action rather than behaviour, where additional factors, for example, misunderstanding, can also be an explanation for lack of performance.

3 The Russian word *obuchenie* is used to describe this teaching tradition. The expression teaching-learning is used to express the idea that both meanings are associated with the word in everyday Russian usage.

REFERENCES

Aidarova, L. (1982) *Child Development and Education* (L. Lezhneva, trans.), Moscow: Progress.

Bozhovich, L.I. (2004) 'Developmental phases of personality formation in childhood (II)', *Journal of Russian & East European Psychology*, 42(4): 55–70 (original work published 1979).

Chaiklin, S. (2001a) 'The category of "personality" in cultural-historical psychology', in S. Chaiklin (ed.) *The Theory and Practice of Cultural-Historical Psychology* (pp. 238–59), Aarhus: Aarhus University Press.

Chaiklin, S. (2001b) 'The institutionalisation of cultural-historical psychology as a multinational practice', in S. Chaiklin (ed.) *The Theory and Practice of Cultural-Historical Psychology* (pp. 15–34), Aarhus: Aarhus University Press.

Chaiklin, S. (2003a) 'Psychological function' in Vygotsky: Fundamental, Vague and Underexplored, in N. Veresov (Organizer) *Multiple Readings of Vygotsky*, Invited Symposium conducted at the XIth European Conference on Developmental Psychology, August, Milan, Italy.

Chaiklin, S. (2003b) 'The zone of proximal development in Vygotsky's analysis of learning and instruction', in A. Kozulin, B. Gindis, V. Ageyev and S.M. Miller (eds.) *Vygotsky's Educational Theory in Cultural Context* (pp. 39–64), Cambridge: Cambridge University Press.

Danziger, K. (1997) *Naming the Mind: How Psychology Found its Language*, London: Sage.

Davydov, V.V. (1988) 'Problems of developmental teaching', *Soviet Education*, 30(9): 3–83 (original work published 1986).

Davydov, V.V. (1990) *Types of Generalization in Instruction: Logical and Psychological Problems in the Structuring of School Curricula* (Soviet studies in mathematics education, Vol. 2; J. Kilpatrick, ed.; J. Teller, trans.), Reston, VA: National Council of Teachers of Mathematics (original work published 1972).

Davydov, V.V. (2008) *Problems of Developmental Instruction: A Theoretical and Experimental Psychological Study* (P. Moxhay, trans.), Hauppauge, NY: Nova Science (original work published 1986).

Domjan, M. (2015) *The Principles of Learning and Behavior* (7th edn), Stamford, CT: Cengage Learning.

El'konin, D.B. (1961) 'A psychological study in an experimental class', *Soviet Education*, 3(7): 3–10.

El'konin, D.B. (1999) 'Toward the problem of stages in the mental development of children', *Journal of Russian and East European Psychology*, 37(6): 11–30 (original work published 1971).

Gal'perin, P. (1967) 'On the notion of internalization', *Soviet Psychology*, 5(3): 28–33 (original work published 1966).

Gal'perin, P.I. (1992) 'Stage-by-stage formation as a method of psychological investigation', *Journal of Russian and East European Psychology*, 30(4): 60–80.

Hedegaard, M. (2008) 'Children's learning through participation in institutional practice: A model from the perspective of cultural-historical psychology', in B. van Oers, W. Wardekker, E. Elbers and R. van der Veer (eds.) *The Transformation of Learning: Advances in Cultural-Historical Activity Theory* (pp. 294–318), Cambridge: Cambridge University Press.

Hedegaard, M. and Chaiklin, S. (2005) *Radical-local Teaching and Learning: A Cultural-Historical Approach*, Aarhus: Aarhus University Press.

Hedegaard, M., Edwards, A. and Fleer, M. (eds.) (2012) *Motives in Children's Development: Cultural-Historical Approaches*, Cambridge: Cambridge University Press.

Iakimanskaia, I.S. (1996) 'Problems of instruction and development in the works of N.A. Menchinskaia', *Russian Education and Society*, 38(3): 74–96.

Keiler, P. (2012) '"Cultural-historical theory" and "cultural-historical school": From myth (back) to reality', *PsyAnima, Dubna Psychological Journal*, 1: 1–33.

Leontiev, A.N. (1978) *Activity, Consciousness, and Personality* (M.J. Hall, trans.), Englewood Cliffs, NJ: Prentice-Hall (original work published 1975).

Leontiev, A.N. (1981) *Problems of the Development of Mind* (M. Kopylova, trans.), Moscow: Progress (original work published 1959).

Leontiev, A.N. and Luria, A.R. (2005) 'The problem of the development of the intellect and learning in human psychology', *Journal of Russian and East European Psychology*, 43(4): 34–47 (original work written 1937).

Lompscher, J. and Giest, H. (2006) *Tätigkeit – Lerntätigkeit – Lernstrategie: Die theorie der Lerntätigkeit und ihre empirische erforschung*, Berlin: Lehmanns Media.

Luria, A.R. (2002) 'Psychoanalysis as a system of monistic psychology', *Journal of Russian & East European Psychology*, 40(1): 26–53 (original work published 1925).

Markova, A.K. (1979) *The Teaching and Mastery of Language* (M. Vale, trans.), White Plains, NY: M.E. Sharpe (original work published 1974).

Menchinskaya, N.A. (1968) 'Fifty years of the Soviet psychology of learning', *Soviet Education*, 10(6): 181–96 (original work published 1967).

Repkin, V.V. (2003) 'Developmental teaching and learning activity', *Journal of Russian and East European Psychology*, 41(5): 10–34.

Talyzina, N. (1981) *The Psychology of Learning* (V. Solovyov, trans.), Moscow: Progress (original work published 1975).

Vygotsky, L.S. (1987) 'Thinking and speech' (N. Minick, trans.), in R.W. Reiber and A.S. Carton (eds.) *The Collected Works of L.S. Vygotsky: Vol. 1. Problems of General Psychology* (pp. 39–285), New York: Plenum Press (original work published 1934).

Vygotsky, L.S. (1997a) 'On psychological systems' (R. van der Veer, trans.), in R. W. Reiber and J. Wollock (eds.) *The Collected Works of L. S. Vygotsky. Vol. 3: Problems of the Theory and History of Psychology* (pp. 91–107), New York: Plenum Press (original work written 1930).

Vygotsky, L.S. (1997b) *The Collected Works of L. S. Vygotsky. Vol. 4: The History of the Development of Higher Mental Functions* (M. Hall, trans.; R.W. Reiber, ed.), New York: Plenum Press (original work published 1931).

Yasnitsky, A. (2011) 'Vygotsky circle as a personal network of scholars: Restoring connections between people and ideas', *Integrative Psychological and Behavioral Science*, 45: 422–57.

Yasnitsky, A., van der Veer, R. and Ferrari, M. (eds.) (2014) *The Cambridge Handbook of Cultural-Historical Psychology*, Cambridge: Cambridge University Press.

Zuckerman, G.A. (2011) 'Developmental education: A genetic modelling experiment', *Journal of Russian and East European Psychology*, 49(6): 45–63 (original work published 2010).

The Post-Human and Responsible Experimentation in Learning

Richard Edwards

INTRODUCTION

Post-humanism has been the subject of much debate in recent decades in many branches of the arts and social sciences (e.g. Braidotti, 2013). Who and what are embraced by the post-human are not always clear, and other related approaches, such as socio-materialism, complexity and actor-network theory have certain resonances with it. However, post-humanism, unlike postmodernism and post-structuralism, has had little attention in the discussion of education and learning. This is perhaps unsurprising given the focus on the human subject and the learning of and by humans at the centre of educational concerns. However, the increasingly non-human participation of technologies and the digital in educational practices, in addition to more traditional objects, artefacts, sentient beings other than humans, and things, such as desks, pens, books, animals and walls, is resulting in a greater interest in materiality in general and post-human theory specifically

(e.g. Lawn and Grosvenor, 2005; Sørenson, 2009; Fenwick et al., 2011). While some, such as Gough (2004), have experimented with post-human possibilities in education, in particular the technological extensions of the human in curriculum and pedagogy, little educational research has addressed the issue of the post-human beyond, for example, metaphorical uptakes of the notions of the cyborg.

The sense of post-humanism informing this chapter does not simply refer to a period *after* humanism and the death of the Renaissance human subject. I am not referring to the new and the now. Nor am I using it simply to refer to those who advocate any form of dys/u-topian future of, for instance, trans-human genetically or technologically modified embodiments, or the supplanting of humans by non-human practices, such as driverless (by humans) cars. It is important then that the post- is not read as an *affirmation*, an *anti-*, nor a *replacement*. The human and humanism are important contributors to the contemporary world in many ways.

Indeed, we cannot consider the post-human without the human, even if the conception of the latter is reframed. For me, as with Lyotard's (1992) reflections on the 'post-' in postmodernism, the post- in post-humanism is constantly at play with precisely that which it deconstructs, that is, the human. It is not *after* in terms of going beyond, but in terms of offering a constant experimentation with or questioning of the human (Badmington, 2003) that could paradoxically enhance the human, but in different ways to that associated with dominant and often essentialised notions of humanism. Certain strands of post-humanism seek to pose the constant question of what it means to be human, without recourse to universal human nature or religious subservience.

In this chapter, therefore, post-humanism refers to an enactment that deconstructs the separation of the human and non-human, subjects and objects, and, with that separation, the centring of the human subject as either a representative of an essentialised human nature or in a state of constant becoming or learning. I will therefore use arguments from post-humanism to pose questions about the limits of human learning as an educational goal and explore possibilities for attaching additional goals that embrace the non-human as well as the human. This entails giving *experimentation* a bigger presence in education in addition to learning, about which I will write more later in this chapter. Here I want to argue that this is not about learning *to* experiment, learning *from* experimentation, or learning *through* experimentation, but that the latter could (and the conditional is important) entail a different, post-human mode of educational existence. It is important to note that while there might be some affinities in this discussion with earlier positions put forward by writers such as Dewey, the latter takes the non-human to be active through interaction with the human and therefore the starting point is purposeful human action. This is not the position adopted here. For me, such approaches already require work to separate the human from the non-human.

The post-human entails the view that action and agency are multiple, relational and distributed and that the non-human, however defined, is integral to the possibilities of and for human social orders (Sayes, 2014).

To question learning as the key goal of education is not in itself new. For instance, Biesta (2004) has pointed to the focus on learning as a limitation upon education and educational discourse, pushing to one side questions about curriculum and pedagogy, and wider social and political purposes. He argues for a reinvigorated discourse *for* education. Others have pointed to the contested nature of learning and the many theories of its occurrence. Here learning is taken to be neither a single homogeneous phenomenon, nor explained through single or simple causal relations. Although over-simplified, Sfard's (1998) distinction of explanations and associated notions of learning into two metaphorical domains makes this clear. She identifies learning by acquisition – learning *about* – and learning by participation – learning *through* – as dominant metaphors and argues for the importance of both. In some ways, these metaphors capture distinctions and tensions between more psychological – having knowledge in the mind – and sociological – becoming knowledgeable through interaction with others – understandings of learning. Practice-based theories of learning – learning *to and through* – add further layers of difference into the discussion of learning and different ways of explaining its occurrence. This suggests that when discussing learning as the goal for education, we are not discussing a single phenomenon and therefore debates can take place about the value of learning based upon very different discursive and material domains. What constitutes learning shapes much educational debate, while what is framed as worthwhile learning and what the limits of a discourse of learning may be are more important questions. However, in such discussions, one thing is central and this is the human subject who learns. Humanism and human-centrism frames much educational discussion of learning.

By contrast, drawing broadly upon certain post-human writings, I wish to suggest that the focus on learning in education is part of a wider set of assumptions and practices that seek to centre the human as the subject of learning and promote a representationalist view of knowledge. In other words, to focus conceptually on learning already assumes certain humanist framings that then enact what they presume. This echoes the work of Rose (1999), who argues that the practices and knowledge produced by modern institutions enact certain forms of subjectivity and humanness rather than being simply responses to human needs, desires and conditions. My argument, following Latour (1993), is that the attempts to position learning as the goal of education are part of modern practices of purification, of separating things into different domains. In other words, to focus education on learning entails a lot of effort to achieve this affect, which modern practices of purification attempt in order to try and overcome the hybrid nature of things. It is a brief discussion of the implications of the latter for education that is the focus of my post-human explorations.

Rather than the modern logic of separation, I want to argue for an additional post-human position of attachment and multiplicity. The use of *additional* is deliberate here rather than perhaps the more conventional notion of *alternative*. Attachment entails conjoining, but this in itself requires things that can be brought together. Such things however may not be pure. Thus, while I argue that purification can never be fully achieved, the practices of separation and attachment are both in play. To be consistent in my argument therefore, I am not dismissing learning as a concern for education, but seeking to attach other concerns, in particular the possibilities for experimentation through the gathering of the human and non-human.

Here, I take experimenting to be collective and distributed rather than individual and subject-centred, gathering the non-human as well as the human. This focus is not human- or subject-centric, but points to the entanglement of the human and non-human, as 'without the non-human, humans would not last a minute' (Latour, 2004a: 91). My argument is not that education is a single set of practices about which there can be multiple perspectives, but that multiple worlds are enacted through the practices of education, as Mol (2002) has argued in relation to the practices of medicine. These worlds are *tinkered* with and *patched* together, themselves conjoined through separation and attachment. Post-human experimentation entails intervening, tinkering and patching through the assemblings of those gathered together. It does not simply entail the attempt to master the natural through representation and manipulation.

The chapter is in three sections. First, I outline what I suggest are some of the presumptions underpinning the focus on learning as the primary goal of education. In particular, I outline the representationalism and forms of separation which I take to be core to this position and the associated enactments of human exceptionalism and mastery of the non-human. Second, I will attach an additional approach based upon experimental forms of intervention. To experiment entails practices of attachment – responding to others and otherness, both human and non-human – conditionality – could rather than should – and fallibility – trial and error, and the possibility of failure. Finally, I shall suggest some of the implications of the argument for educational practices. To illustrate aspects of my argument, I will draw upon different ways of framing the uses of digital technologies in education, as human tool and post-human actor.

SEPARATING, REPRESENTING AND HUMAN LEARNING

It has become commonplace to argue that central to the modern period has been the attempt to create bounded distinctions, categorisations (Bowker and Star, 2000) and domains, purified of the influence of others. It is through separation and attempts to purify that the modern order is made achievable. Latour (1993, 2004a, 2005) has been amongst the most consistent researchers on the work of the moderns to separate and purify, for instance, society from nature, subject from object, meaning from matter, etc. Once purified, these binaries are held to be foundational and structure the ways of theorising and intervening in the world, providing the conditions of possibility for how humans might be human and how they might act.

Hacking's (1983) influential distinction between representing/theorising and intervening/experimenting as general modes of existence in the world is also influential in marking separation as a dominant way of framing. Hacking argued that representing has been separated out and given primacy over intervening, thereby positioning theory as a set of abstract ideas, detached from matter and what matters, and thereby reducing the importance of and possibilities for experimentation. This separation results from, and in, the dividing of matter from meaning, and further divides the material into, for instance, the social, the natural, the technological, the cultural and the economic.

When we add new technologies into this framework of separation, then they act as separate extensions of the human reach, as prosthesis of the subject. We can see this reflected in discourses which emphasise technologies as *tools*. The tool is the dominant metaphor in framing technology: office tools, productivity tools, web tools, authoring tools, apps and Google Web Toolkits. In education, the discourses of hardware, operating systems and software are positioned as extending the possibilities for human learning. The current fetishising of MOOCs and Open Educational Resources is merely a further extension of this logic of computers as tools to support learning. Effectively, computers, their codes, algorithms and standards, are presented as tools for enhancing and extending learning, offering remote and extended ways of representing the world to human subjects. They offer different means through which to learn *about* things. However, for Latour (2004a: 51), 'the social world is no more made up of subjects than nature is made up of objects'. Such distinctions already produce what they assume through the practices enacted. In this framing, the digital is not simply a tool for representing, but offers ways of attaching, which will be addressed in the next section.

In so far as the modern separations are accepted, such distinctions establish the terms of debate with the key question being how to fill the gaps between the distinguished domains, or how they can be related to one another. If the subject is separate from the object, then what is their relationship to each other and how does the subject have secure knowledge of the object? Epistemology has pursued such questions throughout the history of philosophy. In relation to the separation of matter/nature/object from meaning/society/subject, the question arises over how we can represent the former to the latter in meaningful ways. Of course, meaningful is not necessarily truthful in the senses we have come to associate with the practices of the empirical sciences, where knowledge is positioned as a representation of the external world *out there* to the internal world of the mind *in here*. Much space has been given to pursuing the ways in which humans can establish the truthfulness of the meanings through which we represent matter and the non-human.

Barad (2007: 137) argues that 'representationalism takes the notion of separation as foundational. It separates the world into the ontologically disjunct domains of words and things, leaving itself with the dilemma of their linkage such that knowledge is possible … representationalism is a prisoner of the problematic metaphysics it postulates'. In education, this separation is both overcome and reproduced through human subjects who learn *about* objects. It is through learning that human subjects, as *learners*, are able to represent the world to themselves and to others.

Learning is enacted as a mode of existence and way of becoming through such practices. Facts can be established about objects and learnt by human subjects. Both subjects and objects are separated and centred in the process, and it is argued by Rose (1989) that this is supported by the practices of the psy-disciplines, in particular psychology, which precisely focuses on the human subject, mind and consciousness as separate domains to be studied. It is these practices of separation and the representationalist assumptions underpinning them that give traction to human learning as being the critical goal of education.

In Latour's (2005, 2010) terms, this position is both fabricated and real, a 'factish'; the reality of learning is enacted through the practices of separation and representation. In this sense, I am not arguing that learning as a goal for education should be critiqued as mistaken, because it is based upon false assumptions and mystifies or fetishises reality. Nor that it represents unenlightened thinking; something that through unveiling will reveal a further, alternative, better truth to be pursued. To put forward a critique in this manner would itself be consistent with a representationalist view that we can get to the facts and truth of matters. So, while I agree with Barad (2007: 53) that 'representationalism is a practice of bracketing out the significance of practices, that is, representationalism marks a failure to take account of the practices through which representations are produced', for me, this critique does not entail a further work of unveiling. Drawing upon Latour's (2004b) argument that critique as unveiling has 'run out of steam', I am suggesting rather that this work of separation and representation precisely enacts human learning as a real educational priority. However, things could be otherwise through different post-human types of work that require adding rather than replacing. I shall now outline one addition that requires post-human attachments rather than separation and that therefore enacts potentially different educational goals, in particular, that of experimentation.

ATTACHING THE HUMAN AND NON-HUMAN AND EXPERIMENTING

I suggested in the previous section that separation and representationalism were central to establishing human learning as a key concern for education. In this section, attachment will be a crucial concept and I shall argue that it and the underpinning assumptions upon which I draw, point to possibilities for experimenting being an important additional post-human goal for education. I want to suggest that experimenting can be different from learning, entailing practices of post-human attachment.

This line of argument has been influential among writers attempting to develop performative ontologies. Broadly, within such approaches there is an assumption that rather than separation as foundational to enacting a purified human condition, attachment is materially and practically fundamental to a hybridised post-human condition. Objects are not entirely separate entities, but are mixings, gatherings, things; what Latour (1993) refers to as 'quasi-objects' in his argument that we have never been modern, i.e. purified. Humans are themselves hybrids, made up of genes, cells, microbes, atoms, liquids, glasses, pacemakers, etc. In this framing, to think, to reflect, to represent,

> to theorise is not to leave the material world behind and enter the domain of pure ideas where the lofty space of the mind makes objective reflection possible. *Theorising, like experimenting, is a material practice* ... both theorists and experimentalists engage in the intertwined practices of theorising and experimenting ... *experimenting and theorizing are dynamic practices that play a constitutive role in the production of objects and subjects and matter and meaning.* (Barad, 2007: 55–6, emphasis in original)

In a sense, Barad is arguing that this is an alternative approach, which in some senses might suggest she is engaged in an unveiling of representationalism as mistaken and fetishising. On this reading, we should set aside learning, separation and representation, and develop an education about and for attaching, intervening and experimenting. My own view is that this is inconsistent with the argument for experimenting, as representation and separation precisely are made real through such acts; they are forms of experiment in particular practices of knowing and specific ways of being a human subject. Within a representationalist enactment of the world, practices attempt to produce matters of fact through separation and the representation of objects with properties by the knowing human subject. It is clearly related to a familiar focus on learning about the world by human subjects. By contrast, in an experimental enactment of the world, practices attach different things as matters of concern, and engage in trial and error.

Experimentation and attaching assume attachments of the impure human subject with the impure object world. This forms the basis for my argument for viewing experimenting as a crucial educational goal. We may learn about experimenting and learn experimenting through participation, but to experiment is not to learn as such; it is to attach and intervene. The argument here draws from aspects of Latour's (2004a: 195) work, as 'an experiment, as etymology attests, consists in "passing through" a trial and "coming out of it" in order to draw its lessons. It thus offers an intermediary between knowledge and ignorance'. To learn is to transcend ignorance, while to experiment is to sit within the ongoing tension of knowledge and ignorance. Latour's position is part of a bigger argument on the need for collective experimentation to attach humans and non-humans in the composition of a common existence in the face, in particular, of environmental challenges. Experiments require humans and non-human to be attached into certain endeavours, recognising that such trials will enable lessons to be drawn. For me, this is a constant dynamic based upon conditionality – things could be other – fallibility – we approximate until proven otherwise – and responsibility – responsive to others and otherness (Edwards, 2008, 2012). Here knowledge does not precede action, as might be suggested in an approach that says we need to learn about things. Knowledge, ignorance and action are attached through the experimental contributions. Knowledge and understanding become ways of relating *within* the world as well as representations *about* it. Within this situation, there can be good and bad experiments as there can also be good and bad learning.

> A bad experiment is not one that fails, but one from which the researcher has drawn no lesson that will help prepare the next experiment. A good experiment is not one that offers some definitive knowledge, but one that has allowed the researcher to trace the *critical path* along which it will be necessary to pass so that the following iteration will not be carried out in vain. (Latour, 2004a: 196, emphasis in original)

In relation to the digital, to experiment provides the possibilities for different forms of attachment. It is the codes, algorithms and the linking of data, the applications of technical standards, and ways in which decision-making and reasoning are articulated in computer software that (along with the hardware and the electronic infrastructures of networks) make things (like search engines, web applications, e-assessment systems) perform in particular ways and become actors in attaching different elements. Much of this action can be hidden (Edwards and Carmichael, 2012) to the humans who are attached through the webs of technology, when the technologies are taken to be merely tools to contribute to human endeavours. As recent work on code, code/space and algorithms suggest, the non-human is already active in the enactment of the human (e.g. Kitchin and Dodge, 2011; Hamilton and Frieson, 2013; Loveless and Williamson, 2013; Manovich, 2013).

As an example, let us take the work of classification and standardisation associated with the development of digital databases, and the ways in which complex knowledge is represented (Lampland and Star, 2009). While, as Bowker (2005: 140) argues, 'you can't store data without a classification system', in education how this occurs and with what effects, is largely left unexamined, unquestioned and hidden from those using the technology. The technology intervenes in and experiments with all that to which it is attached. With the passing of time and the incorporation of such data into new attachments, the pre-history of data, selections, application of standards, the application of rules can disappear further from view. With the advent of semantic technologies and machine learning, which allow data to be shared, aggregated and reused across a linked web of databases and applications, any act of classification, any assumption encapsulated in a rule expressed in the code of a program, or any decision to exclude certain results from the scope of a search, may have implications far beyond its original setting. There are attachings going on with or without the human through the actions of standards, code and algorithms.

This can be addressed through learning, as we witness in relation to the school curricula in England at the current time and the increased emphasis on the notion of 'learning to code'. However, we can also look at the attachments and experimentation that code is undertaking and the trials to which it is subject, which make them more than tools to extend learning. Barocas et al. (2013) point out that algorithms have a history and geography of what they can and cannot do, so they are not stable nor are they singular units of study or analysis. In line with the wider social scientific research on code, they argue that 'algorithms are invoked as powerful entities that govern, judge, sort, regulate, classify, influence, or otherwise discipline the world' (Barocas et al., 2013: 3). To learn computer programming would not necessarily result in an understanding of the full impact and significance of the work of algorithms. Thus, the suggestion is that there is a need to study not only software but also the availabilities and forms of data, the challenges associated with linking these and the practices within which they are enacted and which they make possible.

Based upon their analysis, Barocas et al. (2013) argue that it becomes impossible to research the precise work of algorithms. They argue that algorithms are elusive and almost unrepresentable; they are *inscrutable*. Here the work of software is not necessarily hidden – by someone or something – but is simply unknowable in the modern sense. The work being done across space and time with different software and datasets can be alluded to but is itself elusive, beyond human representation and learning, but attached to and enabling post-human experimentation. The issue is not whether the work of standards, codes and algorithms can be made visible in representing objects, but of the multiple inscrutable attachments and translations effected by human and non-human actants that are incorporated into educational experiments through the attachment of the digital (Millerand and Bowker, 2009).

It is the sense of attachments, trials and lessons from which to develop further experimentation that, for me, marks a post-human education. This might be said to be learning *through* and learning *to* rather than learning *about*. However, this still starts to centre the human subject, when it is the collective attachments that are gathered in experimenting from which lessons can be drawn that opens up education to something other than learning. In recent work in the sciences, such experimenting has been linked to the materialising and enactment of publics engaging in controversies (e.g. Marres and Lezaun, 2011; Whatmore and Landström, 2011). These are not simply human learnings, as without the non-human attachments there would be no trials or lessons, no experimenting. Attaching enables us to engage and intervene and not simply separate, represent and learn.

The enactment of education as forms of experimenting and attaching does not necessarily sit comfortably with the hegemonic discourse we face in much educational and other research where the knowing subject and learning is privileged. Rather than the human subject representing the non-human object through sense data of, for instance, observation, we enter into the spatio-temporal and materialising practices of attachment and experimentation. It is through the specific forms of boundary-drawing that enactments gather the world as particular trials, things and objects. This form of work is a way of intervening materially within the enactment of the world and not simply another way of representing views about the world. Differences are not simply about matters of opinion and truth, but are ways of experimenting and attaching to address matters of concern.

POST-HUMAN EDUCATION?

The concept of learning has been much represented, debated, discussed and critiqued. The emphasis on learning can be argued itself to have been part of attempts to purify education of additional purposes and to be aligned also with an increasing emphasis on learning *about* associated with representationalism and the separation of human subject from natural object. In some senses then, the emphasis on learning might be said to have limited the educational potential of education in specific ways while expanding certain possibilities. The more challenges and uncertainty in the world, the more one must learn, and this is a lifelong endeavour and not simply for the young. Learning here might be said to reduce unpredictability for humans and is represented as a matter of fact for and by humans, a way of representing the objective world to which separated human subjects must adapt. The human subject is centred as that which must learn about the world in such practices.

The argument in this chapter is that rather than seek to argue for a wider notion of learning, by extending the logic of separation and representationialism, we could more fruitfully attach different post-human sensibilities to education. As argued here, this attachment would focus on practices of experimentation with the human and non-human rather than the more adaptive approaches of human learning. Education would not support learning as defined above alone, but also enable experimenting, attaching and their associated

trials. There may be a learning mode of existence, but this relies, as I have said, on representation and separation. An experimental mode of existence requires attaching the already hybrid human and non-human in forms of trial and error. Both are possible in the enactments of education.

This might mean that multiple goals of education are mutually inconsistent and involve different forms of practice to support learning and experimenting as conceived within this argument, and that education may support a range of practices, including diverse forms of learning. Patching such multiplicity is not easy, as there remain the normative questions of what constitutes worthwhile learning and experimenting. However, it might also mean that in terms of curriculum and pedagogy, educational institutions could be a lot more experimental themselves in what they ask of people and what is valued within them and by the wider orders of which they are part. My concern is that a continued focus on learning will produce an education separated from the concerns of the world and only concerned with the development of a certain form of the human subject through practices that separate the educational institution from the multiple orders within which they are nested and to which they could contribute more responsibly.

Additional to learning therefore, we could pursue experimenting. Experimenting emerges from post-human modes of existence. Thus, while humanism focuses on the mind and learning as a form of reflection, contemplation, abstraction and representation to establish matters of fact, I am suggesting that additionally experimenting and the collective attaching of the human and non-human enact matters of concern and controversy. This provides an additional educational purpose to much of that which is familiar. The difference lies in it not being the human subject who learns through experimenting rather than representing, but the collective that is attached in trial and error, which is an enactment of the post-human. Here there is a decentring of the knowing/learning human subject within educational practices. Where such practices exist, we could seek to expand the senses of experimenting rather than reduce them to ways to support learning.

Experimentation, attaching, fallibility, conditionality and responsibility seem to be ways of engaging with the collective challenges of sustainability, which is central to the post-human challenge. They open up possibilities for enacting matters of concern, but not on the notion of mandating or mastering the future or any strong normative view about what education can achieve or how it can achieve through enhancing the learning of human subjects. We may not want to erase learning as an educational purpose, but add experimenting as a way of placing a question mark over learning as the sole or adequate goal of education. This requires different attachings and the entry of the non-human and material into the experiments of education to a greater extent. The human is already non-human and vice versa. Here education is about more than just learning. It is also about experimenting. And in some ways, perhaps we need less learning in education and more responsible experimenting. This requires different types of educational ecologies to the institutionalisation of learning that tend to be the norm. Given the ecological, economic and social challenges faced, would that be such a bad experiment? It would certainly be a trial.

REFERENCES

Badmington, N. (2003) 'Theorizing posthumanism', *Cultural Critique*, 53: 10–27.

Barad, K. (2007) *Meeting the Universe Halfway*, Durham: Duke University Press.

Barocas, S., Hood, S. and Ziewitz, M. (2013) 'Governing algorithms: A provocation piece', paper prepared for the Governing Algorithms conference, May 16–17, New York University.

Biesta, G. (2004) 'Against learning: Reclaiming a language for education in an age of learning', *Nordisk Pedagogik*, 24: 70–82.

Bowker, G. (2005) *Memory Practices in the Sciences*, Cambridge, MA: MIT Press.

Bowker, G. and Star, S. (2000) *Sorting Things Out*, Cambridge, MA: MIT Press.

Braidotti, R. (2013) *The Posthuman*, Cambridge: Polity Press.

Edwards, R. (2008) 'Education – an impossible practice?', *Scottish Educational Review*, 40(1): 4–11.

Edwards, R. (2012) 'Theory matters: Representation and experimentation in education', *Educational Philosophy and Theory*, 44(5): 522–34.

Edwards, R. and Carmichael, P. (2012) 'Secret codes: The hidden curriculum of the semantic web', *Discourse*, 33(4): 575–90.

Fenwick, T., Edwards, R. and Sawchuk, P. (2011) *Emerging Approaches to Educational Research: Tracing the Sociomaterial*, London: Routledge.

Gough, N. (2004) 'RhizomANTically becoming-cyborg: Performing posthuman pedagogies', *Educational Philosophy and Theory*, 36(3): 253–65.

Hacking, I. (1983) *Representing and Intervening: Introductory Topics in the Philosophy of Natural Sciences*, Cambridge: Cambridge University Press.

Hamilton, E. and Friesen, N. (2013) 'Online education: A science and technology studies perspective', *Canadian Journal of Learning and Technology*, 39(2): 1–21.

Kitchin, R. and Dodge, M. (2011) *Code/Space: Software and Everyday Life*, Cambridge, MA: MIT Press.

Lampland, M. and Star, S. (eds) (2009) *Standards and Their Stories: How Quantifying, Classifying, and Formalizing Practices Shape Everyday Life*, Ithaca: Cornell University Press.

Latour, B. (1993) *We Have Never Been Modern*, Cambridge, MA: Harvard University Press.

Latour, B. (2004a) *Politics of Nature*, Cambridge, MA: Harvard University Press.

Latour, B. (2004b) 'Why has critique run out of steam? From matters of fact to matters of concern', *Critical Inquiry*, 30: 225–48.

Latour, B. (2005) *Reassembling the Social*, Oxford: Oxford University Press.

Latour, B. (2010) *On the Modern Cult of the Factish Gods*, Durham: Duke University Press.

Lawn, M. and Grosvenor, I. (eds) (2005) *Materialities of Schooling*, Oxford: Symposium Books.

Loveless, A. and Williamson, B. (2013) *Learning Identities in a Digital Age: Rethinking Creativity, Education and Technology*, London: Routledge.

Lyotard, J.-F. (1992) *The Postmodern Explained to Children*, London: Turnaround.

Manovich, L. (2013) *Software Takes Command*, New York: Bloomsbury.

Marres, N. and Lezaun, J. (2011) 'Materials and devices of the public: An introduction', *Economy and Society*, 40(4): 489–509.

Millerand, F. and Bowker, G. (2009) 'Metadata standards: Trajectories and enactment in the life of an ontology', in M. Lampland, and S. Star (eds) *Standards and Their Stories: How Quantifying, Classifying, and Normalizing Practices Shape Everyday Life* (pp. 149–76), Ithaca: Cornell University Press.

Mol, A.-M. (2002) *The Body Multiple*, Durham: Duke University Press.

Rose, N. (1989) *Inventing Our Selves*, Cambridge: Cambridge University Press.

Rose, N. (1999) *Powers of Freedom*, Cambridge: Cambridge University Press.

Sayes, E. (2014) 'Actor-network theory and methodology: Just what does it mean to say that nonhumans have agency?', *Social Studies of Science*, 44(1): 134–49.

Sfard, A. (1998) 'On two metaphors of learning and the dangers of choosing just one', *Educational Researcher*, 27(2): 4–13.

Sørenson, E. (2009) *The Materiality of Learning*, Cambridge: Cambridge University Press.

Whatmore, S. and Landström, C. (2011) 'Flood apprentices: An exercise in making things public', *Economy and Society*, 40(4): 582–610.

A Phenomenological Perspective on Learning

David Aldridge

INTRODUCTION

The task I have set myself in this chapter is to situate phenomenology in relation to the range of ways of approaching research into learning. This will necessitate attempting to do justice to the diverse 'phenomenologies' that might be encountered in educational writing (Findlay, 2012; Gallagher, 2012: 7–10). Rather than performing a detailed genealogy, taxonomy or history of ideas, I have focused on a single question – the extent to which phenomenology can be understood as an empirical research methodology. I will also ask what else it might be apart from an empirical methodology, how else could phenomenology constitute a way of seeing learning, and what would be the value of this alternative for understanding learning? Some engagement with these questions will suffice, I think, for an introduction to the phenomenological territory, and in particular a consideration of the

extent to which phenomenology can 'play well with others'.

One study selected as part of a collection showcasing the diversity and application of phenomenological research, attributes an amount of confusion about phenomenology to the fact that it 'is both a philosophy and a methodology' (Ganeson and Ehrich, 2009: 70). This is worth stating early on because a reader's engagement with phenomenology up to this point might be primarily with phenomenology as a social science methodology. Phenomenology is certainly presented as such in many of the major guides to educational research, where it might be offered as part of a taxonomy or a (sometimes chronological) hierarchy of 'qualitative' methodologies that also includes ethnography, grounded theory, symbolic interactionism, etc. (see, for example, Cohen, Manion and Morrison, 2011; Cresswell, 2013). Arguably, the paper I cited at the start of this paragraph treats phenomenology in this way. To the reader acquainted with phenomenological studies of this kind, the claim that phenomenology is also 'a philosophy' might seem unexceptional. All of the available 'methodologies' have distinctive philosophical assumptions that are more or less well developed in the research literature.

Yet there is another reader who might have encountered phenomenology only as a distinctive perspective within philosophy of education; a good example might be the collected papers in the volume 'Heidegger, Education and Modernity', all of which engage with the same 'originary' thinker (Peters, 2002). To this reader, it will not be disturbing to think of philosophers as having their 'methods' (Heidegger, certainly in his earlier work, was insistent on his). But the idea that phenomenology is to be construed as a 'methodology' for any sort of empirical project would perhaps be a surprise. This reader would rather see in phenomenology a way of approaching thinking that could give rise to a substantive body of distinctly 'phenomenological' insights into learning. This already sets phenomenology well apart from other suggested 'methodologies' for qualitative research – ethnography, grounded theory, etc. – about which the same cannot be said. Additionally, however, we will see that this ontology has given rise to a well-developed critique of the value, possibility and even danger of doing certain kinds of empirical research into learning. This means that as well as being susceptible to treatment as an empirical methodology – as part of a social science toolkit from which the researcher can select as appropriate to the nature of the enquiry and the question at hand – phenomenology might also be susceptible to the kind of 'so what' critique that can occasionally be applied to the philosophy of education by those who are operating within an empirical framework.

When we add in the 'phenomenology of practice' that is associated particularly with Max van Manen, we complicate the distinction somewhat. Van Manen has presented phenomenology as a form of 'research into lived experience', and has stressed that this is a qualitative research method that can be taught rather than needing to be learned by 'osmosis' (1990: 2). He has also distinguished the practice of phenomenology from philosophising *about* phenomenology, and argued that while a certain sensitivity to the writing of the originary thinkers inspires phenomenological writing, one does not need to be a philosopher to 'do' phenomenology (2014: 23). However, van Manen has also stressed the 'impossible' nature of doing phenomenological research:

> [Phenomenology] is the project that tries to describe the pre-reflective meaning of the living now. However, phenomenology is also aware that when we try to capture the "now" of the living present in an oral or written description, then we are already too late. The moment that I stop and reflect on what I am experiencing in the present – this moment inevitably becomes objectified – it turns from the subjectivity of living presence into an object of reflective presence. No matter how we try, we are always too late to capture the moment of the living now, whether this now is the micro-moment of the lover's eye, or the macro-moment of living with depression. (van Manen, 2014: 34)

It is characteristic of 'lived experience', van Manen argues, to resist theorisation (or at least a certain narrow understanding of theory that we might find equally in social sciences research or philosophy). So readers might find phenomenological writing of the kind van Manen advocates lacking in the sort of argumentative or other formulaic structures common to other disciplines of research. In fact, the phenomenological techniques to be mastered – if indeed they are appropriately called 'techniques' at all – might have more to do with whatever it is the poet, or the creative writer of fiction, does to make his or her writing more 'truthful'. Phenomenological writing might then appear to alternate highly dense and evasive elaborations of images, situations or episodes with unresolved narratives or anecdotes. It will be marked, van Manen argues, by the absence of a 'punchline' (1990: 13). This kind of writing – improperly understood, or (and this is a significant danger) done badly – is liable to frustrate social science researchers and analytical philosophers alike.

HUSSERL AND THE IDEA OF PHENOMENOLOGY AS SCIENCE

Husserl was working within a disciplinary framework most acknowledge to be philosophical, yet claimed to apply a rigorous 'method'. In the earlier stages of his career, at least, he also claimed for phenomenology the status of a science. The motivation for his project rests primarily on a rejection of a naturalistic or mechanistic account of the world (Carman, 2006: 99). Husserl's contention was that philosophers had lost sight of their purpose by unreflectively accepting the ontological assumptions of the natural sciences, so he sought a genuinely *primordial* philosophy that would be grounded in a certainty and privileged access to entities that the empirical sciences could not attain. Phenomenology is therefore presented as a foundational science *par excellence.* As a scientific approach, it requires a rigorous method that will enable the phenomenologist to focus carefully on the phenomena, the 'things themselves' (*den Sachen selbst*) or the objects of consciousness *purely as they are given to consciousness* and unmediated by opinions or assumptions. The study of the 'phenomena' for Husserl therefore entails elicitation of the form and content of appearances to which we have direct intuitive access. Without needing to question or engage with the reality of transcendent or external objects, we can nevertheless focus on the 'intentionality' of consciousness – that we are always conscious 'of' something.

Four key elements attributed to Husserl's method have become well established as principles or procedures for phenomenology as social research, largely via their codification in the psychological or 'empirical' phenomenology of Amadeo Giorgi and the Duquesne school (Giorgi, 1985) – intentionality, description, reduction and the essences (Findlay,

2012; Ganeson and Ehrich, 2009). An emphasis on description in Husserl's writing served to distinguish his own philosophical work on consciousness from contemporary psychologists whose approach was *explanatory.* Husserl's scientific method sought rigorously to restrict itself to describing the phenomena of consciousness without straying into inference or speculation on the properties of the external objects or psychological mechanisms that might cause such appearances. This rigorous reduction of the phenomenological perspective only to what is available purely to the transparent intuition of the subject is served by a process of 'bracketing' what is known or believed about the properties of mind-independent objects or the mechanistic properties of the world beyond consciousness; in short, the phenomenological reduction requires a bracketing of ontology (Husserl, 2012: 56–60).

Husserl intends the phenomenological method to produce descriptions of the 'essences' of the phenomena of consciousness: the essential properties of particular appearances that are universal to all appearances of that kind, without which each would cease to be the phenomenon under investigation. Essences are to be identified through a process of 'imaginative' or 'eidetic variation'; methodically varying selected elements of the phenomenon to ascertain whether the transformation of that element changes the appearance into a different phenomenon (Husserl, 1973: 341–49).

Although this is not an observation often made by social researchers who attribute their methodology to Husserl, it is surprising that such philosophical considerations gained any kind of foothold in empirical methodology (Neisser, 1959). Aside from the fact that Husserl defined himself *against* the psychologists and was avowedly anti-empirical, his method stressed the *a priori* importance of the pure or direct intuition rather than the gathering of 'data'. In fact, I would argue that the importation of phenomenology into the milieu of social research rests more on the appeal of a rigorous 'scientific' method for areas of enquiry liable to be condemned as irrational or pre-scientific by other disciplinary communities, than any particular interest in the minutiae of Husserl's philosophical assumptions.

Husserl was not sceptical about the existence of other minds, although he acknowledged and wrestled with the significant problem of gaining any knowledge of them through the phenomenological reduction (Husserl, 1960). Any enquiry into the content of other minds could not hope for the kind of certainty or direct intuitive access required in the phenomenological method. However, van Manen argues that the phenomenologist needs *intersubjectivity* in order to 'validate the phenomenon as described' (1990: 11) and Gallagher elaborates that '[my] intentional experience of the world gives me a sense of objectivity that cashes out in terms of inter-subjective accessibility' (2012: 185). In other words, the possibility of presenting phenomenology as an objective science requires that Husserl's descriptions of the essences can be subjected to the critique of his peers for confirmation of their accuracy. The assumption of intersubjectivity is therefore essential for the validity of his philosophical investigations, but does not allow for the gathering of data that could facilitate empirical discovery. This can be seen in Husserl's own criticism of the so-called phenomenological studies of many of his students and contemporaries – that they had neglected the *transcendental* aspects of his philosophy, which focused on ideal essences rather than real or factual contingencies (Neisser, 1959: 199).

The crossing over of phenomenology from philosophy into various areas of social research has been well documented but is not unproblematic. In the study of religion, for example, 'phenomenology' became the methodology *de rigueur* throughout the middle of the twentieth century. What should be noted here, however, is that in attempting to establish the 'essence' of a religion through sociological research, the phenomenological method of bracketing, although it is retained, undergoes a significant transformation. Rather than bracketing ontological assumptions, the use of phenomenology in social sciences contexts often requires that the researcher brackets his or her personal assumptions or prejudices, in favour of the attempt to perceive the phenomenon *as it is perceived by the subject of the study* (Erricker, 1999). This move is often attributed to Husserl's practice of bracketing, but in fact has little precedent in his own description of the phenomenological method. Giorgi identifies in Husserl's project the possibility of establishing qualitative research on a scientific basis. He presents an empirical methodology that aspires to description of the essences of psychological phenomena through the rigorous application of Husserl's method, and has a validity supposedly grounded in the reproducibility of the discovery by other researchers in other contexts (Giorgi, 2009). However, van Manen points out that 'it requires a conceptual leap to move from Husserl's philosophical phenomenology to Giorgi's descriptive analytic procedures' (van Manen, 2014: 211).

Alfred Schutz's attempts to apply phenomenology to social phenomena rather than simply the objects of consciousness potentially offers a way that phenomenology could adopt some of the data gathering methods of the social sciences without compromising Husserl's philosophical motivation. The process of comparing various empirical examples, according to Schutz, could stand in place of imaginative variation, or supplement the potentially limited imaginative capacity of the researcher by offering additional variations. In a phenomenology influenced by Schutz, the process of gathering data through interviews, for example, would not enable the researcher to discover the factual empirical structures of any particular culture, but plays the role of providing intersubjective validity to a description of the *existential* meaning structures of a cultural phenomenon (Schutz, 1970; van Manen, 2014: 347–8). It is difficult to determine whether such a methodology could properly be called empirical. One outcome that seems quite likely, however, is that the exchange between phenomenology and the particular methods of social research would be a one-way street: phenomenologists could borrow methods from other areas of social research as a means of supplementing the practice of imaginative variation, but the empirical social researcher could not 'borrow' from phenomenology. To do so would mean assuming certain ontological relationships between the contents of consciousness and a publicly accessible external world that Husserl would have bracketed as an essential aspect of his 'transcendental' method.

HEIDEGGER AND THE 'PRACTICE TURN'

Heidegger's reading of Husserl is much debated. There is some disagreement among philosophers about the extent to which Heidegger's avowed departure from Husserl represents a radical split from his teacher or is in fact incorporated or anticipated in Husserl's emphasis on the concept of the lifeworld, particularly later in his career. The accuracy of Heidegger's representation of Husserl is not really the focus of this chapter, so rather than speak of firm differences between Heidegger and Husserl I will refer to a 'Heideggerian' turn and remain relatively agnostic about the possible overlaps between the perspectives of the historical individuals. What is important in any case is that radically competing models of intentionality remain influential in the varieties of phenomenological research that are on offer to the reader, and that the choice between them depends on the resolution of the philosophical question of how properly to construe intentionality and the 'natural' attitude. The discussion of phenomenology in educational and social research texts tends to shy away from meeting this philosophical question head-on and present the decision between phenomenologies as a choice about which of a range of diverse tools best fits the problem at hand (see, for example, Garza, 2007).

It is hard to do justice to Heidegger's criticism of Husserl's account of intentionality in such a short piece, so I direct the reader to three sources that have influenced the reading I am about to offer (namely, Dreyfus, 1991; Carman, 2006; Gallagher, 2012). According to Heidegger, Husserl took over a Cartesian ontological assumption about the basic nature of consciousness (1985: 107). Although Husserl had managed to reject a certain subject-object distinction by emphasising that consciousness was always 'of' or 'about' some object, he had nevertheless accepted the Cartesian model of intentionality when he claimed that the natural mode was a state in which objects were purely 'present' to consciousness and could be intuited without theoretical mediation. For Heidegger, the inability to 'bracket' this assumption means that Husserl has not rigorously followed his own method (Carman, 2006: 99). Bracketing this assumption, furthermore, leads to a transformation of the method and its implications. A turn 'to the things themselves' should lead us to a description of the phenomenon of intentionality itself. Heidegger's claim is that Husserl's intentionality is a derivative mode. Entities only occur as 'present-at-hand' – they only present themselves as 'objects' which are susceptible to theoretical examination – when a more foundational and originary mode is interrupted (1962: 102–3).

Our ordinary mode of being, on the other hand, is one of engagement in 'concernful dealings' with things (Heidegger, 1962: 103). We don't see things initially as objects at all (1962: 98). Our intentionality is better understood as being taken up in a project in a 'referential context' or 'totality' (1962: 105). Heidegger opposes this temporality of existential projectedness to a temporality of 'presence'. Our natural mode is one of comportment towards a world of significance rather than the disinterested perception of entities. The classic example is of the craftsman busy in his workshop. He is taken up or absorbed in a particular existential project, and intentionality here can be thought of in terms of the craftsman's *being directed* towards his end product. He interacts with the various objects and tools in his workshop as 'ready-to-hand', as part of a totality in which he has an inexplicit or unreflective mastery. When he reaches out for a hammer that is not in its proper place, and finds instead one which does not have the appropriate size or heft for the job he needs to do, this totality is broken and he is presented with a problem. Now the hammer is present to his consciousness as an object with particular properties (the wrong ones); the problem must be thought through and solved, giving rise to a theoretical mode, before the craftsman can return to his 'natural' state and become absorbed again in his task. Gallagher connects this to the psychologist Gibson's contention that 'we don't perceive the world as a set of objects with certain properties that allow us to infer use-value; we perceive it as a set of affordances that we can act upon' (Gallagher, 2012: 168).

The whole of *Being and Time* is concerned with elaborating the significance of this insight. Firstly, this leads Heidegger to strive toward a new phenomenological vocabulary that would enable him to do justice to intentionality while bracketing all kinds of presuppositions about the 'natural' mode of our engagement with the world. This leads him to replace the human subject with the *Dasein*, the 'being-there', and the phenomenon of 'being-in-the-world'. Dasein is always already 'thrown' into a referential totality or a world of significance. Any theoretical, propositional or reflective thought – any sort of explicit interpretation of entities – presupposes a background of non-thematic mastery or the 'comportment' of Dasein toward the world. This radically changes the transcendence of Husserl's project. Rather than bracketing any considerations about what is 'outside' consciousness, the very distinctions which Husserl implicitly took over, between subject and object or self and world, need themselves to be bracketed. It is of the essence of Dasein to be projected, to be always already

'out there' in the world. This relationality inherent in the basic phenomenon of Dasein is what Heidegger terms 'originary transcendence' (1984).

Against Husserl, then, ontology cannot be bracketed. Heidegger's project is conceived as the attempt to describe how objects or entities are given as such, or to think through the meaning of being (1962: 1). This is radically different from previous ontological projects of describing why there is something rather than nothing, or explaining how entities have come into existence. The phenomenon of the being of beings is the 'thing itself' with which Heidegger's 'fundamental ontology' is concerned, and phenomenology is his means of access to that object (1962: 62). The immense significance and at the same time subtlety of Husserl's mistake, and the fact that this real question of being has been covered over for so long in human history, demonstrates for Heidegger the significance of a further departure from Husserl, in that although Heidegger retains the idea of the 'phenomenon', we never simply perceive or directly intuit our object in Heidegger's phenomenology. Phenomena are not immediately apparent, but have a tendency to become covered over by the history of mankind's attempts to thematise them or render them in propositional thought (1962: 25). Dreyfus (1991: 35) points out that 'we dwell in our understanding like a fish in water'; it is precisely because our everyday or 'average' understanding of being is always presupposed, because it is in fact so close to us, that it is so difficult for us to articulate explicitly. Phenomena therefore must be 'allowed' to show themselves, which leads Heidegger to claim that phenomenology is a fundamentally hermeneutic or interpretive process rather than a matter of intuiting the phenomenon in an unmediated state. This is such a radical departure from the Husserlian reduction that Carman is led to ask whether Husserl touched 'neither the core nor the details of Heidegger's project' (2006: 98).

THE PHENOMENOLOGY OF PRACTICE

We are now in a position to understand how the Heideggerian 'primacy of practice' informs van Manen's 'phenomenology of practice'. The point is to engage with our experience as it is lived rather than as it is conceptualised. This leads to some important restrictions with which van Manen bounds his own conception of the phenomenological project. Theoretical engagement, if there is to be any, must be constituted along the lines of a more 'originary' or ancient Greek understanding of *theoria* that van Manen takes over from Gadamer, which is to do with an attentive contemplation of the matter at hand (van Manen, 2007: 14). The value to the researcher is not to be understood *epistemologically* – in terms, say, of theory-building – but ontologically, in terms of the transformation of self that is brought about through a heightened attentiveness to lived experience. Van Manen plays down the philosophical possibilities of phenomenology in favour of a focus on the individual, and the potential for edification. He therefore views phenomenology as an essentially educational activity in the *Bildung* tradition (1990: 17).

The practitioner is led to phenomenological enquiry through a question about lived experience that emerges from his/her own practice. It is difficult, however, to argue for the gains or outcomes that might arise from the practice of phenomenology as van Manen conceives it. The kind of means–ends thinking that might motivate a researcher to solve a particular 'problem' will not, van Manen argues, give rise to phenomenological thinking. We do not, through a phenomenology of practice, become 'better' at our jobs in the sense of more efficiently accomplishing particular aims. Rather, the promise of engaging in phenomenology is that we return to our practice transformed. As Heidegger argues in his later work, we move towards the possibility of a state of 'dwelling' in our practice that consists of recognising and claiming the possibilities inherent in it. The phenomenologist who enquires into teaching aims to become more attentive to her own experience of becoming a teacher, in the hope of thus becoming more fully. Van Manen (1990: 7) has also popularised the concept of 'tact', that idea that the practitioner approaches her work with a sensitivity or attunement that cannot be reduced or captured in theoretical propositions.

I do not feel as strongly as van Manen about the need to separate out phenomenology from philosophy. Or perhaps van Manen's intention in emphasising this distinction is to avoid discouraging those who might be intimidated by the idea of philosophy from engaging in phenomenological endeavour. Certainly, van Manen's emphasis on the poetic nature of phenomenological writing will rule out certain conceptions of the practice of philosophy, but by no means all. Let us not forget that phenomenologists working in the philosophical tradition have tended to eschew the term philosophy as a description of what they are doing. Certainly, later in his career, Heidegger (2011) wished to distance himself from the metaphysical tradition and preferred to talk about the 'craft of thinking'.

Blattner (2007) sets out an interesting problem in Heidegger scholarship. He takes Heidegger's claim that the background of understanding is 'non-thematic' to mean that the understanding embodied in our 'comportment' is not susceptible to propositional description or expression without reduction, loss or misrepresentation. He then notes Heidegger's project of the 'fundamental ontology' – the attempt to give a phenomenological description of the essential aspects of precisely this originary form of intentionality. These two aims, Blattner argues, might seem to be in opposition, but are in fact only irreconcilable if we accept a third implied premise, that the project of fundamental ontology is to be attempted or communicated propositionally. Blattner resolves this problem by arguing that while Heidegger seems not to have fully accepted these implications in his earlier work, the move in his later career into a more poetic form of writing (away, in fact, even from an explicit emphasis on the practice of phenomenology) represents his ongoing attempt to find a mode of enquiry suitable for the project of fundamental ontology.

It is for this reason that I defend the possibility that phenomenology might offer substantive philosophical insights into learning. The convergence of many of the phenomena of Heidegger's fundamental ontology – understanding, interpretation, thinking, dialogue – with central educational themes, along with the recognition that phenomenology is itself a distinctively educational mode of enquiry, suggest to me that it is possible to strive for an 'ontology of the learning event', even if the means of communicating or expressing such an ontology might stretch conventional disciplinary or stylistic expectations about what properly counts as philosophy.

PHENOMENOLOGY AND THE CRITIQUE OF EMPIRICAL RESEARCH

It is a life's work to sketch out the contours of an ontology of learning. However, in line with my stated aim of bringing phenomenology into dialogue with other forms of research into learning, I will develop some of the resonances that have already been alluded to in the chapter, specifically to the extent that they might furnish or point toward a critique of empirical forms of enquiry.

A starting point here would be the recognition that a preoccupation with learning as an *epistemological* process, concerned with knowledge or even the acquisition of skills or capacities, would be a limited or mistaken conception that would restrict our understanding of learning to a derived or instrumental mode. Heideggerian phenomenology would rather see learning from a broader ontological perspective, as a moment that occurs in dialogue or relation rather than the achievement of an individual subjectivity. Pedagogy is an 'expression of the whole' (van Manen, 1990: 7). Learning might be viewed as an event of becoming in which the self is

transformed in relation to the world (Aldridge, 2013; Barnett, 2004; Dall'Alba and Barnacle, 2007). This would have implications for the assessment or measurement of learning, which would need to take into account the existential orientation of the learner rather than simply the transfer or 'taking in' of new knowledge or capacities that would otherwise leave the learner unchanged (Vu and Dall Alba, 2013). It would acknowledge that more than the learner is transformed in this event: an event of learning occurs in a tradition with which both teacher and learner reflexively interact, and which therefore is itself transformed in the learning event (Gallagher, 1992: 105–7).

A further problem specifically with empirical investigations of learning would be the assumption of educational ends, particularly as they might be linked to explorations into 'what works', or the 'effectiveness' of particular interventions (Standish, 2001). Gadamer makes the distinction between a problem, which strictly bounds the possibility of any enquiry and sets the parameters within which a possible solution might be defined, and the genuine question. The question is open to the indeterminacy of the situation (what Weinsheimer calls 'the hap') and thus allows for the possibility of its own transformation, and the corresponding transformation of the orientation of the enquirer, as an unexpected subject matter 'emerges' (Weinsheimer, 1985: 8). Heidegger's cautioning that appearances can be concealed and must be allowed to show themselves brings to our attention the possibility that the phenomenon we end up describing may be significantly transformed from the one we thought we had originally gone looking for. Thus Munday (2012) has pointed out that the phenomenological approach to the classroom has more in common with the mystery than the problem, and van Manen encourages the use of poetic approaches, calling to mind the power of the great poets to invoke a sense of wonder at everyday circumstances, occurrences and objects.

The empirical aim of gathering 'data' participates in the 'myth of the given' that

Heidegger argues Husserl was not able to shake off (Standish, 2001: 506). For Heidegger, this practice accords with a scientific tendency to attempt to bathe the world in the sterile light of the human subject. The image of the clearing in Heidegger's later thought, an attempt to address the question of being or describe *how it is that things are 'given'*, indicates some of the problems of this endeavour. As light plays across the woodland scene, certain paths and possibilities for human being are illuminated while others are cast into shadow, so that the researcher would do well to consider how it is that 'circumstances *have us*' rather than the other way around (Standish, 2001: 503). There is a serious ethical component to this criticism: the attempt to gather units of data in an ever more complete or total view of learning accords with Heidegger's critique of technological thinking, in which the world comes to be seen as units of generic 'standing reserve' increasingly subject to our manipulation and control (Heidegger, 1977). As Donnelly (1999) argues, instrumental research into learning is in danger of presupposing a conception of our students as 'present-at-hand' rather than doing justice to each child's nature as individual *Dasein*. It rests on an objectification which is one step away from construing our students, also, as so much standing reserve.

CONCLUDING REMARKS

It is not the aim of this chapter to argue against all applications of empirical research. Neither has it been my intention to declaim those enquiries that more closely adopt the trappings of social research methodologies as not properly 'phenomenological'. But certain observations can be made about enquiries of this kind – I am thinking for example of the Ganeson and Ehrich paper cited above, or perhaps a work in psychology by Anderson and Hull Spencer (2013) held up as an example of phenomenological methodology in a popular textbook on approaches to qualitative research. The first observation is that, for all of the attribution of a debt to Husserl, the move into data gathering in the social context would likely not have been recognised as a continuation of his own project, except perhaps through the extension into possibilities for eidetic variation we discussed above.

This is not such a problem, since in any case we have acknowledged that it is the Heideggerian development that has properly brought phenomenology out 'into the world'. It is the Heideggerian turn to ontology, for example, that makes possible Merleau-Ponty's insights into the *embodied* nature of human perception. However, for all of the recognition of the embodiment of lived experience (even 'psychological' studies that have their origins in Giorgi's work do so *through* the work of Merleau-Ponty), these studies seem to remain focused on cognitive representations rather than acknowledging the broader ontological significance of the Heideggerian account of intentionality. The emphasis on bracketing one's own preconceptions in favour of more attentively describing the other's description of the phenomenon, furthermore, seems largely heedless of Heidegger's warning that the phenomenon tends to become covered over and requires interpretation. It is not clear that studies of this kind do the work of letting the phenomenon show itself, so much as the work of categorising and ordering data into appropriate 'boxes' (Standish, 2001: 499).

What I do want to argue is that the validity of these studies, inasmuch as we might construe them as phenomenological, will not rely on the accuracy or extent of the data collection or the rigour with which certain principles or procedures have been followed. It will rather depend on the extent to which the reader finds that he or she can *assent* to the phenomenological description offered. Van Manen (1990: 27) refers to the 'phenomenological nod', the moment of recognition of the *truth* of the phenomenological account, that might possibly be the highest hope of the phenomenologist. There is an attempt at universal truth here. For all that van Manen (ibid.: 22) directs the phenomenology of lived experience towards the edification of the individual practitioner, he carefully points out that we will not find local 'phenomenologies of' particular schools or institutions. The reader might be uncomfortable with this assertion of the general accessibility of the essence of the phenomenon. Is there a conservative element in the claim that the 'truth' of the phenomenological description rests on the possibility of recognition by the reader? Might there not be some elements of the experience of the other that are beyond this possibility of recognition, and thus escape the phenomenologist, however thoughtful or attentive?

Gallagher remarks that Heidegger's thinking on intersubjectivity, the phenomenon of *Mitsein* or *'being with'*, emphasises how being involved in a project that involves others has a tendency to 'pull all of us into specific forms of inauthenticity' (Gallagher, 2012: 203). Although Gallagher feels that Heidegger overstates this danger (and we might temper this with something like Gadamer's advocacy of the ongoing commensurability of human understanding) we do well to remember that 'Participatory sense-making is the result of continuous interactions with others' and that 'The meaning of the world, and the objectivity of entities and events within the world are not established once and for all, or forever guaranteed' (Gallagher, 2012: 204).

But what of the further possibility that a phenomenon is so covered over that it cannot be made to show itself? Heidegger in his later writing seems sensitive to this problem. His original commitment to describing the a-historical essence of *Dasein* is tempered in his later work with a historical element – he accepts that there might be a succession of historical epochs in which being is 'disclosed' differently (Dreyfus, 2006: 346). But this gives rise to a dangerous problem: it is characteristic specifically of the current, 'technological' epoch that the technological 'revealing', conceived as an 'enframing', or total ordering, *conceals its own ontological status as an appearance* and 'drives out every

other possibility of revealing' (Heidegger, 1977: 27). Heidegger is, toward the end of his life, sceptical about the possibility even of phenomenology to resist the totalising tendencies of the technological hermeneutic – famously declaring that 'only a God can save us' (*Der Spiegel/* Heidegger, 1991). What is certain is that, if Heidegger's diagnosis is accurate, empirical methods will not offer the answer; rather they are *definitive of* the technological way of seeing and inextricably implicated in the way that being is revealed as standing reserve. Heidegger seems to suggest that perhaps an originary technological artwork might serve to inaugurate and redeem the technological epoch through disclosing the very essence of technology, and in so doing revealing its status as a form of disclosure (Costello, 2003). In the same way, perhaps the chance of redeeming education from the levelling and controlling tendencies of the current age might come, as Smeyers (2002) and others have suggested, from a poetic evocation of the educational endeavour. This possibility might strengthen the resolve of frustrated social researchers as they struggle with the sometimes seemingly imprecise and elusive attempts of phenomenologists to express the fleeting phenomenon of lived experience before it once more evades their grasp.

REFERENCES

Aldridge, D. (2013) 'The Logical Priority of the Question: R. G. Collingwood, Philosophical Hermeneutics and Enquiry-Based Learning', *Journal of Philosophy of Education*, 47(1): 71–85.

Anderson, E. and Hull Spencer, M. (2013) 'Appendix C: Cognitive Representations of Aids' in J. Cresswell, *Qualitative Inquiry and Research Design: Choosing Among Five Approaches*, 3rd edition, Thousand Oaks, CA: SAGE, pp. 327–46.

Barnett, R. (2004) 'Learning for an Unknown Future', *Higher Education Research and Development*, 23(3): 247–60.

Blattner, W. (2007) 'Ontology, the A Priori, and the Primacy of Practice: An Aporia in Heidegger's Early Philosophy' in S. Crowell and J. Malpas (eds) *Transcendental Heidegger*, Stanford: Stanford University Press, pp. 10–27.

Carman, T. (2006) 'The Principle of Phenomenology' in C. Guignon (ed.) *The Cambridge Companion to Heidegger*, 2nd edition, Cambridge: Cambridge University Press, pp. 97–129.

Cohen, L., Manion, L. and Morrison, K. (2011) *Research Methods in Education*, 7th edition, London and New York: Routledge.

Costello, D. (2003) 'Museum as Work in the Age of Technological Display: Reading Heidegger Through Tate Modern' in D. Arnold and M. Iverson (eds) *Art and Thought*, Oxford: Blackwell, pp. 174–96.

Cresswell, J. (2013) *Qualitative Inquiry and Research Design: Choosing Among Five Approaches*, 3rd edition, Thousand Oaks, CA: SAGE.

Dall'Alba, G. and Barnacle, R. (2007) 'An Ontological Turn for Higher Education', *Studies in Higher Education*, 32(6): 679–91.

Der Spiegel/Heidegger, M. (1991) '"Only a God Can Save Us"; *Der Spiegel*'s interview with Martin Heidegger (1996)' in R. Wolin (ed.) *The Heidegger Controversy: A Critical Reader*, Cambridge, MA: MIT Press, pp. 91–116.

Donnelly, J. (1999) 'Schooling Heidegger: On Being in Teaching', *Teaching and Teacher Education*, 15: 933–49.

Dreyfus, H. (1991) *Being-in-the-World: A Commentary on Heidegger's Being and Time*, London: MIT Press.

Dreyfus, H. (2006) 'Heidegger on the Connection Between Nihilism, Art, Technology, and Politics' in C. B. Guignon (ed.) *Cambridge Companion to Heidegger*, 2nd edition, Cambridge: Cambridge University Press, pp. 345–72.

Erricker, C. (1999) 'Phenomenological Approaches' in P. Connolly (ed.) *Approaches to the Study of Religion*, London and New York: Continuum, pp. 73–104.

Findlay, L. (2012) 'Debating Phenomenological Research Methods' in N. Friesen, C. Henriksson and T. Saevi (eds) *Hermeneutic Phenomenology in Education: Method and Practice*, Rotterdam: Sense, pp. 17–38.

Gallagher, S. (1992) *Hermeneutics and Education*, Albany: State University of New York Press.

Gallagher, S. (2012) *Phenomenology*, Basingstoke: Palgrave Macmillan.

Ganeson, K. and Ehrich, L. C. (2009) 'Transition into High School: A Phenomenological Study' in G. Dall'Alba (ed.) *Exploring Education Through Phenomenology: Diverse Approaches*, Malden and Oxford: Wiley-Blackwell, pp. 66–84.

Garza, G. (2007) 'Varieties of Phenomenological Research at the University of Dallas: An Emerging Typology', *Qualitative Research in Psychology*, 4: 313–42.

Giorgi, A. (ed.) (1985) *Phenomenological and Psychological Research*, Pittsburgh: Duquesne University Press.

Giorgi, A. (2009) *The Descriptive Phenomenological Method in Psychology: A Modified Husserlian Appoach*, Pittsburgh: Duquesne University Press.

Heidegger, M. (1962) *Being and Time*, Oxford: Blackwell.

Heidegger, M. (1977) 'The Question Concerning Technology' in W. Lovitt (trans.) *The Question Concerning Technology and Other Essays*, New York: Harper, pp. 3–35.

Heidegger, M. (1984) *The Metaphysical Foundations of Logic*, Bloomington, IN: Indiana University Press.

Heidegger, M. (1985) *History of the Concept of Time: Prolegomena*, Bloomington: Indiana University Press.

Heidegger, M. (2011) 'What Calls for Thinking' in D. F. Krell (ed.) *Heidegger: Basic Writings*, Abingdon: Routledge, Kegan and Paul, pp. 257–78.

Husserl, E. (1960) *Cartesian Meditations: An Introduction to Phenomenology*, Den Haag: Martinus Nijhoff.

Husserl, E. (1973) *Experience and Judgement*, Evanston, IL: Northwestern University Press.

Husserl, E. (2012) *Ideas*, London and New York: Routledge.

Munday, I. (2012) 'The Classroom: A Problem or Mystery', paper presented at the Philosophy of Education Society Annual Conference, New College, Oxford.

Neisser, H. (1959) 'The Phenomenological Approach in Social Science', *Philosophy and Phenomenological Research*, 20(2): 198–212.

Peters, M. A. (ed.) (2002) *Heidegger, Education and Modernity*, Oxford: Rowman and Littlefield.

Schutz, A. (1970) *On Phenomenology and Social Relations*, Chicago: University of Chicago Press.

Smeyers, P. (2002) 'The Origin: Education, Philosophy and a Work of Art', in M. A. Peters (ed.) *Heidegger, Education and Modernity*, Oxford: Rowman and Littlefield, pp. 81–102.

Standish, P. (2001) 'Data Return: The Sense of the Given in Educational Research', *Journal of Philosophy of Education*, 35(3): 497–518.

van Manen, M. (1990) *Researching Lived Experience: Human Science for an Action Sensitive Pedagogy*, New York: SUNY.

van Manen, M. (2007) 'Phenomenology of Practice', *Phenomenology and Practice*, 1(1): 11–30.

van Manen, M. (2014) *Phenomenology of Practice: Meaning-Giving Methods in Phenomenological Research and Writing*, Walnut Creek: Left Coast Press.

Vu, T. and Dall'Alba, G. (2013) 'Authentic Assessment for Student Learning: An Ontological Conceptualisation', *Educational Philosophy and Theory*, 46(7): 1–14.

Weinsheimer, J. (1985) *Gadamer's Hermeneutics*, New Haven, CT: Yale University Press.

12

Learning, Commognition and Mathematics

Anna Sfard

INTRODUCTION

Humans may not be the only living creatures capable of learning, but the way people learn and the nature and extent of the resulting change are unique. To realize this, it suffices to consider the special type of learning that takes place in school, one that has no obvious counterpart within the animal kingdom. Of all school subjects, mathematics is probably the topic that brings the contrast between human and non-human forms of learning into the sharpest relief. For this reason, mathematics is the illustrative context I will be using in this chapter, while: first, looking for a conceptualization of learning that would help in answering the question of what makes human learning special; second, asking whether the resulting framework is likely to lead to novel insights about learning; and finally, applying understandings thus gained while arguing that it is our special type of learning that gives rise to all things human.

CONCEPTUALIZING LEARNING – THE PARTICIPATIONIST APPROACH

The history of research on learning, although relatively brief, is replete with events which fit the Kuhnian idea of scientific revolution. Ever since its inception, this special domain of study has been a theoretical battlefield, in which different conceptualizations are considered as excluding rather than complementing one another. Whereas everybody seems to agree that learning must be defined as some kind of change, there is no consensus with regard to what it is that changes. In the twentieth century alone, this query has been answered in at least three different ways. At the earliest stages, during the reign of logical positivism, learning was conceptualized as the process of transforming one's *behaviour*. Shortly afterwards, when the entity called 'human mind' had been re-established as an object of inquiry, mental entities such as *schemes*, *internal representations* or *conceptions* were identified as the main object of learning-induced change and the change itself was conceptualized as the 'acquisition' of these entities. More recently, the *acquisitionist* vision was challenged by the approach that can be called *participationist*, since its proponents, inspired mainly by the work of Russian psychologist Lev S. Vygotsky, propose that the learning-defining changes are those that occur in people's *participation* in different kinds of activities. Within this context, the word *activity* is used as referring to culturally specific, tool-mediated, historically established ways of executing various life tasks.

Why this plurality of approaches and the pervasive instability? Research on learning, as any field of study that focuses on people rather than on an unanimated world, is torn between two colliding requirements: to be convincing and useful this research must be scientifically rigorous, whatever the word 'scientific' may mean at the given moment, and to fulfil its mission properly it has to be able to deal with those features of learning that are unique to people. The tension between these two demands is obvious: due to their complexity and inherent messiness, human ways of acting may be scientifically intractable. Indeed, the history of research on learning, so far, makes one wonder whether a single paradigm will ever be capable of fulfilling both these demands.

Behaviourism, when first proposed, could be an object of envy for any biologist or physicist with regard to operationality and rigour, but its findings, although novel and impressive, dealt only with the most basic forms of learning, to be found also in animals. As a result, this strand has been criticized as the science of 'behaviour without mind' (Vygotsky, 1982: 81; quoted in Minick, 1987: 19). Re-establishment of the entity called 'human mind' as an object of inquiry and the use of the computer as a model brought the hope that the problem might have been solved (Bruner, 1990). Gradually, the new science of cognition began to flourish and gained hegemony. Not for long, though. It soon turned out that of the two main strands

that developed within this new line of inquiry, neither the one that followed the computer metaphor of mind, nor the one that focused on the study of learners' (mis)conceptions, could fulfil any of the requirements without compromising the other. The information-processing approach, while relatively high on reliability and rigour, scored disappointingly low on capturing the nature of complex forms of human learning. The reverse proved true for misconceptions research, which, although rich in relevant insights, was not up to the standards of scientific rigour. Its quality was undermined by the constant references to elusive mental entities. It was with this latter issue in mind, among others, that researchers coming from the sociocultural tradition initiated by Vygotsky renounced speculating on what was happening inside the human head and started focusing on what people say and do while participating in daily activities. This 'participationist' line of inquiry brought the study of learning much closer to the pole of the uniquely human. Still, its non-standard methods made some people doubt the 'scientificity' of this type of study.

Its methodological struggles notwithstanding, participationism may be considered as the best option, so far, for those who want to know what makes human learning special. Above all, this approach seems to have succeeded in accounting for the centrally important trait of human learning that the former approaches left unexplained: it provided an answer to the question of how it happens that human activities evolve and grow in complexity from one generation to another. The perpetually changing uniquely human ways of acting, claimed Vygotsky, cannot grow 'from inside' the individual, merely in response to her direct perceptual experiences. If it was so, these activities would remain the same across generations. The uniquely human forms of activity, he said, are something that people learn from other people. In this process of mutual learning some local innovations spread within society, leading to durable, global modifications of activities.

This is how participationism solves the puzzle of historical change. Moreover, if this quandary is cast in the participationist language, it simply disappears. Since participationism removes the ontological divide between individual learning and historical development (both are now seen as changes in prevalent forms of activity), not only ontogenetic but also historical changes may now count as instances of learning. Having agreed on this, one can rephrase the old quandary of *what makes humanity conducive to historical change* as the question of *what it is that makes humans capable of societal learning*. In this rendition, ontogenetic and historical transformations become different levels of one phenomenon occurring within the complex system called human society. To use a metaphor, what appears as two kinds of learning is a pair of images of a single phenomenon, obtained, respectively, by first zooming in on this phenomenon and then zooming out again.

Whereas it is now quite clear that the people's capacity for learning quickly and effectively from one another accounts for societal learning, the question of what it is that makes this mutual learning so powerful and durable remains open. Indeed, how can we explain the fact that the complex, multi-layered activities, painstakingly shaped by humanity over millennia, can be mastered by the child in a matter of years? What is it that makes our ability to accumulate complexity on both individual and societal levels practically limitless? In the rest of this chapter I argue that the answer to this question lies, at least in part, in one particular human activity that mediates whatever else people are doing: the activity of communicating. To make this point, I will take a close look at *discursive learning*, learning that aims at extending and strengthening the activity of communicating. I will be asking about how and why human communication evolves over different timescales – in history and in the course of individual lives – and how it combines with other types of learning, helping to generate, spread and preserve innovation.

DISCURSIVE LEARNING AND ITS FOUNDATIONS

The term *discursive learning* can be interpreted as referring to the activity of becoming able to tell and produce ever new stories about the world, and may thus be seen as the participationist counterpart of the acquisitionist term *knowledge building*. As such, it can be contrasted with *practical learning*,[1] the aim of which is to reorganize and transform concrete objects.[2] Improving practical activities is arguably the most powerful motive that drives the production of ever new stories about the world. As a result, discursive and practical learning are sometimes so tightly intertwined that telling them apart becomes difficult. And yet, while elaborated and treated with caution, this distinction proves useful and eye opening. At the socio-historical level, the main source of the discursive learning is *scientific research*. At the individual level, this type of learning is best exemplified by the study of school subjects such as mathematics, science, history or literature. Admittedly, school is not the only site of the individual discursive learning, but this kind of learning dominates in classrooms. Indeed, it is discursive learning that constitutes the main goal of schooling.

In sum, the term *discursive learning* encompasses activities as different as the young child's getting acquainted with numbers and research mathematicians' creative explorations in the most esoteric regions of advanced mathematics. Learning in school about numbers consists in communicational activities that lead to numerical narratives, such as $2 + 3 = 5$ or 'for all numbers a, b and c, $a(b + c) = ab + ac$'. The value of these stories lies in their potential for mediating and improving a variety of practical, real-life tasks, from the simplest and most common ones, such as cooking or sewing, to the most advanced, such as building computers or travelling in space. Doing research in mathematics, although more creative than the basically reproductive school learning, has similar ends in sight; it aims at new stories about mathematical objects, except that this time the stories will be incomparably more complex and their objects may be too abstract to be easily related to any practical activity.[3]

It is also noteworthy that in both individual and societal discursive learning, the growth of narratives is accompanied by ongoing attempts to improve the tools of the trade, that is, by the efforts to increase the effectiveness of the discourse in which the stories are told. As a result of these meta-level attempts, changes may occur in the *keywords* of the given discourse and in the way they are used, in *visual mediators* the participants employ, and in the *discursive routines* they implement. Whereas in colloquial conversations the role of visual mediators is often played by the material objects around which the conversation evolves, in mathematics this function is fulfilled by symbolic artefacts such as numerals, algebraic expressions and graphs, created specifically to serve as 'representations' of impalpable mathematical objects. Mathematical routines include algorithmically prescribed ways of manipulating mathematical objects, as is the case with different types of calculations, as well as the heuristic procedures of proving, defining or substantiating.

Let me end this section with a historical remark. The idea that both scientific research and school-type learning can be thought of as dealing with discursive activities has its roots in two seemingly independent developments. Thus, this idea was made quite explicit by postmodern philosophers. Consider, for instance, Lyotard's declaration that 'scientific knowledge is a kind of discourse' (Lyotard, 1979: 3), Rorty's reference to knowledge as the 'conversation of mankind' (Rorty, 1979: 389), and Foucault's use of the term 'discursive formations', defined as 'things said … [n]ot books …, not theories …, but those familiar yet enigmatic groups of statements that are known as medicine, political economy, and biology' (Foucault, 1972: blurb).

In the second half of the twentieth century, such were the voices of thinkers interested in society and its historical changes, and thus in societal learning. The idea that also school-type learning is an activity of shaping and extending communication was born even earlier, albeit without being presented in so many words. It followed as an inevitable conclusion from the philosophical writings of Ludwig Wittgenstein and from the psychological musings of Lev Vygotsky. Although these two thinkers might have never heard about one another, they were speaking in unison while dealing with epistemological issues. Above all, both of them repeatedly stressed the inseparability of thought and its expression, either verbal or not. Wittgenstein vehemently rejected the view of thinking as 'incorporeal process which lends life and sense to speaking, and which it would be possible to detach from speaking' (§339, Wittgenstein, 2003 [1953]: 109), whereas participationist ideas about human development professed by Vygotsky implied the equation 'human thinking = a form of communication' as a natural, inevitable corollary.[4] After all, if it is true that any uniquely human competency originates in a historically established, collectively executable activity, then thinking, arguably the most uniquely human of human activities, must also have a developmental predecessor in the form of some historically established, collectively implementable activity. Since communication is the most obvious candidate, one cannot but conclude that *to think means to communicate with oneself.*[5] From here, the claims that *doing mathematics means engaging in a certain well-defined type of communication* and that *learning mathematics is to be interpreted as getting access to that special discourse* follow as the immediate entailment. In the next two sections, I will take a closer look at this learning, as it appears on societal and on individual levels, respectively. While doing so, I will also try to address the question of what makes societal learning possible and how the change in communicating leads to historical changes in other human activities.

SOCIETAL LEARNING OF MATHEMATICS: THE HISTORICAL DEVELOPMENT OF MATHEMATICAL DISCOURSE

Mathematical discourse as practised in today's schools may be centuries old, but in historical terms it is a relatively new invention. To understand the reasons, nature and mechanisms of the far reaching historical transformations, it is important to realize three facts. First, *discourses and other human activities are co-constitutive*: just like the move of one of our legs entails the move of the other, so do changes in the ways we communicate and in the stories we tell induce transformations in whatever else we are doing; and vice versa, our deeds shape the 'whats' and 'hows' of our stories. Second, in this process of co-development, *discourses function as propagators of innovation and as repositories of complexity*. Third, *learning-engendered change of discourse may happen at object-level or at meta-level*. The object-level change expresses itself in the increase in endorsed narratives, whereas in meta-level change the whole discourse undergoes transformation.

CO-CONSTITUTION OF DISCOURSES AND OF OTHER ACTIVITIES

One of the most powerful incentives for trying to change our discourses is the wish to improve familiar activities. Thus, for instance, the development of numerical discourse might well have begun when our ancestors realized that it would be useful to extend the activity of comparing quantities beyond those that could be performed by arranging two sets in a direct one-to-one correspondence. Our distant predecessors, just as the majority of today's children, might well be capable of qualitative choices long before the quantities could be labelled with numbers (Sfard, forthcoming). In the absence of numbers, however, these comparisons could be made only if the sets were simultaneously present and close to one another. In other situations, a person might try to use an auxiliary set that could be compared to each of the original sets separately. With the invention of numerical discourse, such mediating sets could be replaced with numbers.

Due to the fact that discourses and discursive constructs at large, and numbers in particular, travel in space and time with much greater effectiveness than concrete objects, this discursive innovation greatly expanded the range of sets that could be compared. Upon the appearance of numerical discourse, a new way of implementing an old task has been established. As time went by, the idea emerged of extending the activity of comparisons to continuous quantities, such as length. This led to the discourse on *ratios*: whenever two segments, A and B, were to be compared, a third segment, C, would be found with the help of which both A and B could be measured.[6] The comparison between A and B would then be expressed with the help of *the ratio between A and B*, that is, the pair of whole numbers, a and b, showing how many times the 'common measure' C goes into A and B, respectively. After a few centuries, the pairs of integers morphed into a new kind of number, known as *rational*. The new numerical discourse began a new cycle of innovation, transforming existing activities and inspiring the appearance of some new ones.

This historical account may be overly simplified, but it should suffice to instantiate how discourses interact with other human activities to spur their change, and how they develop themselves as a result. It is important to stress that by the twentieth century, incentives for the further development of mathematics were coming from within this discourse no less, perhaps even more, than from any external practical activities. Mathematics was now growing mainly due to the mathematicians' reflection on the existing mathematical discourse and through the activity of exploring abstract mathematical objects already engendered by this discourse.

The phenomenon of this self-generated or *autopoietic* discursive development may not be restricted to mathematics, but in the case of mathematics it stands out in a particularly sharp relief.

DISCOURSES AS PROPAGATORS AND PRESERVERS OF INNOVATION AND AS REPOSITORIES OF COMPLEXITY

The claim about the role of discourse (communication) in disseminating innovation seems self evident. Let me thus devote the rest of this section to the issue of aggregating complexity. So far, I was careful to stress that our communication is not just verbal and that our discourses take shape in multiple modalities, not just in language. Now I wish to stress the all-important contribution of the verbal mode. It is mainly thanks to the linguistic ingredient of human communication that our discourses function as the means for preserving the results of change and accumulating complexity. Below I argue that our capacity for piling one complex innovation upon another stems mainly from the reflexivity of the verbal communication, that is, from our capacity for talking about anything, including the talk itself.

The first fact to consider while trying to explain and substantiate this last claim is that the historical development of mathematics has been guided all along the way by the mathematicians' attempts to say as much as possible in as little words as possible. The best discursive means for saying more with less is the discursive construct known as *mathematical object*, one that appears when we replace talk about processes with talk about things. Thus, for instance, we speak about numbers as if they signified objects existing 'out there', that is, independently of us and our discourses. This way of talking, however, should not be taken for granted. On a closer look, number words do not begin their existence as signifying objects. These words are first learned by the child as mere

labels to be used in the processes of counting. At this point, they are hardly a part of speech, as they do not appear in full sentences. For the child, to reify number means to start using these words within the same language structures as those we apply while speaking about independently existing concrete objects. It is thanks to this kind of use that we can create the brief expression 'five plus four equals nine', which in its symbolic form, $5 + 4 = 9$, becomes even briefer. Here, indeed, the words *five*, *four* and *nine* are used as if they were things, two of which combine together to give the third. As long as number words remain unobjectified, the general fact expressed as $5 + 4 = 9$ would have to be stated in so many words:

> If I have a set of objects which, when counted makes me stop with the number word *five*, and also another set that makes me finish with *four*, then when I put these two sets together and count, I finish with the word *nine*.

No further argument is necessary to show how the act of reifying – of turning talk about processes (in this case, the process of counting) into talk about objects (numbers) – makes the discourse more compact, and thus also more manageable.

In metaphorical terms, mathematical objects function as if they were compact black boxes, to be used without ever considering their complex interiors. Indeed, it is now possible to manipulate these newly constructed mathematical entities and combine them together, something that would have been an awkward thing to do, to say the least, as long as the processes that gave rise to these entities have not undergone reification (think, for instance, about performing any operation on the result of $5 + 4$ when this operation can only be presented with the help of the above long expression). It is also because of this newly attained manageability that mathematicians may now look at the existing numerical discourse 'from above', that is, engage in meta-discourse, in which they can investigate patterns now clearly visible in the existing discourse. They may be intrigued by, say, the operation of squaring numbers and its general properties. Soon, the explorers will be reifying the processes of squaring numbers, perhaps even presenting this process with the help of algebraic formula x^2. The reified operation of squaring will eventually be christened with a new name, *quadratic function*, and will become subject to new operations and new complex processes.

This cyclic procedure of turning processes into objects and then reifying also processes on these new objects is the key to the puzzle of our practically unlimited capacity for aggregation of complexity. The procedure itself would not be possible without our ability to talk, and thus think, about our own ways of talking. This reflexivity is the property that human communication acquires once it turns verbal. One other important conclusion that can be taken from what has been said so far is that numbers, and in fact all other abstract objects, are discursive constructs, that is, they emerge out of talk rather than preceding it. This places abstract objects in sharp contrast with those known as concrete, with the existence of the latter, unlike that of the former, being independent of human discourses.

TWO LEVELS OF DISCURSIVE LEARNING

The changes that happen as a result of discursive learning can be divided into two categories, object-level and meta-level. In mathematics, *object-level* learning is one that expresses itself in the expansion of what is known about the already existing universe of mathematical objects. Object-level growth, therefore, is mainly accumulative. In contrast, *meta-level* developments are those that change the rules of the discursive game rather than simply alter the amount of endorsed narratives. This kind of learning happens when some newly introduced mathematical objects engender apparent contradictions with previously endorsed narratives. A good example of this kind of meta-level

development is one that took place when the introduction of negative numbers led to the revision of the basic epistemological assumption according to which mathematical truths are imposed by the mind-independent reality. In this case, a change in meta-discursive rules was necessary before these new objects were generally accepted. From now on, the only criterion for the acceptance of a new mathematical object would be the inner consistency of the discourse about this object.

The new discourse that constitutes the product of such meta-level change is *incommensurable*[7] with the preceding one: these two discourses use the same words in different ways and produce narratives that may sound mutually contradicting while in fact being incomparable with one another. For instance, after negative numbers were introduced, one could no longer claim that multiplication preserved the order of magnitude between any two numbers (for instance, it's true that $5 > 3$, but if you multiply both 5 and 3 by -1, you get the opposite relation: $-5 < -1$). This, however, did not mean that the participants of the discourse on unsigned numbers were wrong; it only meant that they used the word *number* differently than it was to be used from now on.

INDIVIDUAL LEARNING – THE ONTOGENETIC DEVELOPMENT OF DISCOURSES

The fact that the process of socio-historical development of discourses involves two types of events implies that two kinds of occurrences, object-level and meta-level, exist also in individual learning. In this section, I will argue that these two types of learning-by-a-person take place in different ways and require different forms and amounts of teacher support.

Object-level learning aims at increasing the set of narratives about mathematical objects with which the student is already familiar, and as such can theoretically happen without substantial instructional intervention. Indeed, this kind of learning begins and ends in deriving new narratives from those previously endorsed. Two persons who faithfully follow the rules of deduction must end up constructing the same narratives about the same objects.

In contrast, meta-level learning is supposed to lead to a change that cannot be attained by pure logic. There is an element of contingency and of human choice in every meta-level transformation. For instance, while proceeding from unsigned to signed numbers, mathematicians had to decide which properties of numbers that had been in force so far should be preserved and which of them could be compromised. Historically, these decisions were hard going and time consuming, and when eventually made, they were grounded in the mathematician's strong intuitions with regard to their prospective advantages. These intuitions were by-products of the decision-maker's discursive experience. Only rarely can a novice be guided by such helpful intimations. Moreover, since the new rules or new discursive objects cannot be deduced from anything the students already know, it seems that the only way for the learners to become participants in this discourse is to actually try to participate, even if just peripherally. On the other hand, how can students participate, if they are unable to figure out the reason for its seemingly counter-intuitive meta-rules and cannot yet sense the prospective advantages of all these apparently unlikely innovations?

To break the vicious circle, the learner seems to have no choice but to follow the experts, that is, to engage in *reflective imitation* of those who were there in that discourse before her. Reflective imitation is what Vygotskian scholars would likely call 'instruction of scaffolding': the learner and the teacher work together, whereas the student progresses from mere observation to implementing ever more substantial parts of the task. The student does the latter by an attempt to repeat what was previously done by the expert. The adjective *reflective* has

been added in order to stress that the imitation should be accompanied by the constant effort to understand the expert implementer's reasons for acting the way she did. To put it differently, the learner must try to turn her imitative *ritualized* participation into one that aims at genuine mathematical explorations. This is a demanding task and no learner should be expected to succeed without trying hard.

It can be argued that four conditions are necessary, albeit not sufficient, to ensure the very possibility of meta-level learning. First, there is the need for the learner's exposure to the new discourse. Such exposure will present her, of necessity, with *communicational conflict*, one that arises whenever interlocutors differ in their uses of words, in the manner of looking at visual mediators or in the ways they match discursive procedures with problems and situations. Three additional conditions can be seen as indispensable, if this conflict is to turn from an obstacle to participation into the lever for learning: all the participants of the learning–teaching process need to be of one mind with regard to (a) whose discourse is to be eventually shared, (b) who needs to act as the teacher and who as a learner, and (c) what is the expected form, mechanism and pace of the learning process. Collectively, these last three conditions constitute the participants' unwritten *learning–teaching agreement*. The question of how to create a learning–teaching agreement and whether its existence depends exclusively on what is happening behind the closed door of the classroom merits much additional thinking and empirical research.

CODA: DISCURSIVE LEARNING AS THE ORIGIN OF ALL THINGS HUMAN

As a by-product of their attempts to fathom the nature of school-type learning at large and of the learning of mathematics in particular, discursive researchers arrive at their own answer to the time-honoured question of what it is that makes humans human. The point of departure for their account is the assumption that the gist of humanness is the people's capacity for societal-historical changes. The phenomenon of societal learning cannot be explained by behaviourism and cognitivism, or by any other approach grounded in the vision of knowledge as entity 'acquired' by the individual from the world itself. The interpretation of the term *knowledge building* as developing discourses leads to the conclusion that human communication, and especially communication in language, may be the key to the puzzle. Human languages, with their property of reflexivity, turn discourses into the principal means for transmitting innovation from one generation to another and for the practically unbounded process of storing complexity.

NOTES

1 In choosing this name, I was inspired by Vygotsky's term 'practical intelligence', which he contrasted to 'sign use' (Vygotsky, 1978: 24).

2 This last term, 'concrete object', includes persons, and this means that practical activities include those that transform people's physical and social situations.

3 Because of this, some people doubt the usefulness of advanced mathematical narratives. Most mathematicians, however, seem confident about the applicability of their ideas. The English mathematician A.N. Whitehead was probably speaking for many of his colleagues when making the following statement: 'It is no paradox to say that in our most theoretical moods we may be nearest to our most practical applications' (Whitehead, 1911: 103). Another mathematician, A.R. Forsyth observed that the usefulness of advanced mathematics may sometimes have to wait for a long time to become visible: 'Very many applications of the theories of pure mathematics have come many years, sometimes centuries, after the actual discoveries themselves' (in Moritz, 1942 [1914]: 103).

4 To be sure, Vygotsky never said explicitly as much as that. My claim that he did say all that is needed to make this equation inescapable is based mainly on my reading of his analyses of the relation between thinking and speaking (Vygotsky, 1987).

5 To stress the unity of thinking and communicating, I once proposed to signify them both with one word, *commognition*, a portmanteau that brings together *communication* and *cognition* (Sfard, 2008).

6 In Euclid's *Elements*, the expression 'C measures A' meant that the segment C went into the segment A a whole number of times (without a remainder).

7 My adoption of the terminology introduced by Thomas Kuhn (1962) in the context of 'scientific revolutions' is not accidental. This account of socio-historical learning can be seen as the discursive rendering of Kuhn's vision of the development of science as a sequence of periods of normal science interspersed with those of 'scientific revolution' that lead to paradigms incommensurable with the preceding ones.

REFERENCES

Bruner, J.S. (1990) *Acts of Meaning*, Cambridge, MA: Harvard University Press.

Foucault, M. (1972) *The Archaeology of Knowledge*, New York: Harper Colophon.

Kuhn, T. (1962) *The Structure of Scientific Revolutions* (2nd edn), Chicago: University of Chicago Press.

Lyotard, J.-F. (1979) *The Postmodern Condition: A Report on Knowledge*, Minneapolis: University of Minnesota Press.

Minick, N. (1987) 'Development of Vygotsky's Thought: An Introduction', in R.W. Rieber and A.S. Carton (eds), *The Collected Works of L.S. Vygotsky* (Vol. 1, pp. 17–38), New York: Plenum Press.

Moritz, R.E. (1942 [1914]) *Memorabilia Mathematica: The Philomath's Quotation Book*, New York: The Mathematical Association of America, Spectrum.

Rorty, R. (1979) *Philosophy and the Mirror of Nature*, Princeton, NJ: Princeton University Press.

Sfard, A. (2008) *Thinking as Communicating: Human Development, the Growth of Discourses, and Mathematizing*, Cambridge, UK: Cambridge University Press.

Sfard, A. (forthcoming) 'Creating Numbers: Participationist Discourse on Mathematics Learning', in D. Butlen, I. Bloch, M. Bosch, C. Chambris, G. Cirade, S. Clivaz, S. Gobert, C. Hache, M. Hersant and C. Mangiante (eds), *Rôles et places de la didactique et des didacticiens des mathématiques dans la société et dans le système éducatif. 17è école d'été de didactique des mathématiques. Nantes du 19 au 26 août 2013*, Grenoble: La pensée sauvage.

Vygotsky, L.S. (1978). *Mind in society: The development of higher psychological processes*. Cambridge, MA: Harvard University Press.

Vygotsky, L.S. (1982) 'Consciousness as a Problem in the Psychology of Behaviour', in L.S.Vygotsky (ed.), *Collected Works: Problems of the Theory and History of Psychology*, Moscow: Pedagogica (in Russian).

Vygotsky, L.S. (1987) 'Thinking and Speech', in R.W. Rieber and A.C. Carton (eds), *The Collected Works of L.S. Vygotsky* (pp. 39–285), New York: Plenum Press.

Whitehead, A.N. (1911) *An Introduction to Mathematics*, Cambridge: Cambridge University Press.

Wittgenstein, L. (2003 [1953]) *Philosophical Investigations: The German Text, with a Revised English Translation* (G.E.M. Anscombe, trans. 3rd edn), Malden, MA: Blackwell Publishing.

PART II

Elements of Learning

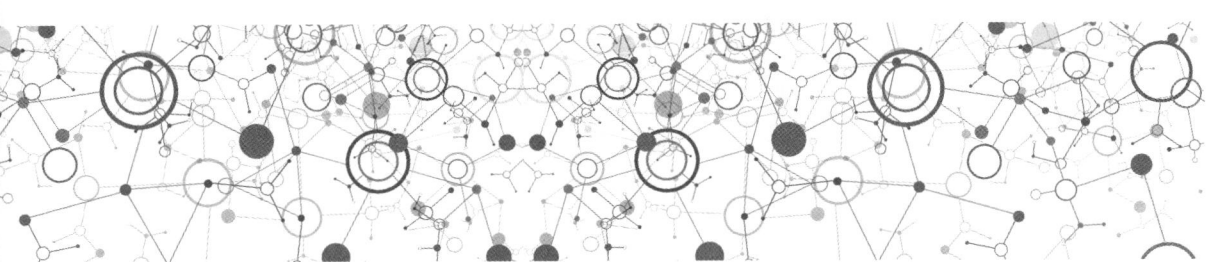

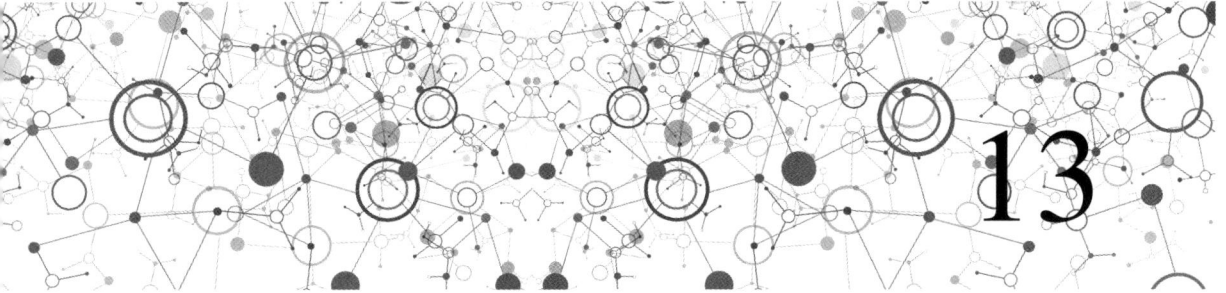

13

Introduction (Part II)

David Scott and Eleanore Hargreaves

This part of the book focuses on two important issues. The first of these is the constitution of a learning environment, comprising elements and the relations between them such as pedagogic arrangements, orientations towards knowledge-sets, skills or dispositions, knowledge framing and knowledge development framing, progression and pacing, relations between the teacher and taught, relations between types of learners, spatial and temporal arrangements, criteria and apparatus for assessment or evaluation, and internal and external relations between its parts. These have been actualised in different ways in a number of influential learning practices: assessment for learning, observation, coaching, goal-clarity, mentoring, peer learning, simulation, instruction, concept-formation, reflection, meta-cognitive learning (cf. Butler in this volume), problem solving and practice. Each of these has been subject to a sustained critique, primarily in relation to their technicist orientation and their embeddedness in forms of technical-rationality. The second issue that concerns us

in this part of the book is the relationships between learning environments and other social practices, such as the curriculum (cf. Moore in this volume), political institutions (cf. Crossouard and Webb in this volume), national and international assemblages, and disciplinary subjects and their boundaries.

For example, in relation to the curriculum, Michael Young (2006: 22) sets out four assumptions of a knowledge-based and learning-centred curriculum (learning being understood here as a knowledge-producing activity):

1 The question of knowledge (what it is that people need to have the opportunity to learn in schools, college or university curriculum) must be central to any educational policy.
2 Knowledge about the world, if it is to be on the basis of the curriculum involves concepts that take us beyond the contexts in which learners find themselves and those in which knowledge is acquired or produced.
3 The crucial implication of this idea of knowledge for the curriculum is that a distinction is essential between the theoretical knowledge produced by

scientists and other specialists, usually within disciplines, and the everyday practical knowledge that people acquire through their experience in families, communities and workplaces. It is the former rather than the latter which is essential and superior to theoretical knowledge for everyday living in all societies.

4   The primary but not only purpose of educational institutions is to take people beyond their everyday knowledge and enable them to make sense of the world and their lives and explore alternatives; the purpose of educational institutions is not to celebrate, amplify or reproduce people's experience. (Young, 2006: 22)

Likewise connections can be made between learning and politics, globalisation and disciplines.

In the Introduction to this book, we made reference to situated-cognition or socio-cultural theories of learning, which view the person and the environment as mutually constructed and mutually constructing. As a result, such theorists identify active, transformative and relational dimensions to learning, indeed they understand learning as contextualised. This last point can be illustrated by an example from the field of informal learning: learning how to be a parent. What characterises this type of learning is that there is as yet no formal type of training which a putative parent has to undergo. It is an example of learning generated from the actual practice itself. More fundamentally, the parent is immersed in particular discourses about parenting which act to close off other possibilities; these discourses reflect the way society is structured. The putative parent has a view about him- or herself and how this relates to parenting. Parenting itself takes place within particular environments, and these are structured in different ways. Single parenting is a qualitatively different experience from parenting by two or more adults. We therefore need to understand learning how to be a parent as situated and as making reference to: discursive structures or significations of gender, sexuality, ethnicity and class; pre-organised meanings about parenting which reflect particular understandings

about knowledge, i.e. views of childhood, adulthood, learning, identity and the like; and other viewpoints, discourses and knowledge structures which act as points of comparison. What this means is that learning is situated and that it has constructed or social features. As a result, it can only be understood by making reference to those knowledge structures, discourses and practices which reflect particular time- and space-bound pre-occupations and values of particular communities.

Furthermore, these communities are stratified in various ways. First, some individuals in society have a greater influence than others in determining what counts as legitimate knowledge and what doesn't. Second, knowledge-gathering takes place in settings and environments in which individuals have different access to resources. The subject matter of learning is in part those differences and this means that power is a necessary element in explanations of social life. Third, there are power dimensions of the learning situation. This is most obvious in formal learning situations where the teacher has a greater opportunity to impose their version of knowledge on the learner than the learner has to construct it for themselves. However, even in the most informal of learning situations there are power dimensions present, as the learner is situated within arrangements of knowledge, how it should be organised and how it should therefore be assimilated, which acts to restrict the capacity of the learner to progress their own learning. Finally, learning acts to fix reality in a particular way which is never entirely justified and cannot be legitimated by reference to a notion of what the world is really like. This act of closure is a part of the reality that the learner is embedded in. By adopting a particular way of working, a particular understanding of knowledge, the learner is rejecting or turning aside from other frameworks, and this itself is an act of power.

However, within this general framework, learners have more control in some settings than in others. The teaching and learning strategy is constructed strongly or weakly, where strong and weak refer to the capacity of the message system to restrict or allow different meanings, interpretations and actions. Each learning moment focuses on a particular aspect of knowledge, whether chosen by a teacher or not. This is made visible by the act of delivery. However, there are always invisible dimensions: what is not chosen and why it was not chosen are invisible. Finally, there are structural dimensions of the learning setting. These comprise in part particular spatial and temporal arrangements. Distance learning approaches are constructed in particular ways so that the learner is allowed some licence over when and where they choose to study. Face-to-face teaching settings are constructed in terms of timetables, sequences of learning, particular relations between teachers and learners and organised places where the teaching takes place. All these various forms of structuring influence what is learnt, how it is learnt, and how that knowledge is used in other settings and other environments. Situated-learning approaches acknowledge that these arrangements for learning are constructed in communities of people. They also suggest that learning is itself a social practice which has the potential to transform the practice itself. What this means is that learning, knowledge and its outcomes have to be understood historically and as being socially embedded.

In this part of the book, Alex Moore writes on knowledge, curriculum and learning, Gunther Kress and Jeff Bezemer on a social semiotic multimodal approach to learning, Rebecca Webb and Barbara Crossouard on the politics of learning, Martin Lawn and Rosario Sergio Maniscalco on learning, governance and the European educational space, and David Scott and Carol Evans on the elements of a learning environment.

REFERENCE

Young, M.F.D. (2006) 'Education Knowledge and the Role of the State: The Nationalisation of Knowledge', in A. Moore (ed.) *Schooling, Society and the Curriculum*, London: RoutledgeFalmer.

14

Knowledge, Curriculum and Learning: 'What Did You Learn in School?'

Alex Moore

INTRODUCTION

In my days as a teacher educator I would often begin my one-year postgraduate course by asking students to share with each other as much as they could immediately remember about what they had learned and been taught during the course of their own compulsory education, which in most cases spanned at least 13 years. Even though I would make it clear that it was not experiences or feelings that I wanted them to recall, but rather the formal curriculum knowledge they had taken away with them and the skills they had formally acquired and developed, it was very common for them to talk instead about the incidental 'life skills' they had developed, or about specific successes they had enjoyed, injustices that still troubled them, or specific lessons or groups of lessons or extra-mural activities that had remained memorable to them over the years. Some would, additionally, talk of the foreign language skills they had acquired; others would recite lines of poetry which still gave them pleasure; and others (a great many others) would repeat, mantra-like, lists of mathematical and scientific algorithms and phrases – 'evaporation causes cooling', 'the side on the hypotenuse is equal to the sum of the squares on the other two sides' – or verbalisations of grammatical and spelling rules, such as 'a verb is a doing, having or being word' or 'i before e except after c'. What was remarkable was how very little disciplinary knowledge or 'factual knowledge' seemed to have lodged itself with any degree of enthusiasm or tenacity in my students' memories, or was drawn upon in adult life other than very rarely. Many would express regret that some of the things they would have liked to have developed more knowledge about – things like gender and race issues, or political education, or philosophy – had not had a more significant presence in the curriculum, or that the research skills and independent thinking demanded of them later on as university students had not been encouraged more.

Whether or not these issues regarding factual recollection (we might say, regarding the accessibility and/or the shelf-life of 'stored knowledge') or of perceived curriculum shortcomings are important depends in no small part on our point of view as to what education is fundamentally *for*, and about what we understand by 'knowledge': in particular, what we understand by such popular terms as 'useful knowledge', 'powerful knowledge' and knowledge that is 'empowering'. These views will themselves be informed by, or perhaps lead us towards, differing understandings of and approaches to *learning*, which in turn are functionally inseparable from our approaches to *teaching*.

It is this relationship between knowledge, learning and pedagogy that I will explore a little in this chapter, contextualising the discussion within differing, sometimes oppositional views as to the purposes of public education more broadly and to the related structure and content of the school curriculum. It is not my intention to present these different approaches as polar opposites, although in practice they may often appear as such, but rather as differing starting-points or default positions which can, depending on circumstances, either compete with one another for supremacy or interact with and complement one another.

KNOWLEDGE AND LEARNING

[Whatever] vagaries there have been in the use of the term ['liberal education'], it is the appropriate label for a positive concept, that of an education based fairly and squarely on the nature of knowledge itself, a concept central to the discussion of education at any level. (Hirst, 1998: 246)

Debates not only about what knowledge *is* but also about which knowledge is important enough to be included in the school curriculum, who should be charged with the responsibility for making such decisions, and on what bases such choices are made continue to exercise philosophers and sociologists of education as well as politicians and policy makers. What is the difference between knowledge and knowing? Or between knowledge and skill(s)? Can we say that some knowledge is more important than other knowledge? Can we, as some have tried to do, 'disaggregate' knowledge into different 'forms' or 'domains' of knowledge? What are we to make, for example, of the English philosopher of education Paul Hirst's identification of 'propositional knowledge' (essentially, factual knowledge), 'procedural' or 'practical knowledge' (for example, 'the 'know-how' kind of knowledge required to ride a bicycle or make a magazine rack) and 'knowledge by acquaintance' – where what is 'known' is an 'object' such as a person, a place or a work of art (Hirst, 1965; Hirst and Peters, 1970)? And what of Hirst's subsequent elaboration of knowledge within various knowledge 'domains': the logico-mathematical, the empirical, the interpersonal, the moral, the aesthetic, the religious and the philosophical (Hirst, 1974; Hirst and Peters, 1970)?

Of particular relevance in considerations of *learning*, do we understand knowledge as, principally, an identifiable body of internalised or internalisable facts and understandings across a range of distinctly different subject disciplines (Mathematics, Languages, Art, Science, and so on), which may be stored for use at some present or future time? Or do we, rather, understand knowledge as the working material through which we develop an appreciation of and expertise in a range of learning skills, so that learning itself, in its many forms and manifestations, becomes the central focus of the education project, with knowledge in a subordinate, supporting role rather than (as is very often the case) the other way round?

This last question has evoked much discussion over the years among scholars of education, where it has become known variously in terms of the 'content-process', 'content-product' and 'process-objectives' debate. In this debate, 'content and 'objectives' curriculum models prioritise lists of 'things' (specified skills, items of knowledge) to be taught and learned, and the means by which such ends are to be achieved are then decided upon by politicians and policy makers, by local authorities, or by schools and teachers. The 'process' approach to curriculum, on the other hand, focuses on teaching and learning as its starting point, and is relatively less concerned to identify clear-cut 'bodies of knowledge'.

The process-objectives debate was perhaps most famously elaborated by Lawrence Stenhouse in his 1975 publication, *An Introduction to Curriculum Research and Development*. Stenhouse began with two important questions:

> Can curriculum and pedagogy be organized satisfactorily by a logic other than that of the means–end model? Can the demands of a curriculum specification ... be met without using the concepts of objectives? (Stenhouse, 1975: 84)

The process model, which Stenhouse offers as a preferable alternative to the more traditional objectives or 'means–end' model, brings with it its own very clear curriculum priorities. However, these are itemised not in terms of detailed skills or required factual knowledge, but in terms of learning-oriented 'activities'. Decisions about what to include in a curriculum and what not to include are then dependent on notions of an activity's actual or potential 'usefulness' to the learner (rather, for example, than on its potential usefulness to the perceived needs of a national economy) – rendering the model learn*ing*-centred as well as learn*er*-centred.

There are no fewer than 12 items on Stenhouse's list for identifying what makes one activity 'more worthwhile than another', the following three of which provide a flavour of his broader thinking. An activity is worthwhile, he suggests if:

> It permits children to make informed choices in carrying out the activity to reflect on the consequences of their choices; it assigns to students active roles in the learning situation rather than passive ones; and it asks students to engage in inquiry into ideas, applications of intellectual

processes, or current problems, either personal or social. (Stenhouse, 1975: 86)

'USEFUL' AND 'POWERFUL' KNOWLEDGE

Stenhouse's emphasis on the identification of 'worthwhile *activities*' clearly prioritises *learning* (we might say, 'active learning') in relation to curriculum selections, rather than a predetermined 'body of knowledge'. Others, however, without necessarily disagreeing with Stenhouse's priorities, speak also of the existence and importance of 'useful' or 'powerful' *knowledge* (see, for example, James et al., 2011: 11): that is to say, knowledge which can be put to use outside (and perhaps subsequent to) schooling, to the benefit of the individual's quality of life, whether in terms of material well-being, or spiritual well-being, or both. Neither of these concepts ('useful knowledge' and 'powerful knowledge') necessarily speaks of learning directly, but this is precisely why they demand a mention in any discussion *of* learning. To make it clear, such approaches, when adopted oppositionally to more learning-centred approaches, have, embedded within them, a particular set of understandings not only about knowledge but about what it is to be human, what it is to be a learner, and what the role of education more broadly should be in relation to wider social, economic and cultural life.

We might begin this brief discussion of useful and powerful knowledge by considering what different people *mean* when they talk of knowledge that is useful and powerful, since these are clearly contested notions, which, to a considerable extent and despite their immediate referencing to theories of learning, clearly align with competing 'traditional' and 'progressive' understandings and approaches to pedagogy. For some, then (we might suggest, 'traditionalists'), useful and empowering knowledge largely comprises what is already included in the traditional school disciplines and their specific syllabuses, in which knowledge tends to be disaggregated into various forms or domains (as in Hirst and Peters' accounts, 1970) which are then located within the traditional subject disciplines. According to this view, mathematical knowledge, scientific knowledge, historical knowledge and so on are potentially useful in that they may, in the long term, help the learner to a prestigious career, or help them in their practical, day-to-day life on leaving school, or enable them to engage in important discussions and decision-making processes with other possessors of such knowledge, and so forth. While some effort may be made to explain to students why and how such knowledge might be useful or empowering, it might equally be presented as if it is useful or empowering *in itself*, simply by way of its 'acquisition' (McCormick and Murphy, 2000; Sfard, 1998). We might say that within this approach, knowledge is understood by both the learner and the teacher as fundamentally 'medicinal'; rather like a pill which one simply has to swallow in order for its healing magic to take effect. There is no pressing need to help students to learn *how* to use the knowledge they have acquired, while the precise nature of such knowledge's usefulness might also be left open; having acquired the knowledge, it is the acquirer's choice and responsibility what to do with it.

For others, useful and empowering knowledge might be constructed somewhat differently, and have a very different purpose. Whereas knowledge within the traditional school disciplines tends to focus on the individual's future well-being (or at least purports to do so) within a wider, unchanging socio-economic system, and indeed might aim also to perpetuate that system in its existing form, this other view of usefulness and empowerment has a more revolutionary aspect. It still emphasises the individual's well-being, but (to anticipate Schiro's 'social reconstruction ideology', below) within a changed socio-economic system in relation to whose development education itself is a key player. Within this understanding of useful and powerful knowledge,

education is seen as a means of raising consciousness in relation to perceived injustices in the wider world, including, perhaps, the ways in which learners themselves may be marginalised or ill treated within the system. The Marxist philosopher, Louis Althusser, in his work *Problèmes Étudiants* (1964, cited in Ross, 1991: xvi), may be seen as one such proponent of this kind of useful and powerful knowledge, regarding mass education as having the potential to empower (hitherto dis-empowered) workers and their children by providing them with knowledge which will give them both the tools (e.g. literacy, and a critical knowledge of how the wider socio-economic system works) and the self-belief to challenge the socio-economic status quo. Within this view of useful and powerful knowledge, it is knowledge of how society (specifically, capitalist society) works to the advantage of some and the disadvantage of others that is prioritised, rather than the kinds of empowerment and usefulness identified in the more traditional approach. We may see, then, within these two different understandings of 'useful' and 'powerful', a fundamental difference as to what education more broadly should be for.

What we do not necessarily see, however, are two different versions of what kinds of *learning* should be encouraged. Despite the difference in intention between the two approaches to useful and powerful knowledge, their pedagogical orientations may differ very little, if at all. Althusser, for example, advises: 'The function of teaching is to transmit a determinate knowledge to subjects who do not possess this knowledge' (Althusser, 1964), suggesting a very traditional, top-down approach to teaching and learning that might be equally at home in the more traditional curriculum and in more 'blank screen' understandings of learning. An alternative to such pedagogical orientations is offered in McCormick and Murphy's 'participation metaphor', with its echoes of Dewey's support for 'inquisitiveness' over 'acquisitiveness' and Stenhouse's 'useful activity' approach. Within all these approaches, the prioritisation of 'knowledge' is replaced by a prioritisation of 'knowing', and the emphasis on 'having knowledge' is replaced by one of 'doing' (McCormick and Murphy, 2000: 213). Within this model, 'empowerment' is understood less in terms of 'stored knowledge', more in terms of one's capacity, effectiveness and enthusiasm for (independent) learning.

In all of these approaches, it is important to bear in mind that knowledge (or for that matter learning capacity) is seldom 'useful' or 'powerful' in its own right, but only potentially so, relying on each individual having the means and the opportunities *to make use of it*. This is an issue of particular importance in societies in which wealth and living standards are subject to wide variations. As Scott and Hargreaves put it in their Introduction to this part of the book, 'communities are stratified in various ways', and knowledge-gathering (to which we might add knowledge-using) 'takes place in settings and environments in which individuals have different access to resources'. It is all very well to talk about useful, powerful, empowering knowledge, but students may be less likely to pursue such knowledge if they remain unconvinced of its capacity to improve their lives, or if circumstances beyond their control will prevent them from putting this knowledge to use.

COMPETING TRADITIONS IN PUBLIC EDUCATION

The identification of useful or powerful knowledge, or worthwhile knowledge, is in itself an important issue for curriculum development and theory. However, at least as important is the matter of who (i.e. the bearers of what ideologies and educational theories) should decide what is useful or powerful or worthwhile.

Michael Apple (1993) is one of many educationalists to comment on the fact that whatever finds its way on to a nation's school curriculum is determined by a politics of

'official knowledge', with education itself being 'deeply implicated in a politics of culture'. That is to say: '[t]he curriculum is never simply a neutral assemblage of knowledge, somehow appearing in the texts and classrooms of a nation. It is always part of a selective tradition, someone's selection, some group's vision of legitimate knowledge' (Apple, 1993: 222; see also Geyer, 1993; Goldberg, 1994).

Apple's view regarding curriculum decision-making is an important one, contradicting an alternative view that curriculum content (the officially mandated knowledge and skills) is self-evident, rational and above politics or ideologies. But if Apple is correct, what are the particular purposes that underpin curriculum selections and (we might add) favoured models of teaching and learning; and what and whose particular interests might they serve? In Apple's account, which specifically though by no means exclusively addresses the case of the USA, public education as it is most widely practised and experienced in the world today is aimed at preserving society's social and economic status quo: preparing young citizens to perpetuate free-market capitalist systems and ideologies within curriculum selections that reflect the interests and expertise of existing dominant classes at the expense of dominated classes, ensuring the perpetuation of an organic society in which some young people are prepared for low status, low paid jobs on leaving formal education while others are prepared for higher status, higher paid jobs, and in which the financial inequity essential for the preservation of capitalist systems is thus also reproduced. Within an almost universally capitalist world, it may make little difference whether or not central governments charged with establishing and developing education policy have been democratically elected.

This understanding of curricular and pedagogic choices in terms of political and social ideologies and power relations offers one way of analysing and making sense of curriculum choices that does not accept fundamentalist views that curriculum selections are simply self-evident and can be arrived at through dispassionate, disinterested rationalism. Another understanding is in terms of competing *theories* of knowledge, teaching and learning, which may have their basis in rationality, but recognise the existence of different theories and the need for some kind of evidence to support this one or that. It is not impossible for two bodies of opinion, both purporting to support an education that is fair and equitable, that is good for young people and good for society, to have very different ideas as to how to bring this about, regardless of more explicitly political or ideological leanings. Some may argue, for instance, that 'traditional', transmissive teacher- and textbook-led pedagogies are the best way to approach learning, regardless of what it is that we want young people to learn, while others may argue that student-centred, 'progressive' pedagogies are more likely to be successful, or that what is needed is a combination of both approaches. Each theory, in turn, will be based on a particular understanding of the human mind, and may well, despite possible claims to the contrary, find itself embedded within a variety of political and ideological orientations, even if these are not its primary drivers. There is nothing, either, to stop politicians selectively appealing to educational theory of various kinds, regardless of the strength or weakness of its argument, or of dipping selectively into a *range* of educational theories, simply because they can find there something that provides a close fit with their existing ideological and political agendas.

In their Introduction to this volume, Scott and Hargreaves have identified two broad, potentially oppositional theories of learning, within each of which there are many variations: that is to say, symbol processing and socio-cultural theories. Symbol processing theory 'understands learning as the sorting, storing and retrieving of coded information from and about the world'. It is a theory that invites traditional, transmissive pedagogies, in which the mind 'is treated as a blank screen' and the learner as passive-receptive.

Theories which emphasise cultural aspects, on the other hand, 'view the person and the environment as mutually constructed and mutually constructing. As a result they identify active, transformative and relational dimensions to learning: indeed they understand learning as contextualised', and thus invite pedagogies which are more progressive, exploratory and student-centred.

It is easy enough to link understandings of learning with the pedagogical orientations most likely to match them. However, we might also understand these contrasting learning theories not just as theories in their own right but as embedded in and perhaps elements or manifestations of wider theories and *traditions* within education, which are simultaneously theories of knowledge, of 'reality' and of the human mind.

KIMBALL'S EDUCATIONAL TRADITIONS

Some years ago, the American writer Bruce Kimball (1986) took precisely this line in elaborating what he called two traditions of education policy in the USA. (As with Apple's ideologies, we should have little difficulty identifying these traditions at work in the histories of the vast majority of public education systems around the world.) These are the 'philosophical tradition' and the 'oratorical tradition', each adopting a particular perspective regarding our understandings of truth and knowledge, and each involved in a seemingly unending, perhaps irresolvable, cyclical battle for supremacy over the other in the field of public educational policy and practice (see Table 14.1).

In terms of the curriculum orientation of education, Kimball argued that the philosophical tradition, because of its orientation to and understanding of 'truth' and 'knowledge' as provisional, contested and constructed, leads to a more future-oriented curriculum in which learners are encouraged to explore questions (their own as well as

Table 14.1   Key differences between the philosophical and oratorical traditions of education, adapted from Kimball, 1986.

The Philosophical Tradition	The Oratorical Tradition
'Truth' is unsettled and elusive	Truth is to be found in the 'great texts' and traditions
The search for 'truth' is an act of *dis*covery	The search for truth is an act of *re*covery
Public education equips learners for an uncertain future	Public education equips learners with certain truths of the past, emphasising the reproduction of the status quo
Curriculum and pedagogy are strong on method (process), weaker on content	Curriculum and pedagogy are strong on content, weaker on method (process)

those that are chosen for them) and in which questioning itself becomes at least as important as the (provisional) answers that the search might throw up: in short, there is an increased emphasis on developing in young learners the desire to – and the knowledge of how to – explore. Authority in relation to truth and knowledge within such a tradition is ideally shared between teachers and learners.

The oratorical tradition, on the other hand, is more concerned with drawing on the past; on identifying cultural artefacts for study and admiration that have stood the national test of time, and also emphasising the collective wisdom and nationally heralded achievements of the past in relation to science, history, mathematics, literature, art, and so forth. Knowledge, like truth, is understood within this tradition as fixed, definable, 'out there'; waiting to be 'found' by the learner rather than constructed or discovered on an academic journey. To return to an earlier discussion concerning content and process curriculum models, the philosophical tradition is more likely to promote process or 'method' (pedagogies enabling students to discuss, to collaborate, to 'discover'), while the oratorical tradition is likely to be weaker on process but stronger on content (the 'knowledge' and its 'truth' that are to be imparted to and internalised by learners).

SCHIRO'S FOUR PHILOSOPHIES

Kimball's two 'traditions' of education map very readily on to the more recent attempt by

Michael Schiro (2013) to disaggregate understandings of and approaches to public education in terms of four 'philosophies', which he also describes as 'ideologies'. Schiro's four philosophies/ideologies are described as: the 'scholar academic', the 'social efficiency ideology', the 'learner centred ideology', and the 'social reconstruction ideology'.

'Scholar academics' believe that '[t]he purpose of education is to help children learn the accumulated knowledge of our culture: that of the academic disciplines' (Schiro, 2013: 4). In policy terms, this means the identification and sanctification of a body of knowledge, an adherence to the division of learning into traditional subject disciplines, and, fundamentally, the 'symbol processing' understanding of learning described by Scott and Hargreaves (in their Introduction to this volume), in which (factual) knowledge is prioritised, and learning is understood essentially in terms of internalisation and storage. Advocates of the 'social efficiency ideology', on the other hand (Schiro, 2013: 5), 'believe that the purpose of schooling is to efficiently meet the needs of society by training youth to function as future mature contributing members of society'; an emphasis, that is, on concerns related to socialisation and the national economy, or to put it another way, an essentially 'reproductive' curriculum aimed at preserving the nation's socio-economic status quo. (This may include emphases on both knowledge and skill[s], and in terms of understandings of and approaches to learning might support either or both symbol processing and socio-cultural approaches.)

In a somewhat sharper contrast with these two rather functional educational and curricular rationales, Schiro offers the 'learner centred ideology' and the 'social reconstruction ideology' (2013: 5–6). Supporters of the first of these focus not so much on 'the needs of society or the academic disciplines, but on the needs and concerns of individuals' – as a consequence of which 'schools should be enjoyable places where people develop naturally according to their own innate natures.' Within this 'ideology', the emphasis is on evolution rather than reproduction: that is to say, the evolution of the individual rather than (necessarily) of the wider society. Here, '[t]he goal of education is the growth of individuals, each in harmony with his or her own unique intellectual, social, emotional and physical attributes'. Such a view clearly supports the socio-critical approach to teaching and learning, suggesting the need for more individualised learning programmes and for a more exploratory approach to teaching and learning which (to return to Kimball) adopts a less rigid 'out there' understanding of 'truth'.

Schiro's final philosophy/ideology, the 'social reconstruction ideology', also, as its name suggests, lends itself more to social-critical approaches to learning than to symbol processing ones; but it does so with a somewhat different inflection, emphasising the developing of a sense of social responsibility in the individual rather than focusing on promoting the individual learner's own well-being. The 'social reconstruction ideology' (Schiro, 2013: 6) suggests that education has, or perhaps should have, as one of its central purposes the development of a critically educated citizenry able to engage reflectively and reflexively with the wider society (and indeed the wider social world), opening up greater possibilities for *societal evolution* or more radical societal change. In relation to learning, such an approach might be seen to promote, along with the development of 'knowledge of' or 'knowledge about', the capacity to *understand*; that is, to understand, within an essentially ethical context, one's self and one's actions in relation to

the wider world, and to take a critical interest in the ways in which such things as poverty and inequity are socially and historically constructed (see also Kliebard, 2004). On a practical level, this might, in turn, suggest a greater emphasis than in symbol processing models on learning development through the discussion and identification of social, economic and environmental *issues*.

Schiro's educational philosophies or ideologies are not necessarily mutually exclusive, and in practice we might expect to find elements of each of them flourishing either easily or with difficulty in public schooling settings. Schiro suggests, however, that, as with Kimball's two educational traditions, they are, on the bigger stage, in perpetual battle for dominance with one another in a political, ideological (and perhaps theoretical) battleground that manifests itself in a variety of localised education 'wars'. Thus, speaking of the case in the USA, though once again the account will be very familiar to many of us living and working in other countries, Schiro observes (2013: 1):

> Seemingly irresolvable disagreements include the reading controversy over whether it is more important to teach decoding (phonics) or comprehension (whole language), the mathematics disputes over whether it is more important to teach mathematical understanding or mathematical skills, and the history conflicts on whether it is more important to teach knowledge of the past or to build strategies for critically analyzing and reconstructing society in the future. [Such disputes] have recently become so fierce that they have become known as the reading wars, the maths wars and the history wars.

QUESTIONS AND ANSWERS: RECALIBRATING A RELATIONSHIP

Thus far we have considered two sets of contrasting positions in relation to education and learning: positions which are not mutually exclusive but are indicative of significantly different prioritisations, each one imbued with and underpinned by contrasting understandings of knowledge, of what it is to be human, and of what education is or should be fundamentally for. The two theories of *learning* – the symbol processing and socio-cultural theories – referenced by Scott and Hargreaves are, for example, likely to be imbued with different understandings of *knowledge* and thus of what knowledge, or, conversely, what learning should be included in the curriculum: in the first case, tending to privilege factual knowledge which can be memorised and stored for future use by absorbent 'blank-screen' learners located within a universe in which all is, ultimately, knowable; in the second case, tending to privilege know-*ing* rather than know-*ledge*, within a universe whose understanding is endlessly incomplete and in which learning is, and can only ever be, an active, agentive process. Kimball's oratorical and philosophical traditions, based initially on orientations to 'truth' (by the *status* of truth, as well as in relation to the authority by which truth is identified and validated) is similarly imbued with understandings of what it means to learn, as much as by how learning best takes place – the oratorical tradition prioritising the absorption of a body of knowledge essentially through acts of memorisation, the philosophical prioritising active meaning-making and knowledge creation. Schiro's four philosophies or ideologies of education illustrate the fundamental *political and policy* differences and tensions underlying public education debates and practice, but also do so across the fields of teaching, learning and curriculum.

In this final section, I want to move away from these accounts, to suggest a distinction or tension of my own, though it is also implicit within Kimball's analysis, which I think may be useful. This concerns the relationships in public education between what I have elsewhere called 'the Question' and 'the Answer' (Moore, 2014). Briefly, I want to suggest that through most of its history, and in the majority of its geographical, cultural and economic locations, formal public education has been overly dominated by an emphasis on answers at the expense of encouraging young learners to be questioners and to develop the necessary skills to pursue and elaborate questions, both of their own choosing and making, and at the invitation or insistence of others.

Answers are undoubtedly very important to us, and experience suggests that their pursuit fulfils an individual and collective human need. However, we should never forget that without questions there would be no answers. Nor should we be too quick to let answers be the 'end' of a question–answer cycle. Rather, we might do better to understand and approach answers as characteristically provisional and emancipatory, acting as the starting points for new sets of questions and new provisional answers to those questions: a learning cycle, that is, which never 'closes' and which is neither presented nor perceived as doing so. When 'the Answer' comes to dominate the educational project – as the nature of still-popular forms of standardised, end-of-course, 'right answer' school tests and examinations suggests that it does – it takes on what I have called a tyrannical aspect (Moore, 2014), that restricts and constrains learning and leads to curricular stagnation. Seen thus, we might liken the question and the answer to notions of 'becoming' and 'being', elaborated by Deleuze (May, 2003) in relation to human desire in the wider socio-economic world, and, more pertinently for us here, perhaps, by Deborah Britzman in relation to education. Learning to teach, Britzman suggests, 'like teaching itself', 'is always a process of becoming: a time of formation and transformation, of scrutiny into what one is doing, what one can become' (Britzman, 1991: 8).

I want to suggest that Britzman's understandings of 'being' and 'becoming' in relation to teacher education and teaching apply equally to curriculum and learning, neither of which should ever seek to stand still or present itself as definitive. If we pursue a project of 'becoming' in relation to formal education more widely, we might well ask ourselves what the implications are for the kind of curriculum, the kind of teaching and the kind(s) of learning and assessment that we consider appropriate. Currently, the most significant assessment of learning, for most school students, seeks to judge how much knowledge the learner has absorbed (whether permanently or temporarily, we can have no sure way of knowing) by a particular point in time (usually at the end of a designated course or perceived developmental phase), and whether they appear to have absorbed more or less in comparison with other learners in similar positions. There may be an extent to which they are required to demonstrate, usually in the form of the written examination, their ability to put such knowledge to use; however, it is unlikely that they will be asked to respond more expansively to such questions as 'How might you put this knowledge to use in future life?'; 'Why do you think this knowledge is important?'; or (even more unlikely) 'Is this knowledge important because it is on the curriculum, or is it on the curriculum because it is important?' Nor are they likely to be assessed on their capacity to ask questions of their own.

If we were to prioritise the development of *learning itself* rather than the knowledge content of the curriculum (effectively, rendering learning itself *the content*), how differently might we assess a student's learning and learning development? And to what uses might we wish our assessments to be put? If we are awarding grades (in the manner of most current high-stakes assessments), might such grades be more or less useful to universities and potential employers than is the case with current knowledge-based testing and examining? Would they be of use to learners themselves? How might we account in our assessments for the fact that, naturally, different people learn – and apply their learning – in different ways, and that there might not be anything such as a learning 'gold standard'? Could we – and how could we – through adopting an end-on assessment regime, prevent learning as a project of 'becoming', of endless questioning and inquisitiveness, slipping back into a debilitating discourse of 'being', one which tells the learner, as if a statement of finality, 'You are a good/poor/average learner'? Or would our approach demand an end to end-on, standardised examinations, to be replaced by a different approach to assessment altogether, based on a different set of ideas about what public education is actually for?

There is no room to explore these questions in this short chapter. They are important ones, however, and they draw us back to the question with which this chapter opened. In the event of a recalibration of the question–answer relationship, in which neither predominates but both are equally valued as part of the learning process, the question, 'What did you learn in school?', might, at the very least, elicit a somewhat different set of responses from ex-students than currently is the case.

REFERENCES

Althusser, L. (1964) 'Problèmes étudiants', in *La Nouvelle Critique:* 152, January. Cited in Ross K. 1991, xvi.

Apple, M. (1993) *Official Knowledge: Democratic Education in a Conservative Age*, New York and London: Routledge.

Britzman, D. (1991) *Practice Makes Practice*, Albany: SUNY.

Geyer, M. (1993) 'Multiculturalism and the Politics of General Education', *Critical Inquiry*, 19 (Spring): 499–533.

Goldberg, D.T. (1994) 'Introduction: Multicultural Conditions', in D.T. Goldberg (ed.) *Multiculturalism: A Critical Reader*, Oxford: Blackwell.

Hirst, P.H. (1965) 'Liberal Education and the Nature of Knowledge', in Hirst, P.H. and White, P. (eds) (1998) *Philosophy of Education: Major Themes in the Analytic Tradition Vol. 1 Philosophy and Education*, London and New York: Routledge, pp. 246–66.

Hirst, P.H. (1974) *Knowledge and the Curriculum: A Collection of Philosophical Papers*, London: Routledge.

Hirst, P.H. (1998) 'Liberal Education and the Nature of Knowledge', in Hirst, P.H. and White, P. (eds) *Philosophy of Education: Major Themes in the Analytic Tradition Vol. 1 Philosophy and Education*, London and New York: Routledge, pp. 246–266.

Hirst, P.H. and Peters, R.S. (1970) *The Logic of Education*, London: Routledge and Kegan Paul.

James, M., Pollard, A., Wiliam, D. and Oates, T. (2011) *Framework for the National Curriculum: A Report by the Expert Panel for* the *National Curriculum Review*, London: Department for Education.

Kliebard, H.M. (2004) *The Struggle for the American Curriculum, 1893–1958* (3rd edition), New York and London: Routledge Falmer.

Kimball, B.A. (1986) *Orators and Philosophers: A History of the Idea of Liberal Education*, New York: Teachers College Press.

May, T. (2003) 'When is a Deleuzian Becoming?', *Continental Philosophy Review*, 36: 139–53.

McCormick, R. and Murphy, P. (2000) 'Curriculum – The Case for a Focus on Learning', in B. Moon, S. Brown and M. Ben-Peretz (eds), *The Routledge International Companion to Education*. London: Routledge, pp. 204–34.

Moore, A. (2014) *Understanding the School Curriculum: Theory, Politics and Principles*, London and New York: Routledge.

Ross, K. (1991) 'Translator's Introduction', in Rancière, J. (ed), *The Ignorant Schoolmaster: Five lessons in intellectual emancipation.* Translated by K. Ross. Stanford, CA: Stanford University Press.

Schiro, M.S. (2013) *Curriculum Theory: Conflicting Visions and Enduring Concerns*, Thousand Oaks, CA: Sage.

Sfard, A. (1998) 'On Two Metaphors for Learning and the Dangers of Choosing Just One', *Educational Researcher*, 27(2): 4–13.

Stenhouse, L. (1975) *An Introduction to Curriculum Research and Development*, London: Heinemann.

15

A Social Semiotic Multimodal Approach to Learning

Gunther Kress and Jeff Bezemer

INTRODUCTION

Semiotics is not usually associated with learning. Some work, most notably the work of Vygotsky (1978) (and that of others of his period, e.g. Bakhtin [1986]) has strong affinities with semiotic thinking. Yet one of Vygotsky's central categories was that of 'concept' – a psychological notion – rather than that of the 'sign' – a semiotic notion. In our approach we take the *sign* as the basic unit of endeavours to account for meaning: learning, of course, being included in that. The aim of the chapter is to show how basic categories of Social Semiotic Multimodality provide essential tools for a distinct understanding of *learning* and what learning is. The categories involved in this are, on the one hand, those of the theory of Social Semiotics; and on the other hand those of Multimodality.

In the term *Social Semiotic Multimodality* inheres a division of labour: 'Social Semiotics' provides a full *theory* of meaning,

while 'multimodality' provides an *account* of the *modes* which are available for making meaning material in a particular community; it elucidates some of the major features of the different modes. Multimodality as such is not a theory; it marks out the field which is relevant for the investigation of meaning. It does, however, have one far-reaching theoretical effect: the claim that all modes, always in combination with other modes, are drawn into meaning-making, which means that the two linguistic modes of speech and writing are treated as two among all modal resources for making meaning. That makes the previously taken-for-granted centrality of speech and writing no longer tenable. If meaning is made in all modes, then the overall meaning of a 'message' is the result of the combination of meanings provided by all modes in use in a 'message'. Each mode is seen to make a *partial* contribution to the overall meaning. That is as true for speech as for writing, as much as for image – still or moving – for gaze, gesture, for objects-as-modes, and so on.

The 'social' in Social Semiotics points to several underlying assumptions. Some of these are that *meaning* arises in 'the social'; that it is the result of work done in social settings; with socially made cultural resources; by socially formed actors/agents. That semiotic work of 'sign-making' produces the basic entities of semiotics: combinations of form and meaning, 'signs'. Multimodality, the other element in *Social Semiotic Multimodality*, points to the fact that meaning is made in many *modes* – socially shaped material resources – beyond those of speech and writing (and a few other 'canonical' resources, *number* for instance). These constitute socially shaped cultural, material, resources for the representation and materialization of meaning. *Meaning*, in other words, is made with many modes beyond speech and writing, always in specific combinations. Increasingly and frequently, in the modal complexes in which meaning is made material, speech or writing are not necessarily central.

The effects of these assumptions for theorizations of *learning* are profound. On the one hand it means that we must attend to *all* signs in *all* modes which are present in and constitute 'learning environments' – whether as designers of these or as those who engage with such environments. We must be aware of what each mode separately and all modes conjointly contribute to the meaning(s) of that environment. On the other hand we must be aware that all *signs* in the modal complex act as – or can potentially be taken as – *prompts* for engagement.

In assessing what has been learned, we can no longer confine our attention to speech or writing as 'central', as 'dominant', or as 'prior' (Kress 2009). The 'documentation' of learning – whether seen as *rating, assessment, evaluation, judging*, etc. – has to take account of *all* the signs in *all* the modes that are present in the materials on which judgements are based. Attention in these documentation activities has to be expanded to encompass all the modal resources available and used in making signs, sign-complexes,

texts – whether in the initial production or in the subsequent response. There is a need for the *recognition* that in the learner's engagement with the learning environment, learning will potentially be based on all modes, and all modes in conjunction.

Conceptions of learning everywhere touch on and draw in 'the social': as agency, as power, as identity/subjectivity, in terms of 'knowing', in all its manifestations. Here Social Semiotic theory makes a distinctive contribution to the issue of learning, in describing the features of the *social* which characterizes a site of learning, whether classrooms, for instance, or any formal site of learning; and in fact all sites which become sites of learning. If we assume that learning is shaped by features of the social environment, then one of the first questions to be posed is just that: 'what are the characteristics of the social in this environment?' and 'are these characteristics relatively similar to those of the wider social environment?' 'Is the social in the process of change right now?' 'Is the social changing at a different pace, with different effects, for different groups (e.g. for groups defined by *age* as a sociological category)?' In answering such questions and in providing descriptions, the combination of *social semiotic theory* (with questions about different kinds of agency, degrees of power, differing interests), combined with an account of the *affordances of modes* involved, is a major attraction of this approach as a means of producing an account of the conditions for learning.

In our discussion of learning we break with a long tradition in 'the West', namely that of making 'the School' (using that term as a generalization, and an abstraction) and its accounts of learning the focus and the point of departure. For the better part of four decades now, learning has been moving beyond the confines – material and conceptual – of 'the school', in all kinds of ways. In trying to keep up with explanations of this expansion of sites of learning, one response to this change has been to invent a plethora of new names – new entities as seemingly new kinds of learning – through the use of adjectival modifiers. These point in (social) directions of all kinds: professional, life-long, adult, life-wide, early, extracurricular, school-based, formal and informal, etc.

These are makeshift solutions. We might ask, somewhat challengingly: 'What *is* learning, and what, or where, is NOT learning?' We therefore start with the issue of learning itself, 'learning-as-such': aware of course that learning necessarily happens in specific environments. We might say that there are some larger-level aspects which characterize and define learning anywhere, and these provide the starting point for us. It then becomes possible to ask: 'How is this issue – let's say, *agency* – realized when it occurs in social environment x, with modes a, b, d?'

The social which had given rise to the long tradition in which school and learning are frequently still discussed, was – broadly speaking – that of the nineteenth-century nation state, with its forms of economy, its bureaucracies, its conceptions of society, its values. All made their specific demands on the institution of the school: to produce *citizens*, with shared understandings of criterial issues, with kinds of knowledge which on the one hand acted as an essential social cement, and were essential to the working of that state, its society and its economy. 'Learning' and 'school(ing)' formed a seemingly indissoluble couple. Now that the coupling has come undone, the conception it produced and which had become naturalized still remains relatively firmly lodged in a collective memory as *the* way to think about learning. In that context, the adjectival modifications can be seen as an attempt to shore up a collapsing edifice.

No new edifice has as yet replaced the older one; nor is one likely to do so in the short- or medium-term future. In its absence a possible point of departure is, as we have suggested, to think about learning-as-such and to do so in the context of salient, central aspects of the social as we might conceive of it at the moment, treating that as a point of reference and departure. We might say, for instance, that the condition of *radical diversity* characterizes all the sites in which

we imagine our account to be useful. In this attempt, a social semiotic and multimodal framework offers an apt framework.

A SOCIAL SEMIOTIC MULTIMODAL ACCOUNT OF LEARNING: FROM TRANSMISSION TO *TRANSFORMATION*

One criterial, defining feature of the social world is (inter)action. 'Communication' is an instance of (inter)action par excellence. From a social semiotic perspective (inter)action/communication constitute *semiotic work*. Meaning arises in social-semiotic (inter)action: it is the result of semiotic work by social actors, acting with socially made cultural resources, to produce *signs*. *Signs* are the product of semiotic work. The sign is the unit in which meaning is made material and evident. In (Social) Semiotics the process of learning is an instance of (inter)action, of communication, of semiotic work. Learning is both an instance and an outcome of (inter)action and/or engagement and sign-making.

Social semiotics requires an apt theory of communication, one that focuses attention on how meaning is made in the making of signs, and by whom. Learning is encompassed in that approach, as an instance of communication. It treats all instances of communication as semiotic work; and all instances of semiotic work as sign-making; and all sign-making as learning. In this approach communication, sign-making, and learning are accounted for in one frame; regardless of the social 'roles' or positions of those engaged in this process: whether as learners, teachers or students, irrespective of status, whether as 'professionals', as 'amateurs' or novices.

The view of communication put forward here has sign-making at its base. A sign is produced by an initial maker for an imagined addressee. This *sign-as-message* is taken as a 'prompt' by an addressee, who responds to (selected elements of) the prompt; in doing so, she or he transforms the elements selected from the initial message, in relation to their interest, and produces a new (inner) sign. (The addressee may be someone intended as such by the maker of the sign, or some other who regards him/herself as addressed.)

COMMUNICATION AS TRANSFORMATION AND INTERPRETATION

In this conception, communication has happened when there has been interpretation. That can serve as a means of accounting for all instances of learning. It supplies an answer to the question: 'What or where is NOT learning'. To complete this, we take a further step, by assuming two kinds of situations. One is that where learners-as-sign-makers are or have been *addressed*: for instance, by teachers, supervisors, curators or any other institution or by any person taking responsibility for the learning of others. The other is where learners are not ('directly') addressed, whether as learners or otherwise. In our examples below, we feature both kinds. The former illustrate *communication*, involving two sign-makers, making and re-making (complex) signs. The latter illustrate learning in the absence of such *communication*.

Considering both, we recognize that *learning results from engagement with the world, irrespective of the degree to which others were involved in shaping that engagement.* What is at issue is the matter of the recognition of the agency of learners.

Recognition of learners' agency also provides the rationale for insisting that sign-makers do not – 'simply', so to speak – copy, or 'acquire', or straightforwardly 'internalize', 'absorb' signs made by others. Just as we reject a simple sender–receiver model as an account for communication, so do we reject this model as an account of learning. Learning, we hypothesize, rests on *principled, transformative engagement*, however or by whomever that engagement is shaped.

As an approach it resonates with other contemporary social theories of learning, such as Lave and Wenger's (1991) theory of legitimate peripheral participation. We share their view that: 'Conventional explanations view learning as a process by which a learner internalizes knowledge, whether "discovered," "transmitted" from others, or "experienced in interaction" with others. ... Learning as internalization is too easily construed as an unproblematic process of absorbing the given, as a matter of transmission and assimilation' (Lave and Wenger, 1991: 47). Instead of measuring the 'transmission' of knowledge, our interest is in the semiotic work done by learners, and the transformative *principles* that learners bring to bear as they engage with the world around them.

Much of what we discuss here also resonates with what Christoph Wulf describes as *mimesis* (2008). He writes:

> Mimetic learning, learning by creative imitation, constitutes one of the most important forms of learning. Mimetic learning does not, however, just denote mere imitation or copying: Rather, it is a process by which the act of relating to other persons and worlds in a mimetic way leads to an enhancement of one's own world view, action, and behaviour. Mimetic learning is productive; it is related to the body, and it establishes a connection between the individual and the world as well as other persons; it creates practical knowledge, which is what makes it constitutive of social, artistic, and practical action. (p. 56)

Wulf and colleagues illustrate 'mimetic learning' with an example of a theatrical performance by school children, involving singing and dancing on stage in front of parents and teachers. Wulf et al. (2010) see their performance as a 'creative imitation' of the performance of a video clip featuring a German musician who hit the charts at the time. Through this mimetic re-enactment of the 'original' body movements in the video clip, the children learn.

Translated to a social semiotic multimodal account of learning, we say that every sign made is new, an 'innovation'; its making is an act of 'creativity'. The on-going, unceasing process of *transformative engagement*, of integration in 'inner' transformation, with a constantly new resultant state, constitutes *learning*. This turns the still largely taken-for-granted power relations (in communication as much as in learning-as-communication) on its head: it is the 'audience' who guarantees that communication has happened, not the 'rhetor'; and it is the *learner* who guarantees that there has been learning, not the 'teacher'.

We always learn, from any form of engagement. In each case the learner decides what that *learning* has been about. The surrounding (often institutional) environments and the power exerted in and by them tend to disguise – or have tended to do so until now – this basic fact about both communication and learning more or less successfully and effectively (Hodge and Kress, 1988; Kress, 2010). Assessment regimes encourage those responsible for the learning of others to measure the outcome of learners' engagement against a yardstick pre-defined by those in power.

Just to be clear, this does not reject the need to orient a given audience to a certain body of knowledge (in institutional educational settings, the 'curriculum'). Rather it is an invitation *both* to take all learning and all means of displaying learning equally seriously. Thus instead of concluding, 'he didn't learn anything', a social semiotic multimodal approach insists on exploring how the learner has *transformed* the signs addressed to her or him; and also insists on exploring those signs that learners made without having been directly addressed as learners. That constitutes a core aim of the framework proposed here: to provide means for making visible that which frequently or usually is or remains (nearly) invisible, unnoticeably minute, and frequently exists beyond 'official' recognition.

INTEREST AND KNOWING

Any and every sign/sign-complex tells us something about how a sign-maker knows and sees the world at the time of the production of the sign. It makes evident a (small) selection of what was learned. Take the following example. A three-year-old, sitting on his father's lap, draws a series of circles, seven to be exact (see Figure 15.1). When he is finished he says: 'this is a car'.

The question arises as to how this is or could be 'a car'. While drawing, he had said: 'here's a wheel, here's another wheel, that's a funny wheel. … This is a car'. In other words, in making the sign, for him the *criterial feature* of a car was its 'wheelness': it had (many) wheels. Wheels were represented by circles; and 'car' was represented by the arrangement of seven circles. To represent wheels by circles rests on a process of analogy: wheels are like circles. The result of this analogy is a metaphor: 'a wheel is (like) a circle'. Similarly with the representation of 'a car': 'a car is something with/that has many wheels'. The sign, and meaning, made here is a sequence of two metaphors: wheels are (like) circles; many circles are (like) a car. For this sign-maker, the signifiers 'circle' and 'many wheels' are *apt* (their material form and their histories of use make them suitable) to be the carriers of the signifieds: 'wheel' and 'car'.

We might ask further why and how, for this three-year-old, a circle could be the signifier for a wheel; and how wheels could be the criterial feature for 'car'. The first question seems self-evident. As far as the second is concerned, if we imagined the eye-level view of a three-year-old, looking at the family car (in this case a 1982 VW Golf, with its prominently visible wheels, especially at the

Figure 15.1 Drawing by a three-year-old child: 'this is a car'

observer's height) we might conclude that his position in the world, literally, physically, but also cognitively and affectively, might well lead him to see cars – at least on occasions – in that way. His drawing/sign represents his 'position' broadly speaking, his 'interest', arising out of his (physical, affective, cultural, social) position in the world at that moment, vis-à-vis the object to be represented. From the perspective of learning we can say that his interest shapes his attention to a part of the world and acts as the motivation for principles of selection (Kress, 1997).

The point is that it is the *interest* (in the sense just given) of the sign-maker/meaning-maker which shapes what is taken as criterial about an entity, at the moment of its representation. The child's drawing suggests and realizes a view of a part of the world that is historically, socially and culturally shaped. What the meaning-maker takes as criterial then determines what (s)he will represent about that entity. The drawing is the result of the child's semiotic work in his *engagement* with a part of the world, embodying his distinct interests.

Two crucial points about this example: the first is that the relation between meaning (signified) and form (signifier) is not an arbitrary one. It is motivated; that is, the form that suggests itself to the sign-maker is the best possible, the apt means, to be the carrier of the meaning of the sign-maker. The signifier (in material form and in the history of its prior uses as this is known to the sign-maker) meets the interest of the sign-maker in seeking an apt means of expressing the signified. The relation of form and meaning is a motivated relation: this sign, like all signs, is *made* on the basis of a motivated relation of form and meaning. The second point is that each sign, in each occurrence, is newly made. We take that to be the case for all signs.

The first of these two points means that we are entitled to make hypotheses about the interest of the sign-maker (in our case here, as learner): his or her choice of signifiers provides an insight into the principles underlying their response. The assumption

that each sign is both motivated and newly made allows us to make hypotheses about the sign-makers' assumptions – and to take their agency seriously: *they have made the sign to express their meaning.*

Any sign is a sign of knowing, and is a sign of the interest of the sign-maker. To explore this further, consider our next example. A medical student is standing at an operating table. The surgeon and he are about to start operating on a small lump on the patient's belly. As the patient lies flat on his back, the lump is not visible. The operating light is focused on the patient's navel. Before the surgeon makes the first incision she points with her left hand to where the (invisible) lump that they will operate on is located and asks the medical student if he wants to have 'a feel of that'. The medical student replies 'yeah', dipping/touching at three different points around the focal area with the swab in his left hand. He then 'feels' superficially with his right hand. He holds his hand flat, putting gentle pressure on various points with the tip of his fingers, covering an area of about 3 inches below the navel. He also makes a sweeping movement in between two pressure points as shown in Figure 15.2a.

The surgeon then joins him in 'feeling', using her left hand. Her hand is slightly tilted, she creates more pressure with the tip of her fingers, reaching deeper into the belly below the navel, shown in Figure 15.2b. The pressure points mark out and make visible the circumference of the lump. This is then followed by a grasping action by the surgeon involving her middle finger and her thumb, which lasts for a couple of seconds.

The surgeon's action – her *touch* – is rather different from the student's. The surgeon's touch is more specific, deeper, firmer, involving (the tip of) a flat though angled hand as well as a grasping action; the student's touch is broader, more superficial, and involves (the tip of) a flat hand only.

The different characteristics of their actions signify different *engagement* with the 'lump', and in that, different interest and knowing. The surgeon's actions were designed to plan

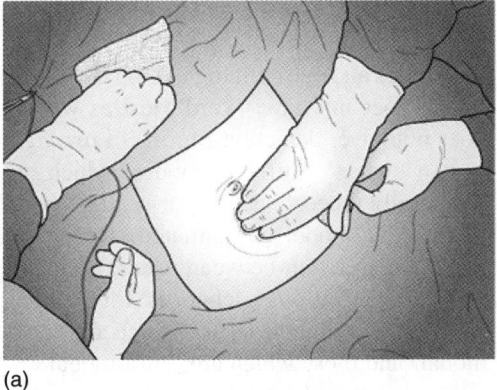

(a)

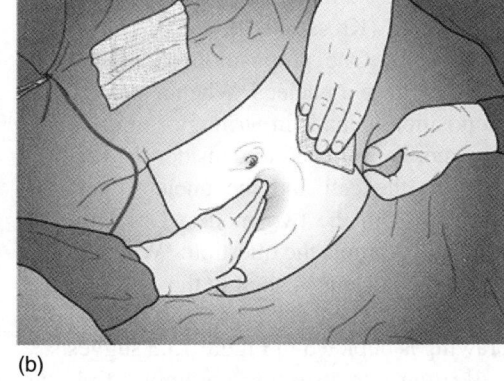

(b)

Figure 15.2a   Medical student touches patient

[Illustrations after video still, Copyright Jeff Bezemer]

Figure 15.2b   Surgeon touches patient

the incision: where to cut with her scalpel. The student's actions were designed to feel the lump. The surgeon knew what to expect, the student didn't. Thus the actions of surgeon and medical student point to different resources, different means of *embodied* knowing, and *demonstrate* different trajectories of prior learning. Their actions, as signifiers, are apt to carry the meanings of each. The signs of both are motivated. At the same time, the actions of both *constitute* learning. With the making of their actions – their *semiotic work*, like the child making marks on paper – they have expanded their resources for making meaning; in this case, for 'reading' lumps of a certain kind, and the specifics of the lump in this patient.

The two have also learned about the other sign-maker from their demonstration of learning: the medical student has *interpreted* how the surgeon touches, and the surgeon has *interpreted* how the student touches. The effects of their interpretations of each other's sign-making have changed their 'inner' resources. The effects of that change in resources will be evident in their subsequent actions; they will transform all future actions. For instance, in these subsequent actions certain features of their actions may be highlighted: foregrounding, through slow motion, say, or attention to the precise direction of a movement. Learning is the effect of such sign-making. With every sign made, the sign-maker's knowing

is transformed; this applies to the student and to the surgeon. Neither could *not* learn from touching the patient.

MODAL SHAPING OF (DEMONSTRATIONS OF) LEARNING AND KNOWING

Modes, through their affordances, suggest potentials, forms and structures, each mode differently so. That has two important implications: first, modes put constraints on *and* provide potentials for *demonstrating* learning; second, modes (and *genres* – which we will not discuss) available to the sign-maker *shape learning*. What the medical student learned by touching the patient will have been different from what he learned by drawing a cross-section of a fatty lump under a skin. Different modes bring a specific lens to an engagement with the world; each mode draws attention differently to features of the signified – that which is to be represented. In doing so, modes shape and structure engagement and potentials for learning. *Speaking* to someone, or *writing*, or *drawing* a map, or *acting out*, all provide distinct potentials for learning, showing and experiencing the world newly, and differently.

In each mode, the potential for learning about an aspect of the world framed is partial.

To give one example, discussed elsewhere in more detail (Kress, 2010), consider learning about cells. One proposition about cells is that they have a nucleus. When a sign of that proposition is made in *writing* or in *drawing*, a learner is prompted to consider the relation between the cell and the nucleus, yet differently so in the two modes. Drawing, for instance, prompts the question: 'Where in the cell is the nucleus?', 'Is it in the centre of the cell, or somewhere else?' as the student whose drawing is depicted in Figure 15.3 suggests.

Writing, or *speech*, prompt different questions, for instance, how is the relation between the cell and the nucleus characterized? As a possessive ('a cell *has* a nucleus'), or as a spatial relation ('there is a nucleus *in* a cell'). The distinct learning potentials of different modes is recognized across different communities. The carpenter's sketch, the architect's 3D model, the police investigator's reconstruction, the researcher's diagrams and transcripts, all 'fix' a specific 'take' on the matter in focus; and in doing so each serves the purpose of *learning*, produces specific forms of what is to be known. Each exploits the distinct potential of modes to provide different insights into the world in focus, the world framed.

The example of the cells shows that as learners make signs, they 'translate' meanings made in one mode or ensemble of modes to meanings made in another mode or ensembles of modes. Given the distinct affordances of different modes, there can never be a 'perfect' translation from one mode to another. Each mode provides its specific 'take', so that

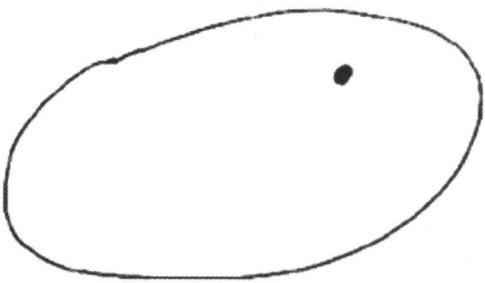

Figure 15.3   Drawing of a Cell

'translations across modes can only ever produce different 'takes' – and indeed different ontologies and epistemologies – on the world. Image does not have 'word', just as writing does not have 'depiction'; forms of *arrangement* ('syntax') differ in modes, which are temporally (speech, action) or spatially (still image, 3D model) instantiated. Hence we make a distinction between re-arrangements and re-organizations – 'changes' for the present want of a suitable term – which are 'inter-modal' and those which are 'intra-modal'.

In the latter, the 'changes', the re-arrangements, deal with whatever the entities/elements/ units of a specific mode are. For these we use the apt term *transformation*: the entities/units/ elements remain the same, though their (re) arrangements differ. Changes from one mode to the other (as in the teacher's 'can someone *tell* me something about a cell?' to 'can you come to the front and *draw* what you have just said?'), that is, *inter-modal* changes – *transduction*s – involve alterations in entities/ units/elements. This is not a matter of re-arrangement. As we pointed out, *writing* has words and syntax; image has depictions and vectors. *Transformation* describes changes in arrangement within one mode. Theoretically, intra-modal transformations are operations on structures within the one mode, in which entities remain the same while structures change. In a transformation, say within the mode of writing, words remain, syntactic/grammatical categories remain those of the mode, as do textual arrangements. What changes is their arrangement. In inter-modal transformation, the change from one mode to another brings with it a change of entities. There are no words in image, there are depictions; semiotic/semantic relations which in speech or writing are expressed in clauses and as verbs are realized through 'vectors' or lines. Other semiotic relations between lexical-syntactic elements – prepositions for instance (on, over, by, etc.) – are realized by spatial means in images, and so on.

Any change, whether inter- or intra-modal, is 'productive': producing changes in meaning and so constituting learning. From the perspective of formal learning this difference holds great potential for exploring precisely such distinctions and their effects in terms of 'knowledge'.

By implication, in institutional settings, when a teacher interprets signs as *signs of learning*, she or he always needs to consider how the learner's *demonstration* of learning was shaped by the *modes* available to the learner/re-maker of the signs or the sign-complex. This has significant implications for evaluation: whether as school teacher or as researcher, if one wants to collect and interpret 'evidence' of learning, the modes provided to the learner to produce that evidence need to be considered carefully (we will not explore the consequences of mis-recognition or lack of recognition in this chapter). Any limitation on the modes available to the learner leads to a limitation on the learner's potential to demonstrate what [s]he has learned. So, for instance, asking science students to demonstrate what they know about cells in *writing* will lead to different accounts and therefore potentially to different assessments of learning than asking them to do so in *image*, or in a 3D model (see Kress et al., 2001). Asking someone to 'write up' what they know puts severe constraints on 'evidencing' their tacit, embodied knowledge.

This is a challenge that those shaping the learning of others are also faced with. In some of our research in clinical settings, *simulation* (in 4D, often) plays a highly significant role. Here too, the kind of simulation used will have crucial effects. Equally, by allowing learners to demonstrate learning in different modes the range of what is and can be recognized can be vastly expanded.

FROM LEARNING ENVIRONMENTS TO SIGNS OF LEARNING

This account of learning can be expanded by exploring the semiotic relations between a sign-complex/text and the environment in (response to) which it was made. Consider visitors to the London Science Museum, where an event has been laid on for an audience of adults, titled, 'How Surgeons Learn to Operate'. In the museum, members of the audience encounter a learning environment designed for them by a 'curator' (in this case, a team of people that included ourselves). Figure 15.4 gives a snapshot of the environment.

The *learning environment* was designed as and focused on a re-enactment of surgical training in the operating theatre. Two surgeons, 'gowned up', were standing on a stage, in front of an operating table with a 'draped' 'patient' on it. A small screen in front of them showed 'laparoscopic' video footage from a simulated operation conducted and recorded earlier. The surgeons enact their roles: one holding the camera, the other holding a grasping instrument; both surgeons look at the screen in front of them, as they would have done in a real operating theatre. On either side of the stage large screens were set up on which the same laparoscopic recording was projected.

During the re-enactment, the museum visitors displayed orientation into varying directions. Some visitors looked at one of the screens; others looked at the surgeons on the stage. That is, their attention was drawn in different directions, and that was rendered visible in the direction of their *gaze*. Through *facial expression* they signified varying responses to what they were attending to. If we tried to 'translate' these expressions into writing, we might say that some signified 'squeamishness', others 'surprise', yet others 'concentrated attention'. There were none who did not 'respond', or, therefore, did not learn. These 'outwardly made' signs give us some initial insight into the experiences of the visitors: what drew their attention, and what did not; and what meaning they attached to what they were orienting to. We take the differences we observe in the signs they make to reflect differences in the interest and experiences of the visitors, leading to different transformations and transductions of what – from the design team's point of view was the 'one' sign complex. So for instance,

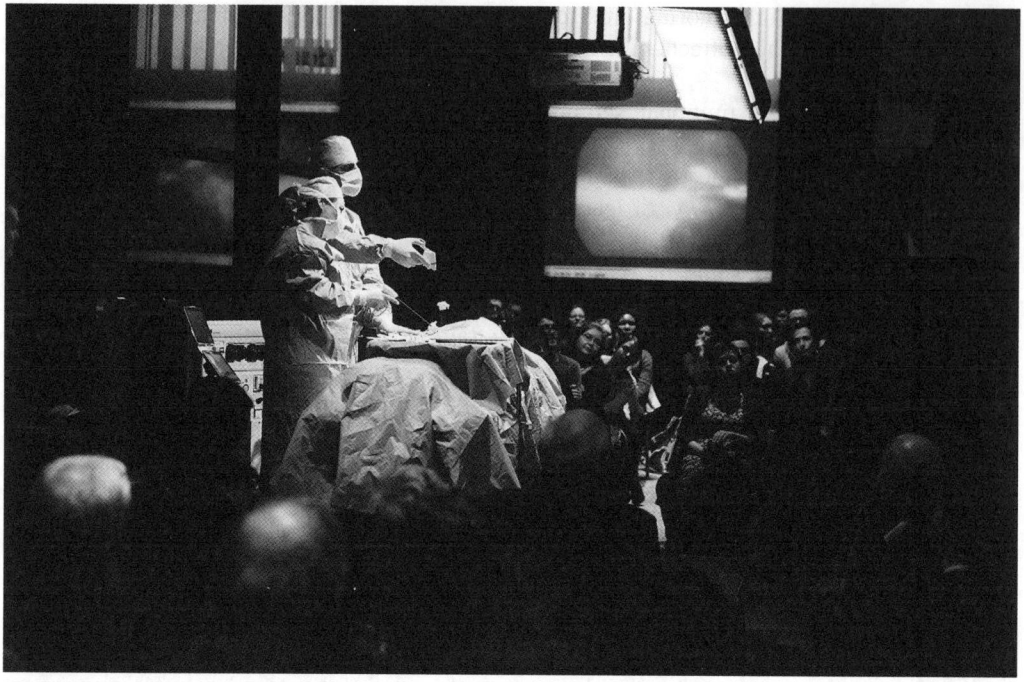

Figure 15.4   Simulation: the design of a learning environment

[Copyright Science Museum London]

a member of the audience, who had recently undergone an operation, would have had a specific interest, which would have shaped how meaning was made on this occasion.

If we then examined what one of the visitors subsequently posted on their blog, such as in Figure 15.5, we could expand that initial account further. We could relate the signs made by the museum visitor in the blog post to the signs made by the 'curatorial team', made in the design of the exhibition. By comparing two complex signs – one made by the curator's team for visitors, and one made by a visitor some time after a visit to the museum, we can begin to gain insight into the visitor/blogger's *transformative engagement* with the exhibition: what in the original sign complex the visitors oriented to, and how those elements were transformed and integrated into new sign complexes. By rendering these transformations and transductions visible, we can get a glimpse of the visitor's learning.

Of course, the signs made by learners only give us 'glimpses', as signs are always *partial* signs of learning, and capture one moment in ongoing inner semiosis. Out of all that which the visitor has learned from the visit, through interpretation, or signs made 'inwardly' and silently, only selections may then, later, be turned into signs made outwardly. Those outward signs are always made for others, shaped by a rhetorical interest. As with sign-making more generally, when looking at signs as signs of learning, we need to attend to the social-rhetorical framing. The curator acted as rhetor, who designed a learning environment for an audience of visitors. On the blogging platform, a different social relation is established: here, the museum visitor-turned-blogger has become rhetor, and her or his sign-making is shaped by their interest in addressing a particular audience. Of all the features that have caught the attention of the visitor, of all the signs made inwardly, a selection is made, in view of the blogger-as-rhetor's

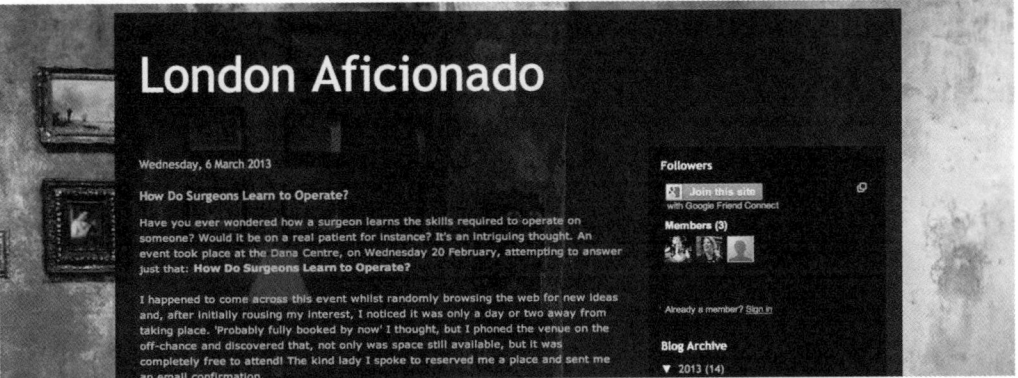

Figure 15.5 Screen shot of a blog post

[Screenshot taken from http://londonaficionado.blogspot.co.uk/]

interest in drawing their audience to some features, while excluding others.

MAPPING TRANSFORMATIONS AND TRANSDUCTIONS

We will now attempt to make some of the *principles* of transformative engagement visible by exploring the semiotic relations between learners' signs and their environments in some detail. We explore these relations in one example, namely how an artist produced a map of a public space. The sign-maker was *unaddressed*; he, as the artist, initiated and organized learning in the absence of 'instructors'.

The example is a map made by an artist, Jan Rothuizen. The map is taken from his 'soft atlas' (2011), a collection of annotated drawings of public and private places in the Netherlands. The places he has mapped out include a prison cell, a circumcision clinic, a living room, a bedroom and a public square. The maps can be interpreted as signs of learning; in this case, learning through 'everyday' engagement with environments that were not designed by anybody for the sign-maker to learn. The maps tell us something about how this artist interpreted the places he visited. Much like an ethnographer, Jan observes these places closely, making 'field' notes and

sketches, and taking pictures. Back in his studio, he draws on these on-the-spot documentations to make what he calls a 'soft map'. Take the map shown in Figure 15.6: a trauma helicopter.

It may be useful to consider the social and semiotic conditions in which the map was made. Jan has tasked himself to draw and write. The semiotic resources he draws on reflect his professional position, his life experiences, resulting in these specific *semiotic repertoires*. Jan addresses a broad, imagined, relatively little known, adult audience. Jan is not 'telling a story'; he represents a spatially organized sign complex: he shows an object. He draws on a specific genre: 'informational', 'illustrational'. All these are evident in this sign complex.

Looking at Jan's map as a sign complex, we can identify the different modes used and how they are used. He uses line *drawing*, *writing* (in block letters, occasionally underlined), and *layout* (not colour, for instance). *Drawings* are mostly re-presentations of what he *saw* (showing, e.g., what the helicopter looked like); *written* elements are re-presentations of what he *saw* ('letters reflect', 'Leo, balding, with small glasses'), of what people *said* to him ('That's where Frans sits. He is a full-time trauma helicopter pilot. Before that he worked for the navy as a pilot'), and what he *smelled* ('smells like fresh car inside').

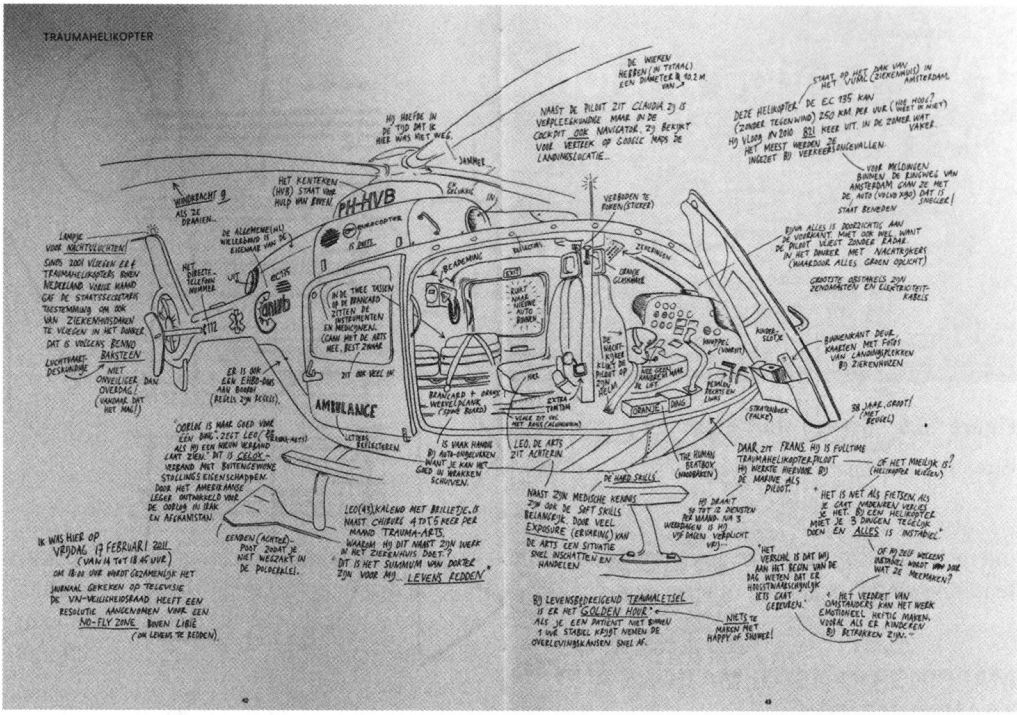

Figure 15.6   Trauma helicopter

[Reprinted from Rothuizen, 2011, p. 42]

As for layout, or the spatial organization of visual elements on the two-page spread (spanning 31cm x 46cm), we note a centre-margin information structure (Kress and van Leeuwen, 2006), with the drawing of the helicopter and its constituent elements placed at the centre, and writing in the periphery. The centre-margin arrangement of image and writing suggests that *seeing* – visual engagement – was prior; *listening* came second. The writing appears as annotations. Most of the written annotations are connected to the drawing with leader lines, naming and describing displayed objects ('fuses', 'lever', 'orange thing'), and elaborating on them ('spine board – comes in handy with car accidents because you can shuffle it well into a wreck'). So, almost all written elements of the text branch out from the centre. Some elements are directly connected to the drawing, others indirectly, via other elements, like rhizomes. The result

is an entirely non-linear text, a non-linear ordering of interpretations.

Making the map, including all the choices described above, such as the centre-margin structure and the use of image and writing, will have shaped Rothuizen's learning. By choosing to draw diagrammatically, topographically, analytically, Jan prompted himself, as it were, to identify and annotate all the constituent parts of the helicopter. Different choices – a left–right structure, use of writing only – would have prompted him to engage differently; it would have led to different selections, arrangements and foregrounding – in short, to a different transformative and transductive engagement. Material and medium choices have epistemological implications too. For instance, Jan has used a pen (a rollerball pen?) that produces fine lines, affording a degree of pictorial detail that is difficult to achieve with, say, a marker.

One question arising from this is why the routes to learning of the kind discussed here are used, promoted, valued in some environments and not, or differently, in others. For us, the answer lies in the ruling ideology of representation. On the one hand, Jan's maps have not abstracted the sign-maker away (as opposed to, say, a 'scientific' diagram). The map is a *personal* account, signified, for instance, in the handwriting and drawing 'style', and in the first person perspective used in writing ('I was here on Friday …'). On the other hand, these maps construe a non-linear ordering (much like picture books and illustration-led 'information books' such as David Macaulay's *The Way Things Work* [2004]), which is regarded as being apt for certain audiences only, and often for outside the institution of the school. Hence, picture books may be found in schools for the very young, while information books, may be kept away from the school.

A multimodal frame of reference, insisting that every mode present contributes to meaning, makes recognition possible, both as a pedagogic and a curricular matter, and as a political matter given the great variety of social/cultural backgrounds of learners. Multimodality makes recognition possible through overt, explicit methods of description and analysis.

Social semiotics insists that signs are constantly newly made, and are 'motivated' in the combination of form and meaning by the sign-maker's interest. This provides a secure route to the recognition of the learner's agency. Through this, the learner's interest becomes apparent in the principles underlying the design of signs and of sign-complexes (texts). The motivated sign forces the recognition of the sign-maker's semiotic work, and requires that to be taken seriously. That is a pre-condition to what might now, at long last, appear as a truly learner-centred view of learning.

IN CONCLUSION

The question we pose ourselves is: 'What does this account provide which is not provided in other quite closely related (socio-cultural) accounts? Without much retracing here we would say that the account overall might provide an essential response to the problems posed by the social condition of profound diversity. Multimodality asks what modes have been used, and what learning is evident in each of the modes used. From the perspective of *diversity*, multimodality demonstrates that design has become an essential practice, given that each instance of communication may need to be designed, modally, in quite specific ways. On principle, there are no longer any canonical or conventional arrangements – especially given that relations of power are also now highly provisional.

Given the condition of diversity, it becomes essential to have means and tools for the recognition of learning in multimodal complexes of highly varying kinds.

REFERENCES

Bakhtin, M. M. (1986) *Speech Genres and Other Late Essays*, Austin: University of Texas Press.

Hodge, R. I. V and Kress, G. R. (1988) *Social Semiotics*, Oxford: Polity Press.

Kress, G. R. (1997) *Before Writing: Rethinking the Paths to Literacy*, London: RoutledgeFalmer.

Kress, G. R. (2009) 'Assessment in the perspective of a social semiotic theory of multimodal teaching and learning', in C. M. Wyatt-Smith and J. J. Cumming (eds), pp. 19–41.

Kress, G. R. (2010) *Multimodality: A Social Semiotic Approach to Contemporary Communication*, London: RoutledgeFalmer.

Kress, G. R. and van Leeuwen, T. (2006) *Reading Images: The Grammar of Visual Design*, 2nd edition, London: RoutledgeFalmer.

Kress, G. R., Jewitt, C., Ogborn, J. and Tsatsarelis, C. (2001) *Multimodal Teaching and Learning: The Rhetorics of the Science Classroom*. London: Continuum.

Lave, J. and Wenger, E. (1991) *Situated Learning: Legitimate Peripheral Participation*, Cambridge, UK: Cambridge University Press.

Macaulay, D. (2004) *The Way Things Work,* 2nd edition, London: Dorling Kindersley.

Rothuizen, J. (2011) *De zachte atlas van Nederland*, Amsterdam: Nieuw Amsterdam.

Vygotsky, L. S. (1978) *Mind in Society: The Development of Higher Psychological Processes*, M. Cole et al. (eds), Cambridge, MA: Harvard University Press.

Wertsch, J. V. (1991) *Culture, Communication and Cognition: Vygotskian Perspectives*, New York: Cambridge University Press.

Wulf, C. (2008) Mimetic learning. *Designs for Learning* 1(1), 56–67.

Wulf, C., Althans, B., Audehm, K., Bausch, C., Gohlich, M., Sting, S., Tervooren, A., Wagner-Willi, M. and Zirfas, J. (2010) *Ritual and Identity: The Staging and Performing of Rituals in the Lives of Young People*, London: Tufnell.

16

Learners, Politics and Education

Rebecca Webb and Barbara Crossouard

INTRODUCTION

This chapter originates in two separate research studies conducted by the authors in markedly contrasting contexts. One focuses upon discourses of human rights in English schooling, and the other on young people's active citizenship in Senegal. As academic colleagues, once we started to present our respective analyses of our projects at research workshops, it became apparent that they both illuminated the intersections of learning and politics, although in ways that implied that education was *not* political; indeed, that it *should* not be political.

Prompted by a post-structural understanding of subjectivity, this chapter draws upon our different project data to problematize 'the political' and 'politics', and the relationship of both to learning. Rather than only policies and practices that govern state or institutional structures, our analysis demonstrates how politics and the political are implicated in the processes of democratization and also

of subjectification. We illuminate the fluidity and contingencies of these processes, and their construction through local, national and global identifications.

The section that follows provides a theoretical backdrop for the chapter. It first addresses the emergence of modern understandings of citizenship, problematizing the assumptions of the human agent that this entails. We consider how such understandings continue to resonate through contemporary conceptualizations of education and international human rights discourses, before turning to post-structural apprehensions of the subject, constructed through 'difference'. This then supports our theoretical interrogations of our two sets of data through which we seek to illustrate how politics and the political are intrinsic to education, subjectification and democratization. We conclude by arguing for an understanding of 'politics' and 'the political' within education that do not posit either a 'required subject' or the foreclosure of 'the domain of the political' (Butler, 1995: 36).

EDUCATION AND THE SUBJECT

As our projects intersect with citizenship and human rights, we start by briefly problematizing the origins of Western understandings of citizenship, where, from its ancient forms we encounter its potential to act in exclusionary ways. In Greek city states, citizenship was reserved for male householders of independent means, their financial and household status underpinning their freedom to engage in civil and political spheres, from which children, women and slaves were excluded (Bingham and Biesta, 2010). In its modern form, this separation of public and private spheres was also assumed in the understandings of citizenship associated with the emergence of Western liberal democracies from the eighteenth century. Many feminist writers (e.g. Honig, 1992; Mouffe, 1992) have critiqued the masculinist ontologies and epistemologies embedded within such thinking, and how this privileged the strong individualism of the rational, autonomous subject, assumed to be male. Women, on the other hand, were presupposed to suffer from inherent frailties, including suspect emotional tendencies, which rendered them unfit to participate outside of the private, domestic sphere. As Butler (1992: 12) eloquently illuminates, the autonomy supposedly achieved through man's rationality has always been illusory: a 'product of a disavowed dependency' and a denial of the very social relations through which the subject and such claims to autonomy have been constituted.

Engaging with the understandings of the subject in Kant (1992 [1784]), Bingham and Biesta (2010: 28) draw out the powerful assumptions that have been sedimented together in Enlightenment thought, i.e. man (sic) had a duty to use his reason to transcend his (unenlightened) state of immaturity, with education as the 'lever' through which to achieve this emancipation. The use of reason to arrive at 'truth' and emancipation has also depended crucially upon the premise that this could allow a separation of knowledge and power, and indeed that 'knowledge can only exist where the power relations are suspended' (Foucault, 1975: 27). On the contrary, rather than being 'outside power', or 'the reward of free spirits', Foucault has pointed to truth as being 'a thing of this world', produced through and within regimes of truth, each with 'its "general politics" of truth' (Foucault, 1984: 72–3).

Despite this, the logic of individual empowerment within liberal thought remains important in contemporary discussions of education. Liberal thought also permeates the international human rights regimes developed in the aftermath of World War II, which have included the rights of the child and the right to education. However, whilst these claim to attend to the agency of the child (and of youth), critics are concerned that the spaces opened may 'domesticate' child and youth citizenship, confining education to a process of mere socialization, rather than allowing for contestation and the revision of existing norms (Biesta, 2013). Pyckett (2007) similarly draws our attention to the instrumentalities which pervade 'Common Sense', consensual constructions of learner discourses, and how these work to de-politicize the global, national and local policy contexts of education.

As Mouffe (1992: 370) points out, the rationalities of Enlightenment thought and its understandings of the subject as a 'transparent entity' have been thoroughly critiqued by many writers from different traditions during the twentieth century. She draws instead on post-structural theories of discourse which see the subject as being produced through demarcations of difference, within which some ways of being, speaking, doing and thinking are recognized as legitimate, while others are not, within the 'politics of truth' of any society. This makes subject formation inherently political, shot through with contested, agonistic relations, in which constituent 'others' are always implicated. Butler's concept of performativity is particularly valuable here. It allows us to consider the subject that is constantly in process, and indeed brought into being as an 'effect' of the re-citation of linguistic norms and signifying practices, rather than as s(he) who originates from a stable or essential subject, i.e. 'a doer before the deed' (Butler, 2006: 34).

Rancière is likewise concerned with the political as an integral dynamic of subject formation. He describes this as a process of subjectification, which is always about a 'disidentification, [a] removal from the naturalness of place' (Rancière, 1995: 36, in Bingham and Biesta, 2010: 32). It requires the shifting of 'a body' from 'the place assigned to it [so that] it makes visible what had no business being seen and makes heard a discourse where once there was no place for noise' (Rancière, 1999: 30 in Bingham and Biesta, 2010: 34). Crucially, this idea embraces politics as a discourse of 'dissensus', which challenges consensus as an order in which everyone already has a place and an identity. Like Butler, who resists the claim of foundational philosophies as requiring a political 'stable subject' (Butler, 1995: 36), Rancière suggests dissensus as a *process* that is generative of subject formation. In common with other post-structural theorists, he sees such a process as one that 'does not happen before the act of politics but rather in and through it' (Rancière, 1999: 40). For Rancière subjectification and dissensus are *always* momentary, fleeting and re-constituted processes within new political acts.

Overall, these theorists call attention to the 'mutually constitutive' relations between language and social life' (Dunne et al., 2005: 93), so discourse analysis informed our engagement with our data. As discourse itself is as much about creating the speaker as vice versa, discourse analysis allows for *more than* language. Rather, it attends to what language does and what it makes possible; as well as its confusions and its contradictions. This presupposes different institutional positions from which people speak, with power relations suturing subjects to these positions. It sees both researcher and researched as constituted within these dynamics. Our recognition of the power of language and our constitution through discursive relations provokes in us a concern to disrupt common-sense, taken-for-granted constructions (MacLure, 2010). We therefore engage in 'thinking *with* theory' in our data analysis (Jackson and Mazzei, 2012). Following their examples, we construct vignettes from our data to invite theory in to open up the possibilities of what can be said.

PROBLEMATIZING THE CONSTRUCTION OF EDUCATION, LEARNING AND POLITICS

Exploring Youth as Active Citizens in Senegal – Barbara's Research Data[1]

The research project in which I was involved explored how the work of an international non-governmental organization (INGO) in Senegal supported youth as active citizens, particularly with respect to their rights to education and to sexual and reproductive health (Crossouard and Dunne, 2015; Dunne et al., 2014). It was a particularly interesting time to investigate youth citizenship in Senegal as fieldwork took place soon after the election of a new president and government. However, even if in the end the elections unfolded peacefully, this was after widespread demonstrations against constitutional abuse (in which youth had been highly active).

The research included interviews with adult stakeholders in education programmes related to youth citizenship, focus group interviews with youth participants, and other youth who had been active in these protests. At the behest of the INGO, I was accompanied by two 'youth researchers', one male and one female, with the aim of privileging youth voices. Although they had no previous involvement in research, their educational experiences gave them many insights relevant to the research. They had completed their schooling through an alternative education programme (AEP) whose approach to citizenship education had stressed the peaceful, consensual resolution of conflict, alongside respect for traditional family values. The youth researchers had also participated as peer educators in a HIV/AIDS education project, and a further project again through the AEP that had involved youth throughout Senegal in monitoring the recent election processes. Youth from the AEP (including the youth researchers) saw it as imperative that their participation was politically neutral – their politics was a private concern.

Despite the frequent construction of youth as 'agents of change' by adult respondents, youth's active citizenship quickly showed that it involved very diverse positions on politics, and the political. This distinction takes up Mouffe (2005: 9), where '*politics*' refers to the ensemble of institutional practices that seek to organize human coexistence, such as spheres of public party politics and government, and '*the political*' refers to 'the dimension of antagonism that [is] constitutive of human societies', which therefore takes up the agonistic understandings of subject formation outlined above.

Youth's different positions were strikingly illuminated in a focus group conducted by myself and the youth researchers with youth activists who had been central within the anti-government demonstrations described above. The youth activists constructed their actions as being in defence of Senegal's democratic constitution. They voiced open criticism of the 'monarchical ambitions' of the previous president and expressed pride in having contributed to his eventual defeat through democratic processes. However, being deeply opposed to such protests, and the violence that had sometimes ensued, both youth researchers abandoned the interview schedule and addressed participants using language such as '*what I deplore is …*'. The respondents were taken aback, but countered these accusations by vigorously asserting the importance of defending the principles of free speech and democracy; already this was therefore a profoundly agonistic and political encounter.

However, in our post-interview debrief immediately afterwards, when questioning how they had conducted the interview, the male youth researcher responded to me angrily, saying of one female respondent: '*elle me faisait de la politique, elle essayait de me convainçre, elle n'a pas le droit de faire ça*' (*she was arguing politics with me, trying to win me over – she has no right to do that*). Although youth's disengagement from 'politics' (understood in terms of spheres of public party politics and government) has been identified in many different contexts, in this striking reversal of the rights to free speech, participation in politics seems to be reduced to a procedural compliance with the mechanisms of government. The legitimacy of political contestation and of engaging across issues of difference is challenged, implying therefore a silencing of the political.

The previous section discussed how subject positions are produced through demarcations of difference. A further key differentiation made during this focus group involved the articulation of how gender and sexuality related to politics, and to youth. Within the heated discussions described above, the female youth researcher (who had a strong commitment to sexual and reproductive health education) made a sharp differentiation between the political sphere (*le volet politique*) and things that were of *real* concern to youth, these being youth unemployment, incest, youth indiscipline, irresponsibility, rape, sexual abuse – the focus group participants were asked why their focus was only on politics, rather than these more important issues. The respondents agreed these were important, and that they were still discussing their post-election priorities, *without* however challenging this relationship to politics. Given the concern for SRH rights in the research, young people's articulation of these positions on issues such as incest, rape and sexual abuse as *not* belonging within politics (drawing on Mouffe, 2005), is remarkable, in particular for the ways it undermines youth as 'agents of change'; although it would align with republican understandings of citizenship associated with Senegal's colonial past. At the same time, the encounter was deeply agonistic and political, and, even if surrounded by many ambiguities, it could be seen as an eruption of dissensus, generative of subject formation (Rancière, 1995). These ambiguities are taken up further in Rebecca's research, to which we now turn.

Engaging 'Rights' Processes and Subjects of Schooling in England – Rebecca's Project

My research explored the implications of adopting a discourse of 'Rights', utilizing the UNICEF UK's 'Rights Respecting Schools' framework (the RRS),[2] to guide both the policy and practices of a large state primary school in England. I wanted to engage with the way in which such a discourse shaped what went on in school on an 'everyday' basis. More than this, however, I sought to find out what might be expected of the 'Rights' subjects of the discourse, as well as to ascertain what was claimed for a 'values-based' project of democratic schooling of this nature. The school had achieved 'Level 1' of the RRS award and was working towards 'Level 2', which required it to instrumentally demonstrate a range of 'common-sense' rationalities, such as: 'The school has an inclusive and participatory ethos based on the Convention of the Rights of the Child (CRC).[3]

This research involved me conducting fieldwork over a period of ten months in a variety of different school spaces: some official, such as classrooms and the assembly hall, and others less formal, such as corridors, play areas and meeting rooms. On occasions, I was a participant-observer variously joining in with a range of school activities, such as working with groups of children on learning tasks, conducting 'playground duty', and generally helping with ancillary tasks. At other times, I had the leisure and privilege of watching. I documented my time in school with copious field-notes, fiercely scribbled at the time, and refined away from the field soon after. Towards the end of my fieldwork, I conducted some informal, semi-structured

individual and group interviews with a selection of research subjects that built on conversations we had had in the course of previous day-to-day interactions. My aim was to scrutinize everyday occurrences of school life, acknowledging that they can be understood in many different ways, all and none of which can be seen as 'true' (Laws, 2011: 15). Like Laws, I also wanted to achieve a way of 'reading' the school in new ways in order to see things that may have been taken for granted previously.

I used post-structuralism to contest, but not dismiss, the limits of Enlightenment theories that we set out in our Introduction. In making sense of my fieldwork, I drew on a 'bundle of theorizations' that enabled me to recognize my own investments in the texts I constructed. In what follows, I draw upon three vignettes (MacLure, 2010) of data in order to 'trouble' the RRS discourse in three separate incidents, all of which call into question *processes* of democratization and subjectification at work as part of this schooling enterprise, again constituted variously by research subjects as *beyond* politics.

The first incident was the occasion of an interview between me and a senior manager with responsibility for the RRS initiative who explained to me that she was '*passionate*' about the '*Rights*' and '*Equality and Diversity… "journey"*' that the school was on, although this was '*not political, you know …*'. I interpreted her comments as understandably defensive. I heard what she said as a way of being accountable both to me, but also perhaps to a wider, imagined public audience (governors; parents; Ofsted – stakeholders and surveyors of schooling practices). I saw this linked to 'accountability discourses' which required on-going measurements, standardizing, auditing, and the presenting of oneself and one's professional actions in particular ways – '*don't worry, they're not political you know … we are a "safe pair of hands"*'. In Foucauldian terms, we might read here the productive effect of the power of the other dominant schooling discourses, seeping into the senior manager's need to remonstrate – albeit unconsciously perhaps – her defence of the '*journey*' that she and her school community were on; a journey along a non-contentious, rational and dispassionate path and one that elevates human agency. This senior manager was required to negotiate, effectively and affectively, multiple discursive regimes which could not, and did not, stack up.

More than this, however, I read the RRS 'political' rhetoric as occupying the proclamatory terrain of what is termed a 'post-ideological era' of politics, a national, strategic claim of the UK government (Hall and O'Shea, 2013). This means that education is required to be, as much as for any other public body, about seemingly 'common-sense' goals, sound managerialism and a 'fair society' (Hall and O'Shea, 2013); a consensus that for Rancière (2004) can only ever be about getting rid of the allure of politics – a 'closing the gap': '… consensus … as the reduction of democracy to the way of life of a society' [as the 'already declared'] (Rancière, 2004: 306). Considered in these terms, the discourse became incontestable, about 'the Bleeding Obvious' (MacLure, 2010). It worked as an empty unmarked sign of unity or sameness that didn't need to be contested, that simply 'was', that belonged to nothing or no one and that simply stood for everyone (Gedalof, 2013: 9). It worked to foreclose definitions and differentiation, so that '*equality* and *diversity*' are left unexplained apart from the information she gave me that '*feedback from children and parents*' suggested that it made a '*difference*'.

The second incident was connected to my attendance at a formal event of democratic schooling, that of a Student Council Meeting to which I had been invited by the councillors, 18 or so children between 6 and 11 years of age; and the Chair, the head teacher. I found myself focusing upon the subjectivities of those constituted within the meeting, which seemed to me to be 'fixed' by particular identity constructions. In the first instance, I was struck by the prowess of one young boy in 'holding the floor' to speak of the need for better outdoor play equipment. At one point he addressed a young girl next to him to ask her if she wanted to add anything to what he had said. Through her silence, and the shaking of her head, she made it clear that she did not wish to contribute. Towards the end of the meeting, an older boy raised another issue of equipment (this time for indoor 'Golden Time')[4] through 'Any Other Business', again signalling appropriately his desire to speak by half raising his hand to an attentive audience. On this occasion two older girls posited solutions to the queries he raised: how about sharing the existing play equipment more effectively between classes of children? or, why not 'pool' the resources in one area so that their use could be more effectively monitored?

I found myself pondering the 'politics' of difference by engaging with Butler to think through what I had seen: who is she, this child citizen subject of the Student Council, I asked myself? In simple terms, we could say that, on this occasion, the 'she' was a 'he': it was boys who spoke and girls who listened and served. The 7-year-old boy performed – at length – with considerable acumen; the older boy responded to 'Any Other Business' and solicited the reactions of the girls around him who then provided the answer. It was boys who constituted the participatory '*voices*' of the '*active citizen*' of this liberal discourse. Here we had 'power forming the subject' (Butler, 1997: 2) in such a way that it was masculine identities that prefigured the citizen subjectivities of this space so as to constitute them as foundational.

We could suggest that in a process of subject formation here, that mutual acts of recognition 'through which subjects accord each other the status of the viable subject' (Davies, 2006: 427) meant that the boys were, unwittingly, encouraged to speak up and perform a masculinity with which they identified, and which was readily apprehended and taken up by the head teacher. However, I found myself amused by the behaviour of the 7-year-old girl who seemed to me to enact her agency on her own terms. Perhaps she had to listen to this charming young boy all too often and perhaps – for her – her silence and enjoyment of her lunch and her refusals were her way of ensuring the accomplishment of herself as a 'recognisable and thus viable subject' (Davies, 2006: 427). Conversely, the two older girls seemed to fall into what Butler herself describes as 'temporal modalities' (Butler, 1997: 14). Firstly, they conformed to a modality of gendered behaviour as demure, passive and polite which gave way to the older boy in raising the issue of the play equipment, which is 'always prior, outside of itself, and operative from the start' (Butler, 1997: 14). Then, in responding as gendered 'fixers-of-problems' and 'do-ers', they came up with constructive suggestions of how to solve the matter of the lack of toys. In this way, they moved in to a second modality, which was the 'willed effect of the subject [so that] subjection is a subordination that the subject brings on itself' (Butler, 1997: 14). Within such subjection, Butler reminds us, lies the *possibility* for 'resistance and opposition'. But, I have to confess, that I failed to pick it up on this occasion.

However, by contrast in a semi-official space of schooling on a separate occasion, I was party to a focus group discussion between a group of eight 10- and 11-year-olds. I had asked them what they made of the RRS initiative. To begin with they looked fidgety and embarrassed and a little bored. I then referred specifically to several posters and displays that we could see and in particular to the 'Rights Charters'[5] around the walls in order to generate dialogue. It was as though I had lit a 'touch-paper'. One child announced that *'Toilet Charters'* had started to appear on the doors to the junior school toilets. He pronounced this as *'a joke'*. Another child remarked that she thought that someone had flushed one of the Toilet Charters, *'down the toilet'*. This was greeted with barely contained delight by the assembled group, and a different child suggested gleefully: *'I mean ... some of them* [the statements on the Toilet Charter] *are just so funny ... "You have a right to feel safe and secure" ... it*

doesn't really happen so often that you need to put a charter up!'

At the time, I was struck by the ready wit and wry humour of this group; their ability to banter, including with me, and to poke fun (gently), to challenge one another (pretty kindly), to defend, and what is more, to pour scorn (in bucket loads) on a very well intentioned (and no-doubt, time and labour intensive) scheme designed to manage behaviour. ... This was clearly a 'performance' and a very well-crafted and choreographed one at that. In Butlerian terms, here were alternative citational acts being played out which clearly constituted and contested 'the coherence of that "I"' (Butler, 2004: 376). These seemed to be of a different order to some of the gendered performative acts of the citizen subject that I had witnessed in the Student Council meeting. In this regard they amplified the way in which gender is neither a 'stable identity [n]or a locus of agency from which various acts proceed' (Butler, 1988: 519). For example, it was a 10-year-old girl who asserted that the Toilet Charter didn't need to be written down, and who then continued to take part in the ensuing banter: *'it sounds like a joke but they – the teachers – mean it to be really serious'*. This was an assertive and subversive interjection in which she presumed to know better than the adults, who, she indicated, had been enacting 'Rights' on her behalf. Here her 'power pervades the very conceptual apparatus that seeks to negotiate its terms' (Butler, 1995: 39), including that of her own subject position. Another girl was equally gleeful in her command that: *'we know how to go to the toilet!'* With its satirical and sardonic overtones and light yet purposive enactment, this felt to me to be, again, in Butler's own words, 'the very precondition of a politically engaged critique' (1995: 39) of a very different quality to that which we met in the formal space of the council meeting.

These children did not wish to recognize this charter as theirs; they were delighted that one child had, allegedly, taken it upon herself to *'flush it down the toilet'*. On that basis, at least, this seemed to be citizenship as a signifying 'political' act, which in Rancièreian terms could be said to be one of disidentification. This appeared to me to be, therefore, 'dissensus' which challenged consensus as 'an order' that was *all-inclusive* ...; [so] that there is an identity for everyone' (Bingham and Biesta, 2010: 34). Rather, dissensus emerged here as a *process* which generated subjectivity. It was fleeting and re-constituted within new political acts, which, for Rancière, are always about 'undetermined political processes' (Biesta, 2011: 141). It emanated from an epistemological construction of these children as speakers who could speak up for themselves on their own terms and in their own right. And crucially, it shifted the balance of this Rights Respecting School (momentarily) from one of mere generator of citizenship identities to one of 'producer of political subjectivities' (Biesta, 2011: 150).

CONCLUSION

This chapter grew out of two research projects in entirely different contexts. One focused upon discourses of human rights in an English school and the other on youth's active citizenship in a West African context. As research colleagues working on these projects separately, we were drawn to the commonalities in our respective readings of our data. The projects suggested to us contemporary discourses of learning and schooling as those which are, and ought to be, beyond 'the political' and 'politics', where both are to be conceived as non-contingent and necessitated upon the engagement of already imagined identities. We were struck by the ways in which United Nations frameworks travel through different spaces and temporalities to become 'plugged in' (borrowing an expression coined in Jackson and Mazzei, 2012) to predominant and commonsensical ideas of democratic education as rational, consensual and predetermined. On the contrary, our methodological engagements suggest that there is an imperative to

ask questions of the *process* of the construction of the subject (Pelletier, 2009), as well as the political and educational meanings of these discourses. In other words, we should address seriously the 'consequentiality of taking the subject as a requirement or presupposition of theory' (Butler, 1995: 36), which runs the risk of silencing youthful voices, especially in democratic contexts where they are actively 'invited' to speak and be heard.

Rather than 'agents of change', there were clearly points in our data where youth as citizen subjects acted in ways that attempted to close down what could be spoken of, and in what spheres, even questioning the legitimacy of political contestation. Nonetheless, we are also somewhat encouraged by how our data suggests that there is *always* some youthful scope for dissensual 'breaking out' in ways that mean that: '[t]he deconstruction of identity is not the deconstruction of politics; rather, it establishes as political the very terms through which identity is articulated' (Butler, 2006: 203).

In concluding this chapter, we take forward some implications of the argument that politics (or as Mouffe would say, the political) is intrinsic to learning, as a process of subjectification. Firstly, however, having critiqued the instrumentalities of a discourse of learning which pretends to be outside of politics, we neither seek to provide recipes for action, nor to deny the possibility of agency. Rather than giving primacy to theories of learning, which aim to facilitate 'learning processes' and make these more effective, we argue with others such as Biesta (2013) and Pyckett (2007) for the importance within 'educational' processes of taking the work of social construction seriously. This implies in turn that we problematize the 'naturalness' of learning and its contemporary allure of innocent beneficence. This also requires a recognition of the agonistic rather than consensual relations through which our subjectivities are constructed. And finally, it may also mean that alongside attention to the structures of inequality through which differences are articulated (such as gender, social class, age relations), the moments of dissensus rather than consensus are those that hold the more fertile possibilities for educational action, for the disruption of the taken-for-granted, the 'bleeding obvious', and for the coming into being of new subjectivities.

NOTES

1   The Senegal case study was conducted by Barbara within a wider research project, entitled 'Youth as Active Citizens: youth working towards their rights to education and sexual reproductive health'. This was funded by Oxfam Novib and the Swedish International Development Agency, and lead by Professor Mairéad Dunne, Director, Centre for International Education, University of Sussex. The support of the funders and of Professor Dunne, Dr Naureen Durrani and Dr Kathleen Fincham is gratefully acknowledged.
2   The Rights Respecting School (RRS) initiative is an award developed by UNICEF to put children's rights at the heart of schools' policies and practices. The award can be achieved at Level 1 and Level 2.
3   The Convention on the Rights of the Child (CRC) was adopted by the United Nations in 1989 as a way of enshrining 54 universal articles to protect the rights of all young people under the age of 18.
4   This is a play period traditionally coming at the end of the school week, which is designed as a collective reward for hard work and good behaviour. Very often children are able to choose an activity to undertake for an hour or so.
5   These were charters that the school institution had developed from the UNICEF UK RRS framework that reminded the children of ways they should behave and treat one another. They focused upon rights as well as upon responsibilities.

REFERENCES

Biesta, G. (2011) 'The Ignorant Citizen: Mouffe, Rancière, and the Subject of Democratic Education', *Studies in Philosophy and Education*, 30(2): 141–53.

Biesta, G. (2013) 'Interrupting the Politics of Learning', *Power and Education*, 5(1): 4–15.

Bingham, C. and Biesta, G. with Rancière, J. (2010) *Jacques Rancière: Education, Truth, Emancipation*, London and New York: Continuum.

Butler, J. (1988) 'Performative Acts and Gender Constitution: An Essay in Phenomenology and Feminist Theory', *Theatre Journal* (December), 49(1): 519–31.

Butler, J. (1992) 'Contingent Foundations: Feminism and the Question of "Postmodernism"', in J. Scott and J. Butler (eds) *Feminists Theorize the Political*, New York: Routledge, pp. 3–21.

Butler, J. (1995) 'Contingent Foundations: Feminism and the Question of "Postmodernism", in S. Benhabib, J. Butler, D. Cornell and N. Fraser (eds) *Feminist Contentions: A Philosophical Exchange*, New York: Routledge, pp. 35–57.

Butler, J. (1997) *The Psychic Life of Power*, Stanford, CA: Stanford University Press.

Butler, J. (2004) *Undoing Gender*, New York: Routledge.

Butler, J. (2006) *Gender Trouble* (2nd edn), Abingdon: Routledge.

Crossouard, B. and Dunne, M. (2015) 'Politics and youth citizenship in Senegal: the policing of dissent and diversity'. *International Review of Education,* 61(1): available on iFirst at http://link.springer.com/article/10.1007/s11159-015-9466-0 (Accessed 5 June 2015).

Davies, B. (2006) 'Subjectification: The Relevance of Butler's Analysis for Education', *British Journal of Sociology of Education*, 27(4): 425–38.

Dunne, M., Pryor, J. and Yates, P. (2005) *Becoming a Researcher*, Buckinghamshire: Oxford University Press.

Dunne, M., Durrani, N., Crossouard, B. and Fincham, K. (2014) Youth as Active Citizens Report. Youth Working Towards their Rights to Education and Sexual and Reproductive Health. *Oxfam Novib*, The Netherlands, University of Sussex.

Foucault, M. (1975) *Discipline and Punish: The Birth of the Prison*, New York: Vintage Books.

Foucault, M. (1984) 'Truth and Power', in P. Rabinow (ed.) *The Foucault Reader*, London: Penguin, pp. 51–75.

Gedalof, I. (2013) 'Sameness and Difference in Government Equality Talk', *Ethnic and Racial Studies*, 36(1): 117–35.

Hall, S. and O'Shea, A. (2013) 'Common Sense Neoliberalism', *Soundings* (Winter), 52: 1–18.

Honig, B. (1992) 'Toward an Agonistic Feminism: Hannah Arendt and the Politics of Identity', in J. Butler and J. Scott (eds) *Feminists Theorize the Political*, New York: Routledge, pp. 215–35.

Jackson, A.Y. and Mazzei, L.A. (2012) *Thinking with Theory in Qualitative Research: Viewing Data across Multiple Perspectives*, Abingdon: Routledge.

Kant, E. (1992 [1784]) 'An Answer to the Question: What is Enlightenment?', in P. Waugh (ed.) *Postmodernism: A Reader*, London: Edward Arnold, pp. 89–95.

Laws, C. (2011) *Poststructuralism at Work with Marginalised Children*, Bentham Books (ebook).

MacLure, M. (2010) 'The Offence of Theory', *Journal of Education Policy*, 25(2): 277–86.

Mouffe, C. (1992) 'Feminism, Citizenship and Radical Democratic Politics', in J. Butler and J. Scott (eds) *Feminists Theorize the Political*, New York: Routledge, pp. 367–84.

Mouffe, C. (2005) *On the Political*, London and New York: Routledge.

Pelletier, C. (2009) 'Rancière and the Poetics of the Social Sciences', *International Journal of Research and Method in Education*, 32(3): 267–84.

Pyckett, J. (2007) 'Making Citizens Governable? The Crick Report as Governmental Technology', *Journal of Education Policy*, 22(3): 310–19.

Rancière, J. (1995) *On the Shores of Politics*, London and New York: Verso.

Rancière, J. (1999) *Disagreement*, Minneapolis and London: University of Minnesota Press.

Rancière, J. (2004) 'Who Is the Subject of the Rights of Man?', *The South Atlantic Quarterly*, 103(2/3): 297–310.

Learning, Governance and the European Educational Space

Martin Lawn and Rosario Sergio Maniscalco

INTRODUCTION

Education as a policy area has a history in the European Union but it is an indistinct one, especially in its early decades, and it has been transformed through the overall policy aim of a knowledge economy, and, since 2000, by constant and systematic comparison. Most of all, the field of Education has metamorphosed into a space of Learning. As 'Education' has changed, from the 1980s to today, moving from patrimony to a space of comparison, so its direction has increased in sophistication and purpose. 'Learning' is now a powerful and omnipotent discourse. But the European Union is unable to control its formation by direct employment policies, political influence and direct funding (in the way that older nation states did with their systems) and to manage or overcome multiple players. In the field of education in particular, the governing of education in Europe relies upon Treaty, Law and Innovation, and a linked set of old and new public, semi-public and private actors for its emergence. Networks of actors

of many kinds are producing, translating, comparing or imagining a new European Learning Space. Lifelong learning, citizenship and the knowledge economy are shaping and being shaped together as the determining characteristics of this space. The gradual shift from an indiscernible series of activities in the field of culture and education to a regulated space of learning via benchmarks and indicators is also a narrative about a shift in governance in Europe.

THE EMERGENCE OF A EUROPEAN EDUCATION SPACE

It is possible to approach the European Education Space (EES) as a single and relatively well defined geopolitical space in which policies are made and education is promoted according to ideological and political biases, and governed and administered according to the different states' capacity. It is also possible to address this concept in terms of common

(European) cultural roots, similar educational practices and pedagogical models, comparable key actors and stakeholders across European countries. Comparative educational research shows, in effect, many correlations and a deep interdependence amongst European national educational systems; for example, in terms of institutional forms and policy-making (Antunes, 2006), teacher education (Center for Social and Economic Research, 2009), opportunities for adult and continuing education (European Commission, 2013), learning curricula, objectives and trajectories (Green, 2007; Moutsios, 2007).

Less obviously, it is possible to discuss a *European Education Space* as a result of the European nation states' political will (and consequent formal commitment) to uniform educational paths and diplomas in order to ensure mutual recognition of educational trajectories and in the perspective of supporting and facilitating the mobility of citizens/workers. De facto, EU Treaty articles and intergovernmental agreements signed by European States are increasingly binding them to processes of standardization. Moreover, in EU policy statements it is possible to find several references to a 'European Education Space', although there is no unambiguous formal definition for it. As Roger Dale pointed out, for example, the European Commission (EC) wrote about a 'European *Space* of Education' and a 'European *Area* of Education' in quite vague terms (Dale, 2009a: 31, referring to Hingel, 2001: 4, 9). Furthermore, there are references to a 'European Research Area' (ERA), the 'European Higher Education Area' (EHEA) and to the 'European Education and Training Area' (EETA) in the statements of the Bologna and Copenhagen processes, while a European Learning Area (ELA) is mentioned in the European Commission's *Memorandum for Lifelong Learning* (EC, 2000a). Finally, the Communication from the EC entitled *Making a European Area of Lifelong Learning a Reality* devoted a whole paragraph (1.3) to 'a European area of lifelong learning' (EC, 2001a: 3). This Space *is* indistinct, ambiguous and without clear structures, and yet it is also discursive, governmental and expansive. It has shape and direction and should be treated as a necessary governing feature in a Europe that has to act by standards and persuasion in education.

Launched at the EU Lisbon summit in 2000, the so-called 'Lisbon Agenda' rapidly gained significant importance and started attracting the interest of scholars in educational research, with a number of thorough studies focusing specifically on the opportunities for coordination it provided in the educational policy area (e.g. Nóvoa and Lawn, 2002; Phillips and Ertl, 2003; Kuhn and Sultana, 2005). Drawing on the macro-economic terms established in 1992 by the Maastricht Treaty, and in the perspective of joining national forces to respond to the challenges of globalization cooperatively, the 'Lisbon strategy' pursued the goal of developing the European Union, by 2010, as 'the most dynamic and competitive knowledge-based economy in the world, capable of sustainable economic growth, with more and better jobs, greater social cohesion and respect for the environment' (European Union, 2000). This ambitious project for the construction of a 'Europe of knowledge' through a ten-year strategy for economic and social renewal was intended to make EU economies more competitive worldwide, eradicate unemployment and transform the Union into a true knowledge society by encouraging investment in knowledge, research and development, technological and scientific innovation as sources of higher productivity and profitability.

As a consequence of Article 7 of the Lisbon Council Presidency Conclusions, an ambitious work programme was designed, and was expected to be 'achieved by improving the existing processes, introducing a *new open method of coordination* at all levels, coupled with a stronger guiding and coordinating role for the European Council to ensure more coherent strategic direction and effective monitoring of progress' (EU, 2000, Para 5, original emphasis). With the Lisbon Strategy the EU was calling on the Member States to develop the European peoples' competences, in order to support the 'European economic project' and to foster European economic growth and competitiveness (Horsdal, 2007; Moutsios, 2007).

BUILDING THE EUROPEAN EDUCATIONAL POLICY SPACE

The European Union has undergone distinct impulses and momenta correlated with the establishment of new legal bases, especially through the progressive consolidation and reform of the EU Treaties (Shaw, 1999; Grek and Rinne, 2011). John West associated this metamorphosis with the broadening of the EU's policy influence and reach, notably with the European Commission trying to 'test the limits' of the new governance tools provided, in particular, by the Treaty of Maastricht signed in 1992 (the Treaty on the European Union, henceforth TEU), which set the legal basis for a common European framework in the area of education and training:

> This formative period for policy was thus essentially one of experimentation, with the Commission attempting to widen the scope of its activities into education proper, testing the limits of central actions which were acceptable to Member States, establishing some democratic credentials for its activities in education and training through reaching directly to a number of the stakeholders within Member States. (West, 2012: 10)

The Maastricht Treaty gave a strong impulse to move forward from the simple economic dimension of the European Economic Community and led to the creation of the European Union and its single currency. It established freedom, democracy and human rights as founding principles of the newborn EU (Art. 6, Para. 1), and included for the first time education among its policy competences, dedicating special attention to mobility, the acquisition of languages and cooperation in the form of information and experience exchange between educational institutions of the EU countries. The most important goal of Article 126 of the TEU (Article 149 of the consolidated Treaty of Amsterdam) was thus the development of a 'European dimension in education, particularly through the teaching and dissemination of the languages of the Member States', while Article 127 (Article 150 of the Amsterdam Treaty) aimed at improving 'initial and continuing vocational training in order to facilitate vocational integration and reintegration into the labour market'. Also, an important role was played by the mutual recognition of diplomas, certificates and study periods among the Member States in order to 'encourage mobility of instructors and trainees and particularly young people' (Article 150).

The launch of the Lisbon Agenda in year 2000 is considered by many scholars a 'turning point' in education policy (Ertl, 2006; Grek, 2008: 212; Dale, 2009a, 2009b). With the Lisbon Strategy, education and training were actually put at the heart of the EU's mainstream policy. Contextually, the 'Education and Training 2010' work programme was launched, and a European 'soft governance' approach was developed through the Open Method of Coordination (OMC) and its implementing techniques: the setting of standards, indicators and benchmarks, and increased peer pressure (country rankings and occasions for the sharing of best practices). Hence, the breadth and scale of the education domain took a significant turn following European Council meetings, in Lisbon and Stockholm, with the adoption of the target to become the 'most competitive and dynamic knowledge-based economy in the world' (Beukel, 2001: 6; Hingel, 2001). For education, this meant a focus on the internal creation of a strengthened area of policy, including measurable objectives – the 'Lisbon goals' (EC, 2003) – and a new emphasis on managing the education policy area in Europe under globalization, with its emerging world markets in education services. Intensification involved a wider range of actors. New agents moved freely across Europe (Hiatt, 2000) offering products and opportunities so as to extend their 'influence' and 'brand identity' with new consumers. New 'learning businesses' delivered education as a commodity and searched for new markets. So, when the EU now promoted a new policy, on *eLearning*, for example, it used private/public partnerships to manage project delivery and increase the range of partners and capital in this task (EC, 2001d). Its new partners were Nokia, IBM and Cisco. The European Education Partnership, a commercial group, refers to this as the 'pan-European learning market' (EEP, 2001).

The EU intended to expand distance learning, double the rate of student and teacher mobility and increase the transferability of qualifications (Kokosalakis, 1998; Slowinski, 1998). The area of education began to metamorphose into 'lifelong learning systems', connected to the other policy domains of employment, science, technology and information and communication technologies. This new world trade in education services, often referred to as 'borderless education', describes distance learning, mobility of students, commercial companies and provider mobility (teachers), and is aimed at providing a 'level playing area' for supply (Hiatt, 2000).

Trade needs common standards, for instance, common definitions, shared objects and technologies, and working connections. This applies to the business of education just as much as to the communications or food industries. Throughout the last half century the development of projects for comparison, data collection and convergence, was being sustained by projects on cross-institutional collaboration, documentation and statistics, recognition of qualifications and key organizations, like EuroStat, EuroBarometer, Eurydice or the European Education Thesaurus. In effect, these agencies provided the standardization processes upon which a common market in education and processes of comparative analysis and action could be built. Under the auspices of the European Statistical System (ESS) a special task force on lifelong learning and statistical data (Eurostat, 2001) was created to bring together all the current demands for numerical information and indicators from within European programmes, and those demanded by new intentions for social and economic development (EC, 2001a). This sophisticated monitoring system required the member states to build or enhance adequate administrative capacity in order to deal with the reporting needs of the OMC (Borrás and Radaelli, 2010: 8). In this way, the policy agenda reorganized the process of data accumulation and in turn was able to act more effectively on its lifelong learning agenda. Learning within systems and as an individual obligation could be viewed, and become transparent. It could also be more clearly shaped and constructed.

LIFELONG LEARNING

Prior to the intensification of the EU internal management, by means of Open Coordination, the adoption of the goal of a learning society in the Commission's White Paper on Education and Training, *Teaching and Learning: Towards the Learning Society* (EC, 1995), signalled a major reworking of its goals for the domain of education. It presented the guidelines for lifelong learning and launched, in 1996, the European Year of Lifelong Learning in order to promote the recognition of an integrated European education policy. Since then, 'lifelong learning' has become the core ideal of EU policy in education, clearly expressed in the Communication from the Commission, *Making a European Area of Lifelong Learning a Reality*, which aimed at creating a 'European space for lifelong learning' (EC, 2001a). According to this policy document, people of all ages should have equal and unlimited access to high quality learning within the entire EU, in order to achieve competitiveness, employment, social inclusion, citizenship and personal development.

The idea of learning (and not education) has significance as it led to a powerful drive linking lifelong learning (LLL) and a knowledge economy, combining citizenship and work. Making the link between knowledge and lifelong learning was seen as a necessary solution to the problem of invisibility and the lack of institutional power over the education domain by the European Union. In this way, education could be redefined as an individual necessity, rather than as patrimony or as part of community systems. Europeanization could be achieved through this distinctive European way, as a governance strategy and as a mission (EC, 1996). The discourse was aimed directly at the individual; it was to offer a vision to them and produce a responsibility for them. The vision made sense of the European project and created a programme in which the citizens of Europe were both appealed to and constructed. Europe was about competitiveness and decisiveness and the individual was the place in which this could be situated. They were to be given the task of managing the future by acquiring the capacity to exercise responsibility for their own education and training choices. Learning was the key.

A Commission Study Group's vision on education sketched out, in a preparatory document, the new policy in this area (EC, 1996) and the idea of producing Europe through learning, and clearly expressed, by overcoming a list of oppositions, the envisioned future for Europe. The future Europe was to be built by a shift from objective to constructed knowledge: from an industrial to a learning society, from instruction to personal learning, and from formal educational institutions towards new organizational structures for learning. Learning citizens would have to constantly renew their fund of knowledge, extend their citizenship through active solidarity and on a lifelong basis, develop creativity, flexibility, adaptability, the ability to 'learn to learn' and to solve problems. Lifelong learning emerged as the vision of Europe and, in its governance, the individual is relocated from the nation state into a new space and mobility in which 'learning' is to be situated in them. As the Eurostat Taskforce on lifelong learning pointed out:

> Responsibility for education and learning shifts from the public (state) to non-governmental organizations as well as to the individuals themselves. ... While traditional educational institutions have been (and still are) primarily concerned with transmitting knowledge, modern learning opportunities and the LLL approach put the emphasis on the development of individual capabilities and the capacity of the person to learn. At the heart of the LLL concept lies the idea of enabling and encouraging people 'to learn how to learn'. (EC/Eurostat, 2002: 18)

Lifelong learning reconstituted education, widening its field, integrating its functions, centring the 'individual learner', and stressing performance and comparison (EC, 2001a, 2001c).

In the above light, Table 17.1 exemplifies the distinct stages of the building of the European Education Space and the parallel evolutionary phases of the European Education Partnership.

GOVERNING A POLICY SPACE

The fabrication of a European policy space has been approached and described from different angles. The Open Method of Coordination has been defined as a 'soft' mode of governance of a 'non-legislative nature' (Borrás and Radaelli, 2010: 10), which provided a new framework for cooperation between the European Union and Member States that would include coordination activities, action programmes, benchmarking and sharing of best practices. Its liturgy pushed national policies to agree on common objectives (Nóvoa and Lawn, 2002) with the intention of reforming national educational systems (Baker and LeTendre, 2005) under the impulse of the globalization of cultural, economic and political structures (Kamens and McNeely, 2009). Overall, the Lisbon Strategy, complemented by a set of well-defined benchmarks of 'policy performance' and indicators monitoring the progress towards measurable objectives, is one clear example of this kind of soft governance, defined by Rose (1991: 673) as 'governing by numbers' (with a clear reference to the abundant use of 'rough quantitative data'). In line with this definition, the

Table 17.1 Periodization of the Education Policy Space and its actions

Years	Phase	Legal basis	Principal influences on the EEP
1951–1957	I. European culture and common values	Treaty of Paris (1951)	Dominance of economic integration in policy agendas; setting of common identity and cultural values; launch of common vocational training policy (EU, 1963)
1957–1987		Treaty of Rome (1957)	
1986–1992	II. Educational cooperation and mobility	Single European Act (1986)	Reinforcement of educational cooperation with the first action programme (EU, 1976); projects on language learning and student mobility
1992–1997	III. Subsidiarity and VET	Treaty of Maastricht (1992)	Subsidiarity principle and common European framework in the area of education and training (Art. 149 and Art. 150 of the consolidated Treaty of Amsterdam); action programme for the implementation of a European Community vocational training policy (EU, 1994)
1997–2000		Treaty of Amsterdam (1997)	
2000–2007	IV. OMC, EEP and EES	Bologna Declaration (1999), Lisbon Agreements (2000), Copenhagen Declaration (2002)	Education and training are put at the heart of the EU's mainstream policy; the 'Education and Training 2010' work programme is launched; (lifelong) learning becomes pivotal in the EEP; the OMC in E&T is boosted through inter-governmental agreements and the strengthening of the European Education Space (EU, 2000; 2001; EC, 2001a); European soft law is developed by setting of standards, indicators and benchmarks, and through increased peer pressure (rankings and sharing of best practices)
2007–present		Treaty of Lisbon (2007) and on the Functioning of the European Union	

EEP has been described as a mode of 'governing by statistics' or 'governing through data' (Ozga, 2009), 'governing by standards' (Lawn, 2006; Lawn and Grek, 2012), 'by blueprints' (Borrás and Radaelli, 2011) and 'governance by persuasion' (Noaksson and Jacobsson, 2003), which stresses the 'multilateral surveillance' through a very thorough examination and long preparation process, and occasions for consultation and dialogue with the stakeholders.

EU governance in education not only involves a mixture of state and non-state agencies, and the coordination of non-governmental and non-legislative policy tools, but is being undertaken by independent agencies and actors not formally involved (in the sense of being funded or coordinated) in EU-sponsored projects. Learning operates as a discourse across areas of policy, through its close association with ICT, and it operates as a commodity, marketed across Europe by private companies and entrepreneurial

organizations. It has another aspect, an important one, which it is important to recognize. 'Learning' is a persuasive and useful idea to many European actors – experts, professionals and citizens.

The 'imagined community' of European education may be discursively bound together by objectives and indicators, but it is shaped by constant interaction between groups of linked professionals, managers and experts. This space is formed between state and EU offices, between agencies and sub-contractors, between academics and policy managers, between experts and officials, and between voluntary and public sector workers. It is a growing *culture*, which exists in formal operations, and the interstices between them, in the immaterial world. Networks are constantly mobilized to deliver or effect 'learning' in many ways, and use 'learning' to find new possibilities.

Hence, in the fabrication of the European policy space, soft governance has been based on persuasive power, and the construction of non-threatening standards, and has been a very distinctive aspect of governing in the EU:

> The European Space is more than an ill-defined space of regulation or flows; it is a space of attraction and meaning, in which soft power is at work, creating a space in which actors are drawn to work within and produce it. The construction of Europe is taking place through the cultivation of support and the creation of meaning, just as much as by trade, regulation, soft law or cross-border agreement. A key element has been the production of an attractive idea; the ambiguous, modernizing and mobilizing idea of a project, and a concomitant 'space' to be created. (Lawn, 2006: 272)

The EU relies fundamentally on *policy learning*, especially since the Lisbon Strategy, which inaugurated a role of coordination for the EC (*ipso facto*, the OMC) in the educational policy area. Mutual learning from other Member States and through expert networks, peer learning activities and thematic reviews and conferences became the education policy space's core. Moreover, as the Commission emphasized in the White Paper on European Governance, the 'confidence in expert advice' is considered an indispensable complement to the evidence base for EU policy-making:

> Scientific and other experts play an increasingly significant role in preparing and monitoring decisions. From human and animal health to social legislation, the Institutions rely on specialist expertise to anticipate and identify the nature of the problems and uncertainties that the Union faces, to take decisions and to ensure that risks can be explained clearly and simply to the public. ... Such structured and open networks should form a scientific reference system to support EU policy-making. (EC, 2001b: 19)

In relation to the Lisbon Strategy, Ozga et al. (2011: 89) also stressed that:

> the involvement of the European Commission in a growing range of education-related steering actions has meant a rise in necessary support activities; these are evidenced in expert exchanges, secondment of experts, observatories, advisory committees and working groups, information networks and gateways, consultation of stakeholders, ... consortia in framework programmes,

peer reviews, conferences, seminars and symposia, monitoring, evaluation and focused research.

Alongside all the policy documents, regulations, projects and Ministers' meetings, there has been a significant growth in the work of internal and external experts and professionals contributing to the 'fabrication' of the policy infrastructure:

> The governing of Europe depends on the activity [of] a new elite of technocrats, professionals and academics, with expert knowledge or skills, who are working in public or private organizations. They meet in associations or through projects or networks. They are solving problems, problems in the governing of Europe, through the collection, classification, and analysis of data, the parallel creation of standards or the accumulation of knowledge about problems and development. The microclimates in which these technocrats flourish have their own imaginaries, combine technical possibilities and software-driven visions, professional associations, expert networks and embedded common sense meanings and values. Since the turn of the millennium, data collection activity has grown very fast, and the Lisbon Open Method of Coordination (OMC) process has driven it along with its targets, benchmarks and indicators. (Lawn, 2013: 20–1)

Learning, and its observation, shaping and growth, and its transparency through data, has become the key signifier of European education policy.

CONCLUSIONS

The creation of a distinctive and useful European education policy space is a necessary part of the project of Europeanization in the EU. A 'European Education Area' is fundamental to the contemporary structuring of the Union; it announces the arrival of a major discursive space, centred on education, in which the legitimation, steering and shaping of European governance is being played out. This chapter has explored the problem of governance and education, through its first stage, the construction of a European education project, and then it examined, in the second stage, the determination of a new policy of lifelong learning. This new policy shifts the emphasis from formal institutional influence and centres on the individual learner, stressing performance and comparison.

The situatedness of lifelong learning as the vision of Europe and its governance continues as the individual is relocated from the nation state into a new space and mobility, and at the same time, they are viewed/imagined as learning citizens. The terminological transition from 'education' to 'learning' has deeply affected the definitions of lifelong education and learning. Tuijnman and Broström (2002: 103) noted that 'the emphasis on "learning" rather than "education" is highly significant because it reduces the traditional preoccupation with structures and institutions and instead focuses on the individual'. In this respect, Karin Filander argues that lifelong learning can be interpreted as a 'shift of responsibility' from the state to the individual, which corresponds to a withdrawal of the public authorities' role in educating their citizens:

> The rhetoric of lifelong learning subjectivizes individuals themselves to be responsible for their success and failure. Self-directed, active learners carry the main responsibility for their own learning and continuous renewal in the different phases of their lives. ... Individuals carry on their own choices and responsibilities as self-directed customers in the markets of education. As customers of the education systems, individual students choose from several alternatives of the supermarket of educational institutions their own paths and their own individual study plans. School-based study plans and teacher-centred models of teaching and knowledge structures belong to the old times of the centralized welfare state. (Filander, 2007: 262–3)

Analogously, Ozga et al. (2011: 86) pointed out that, as education was redefined as learning, this theme has become 'the centre of European Union policy-making, as well as a new field of commercial activity' in the knowledge economy. In this new form, according to Ozga et al. (2011: 26–7), learning becomes one of the key policy domains of the EU, whereas education continues to be largely characterized as contained within state borders.

The focus on the political, administrative and economic form of the new Europe has obscured this kind of cultural analysis, which emphasizes the processes of production and consumption of policy. The necessity to produce a governing discourse, in which a unity is created and projected into an identified future, is vital to governing Europe, and education/learning is now central to it. While regulation and open coordination methods can intensify and attempt to control European agents of varying kinds, network governance, attracting with different intensities mobile actors who are freely engaged in European processes, allows a soft governance to emerge, none more so than in education/learning: learning in EU governance tries to overcome the problem that a language of managerial performance benchmarks cannot substitute for a collective project of change (Laidi, 1998: passim).

REFERENCES

Antunes, F. (2006) 'Globalisation and Europeification of Education Policies: Routes, Processes and Metamorphoses', *European Educational Research Journal*, 5(1): 38–55.

Baker, D.P. and LeTendre, G.K. (2005) *National Differences, Global Similarities: World Culture and the Future of Schooling*, Stanford, CA: Stanford University Press.

Beukel, E. (2001) 'Educational Policy: Institutionalization and Multi-Level Governance', in S. Andersen and K. Elliassen (eds) *Making Policy in Europe*, 2nd edn, London: Sage.

Borrás, S. and Radaelli, C.M. (2010) *Recalibrating the Open Method of Coordination: Towards Diverse and More Effective Usages*, Report n. 7, Stockholm: Swedish Institute for European Policy Studies.

Borrás, S. and Radaelli, C.M. (2011) The 'Politics of Governance Architectures: Creation, Change and Effects of the EU Lisbon Strategy', *Journal of European Public Policy*, 18(4): 363–84.

Center for Social and Economic Research (2009) *Key Competences in Europe: Opening Doors for Lifelong Learners Across the School Curriculum and Teacher Education*, Warsaw: Center for Social and Economic Research.

Dale, R. (2009a) 'Contexts, Constraints and Resources in the Development of European Education Space and European Education Policy', in R. Dale and S. Robertson (eds) *Globalisation and Europeanisation in Education*, Oxford: Symposium Books, pp. 23–43.

Dale, R. (2009b) 'Studying Globalisation and Europeanisation in Education: Lisbon, the Open Method of Coordination and Beyond', in R. Dale and S. Robertson (eds) *Globalisation and Europeanisation in Education*, Oxford: Symposium Books, pp. 121–40.

Ertl, H. (2006) 'European Union Policies in Education and Training: The Lisbon Agenda as a Turning Point?', *Comparative Education*, 42(1): 5–27.

European Commission (1963) Decision 63/266/EEC of 2 April 1963 of the Council laying down general principles for implementing a common vocational training policy.

European Commission (1976) Resolution of the Council and of the Ministers of Education, meeting within the Council, of 9 February 1976 comprising an action programme in the field of education.

European Commission (1994) Council Decision 94/819/EC of 6 December 1994 establishing an action programme for the implementation of a European Community vocational training policy.

European Commission (1995) White Paper COM (95) 590-final of 29 November 1995 on Education and Training, *Teaching and Learning: Towards the Learning Society*, Brussels: European Commission.

European Commission (1996) *Accomplishing Europe through Education and Training*. Report by Study Group on Education and Training, Luxemburg: Office for the Official Publications of the European Communities.

European Commission (2000a) Commission Staff working document SEC(2000)1832 *A Memorandum on Lifelong Learning*.

European Commission (2000b) Presidency Conclusions of the Lisbon European Council of 23–24 March 2000.

European Commission (2001a) Communication from the European Commission COM(2001)678 final, *Making a European Area of Lifelong Learning a Reality*.

European Commission (2001b) White Paper COM(2001)428 final, *European Governance* of 25 July 2001.

European Commission (2001c) *Lifelong Learning, Practice and Indicators*, Brussels: European Commission.

European Commission (2001d) *The E-learning Action Plan, Designing Tomorrow's Education*, Brussels: European Commission.

European Commission/Eurostat (2002) *Measuring Lifelong Learning*, Report of the Eurostat Taskforce on Measuring Lifelong Learning, pp. 15–38, Luxembourg: European Commission.

European Commission (2003) Conclusions of the Council of the EU 2003/C 134/02 of 5 May 2003 on the Reference Levels of European Average Performance in Education and Training (Benchmarks).

European Commission (2013) *Adult and Continuing Education in Europe: Using Public Policy to Secure a Growth in Skills*, Luxembourg: Publications Office of the European Union.

European Education Partnership (EEP) (2001) *Partnerships in Practice*, Brussels: European Education Partnership.

European Union (2000) Presidency Conclusions of the Lisbon European Council of 23–24 March 2000.

Eurostat (2001) *Report of the Eurostat Task Force on Measuring Lifelong Learning*, Brussels: Statistical Office of the European Communities.

Filander, K. (2007) 'Deconstructing Dominant Discourses on Vocational Education', in R. Rinne, A. Heikkinen and P. Salo (eds) *Adult Education: Liberty, Fraternity, Equality? Nordic Views on Lifelong Learning*, Turku: FERA, pp. 261–74.

Green, A. (2007) 'Models of Lifelong Learning and the "Knowledge Society" in Europe', in H.-G. Kotthoff and S. Moutsios (eds) *Education Policies in Europe: Economy, Citizenship, Diversity*, Berlin: Waxmann, pp. 27–46.

Grek, S. (2008) 'From Symbols to Numbers: The shifting technologies of education governance in Europe', *European Educational Research Journal*, 7 (2): 208–18.

Grek, S. and Rinne, R. (2011) 'Fabricating Europe: From Culture to Numbers', in J. Ozga, P. Dahler-Larsen, C. Segerholm and H. Simola (eds) *Fabricating Quality in Education: Data and Governance in Europe*, London and New York: Routledge, pp. 19–31.

Hiatt, N. (2000) 'The Millennium Round and the Liberalisation of the Education Market', *Education and Social Justice*, 2(2): 12–8.

Hingel, A. (2001) *Education Policies and European Governance*, Brussels: European Commission, Directorate General for Education and Culture, Policy Unit A1.

Horsdal, M. (2007) 'The Discourses of Lifelong Learning in a Knowledge Economy', in R. Rinne, A. Heikkinen and P. Salo (eds) *Adult Education: Liberty, Fraternity, Equality? Nordic Views on Lifelong Learning*, Turku: FERA, pp. 33–45.

Kamens, D.H. and McNeely, C.L. (2009) 'Globalisation and the Growth of International Educational Testing and National Assessment', *Comparative Education Review*, 54(1): 5–25.

Kokosalakis, N. (1998) *Non-official Higher Education in the European Union*, Athens: Centre for Social Morphology and Social Policy.

Kuhn, M. and Sultana, R. (eds) (2005) *Homo Sapiens Europæus? Creating the European Learning Citizen*, London: Peter Lang.

Laidi, Z. (1998) *World without Meaning – the Crisis of Meaning in International Politics*, London: Routledge.

Lawn, M. (2006) 'Soft Governance and the Learning Spaces of Europe', *Comparative European Politics*, 4(2): 272–88.

Lawn, M. (2013) 'The Understories of European Education: The Contemporary Life of Experts and Professionals', *Sisyphus Journal of Education*, 1(1): 18–35.

Lawn, M. and Grek, S. (2012) *Europeanizing Education: Governing a New Policy Space*, Providence, RI: Symposium Books.

Moutsios, S. (2007) 'The European Union and its Education Policy', in H.-G. Kotthoff and S. Moutsios (eds) *Education Policies in Europe: Economy, Citizenship, Diversity*, Berlin: Waxmann, pp. 15–25.

Noaksson, N. and Jakobsson, K. (2003) *The Production of Ideas and Expert Knowledge in the OECD: The OECD Jobs Strategy in Contrast with the EU Employment Strategy*, 7, Score Rapportserie.

Nóvoa, A. and Lawn, M. (eds) (2002) *Fabricating Europe: The Formation of an Education Space*, Dordecht: Kluwer Academic Publishers.

Ozga, J. (2009) 'Governing Education through Data in England: From Regulation to Self-evaluation', *Journal of Education Policy*, 24(2): 149–62.

Ozga, J., Segerholm, C. and Simola, H. (2011) 'The Governance Turn', in J. Ozga, P. Dahler-Larsen, C. Segerholm and H. Simola (eds) *Fabricating Quality in Education: Data and Governance in Europe*, London and New York: Routledge, pp. 85–95.

Phillips, D. and Ertl, H. (eds) (2003) *Implementing European Union Education and Training Policy: A Comparative Study of Issues in Four Member States*, Dordecht: Kluwer Academic Publishers.

Rose, N. (1991) 'Governing by Numbers: Figuring Out Society', *Accounting Organisation and Society*, 15(7): 673–92.

Shaw, J. (1999) 'From the Margins to the Centre: Education and Training Law and Policy', in P. Craig and G. de Búrca (eds) *The Evolution of EU Law*, Oxford: Oxford University Press.

Slowinski, J. (1998) 'SOCRATES Invades Central Europe', *Education Policy Analysis Archives*, 6(9).

Tuijnman, A.C. and Broström, A.-K. (2002) 'Changing Notions of Lifelong Education and Lifelong Learning', *International Review of Education*, 48(1–2): 92–110.

West, J. (2012) *The Evolution of European Union Policies on Vocational Education and Training*, Research Paper no. 34, London: Centre for Learning and Life Chances in Knowledge Economies and Societies.

18

The Elements of a Learning Environment

David Scott and Carol Evans

INTRODUCTION

In the Introduction to this book, David Scott and Eleanore Hargreaves characterised learning as a process, with a range of characteristics. It has a set of pedagogic relations, that is, it incorporates a relationship between a learner and a learning object, which could be a person, a text, an object in nature, a particular array of resources, an artefact, an allocation of a role or function to a person, or a sensory object. A change process is required for this, and is either internal to the learner or external to the community of which this learner is a member. In addition, there are temporal and spatial arrangements, and these can be understood in two ways: learning is internally structured, and also externally located in time and space.

Further to this, and as an element of a general meta-theory, learning is conditioned by an arrangement of resources. These arrangements are embodied, discursive, institutional, systemic or agential, and each learning episode therefore has socio-historical roots. What is learnt in the first place is formed in society and outside the individual. It is thus both externally and internally mediated, and this means that it has an internalisation element, where what is formally external to the learner is interiorised by the learner, and a performative element, where what is formally internal to the learner is exteriorised by the learner in the world. A theory of learning then pivots on the idea that there is an entity called for the sake of convenience a human and that this entity has a relationship (both inward and outward) with an environment (for some, this entails a post-humanising and materialising process).

Knowledge then is transformed at the pedagogic site, so it is possible to suggest that modes of progression and pacing, the relations that are adopted between teachers and learners and between types of learners, the spatial and temporal arrangements that are made, the criteria used for evaluation, the degree and type of simulation of the object under consideration, and the performative element of the learning process, are fundamental components of this pedagogic transformation.

For example, this pedagogic transformation comprises in part a degree and type of simulation. In a simulation a new medium is chosen which gives the learning object a new form, these media being virtual, graphic, enumerative, enactive, symbolic or oral. Indeed, depending on the new form, there is a distance between the original object and the mediated object, and this varies in strength. This doesn't mean that the object is better or less well represented in its new form, only that it takes on a new guise; it is pedagogically formed. And this means that its potential impact is likely to be different. A simulation might involve, for practical purposes, a computer representation of something in nature that cannot be experienced by the learner. Inevitably, the elements of the object and the relations between those elements are both reduced and changed in the simulation; and what this means is that any reaction or response to the object by a learner is influenced by its new media as well as the shape and form it now assumes. The response is always to the mediated object. And, the implication of this is that the pedagogical relation between the learner and the world is never direct but is realised through the mediated object, with the process of knowing the unmediated object a retroductive one, although this may be understood in a different way by the learner.

In trying to understand learning, we need to understand the constitution of the learning object (i.e. its structure and grammar), which is then animated by the learning process. We can categorise a learning object's effect and history in four ways: the capacity of the object to change the present state of affairs, the sustainability of the integrity of the object during the process, the malleability of the receiving schema (cf. Piaget, 1962), and the transformative potential of the learning experience. All of this amounts to a set of relations between a cognising subject and the social and natural worlds.

The first of these is the capacity of the learning object to change the status quo. This refers to the structure of the learning object or the way it is constituted. Some of these learning objects are crafted so that, even given the state of the schema into which they are being introduced, they have a more fundamental impact than other forms of learning. The second is the sustainability of the integrity of the object over time. What is being referred to here is the capacity of the learning object to retain its original shape, form and content in the learning process. When we refer to the integrity of a learning object, we should not understand this in an ideal sense. A learning object is always an amalgam of different ideas, values and prescriptions, which is never completely coherent. What this suggests, however, is that in the long process of formulation, to internalisation, through to realisation, and thence to performance, the original integrity of the learning object is either strongly or weakly realised.

The third feature is the malleability of the receiving schema, and this in turn points to the degree of resilience of the schema, or the capacity to resist or allow learning to take place. Learning has a greater or lesser capacity to impact on and change these schemas, and in part this refers to how it is going to be introduced, but also to the constitution of the learning object. Its penetrative power (though this may not be realised) or capacity to effect change is different in different learning episodes. We might want to call this the intensity of the learning object, and clearly its obverse is the resilience or otherwise of the current arrangements within the individual's mind. This is the malleability of these arrangements. Then there are the performative elements of the learning experience, and these refer to the capacity of the learning process to feed back into the environment, both the natural and social worlds and the learning process itself.

Jean Piaget (1962) suggested a number of interactive mechanisms between the stimulus and the person that characterise learning. The first of these is accumulation, and this is where there is little schematic formation in the individual (usually due to age) and learning consists of recall and applications in situations that are similar to those which were originally absorbed. The second is assimilation, and this is where a new element has to be addressed and made sense of by the individual; but this process is still essentially passive. The new elements are easily absorbed, indeed assimilated, into the existing schema of the individual and easily applied when directed to the field in question. The third element is accommodation and this is where the new element cannot easily accommodate to the new schema and thus a process of transformation of both takes place, i.e. the original stimulus or object of learning and the schema that is attempting some form of accommodation with it. In Piaget's terms it has been internalised.

LEARNING MODELS

Theoretical and contextual considerations impact, then, on how elements of teaching and learning are realised. Acknowledging this allows us to distinguish between a number of learning models: assessment for learning, observation, coaching, goal-clarification, mentoring, peer-learning, simulation, instruction, concept-formation, reflection, meta-cognitive learning, problem-solving and practice. These models give different emphases to the various elements of a learning environment that we have identified above.

The first of these models is the assessment for learning model. Assessment for learning can be presented as five key strategies and one cohering idea (see also Waring and Evans, 2015). The five key strategies are: engineering effective classroom discussions, questions and learning tasks; clarifying and sharing learning intentions and criteria for success; providing feedback that moves learners forward; activating students as the owners of their own learning; and activating students as instructional resources for one another (Wiliam and Thompson, 2008). And the cohering idea is that evidence about student learning is used to adapt instruction to better meet learning needs; in other words, teaching is adaptive to the student's learning

needs and evidence from the assessments is used by teachers, learners, or their peers to improve instruction (Wiliam and Thompson, 2008).

An important aspect of this model is the active engagement of the learner in the learning process as both an initiator and user of feedback (Waring and Evans, 2015). The key then is the relationship between assessment (designed as formative and developmental) and learning. As noted by Boud (2000: 221), '[f]or assessment to be formative, it has to be used'; an important element of any assessment for learning model is that students are given opportunities as part of the assessment design to use feedback to improve their work. Evans (2013) has suggested that this forms an important part of an holistic assessment design and that it also includes a number of key principles: feedback is ongoing and an integral part of assessment; assessment feedback guidance is explicit; greater emphasis is placed on feedforward compared to feedback activities; and learners are engaged in, and with, the process. The assessment for learning movement has been criticised on three grounds: the focus on formative assessment has inevitably marginalised processes of learning; as a result, some of the strategies are both misapplied and misunderstood (for example, peer learning does not amount to asking students to make quantitative judgements about their colleagues' work in relation to a set of criteria); and the reductive process for the purposes of quantifying and comparing results may have led to a distorted understanding of the process of learning.

Torrance and Pryor (1998) have identified a range of assessment approaches with 'convergent assessment' at one end of the spectrum and 'divergent assessment' at the other, where convergent assessment demands correct answers from students and divergent assessment explores what students can and cannot do and how they make connections between ideas. They suggest that divergent assessment leads to students choosing to engage with subject knowledge to a greater extent and to make new connections between ideas, while convergent assessment tends to be an end in itself. Feedback within a convergent framework focuses on the elicitation of correct answers and identifies errors in a student's performance (see also, Black and Wiliam's 'directive' feedback (1998) and Hattie and Timperley's 'task-focused feedback' (2007)), while within a divergent framework, feedback is 'exploratory, provisional or provocative' (Torrance and Pryor, 1998: 4), often encouraging students to reconstruct their thinking about the subject domain or learning process (see also, Black and Wiliam's (1998) 'facilitative feedback'; and Hattie and Timperley's (2007) 'process-focused/self-regulation-focused feedback').

Underpinning student involvement in assessment is Boud's (2000) concept of sustainable assessment, which is defined as practices which meet students' immediate assessment needs, but do not marginalise the knowledge, skills and dispositions they require to develop lifelong learning practices. Building on this work, Hounsell (2007) has outlined three key areas of sustainable feedback practice: provision of 'high value' feedback carrying impact beyond a task; enhancing the student's role in generating, interpreting and engaging with feedback; and constructing teaching and learning environments in which productive dialogue between the learner and the teacher is generated. For feedback to be sustainable, students need to be supported in the self-monitoring of their work, independently of the teacher (cf. Carless et al., 2011). Repositioning assessment feedback, it is suggested, emphasises: the co-constructed nature of feedback as dialogue between students and teachers; the use of multiple sources of feedback, with the teacher not necessarily being the dominant source of feedback but more the facilitator of student access to sources for learning; a move from individualistic to collectivist styles of learning through, for example, peer feedback mechanisms; and assessment feedback as a fully integrated element of assessment rather than as a series of isolated events (Boud and Molloy, 2013).

The second learning set is an observation model. Here the teacher displays the action which the learner is required to imitate in the classroom, and then later in the context of application. There are three principal types: a live model involving a demonstration or acting out of the behaviours to be learnt; a verbal instructional model where this comprises descriptions and explanations of behaviours; and a symbolic model, examples of which are scenarios and expressive performances. These are stimuli for learning. The learning skills required of the learner are: observing a performance by the teacher, whether this comprises live modelling, verbal instruction or symbolic modelling; comparing the performance with an embodied form of that display already held by the learner; adjusting their current construct through modification or substitution; practice by the learner whilst being supported within the artificial environment; practice by the learner without support within the artificial environment; transferring the skill to the real environment whilst being supported; and consolidation without support through use in the real environment (cf. Bandura, 1977). The importance of appropriate scaffolding to support learning is a key aspect of this model.

The third of these is a coaching model. Here the focus is on a series of steps: modelling by the expert; coaching whilst the learner practices; scaffolding where the learner is supported during the initial stages, with that support gradually being withdrawn as the learner becomes more proficient (coaching here involves the teacher in identifying for the learner deviations from the model in the performance of the learner, and then supporting the learner as they make attempts to correct this performance); articulation by the learner of that process; reflection on those processes and comparison with the expert's reasons for action; and exploration where the learner undertakes the various activities without support (cf. Collins et al., 1989). Coaching can be seen as a one-to-one activity, or as part of team and organisational development, and especially as part of peer learning activities within communities of practice.

A fourth model involves clarifying and sharing learning intentions and criteria for success with the student over a period of time. To this end, teachers provide learners with explicit statements and explanations about the instructional objectives in a lesson or series of lessons (Zimmerman and Schunk, 2011). Goal clarity has three learner-focused aspects: explanations about how they are expected to perform the tasks assigned to them; opportunities for them to grasp what is expected of them; and reflections about their capacity as self-directed learners in the completion of the task. This mechanism comprises a number of processes: identifying the standard and interpreting its meaning; providing a description with the learner of their mastery of that standard, which should allow the identification of weaknesses in their capacity and the means for ameliorating these weaknesses; record-keeping for further identification of the learner's current capability; reflection on this and the identification of the means of improving; and a meta-reflective record of progress in the curriculum (Meece et al., 2006).

A fifth model is mentoring. This supports the informal transmission of content knowledge, social capital or resources with a psycho-social function. It is usually conducted face-to-face and involves a relationship between two people, one of whom is considered to have greater knowledge, wisdom or experience. Five possible mentoring techniques have been identified (cf. Aubrey and Cohen, 1995): supporting the learner and taking part in the same activity and learning side-by-side with them; preparing the learner for the future even if they are not ready or able to learn what is being offered to them in the present; catalysing learning so that it provokes a different way of thinking, a change in identity or a re-ordering of values; showing through personal example; and finally, helping and supporting the learner in reflecting back on their previous learning. The terms coaching and mentoring are often used synonymously but important distinctions between these two approaches have been identified. In distinguishing between these two terms,

Clutterbuck and Megginson (2005) identify three specific differences in terms of emphasis: time-scale, approach and context. For example, coaching is focused on performance change whilst mentoring is focused on managing the life-course; and coaching is focused on the immediate context whereas mentoring involves enlarging a learner's networks. In addition, coaching is typically seen as being of much shorter duration and in response to a specific goal, whereas mentoring considers immediate issues as part of long-term change. Both mentoring and coaching are about achieving change, and place a strong emphasis on the development of learner self-regulation through the use of appropriate tools, such as critical reflection and appropriate scaffolded support.

A sixth model of learning is peer learning. The other forms of learning comprise unequal relations between the teacher and the learner. Here the assumption is made that the learning relationship is between equals, and thus a different form of learning is implied. Examples of this type of learning include: being offered emotional support if learning proves to be difficult – always a better form of support if given by someone who is going through the same learning process; dyadic performance confrontations, where learning is provoked by confrontational exchanges between learners so that each individual can test their theories, ideas and constructs against those held by other learners engaging in the same type of learning; pair-problem-solving, where learning is enabled through cooperation between two learners of roughly equal standing, so that in a problem-solving exercise better solutions are forthcoming because there are two problem-solvers rather than one; reciprocal peer tutoring, where non-expert tutoring between equals has the advantage of each person being able to make their own evaluation of the advice being offered unencumbered by status or hierarchy; and scripted cooperative dyads, where peer engagement is focused on the joint production of a script, artefact, performance or text with the advantage that alternative and new interpretations/readings are forthcoming (cf. Falchikov, 2001). The efficacy of peer feedback depends on the extent to which students are proactive in their receipt, use and giving of feedback (cf. Evans, 2013).

A seventh model of learning involves simulation. Simulation is a reproduction of an event or activity, conducted outside the environment in which that event or activity usually takes place. Simulations can be produced through computer games, role-plays, scenarios, presentations and affective and conceptual modelling. The purpose of this learning process is to simulate a real event, and this is to allow the person or persons taking part in that simulation to explore it, to experiment within it, to understand the process, to begin the process of internalisation, to experience albeit in a limited way the emotions and feelings that would normally accompany the experience in real-life, and fundamentally, to allow learning to take place through trial and error and making mistakes in safe situations, which do not have the consequences they would have in real-life situations. Simulations compress time and remove extraneous detail. They are immersive learning experiences, where skills and performances can be enhanced in a way that is not possible outside the simulation.

With instruction, the teacher needs to: gain the attention of the group of learners; inform the learners of the objectives of the learning exercise; stimulate recall of prior learning amongst the group of learners, so that the new information is related productively to previous and current learning; present content to the learner; implement appropriate scaffolding processes; stimulate a performance by the learner; provide feedback to the learner which is a comment on their performance and allows corrective action to take place; and evaluate the corrected performance (cf. Gagne, 1985).

A concept-formation learning process focuses on the re-forming of conceptual schema held by the learner. Learning is complex and potentially rich and rewarding, where the learner is presented with a mass of information, ideas and opinions from a number of different sources (i.e. books, articles, lectures, seminars, emails, e-seminars, personal communications, and so on). What the learner does is shape this mass of information, and this shaping can take a number of different forms: partial shaping, complete shaping, discarding with no replacement, confusion, on-going, going backwards and forwards, and so on. Shaping takes place against a scholarly background, aspects of which may or may not be implicit and where some but not all of its aspects can be surfaced for deliberation. Conceptual learning is irredeemably social, embedded and selective. So the learner has to absorb some of the ideas they are presented with and discard or partially discard others.

Reflection is a seminal form of learning. It has been variously described as critical reflection, reflective practice, reflective thinking and reflexivity. Whereas some see these terms as interchangeable and as having similar meanings, others have sought to differentiate between different types and levels of reflective activity (cf. Black and Plowright, 2010). For example, Harvey et al. (2010) have argued that not all reflection is critical reflection. Bolton (2010: 13) defined reflection (single loop activity) as 'an in-depth consideration of events or situations outside of oneself: solitary or with critical support', and reflexivity as a double loop process which includes reflection and reflexivity and is focused on 'finding strategies to question our own attitudes, thought processes, values, assumptions, prejudices and habitual actions, to strive to understand our complex roles with others'. Wilson and Demetriou (2007: 224) have highlighted the varying quality of different types of reflection, drawing on the work of Schön (1983) and Eraut (2004). They differentiate between three types of reflective practice: intensive action reflection which is seen as tacit, implicit and occurring on a daily basis in practice where individuals use intuitive tacit knowledge to inform practice (reflection-in-action); reactive or reflective learning (knowledge of action) involving immediate reactive reflection on events that have already taken place; and deliberative reflection (knowledge for action) involving the conscious management of thoughts and activity and the deliberate setting aside of time to ensure that judgements are based on a deep understanding of a particular issue.

Critical reflection is seen as a precursor to transformative learning (cf. Mezirow, 1990) by supporting the development of metacognition through the use of critical reflective practices (Eames and Coll, 2010). It is widely recognised as a key component in the learning processes of individuals and organisations (Brookfield, 2009). There is a wide variation in the techniques and approaches used in the practice of critical reflection (see Waring and Evans (2015) for an overview). There is, however, general agreement that the process of critical reflection needs to be facilitated, with approaches ranging from informal discussions to highly structured formats (Moon, 2006). There are a number of models of reflection based on specific philosophical approaches (e.g. Dewey (1938) or Habermas (1981)) that are in common use. To facilitate critical reflection, a range of tools and practices have been developed, and these include, for example, the use and analysis of critical incidents (Tripp, 1995), Brookfield's (1995) lenses, and the much used Kolb learning cycle (1984).

The learning cycle, developed by David Kolb (1984), is based on a belief that deep learning (learning for real comprehension) comes from a sequence of experience, reflection, abstraction and active testing. Reflection is a form of evaluative thinking. It is applied to ideas for which there is no obvious solution and is largely based on the further processing of knowledge and understanding and possibly emotions that the learner already possesses. It is thus a second-order internal activity, which can in certain circumstances be transformed into a learning strategy. There are some optimum conditions for reflection: time and space, a good facilitator, a supportive curricular or institutional environment, and an emotionally supportive locale for learning.

Meta-cognitive learning refers to learners' awareness of their own knowledge and their ability to understand, control and manipulate their own cognitive processes. However, most meta-cognitive processes can be placed within three categories (cf. Harris and Graham, 1999).

The first is meta-memorisation. This refers to the learners' awareness of their own memory systems and their ability to deploy strategies for using their memories effectively. The second is meta-comprehension. This refers to the learners' ability to monitor the degree to which they understand information being communicated to them, to recognise failures to comprehend, and to employ repair strategies. And the third is self-regulation. This term refers to the learner's ability to make adjustments in their own learning processes. The concept of self-regulation overlaps with meta-memorisation and meta-comprehension; its focus is on the capacity of the learners themselves to monitor their own learning (without external stimuli or persuasion) and to act independently. These regulatory processes may be highly automated, making articulation of them difficult for the learner.

Self-regulated learning has been conceptualised in a number of different ways; notable examples are Boekaerts (1999) and Vermunt and Verloop (1999). Both approaches stress the importance of three regulatory processes: regulation of the self; regulation of the learning process; and regulation of information processing modes. The efficacy of the self-regulation process depends on the aggregated effect of cognitive, meta-cognitive and motivational elements. The interrelated nature of self-regulatory processes is also evident in Zimmerman's (2002) three-phase cyclical model, involving forethought, performance and self-reflection. Forethought involves task analysis (i.e. goal setting and strategic planning) and self-motivational beliefs (i.e. self-efficacy, outcome expectancies, intrinsic valuations and learning goal orientations); performance involves self-control (i.e. self-instruction, attention focusing and task strategising) and self-observation (i.e. self-recording, self-experimentation and self-reflection); and self-reflection involves self-judgement (i.e. self-evaluation and causal attribution) and self-reaction (i.e. self-satisfaction and affect).

A number of strategies have been proposed to support learner self-regulatory skill development by stimulating students to employ cognitive, meta-cognitive and affective activities in learning. Of note is the work of Vermunt and Verloop (1999) who have focused on the efficacy of strong, loose or shared teacher control of the learning environment. In the case of strong teacher control, there is a limited opportunity for learners to develop their self-regulatory capacity as the teacher performs the tasks for them. In a loosely controlled setting, the teacher hands over the responsibility for performing to the learners, which is a high-risk strategy for those learners with a limited capacity to self-regulate. In a shared or co-regulated control situation learners are encouraged and supported to employ specific strategies to support their learning through the generation of constructive friction, whereby learners are sufficiently challenged and supported to increase their skills, as opposed to destructive friction which causes a decrease in learning skills, for example where learning and thinking skills are not called upon or skills are not developed. In the development of co-regulatory and process-oriented practice, the role of the teacher is reconceptualised as one where the teacher fulfils a number of inter-related roles, such as diagnostician, challenger, model learner, activator, monitor and evaluator.

A problem-solving approach is where the learner finds out for themselves rather than being given answers to problems. The learner is required to engage in a series of interrogative processes with regards to texts, people and objects in the environment, and come up with solutions to problems. The learner is also required to use the skills of information retrieval, information synthesis and analysis, and knowledge organisation. The learner may come up with inadequate, incorrect and faulty syntheses and analyses. However, this is acceptable because the learning resides in the process rather than in the end-product. Problem-solving learning involves the learner in judging their own work against a curriculum standard and engaging in meta-processes of learning, that is, understanding about processes related to their own learning; the

development of learning pathways; the utilisation of formative assessment processes; the development of personal learning strategies; and the internalisation of the curriculum.

Finally, there is practice. Practice is the act of rehearsing a behaviour over and over again, or engaging in an activity again and again. This reinforces, enhances and deepens the learning associated with the behaviour or activity.

INTERNALITY, EXTERNALITY AND VERTEXICALITY

These learning models are all characterised by a relation between an internal and an external process. To this end, Lev Vygotsky (1978: 45) suggested that:

> Child logic develops only along with the growth of the child's social speech and whole experience. It is through others that we develop ourselves and … this is true not only with regard to the history of every function … Any higher mental function was external because it was social at some point before becoming an internal, truly mental functioning.

Thus learning is social, both in the sense that learning takes place in society and with people in society, but more fundamentally, because the contents and processes of learning are social phenomena. We are therefore confronted in relation to learning with a particular set of relations between external structures and internal or agential processes, and it is the vertexical relations between the two that produces learning. These structures (i.e. embodied, discursive, agential, institutional and systemic) are fluid, transitive and at times contradictory (but not in equal measure), and the learner is inserted in them, though never so that their freedom of action and re-creation is absolutely circumscribed. Examples of discursive formations expressed in narrative mode are: mastery, coping, expansion, autonomy, self-actualisation and performance. Each of these discursive formations is temporally sequenced, though in different ways, so, for example, a learning narrative might consist of exchanges between teachers and learners where the purposes of these exchanges is to dissolve, fragment or otherwise disrupt the model of knowledge held by the learner. This implies a non-linear learning narrative and thus it has implications for an understanding of how time impacts on learning. All learning sequences then are characterised by movement from one time moment (T_a) to another (T_b), and onwards to a series of other time moments (T_c to T_n). However, this sequence should not be understood as exclusively linear or non-recursive.

In any learning sequence, the learner is confronted with a set of ideational resources or structured discourses, and, in addition, they are embedded in another set of structures, i.e. structures of agency. These structures of agency mediate, for the individual learner, entry into those discursive structures which act as a resource for their belief systems; as a result, learning theorists have to confront notions of formal and informal learning and therefore of assimilation, discarding, layering, organising, synthesising, selecting and meta-processes connected to learning. Discursive structures may be characterised as those ideational resources which sustain the learner, and they include a range of stories, narratives, arguments and chronologies that have a number of distinctive features: they have a specific time-place location, and thus are subject to change and amendment; they are structured in turn and thus different patterns of story-telling or narrative genre are possible; and they compete with other genres. In addition, they play a role in the construction and maintenance of structures of agency.

It is this relationship then between these structures and the agential capacity of the learner, which determines whether and in what way learning can take place. These vertexical modes have five forms. The first refers to the knowledgeability of the learner, that is, the amount and type of knowledge held, with this type of knowledge comprising cognitions, skills and dispositions. The second vertexical mode again refers to the agential learner but

this time to those factors which impact on the knowledgeability of the agent, i.e. unconscious beliefs, unacknowledged conditions of action, tacit knowledge and unintended consequences. The third vertexical mode refers to the degree and type of give in the structure. We have identified above five types of structure (embodied, discursive, agential, institutional and systemic), and each of these has a different type of give, or a different shaping capacity. An embodied structure such as a notion of sexuality, compared with a discursive structure is an example of this, and this is in part because the discursive structure can in certain circumstances be ignored, though there are consequences or sanctions as a result. The fourth vertexical mode refers to the degree and type of give in the agent, or in those structures of agency, which provide the conditions for those agents to make the decisions they do. And finally, the fifth mode relates to the consequences of that vertexical relation in learning. There are different consequences depending on the type of vertexical relation that is implicated in each and every learning episode.

REFERENCES

Aubrey, B. and Cohen, P. (1995) *Working Wisdom: Timeless Skills and Vanguard Strategies for Learning Organizations*, San Francisco: Jossey Bass.

Bandura, A. (1977) *Social Learning Theory*, New York: General Learning Press.

Black, P. and Plowright, D. (2010) 'A multidimensional model of reflective learning for professional development', *Reflective Practice*, 11(2): 245–58.

Black, P. and Wiliam, D. (1998) 'Inside the black box: raising standards through classroom assessment', *Phi Delta Kappan*, 80(2): 139–48.

Boekaerts, M. (1999) 'Self-regulated learning: where we are today', *International Journal of Educational Research*, 31: 445–57.

Bolton, G. (2010) *Reflective Practice*, London: Sage.

Boud, D. (2000) 'Sustainable assessment: rethinking assessment for learning society', *Studies in Continuing Education*, 31(2): 219–33.

Boud, D. and Molloy, A. (2013) 'Rethinking models of feedback for learning: the challenge of design', *Assessment and Evaluation in Higher Education*, 38(6): 698–712.

Brookfield, S. (1995) *Becoming a Critically Reflective Teacher*, San-Francisco: Jossey-Bass.

Brookfield, S. (2009) 'The concept of critical reflection: promises and contradictions', *European Journal of Social Work*, 12(3): 293–304.

Carless, D., Salter, D., Yang, M. and Lam, J. (2011) 'Developing sustainable feedback practices', *Studies in Higher Education*, 36: 395–407.

Clutterbuck, D. and Megginson, D. (2005) *Making Coaching Work – Creating a Coaching Culture*, London: Chartered Institute of Personnel and Development.

Collins, A., Brown, J. and Newman, S. (1989) 'Cognitive apprenticeship: teaching the crafts of reading, writing, and mathematics', in L.B. Resnick (ed.), *Knowing, Learning, and Instruction: Essays in Honour of Robert Glaser* (pp. 453–94), Hillsdale, NJ: Lawrence Erlbaum Associates.

Dewey, J. (1938) *Experience and Education*, New York: Touchstone.

Eames, C. and Coll, R.K. (2010) 'Cooperative education: integrating classroom and workplace learning', in S. Billett (ed.), *Learning through Practice* (pp. 180–96), Dordrecht, The Netherlands: Springer.

Eraut, M. (2004) 'Informal learning in the workplace', *Studies in Continuing Education*, 26: 247–73.

Evans, C. (2013) 'Making sense of assessment feedback in higher education', *Review of Educational Research*, 83(1): 70–120. Available online at http://rer.sagepub.com/cgi/reprint/83/1/70?ijkey=x/CimNd6vjZWl&keytype=ref&siteid=sprer (accessed 6 June 2014).

Falchikov, N. (2001) *Learning Together: Peer Tutoring in Higher Education*, London: RoutledgeFalmer.

Gagne, R. (1985) *The Conditions of Learning*, New York: Holt, Rinehart and Winston.

Habermas, J. (1981) *The Theory of Communicative Action, Volume 1*, Thomas McCarthy (trans.), Boston: Beacon Press.

Harris, K.R. and Graham, S. (1999) 'Programmatic intervention research: illustrations from the evolution of self-regulated strategy development', *Learning Disability Quarterly*, 22: 251–62.

Harvey, M., Coulson, D., Mackaway, J. and Winchester-Seeto, T. (2010) 'Aligning reflection in the cooperative education curriculum', *Asia-Pacific Journal of Cooperative Education*, 11(3): 137–52.

Hattie, J. and Timperley, H. (2007) 'The power of feedback', *Review of Educational Research*, 77(1): 81–112.

Hounsell, D. (2007) 'Towards more sustainable feedback to students', in D. Boud and N. Falchikov (eds), *Rethinking Assessment in Higher Education* (pp. 101–13), London, UK: Routledge.

Kolb, D.A. (1984) *Experiential Learning Experience as a Source of Learning and Development*, New Jersey: Prentice Hall.

Meece, J., Anderman, E. and Anderman, L. (2006) 'Classroom goal structure, student motivation, and academic achievement', *Annual Review of Psychology*, 57(1): 487–503.

Mezirow, J. (1990) 'How critical reflection triggers transformative learning', *Fostering Critical Reflection in Adulthood*, 1–20.

Moon, J.A. (2006) *Learning Journals: A Handbook for Reflective Practice and Professional Development* (2nd edn), London and New York: Routledge.

Piaget, J. (1962) *The Language and Thought of the Child*, London: Routledge and Kegan Paul.

Schön, D.A. (1983) *The Reflective Practitioner: How Professionals Think in Action*, London: Avebury.

Torrance, H. and Pryor, J. (1998) *Investigating Formative Assessment*, Buckingham: Open University Press.

Tripp, D. (1995) *Critical Incidents in Teaching*, London: Routledge.

Vermunt, J. and Verloop, N. (1999) 'Congruence and friction between learning and teaching', *Learning and Instruction*, 9: 257–80.

Vygotsky, L. (1978) *Mind in Society: The Development of Higher Psychological Processes*, M. Cole, V. John-Steirner and S. Scribner (eds), Cambridge MA: Harvard University Press.

Waring, M. and Evans, C. (2015) *Understanding Pedagogy: Developing a Critical Approach to*

Teaching and Learning, Abingdon, Oxon: Routledge.

Wiliam, D. and Thompson, M. (2008) 'Integrating assessment with instruction: What will it take to make it work?', in C.A. Dwyer (ed.), *The Future of Assessment: Shaping Teaching and Learning* (pp. 53–82), Mawah, NJ: Lawrence Erlbaum Associates.

Wilson, E. and Demetriou, H. (2007) 'New teacher learning: substantive knowledge and contextual factors', *The Curriculum Journal*, 18(3): 213–29.

Zimmerman, B. (2002) 'Becoming a self-regulated learner: an overview', *Theory into Practice*, 41(2): 64–71.

Zimmerman, B. and Schunk, D. (2011) *Handbook of Self-regulation of Learning and Performance*, New York: Routledge.

Curriculum, Pedagogy and Assessment

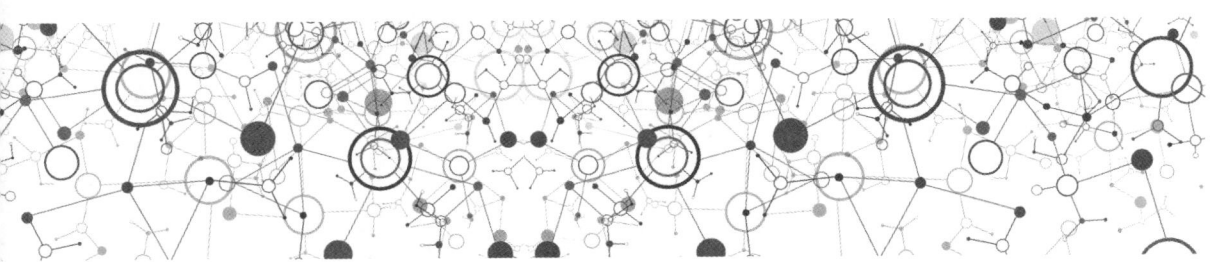

19

Introduction (Part III)

Eleanore Hargreaves and David Scott

Part III of this Handbook focuses on teachers and their role in supporting, inspiring or restricting learning in classrooms and beyond. For example, Vicki Vescio and Alyson Adams consider the kind of learning that teachers engage in as members of Professional Learning Communities and their relationship with students' classroom learning. Clive Harber's chapter, using international examples, examines the school as a model of authoritarian teaching for socialisation, where the voice of learners is restricted. Lisa Smulyan explores in her chapter the hidden impacts of local, national and global communities of practice on what happens in the classroom. Aki Murata focuses on the degree to which teachers sustain classroom discussion by incorporating different student ideas, and how this affects the ways students learn mathematics. Alina Reznitskaya and Ian Wilkinson consider dialogic teaching as a pedagogical approach that capitalises on the power of talk to foster students' thinking, understanding and learning. John Pryor theorises a dialogic pedagogy of convergent and divergent response as an alternative basis for formative assessment while Bethan Marshall considers language learning and teaching within Assessment for Learning.

All these contributions suggest that the traditional patterns of interaction among teachers and learners can, and perhaps need to, be challenged. One key area for provocative thought in this sense is teachers' 'feedback'. Teacher 'feedback' is currently considered by many as a key means for improving pupils' learning (Higgins et al., 2011), but this assumption needs to be examined with reference to the pedagogic relationships within which feedback is given. By 'feedback', we refer to responses made by a teacher to the behaviour of a learner, including learning behaviours.

Most classrooms are currently framed by an authoritarian relationship between the learner and the teacher. That is, the teacher, supported by his/her senior colleagues and the hierarchical structures of which they are a part, takes most decisions about what learners do, how they do it, when they do it *and* how and where they are placed physically. An authoritarian system is one with a 'dependence relationship in which one person is dominant and another or others dependent' (Meighan and Harber, 2007: 238). Different embodiments of authoritarianism reflect the teacher's dominance in stronger or weaker ways. Meighan and Harber (2007, based on Lippitt and White, 1958) distinguished between six versions of authoritarianism, each of which allowed progressively more dialogic means for establishing order in classroom learning and depended increasingly less on the teacher's dominance. Their spectrum of authoritarianism included categorisations such as: autocratic, parental, charismatic, organisational, expert and consultative. Teachers could exercise an authoritarian approach in any or all of these senses in one classroom. In each of these, the relationship was ultimately one of *dominant/passive* to greater or lesser degrees.

Flink, Boggiano and Barrett's (1990) research findings indicate a clear and negative connection between teachers' over-use of controlling strategies and pupils' creativity, autonomy and criticality. Studies in Self Determination Theory suggest that children need to feel autonomy and relatedness to others, as well as competence, in order to learn creatively and critically (Niemiec and Ryan, 2009). In a relationship where the teacher is overly dominant in terms of acting as the *primary knower* and the *monitor* or *judge* of value (Nassaji and Wells, 2000), the autonomy, competence and relatedness of the learner is threatened. Lin (2007) describes how the Initiation Response Feedback (IRF) sequence, common to many traditional classrooms, helps teachers in their role as classroom managers and as primary knowers by embracing two functions: the *converging function* and the *certifying function*. The converging function of IRF helps the teacher to 'maintain tight control and minimise digression' (Lin, 2007: 88); while the certifying function 'work[s] students' input into acceptable answers to exam-type questions, that is, to certify it as correct and model answers' (Lin, 2007: 88). Within this process, certifying information takes priority over personal

information, such as a child's opinion, and the teacher may not trust the class to reach the required information level through pupil-led dialogue. The pace of the IRF classroom tends to be fast, allowing little time for pupils or their teacher to pause and reflect, sometimes resulting in talk moving from one focus to another non-sequentially. Lin (2007) comments that both convergence and certification function primarily through the teacher's 'feedback', the 'F' in the IRF sequence.

Thus the concept of 'feedback' that has developed within this context of the authoritarian classroom takes both a converging and certifying function, leaving less room for learners' initiatives or critical, divergent responses. The term 'feedback' itself stems from engineering and a mechanical response to a particular stimulus. The constraining and judgemental feedback characteristic of the authoritarian classroom can also take the form of a rather mechanical response to a student's behaviour. Given the alternative suggestions for the teacher–student relationship in this part of the book, it is useful to ask how valuable it is for educators to continue to focus on 'feedback'. Has the time come for a different approach? Is the concept itself outdated in more symmetrical, more human, more collaborative, more dialogic classrooms?

Based on the theories of Lev Vygotsky, Storch (2002) categorised some alternative ways of thinking about the teaching relationship, in addition to the *dominant/passive* pattern. In the *expert/novice* relationship described by Storch, the teacher dominates but their aim is to initiate the learner into their own expertise and help them learn, like an apprentice. As illustrated in Flink et al.'s (1990) study, because there is a desire here for learning by both parties rather than an exterior motivation, this relationship may help both partners in learning. In Storch's *collaborative* relationship, both teacher and learner support and initiate contributions and build on the other's. Authority in relation to truth and knowledge are shared between teacher and learner in such a relationship. Damon and Phelps (1989) emphasised, in a similar vein, two aspects of a pedagogic relationship which support both the teacher and the learner: *mutuality*, which depends on *each partner* responding to/ engaging with/acting on the other's input; and *equality*, which depends on learners and teachers sharing the responsibilities for learning, making similarly plentiful contributions and assuming authority in comparable ways.

These earlier studies of learning relationships suggested that the most productive learning, in terms of creative, autonomous and critical thought, resulted from *collaborative* or *expert/novice* relationship patterns, in which both mutuality and equality were high. On this basis, a classroom run along the lines of the *dominant/passive* relationship with low mutuality and low equality is likely to be least promising in terms of nurturing learning; especially learning related to Schiro's 'learner centred ideology' and the 'social reconstruction ideology' (see Moore, this volume).

In terms of scholarship on teacher 'feedback', Kluger and De Nisi's (1996) well-known 'feedback' review has been particularly useful in reminding teachers that 'feedback' can have negative effects for up to 40 per cent of the time, which might include pupils developing a dependency on teachers rather than becoming more creative, autonomous and critical. And yet, in their introduction, Kluger and De Nisi (1996: 255) define 'feedback' as 'actions taken by (an) external agent(s) to provide information regarding some aspect(s) of one's task performance'. This definition, including the word 'information', places the conceptualisation towards the *dominant/passive* extremity of the teacher/learner relationship spectrum. Kluger and De Nisi (ibid.) go on to focus on the question of 'what effects can a teacher, manager, boarding school counsellor, or computer-program designer expect to obtain from an FI ['feedback' intervention]'? This suggests that in conceptualising learning, they do not pay attention to the nature of the human relationship between teacher and learner but rather refer to a linear and predictable process that can be drawn out of learners by teachers, regardless of the learners' agentic characteristics. This is indeed a *dominant/*

passive scenario. Similarly, in her very expansive review of formative 'feedback', Shute (2008) talks of 'feedback' itself being *delivered* by teachers, rather than constructed or indeed co-constructed with pupils, reinforcing the authoritarian tendencies built into such models where one party is *dominant* and the other *passive.* Henderlong and Lepper (2002), in their review, have questioned the long-term benefits of praise as 'feedback'. Praise can be connected to coercion on the part of an authoritarian teacher who uses it to try to reinforce certain behaviours. Storch (2002) noted that collaborating teaching–learning partnerships, whose mutuality and equality were high, did praise each other but only as part of an ongoing negotiation of each other's learning, and praise was always genuine and given to both partners within the relationship. This is in stark contrast to praise from an authoritarian teacher, for whom praise can often be the more palatable side of their 'normalising judgement' (Foucault, 1979), whereby they judge their pupils at all times and correct or punish them when the judgement is negative.

Within a 'divergent' assessment framework, Pryor and Crossouard (2008: 4) write of 'feedback' as 'exploratory, provisional or provocative', often encouraging children to reconstruct their thinking about the subject domain or learning process. Hattie and Timperley (2007) define 'process-focused/ self-regulation-focused feedback' as teacher comments that support the learner to reconsider their learning processes and how they might be made more effective. These authors, along with Butler and Winne's exploration of feedback within self-regulated learning (1995), are envisaging the feedback dialogue more along *collaborative lines* or in terms of *expert/novice*, reflecting some of the alternative models described by authors in this book. More recently, James (2006) illustrates a *collaborative* learning relationship, in which she depicts 'feedback' within a socio-cultural approach as responses emanating from the audience, to the authentic learning products designed and processed by learners collaboratively. In this model, the community of learners takes the principal responsibility for constructing 'feedback' together, which might be as simple as showing spontaneous appreciation. The 'feedback' relates to how well a task is received by its intended audience, including experts and novices, but the intended audience has been nominated by the learner as s/he constructed his/her own goals in order to build up the identity s/he valued.

How valuable is it for such a response still to be defined as 'feedback'? This response is not *feeding back* so much as widening or enriching learning in an ongoing way. Critically analytic, responsive, responsible, risky and inspiring interactions perhaps replace 'feedback' in teaching situations that are no longer *dominant/passive*. As readers enjoy this part of the book where non-traditional aspects of pedagogy are explored from a range of angles, we suggest that 'feedback' should continue to be problematised in relation to its new purposes.

REFERENCES

Butler, D. and Winne, P. (1995) 'Feedback and self-regulated learning', *Review of Educational Research*, 65(3): 245–81.

Damon, W. and Phelps, E. (1989) 'Critical distinctions among three approaches to peer education', *International Journal of Educational Research*, 13(1): 9–19.

Flink, C., Boggiano, A. and Barrett, M. (1990) 'Controlling teaching strategies: Undermining children's self-determination and performance', *Journal of Personality and Social Psychology*, 59(5): 916–24.

Foucault, M. (1979) *Discipline and Punish: The Birth of the Prison*, New York: Random House.

Hattie, J. and Timperley, H. (2007) 'The power of feedback', *Review of Educational Research*, 77(1): 81–112.

Henderlong, J. and Lepper, M. (2002) 'The effects of praise on children's intrinsic motivation: A review and synthesis', *Psychological Bulletin*, 128(5): 774–95.

Higgins, S., Kokotsaki, D. and Coe, R. (2011) *Toolkit of Strategies to Improve Learning*, London: Sutton Trust.

James, M. (2006) 'Assessment, teaching and theories of learning', in J. Gardner (ed.), *Assessment and Learning*, London: Sage, pp. 47–60.

Kluger, A. and DeNisi, A. (1996) 'The effects of feedback interventions on performance: A historical review, a meta-analysis, and a preliminary feedback intervention theory', *Psychological Bulletin*, 119: 254–84.

Lin, A.M. (2007) 'What's the use of "triadic dialogue?": Activity theory, conversation analysis, and analysis of pedagogical practices', *Pedagogies: An International Journal*, 2(2): 77–94.

Lippitt, R. and White, R. (1958) 'An Experimental Study of Leadership and Group Life', in E. Maccoby, T. Newcomb and E. Hartley (eds.) *Readings in Social Psychology*, New York: Holt, Rinehart and Winston.

Meighan, R. and Harber, C. (2007) *A Sociology of Educating*, New York: Continuum.

Nassaj, H. and Wells, G. (2000) 'What's the Use of Traidic Dialogue? An Investigation of Teacher–student Interaction', *Applied Linguistics*, 21, 3: 376–406.

Niemiec, C. and Ryan, R. (2009) 'Autonomy, competence, and relatedness in the classroom: Applying self-determination theory to educational practice', *Theory and Research in Education*, 7(2): 133–44. DOI: 10.1177/1477878509104318.

Pryor, J. and Crossouard, B. (2008) 'A sociocultural theorisation of formative assessment', *Oxford Review of Education*, 34(1): 1–20.

Shute, V.J. (2008) 'Focus on formative feedback', *Review of Educational Research*, 78(1): 153–89.

Storch, N. (2002) 'Patterns of interaction in ESL pair work', *Language Learning*, 52(1): 119–58.

20

Formative Assessment: A Success Story?

John Pryor

INTRODUCTION

Formative assessment seems to be universally acknowledged as a good idea, and in the last twenty years it has become a major consideration of practitioners and researchers across the world. It is an idea that promises to transform teaching and learning in the interests of all. However, in this chapter I will argue that the success of formative assessment has been illusory. Although it has received official sanction and has been 'implemented' widely, especially in its guise as assessment for learning, I am critical of the way the concept has been adopted and the practices that this has produced. When innovations in education, and indeed in many other fields, are analysed, the claim is often made that the idea was good in theory, but that the practice fell short. By contrast I will argue that the reason why the promise of formative assessment remains largely unfulfilled lies not so much with inadequate practice of a good theory, but with the theory that underpins it. In suggesting an alternative theoretical understanding I will draw on research conducted both in schools and in higher education to suggest an approach to formative assessment which, whilst remaining problematic, might enable it to fulfil its promise.

THE DEVELOPMENT OF FORMATIVE ASSESSMENT

The practices now seen as formative assessment must have been a part of teaching and learning encounters for as long as these have taken place. However, as a term, it emerged in the 1960s when Scriven (1967) distinguished between the two different purposes of the evaluation of educational programmes: *summative* which was about judging or measuring them and *formative* which sought mainly to improve them. This distinction was soon carried over into thinking about students' academic work and achievement, with Bloom et al. (1971: 117) defining formative assessment as involving 'the process of curriculum construction, teaching, and learning for the purpose of improving any of these three processes'. For these researchers and for other early users of the term, only the purpose of the assessment was different, while the processes of formative and summative assessment remained the same. However, as formative and summative purposes have been pursued over more than forty years, thinking and practices have changed. Particularly in contexts where there has been a concerted attempt to develop it, formative assessment acquired distinctive attributes, alongside those features held in common with summative assessment. Moreover, what seems appropriate and useful in one context does not necessarily suit others, which has led to a further broadening out of the term (Black and Wiliam, 2003; Pryor and Crossouard, 2008). Brookhart (2005) sees this as a gradual expansion and evolution of definitions of formative assessment, in which the work of Royce Sadler (1989) in Australia was especially influential. From the original focus on testing it came to include the way that teaching and learning activities or instructional systems are designed so as to optimize opportunities for judging and reflecting on work. Most crucially, Sadler offered a more elaborate view of assessment criteria, which emphasized the development of a shared understanding between teachers and learners of the standard of work required. This had the effect of making the student 'more actively a subject as well as an object of formative assessment' (Brookhart, 2005: 2).

Formative assessment emerged most strongly in the UK. As part of the planning of the English National Curriculum in the 1980s, a Task Group on Assessment and Testing chaired by Paul Black also elaborated on formative assessment and its possibilities, in particular underlining that it could be embedded within teaching, as an 'integral part of the educational process, continually providing both "feedback" and "feedforward"' (TGAT, 1987: Para 4). Although its proposals were not fully acted upon, TGAT concentrated interest from academic researchers

many of whom joined the British Educational Research Association's (BERA) Assessment Policy Task Group. It held regular seminars on assessment reform, and it was this group that commissioned a literature review of research on formative assessment from Black and his colleague Dylan Wiliam.

The review, the most influential single piece of work on formative assessment, was published as an article in a special edition of *Assessment in Education* in 1998, along with several responses. It chose to use what was seen then as a wide definition of formative assessment, interpreting it as 'encompassing all those activities undertaken by teachers, and/or by students, which provide information to be used as feedback to modify the teaching and learning activities in which they are engaged' (Black and Wiliam, 1998a: 7–8). This definition allowed it to include amongst the 250 texts reviewed works by authors who had not actually used the term and thus to reconstruct the field of formative assessment. The article acknowledged both the psychological complexities and the potential and actual problems of social context and included research critical of formative assessment and studies showing how little formative assessment takes place in classrooms. However, its most striking finding was the claim that there was solid evidence associating formative assessment with strong academic performance, having 'particular benefit to the disadvantaged and low-attaining learners' (Black and Wiliam, 1998a: 59). It ended by considering how formative assessment might be developed both practically and theoretically.

The academic review was followed by a booklet aimed at teachers, summarizing its findings and widely distributed in the UK (Black and Wiliam, 1998b). It was also reproduced in the US in a professional journal. Named *Inside the Black Box*, it promoted formative assessment as a way of making clear what are often the hidden parts of teaching and learning. Gipps (1994) had made the point that dominant forms of summative assessment, while according well with behaviourism, were not easily compatible with constructivist learning theories, whereas formative assessment fitted much more easily. She made a distinction between summative assessment as assessment *of* learning and formative assessment as assessment *for* learning. As part of the response to *Inside the Black Box* and subsequent booklets, this latter term was taken up. This started what might be called the Assessment for Learning (AfL) movement, joined initially in the UK but subsequently in the rest of the Anglophone world (see for example, Crooks, 2011).

Assessment for Learning was initially very popular as an idea with teachers at an individual and school level, but in the UK it also attracted the attention of policy makers. Given the strong commitment of successive governments to summative testing, this may seem surprising. However, AfL may be seen in part as an educational sweetener for teachers, since the recently introduced national tests were so unpopular with practitioners. Also, policy makers were attracted by Black and Wiliam's (1998a) claim that, if implemented widely, it might raise the mathematics attainment score of an average country like England or the United States to that of a top performing country like Singapore. AfL promised to eliminate the 'long tail of underachievement', which popularly affects performance in the reductive statistics used to compare education at national and international level. UK governments have adopted what Gewirtz (2003: 7) describes as a 'hyper-rationalist engineering model', characterized by frequent assertions that 'what counts is what works'. Formative assessment packaged as AfL was seen as reducible to simple procedures which would 'work' in absolute and generalizable ways.

AfL was adopted as an official discourse with development sponsored by the government. AfL materials were produced and an official *Assessment for Learning Strategy* 'rolled out' across the country. In contrast to smaller development projects, the main text of the associated document (DCSF, 2008) took a simplistic view of AfL. It seemed to include both summative and formative assessment,

talking of 'rigorously monitoring all pupils' progress' (p. 4) and stressing ideas such as 'accuracy, fairness and reliability' (p. 5). AfL was presented as a straightforward technology governed by a set of rules applicable to any learning situation in order to create improvement. A more nuanced view was not totally absent but appeared only in the Annex, where AfL emerged as a more complex set of interactions, which teachers and learners needed to explore in different contexts.

Meanwhile formative assessment/assessment for learning had become not just a British phenomenon. Its development in the USA was strongly influenced by and aligned with British work at a theoretical level (Shepard, 2000; Stiggins and Chappuis, 2005). However, as Shepard (2005) notes, it came at a bad time, when there was an increasing emphasis on accountability and standards-based testing. This has resulted in mechanistic interpretations of formative assessment at the level of practice, where it has been strongly associated with the plethora of commercial, interim and benchmark tests. Similar accountability pressures influenced its adoption in Australia (Klenowski, 2011).

In contrast to English-speaking countries, in French-speaking countries the development of formative assessment has actually received somewhat less attention in recent years. This is partly because the extension of formative assessment as a concept and a way of developing pedagogic practice took place rather earlier, and through the work of researchers such as Allal (1988) and Perrenoud (1998). The notion of formative assessment was linked to and has subsequently to a certain extent been overtaken by the idea of *régulation* – usually translated, though possibly not fortuitously, as regulation (Allal and Mottier Lopez, 2005). This notion was to emphasize the idea that the point of formative assessment is not to perform a set of techniques but to have a dynamic effect on, that is to regulate, both teaching and learning and thus be formative in the sense mentioned above by Black and Wiliam (1998a); also it keys in with psychological ideas such as that of the self-regulated learner (Boekaerts and Corno, 2005).

Elsewhere in the world, the emergence of formative assessment as a way of conceptualizing a potentially very powerful approach to part of the teaching and learning process has been slower but continues to gain ground. There have been several major international studies of formative assessment in developed countries (OECD, 2005; Shute, 2008) and the term now features in the many new national competence-based curricula that are being introduced in the Global South (Chisholm and Leyendecker, 2008). Formative assessment has also been embraced by further and higher education sectors (e.g. Ecclestone, 2002; Knight and Yorke, 2003; Nicol and Macfarlane-Dick, 2006; Torrance et al., 2005).

However, at the same time as the success of formative assessment/AfL as a policy discourse was gathering momentum, doubt was also beginning to be expressed. Some of this involved questioning its instrumental effectiveness. An article by Smith and Gorard (2005) suggested that in the school where they conducted research comparing an AfL group with a control group, it was the latter which performed better, leading them to claim that the wider application of AfL 'can lead, inadvertently, to student and school disimprovement' (Smith and Gorard, 2005: 37). Black et al. (2005) responded that in the school in question there was no evidence that, despite this school's embrace of AfL, any formative assessment had actually taken place. Their definition was reiterated by Black and Wiliam (2009: 9), who held that assessment was only formative:

> to the extent that evidence about student achievement is elicited, interpreted, and used by teachers, learners, or their peers, to make decisions about the next steps in instruction that are likely to be better, or better founded, than the decisions they would have taken in the absence of the evidence that was elicited.

A recent US-based review by Bennett (2011: 5) also claims that 'the magnitude of commonly made quantitative claims for effectiveness is suspect, deriving from untraceable, flawed,

dated or unpublished sources'. Torrance (2007) suggests that research reviews have established that formative assessment can improve learning and achievement, not that it will.

Other critics, most prominent amongst them researchers involved in its development, have focused on the reductive or instrumental application of AfL, whose 'spirit' is misunderstood (Marshall and Drummond, 2006). This has led to some of its original proponents in the UK distancing themselves from Assessment for Learning, preferring again the original term, formative assessment. Conversely Swaffield (2011) makes a number of distinctions between Assessment for Learning and formative assessment, mainly concerned with applying the former to activities embedded more closely in classroom interactions and with the learning moment, while seeing the latter as having a longer time scale and being more focused on the use of testing. She uses this distinction to show that AfL has become confused with the formal aspects of formative assessment and has been misappropriated in official UK sources.

Much of the academic criticism derives from empirical studies of formative assessment in different contexts. Contrary to the claim in OECD (2005) that what is most problematic is the lack of connection between systemic, school and classroom approaches to assessment, these suggest that teachers are all too well attuned to the instrumental view of formative assessment and its focus on criteria compliance. Early work of my own with Harry Torrance (Torrance and Pryor, 1998) found that despite some adherence to constructivist understandings of learning, behaviourist assumptions remained important for primary school teachers and behaviourist practices were their default position. This involved specifying objectives and assessment criteria and providing feedback that was ostensibly transparent, but which very often in the context of child-centred intentions was not so clear, about how their work met with prescribed criteria. Highlighting the gap between desired and actual performance to reinforce desired behaviour was all part of this.

After over a decade of developmental work on formative assessment, Crossouard (2011) describes something similar. Although the tasks which they were setting were part of an innovation on authentic and contextualized learning, teachers in her Scottish research were carrying out formative assessment in terms of identifying 'specific observable behaviours', and formative assessment was a 'technique' to be applied (Crossouard, 2012: 900). Returning to the teachers in the Smith and Gorard (2005) case one might conclude that their assumptions of the process were also consistent with the expectation of AfL as a simple technology. Similar observations have been made in other school-based research (e.g. Hargreaves, 2012, 2013; Hume and Coll, 2009; Swaffield, 2011). Indeed Hume and Coll take up Torrance's (2007) notion derived from work in further education that formative assessment as practised is less assessment *for* learning than assessment *as* learning. Here 'transparency of objectives, coupled with extensive use of coaching and practice to help learners meet them' means that assessment procedures and practices may come completely to dominate the learning experience, and 'criteria compliance' comes to replace 'learning' (Torrance et al., 2005: 10).

The assumption that formative assessment is always benign has also been called into question. A central claim of Torrance and Pryor (1998: 167) was that

all assessment practices will have an impact on pupils' learning, but that this impact can be negative as well as positive ... [as] the inter-relation of teaching, learning and assessment is not a set of procedures that can be unilaterally invoked by teachers, but a social interaction which takes place between them and their pupils.

This is echoed in other work (e.g. Elwood, 2006; Hargreaves et al., 2002) and is taken up in more detail in Torrance's (2012) notion of 'deformative assessment' and in Crossouard's (2012) account of pupils' mortification. Ball et al.'s (2012: 518) study of assessment in secondary schools makes a similar point, describing AfL as part of an infrastructure of technical methods driving the 'totalising and individualising of performance'. What these analyses are highlighting is that within assessment for learning, power relations are at play and formative effects are neither purely cognitive nor necessarily those intended by policy makers or teachers.

THEORY FOR FORMATIVE ASSESSMENT

The development of formative assessment was supposed to involve a paradigm shift (Gipps, 1994), but it is clear that this has not occurred. It would be wrong to claim development work on formative assessment has been inspired by behaviourism. Almost all those involved have explicitly rejected this approach and indeed much emphasis has been placed on social constructivism, with learning in formative assessment seen as a joint activity. However, formative assessment exists as an idea and as a set of practices within the lifeworld of schooling and education and the people who participate in it. As such it is implicated in issues of knowledge, reality and power, how these are construed and enacted and what theory is at stake. The policy focus on formative assessment as an instrumental means to achieve the specified outcomes of outcomes-based curricula has conspired with the familiarity and safety of behaviourist approaches. As a result the theory which seems to animate teachers' and learners' practices is problematic. Elwood (2006: 230) points out that, even within more constructivist understandings, learning is often conceptualized as something happening 'inside the head' of the student. She argues for a view of learning where learning cannot be viewed in isolation, as something that the student possesses and that formative assessment seeks to uncover:

assessment can only describe the relationship between the learner, the teacher and the assessment task in the social, historical and cultural context in which it is carried out. If we look to within the student for their learning we are looking in the wrong place. (Elwood, 2006: 230)

In response to Edwards's (2009) call for considering how theory matters in educational settings, Barbara Crossouard and I have pursued this question in some detail, in particular considering what a performative, rather than a representational, view of knowledge brings to the understanding and practice of formative assessment (see Crossouard and Pryor, 2012). Drawing on the work of Barad (2003, 2007) this defines knowledge as something that is performed in particular settings and therefore shifts attention to learning as the dynamics of the practices which produce knowledge. Barad (2003: 817) contends that 'reality is not composed of things-in-themselves or things behind-phenomena but "things"-in-phenomena'. That is phenomena are enacted in settings where there are arrangements of people and of things, what she calls apparatuses, and where the representation is part of the enactment (Edwards, 2009). With a background in physics, she uses the example of experiments on light where one configuration gives meaning to the notion of light as a wave, while another gives meaning to the notion of particle:

> The notions of 'wave' and 'particle' do not refer to inherent characteristics of an object that precedes its intra-action. *There are no such independently existing objects with inherent characteristics.* (Barad, 2003: 816, original emphasis)

Thus the contingencies of a particular setting and the interactions of people, or as Barad would have it, the intra-actions of the different elements that make up the apparatus, are what constitute reality. Barad (2003: 802) questions the separation of 'language' and 'things', and the 'unexamined habits of mind that grant language and other forms of representation more power in determining our ontologies than they deserve'.

Formative assessment considered in this light might potentially avoid the problems of representation that are almost necessarily implicated in summative assessment.[1] As its purpose is learning, the production of knowledge, it is concerned not with discovering an already existent knowledge in the heads of individuals but with bringing knowledge into existence. Formative assessment then becomes a dialogic encounter, a pedagogy of response, where knowledge is created by teachers responding to students and students responding to their responses. Moreover, it is no longer individualized, but is jointly accomplished by all those participating in the task at hand. Nevertheless, its local positioning does not remove it from institutional, social and disciplinary discourses, rather these are part of the setting, things in the phenomenon. Formative assessment here is dialogic, not only in the sense that it acknowledges the way that teachers and students are mutually engaged, but also in the Bakhtinian sense, whereby what is said and done is a response to what has already been said and done (Bakhtin 1981).[2] Thus, eschewing the separation of words from the materiality of things and people, we can focus on the productive nature of formative assessment encounters, 'how these bring into being particular material worlds' (Crossouard and Pryor, 2012: 253). By looking to produce knowledge within the task and the context rather than to identify it in individual students it thus avoids, in Elwood's (2006) words, looking in the wrong place.

A Model for Formative Assessment

This theoretical position opens up the possibility for an emergent model of formative assessment, which will now be described based on research and development which I have been involved with over the last twenty years. At the centre of this have been the ideas of convergent and divergent assessment. These were developed initially as categories from empirical observation in early years classrooms but have subsequently been invoked in diverse educational settings from primary schools through to doctoral education (Pryor and Crossouard, 2008, 2010; Torrance and Pryor, 1998, 2001). Rather than always being discrete categories they can be seen as ideal types at different ends of a spectrum of practice, which are constantly in tension.

Convergent assessment is about the student being able to do a specific thing in a specified way. It involves a response that relates to normative 'official' criteria with a primary concern to address the 'relay of the curriculum' (Crossouard and Pryor, 2012). It is initiated and controlled by the teacher posing closed questions and tasks where there is clearly, for the teacher, a single or very limited range of correct responses. This means that there is a tight focus for observation with teachers able to note and to act on the achievement of objectives via a literal or mental checklist. They give feedback that is authoritative, judgmental or quantitative, and errors can be contrasted with correct responses leading to a range of suggestions for improvement. Successful convergent assessment will seem to have taken place on completion of a task in hand in ways which comply with the normative criteria. In this account the notion of compliance and 'relay' demonstrates the resilience of representationalism, even when the unknowability of responses to convergent assessment has been considered and a performative understanding of signification is attempted (see Pryor and Crossouard (2010) for examples).

At the other pole is divergent assessment where the point of departure is a more open concern with what students can do. Responses are much more overtly dialogic in form and are often couched in language that more nearly approximates to conversation, unlike convergent questions where the questioner 'knows' the answer they require. Feedback may be provisional, exploratory or provocative, prompting further engagement where disagreement may be seen as a means of opening debate and prompting thinking rather than correcting errors. Divergent assessment may also be initiated by students as well as teachers.

In empirical work in various settings both types have been noted, though generally it is convergent assessment which dominates and an exclusive reliance on the convergent would characterize the kind of instrumental, criteria-compliant coaching that has been

critiqued above. Indeed when these categories are invoked in critical work, particularly in the context of developing 'autonomous' learners, it is frequently to indicate the necessity of the divergent for good formative assessment (see for example, Hargreaves, 2013; Yorke, 2003). However, to see convergent as bad and divergent as good is not helpful. Nevertheless, in order for assessment interactions to be most formative in ways that are intended and positive for the student, they need to be seen as more than a means to accomplish the task in hand, which involves thinking about, reflecting on and understanding their 'regulative' purpose. This may in part be a cognitive issue, which metacognitive 'thinking about thinking' questions address. However, if we see learning as a jointly achieved social performance, it is critically about gaining a social understanding of how what is going on the classroom produces the knowledge at hand and how this relates to and is produced by wider discourses.

Divergent formative assessment obviously is therefore necessary to open up opportunities for these questions to be addressed and indeed allows the possibility of difference amongst students in their responses. It also signals a teacher's interest in and acceptance of diversity within a teaching group. However, with a totally divergent approach the official, public criteria would be missing, and thus this discursive meta-perspective would not be available. Movement then is needed *between* the convergent – what is normatively valued, and the divergent – what is valued by students in this situation. The best possibilities for dialogue, where teachers and students might address the sociological problems of learning, and problematize and clarify the social rules which govern the learning context, are offered then by a combination of the convergent and divergent. This enables formative assessment to aim for much more than just the highlighting and removing the gap between the students' knowledge and curricular criteria; it becomes a means to 'explore and exploit the gaps between teacher and student, and between students' present and developing understanding through pedagogic action, so that learners come to understand what are the issues at stake, and what learning means for them' (Torrance, 2007: 333–4).

Instead of formative assessment being a technique, which can be used instrumentally to prompt a specified response to curriculum content, it involves a more explicit recognition of the teacher's position and the educational context in their dialogue with students. It brings a social and political dimension to formative assessment. Moreover, rather than separating the knowing subject from knowledge, the positionality of teacher and students and the particular spaces of their interactions become salient. This brings with it an invocation of issues of identity and marks a move from an epistemological understanding of learning as knowledge that is acquired and individually possessed, to an ontological one, which emphasizes its performative nature, whereby knowledge has to be brought constantly into being.

This in turn has implications for when and where formative assessment takes place and for the design of tasks where there are relational spaces available. Although formative assessment may also take place opportunistically it cannot be assumed that sufficient opportunities for response will occur spontaneously. Teachers' curriculum planning will need to make suitable spaces for them. Tasks are needed that allow for connected encounters rather than discrete learning units, so that both the *nature* of the task and its *structuring* allow opportunities for engagement with wider disciplinary and institutional structures. What this looks like in practice will clearly depend on a number of factors including the subject area and the age and level of the students. Examples of this in a higher education context are given in some detail in Pryor and Crossouard (2010)[3] where an assessment task involving methodological reflections on the process of developing a research proposal and the piloting of a research instrument afforded students opportunities to experience and reflect upon the processes of conducting research. However, similar opportunities can occur with younger students where work goes

through stages of preparation and drafting before being finalized, with opportunities for response in between (see Crossouard (2009) for further consideration at primary school level[4]). However, it is not only a question of the sequencing of a series of procedures or activities, but also of enabling relational spaces, considering their temporal, spatial and social dimensions.

This will involve building in both convergent and divergent opportunities at a collective, class or group level whereby the dominant pattern of teacher-initiated discourse is extended to one where students are encouraged to bring forward issues from the task in hand. Students respond to the task and the process of accomplishing it and the teacher then responds to students. What occurs is not completely predictable, but will be strongly relevant to students' concerns. The actual accomplishment of this will inevitably be demanding within almost all educational settings, for it requires a teacher to respond in a way that both opens up and closes down; they constantly need to make nice judgements about which type of response to use.

When we talk about the formative purpose of these interactions, the intention is that learning takes place and that knowledge is created. However this goes beyond the practical and procedural completion of the task in hand to wider discursive and existential issues. Figure 20.1 shows an expanded version of what these formative purposes might entail. Teachers and students move up and down the diagram. Interaction in-the-moment involving commenting on and completing the task is at the top. Here formative assessment makes connections with summative criteria, both specific and more general. Students' and teachers' interactions are strongly framed by the task which needs to be accomplished.

Though it is important for formative assessment to consider longer-term prospective and reflective agendas, it cannot focus exclusively on them, so in terms of frequency and length of time, the concrete and reflective elements higher in the table are always likely to predominate. Nevertheless, the argument in this chapter

Joint activity		Response category	Description
Completing the task in hand	↓↑	How can I/we get this done?	Concrete/procedural
	↓↑	How can I get this done well?	
Thinking about improvement	↓↑	How might I do this better	
	↓↑	How did I do that?	
	↓↑	What does better mean?	Reflective/discursive
Making sense of criteria	↓↑	Who decides that?	
	↓↑	Why do they think it is better?	
	↓↑	How does this relate to power issues?	
Invoking learner identities	↓↑	How am I implicated in this?	
	↓↑	How does this relate to my identities (past present and future)?	Discursive/Existential
	↓↑	Who am I? Who do I wish to be?	

Figure 20.1   Expanded purposes of formative assessment

Source: Pryor and Crossouard (2010: 270)

stresses the importance of the lower elements, so that rather than the formative assessment task being the sole end, it potentially also becomes a means to access deeper discursive and existential issues. These will include responses which invite or provoke students into considering their activity in relation to questions of power: the ways of being, thinking and doing that are privileged in their particular institutional context and how this relates to a wider regulative or disciplinary order.

Beyond this 'meta-social' discourse is the possibility to relate this to their own received or desired identities. These moves may be explicitly invoked less frequently during teaching and learning, and may often remain tacit, but they are powerful for students, and feature strongly in accounts of the learning that is important to them (Pryor and Crossouard, 2010; Whitelock et al., 2008). This is not to suggest that fundamental ontological issues for the learner could or should be constantly raised by formative assessment, nor indeed that the teachers' intention should be either to confirm or destabilize student identities. However, within formative assessment as dialogic pedagogy it is about acknowledging the affective nature of learning and assessment and of opening up possibilities for students to respond at this level.

CONCLUSION

The notion of formative assessment as a technology which can be applied to students has an obvious attraction, for no matter how sophisticated the techniques might become, the approach has a simplicity and familiarity. It assumes that language is separate from but directly signifies the material world so that formative assessment can seek and transparently comment on stable knowledge. I have argued that this assumption tied to an instrumental view of formative assessment as a technique means that it cannot do what its proponents claim for it – to be an assessment for learning. Instead I have argued that a performative approach to learning, which recognizes knowledge as both epistemological and ontological is a starting point for a model of formative assessment, based around a dialogic pedagogy of convergent and divergent response. Bringing this about in the classroom is not to be underestimated, as it demands much from teachers and runs counter to what is familiar to them. Whereas they may be coerced into applying a technology, such an approach would be neither desirable nor possible in this case. However, the main conclusion of earlier work with teachers which has influenced this analysis, was that one can interact with teachers and engage with their premises about learning and teaching, education and social justice (Torrance and Pryor, 2001). This may begin a process which leads to more responsive encounters that are in tune with a performative notion of knowledge and learning and begin to fulfil the promise of formative assessment.

ACKNOWLEDGEMENTS

Much of my thinking and discussion on formative assessment has taken place with my collaborators, initially Harry Torrance and in recent years Barbara Crossouard. Although they were not involved in the actual writing of this chapter, their influence on it has been great.

NOTES

1 Generally speaking summative assessment is about taking a performance as representative for standing for a competence. Even in 'performance assessments' such as a practical driving test what happens on the day is considered indicative of a more generalized experience and it is on this basis that certification is given – though it is often recognized to be problematic.
2 For recent noteworthy applications of Bakhtin's ideas to educational settings, see Cuenca (2011) and Sutherland (2013).
3 This section draws strongly on this text which gives further specific examples.
4 A good example of this kind of structuring in a US first grade class is shown on YouTube (https://www.youtube.com/watch?v=hqh1MRWZjms).

REFERENCES

Allal, L. (1988) 'Vers un élargissement de la pédagogie de la maîtrise: processus de régulation interactive, rétroactive et proactive', in M. Huberman (ed.) *Assurer la réussite des apprentissages scolaires, Les propositions de la pédagogie de maîtrise* (pp. 86–126), Paris: Delachaux et Niestlé.

Allal, L. and Mottier Lopez, L. (2005) 'Formative evaluation of learning: a review of publications in French', in: Organization for Economic Co-operation and Development, *Formative Assessment Improving Learning in Secondary Classrooms: Improving Learning in Secondary Classrooms* (pp. 241–64), Paris: OECD.

Bakhtin, M. (1981) *The Dialogic Imagination: Four Essays by M.M. Bakhtin*, Austin, TX: University of Texas Press.

Ball, M., Maguire, M., Braun, M., Perryman, J. and Hoskins, K. (2012) 'Assessment technologies in schools: "deliverology" and the "play of dominations"', *Research Papers in Education*, 27(5): 513–33.

Barad, K. (2003) 'Posthumanist performativity: toward an understanding of how matter comes to matter', *Signs, Journal of Women in Culture and Society*, 28(3): 801–31.

Barad, K. (2007) *Meeting the Universe Halfway*, Durham: Duke University Press.

Bennett, R. (2011) 'Formative assessment: a critical review', *Assessment in Education: Principles, Policy and Practice*, 18(1): 5–25.

Black, P. and Wiliam, D. (1998a) 'Assessment and classroom learning', *Assessment in Education. Principles, Policy and Practice*, 5(1): 7–73.

Black, P. and Wiliam, D. (1998b) *Inside the Black Box: Raising Standards through Classroom Assessment*, London: Kings College.

Black, P. and Wiliam, D. (2003) '"In praise of educational research": formative assessment', *British Educational Research Journal*, 29(5): 623–37.

Black, P. and Wiliam, D. (2009) 'Developing the theory of formative assessment', *Educational Assessment, Evaluation and Accountability*, 21(1): 5–31.

Black, P., Harrison, C., Hogden, J., Marshall, B. and Wiliam, D. (2005) 'Dissemination and evaluation: a response to Smith and Gorard', *Research Intelligence*, 93(7).

Bloom, B., Hastings, J. and Madaus, G. (1971) *Handbook on Formative and Summative Evaluation of Student Learning*, New York: McGraw-Hill.

Boekaerts, M. and Corno, L. (2005) 'Self-regulation in the classroom: a perspective on assessment and intervention', *Applied Psychology: An International Review*, 54(2): 199–231.

Brookhart, S. (2005) *Research on Formative Classroom Assessment: State-of-the-Art,*

Paper given at the Annual Meeting of the American Educational Research Association, Montreal, Canada.

Chisholm, L. and Leyendecker, R. (2008) 'Curriculum reform in post-1990s sub-Saharan Africa', *International Journal of Educational Development*, 28(2): 195–205.

Crooks, T. (2011) 'Assessment for learning in the accountability era: New Zealand', *Studies in Educational Evaluation*, 37(1): 71–7.

Crossouard, B. (2009) 'A sociocultural reflection on collaborative challenges and formative assessment in the states of Jersey', *Research Papers in Education*, 24 (1): 77–93.

Crossouard, B. (2011) 'Supporting complex learning in conditions of social adversity: formative assessment in collaborative challenges', *Assessment in Education: Principles, Policy and Practice*, 18(1): 59–72.

Crossouard, B. (2012) 'Pupil mortification: digital photography and identity construction in classroom assessment', *British Journal of Sociology of Education*, 33(6): 893–911.

Crossouard, B. and Pryor, J. (2012) 'How theory matters: formative assessment theory and practices and their different relations to education', *Studies in Philosophy and Education*, 31(3): 251–63.

Cuenca, A. (2010) 'Democratic means for democratic ends: the possibilities of Bakhtin's dialogic pedagogy for social studies', *The Social Studies*, 102(1): 42–8.

DCSF (2008) *The Assessment for Learning Strategy*, London: DCSF.

Ecclestone, K. (2002) *Learning Autonomy in Post-16 Education: The Policy and Practice of Formative Assessment*, London: RoutledgeFalmer.

Edwards, R. (2009) *Materialising Theory: Does Theory Matter?* Paper presented in Keynote Symposium on 'The Theory Question in Education' at the Annual Meeting of the British Educational Research Association, University of Manchester, 2–6 September.

Elwood, J. (2006) 'Formative assessment: possibilities, boundaries and limitations', *Assessment in Education: Principles, Policy and Practice*, 13(2): 215–32.

Gewirtz, S. (2003) *Enlightening the Research–Policy Relationship: Issues and Dilemmas for Educational Researchers*, Paper presented at the European Conference on Educational Research, Hamburg, September.

Gipps, C. (1994) *Beyond Testing: Towards a Theory of Educational Assessment*, London: Falmer Press.

Hargreaves, A., Earl, L. and Schmidt, M. (2002) 'Perspectives on alternative assessment reform', *American Educational Research Journal*, 39(1): 69–95.

Hargreaves, E. (2012) 'Teachers' classroom feedback: still trying to get it right', *Pedagogies: An International Journal*, 7(1): 1–15.

Hargreaves, E. (2013) 'Inquiring into children's experiences of teacher feedback: reconceptualising Assessment for Learning', *Oxford Review of Education*, 39(2): 229–46.

Hume, A. and Coll, R.K. (2009) 'Assessment of learning, for learning, and as learning: New Zealand case studies', *Assessment in Education: Principles, Policy and Practice*, 16(3): 269–90.

Klenowski, V. (2011) 'Assessment for learning in the accountability era: Queensland, Australia', *Studies in Educational Evaluation*, 37(1): 78–83.

Knight, P.T. and Yorke, M. (2003) *Assessment, Learning and Employability*, Maidenhead: Society for Research into Higher Education and the Open University Press.

Marshall, B. and Drummond, M.J. (2006) 'How teachers engage with Assessment for Learning: lessons from the classroom', *Research Papers in Education*, 21(2): 133–49.

Nicol, D.J. and Macfarlane-Dick, D. (2006) 'Formative assessment and self-regulated learning: a model and seven principles of good feedback practice', *Studies in Higher Education*, 31(2): 199–218.

Organisation for Economic Co-operation and Development (OECD) (2005) *Formative Assessment Improving Learning in Secondary Classrooms: Improving Learning in Secondary Classrooms*, Paris: OECD.

Perrenoud, P. (1998) 'From formative evaluation to a controlled regulation of learning processes: towards a wider conceptual field', *Assessment in Education, Principles, Policy and Practice*, 5(1): 85–102.

Pryor, J. and Crossouard, B. (2008) 'A sociocultural theorisation of formative assessment', *Oxford Review of Education*, 34(1): 1–20.

Pryor, J. and Crossouard, B. (2010) 'Challenging formative assessment – disciplinary spaces and identities', *Assessment and Evaluation in Higher Education*, 35(3): 265–76.

Sadler, D.R. (1989) 'Formative assessment and the design of instructional systems', *Instructional Science*, 18: 119–44.

Scriven, M. (1967) 'The methodology of evaluation', in R. Tyler, R. Gagné and M. Scriven (eds) *Perspectives on Curriculum Evaluation*, Chicago: Rand McNally.

Shepard, L. (2000) 'The role of assessment in a learning culture', *Educational Researcher*, 29(7): 4–14.

Shepard L (2005) 'Formative assessment: caveat emptor', Keynote address, ETS Invitational Conference, The Future of Assessment: Shaping Teaching and Learning, New York, October. Accessed online 30/11/11 at http://www.csai-online.com/sites/default/files/resource/imported/shepard%20formative%20assessment%20caveat%20emptor.pdf

Shute, V. (2008) 'Focus on formative feedback', *Review of Educational Research*, 78: 153–89.

Smith, E. and Gorard, S. (2005) '"They don't give us our marks": the impact of formative assessment techniques in the classroom', *Assessment in Education*, 12(1): 21–38.

Stiggins, R. and Chappuis, J. (2005) 'Student-involved Classroom Assessment to close achievement gaps', *Theory into Practice,* 44(1): 11–18.

Sutherland, J. (2013) 'Going "meta": using a metadiscoursal approach to develop secondary students' dialogic talk in small groups', *Research Papers in Education*, DOI: 10.1080/02671522.2013.850528.

Swaffield, S. (2011) 'Getting to the heart of authentic Assessment for Learning', *Assessment in Education: Principles, Policy and Practice*, 184: 433–49.

Task Group on Assessment and Testing (TGAT) (1987) *A Report*, London: Department of Education and Science.

Torrance, H. (2007) 'Assessment *as* learning? How the use of explicit learning objectives, assessment criteria and feedback in post-secondary education and training can come to dominate learning', *Assessment in Education: Principles, Policy & Practice*, 14(3): 281–94.

Torrance, H. (2012) 'Formative assessment at the crossroads: conformative, deformative and transformative assessment', *Oxford Review of Education*, 38(3): 323–42.

Torrance, H. and Pryor, J. (1998) *Investigating Formative Assessment: Teaching, Learning and Assessment in the Classroom*, Buckingham: Open University Press.

Torrance, H. and Pryor, J. (2001) 'Developing formative assessment in the classroom: using action research to explore and modify theory', *British Educational Research Journal*, 27(5): 615–31.

Torrance, H., Colley, H., Ecclestone, K., Garratt, D., James, D., Jarvis, J. and Piper, H. (2005) *The Impact of Different Modes of Assessment on Achievement and Progress in the Learning and Skills Sector*, London: Learning and Skills Research Centre.

Whitelock, D., Faulkner, D. and Miell, D. (2008) 'Promoting creativity in PhD supervision: tensions and dilemmas', *Thinking Skills and Creativity*, 3(2): 143–53.

Yorke, M. (2003) 'Formative assessment in higher education: moves towards theory and the enhancement of pedagogic practice', *Higher Education*, 45(4): 477–501.

21

Professional Development in Dialogic Teaching: Helping Teachers Promote Argument Literacy in Their Classrooms

Alina Reznitskaya and Ian Wilkinson

INTRODUCTION

The demands placed on teachers of every grade level today far exceed instructing students in basic skills and knowledge. From major policy documents in the US, academic publications and popular press, we read that teachers must prepare their students to make well-reasoned judgments about complex, open-ended problems (Goodnough, 2010; Kuhn, 2010; Lipman, 2003; National Governors Association Center for Best Practices and the Council of Chief State School Officers, 2010; Partnership for 21st Century Skills, 2012; Postman, 1995). The latest Common Core State Standards Initiative in the US, for example, places heavy emphasis on the development of students' argumentation skills, explaining that students must learn to 'think critically and deeply, assess the validity of their own thinking, and anticipate counterclaims in opposition to their own assertions' (National Governors Association Centre for Best

Practices and the Council of Chief State School Officers, 2010: 24).

These are commendable goals, and they require new approaches to instruction. Fortunately, there is now strong theory, as well as sufficient research, to inform us about pedagogically productive ways to support the development of students' argumentation (e.g. Alexander, 2006; Lipman, 2003; Reznitskaya et al., 2009; Soter et al., 2008; Wegerif et al., 1999; Wells, 1999). In this chapter, we describe one approach to instruction – *dialogic teaching* – that capitalizes on the power of talk to further students' thinking, understanding and problem solving (Alexander, 2006; Burbules, 1993; Mercer and Dawes, 2008). In dialogic teaching, teachers are aware of different patterns of classroom discourse and can strategically choose ways of organizing instruction to meet specific pedagogical goals.

This chapter describes the use of dialogic teaching in upper-elementary language arts classrooms in the US, with the goal of advancing teachers' knowledge, skills, and disposition in argumentation and, ultimately, students' argument literacy. Following Graff (2003), we define *argument literacy* as the ability to comprehend and formulate arguments through speaking, listening, reading and writing. When working on the goal of supporting the development of argument literacy, teachers use the discussions of assigned readings to engage students in a special kind of talk, called *inquiry dialogue*. During inquiry dialogue, students take part in discussions of complex, contestable questions raised by the texts they read. They are expected to take on responsibility for instructional functions traditionally reserved for the teacher, such as managing participation and evaluating answers.

Following Walton (1992), we distinguish inquiry dialogue from other dialogue types, such as negotiation or persuasion. For example, persuasion dialogue is focused on convincing someone to accept a given position, whereas inquiry dialogue is a collaborative attempt to reach a sound conclusion (Walton and Macagno, 2007). This difference in goals is important because it affects normative protocols (i.e. rules of what is considered appropriate in the dialogue), the standards used to evaluate the strength of proposed arguments, and the pedagogical approaches to teaching argumentation (Nussbaum and Ordene, 2011; Walton, 1992).

The use of inquiry dialogue requires practitioners to move away from the centuries-old role of 'a sage on the stage' and become skilful facilitators of a collaborative and rigorous intellectual engagement.

> To invite students to articulate and explore their ideas … is to require that teachers hear those ideas, diagnose their virtues and weaknesses, and incorporate them into the substance of instruction … This is a new role for teachers whose practice has been defined by traditional goals and methods, and it comes with different and strenuous intellectual demands. (Hammer and Schifter, 2001: 442)

In fact, transitioning to this new role presents a serious challenge for new and experienced teachers (Alvermann and Hayes, 1989; Juzwik et al., 2012; Nguyen et al., 2007). For example, in a carefully planned study designed to improve classroom practices, researchers worked with practitioners for the period of six months, during which teachers took part in videotaped observations, reflection and planning conferences (Alvermann and Hayes, 1989). Regrettably, the authors concluded that teacher participants 'exhibited a marked stability in their patterns of verbal exchanges' and that the 'attempts to modify teacher and students' verbal exchange patterns were largely unsuccessful' (Alvermann and Hayes, 1989: 331). The difficulties with improving classroom instruction are also evident from numerous studies that show typical teacher practices to be generally unaffected by new educational goals that emphasize students' independent and critical thinking (Alexander, 2005; Nystrand et al., 2003; Smith et al., 2004). Instead of engaging students in argumentation about complex problems, teachers continue to dominate classroom discussions, avoid contestable issues, and require students 'to report on someone else's thinking rather than to think for themselves' (Alexander, 2008: 93).

In this chapter, we discuss our recent efforts to address the disparity between the advocated pedagogical approaches and the reality of typical classroom practices. First, we explain key principles of dialogic teaching, relating them to the goals of our professional development programme. Second, we discuss previous attempts to change teachers' discourse practices, situating our current project within the relevant literature on teacher learning and reviewing work on effective practices in professional development. Third, we describe a research programme designed to identify and evaluate instructional activities and materials that support teachers' knowledge and use of dialogic teaching to promote argumentation. We conclude with a description of general principles for professional development in dialogic teaching.

DIALOGIC TEACHING

Dialogic teaching is a general approach to instruction that centres around strategic use of classroom talk to support student learning (Alexander, 2008). It is consistent with social-constructivist theory that views language as fundamental to thinking and learning (Mercer and Littleton, 2007; Vygotsky, 1968; Wells, 1999). According to this theory, talk helps us to develop and organize our thoughts, to reason, to plan and to reflect on our actions. Vygotsky (1968), who emphasized the primacy of language in thinking, wrote that 'thought is not merely expressed in words; it comes into existence through them' (Vygotsky, 1968: 218).

In addition, learning is seen as a process of internalization of cultural tools, or ways of acting and thinking (Mercer and Littleton, 2007; Vygotsky, 1968; Wells, 1999). Students need to encounter or *use* these tools to develop their mental capacities. Language is the 'tool of tools' that not only helps us formulate our thoughts, but also fundamentally transforms individual cognition (Cole and Wertsch, 1996). During productive class discussions, students develop their cognitive capacities, as they internalize language practices from a social, external, plane to an individual, internal plane (Vygotsky, 1978). For instance, a student who says something vague during a dialogue with peers will at first only recognize that vagueness when someone else in the classroom community pushes her for clarification. Eventually, the student anticipates this reaction from her peers and self-edits her ideas before communicating them to the group. What began as interpersonal interaction becomes an intrapersonal cognitive habit.

Using language to interact with others also offers unique opportunities for a 'social mode of thinking' or 'interthinking' (Mercer and Littleton, 2007). That is, exchanging ideas in a public forum gives students a means for combining their intellectual resources to collectively make sense of their experiences and to solve problems. In a dialogic setting,

participants will spontaneously react to each other's ideas, adding detail to given reasons, qualifying general statements, or finding flaws in each other's arguments (Kennedy, 2013; Lipman et al., 1980). Thus, the multiplicity of voices in a dialogic discussion provides for a self-correcting mechanism that helps to improve the quality of argumentation.

It is important to note that, despite its name, dialogic teaching does not imply exclusive use of a dialogue in a classroom. Instead, it entails having a broad pedagogical repertoire of language patterns (Alexander, 2008; O'Connor and Michaels, 2007). Depending on specific instructional goals, teachers should be able to flexibly use different kinds of talk including recitation, exposition or discussion. At the same time, theory and research suggest that dialogic inquiry into complex questions is a type of classroom interaction that is well suited to support the development of higher-order thinking skills, such as argument literacy (Nystrand et al., 2003; Reznitskaya et al., 2009; Soter et al., 2008; Wegerif et al., 1999; Wells, 1999). Furthermore, it is now well-documented that discussions about contestable questions rarely happen in today's classrooms across school subjects, age levels, and national borders (Alexander, 2008; Applebee et al., 2003; Nystrand et al., 2003; Smith et al., 2004). Thus, while recognizing the importance of flexible language use in a classroom, our professional development programme largely focuses on helping teachers learn how to make their interactions with students more dialogic.

The use of inquiry dialogue requires teachers, and eventually their students, to develop views of knowledge and knowing that are congruent with this type of classroom practice (Kuhn and Udell, 2003; Windschitl, 2002). Specifically, participation in inquiry dialogue relies on an underlying commitment to rational thinking as a mechanism for formulating better judgments. Models of epistemological development suggest that people progress from a simple view of knowledge as static and known by authorities to a more nuanced understanding of knowledge as socially constructed through the use of reasoning (for review, see Hofer, 2001). Kuhn (1991) offers a useful classification of individual theories of knowledge, proposing three stages of development: absolutist, multiplist and evaluatist. Absolutists view knowledge as fixed, certain and existing independently of human cognition. Multiplists see knowledge as entirely subjective, denying the role of reason and expertise and considering all opinions to be equally valid. At the most advanced stage, evaluatists accept the subjective nature of knowledge, while also recognizing that we can engage in a rational evaluation of different viewpoints and, as a result, consider some judgments to be more reasonable than others.

Teachers who subscribe to an evaluatist epistemology are more likely to successfully use inquiry dialogue because they view knowledge as 'the product of a continuing process of examination, comparison, evaluation, and judgment of different, sometimes competing, explanations and perspectives' (Kuhn, 1991: 202). Supporting the important role of epistemology in teaching, research has shown that teachers' epistemological beliefs are typically aligned with their instruction, influencing power relations and interactional patterns between teachers and students (e.g. Johnston et al., 2001; Richardson et al., 1991; Sinatra and Kardash, 2004; Stipek et al., 2001). Notably, the relationship between beliefs and practices is not simple, as subscribing to more sophisticated ideas about knowledge and knowing may not always translate into effective use of dialogue-based practices during instruction (Alvermann et al., 1990; Schraw and Olafson, 2002). This is why we designed our professional development programme to help practitioners integrate theoretical, epistemological and practical understandings.

To illustrate the use of inquiry dialogue and review its key features, let us consider a short excerpt from a discussion in a fifth-grade classroom. The teacher in this excerpt participated in our professional development programme in dialogic teaching for a period of seven months. The students had read an article entitled 'Deadly Hits' about a boy named Zack, who was paralysed after getting a concussion during a football game. Students are discussing a question, 'Who is responsible for Zack's injury?'

Teacher:	So who would like to start us off this morning? Okay, Jerry.
Jerry:	Well, I think the one responsible for Zack's injury would be the coach, because he was the one who let Zack play when he shouldn't, because he knew that he already had an injury.
Andrew:	I disagree with Jerry because it actually said in the passage that Zack thought that his team needed help, so he decided to go in, 'cause the coach wasn't trained to find a concussion. So, he decided to go in on his own, without the coach telling him to. 'Cause the coach wasn't trained to see a concussion.
Lily:	I agree with Andrew because … you wouldn't let … If you know we got hurt and we insisted to go back into something like that, you would at least make sure that we're okay. And I think Zack's coach probably did that … I think Zack's coach probably made sure that he was okay, so it's not all of his fault. He as an adult should say 'No, maybe you could go back in next time'. But it's not only his fault.
Teacher:	So wait, how is that agreeing with Andrew? 'Cause Andrew says it's not the coach's fault, but you're …
Lily:	Yeah, I don't think it's the coach's fault either.
Teacher:	But you said, 'As an adult he should know'. I'm just … I want you to just clarify.
Lily:	Well okay, I agree with Andrew, like everything that he said, but it's not complete … Okay, I just agree with Andrew, like what he said. … The coach didn't say 'Zack, get back in here'. Zack wanted to and he went in on his own.
Kate:	I disagree with Jerry. I don't find that it's the coach's fault because in the paragraph it says they, the coaches weren't trained at that time to know what brain concussion looks like. 'Cause brain concussions are invisible injuries, it says it in this story, so, I don't find that it's the coach's fault and …

Jerry: But Zack was hurt …
Kate: Yeah, but he said he was all right, so how is the coach supposed to know?
Teacher: OK, so let's let him respond to that. They challenged you, right? So now let's let Jerry respond … We had a few challenges, so let's let Jerry maybe respond to that challenge, and maybe, I don't know …
Jerry: But if you see someone fall down very hard on their head and come back to the bench, saying that they're alright, the coach should know that they've been in an injury, and the coach should not let them play.

The discussion is centred on an open-ended, contestable question that does not have a single right answer. During the discussion, the teacher largely releases control over the flow of discourse to the students. We see students asking questions, self-nominating, and evaluating each other's answers. There are exchanges with consecutive student turns without teacher interruption. As students discuss their positions on the question of who is responsible for the injury, they provide elaborated explanations of reasoning behind their views and refer to story information for evidence. The teacher does not dominate the discussion, speaking less than the students. Her deliberately chosen questions serve to advance the inquiry further, as she asks students to clarify how their ideas connect with those of other group members ('So, wait, how is that agreeing with Andrew?') and encourages the discussion of an opposing perspective ('They challenged you, right? So now let's let Jerry respond').

The excerpt above demonstrates the demands placed on teachers and students in a more dialogic classroom. During inquiry dialogue, students need to work on two major goals: (1) to collaborate with each other, and (2) to engage in rigorous argumentation. When students are not achieving these goals independently, the role of the teacher is to intervene, to model and support good reasoning. Teacher contributions during the discussion change from telling students what to think to helping them improve their

thinking. In other words, teachers need to be 'procedurally strong, but substantively self-effacing' (Splitter and Sharp, 1996: 306). Instead of feeding students the right answers, they model and support effective use of talk to help students to co-reason together.

The focus on procedural teacher intervention used to improve student reasoning implies that practitioners need to understand the processes and criteria of quality argumentation (Hammer and Schifter, 2001; Splitter and Sharp, 1996). Moreover, teachers need to apply this understanding, reacting to student arguments as they are being developed – in real time – during the discussion. This is a challenging task that requires a sharp focus on discussion content, as well as the ability to track and analyse it:

> It takes a thoughtful teacher to set up the environment, to identify, model and coach, not just its reasoning moves, but its group rules and practices, to help it stay on-track and focused, and to work to provide just enough structure – not more and not less – for its own inherent structure to emerge … The teacher must learn – through paying careful and thorough attention to what children are saying – to recognize [the] reasoning moves in everyday language, and to feed that recognition back to her students. (Kennedy, 2013: 4)

To conclude, dialogic teaching requires that practitioners develop knowledge and skills that differ significantly from those that prevail in more traditional classrooms. First, teacher pedagogical and epistemic views need to be consistent with socio-constructivist theories and evaluatist perspectives that underlie dialogue-intensive practices (Windschitl, 2002). Second, teachers have to develop an awareness of different kinds of talk and use language flexibly and strategically in relation to given pedagogical goals. Third, for the purpose of promoting students' argument literacy through inquiry dialogue, teachers need to: (1) understand the processes and criteria of quality argumentation; (2) be able to recognize strengths and weakness in student reasoning; and (3) have a repertoire of moves to model and support good reasoning. These are ambitious goals that entail a serious transformation in beliefs and practices of many practitioners (Alexander, 2008; Nystrand et al., 2003; Windschitl, 2002). In the next section, we review previous research on teacher education and professional development and identify features that potentially support teachers' use of dialogue-intensive pedagogies.

CHANGING TEACHERS' DISCOURSE PRACTICES

There have been numerous efforts to help teachers make the transition to more dialogic discourse practices (see Murphy et al., 2011) and a few concerted attempts to systematically study the professional development needed to support them in that process (e.g., Adler et al., 2004; Michaels et al., 2008; Saunders and Goldenberg, 1996). The days of traditional one-shot professional development workshops have passed as it is now well documented that they seldom produce substantial or sustained shifts in teachers' practices (Cochran-Smith and Lytle, 1999; Englert and Tarrant, 1995). Indeed, there is an emerging consensus that effective professional development for teachers needs to, among other elements, be grounded in the daily lives of teachers, be intensive and sustained, involve the collective participation of teachers, and provide both conceptual and procedural knowledge about teaching and learning (Wei et al., 2009; Yoon et al., 2007). Dialogue-intensive pedagogies impose an additional order of complexity on teaching and learning, and the supports needed to help teachers make the transition to more dialogic practices are not so readily defined. In this section, we review the little that is known about professional development in dialogic teaching and related pedagogies.

We begin with the observation that engaging teachers in reflection on their discourse practices appears to be necessary but not sufficient for changing their practices. As noted previously, Alvermann and Hayes's (1989) efforts to improve the discussion practices of five high school teachers proved largely unsuccessful. Despite engaging teachers in repeated cycles of videotaped observations, reflection on the videos, and planning conferences over a six-month period, teachers' discourse practice remained essentially unchanged. In their conclusion, Alvermann and Hayes (1989: 333) noted that 'merely asking teachers to reflect upon entrenched patterns of classroom discussion is obviously insufficient to change those patterns'.

Subsequent professional development efforts to modify teachers' discourse practices have combined opportunities for reflection with more deliberate forms of co-inquiry into teachers' practices. For example, Kucan (2007, 2009) asked 12 teachers in a Masters-level methods course in reading comprehension to record, transcribe and analyse excerpts of their own discussions and then engaged the teachers in analysis of the transcripts. The categories used to code teachers' questions and responses, in conjunction with instruction in how to conduct discussion to foster students' comprehension of text, provided the impetus for teachers to make improvements, albeit modest, in their discourse practices. In a similar fashion, Juzwik and colleagues (Heintz et al., 2010; Juzwik et al., 2012) prompted teacher candidates in a secondary English teacher preparation course to reflect on videos of their teaching to help them engage in more dialogically organized instruction. The videos were posted to an online social networking site to enable teacher candidates to comment on each others' practices and to reflect on how they might implement the feedback they received from their peers and their instructors.

Other researchers of professional development have sought to arm teachers with a repertoire of discursive moves to enhance their discourse practices. Beck et al. (1996) trained teachers to implement Questioning the Author (QtA), an approach to conducting text-based discussion in social studies and language arts classes that focuses on having students grapple with what an author is trying to say to foster a more coherent understanding of the text. In QtA, the teacher poses *Queries* such as 'What is the author trying to say?', 'What do you think the author means by that?', or 'How does that connect with what the author already told us?' In later work, McKeown and Beck (2004) developed a set of 'Accessibles', one-page descriptions of pedagogical cases to support teachers' implementation of QtA. Similarly, Michaels and O'Connor (2015) identified a set of *talk moves* to help teachers facilitate substantive and rigorous discussions (e.g. 'Can you say more?', 'Why do you think that?'). These talk moves are conceptualized as tools to help teachers engage students in high-level thinking and reasoning. They provide the basis for professional development in Accountable Talk (Michaels et al., 2002, 2008), an approach to conducting academically productive discussions in various content areas (see also, Hillen and Hughes, 2008).

Still more ambitious attempts to change teachers' discourse practices have incorporated reflection, co-inquiry and discursive moves within a more expansive teacher-learning context. These efforts seem to have yielded more sustained shifts in teachers' discourse practices. Notable among these efforts are: Goldenberg and colleagues' professional development work with primary-grade language arts teachers to help them conduct Instructional Conversations (Goldenberg, 1993; Goldenberg and Gallimore, 1991; Saunders and Goldenberg, 1996; Saunders et al., 1992); Adler et al.'s (2004) work with middle school teachers to foster more dialogic discussions in their language arts classrooms; and Hennessy et al.'s (2011) work with teachers in various grades and content areas to help them adopt a more dialogic pedagogy when using interactive whiteboards. What distinguishes these professional development efforts from others is that they adhered to many of the principles known to characterize effective professional development. For example, the professional

development was firmly grounded in the realities of teachers' daily work, took place over an extended period of time (in some cases, involving a weekly meeting over a year), and helped teachers acquire both conceptual and procedural knowledge of the pedagogy. Another distinguishing feature was that researchers offered opportunities for teachers to co-plan lessons in meetings. These lessons provided the basis for subsequent co-inquiry and reflection through analysis of videos or transcripts. Yet another feature was that the process of co-inquiry was itself dialogic. For example, in Goldenberg's work, weekly meetings with teachers took on many of the qualities of Instructional Conversations; in Hennessy et al.'s work, the co-inquiry was dialogic inquiry (Wells, 1999) such that dialogue served as the central means by which teachers constructed their understanding of the new pedagogy.

In sum, research on professional development in dialogic pedagogy is relatively inchoate. Reflection on discourse through analysis of video and transcripts, teacher learning through a process of co-inquiry, and a focus on discursive moves to promote productive talk appear to be core features of most programmes. Providing opportunities for co-planning and using dialogic pedagogy as a vehicle for achieving professional development goals also seem to be important. These features helped to guide the design of our own professional development programme to support teachers' knowledge and use of dialogic teaching to promote students' argument literacy.

PROFESSIONAL DEVELOPMENT IN DIALOGIC TEACHING

Overview of a Dialogic Teaching Programme

We are currently working on a three-year project to design and evaluate a comprehensive professional development programme in dialogic teaching. The project is being conducted largely as a design study (Collins et al., 2004), during which we work collaboratively with teachers to identify and organize instructional content and activities that support teachers' use of dialogic teaching to promote argument literacy. Each year, we implement a version of the programme and collect data from teachers and students to assess programme effectiveness and inform its revisions. In other words, each year comprises a new iteration of the programme. At the time of writing, we are nearing the conclusion of the second year of the project.

Study participants came from school districts in two states in the US, Ohio and New Jersey. In Year 1, we worked with a total of ten Grade 5 teachers and their students (six in Ohio and four in New Jersey). In Year 2, 13 fifth-grade teachers participated at both sites (six in Ohio and seven in New Jersey). The teaching experience of participants ranged from two to 26 years.

First Year

The project in Year 1 was conducted in three stages: pre-testing, implementation of the professional development programme, and post-testing. During the pre-testing stage (September), we videotaped two discussions in each classroom to collect baseline information about typical teacher practices. We also interviewed teachers about their background and experience, as well as assessed their epistemological beliefs using the interview measure developed and validated by King and Kitchener (1994).

From October through May, we implemented our professional development programme. The programme included a variety of activities, such as study group meetings, focus group interviews and in-class coaching. All project activities were similar at both sites, but with some variations to test the viability and effects of different instructional approaches or sequences of approaches. During the post-testing period (May), we

again interviewed teachers about their epistemological beliefs. We also piloted measures designed to assess students' argument skills when speaking, reading, and writing to be used in subsequent years to evaluate programme effectiveness.

By the end of our first year, we had developed initial materials for the programme, such as PowerPoint slides, instructional activities, and videos for illustrating inquiry dialogue. We also collected data from multiple sources, including study group meetings, focus group interviews and coaching sessions. We conducted content analysis of the data to inform the revisions of the professional development programme for Year 2.

Second Year

In Year 2, the study was structured using the same three stages as in Year 1. The pre- and post-testing stages were identical to Year 1. However, stage two – the implementation of the professional development programme – was revised based on the data collected and analysed in Year 1. In Year 2, project activities were similar at both sites, with variation in materials and programme delivery methods only to accommodate specific needs of teachers at the two sites. The activities in Year 2 consisted of: (1) a two-day workshop; (2) eight study group meetings, including three focus-group interviews; and (3) six individual coaching sessions.

The programme in Year 2 began in October, with a two-day workshop on dialogic teaching, lasting approximately 12 hours in total. There was a short, one- to two-week interval between Day 1 and Day 2. After the first day of the workshop, we asked teachers to conduct inquiry dialogue with their students before the next meeting, and at least once per month through the rest of the academic year. The teachers conducted the discussions during language arts lessons, and we videotaped their discussions.

Following the two-day workshop, we met with teachers every two weeks in

November and December in teacher study groups. Starting in January, study group meetings were conducted once per month. Study groups lasted about two hours, totalling approximately 14 hours per year. During these study-group meetings, participants engaged in mini-lessons, collaboratively analysed transcripts and videos of classroom discussions, and took part in activities on topics related to dialogic teaching, inquiry dialogue and argumentation. Teachers also read and discussed several short digests that we wrote on these topics.

In addition to taking part in workshops and study groups, teachers received individual coaching in how to conduct discussions to promote argumentation. During these sessions, teachers viewed and critiqued their own classroom interactions with the help of an experienced discourse coach, who supported the teachers' on-going development and reflection. They also rated the quality of their discussion using a carefully researched observational rating scale. Another coaching activity was a demonstration of inquiry dialogue with fifth-grade students conducted by the discourse coach in the teachers' own classrooms. Each teacher participated in six coaching sessions, lasting about 30–40 minutes each.

Finally, during study group meetings in November, February and May, we conducted focus-group interviews with teacher participants. The purpose of these focus-group interviews was to identify what teachers found valuable (or not) in learning about dialogic teaching and argumentation. All workshops, study group meetings, focus-group interviews and coaching sessions were audio-recorded, transcribed, and analysed to inform revisions of the professional development programme.

Examples of Instructional Activities for Teachers

By the end of Year 2, we had identified key instructional priorities and related activities

of the professional development programme in dialogic teaching. Consistent with previous research on the classroom talk and related professional development efforts (Alexander, 2005; Alvermann et al., 1990; Mehan, 1998; Nystrand et al., 2003; Smith et al., 2004), our teachers needed considerable support with learning how to effectively facilitate inquiry dialogue in their classrooms. This is why the majority of instructional time in our programme was spent on helping teachers acquire the necessary skills and knowledge to become effective facilitators of inquiry dialogue. When designing the programme, we chose instructional activities that were themselves aligned with dialogic teaching and, more generally, with evaluatist epistemological perspectives and social-constructivist theories of learning. This was done in order to help teachers experience, and eventually adopt, classroom practices consistent with contemporary theories of knowledge construction.

An example of an instructional activity we used during our study-group meetings was debriefing. During this activity, teachers discuss the successes and challenges they have experienced with implementing inquiry dialogue in their classrooms. This created opportunities for collegial support, promoted teacher engagement, and allowed sharing of effective classroom practices among teachers. Thus, teachers were learning about dialogic teaching 'through social interaction around problems of practice' (Elmore, 2002: 17), a feature of professional development that is consistent with our approach to instruction and that supports teacher use of new instructional methods (Elmore, 2002; Wei et al., 2009).

Another effective practice that emerged in our professional development programme was co-planning. During co-planning, teachers collaboratively constructed an entire unit around a text to be read by their students (i.e. the 'Deadly Hits' article cited earlier). Teachers identified key topics or themes in the text and turned them into contestable questions to be used during inquiry dialogue (e.g. 'Who is responsible for Zack's injury?'). Next, teachers participated in inquiry dialogue, led by an expert facilitator. Being participants in the inquiry dialogue allowed teachers to explore central themes in a given student text on a deeper level, thus becoming more prepared to discuss the same text with their students. In addition, it enabled teachers to experience the rewards and demands of examining complex questions in a collaborative and structured environment, where each member was accountable for helping the group to reach the most reasonable judgment. As they engaged in inquiry dialogue, teachers adopted new roles and participation structures, and experimented with new discourse practices. Teachers also observed and reflected on the facilitation of the inquiry dialogue modelled by an expert.

In addition to participating in inquiry dialogue during co-planning, teachers collaboratively worked on designing pre-discussion and post-discussion activities around a given text. Pre-discussion activities were used to promote students' cognitive and affective engagement with the text. For example, before gathering for a discussion, students took notes about their reactions using post-it notes or selectively highlighted ideas in the text that resonated with them. On the other hand, the goal of post-discussion activities was to help students transfer the argument skills and dispositions learned in the group to their individual efforts in speaking, hearing, reading and writing arguments. For example, during a post-discussion activity students wrote a letter to a relevant party (e.g. the protagonist in a story) explaining their group's position on the issue.

As noted earlier, although dialogic teaching is centred on inquiry dialogue, it requires that teachers flexibly use multiple teaching strategies to help students develop and transfer their argument literacy skills. From observation and teacher feedback, we learned that engaging teachers in debriefing and co-planning was useful for helping them to acquire procedural knowledge about dialogic

teaching and to connect it to conceptual knowledge about the role of talk in learning. Co-planning also offered teachers a shared experience that they were able to take back to the classroom, thus grounding their learning in practice.

CONCLUSION

Informed by prior work in professional development and dialogic teaching, and our own ongoing study, we are developing a set of design principles to guide future iterations of our programme. The emerging principles include:

- Professional development in dialogic teaching should exemplify dialogic teaching. In particular, teachers should have multiple opportunities to engage in and be exposed to inquiry dialogue;
- Teachers should have multiple opportunities to reflect on their discourse practices through analysis of video and transcripts of discussions;
- Teachers' use of discourse-moves to promote argumentation is contingent on the quality of student arguments and should be taught in the context of an analysis of argumentation;
- Instruction should be situated in authentic activity and proceed from whole to part (e.g. co-planning provides a context for learning about pre- and post-discussion activities and orchestrating inquiry dialogue; inquiry dialogue provides a context for learning about parts of an argument);
- Connections to standards and curricular content for which teachers are responsible should be readily apparent.

As we have indicated, making the transition from teacher-dominated classroom practice to a more dialogic pedagogy requires a substantial shift in teachers' beliefs about knowledge construction and about the role of talk in learning. Research on professional development in dialogic pedagogy is not well developed, and it remains to be seen whether our current instantiation of these design principles is sufficient to support teachers in making the transition to dialogic teaching to promote argument literacy. Our analyses of videotaped discussions at the beginning and end of each year of our study suggest that teachers made substantial improvements in their facilitation of inquiry dialogue and in the quality of students' argumentation. Although our initial results are promising, considerable research remains to be done to identify and test innovative strategies to help practitioners learn about the theoretical, epistemological and procedural knowledge needed to successfully implement dialogic teaching in classroom settings.

REFERENCES

Adler, M., Rougle, E., Kaiser, E. and Caughlan, S. (2004) 'Closing the gap between concept and practice: Toward more dialogic discussion in the language arts classroom', *Journal of Adolescent and Adult Literacy*, 47(4): 312–22.

Alexander, R. J. (2005) *Culture, Dialogue and Learning: Notes on an Emerging Pedagogy*, Paper presented at the Conference of the International Association for Cognitive Education and Psychology, July, University of Durham, UK.

Alexander, R. J. (2006) *Towards Dialogic Teaching: Rethinking Classroom Talk* (3rd edn), York, UK: Dialogos.

Alexander, R. J. (2008) *Essays on Pedagogy*, New York: Routledge.

Alvermann, D. E. and Hayes, D. A. (1989) 'Classroom discussion of content area reading assignments: An intervention study', *Reading Research Quarterly*, 24: 305–35.

Alvermann, D. E., O'Brien, D. G. and Dillon, D. R. (1990) 'What teachers do when they say they're having discussions of content area reading assignments: A qualitative analysis'. *Reading Research Quarterly*, 25: 297–322.

Applebee, A. N., Langer, J. A., Nystrand, M. and Gamoran, A. (2003) 'Discussion-based approaches to developing understanding: Classroom instruction and student performance in middle and high school English',

American Educational Research Journal, 40(3): 685–730. DOI: 10.3102/00028312040003685.

Beck, I. L., McKeown, M. G., Sandora, C., Kucan, L. and Worthy, J. (1996) 'Questioning the author: A year-long classroom implementation to engage students with text', *The Elementary School Journal*, 96(4): 385–414.

Burbules, N. (1993) *Dialogue in Teaching: Theory and Practice*, New York: Teachers College Press.

Cochran-Smith, M. and Lytle, S. (1999) 'Relationship of knowledge and practice: Teacher learning in communities', in A. Iran-Nejad and P. D. Pearson (eds), *Review of Research in Education* (Vol. 24, pp. 249–306), Washington, DC: American Educational Research Association.

Cole, M. and Wertsch, J. V. (1996) 'Beyond the individual-social antimony in discussions of Piaget and Vygotsky', *Human Development*, 39: 250–6.

Collins, A., Joseph, D. and Bielaczyc, K. (2004) 'Design research: Theoretical and methodological issues', *Journal of the Learning Sciences*, 13: 15–42.

Elmore, R. F. (2002) *Bridging the Gap Between Standards and Achievement: The Imperative for Professional Development in Education*, Washington, DC: Albert Shanker Institute.

Englert, C. S. and Tarrant, K. L. (1995) 'Creating collaborative cultures for educational change', *Remedial and Special Education*, 16(6): 325–36.

Goldenberg, C. (1993) 'Instructional conversations: Promoting comprehension through discussion', *The Reading Teacher*, 46: 316–26.

Goldenberg, C. and Gallimore, R. (1991) 'Changing teaching takes more than a one-shot workshop', *Educational Leadership*, 49(3): 69–72.

Goodnough, A. (2010) 'The examined life, age 8', *The New York Times*.

Graff, G. (2003) *Clueless in Academe*, New Haven, CT: Yale University Press.

Hammer, D. and Schifter, D. (2001) 'Practices of inquiry in teaching and research', *Cognition and Instruction*, 19(4): 441–78.

Heintz, A., Borsheim, C., Caughlan, S., Juzwik, M. M. and Sherry, M. B. (2010) 'Video-based response and revision: Dialogic instruction using video and web 2.0 technologies',

Contemporary Issues in Technology and Teacher Education, 10(2): 175–96.

Hennessy, S., Mercer, N. and Warwick, P. (2011) 'A dialogic inquiry approach to working with teachers in developing classroom dialogue', *Teachers College Record*, 113(9).

Hillen, A. F. and Hughes, E. K. (2008) 'Developing teachers' abilities to facilitate meaningful classroom discourse through cases: The case of Accountable Talk', *AMTE Monograph 4, Cases in Mathematics Teacher Eduation: Tools for Developing Knowledge Needed for Teaching*, pp. 73–88.

Hofer, B. K. (2001) 'Personal epistemology research: Implications for learning and teaching', *Educational Psychology Review*, 13(4): 353–83. DOI: 10.1023/A:1011965830686.

Johnston, P., Woodside-Jiron, H. and Day, J. (2001) 'Teaching and learning literate epistemologies', *Journal of Educational Psychology*, 93(1): 223–33. DOI: 10.1037/0022-0663.93.1.223.

Juzwik, M. M., Sherry, M. B., Caughlan, S., Heintz, A. and Borsheim-Black, C. (2012) 'Supporting dialogically organized instruction in an English teacher preparation program: Video-based, web 2.0-mediated response and revision pedagogy', *Teachers College Record*, 114 (3): 1–42.

Kennedy, D. (2013) 'Developing philosophical facilitation: A toolbox of philosophical moves', in S. Goering, N. Shudak and T. Wartenberg (eds), *Philosophy in Schools: An Introduction for Philosophers and Teachers*, New York: Routledge.

King, P. M. and Kitchener, K. S. (1994) *Developing Reflective Judgment: Understanding and Promoting Intellectual Growth and Critical Thinking in Adolescents and Adults*, San Francisco, CA: Jossey-Bass.

Kucan, L. (2007) 'Insights from teachers who analyzed transcripts of their own classroom discussions', *The Reading Teacher*, 61(3): 228–36.

Kucan, L. (2009) 'Engaging teachers in investigating their teaching as a linguistic enterprise: The case of comprehension instruction in the context of discussion', *Reading Psychology*, 39: 51–87.

Kuhn, D. (1991) *The Skills of Argument*, Cambridge, UK: Cambridge University Press.

Kuhn, D. (2010) 'Teaching and learning science as argument', *Science Education*, 94(5): 810–24. DOI: 10.1002/sce.20395.

Kuhn, D. and Udell, W. (2003) 'The development of argument skills', *Child Development*, 74(5): 1245–60. DOI: 10.1111/1467-8624.00605.

Lipman, M. (2003) *Thinking in Education*, New York: Cambridge University Press.

Lipman, M., Sharp, A. M. and Oscanyon, F. S. (1980) *Philosophy in the Classroom*, Philadelphia, PA: Temple University Press.

McKeown, M. G. and Beck, I. L. (2004) 'Transforming knowledge into professional development resources', *Elementary School Journal*, 104(5): 391–408.

Mehan, H. (1998) 'The study of social interaction in educational settings: Accomplishments and unresolved issues', *Human Development*, 41(4), 245–69. DOI: 10.1159/000022586.

Mercer, N. and Dawes, L. (2008) 'The value of exploratory talk', in N. Mercer and S. Hodgkinson (eds), *Exploring Talk in School* (pp. 55–71), London: Sage.

Mercer, N. and Littleton, K. (2007) *Dialogue and the Development of Children's Thinking: A Socio-cultural Approach*, London: Routledge.

Michaels, S. and O'Connor, C. (in press) 'Conceptualizing talk moves as tools: Professional development approaches for academically productive discussion', in L. B. Resnick, C. Asterhan and S. N. Clarke (eds), *Socializing Intelligence through Talk and Dialogue* (pp. 347–362). Washington DC: American Educational Research Association.

Michaels, S., O'Connor, C. and Resnick, L. B. (2008) 'Deliberative discourse idealized and realized: Accountable Talk in the classroom and in civic life', *Studies in Philosophy and Education*, 27(4): 283–97.

Michaels, S., O'Connor, M. C., Hall, M. W. and Resnick, L. B. (2002) *Accountable Talk: Classroom Conversation that Works* (3 CD-ROM set), Pittsburgh, PA: University of Pittsburgh.

Murphy, P. K., Wilkinson, I. A. G. and Soter, A. O. (2011) 'Instruction based on discussion', in R. E. Mayer and P. A. Alexander (eds), *Handbook of Research on Learning and Instruction*, New York: Routledge.

National Governors Association Center for Best Practices and the Council of Chief State

School Officers (2010) *Common Core State Standards: Appendix A. Research Supporting Key Elements of the Standards.*

Nguyen, K., Anderson, R. C., Waggoner, M. and Rowel, B. (2007) 'Using literature discussions to reason through real life dilemmas: A journey taken by one teacher and her fourth-grade students', in R. Horowitz (ed.), *Talking Texts: Knowing the World through the Evolution of Instructional Discourse* (pp. 187–206). Hillsdale, NJ: Erlbaum Associates.

Nussbaum, E. M. and Ordene, V. (2011) 'Critical questions and argument stratagems: A framework for enhancing and analyzing students' reasoning practices', *Journal of the Learning Sciences*, 20(3): 443–88.

Nystrand, M., Wu, L., Gamoran, A., Zeiser, S. and Long, D. A. (2003) 'Questions in time: Investigating the structure and dynamics of unfolding classroom discourse', *Discourse Processes*, 35(2): 135–200.

O'Connor, C. and Michaels, S. (2007) 'When is dialogue "dialogic"?', *Human Development*, 50(5): 275–85.

Partnership for 21st Century Skills (2012) *A Framework for 21st Century Learning*, Retrieved from http://www.p21.org/index.php

Postman, N. (1995) *The End of Education: Redefining the Value of School*, New York: Knopf.

Reznitskaya, A., Kuo, L., Clark, A., Miller, B., Jadallah, M., Anderson, R. C. and Nguyen-Jahiel, K. (2009) 'Collaborative Reasoning: A dialogic approach to group discussions', *Cambridge Journal of Education*, 39(1): 29–48. DOI: 10.1080/03057640802701952.

Richardson, V., Anders, P., Tidwell, D. and Lloyd, C. (1991) 'The relationship between teachers' beliefs and practices in reading comprehension instruction', *American Educational Research Journal*, 28(3): 559–86.

Saunders, W. and Goldenberg, C. (1996) 'Four primary teachers work to define constructivism and teacher-directed learning: Implications for teacher assessment', *The Elementary School Journal*, 97(2): 139–61.

Saunders, W., Goldenberg, C. and Hamann, J. (1992) 'Instructional conversations beget instructional conversations', *Teaching and Teacher Education*, 8(2): 199–218.

Schraw, G. and Olafson, L. (2002) 'Teachers' episitemological world views and educational practice', *Issues in Education*, 8(2): 99–149.

Sinatra, G. M. and Kardash, C. M. (2004) 'Teacher candidates' epistemological beliefs, dispositions, and views on teaching as persuasion', *Contemporary Educational Psychology*, 29(4): 483–98. DOI: 10.1016/j.cedpsych.2004.03.001.

Smith, F., Hardman, F., Wall, K. and Mroz, M. (2004) 'Interactive whole class teaching in the National Literacy and Numeracy Strategies', *British Educational Research Journal*, 30(3): 395–411. DOI: 10.1080/01411920410001689706.

Soter, A., Wilkinson, I. A. G., Murphy, P. K., Rudge, L., Reninger, K. and Edwards, M. (2008) 'What the discourse tells us: Talk and indicators of high-level comprehension', *International Journal of Educational Research*, 47: 372–391. DOI: 10.1016/j.ijer.2009.01.001.

Splitter, L. J. and Sharp, A. M. (1996) 'The practice of philosophy in the classroom', in R. F. Reed and A. M. Sharp (eds), *Studies in Philosophy for Children: Pixie* (pp. 285–314). Madrid: Ediciones De La Torre.

Stipek, D. J., Givvin, K. B., Salmon, J. M. and MacGyvers, V. L. (2001) 'Teachers' beliefs and practices related to mathematics instruction', *Teaching and Teacher Education*, 17(2): 213–226. DOI: 10.1016/S0742-051X(00) 00052-4.

Vygotsky, L. S. (1968) *Thought and Language (Newly Revised, Translated, and Edited by Alex Kozulin)*, Cambridge, MA: MIT Press.

Vygotsky, L. S. (1978) *Mind in Society: The Development of Higher Psychological Processes*, Cambridge, MA: Harvard University Press.

Walton, D. (1992) 'Types of dialogue, dialectical shifts and fallacies', *Argumentation Illuminated*, pp. 133–47.

Walton, D. and Macagno, F. (2007) 'Types of dialogue, dialectical relevance and textual congruity', *Anthropology and Philosophy: International Multidisciplinary Journal*, 8: 101–19.

Wegerif, R., Mercer, N. and Dawes, L. (1999) 'From social interaction to individual reasoning: An empirical investigation of a possible sociocultural model of cognitive development', *Learning and Instruction*, 9(6): 493–516. DOI: 10.1016/S0959-4752(99)00013-4.

Wei, R. C., Darling-Hammond, L., Andree, A., Richardson, N. and Orphanos, S. (2009) *Professional Learning in the Learning Profession: A Status Report on Teacher Development in the United States and Abroad*, Dallas, TX: National Staff Development Council.

Wells, G. (1999) *Dialogic Inquiry: Toward a Sociocultural Practice and Theory of Education*, Cambridge, UK: Cambridge University Press.

Windschitl, M. (2002) 'Framing constructivism in practice as the negotiation of dilemmas: An analysis of the conceptual, pedagogical, cultural, and political challenges facing teachers', *Review of Educational Research*, 72(2): 131–75. DOI: 10.3102/00346543072002131.

Yoon, K. S., Duncan, T., Lee, S. W.-Y., Scarloss, B. and Shapley, K. (2007) 'Reviewing the evidence on how teacher professional development affects student achievement', *Issues and Answers Report*, 33.

22

Interactions between Teaching and Learning Mathematics in Elementary Classrooms[1]

Aki Murata

INTRODUCTION

In classrooms all over the world, students are learning mathematics daily. With increased international communication and access, we can now observe efforts to support students' learning in each culture, sometimes in similar ways, sometimes differently, based on unique local contexts. One commonality across different global educational communities is the effort to meet the differing needs of our increasingly diverse student population (OECD, 2010). The understanding of mathematics teaching and learning has also shifted from a purely cognitive process to a more social process. A new framework to conceptualize mathematics teaching and learning is essential if we want to support our teachers and students to do well. In this chapter, I will explain the interaction model of mathematics teaching and learning in the effort to illustrate current issues in the field of mathematics education and to propose a possible framework for a solution. After a brief framing of current issues, I will present and discuss the interaction model to support our teachers and students in the classrooms for the changing world.

LEARNING AS SOCIAL INTERACTIONS

As explained in the Introduction to this book (Scott and Hargreaves, this volume), our thinking about learning has shifted from a purely individual mechanistic process to a social process in recent decades. Vygotsky (1978) argued that learning is essentially a social activity and best thought of as developing through interaction with the social world, or its inhabitants and their objects. Human learning and development happens through social activities, interactions with others, tools and the environment. Ideas generated during initial interactions between the learner and his/her environment, are then internalized by the learner and become a part of his/her future independent thinking.

Several scholars focus their investigations on how individual learning is supported by social interaction (Boaler, 2008; Cobb, 1994; Cobb and Bower, 1999; Hatano, 1993; Palincsar, 1998; Rogoff et al., 1995; Saxe, 1991). Cobb (1994) explains how constructivist and sociocultural perspectives are complementary to each other; sociocultural theories inform the conditions for learning and constructivist theories focus on how students learn in the environment. Both perspectives are necessary for an understanding of the learning system at the individual and group levels of analysis, and how instruction works within the system. In describing the development of mathematical practices in the classroom, Cobb et al. (2001) state how an individual student's act of reorganizing her reasoning (psychological perspective) for linear measurement is simultaneously an act of participation in the mathematical practice (social practice). The student's learning was 'supported by her participation in the emergence of the very practice to which she contributed by learning' (Cobb et al., 2001: 145). This reflexibility of social settings and individuals is crucial to understanding and designing an effective learning environment. In seeing individual activities as acts of participation in a system of practices that are themselves evolving simultaneously, the dynamic and ever-changing relationships between individuals and social settings become the key to understanding human learning.

CLASSROOM ZONE OF PROXIMAL DEVELOPMENT

As a learner bridges his/her current and potential levels of understanding in interaction with others, he/she moves along a distance in what Vygotsky called the *Zone of Proximal Development* (ZPD). An extension of this theory may suggest that when multiple students' individual ZPDs overlap in a classroom, learning can be orchestrated by connecting and extending multiple student ZPDs (Figure 22.1). With differences among students, the classroom ZPD can stretch far longer than each individual ZPD (within the classroom). Classrooms can be considered a place where students' differing needs for assistance interact, and by carefully facilitating such needs, students can assist in each other's learning.

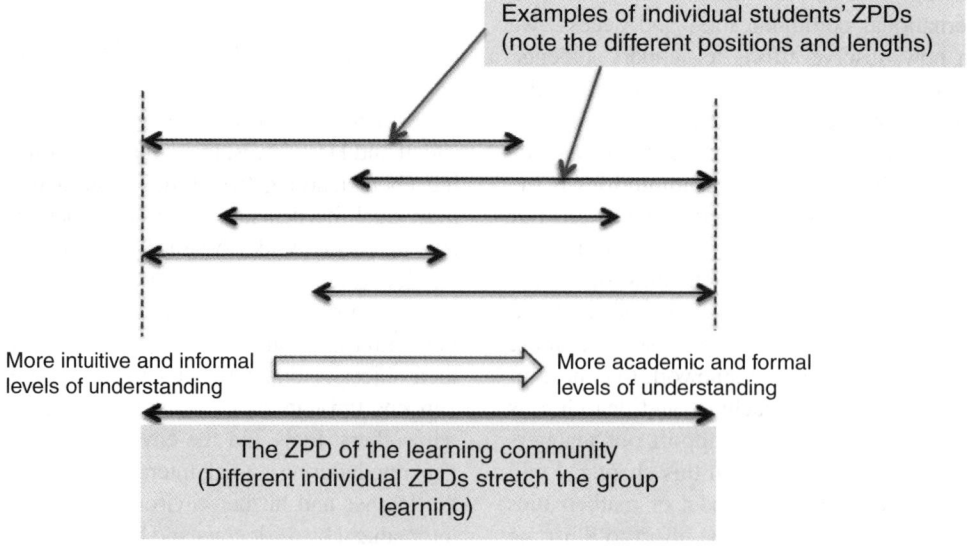

Figure 22.1   Individual ZPDs and classroom ZPD

Source: Murata, A. (2013) 'Diversity and high academic expectations without tracking: Inclusively responsive instruction', *The Journal of Learning Sciences*, 21(2): 312–335.

For example, in a typical Grade 2 classroom with a diverse range of students, students are likely to have different levels of understanding and approaches to solving a multi-digit subtraction problem. For the subtraction problem 46 – 19, some students may use a mathematical drawing of 46 circles, cross out 19, and count the rest to find the answer, 27. Other students may use manipulatives (e.g. base-ten blocks) to aid their thinking about numbers in tens and ones by regrouping. They place four ten rods and six unit cubes to show 46, trade one of the ten rods for ten units to make the representation into 3 tens and 16 ones, and from there, subtract 1 ten (30 – 10 = 20) and 9 unit cubes (16 – 9 = 7), and group the remaining blocks to find the answer 27. Yet, there may also be students who set up a vertical algorithm to find the answer by subtracting by places and decomposing. These students have different ZPDs regarding the level of abstraction. In solving the problem, sharing, articulating, being exposed to and understanding different approaches (such as these) in the classroom, the students who are at the most concrete level can get a glimpse of the abstract thinking, while the students who are at the most abstract level can be reminded conceptually (and concretely) why the algorithm works the way it does. All students can go through these levels together in a classroom when the range of student methods are laid out and the teacher helps students discuss the connections among the ideas.

By combining these different ZPDs together, the ZPD of the classroom stretches farther and challenges all the students to move beyond the distance they may achieve individually. This is important because having a longer ZPD means the classroom has the potential to learn more based on individual differences among students. In other words, in a homogeneous classroom where students' ZPDs are similar, classroom learning does not stimulate individual learning as much. However, in a heterogeneous classroom with students with differing levels of mathematics understanding, while it is not necessarily true that all individuals in the classroom reach the same learning destination (end of the ZPD of the classroom) at the end of the instructional period, they will be stimulated to learn more than they can individually with a teacher.

In Figure 22.1, the length of an individual ZPD depends on the student's intellectual readiness to learn, but the potential to go beyond the ZPD may depend on his/her intention to learn. Intellectual readiness may be defined by the student's cognitive capacity and developmental level, but the intention may be influenced by other social and affective factors. If students do not feel that their ideas are valued, if they somehow feel threatened by the classroom or school environment, they may not be willing to go beyond what they feel safe to learn (their own ZPD). Students constantly negotiate their intellectual readiness and social intentions, and change their perceptions of themselves as learners. Learning environments help determine whether or not individuals may go beyond their ZPDs in a group. In the following section, the interaction model of mathematics teaching and learning will be illustrated, which makes such learning possible.

INTERACTION MODEL OF MATHEMATICS TEACHING AND LEARNING: TAKING ADVANTAGE OF DIVERSITY

I propose an instruction model for teachers to maintain high expectations for all students while remaining responsive to varied students' learning needs by taking advantage of the existing diversity in their classrooms.

Figure 22.2 illustrates the *interaction model of teaching and learning*. The smaller grey core in the centre of the cylinder-like shape indicates the formal learning goals of the instructional unit. For mathematics, the formal goals may include mathematically-desirable and efficient solution methods that may not be intuitive and accessible by students at the beginning of an instructional unit (e.g. accessible variations of standard algorithms). The larger pale grey outer cylinder

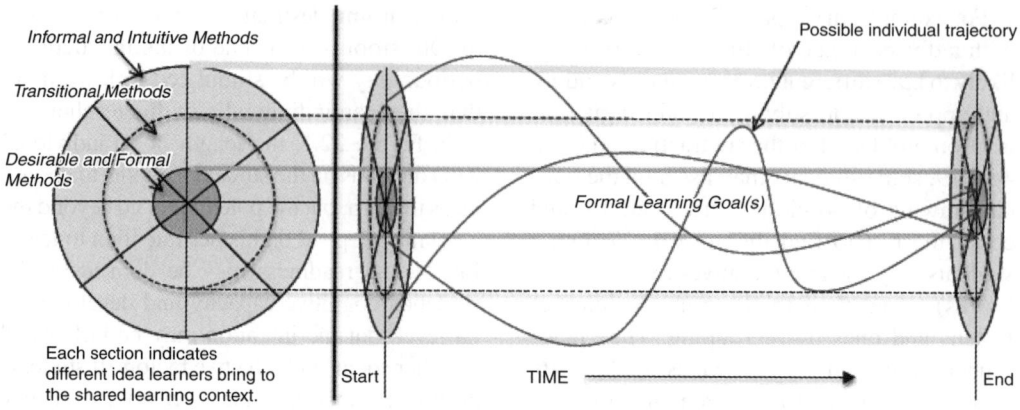

Figure 22.2   Interaction model of teaching and learning

Source: Murata, A. (2013) 'Diversity and high academic expectations without tracking: Inclusively responsive instruction', *The Journal of Learning Sciences*, 21(2): 312–335.

shows classroom instruction, within which smaller embedded concentric circles indicate different levels of students' approaches and methods (labelled *informal and intuitive methods* and *transitional methods*) in relationship to the formal learning goals. The methods in the outer circles are not central learning goals, but important goals to address as students make their own connections.

The sections of the slice of the circle (see the left side of the diagram) indicate different ideas learners bring to the shared environment. For example, in learning multiplication, a section may represent the students' understanding of other operations (e.g. addition, subtraction) or different ways students represent their ideas. Each section has some relevance to the formal learning goals (see the dark grey centre), but different learners may make different connections, and their contributions to the group learning in a section may vary.

Each thin arrow on the right is an example of how a hypothetical individual learning trajectory can be observed. These trajectories interact with one another (often through sharing and discussing different ideas) as they move forward (left to right in the figure) in the shared learning journey. Each learning trajectory brings (and touches on) different ideas (sections) in the shared context, and this inclusive setting helps expose students to diverse perspectives.

ACADEMIC AND SOCIAL DEVELOPMENT THROUGH CLASSROOM INTERACTION

The space inside of the cylinder (the right side of the diagram) is where different ideas interact, merge, and/or split, to help develop the shared understanding of the group as well as individual understandings within the group. This space is important not only for students' academic learning but for how they come to position themselves as knowers in the social (classroom) setting. Gutierrez (Gutierrez et al., 1995) uses the term 'third space' to describe the space where the teacher's script and students' counterscript intersect, creating the potential for authentic interaction to occur. Moje et al. (2004) and Barton and Tan (2009) also describe a navigational space where different kinds of discourses coalesce to destabilize and expand the boundaries of the official school discourse; learners gain competency and expertise through negotiation. Such spaces are especially important when learners come from outside of the mainstream academic culture. Their learning may be influenced by how a variety of student thinking is taken up within a whole group discussion.

As students position themselves as possible knowers in academic settings (Aukerman, 2007), they experience constant intellectual negotiation. While they may feel rewarded for efficiency in using formal methods (i.e. the instructional goal, or the centre of the cylinder, Figure 22.2), informal approaches and ideas (i.e. the outer circles of the cylinder) may be more closely and meaningfully tied to the original and personal understanding, which can be difficult for students to let go. When the classroom considers and privileges multiple learning trajectories, individual students may pass through multiple layers of these concentric circles, thus being exposed to various ways of thinking. It is by encouraging students to make non-linear movements that they develop a deeper understanding of the material. Individuals may even move away from the core of the cylinder at times, but such movements serve to add extra dimensions to an individual's learning. Thus, the space needs to be sufficiently large (wide) in order to allow different movements. This space for possible conceptual movements is referred to as the *width* of instruction.

INSTRUCTIONAL WIDTH

In a more traditional classroom where learning goals are strictly specified and solution methods are prescribed (i.e. focusing only on the dark grey centre), students still follow their own trajectories by making different connections (see the curvy arrows in Figure 22.2). However, their ideas are not taken up by the teacher nor shared. Gutierrez et al. (1995) discusses how different scripts may exist and conflict in a classroom: the teacher's monologic script and the students' counterscripts. In such an environment, students could consider school learning to be disconnected from what they know outside of the classroom and develop separate knowledge bases (Boaler, 2002). When incorporating different ideas and methods, school mathematics opens up and becomes more connected to the students' everyday world (Angier and Povey, 1999; Boaler, 2002; Gutierrez et al., 1995).

In a recent study (Murata et al., 2015), my colleagues and I compared classroom and individual learning trajectories in two Grade 1 classrooms by tracing the student methods shared in classroom discussion (classroom trajectory) and during individual interviews (individual student trajectories). Our results showed that one teacher tightly controlled the classroom trajectory by focusing primarily on target methods (dark grey centre of the cylinder, Figure 22.2) in classroom discussions. While the students appeared to use the target methods in the classroom context, they were more likely to hold on to concrete and basic methods (outer rings of the cylinder, Figure 22.2) in individual interviews. In contrast, the other teacher incorporated a variety of student methods from all parts of the circle in classroom discussions. This teacher did not necessarily address the target method in every lesson, but students focused in on this more formal method in interviews relatively quickly over time. This contrast demonstrated that *instructional width*, the degree to which teachers maintain a narrow or wide classroom discussion, by incorporating different student ideas (Figure 22.2, cylinder), affected the ways students learned mathematics. Narrowing the instruction too early, before students had experiences relating their own ideas with the target content, can create and maintain a distance between students and the mathematics they are learning. If discussion was inclusive of different student ideas and provided opportunities for students to grapple with these ideas without being hurried to use the target method, they made the connection between their ideas and the target content, even though the process could be messy and unpredictable for the teacher at times.

Wide instruction offers space for students to experience themselves as possible learners within the academic context. When students come from families and communities whose values differ from mainstream school values, it can be an alienating experience simply to be in schools, knowing that expectations are different from those in the home community. It can become a constant struggle even if students are willing to adhere to school norms.

A small academic or social success in the formal school context may motivate the student to start developing the self-identification of a possible learner, however, he/she may then need to confirm the connection with the non-academic community to feel safe and regroup, before moving farther forward into academic membership. It requires a synergistic combination of social and academic experiences for sustaining change. During any part of this process, a small drawback can happen, and past gains may unravel. As discussed earlier in the chapter, each student can reach the extremes of his or her ZPD intellectually, but going beyond their own ZPD to join the classroom ZPD takes personal commitment to the classroom community. Narrow instruction will keep individual students within their own limited capacities. If all students work only within their own ZPDs, teachers will be overwhelmed by having to attend to each student's needs separately. Classrooms are a social context for a reason; teachers can take advantage of the already-existing diversity in the classroom to stretch every student's learning simultaneously, while making their own work more manageable. Students need wide enough instruction to do this and teachers need specific supports to make sense of instructional width. The following section will provide examples of such supports for teachers.

TEACHING SUPPORTS FOR WIDE INSTRUCTION

In focusing on the interaction of the group *and* the individuals, it is possible to design *wide* instruction in which a variety of individual student learning trajectories is embedded. But teachers need support in order to do this well. Cobb et al. (2001) states that in the hands of a skilled teacher, diversity is a primary motor of the collective mathematical learning of the classroom community. The difference between the case Cobb and colleagues present and the case I am discussing

in the current chapter is that in some societies, resources are available to help all teachers understand and gain the skills to take advantage of individual differences to drive collective learning, while in other societies (e.g. the United States), this kind of teaching is often considered only possible for a few talented teachers.

In the following sections, I will outline possible teaching supports to increase instructional width. This is not an exhaustive list, and it is important to note that these supports are interdependent, so attending to one support will help other supports to also work better.

CONCEPTUAL CURRICULA THAT SUPPORT STUDENTS AND TEACHERS TO LEARN

In many cultures where students show relatively high performance levels in international achievement examinations, coherent and conceptual curricula exist (OECD, 2004; Schmidt et al., 1997). These curricula are often products of the synergy between theory and practice, and teachers embrace and benefit from them. For example, in Japan, each time the course of study is revised by the ministry of education, teachers refine the vision, and textbook publishers create textbook curricula based on the teachers' vision. Teachers often take these new, rather abstract ideas presented by policy makers, and make them come to life in actual lessons through lesson study, a collaboration-based professional development. During national-level lesson study, which may attract hundreds of people to a public demonstration lesson, teachers play a central role in shaping lessons based on the new educational vision. They help define the vision for the future through teaching, and by discussing and refining ideas together in the educational community. Textbook publishers often take these lessons and use them as a part of the published textbook curriculum. In these ways, textbooks reflect teachers' ideas, are coherently structured, and are used across different school districts and grade levels throughout the country.

In Japanese teachers' manuals, students' typical learning trajectories of mathematics topics are often clearly outlined, with explanations of how and why variations can happen. Thus, teachers are supported to understand how their students think, how their learning can take different trajectories, and why. Based on this information, teachers facilitate student learning through classroom problem solving and discussions. In the textbooks, each new instructional unit typically begins with a contextualized problem that is carefully designed to invite students' prior understanding and to make it easier for teachers to facilitate different student thinking in classroom learning.

A strong and coherent curriculum supports teacher learning. The United States has been an unfortunate exception where disconnected and varied standards have made teachers' work confusing and difficult for many decades. The new Common Core State Standards (CCSS, 2010) focuses on a coherent set of curricular goals, aligned with typical student learning trajectories of different mathematics topics, and it is meant to lead the education community in a similar direction to other countries. With these efforts, the United States is trying to remedy the *mile wide and inch deep* curriculum, and provide extra time and space for teachers and students to make sense of the learning happening in classrooms. There are research-based textbook curricula that are designed to support teacher learning in similar fashion, too. For example, *Math Expressions* (Houghton Mifflin, 2014) is a curriculum that focuses on a few core mathematics concepts that are organized in a linear progression for student learning (Fuson and Murata, 2007). The activity-based and discussion-focused lessons are outlined with possible student responses and thinking to help teachers develop a better understanding of student learning as they teach the textbook curriculum.

VISUAL REPRESENTATIONS: MATHS DRAWINGS AND MANIPULATIVES

Visual representations are an effective tool to make mathematics concepts accessible to students, and to connect different mathematics topics for students. With visual representations, such as maths drawings and manipulatives, students become more aware of their own thinking, and how mathematics works. Although there is a wealth of visual representations and manipulatives available for instruction, curriculum designers' purposeful selection of them, careful planning for how to use them in the course of lessons, and clear descriptions for teachers to make connections between the representations and student learning, will make wider instruction possible and manageable. For example, when students share different ideas to solve a problem, the teacher may use a common representation to show these ideas, highlighting the commonality among them, thus making the connections visible. The representation becomes an effective support for facilitating a student discussion of mathematics. Also, a common representation or mathematical notation that shows different mathematics content topics will help bridge different topics. For example, in solving a word problem, '*There are 19 students on the school bus. Some more came onboard, and now there are 46 students in total. How many students came onboard the bus in the middle?*' a teacher may represent the problem situation by writing $19 + \square = 46$. As another student shares his/her solution as subtraction, the teacher may write $46 - 19 = \square$ right next to the original number sentence. In doing so, students can see how addition and subtraction are related. It is also crucial to connect visual representations with formal mathematical notations because students use these abstract mathematical expressions in future learning. Thus, textbook designers should carefully select visual representations that can be generalizable and extendable to more complex mathematics content, larger numbers and formal equations.

DISCUSSION NORMS AND CLASSROOM EXPECTATIONS

Classroom norms that encourage, welcome and demand sharing of students' developing ideas will support *wide* instruction. Teachers should communicate early on that learning is social, and everyone is expected to contribute to the shared learning journey. Students must be supported to understand that it is their responsibility to share their developing ideas, listen to each other's ideas, give feedback, ask questions, and work together to develop a shared understanding. This process will help students develop and nurture a sense of belonging. Appropriate design of the learning activities can lay the foundation for community building, but it is the ongoing and shared participation in activities that are mathematically engaging that nurtures this sense of belonging.

Through classroom interactions, teachers need to emphasize that finding the correct answer is not the sole purpose of shared learning experiences. On the contrary, sharing and discussing different ideas, questioning and refining each other's approaches, and creating a common understanding are the central learning goals in the classroom community, and all members of the community invest time and effort in this process. The teachers can model this by probing students' thinking through discussions, allowing them time to ponder mathematical ideas, recognizing and praising students who share mistakes in public, and being excited about the process of building a common understanding. Such practices will help students develop a sense of community, which becomes a motivation for students to keep trying in the face of difficult problem solving.

SUMMARY

The interaction model of teaching and learning presents a new perspective to understand the current mathematics classrooms as we investigate and help improve classroom practices. Moving away from seeing learning as a purely cognitive process, the interactional perspective shifts the focus to how social interactions drive learning. Once teachers understand and use a variety of student ideas in their instruction, to make their practice wider and more inclusive, more students will learn. The interaction model described in this chapter helps meet students' diverse needs by including a variety of approaches in the classroom. Instead of treating student diversity as an obstacle, we can work directly *with* the diversity and take advantage of differing student approaches to benefit everyone.

As we discover more about the ways in which classroom learning and individual student learning interact and support each other, we can further investigate how students' contributions to the group discussion frame and reframe classroom learning. Prior research primarily investigated how social experiences influence individual learning, but we are also interested in better understanding how individual actions help change and reframe the larger community's collective learning. In Figure 22.2, the width of the cylinder helps define how student learning is framed, but student learning also changes the shape of the cylinder in the process. For example, the student solutions of the problem may change the direction of the classroom discussion, which can require the teacher to reroute the instruction. My previous work (Murata, 2004, 2013; Murata and Fuson, 2006; Murata et al., 2004) investigated the interaction between teaching and learning in Japanese Grade 1 classrooms as students learned to add two numbers with totals in the teens. After having become familiar with larger addend + smaller addend problems (e.g. 9 + 4) using the Break-Apart-to-Make-Ten (BAMT) method (recomposing addends to make a ten; e.g., $9 + 4 = 9 + (1 + 3) = (9 + 1) + 3 = 10 + 3 = 13$), the teacher introduced a set of smaller addend + larger addend problems (e.g. 4 + 9) in a lesson. When most students changed their solution approach and reverted to counting, the teacher shifted his instruction back to provide more support so they would understand how to use the more efficient BAMT method again with this new problem type. Experiencing a variety of problems and methods will strengthen students' understanding of the mathematics concept; the teachers' sensitivity to student thinking with new problems will allow teachers to modify their teaching, to support students to navigate smoothly their own learning trajectories.

We may also investigate, examine existing mathematics curricula, and develop new curricula that effectively support teachers' understanding of wide instruction. As mentioned above, there are ways to support teachers to understand effective facilitation of student discussions by incorporating diverse student ideas. Having 30 students in a classroom does not mean the teacher needs to facilitate 30 different learning trajectories. For any core mathematics topic, there are generally three to five most likely trajectories based on students' prior learnings of related concepts, and typical challenges specific to the new concept. These trajectories can be outlined, examined and summarized in the teachers' manuals, so teachers can see the relationships and not feel overwhelmed by the possibilities. Even when students appear to have different ideas, these ideas have likely stemmed from a few common patterns of general mathematical thinking, and knowing these patterns will help teachers facilitate discussions. When this type of curriculum becomes the norm, it frees teachers from the overwhelming task of teaching 30 students in 30 different ways, and they can focus their attention on typical learning trajectories and how best to facilitate them.

Another important future investigation will be on the social and affective aspects of learning. Wide classroom discussions can help create expanded membership in the learning community, but students' social and emotional development must go hand in hand with academic learning in order to produce sustained growth. Examining how students develop a sense of belonging in the classroom while building an academic identity provides insight into the complex personal process of becoming a successful student, when the definition of *success* may vary across students and change over time.

When educators see teaching and learning as a set of interactions, they share and welcome different ideas. The width and inclusiveness of discussions are not only important for elementary mathematics classrooms, but also in the larger education community. The interaction model could potentially change the way we understand how people learn, and how we develop and nurture knowledge. The model presents a vision of future learning communities where diversity is the driving force of learning.

NOTE

1   Parts of this chapter previously appeared in Murata (2013).

REFERENCES

Angier, C. and Povey, H. (1999) 'One teacher and a class of school students: Their perception of the culture of their mathematics classroom and its construction', *Educational Review*, 51(2): 147–60.

Aukerman, M. (2007) 'When reading it wrong is getting it right', *Research in the Teaching of English*, 42(1): 56–103.

Barton, A. C. and Tan, E. (2009) 'Funds of knowledge and discourses and hybrid space', *Journal of Research in Science Teaching*, 46(1): 50–73.

Boaler, J. (2002) *Experiencing School Mathematics: Traditional and Reform Approaches to Teaching and their Impact on Student Learning*, New York: Routledge.

Boaler, J. (2008) 'Promoting "relational equity" and high mathematics achievement through an innovative mixed ability approach', *British Educational Research Journal*, 34(2): 167–94.

Cobb, P. (1994) 'Where is the mind? Constructivist and sociocultural perspectives on mathematical development', *Educational Researcher*, 23(7): 13–20.

Cobb, P. and Bower, J. (1999) 'Cognitive and situated learning perspectives in theory and practice', *Educational Researcher*, 28(2): 4–15.

Cobb, P., Stephan, M., McClain, K. and Gravemeijer, K. (2001) 'Participating in classroom mathematical practices', *Journal of the Learning Sciences*, 10(1/2): 113–63.

Common Core State Standards Initiative (2010) *Mathematics Standards*. Retrieved from http://www.corestandards.org/Math/

Fuson, K. and Murata, A. (2007) 'Integrating the NRC principles and the NCTM process standards: Cognitively guided teaching to individualize instruction within whole-class activities and move all students within their learning paths', *National Council of Supervisors of Mathematics Journal*, 10(1): 72–90.

Gutierrez, K., Ryes, B. and Larson, J. (1995) 'Script, counterscript, and underlife in the classroom: James Brown versus *Brown v. Board of Education*', *Harvard Educational Review*, 65: 445–72.

Hatano, G. (1993) 'Time to merge Vygotskiian and constructivist conceptions of knowledge acquisition', in E. A. Forman, N. Minick and C. A. Stone (eds) *Contexts for Learning: Sociocultural Dynamics in Children's Development*, New York: Oxford University Press, pp. 153–66.

Houghton Mifflin (2014) *Math Expressions*, Boston, MA: Houghton Mifflin.

Moje, E. B., Ciehanowski, K. M., Ellis, S., Carrillo, R. and Collazo, T. (2004) 'Working toward third space in content area literacy: An examination of everyday funds of knowledge and discourse', *Reading Research Quarterly*, 39(1): 38–70.

Murata, A. (2004) 'Paths to learning ten-structured understanding of teen sums: Addition solution methods of Japanese Grade 1 students', *Cognition and Instruction*, 22(2): 185–218.

Murata, A. (2013) 'Diversity and high academic expectations without tracking: Inclusively responsive instruction', *The Journal of Learning Sciences*, 21(2): 312–35. DOI:10.1080/10508406.2012.682188.

Murata, A. and Fuson, K. C. (2006) 'Teaching as assisting individual constructive paths within an interdependent class learning zone: Japanese first graders learning to add using ten', *Journal for Research in Mathematics Education*, 37(5): 421–56.

Murata, A., Otani, N., Hattori, N. and Fuson, K. C. (2004) 'The NCTM Standards in a Japanese primary classroom: Valuing students' diverse ideas and learning paths', in R. Rubenstein (ed.) *National Council of Teachers of Mathematics 2004 Yearbook: Perspectives on the Teaching of Mathematics*, Reston, VA: National Council of Teachers of Mathematics, pp. 82–95.

Murata, A., Siker, J., Kang, B., Kim, H.-J., Baldinger, E., Scott, M. and Lanouette, K. (2015) 'Classroom group learning and individual student learning: Case of two first grade number talk lessons' (under review).

OECD (2004) *What Makes School Systems Perform? Seeing School Systems through the Prisms of PISA*, Paris: OECD.

OECD (2010) 'Educating teachers for diversity: Meeting the challenge', Paris: OECD.

Palincsar, A. (1998) 'Social constructivist perspectives on teaching and learning', *Annual Reviews of Psychology*, 49: 345–75.

Rogoff, B., Radziszewska, B. and Masiello, T. (1995) 'Analysis of developmental processes in sociocultural activity', in L. Martin, K. Nelson and E. Toback (eds) *Sociocultural Psychology: Theory and Practice of Doing and Knowing*, Cambridge, England: Cambridge University Press, pp. 125–49.

Saxe, G. (1991) *Culture and Cognitive Development: Studies in Mathematical Understanding*, Hillsdale, NJ: Erlbaum.

Schmidt, W. H., McKnight, C. C. and Raizens, S. A. (1997) *A Splintered Vision: An Investigation of U.S. Science and Mathematics Education*, Boston, MA: Kluwer.

Vygotsky, L. S. (1978) *Mind in Society: The Development of Higher Psychological Processes*, Cambridge, MA: Harvard University Press.

23

Violence in Schools: The Role of Authoritarian Learning

Clive Harber

INTRODUCTION

I have come to a frightening conclusion: I am the decisive element in the classroom. It is my personal approach that creates the climate. It is my daily mood that makes the weather. As a teacher I possess tremendous power to make a child's life miserable or joyous. I can be a tool of torture or an instrument of inspiration. I can humiliate, humour, hurt or heal. In all situations it is my response that decides whether a crisis will be escalated or de-escalated, and a child humanised or dehumanised. (Ginott, 1972: 15–16)

Not all learning is good. This chapter examines violence in schools internationally and focuses on the authoritarian contexts of learning that can help to explain its presence. 'Violence' here is understood in the manner of the Gulbenkian Foundation's Commission on Children and Violence – 'Violence is defined as behaviour by people against people liable to cause physical or psychological harm' (1995: 4). The World Health Organization further defines violence as:

The intentional use of physical force or power, threatened or actual, against oneself, another person, or against a group or community, that either results in or has a high likelihood of resulting in injury, death, psychological harm, mal-development or deprivation. (WHO, 2002: 5)

There are many complex and contested definitions and understandings of school violence. De Wet (2007: 249), for example, states that:

Violence in schools is present in any situation where a member of the school community (teacher, student, other education worker, parent or visitor) is intimidated, abused, threatened, or assaulted, or their property deliberately damaged by another member of that community or the public, arising out of their activities in a school.

Violence in schools such as bullying, physical violence and sexual abuse can, and often does, have negative effects on mental health, physical health, sense of well-being, sense of social isolation, depression, frustration and, importantly for the present context, academic achievement and learning (Johnson et al.,

2011; Strom et al., 2013: 244). In South Africa, for example, where violence in school is a widespread problem, the National School Violence Study (CJCP, 2013) argued that school violence resulted in truancy, a decrease in educational performance, depression, fatigue, reduced trust, and the victim becoming more aggressive, as well as reinforcing the message that violence is the most appropriate way of resolving conflict and instilling discipline. It can also 'erode young people's sense of hope and optimism in their future and, consequently, their ability to cope with any adversity and difficulties they may face in growing up in a social and economic environment that is, at best, challenging' (2013: 4).

It was also clear from the respondents in the study of school violence in six provinces of South Africa by Mncube and Harber (2012) that violence in schools has serious and negative consequences for school attendance, learning and achievement among a significant proportion of learners. When asked the consequences of violence, 14% of the total sample said that it had resulted in missing days at school, 8% said that they had been unable to learn, 6% that they had failed courses and 1% that they had dropped out of school. Thirty-one per cent of girls in the sample said that they would not return to school. This experience of violence has serious implications for the future health and productivity of South African society and the economy.

It is important therefore to examine the nature and sources of violence that occur in schools internationally. It is particularly important to differentiate between different types of violence and examine their sources and the role of the school in each case, as well as how they might exist and originate outside of the school but intrude on it (external). The school might also play a role in reproducing them inside the school through omission, i.e. by not doing something (internal indirect) or by actively encouraging or perpetrating violence itself (internal direct). Table 23.1 sets out a typology of violence in schools and their sources.

There is now a large literature on schools and violence. Harber (2004 and 2009), Harber and Mncube (2015, forthcoming), Bush and Salterelli (2000), Pinheiro (2006) and PLAN (2008), for example, contain many, often shocking and distressing, detailed international examples of each type of school violence set out in Table 23.1. Perhaps the main point to stress here is that violence in schools is now more widely recognised as a global problem than it was and it is also more widely recognised that more of the violence that exists in schools is internally generated and facilitated than has tended to be acknowledged in the past. In Harber and Mncube (2015, forthcoming) we develop a threefold theoretical explanation of *why* schools reproduce violence (i.e. internal indirect) and actively perpetrate violence (direct). These refer to the role of schooling in reproducing both social and economic inequality and a dominant social construction of masculinity that leads to a proclivity towards violence as well as authoritarian forms of socialisation. Given the limited space available for present purposes, this chapter will focus on perhaps the most salient factor in why schools actually play a significant part in creating and perpetuating violence in society and that is its role in authoritarian socialisation as a form of learning.

SCHOOLING AND AUTHORITARIAN SOCIALISATION

A band of efficient schoolmasters is kept at much less expense than a body of police or soldiery. (H. L. Bellairs, Victorian author of a report on the South Wales coalfield, cited in Williams, 2003)

State Parties shall assure to the child who is capable of forming his or her own views the right to express those views freely in all matters affecting the child, the views of the child being given due weight in accordance with the age and maturity of the child. (Article 12, UN Convention on the Rights of the Child, signed by every country in the world except America and Somalia)

One important reason as to why violence occurs in schools that are supposed to nurture

Table 23.1   Types and sources of violence in schools

Type of violence	External	Internal/Indirect by omission	Internal/Direct
Violent incursion of schools from armed force in international or civil conflict (e.g. ideological, religious or ethnic)	Army or militia attacks school buildings and staff and students	Does school teach about peace/ actively promote inter-communal respect and democratic values and behaviours?	Does school teach hatred of the 'other' through the curriculum and teacher attitudes and behaviour? Does the school promote militarisation?
Physical violence between individuals e.g fighting, physical beatings and shootings, including gang violence	Violent conflicts and rivalries that originate outside the school spill over and are continued in the school. The ease of obtaining guns (and knives) in the wider society increases the chance of their use in disputes in school. Violent attitudes and behaviour learnt at home are brought to school by learners, and violence is carried out against both teachers and other learners.	Does the school actively provide an organisational climate and physical structure that fosters loyalty to the school and a desire to protect it? Does the school have a clear non-violence and conflict resolution policy and an active conflict resolution committee? Do teachers consider violence prevention, including why students might want to use violence, a part of their job and a priority? Is violence considered in the curriculum? Is restorative justice practised? Does teacher absenteeism and lateness to class facilitate fighting?	Is the school left unprotected by fencing and security? Do teachers physically beat students – corporal punishment and slapping, pinching etc.?
Bullying	Is bullying (physical, verbal and cyber) learnt by students in the family and the community then practised in the schools?	Does the school have an anti-bullying policy and is it actively pursued? Does the school itself exhibit qualities of a bullying culture by forcing students to obey and conform to unnecessary and arbitrary rules?	Do teachers bully students by verbally abusing and humiliating them?
Sexual harassment and violence	Do girls suffer sexual harassment in school because male practices and expectations in the wider society intrude into school?	Do schools do anything to prevent sexual harassment of female students by male students by rules and disciplinary procedures and by educating about gender and gender equality?	Do teachers themselves sexually harass female students (and staff)?
Examination stress and illness	Do the competitive nature of educational selection and the labour market demands of the wider society (and its families) create harmful stress (and thus physical and psychological illness) in schools?	Do schools try to do anything to ameliorate such pressures through discussing the nature of examinations and providing support and encouragement for all? Do higher achieving students help less achieving ones? Where possible, do schools encourage cooperative as well as competitive learning?	Do schools make matters worse by an exaggerated emphasis on examinations and over-preparation via testing? Do they further promote competition, winners and losers, via class rankings, prizes, streaming etc.

learning in a safe and caring environment is that, despite most countries having signed the UN Convention on the Rights of the Child, for the majority of pupils schooling is an essentially authoritarian experience. They are institutions where curriculum and management priorities are set by those above the learners, in Ministries of Education, in local or regional authorities and by the school head teacher and staff. The voice of learners is not heard or not sufficiently heard. As a result, the priorities, needs, rights and feelings of learners can be ignored, downplayed or supressed. It is also difficult for teachers or pupils to act independently and to critique and challenge dominant social and political orthodoxies, including those that lead to violent behaviour and conflict. Authoritarian schools are therefore schools that reproduce and perpetuate, not only the socio-economic and political inequalities of the surrounding society, including gender relationships, but also the violent relationships that often go with them.

A useful theoretical framework for understanding schools as systems of control and surveillance that help to maintain existing power relationships was provided by Michel Foucault (1977). Foucault questioned whether historical development was taking a linear path towards rationality, enlightenment and progress. He believed that, on the contrary, modern society had developed into a more limiting and inherently 'violent' form of rationality. He argued that the regulatory practices of contemporary institutions, including schools, are even more oppressive because they are more subtle and hidden. Schools, as other forms of modern institution, control through their bureaucratic, routinised authoritarianism; constantly measuring, categorising, ordering and regulating so that control and surveillance becomes accepted by the majority as normal and natural. The intended result is increased docility and obedience: the bells, timetables, rules, hierarchies and punishments that form part of daily reality in most schools internationally.

Indeed, it has been argued that socioeconomic control and reproduction of the status quo has been a feature of formal schooling since its inception. Green's historical study of the origins of formal schooling systems in England, France, the United States and Prussia in the nineteenth century argues that a key purpose of their construction was the formation and consolidation of national consciousness but with different implications for different levels of the social order:

> The nineteenth-century education system came to assume a primary responsibility for the moral, cultural and political development of the nation. It became the secular church. It was variously called upon to assimilate immigrant cultures, to promote established religious doctrines, to spread the standard form of the appointed national language, to forge a national identity and a national culture, to generalise new habits of routine and rational calculation, to encourage patriotic values, to inculcate moral disciplines and, above all, to indoctrinate in the political and economic creeds of the dominant classes. It helped construct the very subjectivities of citizenship, justifying the ways of the state to the people and the duties of the people to the state. It sought to create each person as a universal subject but it did so differentially according to class and gender. (Green, 1990: 80)

With certain exceptions, there is widespread evidence that the dominant or hegemonic model globally remains authoritarian rather than democratic (Harber, 2004, 2009; Harber and Mncube, 2012). Education for and in democracy, human rights and critical awareness is not a primary characteristic of the majority of schooling. Whilst the degree of harshness and despotism within authoritarian schools varies from context to context and from institution to institution, in the majority of schools power over what is taught and learned, how it is taught and learned, where it is taught and learned, when it is taught and learned and what the general learning environment is like is not in the hands of pupils. It is predominantly government officials, head teachers and teachers who decide, not learners. Most schools are essentially authoritarian institutions, however benevolent or benign that authoritarianism is and whatever beneficial aspects of learning are imparted. In this authoritarian situation of relative powerlessness and neglect of their human rights pupils can be mistreated violently or be influenced by potentially violent beliefs because the dominant norms and behaviours of the wider society are shared, not challenged, by many adults in the formal education system.

In an authoritarian setting with an expectation on obedience, with low levels of concern for social justice and with no other ways of dealing with dissent or difference, then individuals or groups who reject what is happening to them may well resort to physical violence because there is no other way to respond or because they have learned that this is the normal way to behave and respond; violence may be an inevitable reaction to violent structures. Students in Canada, for example, were asked in focus groups to identify what it was about schools that made them angry. Students listed hundreds of things that made them angry, but at the crux of the matter were power relationships and matters of equity (Ross Epp, 1996: 8).

Historically, schooling provided a means of social and political control, in particular to counter the threat to the state of increasingly industrialised, urbanised and potentially organised working populations in North America and Europe. As Green's study argues, '[t]he task of public schooling was not so much to develop new skills for the industrial sector as to inculcate habits of conformity, discipline and morality that would counter the widespread problems of social disorder' (1990: 59).

Schooling for the majority would be organised accordingly to prepare future workers with the subordinate values and behaviours necessary for the modern bureaucratic, mass production workplace and the existing social order: regularity, routine, monotonous work and strict discipline. Its organisational form would therefore need to be authoritarian in order to inculcate habits of obedience and conformity. As Marten Shipman puts it in his study of the history of education and modernisation:

Punctuality, quiet orderly work in groups, response to orders, bells and timetables, respect for authority, even tolerance of monotony, boredom, punishment, lack of reward and regular attendance at place of work are the habits to be learned at school …

Education not only prepares for new ways of living it also stresses attitudes to authority that help to preserve the existing distribution of power. (1971: 47, 54–55)

These relationships essentially remain in place in contemporary industrialised countries. In terms of surveillance, for example, schools in England regularly use CCTV cameras to spy on pupils and ensure teachers are working hard enough. In many cases teachers cannot turn the camera off, even when they are having a sensitive and personal conversation with an individual pupil. A report in 2012 suggested that at least 100,000 such cameras were installed in classrooms and corridors across Britain, with 90% of secondary schools using them. One teacher union commented that 'Lab rats have more privacy' (Paton, 2014). Also, despite a growth in school councils dealing with other matters, pupils in England still have very little say over the core purpose of schooling, that is, the curriculum and teaching and learning methods. Indeed, in many ways the introduction of a subject aimed at education for democratic citizenship has merely highlighted gaps between the stated aims and practices of this area and the rest of what happens in schooling in terms of a centrally prescribed curriculum, testing and competitive league tables (Harber, 2010). Research on school pupils themselves has also tended to support this. A survey of 15,000 British pupils in 2001 on the topic of 'The School That I'd Like' (Burke and Grosvenor, 2003) found that pupils felt that schools were not happy places, that pupils' views were not listened to, that they weren't treated and respected as individuals, and that schools were rigid and inflexible institutions. This echoed earlier work by Rudduck et al. (1996), which found that listening to pupils' views could be very helpful for school improvement, though in practice it rarely occurred.

A study of primary school children in Ireland found that:

[I]n general children defined their relationships with their teachers in terms of control and regulation … school was experienced as something that was done to them and over which they exercised little control … The children's talk was replete with examples of adult power. They remarked on the absence of consultation with them over curricular, pedagogical and evaluative practices in schools ... adults decided what and how children would learn. (Devine, 2003: 138–40)

In America a book on pupil perspectives on schooling was entitled *Fires in the Bathroom.* It is called this because:

It's a safe bet that in random high schools across the United States, some kid has just set the bathroom wastebasket on fire. And deep down, all of us know why. Anyone who has made it out of their teens most likely remembers the feeling of anonymity and captivity that even the best high schools can convey. (Cushman, 2003: ix)

Cushman's book is based on a survey of pupils' views about what can be done to improve schools, classrooms and learning and avoid violence and conflict. Again there is a clear message about the need to genuinely listen, consult and discuss with students about their education and a clear message that school organisation and priorities do not currently encourage or facilitate this.

This authoritarian model of schooling with its origins in state formation, modernisation and social and political control gradually extended globally from European societies through colonisation, where the key purpose of schooling was to help to control indigenous populations for the benefit of the colonial power. By the 1930s colonialism had exercised its sway over 84.6% of the land surface of the globe (Loomba, 1998: 15). When formal education was eventually provided, missionary schools and those of the colonial state were used to control local populations by teaching the superiority of the culture of the colonising power and by supplying the subordinate personnel necessary for the effective functioning of the colonial administration (Altbach and Kelly, 1978). Even if it was not always entirely successful in this, and indeed in the end helped to sow the seeds of its own destruction, the organisational style of schooling bequeathed by both the needs of industrialised mass production and then colonialism remains as a firm legacy in many post-colonial societies.

In a study of the ex-British colony of Trinidad and Tobago, for example, the author argues that:

Schooling was intended to inculcate into the colonised a worldview of voluntary subservience to the ruling groups, and a willingness to continue to occupy positions on the lowest rungs of the occupational and social ladder. A number of effective strategies were used in the process, but the most significant among these was the instructional programmes and teaching methodologies used in colonial schools ... Values, attitudes and behaviour were highlighted such as the habits of obedience, order, punctuality and honesty. (London, 2002: 57)

Some of the characteristics of colonial schooling in Trinidad and Tobago outlined by London include mindlessness, verbatim repetition, character development, mastery of rules as a pre-requisite for application, use of abstract illustrations, monotonous drill, inculcation of specified norms for cleanliness and neatness and harsh discipline. He concludes by arguing that schooling is one of the places where colonial forms and practices have persisted and remained essentially the same throughout the post-colonial period.

A similar authoritarian stress on conformity and obedience existed, for example in British India (Alexander, 2000: 92), Francophone Africa (Moumouni, 1968) and Portuguese Mozambique (Barnes, 1982). In a study of contemporary schooling in India, Mali, Lebanon, Liberia, Mozambique, Pakistan, Mongolia, Ethiopia and Peru for DfID/Save the Children the authors note that:

Almost all the systems were essentially modelled on those of the colonial powers (Britain, France, Portugal and Spain) and still use styles of classroom discipline and teaching methodology that were current a hundred years ago or more in the colonial country. (Molteno et al., 2000: 13)

A detailed review of evidence of schools in developing countries in terms of whole school ethos and culture, school discipline and corporal punishment, classroom methods and assessment, teacher education and politics, resources and culture also suggests that, despite some positive exceptions, there remain formidable obstacles to the introduction and maintenance of more democratic forms of schooling (Harber and Mncube, 2012: Ch. 4).

For example, stating that most education systems in Arab states exist in the context of authoritarian political regimes, Massialas and Jarrar comment that '[t]he Arab classroom teaches reverence to authority figures and complete submission to their will; it teaches not to question traditional sources of knowledge and wisdom' (1991: 144–5).

Despite the 'Arab Spring' of 2011, it will be some time before the majority of schools in North Africa help to build, develop and sustain democracy, even if the authoritarian states above them are reformed in a more democratic direction. While Herrera and Torres (2006: 8) cite some positive examples of educational projects grounded in a more critical pedagogy in the Arab region, a nevertheless recurrent theme in almost all chapters of this book on Egypt is the overwhelmingly authoritarian nature of relationships in schools and universities based on control and submission. As one contributor put it, schools are characterised by '[t]he inflexible state curricula, rigid examination processes, heavily bureaucratic school administration and constant inspections, all (of which) reflect the authoritarianism school governance'.

Similarly, in a study of the potential of shared decision-making involving pupils in schools in Egypt, Hammad (2010) found that the egalitarian ethos necessary to promote democratic decision-making was not there. The centralised, hierarchical control, lack of trust, excessive emphasis on enforcing rules and regulations, the bureaucratic and authoritarian mode of teacher education and autocratic style of head teachers, were all part of a school culture of compliance and passivity and were serious obstacles to progress.

A study of schooling and violence in Colombia for UNESCO's International Bureau of Education argued that the function of schools was control, homogenisation and reproduction. Time is controlled by strict timetables where everyone does the same thing at the same time and physical space is used as a means of controlling and watching over all of the activities undertaken at the school. Absolute power is incarnated in the image of the teacher, and this fluctuates between the strict application of the rules to the administration of judgements and condemnation of the students' attitudes, behaviours, feelings and abilities at times at the teacher's whim. Students have no say in the curriculum which is taught in a dogmatic and authoritarian manner generating discrimination, school failures and drop out (Bernal, 1997: 36–7).

In Vietnam, Saito et al. (2008) found that although government policy was entitled 'child-centred education', there was a huge gap between the policies and the actual practices:

> In reality, children who need to be at the centre of the educational policies were still oppressed and regarded as marginal. Moreover, there was a severe lack of trust among colleagues in schools despite the fact that it was imperative to develop teacher collegiality; without professional collegiality in schools it would be impossible to promote child-centred education. In sum, based on what was observed, primary schools tended to be institutions which lack a certain amount of care and concern pertaining to the students. (2008: 101–2)

A key figure in creating the processes and ethos of a school is the head teacher. The immediate concern is with analysing why violence takes place in some schools and it is of significance that the role of the head in schools in many developing countries has been described as that of a 'despot' (Harber and Davies, 1997: Ch. 4). Using examples from Nigeria, Malaysia, Thailand, Indonesia, South Africa, Kenya and Latin America, Harber and Davies (1997: 61) argued that:

> … in developing countries head teachers emerge from the teaching population and have had little or no training for the job. Classroom teaching experience is the key factor in the selection of heads … evidence from a wide range of developing areas strongly suggests that classroom teaching is overwhelmingly authoritarian in style. Given the nature of school organisation, their own identities as teachers and the top-down, highly centralised

systems of education in most developing countries, it would be unlikely for the majority of head teachers to be anything other than despots, benevolent or otherwise.

Likewise, in a section of a review of a wide range of published literature on school principalship in developing countries entitled 'A King in His Realm?' Oplatka (2003: 437) argued that:

> A major ideal characteristic of principalship in developed countries is a participative, democratic leadership style ... Conversely in many developing countries the degree of autocratic leadership style displayed by the principal is relatively high.

These autocratic styles range from 'army-like' control where principals demand from subordinates unquestioning obedience to authority, to a pseudo-participative leadership style where the last word always belongs to the principal. Citing studies from Singapore, Mexico, Thailand and China, Oplatka also partly attributes this to cultural scripts based on a high level of 'power distance values' (Hofstede, 1991) where the expectations of the less powerful is to accept that power is distributed unequally. In Tanzania, Van Der Steen (2011: 35) comments that:

> In terms of management, state primary schools are hierarchically organised, with headteachers as the highest authority as well as personally accountable with regard to running the school as required by ward and district education officers ... They can hardly diverge therefore from the 'top-down' directives, guidelines and values imposed by education officers and school inspectors.

In a study of both public and private schools in Pakistan, Nazir (2010: 339) found that power was very much concentrated in the hands of the 'higher-ups', the headteachers and, in the case of private schools, also the owners, and that:

> In both cases the tendency of the teachers is to accept the authority without challenging it. In private schools, this submission seems to come from job insecurity, and in government schools, from the fear of transfer to undesirable areas and schools. The teachers have not reported any democratic practice to legitimise authority in educational settings.

Also in Pakistan, an in-service education project to develop teachers who used more participative classroom styles and worked with other teachers to help them diversify their teaching was hampered by school managements who saw the teachers as a threat (Shamim and Halai, 2006: 62). Moreover, in the same project one teacher stated that:

> Once my students were busy in discussion and there was noise in the class, the head entered the class and scolded the students about discipline and asked me to stop this game and start to teach as before. (cited in Dean, 2006: 97)

Hawkins (2007) argues that the traditional, non-democratic model of schooling persists, is dominant and is taken for granted. In discussing what he terms 'The Intractable Dominant Educational Paradigm', he recounts a research project in Ethiopia where he was regularly reminded by Ethiopians that they were one of the only African nations never to be colonised by the West and that therefore they did not suffer from many of the post-colonial legacies found in other African and developing countries. Yet visits to schools and colleges revealed little that was truly Ethiopian; indeed, they were like schools anywhere in the world, only poorer: 'When pressed as to the rationale of models from the West (or global north), the answer almost invariably was "so we can develop like them"' (Hawkins, 2007: 137).

Hawkins argues that the features of this dominant paradigm which exists almost everywhere despite the political nature of the regime are that:

- An authoritarian relationship often lies at the core of the teacher–learner interaction;
- Teachers are generally insecure because of a lack of training and poor remuneration;
- Teaching methods do not generally benefit from knowledge of cognitive psychology and child development;
- Teachers generally discourage discussion and questioning, and adhere to textbooks;
- A principal function of schooling is to select entrants to the next educational level;

- The selection is through a highly competitive examination system which requires the reproduction of rote learning rather than critical thought;
- The main activities of the formal school system are directed towards preparing pupils for these examinations; and
- Students and parents are preoccupied with certificate-status rather than with the essence of what is taught. (Hawkins, 2007: 150–1)

The problem, according to Hawkins, is that this model of schooling has come, almost universally, to be regarded as the only possibility, the only model of a 'real' school.

The net result of this is the creation of education systems and schools which, too often, have a major function in social and political control. In reflecting on his detailed empirical five-nation study of culture and pedagogy, Alexander (2000) was struck by the pervasive sense of control in all five schooling systems. The mechanisms, he argues, are universal: structure, curriculum, assessment, inspection, qualifications, school organisation and teaching. The controlling function is exercised at different levels:

> At national level … governments devise policies and structures, allocate budgets, determine goals, define curricula and institute mechanisms for assessing and policing what goes on at the system's lower levels. At regional and local levels such systems may be replicated or, depending on the balance of control over what goes on in the classrooms, they may simply be implemented. At school level, heads exercise varying degrees of influence or direct control over what goes on in classrooms; and at the end of the line, in classrooms, children are every day subjected to the pedagogic controls of teaching and curriculum. These controls extend into the furthest recesses of task, activity and interaction, and are mediated through routine, rule and ritual. Comparative macro-micro analysis illuminates the way these stack up and cumulatively impact on the child. (Alexander, 2000: 562)

CONCLUSION

This chapter has addressed a key problem for contemporary schooling and learning, that of physical and psychological violence. It has argued that violence in schooling is widespread, that a number of different types of violence exist and that these can have their origins either inside or outside school. It has also focused on the globally dominant, authoritarian nature of schooling to help to explain why violence in schools is so widespread and persistent. The answer to this is more democratic forms of school organisation, learning and teaching, and this has been the subject of much writing and discussion (including by the present author) but, as yet, insufficient actual practice.

REFERENCES

Alexander, R. (2000) *Culture and Pedagogy: International Comparisons in Primary Education*, Oxford: Blackwell.

Altbach, P. and Kelly, G. (1978) *Education and Colonialism*, London: Longman.

Barnes, B. (1982) 'Education for Socialism in Mozambique', *Comparative Education Review*, 26(3): 406–19.

Bernal, E. C. (1997) 'Colombia: Country and Schools in Conflict', in *Final Report and Case Studies on the Workshop on Educational Destruction and Reconstruction in Disrupted Societies*, Geneva: International Bureau of Education and the University of Geneva.

Burke, C. and Grosvenor, I. (2003) *The School That I'd Like*, London: RoutledgeFalmer.

Bush, K. and Saltarelli, D. (eds) (2000) *The Two Faces of Education in Ethnic Conflict*, Florence: UNICEF.

CJCP (Centre for Justice and Crime Prevention) (2013) *School Violence in South Africa: Results of the 2012 School Violence Survey*, Cape Town: CJCP.

Cushman, K. (2003) *Fires in the Bathroom*, New York: The New Press.

Dean, B. (2006) 'Creating a Critical Mass: the Visiting Teacher Programme', in I. Farah and Jaworski, B. (eds) *Partnerships in Educational Development*, Oxford: Symposium Books.

Devine, D. (2003) *Children, Power and Schooling*, Stoke on Trent: Trentham Books.

De Wet, N. N. (2007) 'Free State Educators' Perceptions of the Causes and the Scope of School Violence', *Education as Change*, 11(1): 59–85.

Foucault, M. (1977) *Discipline and Punish*, London: Penguin Books.

Ginott, H. (1972) *Teacher and Child*, New York: Macmillan.

Green, A. (1990) *Education and State Formation*, London: Macmillan.

Gulbenkian Foundation (1995) *Children and Violence*, London: Calouste Gulbenkian Foundation.

Hammad, W. (2010) 'Teachers' Perceptions of School Culture as a Barrier to Shared Decision-Making in Egypt's Secondary Schools', *Compare*, 40(1): 97–110.

Harber, C. (2004) *Schooling as Violence: How Schools Harm Pupils and Societies*, London: RoutledgeFalmer.

Harber, C. (2009) *Toxic Schooling: How Schools Became Worse*, Nottingham: Educational Heretics Press.

Harber, C. (2010) 'Long Time Coming: Children as Only Occasional Decision-Makers in Schools', in S. Cox, A. Robinson-Pant, C. Dyer and M. Schweisfurth (eds) *Children as Decision Makers in Education*, London: Continuum.

Harber, C. and Davies, L. (1997) *School Management and School Effectiveness in Developing Countries*, London: Cassell.

Harber, C. and Mncube, V. (2012) *Education, Democracy and Development*, Oxford: Symposium Books.

Harber, C. and Mncube, V. (2015, forthcoming) *Schools and Violence in South Africa: Causes, Reduction and Prevention*, Pretoria: UNISA Press.

Hawkins, J. (2007) 'The Intractable Dominant Educational Paradigm', in M. Mason, P. Hershock and J. Hawkins (eds) *Changing Education: Leadership, Innovation and Development in a Globalizing Asia Pacific*, Hong Kong: Comparative Education Research Centre.

Herrera, L. and Torres, C. A. (eds) (2006) *Cultures of Arab Schooling*, New York: State University of New York Press.

Hofstede, G. (1991) *Cultures and Organizations: Software of the Mind*, Maidenhead, UK: McGraw-Hill.

Johnson, S. L., Burke, J. and Gielen, A. (2011) 'Prioritising the School Environment in School Violence Prevention Efforts', *Journal of School Health*, 81(6): 331–40.

London, N. (2002) 'Curriculum Convergence: An Ethno-historical Investigation into Schooling in Trinidad and Tobago', *Comparative Education*, 38(1): 53–72.

Loomba, A. (1998) *Colonialism/Postcolonialism*, London: Routledge.

Massialas, B. and Jarrar, S. (1991) *Arab Education in Transition: A Source Book*, New York: Garland.

Mncube, V. and Harber, C. (2012) *The Dynamics of Violence in South African Schools*, Pretoria: UNISA.

Molteno, M., Ogadhoh, K., Cain, E. and Crumpton, B. (2000) *Towards Responsive Schools: Supporting Better Schooling for Disadvantaged Children*, London: Department for International Development/Save the Children.

Moumouni, A. (1968) *Education in Africa*, London: Andre Deutsch.

Nazir, M. (2010) 'Democracy and Education in Pakistan', *Educational Review*, 62(3): 329–42.

Oplatka, I. (2003) 'The Principalship in Developing Countries: Context, Characteristics and Reality', *Comparative Education*, 40(3): 427–48.

Paton, G. (2014) 'Classrooms Put Under "Permanent Surveillance" by CCTV', *The Telegraph*, 20 April.

Pinheiro, P. (2006) *World Report on Violence Against Children*, Geneva: United Nations.

PLAN (2008) *The Global Campaign to End Violence in Schools*, Woking: PLAN.

Ross Epp, J. (1996) 'Schools, Complicity and Sources of Violence', in J. Ross Epp and A. Watkinson (eds) *Systemic Violence: How Schools Hurt Children*, London: The Falmer Press.

Rudduck, J., Chaplain, R. and Wallace, G. (eds) (1996) *School Improvement: What Can Pupils Tell Us?* London: David Fulton.

Saito, E., Tsukui, A. and Tanaka, Y. (2008) 'Problems of Primary School-Based In-Service Training in Vietnam: A Case Study of Bac Giang Province', *International Journal of Educational Development*, 28(1): 89–103.

Shamim, F. and Halai, A. (2006) 'Developing Professional Development Teachers', in I. Farah and B. Jaworski (eds) *Partnerships in*

Educational Development, Oxford: Symposium Books.

Shipman, M. (1971) *Education and Modernisation*, London: Faber.

Strom, I., Thoresen, S., Wentzel-Larsen, T. and Grete, D. (2013) 'Violence, Bullying and Academic Achievement: A Study of 15-Year-Old Adolescents and their School Environment', *Child Abuse and Neglect*, 37: 243–51.

Van Der Steen, N. (2011) *School Improvement in Tanzania: School Culture and the Management of Change*, PhD thesis, London University Institute of Education.

WHO (World Health Organization) (2002) *World Report on Violence and Health*, Geneva: WHO.

24

Learning, Pedagogy and Assessment

Bethan Marshall

INTRODUCTION

In English we have two words that describe what happens in a classroom. We talk of teaching and learning. In some respects the two are united in the word *pedagogy* – one of the words that appears in the title of this chapter – and yet it is insufficient to describe what's going on and so the word learning, typically, has to be added, as it has been done here. That is because, traditionally, we think of teaching being executed by the lone adult in the room and the learning being undertaken by the pupils. But that assumption has been challenged by those who believe in a socio-constructivist classroom where teachers and pupils learn from each other. Dialogue between the teacher and pupil becomes essential in this kind of classroom. Dialogic teaching (Alexander, 2010; Mercer and Littleton, 2007) highlights the potential of talk and dialogue in bringing about effective learning. Alexander (2010: 8) identified five major principles of effective classroom talk:

'collective, reciprocal, supportive, cumulative and purposeful'.

This fourth principle of dialogic teaching 'cumulative' links to the idea of Assessment for Learning (AfL) and the final word in our title, assessment. It is connected to AfL because when talking cumulatively participants not only react to each other, but also build on one another's contributions. A coherent line of reasoning develops, therefore, between the participants and thus they improve on their initial response. And this is formative assessment, a term we will use interchangeably with AfL.

In their seminal article on formative assessment, Black and Wiliam argued that, '[w]hat is essential is that any dialogue should evoke thoughtful reflection in which all students can be encouraged to take part, for only then can the formative process start to work' (Black and Wiliam: 1998a: 8), and added, '[a]ll such work involves some degree of feedback between those taught and the teacher, and this is entailed in the quality of the interaction which is at the heart of pedagogy' (1998a: 16). Assessment then, in this sense, is about dialogue and this is what we will focus on in this chapter rather than written feedback (Marshall, 2007).

UNDERPINNING PRINCIPLES

When contemplating the nature of formative assessment in English (Marshall, 2005) I changed the categories under which AfL would take place to include a section on talk. In both their original pamphlet and in their book, Black and Wiliam (1998b; Black et al., 2003) had a section on questioning. They felt that by asking rich, often pre-planned questions, as opposed to closed questions, this might stimulate pupils into 'thoughtful reflection'. I changed the heading to 'Classroom Talk' (Marshall, 2005). This was because in the lessons I observed as part of the King's Medway Formative Assessment Project (KMOFAP), English teachers who practised formative assessment (AfL) exchanged ideas with pupils in a spontaneous, un-preplanned manner. Essentially what these teachers did was to listen to and engage in what the pupils were saying and then build on their response in the type of reply or feedback that they gave. This was formative assessment because in their response teachers were asking the pupils to reconfigure and so improve their initial response, rather like the idea of cumulative dialogue.

The presence of classroom talk or dialogue, especially in English classrooms, owes much to the work of Vygotsky (1978a, 1978b). In essence, AfL could, in certain circumstances, when the principle of dialogue is involved, be seen to be akin to Vygotsky's zone of proximal development (ZPD) where a child moves through his or her ZPD with the help of a 'more able other' (Cordon, 2000: 8). Although people can move through the zone of proximal development using scaffolding, this dialogue does not conform to Bruner-style scaffolding because

scaffolding tends, in English classes, to be pre-planned.

One teacher called the kind of interaction whereby pupils were being asked to reconfigure their answer 'social' (Marshall, 2011). 'It's like being in a conversation' (2011: 96). To this extent then AfL is a Vygotsian social construct, '[a]n environment in which people can be stimulated to think and act' and where 'learning is by definition a social and collaborative activity in which people develop their thinking together' (James, 2009: 57).

But this is where dialogic teaching or dialogism is also important. The theorist, Bakhtin, wrote *The Dialogic Imagination* (1981) in which he talks of heteroglossia – the interaction of multiple voices. And this idea can also be found in the notion of dialogic teaching. Robin Alexander cites Bakhtin in his booklet *Towards Dialogic Teaching: Rethinking Classroom Talk* (Alexander, 2010). In it he writes that good classroom dialogue requires

> willingness and skill to engage with minds, ideas and ways of thinking other than our own; it involves the ability to question, listen, reflect, reason, explain, speculate and explore ideas … [it] lays the foundations not just of successful learning but also social cohesion, active citizenship and the good society. (Alexander, 2010: 5)

The nature of effective classroom dialogue, creating successful learning but also social cohesion, is most evident in Lefstein and Snell's book *Better than Best Practice* (2014), where they analyse lessons using discourse analysis, looking for dialogic teaching which enhances learning.

Significant also, however, is Dewey's (1966) definition of 'progressive' education as 'high organization based upon ideas' (pp. 28–9) in which the emphasis is less based on the dialogue between teacher and student, or between students, and more on the progress that students make in their learning: in that it is about progression, about the student constantly moving forward, it too is about AfL. The challenge for Dewey is, 'to discover and put into operation a principle of order and operation which follows from understanding what the educative experience signifies' (p. 29). He acknowledges that it is 'a difficult task to work out the kinds of materials, of methods, and of social relationships that are appropriate' (1966: 29).

In a sense this is what a teacher – be they applying the principles of formative assessment or dialogic teaching – attempts. A good teacher will consider the 'social relationships' they have built in order that a dialogue can take place and the student can progress. The implementation of AfL or dialogic teaching in the classroom, then, becomes about much more than the application of certain procedures – questioning, feedback, sharing the criteria with the learner and peer and self-assessment. It is about the realization of certain principles of teaching and learning.

The notion of language being essential to learning builds on the work of Vygotsky and Bruner. Within the ZPD, they suggested, pupils need to interact with those who are 'more capable'. This interaction with peers and teachers provides a 'scaffolding' for the learner, through which the learner develops the capabilities themselves.

In practical terms, this involves teachers in carefully devising and creating tasks that maximise opportunities for pupils to think through and develop their ideas as an aid to understanding and writing. The richer the task, the more meaningful the teachers' feedback, for within this model of teaching and learning the most frequent form of feedback will be oral – characteristically, based on the research evidence of KMOFAP, a follow-up question that prompts further thinking.

GUILD KNOWLEDGE

The one other area pupils need to be apprenticed to in order to progress is what Royce Sadler describes as 'guild knowledge'(1989). This means that they need to learn to develop judgement about the quality of work they and others produce in relation to the core concepts and processes of the subject.

Significantly, Sadler suggests that simply providing lists of criteria for what makes for a good piece of writing or performance is insufficient to help pupils to progress because: the whole is always more than the sum of its constituent parts; the inter-relationship between all the constituent components is always too complex to be meaningfully itemised; and the diversity of potential outcomes makes the use of criteria too restrictive to be helpful in suggesting progression.

Instead, he argues that pupils need to be apprenticed to the guild through the assessment process. Dylan Wiliam has suggested that UK English teachers, for example, develop – principally through assessing pupils' work and through attending standardising meetings – a shared construct of what a particular grade looks like (Wiliam, 2000). Observation of these standardisation meetings illustrates the point (see Marshall, 2011). In these meetings the use of criteria is always subordinate to the teacher's overall impression of the quality of the candidates' work. In one exchange, for example, a moderator rejects the idea that the grade should be determined from a simplistic assessment against analytic criteria because 'this screams D at me' (Marshall, 2011). What is vital to the process is the way in which the teachers learn to interpret the evidence.

Peer and self-assessment enables pupils to begin the development of a similar understanding of the construct that the community of teachers already shares. Discussion about their own writing and that of others enables them to gain insight into what is involved in, for example, a good essay, and thus apprentices pupils into the guild. In so doing it extends the range and scope of their repertoire by helping them see what quality looks like.

None of these principles matter, however, unless it is realised that it is the relationship between the teacher and pupil that is crucial in developing a formative classroom. As we have already seen, Black and Wiliam observe that, 'the quality of the interaction [between pupil and teacher] … is at the heart of pedagogy' (Black and Wiliam, 1998b: 16). There is, in the end, no substitute for the teacher actually being interested in what the pupils have to say. At the heart of all true dialogue lies the relationship between the participants.

PRINCIPLES IN PRACTICE

If we consider a history lesson, taught to a mixed ability group of 12–13-year-olds, we will see all of these principles in practice: Vygotsky's need for language as a means of learning; Dewey's 'high organisation based on ideas' and Sadler's 'guild knowledge'. We will also note the way in which dialogic teaching and formative assessment or AfL intertwine and overlap to create a good lesson.

A History Lesson

To begin with the lesson illustrates the importance of rich tasks, which develop the pupils' thinking as a vehicle towards independence, both through the nature of the tasks themselves and through the way in which they are sequenced. Progression is brought about within the task through dialogue, and between tasks – one arising out of, and so building on the previous one. David, the history teacher, used questioning and feedback as the most prominent formative procedures or strategies throughout the lesson to extend the pupils' historical understanding and skills and yet much of the dialogue he engages in is like a conversation (Marshall, 2011).

The main curriculum content of the lesson was concerned with the slave trade triangle of the late eighteenth, early nineteenth centuries between England, Africa and the Caribbean but certain core concepts and key skills were also being taught which apprenticed pupils into the subject community or 'guild knowledge'. In this instance pupils were being asked to consider what type of evidence certain sources might proffer, how

to use such sources, and also the role of chronology. Towards the end of the lesson they also began to consider the type of language and register necessary for writing about historical sources.

The lesson was divided into three main activities, each building on the other, to achieve David's broadly stated aim of the lessons, which was to 'deepen their [the pupils'] understanding of how the slave trade operated' and how to use sources to do so. This dual aim was clearly articulated in the learning outcomes he placed on the inter-active whiteboard at the start of the lesson He told the pupils that by the end of the hour they would, 'be able to explain how the slave trade operated and demonstrate this by sequencing, categorising and inference from visual sources'.

The first activity recapped on what they had learned in previous lessons. This could have been done by simply asking pupils to list the main 'facts' they had learned the day before. Instead, David asked five multiple-choice questions pertaining to the slave trade where pupils had to identify the odd one out from a list of four. Each question contained information that they would need to be reminded of for the next stage of the lesson, but what was important was less the answer than how they justified their ideas, an aim he pointed out on a number of occasions during this section of the lesson.

The pre-eminence of justification as an aim was most evident in an exchange on the question about factory workers, construction workers, servants, farm workers. The pupils displayed their answers simultaneously on small white boards so that David could, at a glance, see the range of responses. The pupils were divided in their answers between the first two – factory and construction workers. It was evident that the teacher had had in mind the first factories in the main being UK-based and employing the English working class, but a boy pointed out that there were sugar cane factories on some islands. The exchange was cumulative (Alexander, 2010) in that when asked to justify his views the pupil acknowledged that there were factories in Britain, thus recognising the standard arguments, but in addition building on that information by adding something else to the answer – there were factories on some of the islands as well. The exchange reinforced the idea that history was not simply about the recall of facts, but about those facts being used as evidence in an argument to justify a historical interpretation (see Masterman and Sharples, 2002; Hayden, 2004).

It also connoted that the classroom was a community of learners in which all voices, not just that of the teacher, were valued, a view emphasised in the last phase of this section of the lesson. This was reinforced when a pupil, rather than David the teacher, talked to an overhead slide of the slave triangle to recap on what occurred at each stage (Bakhtin, 1981; James, 2009; Alexander, 2010).

In the second and main activity of the lesson the pupils were given first five, and later four more, contemporaneous pictures that illustrated aspects of the slave trade. Again David explained that studying these pictures would deepen their understanding (Dewey, 1966). The pupils worked on these in pairs. The dialogue between the two girls below is again suggestive of the way the activity enabled pupils to think about both the historical content and processes for themselves and develop their ideas by doing so.

P2:   Shall we put them in the triangle? (Pause-looking at pictures). That's when they're captured.
P1:   They're all wearing very nice clothes or OK clothes in this picture. Do you think that could have been in Africa?
P2:   Um
P1:   Because the clothes there are very different aren't they?
P2:   Maybe that's after this one.
P1:   Think that one.
P2:   So that goes like that.
P1:   But they're working there in the plantations.
P2:   Yeh. So maybe it's like that (moving pictures around).
       I think that's just before they get on this boat and this is when they're captured and that could go there.
P1:   Mmm. What do you think this is?

In order to engage with the task the pupils needed both to build on the knowledge they had gained on the slave trade (which had been explored in the first activity and the previous lesson) and to attend to the detail of the pictures to give them evidence to sequence. In this respect it was very like Dewey's 'high organisation based on ideas' in that the lesson had a 'cumulative' nature, one phase building towards and into the next.

This need for synergy of activity was particularly clear in one of the pictures and significantly it was on this picture that David focused as he went around listening to the pupils and then used this in the whole-class feedback on the activity. In this way his actions were formative because he used the evidence of the way the pupils engaged with a task to further the understanding of the whole class (Marshall, 2011). The picture showed two groups of Africans, one with guns, the other with spears. Most had placed this at the beginning of their sequence, seeing it as evidence of the part that certain tribes played in the slave trade. The teacher's prompting through questions, however, led the pupils to see that in order for them to have guns, they must already have traded so that another picture must come before this one. Significantly, however, at no point did he dictate which one this should be and the pupils proffered at least two suggestions, both of which were accepted.

In this respect the dialogue was formative, in that AfL looks to dialogue as a means to an assessment end. Its main aim is assessing the learning that is going on. Dialogic teaching does not necessarily do this. It looks more at the learning, the exchange in understanding that takes place. It could be said, then to have a different epistemology. Nevertheless, as we have already seen, they are related in that dialogue is essential to AfL, especially the 'cumulative' kind. In some instances a teacher may have an end point at which they want to enable the pupil to arrive; at others it may be more like being in 'a conversation' (Marshall, 2011: 96). In this instance, although he did not say that one explanation was preferable, he did nevertheless suggest an order.

The delicate balance between openness of decision making ('it's how you justify it'; 'there's a lot in what you say'; 'there isn't a right answer') and the improbability of certain choices in the sequencing of the pictures (as in the picture with guns), began to induct pupils into the significance of causal reasoning within history and the limits source evidence places on interpretation. In this way the activity apprenticed pupils into the 'guild knowledge' necessary to progress within the discipline. The nature of the dialogue, oral feedback and questioning between peers and between pupils and teacher, all contributed to this broad horizon. The particular content of the lesson contributed towards the more general historical aim. Here then we see Royce Sadler's 'guild knowledge' as students are learning the curriculum particulars of the slave trade but are also being apprenticed into a historical way of thinking.

The final activity of the lesson both reinforced what had been achieved so far and developed it. Pupils were asked to write captions underneath each of the pictures. The teacher modelled the type of writing required before they embarked on the task. Taking what was arguably the first picture of the sequence he asked for contributions, which he developed and refined. He began with

T: Why would you not write 'Slaves walking across a field'?
P: Because they could be anywhere.
T: So?
P: Captured Africans taken to a ship.
T: Can we see a ship? How else could we add to it?
P: Captured Africans being marched to a ship on the West African coast.
T: Have we left anything else out?
P: Fellow African tribes capturing and taking their own people to captivity.

What is interesting about this exchange was the way that through questioning the teacher pushed the pupil to develop the density and precision of the caption and in this respect the exchange is cumulative (Alexander,

2010). David set up an initial response, such as a pupil might make, to be critiqued and developed. Again through the model he makes the criteria for a good caption clear. But this was done less in terms of what was right and wrong and more by what would make for quality in a caption – in this case evidential and inferential density about the slave trade from a visual source. In this way subject content and processes were blended in the articulation of a caption. Moreover, the use of a caption is, in itself, a stepping-stone to enable pupils to use this type of language or discourse within an essay. It provides students with, to cite James again, 'an environment in which people can be stimulated to think and act' and one in which 'learning is by definition a social and collaborative activity in which people develop their thinking together' (James, 2009: 57).

David then developed their language or discourse capacity as he went around the class listening to and reading their attempts, again selecting one caption and exchange, as a result of his sampling of pupil engagement, in the whole-class feedback to reinforce it. Moreover in doing so he added what might be called a moral dimension to the exercise. As he went around he had found two girls who had written of a picture, 'Slaves being sold at auction'.

T: How can you tell they are being auctioned?
P: Because there's a sign that says 'Horses, negroes, cattle'.
T: What's so bizarre and shocking about how that's set up?
P: They're being sold as if they are cattle.

In the whole class feedback, using the same two girls, he rehearsed this exchange for the rest of the pupils, having focused their attention on the relevant picture.

T: What does that sign tell you?
P: That they think of people in the same way as they do cows and horses.
T: What else might you add to the caption, 'Slaves sold at auction'?
P: Slaves who are sold at auction are treated like items not people.

The teacher used the girls as experts to enable the rest of the class to develop their own understanding. In this way, although he was orchestrating the commentary, by focusing attention on the girls' observations, he reinforced the sense of the classroom as a community where all learned from each other, which highlights the socio-constructivist nature of the classroom (Vygotsky, 1978a, 1978b; James, 2009)

The lesson ended with both a pointer to what was to come next and a reinforcement of what had been learned in the lesson so far – what can be learned from visual sources and their limitations.

T: What other evidence would we need to have to understand the slave trade other that these pictures?
P1: Written documents.
T: What kind of written documents?
P2: First-hand accounts of someone who is a slave.
P3: Or a slave owner. Get different points of view.
T: What other kinds of things would you need to know about the triangle?
P4: Facts and figures of the numbers of people involved.

This last exchange both demonstrates the pupils' existing knowledge of the importance of primary sources in building historical evidence and gives them a clear indication of how this will be used in extending their understanding of the topic in which they are currently engaged. In so doing the lesson exemplifies Dewey's notion of progressive education As we have seen he wanted classrooms 'to discover and put into operation a principle of order and operation which follows from understanding what the educative experience signifies' (Dewey, 1966: 29).

CONCLUSION

This chapter has concentrated on the day-to-day business of the classroom rather than on

written feedback on assignments. It should be noted though, that as with oral feedback, written comments are of little or no value if they do not take the pupils' performance forward and if there is no opportunity for the pupil to act upon them. This is because, in the main, the efficacy of any written comments will largely depend on the extent to which the tasks have been set up and understood by the pupil. But it is also because this is where dialogic teaching and most formative assessment takes place, in the cut and thrust of the exchanges between pupil and pupil and teacher and pupil and the relationship this creates. It is during lessons that teachers have the most opportunity to engage with their pupils and help them progress by developing their thinking and their ability to articulate this within the subject discipline.

Teachers in the arts and humanities use procedures such as questioning and feedback to develop and extend pupils' thinking in much broader terms than in, for example mathematics and science. (In these subjects questioning and feedback are used almost diagnostically – first to identify and then to close a very specific gap in knowledge or conceptual understanding (Harlen, 2006).) The interventions of teachers are, moreover, often impromptu, arising directly out of the pupils' contributions, much in the way ordinary, non-classroom dialogue takes place. The effectiveness of these interventions, in developing thinking, is entirely dependent on the richness of the tasks and the way they link together as the lesson progresses.

Similarly, sharing the criteria with the learner and peer and self-assessment need approaches and tasks which apprentice pupils build into a 'guild knowledge'. This is more complex than a set of narrowly defined goals and better understood as a horizon towards which the pupils are taking varied paths, which the teacher helps them negotiate. In this way AfL demands Dewey's 'high organization based on ideas' if it is going to help pupils become independent learners because the nature of the tasks affects all subsequent interactions within the class.

The lesson we have analysed is illustrative of the way in which both dialogic teaching and formative assessment are far more than a set of procedures. The type of lesson that relies on procedures has been called the letter of AfL whereas the lesson cited above encapsulates the spirit (Marshall and Drummond, 2006). This is because it instantiates the way English and Humanities teachers conceptualize and sequence the tasks undertaken by pupils in the lesson. Define the scope of the tasks too narrowly and opportunities are missed.

If Dewey gives us an overarching principle for understanding what we are aiming for in AfL, Perrenoud's concept of the regulation of learning provides a helpful way of comprehending the dynamic of the classroom. For Perrenoud formative assessment is really about the way teachers regulate learning (Perrenoud, 1998). He describes different types of classrooms. In some of these classrooms learning is highly regulated and prescribed. The scope of the activities is tightly defined. The outcomes of the learning are largely content driven and predetermined and pupils complete a series of narrow activities, which are designed to cover the prescribed learning objectives. There is little opportunity for the pupils to own their own learning and the only information it gives the teacher is a deficit model of what they cannot do according to the narrowly defined terms of reference.

In another type of classroom (as in the one discussed above) the tasks are more open ended, thus, the scope for pupils to govern their own thinking is greater, the possibility for the teachers to give feedback and engage in constructive, cumulative dialogue is meaningfully enhanced. For in this type of classroom, 'regulation does not include setting up activities suggested to, or imposed on the pupils but their adjustment once they have been initiated' (Perrenoud, 1998: 88). This is the kind of classroom we want if learning is truly to take place.

REFERENCES

Alexander, R. J. (2010) *Towards Dialogic Teaching: Rethinking Classroom Talk*, York: Dialogos UK Ltd.

Bakhtin, M. (1981) *The Dialogic Imagination: Four Essays*, Austin, TX: University of Texas Press.

Black, P. and Wiliam, D. (1998a) Assessment and Classroom Learning, Assessment in Education: Principles, Policy and Practice. 5(1): 5–130.

Black, P. J. and Wiliam, D. (1998b) *Inside the Black Box: Raising Standards Through Classroom Assessment*, London: NFER, Nelson.

Black, P. J., Harrison, C., Lee, C., Marshall, B. and Wiliam, D. (2003) *Assessment for Learning: Putting It into Practice*, Buckingham: Open University Press.

Black. P., McCormick, R., James, M. and Pedder, D. (2006) 'Learning how to learn and Assessment for Learning: a theoretical inquiry', *Research Papers in Education*, 21(2): 119–32.

Corden, R. (2000) *Literacy and Learning Through Talk: Strategies for the Primary Classroom*, Buckingham: Open University Press.

Dewey, J. (1966) *Experience and Education*, London: Collier Books.

Harlen, W. (2006) 'Formative assessment in science and maths classrooms', in J. Macmillan (ed.), *Formative Classroom Assessment: Theory into Practice*, New York: Teachers College Press.

Hayden, T. (2004) 'History', in J. White (ed.), *Rethinking the School Curriculum: Values, Aims and Purposes*, London: RoutledgeFalmer.

James, M. (2009) 'Assessment teaching and theories of learning', in J. Gardener (ed.), *Assessment and Learning*, London: Sage.

Lambert, D. (2004) 'Geography', in J. White (ed.) *Rethinking the School Curriculum: Values, Aims and Purposes*, London: RoutledgeFalmer.

Lefstein, A. (2010) *Dialogue in Schools: Towards a Pragmatic Approach*, Working Papers in Urban Language and Literacies, King's College Papers 33.

Lefstein, A. and Snell, J. (2014) *Better than Best Practice: Developing Teaching and Learning through Dialogue*, London: Routledge.

Marshall, B. (2005) *English Inside the Black Box*, London: NFER Nelson.

Marshall, B. (2007) 'English teaching', in J. Macmillan (ed.), *Formative Classroom Assessment: Theory into Practice*, New York: Teachers College Press.

Marshall, B. (2011) *Testing English: Summative and Formative Assessment in English*, London: Continuum.

Marshall, B. and Drummond, J. (2006) 'How teachers engage with formative assessment: lessons from the classroom', *Research Papers in Education*, 21(2): 133–50.

Masterman, L. and Sharples, M. (2002) A theory-informed framework for designing software to support reasoning about causation in history. *Computers and Education*, 38(1–3): 165–85.

Mercer, N. and Littleton, K. (2007) *Dialogue and the Development of Children's Thinking: A Sociocultural Approach*, Oxford: Routledge.

Perrenoud, P. (1998) 'From formative evaluation to a controlled regulation of learning processes: towards a wider conceptual field', *Assessment in Education: Principles, Policy and Practice*, 5(1): 85–102.

Sadler, R. (1989) 'Formative assessment and the design of instructional systems', *Instructional Science*, 18: 119–44.

Vygotsky, L. (1978a) *Thought and Language*, Cambridge, MA: MIT Press.

Vygotsky, L. S. (1978b) *Mind in Society: The Development of Higher Psychological Processes*, Cambridge, MA: Harvard University Press.

Wiliam, D. (2000) 'The meanings and consequences of educational assessments', *Critical Quarterly*, 42(1): 105–27.

25

Teaching and Learning in a Global World

Lisa Smulyan

INTRODUCTION

The principal of the Taktse International School in Sikkim, India, explains to me that he is constantly balancing his own lived respect for local historical, spiritual and indigenous practices and values with his desire to bring collaborative, inquiry-based (identified as Western) learning and teaching practices to the school. He questions his own practice: How can I bring change to this school and this community without pushing teachers and students into negative feelings (often experienced as colonial) of inferiority or lacking in value? How can I balance parents' desire for English instruction that will make their children economically successful with the school's goals of engaging children in an understanding of their own cultural heritage and teaching critical thinking skills that are not currently part of most Indian education?

This story exemplifies the deep influence of intersecting multiple contexts on teaching and learning. The local context – influenced by Buddhist tradition and a growing tourist economy – intersects with a national historical and institutional context, and both are affected by global shifts in education. It is almost impossible to separate these contexts given that each is so closely influenced by the others.

While we know that context impacts learning, many prior studies focus on how a specific single context impacts on individuals as learners. This understanding has led researchers to explore, for example, how home culture influences student learning (Moll and Amanti, 2005; Street, 1999) and how communities of practice can be social contexts that scaffold learning (Lave and Wanger, 1991). Wenger (2009) argues that we are all participants in *multiple* communities of practice at any given time, each of which creates a social context within which participation leads to different processes of learning and knowing. Participation in these communities shapes what we do, how we think about ourselves, and what meaning we make of our interactions and experience. Wenger (2009: 212) points out that these multiple communities of practice in which we participate 'are so informal and so pervasive that they rarely come into explicit focus', and that they shift over time as our lives and contexts change.

Wenger's communities of practice tend to be the immediate social contexts in which we work and live – our families, our workplaces, our schools. He also includes the less formal communities, those that do not have a name and do not issue membership cards (2009: 213), within which we learn. In this chapter, I will argue that communities of practice also include the local, national and global contexts that shape our interactions, our identities and the meanings we make. While teachers and students may not interact directly with national policy makers or global counterparts, these often invisible communities impact the engagement, knowledge, and meaning made by those who participate in any form of schooling today.

In the sections that follow I will begin to explore how intersections of multiple contexts affect learning and teaching. In the process, I will examine questions such as: What are some of these multiple contexts and how does each influence the learning process? When are the contextual boundaries firm and when and how do they intersect? When is power and position a factor in the intersection of contexts? How can we maintain a focus on the individual learner and the learning process and simultaneously embed that process in the fluid multiple contexts within which it occurs? While the chapter does not provide definitive answers to these questions, it explores prior work that helps us articulate the questions and begin to engage with them.

WHAT ARE THE MULTIPLE CONTEXTS THAT FRAME/IMPACT SCHOOLING?

'We can't summarize'. At Taktse, several teachers and administrators tell me that they have recently had a helpful professional development workshop on summarizing – a skill that both they and their students need to

learn. In India, students generally learn content through pedagogies that emphasize rote learning and exam-based regurgitation of facts. They don't need to summarize; they just need to know what they have been taught and repeat it back in order to succeed on exams that determine placement in the next level of education. One teacher also explains to me that in the specific local context within which the school is located, one grounded in Buddhist beliefs and values, all facts, ideas and concepts carry equal weight. It is difficult to summarize, to give priority to some ideas over others, when all details and ideas are valued equally. But the school wants its students to be able to 'think critically', and, if they choose, to attend colleges in the United States where they will need to be able to summarize as a step to other ways of knowing. So teachers in this school enlist support and have professional development workshops on how to summarize and how to teach students to summarize.

Learning at this school is framed by its specific local context and values (a Buddhist understanding of interdependence, harmony and mindfulness – or Dharma), by a national system of education (testing to move ahead in the system), and by a global (often interpreted as Western) expectation of what constitutes critical thinking and knowing. While there are other contexts that impact learning, scholars in the field of comparative education focus on local, national and global contexts as central to our understanding of learning and teaching around the world. Those who focus on local contexts often explore the role of indigenous culture in the process of learning (e.g. Semali, 1999). Those who focus on the nation state examine the role of historical and cultural expectations of the role of education and its impact on the development of citizens (e.g. Carnoy, 2007; Horsky and Chew, 2004). And researchers who examine the impact of globalization often explore the dominance/imposition of Western notions of childhood and learning in schooling around the world (e.g. Kellner, 2005; Reimers, 2006) and compare the effectiveness of different approaches to teaching and learning. Although I first present these three contextual frames separately below, it is quite clear that it is almost impossible to talk about each without drawing on the intersections that exist between them.

LOCAL CONTEXTS

In a world dominated by nation states, much of the research examining the impact of local context on schooling explores the possibility of integrating, or re-integrating, indigenous beliefs, norms, culture and history into curriculum and pedagogy. Another locally oriented focus is on the use of community schools to reach children and families who are underserved by failing or ineffective national systems of education. In some cases, community schools draw on indigenous knowledge as a way of collaborating with local families in the development of an appropriate and effective educational system.

Indigenous knowledge is, itself, a complicated and sometimes contested term. Semali (1999: 307) explains that:

> Indigenous (local) knowledge does not derive its origins or meaning from the individual but from the collective epistemological understanding and rationalization of the community. ... It is about what local people know and do, and what local communities have known and done for generations – practices that developed through trial and error and proved flexible enough to cope with change.

Semali also points out, however, that communities often lack consensus about what constitutes indigenous knowledge; people living in a particular community or culture may not share the same knowledge base for decision-making, and the invisibility of indigenous knowledge may make it hard to articulate and codify into curriculum and pedagogy. And, as discussed more explicitly below, indigenous knowledge never exists in a vacuum but always in conversation with national, historical and global epistemologies.

In several countries in South America, including Peru and Bolivia, the re-incorporation of indigenous knowledge in schools began with the official inclusion of indigenous languages into (especially) rural schools and eventually shifted to include policies supporting intercultural bilingual education (Aikman, 1999; Hornberger, 2003). The latter provides education in students' first (non-Spanish) language in primary school and also encompasses a curriculum and pedagogy that is relevant to and validates students' socio-cultural identities (Aikman, 1999). These programmes continue to struggle, however, given the lack of concrete governmental support, insufficient teacher training in indigenous languages or alternative pedagogies, the vagueness of locally based curriculum and pedagogy, and, at times, community resistance from parents who want their children to become proficient in the language and culture of power.

Community schools, often developed and supported by either international or indigenous non-governmental organizations (NGOs), both respond to a gap in educational services and incorporate more locally focused and needs-based curriculum and pedagogy. Wood (2007: 4), for example, explains that in some communities in Africa, community schools are 'the only educational opportunity on offer', given that national systems of education may not be able to provide even basic education in small, rural communities. At the same time, community schools allow local groups to have a say in what they believe is the most appropriate education for their children. Shizha (2005: 75) argues that the indigenization of education draws on the knowledge and strength of the local community.

> The local people are the vital source of indigenous knowledge and their contribution cannot be over-emphasized. The school and the community are cultural circles, which should engage in constant dialogue to promote indigenous ways of explaining what students experience and what schools should promote as relevant ways of explaining community problems. The community provides alternative ways of explaining social phenomenon [sic] and this is critical in fostering understanding among students.

In Mali, for example, community schools supported by Save the Children teach classes in the local language (Bamanakan) and organize a curriculum around

> village life, agriculture and natural resource management, health and basic business schools, in addition to the 'three Rs', history, geography and observation of nature. Functional literacy and numeracy skills were combined with life skills and with knowledge that would enable village children to make better use of local resources and improve their health and their ability to function effectively in the village setting and in the commercial world. (Glassman and Millogo, 2007: 18)

Local community members participate in school management committees that help get schools built and running and then help to make and carry out community action plans.

Those who describe communities of practice as sites of learning often seem to conceptualize these communities as existing entirely within the local context. Learning and teaching in the local context are grounded in immediate, lived realities, identities and meaning. Local learning incorporates language, knowledge and community voice and understanding. An emphasis on the incorporation of indigenous and/or local curriculum and pedagogy is often, however, an attempt to push back against national, colonial and global efforts to shape educational goals and systems. It is, therefore, almost impossible to talk about the local context without reference to national and global contexts; the local is always in interaction with these other, often less visible, contexts, usually in ways that reflect politics, power and identity.

NATIONAL CONTEXTS

Many researchers have explored the role of the nation state in what constitutes learning in schools. Around the world and across time, learning has been used to foment national revolution (Hirshon, 1983); consolidate power shifts within a country (Harber, 1997; Kirk, 2011; Levers, 2006); shape national citizens (Kaplan, 2006); and contribute to a nation's economic growth (Harber,

2002). Clearly nation states differ in structure and function in ways that create unique contexts for learning and teaching. Cowen and Shenton (2003), for example have developed a typology of states that focuses on a developmental acceptance of modernism and the state's relationship to capitalism. The way in which each state organizes its economy impacts its organization of other social sectors, including the role it assigns to education. Carnoy (2007), for example, explains how the state, through policies that impact everything from health care to teacher training, creates a national political and social context that in turn influences the learning that occurs in classrooms. Thus, Cuba, an authoritarian socialist state, has produced a national context in which all children have a relatively equal opportunity to learn. In contrast, in Chile and Brazil, citizens have greater individual freedom and less centralized government support for health, education, employment, etc. The socio-political context in Chile and Brazil leads to a greater inconsistency in the availability of good schooling for children and many more inequalities in the amount and kinds of learning that occur in schools across these countries. The national context, then, can create or limit the opportunities children have to learn (Carnoy, 2007).

The national context also impacts the content and pedagogy available to students. Tobin et al. (2009), in *Preschool in Three Cultures*, examine the deeply rooted national cultural factors that influence schooling in China, Japan and the United States. In contrast to Carnoy's (2007) emphasis on explicit government policies that create a national context for learning, Tobin et al. (2009: 242) explain that implicit cultural logics, those that are not 'mandated in government documents, written down in textbooks, taught in schools of education, given a formal name, and otherwise made explicit' frame both curriculum and pedagogy in the three countries they studied. These deeply held logics of what comprises learning, how individuals should interact within a group, and what constitutes a citizen of the state influence teaching and learning. These logics can also buffer schools, teachers and students from historical changes and globalized trends. Japanese preschool educators, for example, have a deeply held belief that preschool should recognize and support children as children rather than as individuals on a developmental path of childhood and learning. They also believe that, in a rapidly changing world, schools should help children maintain traditional Japanese values, such as empathy, social-mindedness, and the ability to change one's behaviour according to the context (Tobin et al., 2009: 240). Japanese preschools provide a context that both draws on and perpetuates a particular national and cultural ideology.

Kaplan (2006) focuses less on culture and more on the concept of citizenship in his examination of the importance of schools in shaping national citizens in Turkey. He argues that education is a national project used by all nation states to create citizens who, in turn, support and contribute to that state. Curriculum content and pedagogy help students internalize values and beliefs, thus reinforcing and reproducing a hegemonic political and social system. Kaplan acknowledges that citizens are diverse in multiple ways, and that as they respond to and interact with the state they constantly define and redefine the state. But he makes a strong argument, supported by many others in the field of comparative education, for schools as sites for the development of national citizenship, and for learning as both framed by and contributing to national social and political agendas (cf. Harber, 2002; Horsky and Chew, 2004; Kirk, 2011).

The national context, like the local context, always consists of multiple, overlapping and sometimes competing frameworks for learning and teaching. Just as local communities of practice are multiple and pervasive, so are the national communities and practices that impact on learning and teaching. These national communities may be less visible, more imaginary, than the localized communities of practice envisioned by Lave and Wenger (1991), but they still impact teaching and learning in substantive ways. The national context of India, for example, in which the Taktse International School functions, includes an examination system of government schools and universities which influences school practices, definitions of what constitutes knowing, and student identities. India's national context also includes a social system which values certain approaches to behaving and making meaning, one that, for example, privileges the English language as a means for economic and social advancement.

National contexts constantly interact with local and global contexts. For example, the emphasis on national approaches to education has been supported by international organizations, including USAid, the World Bank and various United Nations agencies as they develop and implement educational policies. These organizations share a common belief in modernization, which suggests that national economic development depends on the acceptance and implementation of Western capitalist policies and structures (Samoff, 2013). Funding for education emphasizes the link between investing in human capital and growing the national economy; these agencies have, in some cases, wielded a great deal of power over what curriculum and pedagogy should look like in so-called underdeveloped countries. The national, in these cases, is clearly influenced by global forces that guide policy and practice.

GLOBAL CONTEXT(S)

There is debate in the field of comparative education about what constitutes the global context and what impact that context has on learning and schooling. Globalization involves economic, political, social and cultural forces, all of which influence educational institutions, goals and processes. Some globalization discourses emphasize the imposition of educational practice through power that has arisen through conquest and colonialism. This discourse divides the world into west/east, north/south, core/periphery regions (Samoff, 2013) and describes the impact of the former on the latter. Samoff (2013: 54) explains that:

> In the modern era, with few exceptions, the direction of influence is from European core to southern periphery. Institutional arrangements, disciplinary definitions and hierarchies, legitimizing publications and instructional authority reside in that core, which periodically incorporates students and professors from the periphery, of whom many never return home.

World systems theorists explain the worldwide convergence of educational organizations and curriculum standards through this lens, identifying a global convergence in education that results from a neoliberal agenda promoted (and funded) by Western and multinational organizations, including the United Nations, USAid, and the World Bank as well as international NGOs.

World culture theorists have a somewhat more benign view, explaining that the global convergence of educational systems and processes results from a voluntary adoption of similar (Western) educational practices. This process emerges from the gradual diffusion and acceptance of a specific model of the nation state, one which includes structures for organizing government, health care systems, militaries and other institutions (Anderson-Levitt, 2003). This perspective assumes more agency on the part of local and national actors who make active choices, and, in the process, modify and challenge global initiatives in ways that are appropriate for and respectful of their local needs. Despite these national differences, however, there is a convergence of school structures (age-based classrooms and schools), curriculum (languages, mathematics, natural science, social science, arts, physical education), and pedagogy (whole-class lecture, recitation and seatwork), which suggests movement towards a global system of schooling (Anderson-Levitt, 2003).

Some have gone so far as to suggest that a global approach *should* be used to shape curriculum and pedagogy. Reimers (2006: 276), for example, argues that the goal of schooling world-wide should be global citizenship:

> This public purpose should support the development of a political culture that fosters the rule of national and international law and respect of human rights, the development of understanding to support trade and economic and peaceful bilateral and international diplomacy as the preferred means to solve international disputes, the development of the capability to understand and address the serious environmental challenges facing humanity and to collaborate across national boundaries in the creation of sustainable forms of human–environmental interactions and in the development of the skills to promote rationality in deliberation and action, and to advance science and technology as means to improve human health and well being.

Reimers describes local and national goals, curriculum and pedagogy as relativistic rather than aligned with universal, global values, needs and expectations. Others, however, question the universality of Reimers's global values and needs, suggesting that they map clearly onto Western notions of democracy and capitalism and imply content and pedagogy that may not reflect or respect local or national expectations and desires.

Kellner (2005) points out that contradictions emerge even within the concept of globalization. He argues that globalization 'involves the proliferation of the logic of capital, but also the spread of democracy in information, finance, investing, and the diffusion of technology' (2005: 34). These two forces may be complementary but may also be contradictory, in that globalization can contribute to the growth of small-scale, local movements that may or may not support Western views of capitalism or democracy. Kellner thus describes what he calls 'globalization from below', movements in which less-empowered groups and individuals can draw on global resources to bring attention to their work.

> Such potentially positive effects of globalization include increased access to education for individuals excluded from sharing culture and knowledge and the possibility for oppositional individuals and

groups to participate in global culture and politics through gaining access to global communication and media networks and to circulate local struggles and oppositional ideas through these media. (2005: 36)

Given this contested and complex version of globalization, Kellner (2005: 49) argues that critical educators 'need to develop transformative educational strategies to counter the oppressive forces and effects of globalization in order to empower individuals to understand and act effectively in a globalized world and to struggle for social justice'. Although he does not make explicit exactly what this education might look like, one could imagine that the incorporation of local and national values, beliefs, content and pedagogy could help provide some of the resistance he calls for.

Although it is characterized by what appears to be some convergence, imposed or chosen, of educational values, beliefs, curriculum and pedagogy, the global context is multiple within itself and always in conversation with – challenged by or modified by – the local and national contexts within which teachers and students learn and teach. And yet it clearly constitutes a community of practice – or communities of practice – within which learners make meaning and develop a sense of who they are as knowers and what is valued as knowledge.

INTERSECTION OF MULTIPLE CONTEXTS WITHIN RELATIONSHIPS OF POWER

As suggested above, local, national and global contexts for teaching and learning never exist independently; each informs and is informed by the other. Taktse International School, for example, wants to promote and celebrate local culture and values – a goal strongly encouraged by the school's founders and board. It also wants students to do well in the national examinations that will allow students to pursue higher education.

Parents want their children to excel in English because it is seen as the language of economic mobility in India and the world. The school head and teachers want to engage students in what is seen as a more Western approach to learning, one that encourages critical thinking and is activity- and inquiry-based rather than rote- and purely content-based. Some involved with the school are concerned that the latter reflects an acceptance (imposition) of Western/colonial/global norms that may conflict with the celebration of local ideas. For Taktse teachers and students, negotiating these overlapping local, national and global contexts results in content, pedagogy and expectations about learning that are unique to this particular school.

Anderson-Levitt (2003) and others suggest that while there may be global similarities at one level of schooling, debates or dialogues occur within this global framework that suggest other contextual levels at work. The case studies she includes in *Local Meanings, Global Schooling* illustrate some of the patterns of interaction between competing and overlapping global, national and local contexts for learning.

First, our examples raise the possibility that local actors find multiple, competing models out there in the larger world. Second, we are not convinced that local educators borrow models freely; hints of resistance by ministries of education suggest otherwise, and even where ministries import willingly, teachers often experience reforms as imposed from above. Third, our cases show that enacted policy differs from official policy and that this difference matters. … We show that educators on the ground transform the meanings of the common talk or, as noted, resist it entirely. (Anderson-Levitt, 2003: 17)

One example of this complicated interaction of the impact of global, national and local contexts on teaching and learning is Japan's Integrated Studies reform, a national policy designed to increase local teacher autonomy and engage students in meaningful individual learning (Bjork, 2009). Japan has a strongly nationalized system of education in which curriculum and pedagogy are standardized and student educational (and occupational) success is determined through a hierarchical system of exams. Despite a world-wide movement for centralized national schooling (Anderson-Levitt, 2003), many Asian countries have experimented in the last decade with curricular decentralization in order to shift some governmental control to local agencies, respond to local needs, and prepare students to lead 'rewarding and meaningful lives' (Bjork, 2009: 25). The call for a more 'relaxed' approach to education in Japan also emerged, in part, from international evaluation and critique of Japan's highly intense system of education. In this example, then, there are competing global movements (centralization and decentralization, standardized and student-centred approaches) in the development of a national policy. There is also an attempt to become more responsive to local contexts and individual student needs. The Integrated Studies programme, developed and implemented by Japan's ministry of education (MEXT) encourages teachers to design locally-based curriculum and instruction that engages students in thinking and learning outside of the exam preparation framework of schooling.

In his evaluation of this programme at the local level, Bjork (2009) notes that the local and student-centred aspects of this programme are often overpowered by other aspects of the national system of education and by local teacher, student and parent beliefs (reflecting national and global communities of practice) about what constitute teaching and learning. While younger students enjoyed the Integrated Studies programme, older students had a more varied response, depending on their ability to negotiate independent learning experiences. Teachers often struggled with the ambiguous instructional approaches included in Integrated Studies; they also continued to feel pressure from students, parents, their schools and the national system to prepare students to succeed in the national exams. Time taken for Integrated

Studies was time taken away from the latter. Bjork (2009: 42) concludes that:

> Considerations rooted in the local community exerted a more direct and powerful influence over educators as they responded to policy directives than did concerns about conforming to Ministry expectations. Teachers made decisions with careful attention to the factors that determined their students' immediate educational prospects; classroom experience and parental opinion, rather than MEXT [Ministry of Education, Culture, Sports, Science and Technology in Japan] priorities, guided their actions.

In this case, we can see that local definitions of teaching and learning create a context within which teachers and students interpret and experience national directives. The national reforms are, themselves, informed by competing global discourses. And those local definitions are rooted in a historical and cultural national context that influences what constitutes teaching and learning. Even when local actors control some aspects of schooling, they may be influenced by national and global systems of belief and value.

As described at the beginning of this chapter, Wenger (2009) argues that we all belong to multiple communities of practice. I argue here that these communities exist at local, national and global levels that impact interactions, identity, teaching and learning. I also argue that interactions among the multiple communities of practice are rarely neutral; they exist within relationships of power that shift over time. In the Integrated Studies programme described above, for example, the national examination system and its impact on students' academic and economic success trumped parent, teacher and student interest in more localized and student-centred approaches to learning. In a different kind of analysis, Swift-Morgan (2006) challenges what local participation in schools really means. While some have suggested that community schools can increase the focus on indigenous teaching and learning, in her study of community-based schools in Ethiopia, Swift-Morgan shows that community participation often means monetary contributions to schooling rather than involvement in decision-making or teaching and learning. Community members who were 'involved' (beyond contributions) in the schools she studied tended to participate in occasional community meetings and to monitor their own children's work outside of the school. Few were involved in school organization, fewer yet in curriculum and teaching. Community participants tended to be men from higher socio-economic classes; women and the poor rarely engaged. The NGOs and government actors who helped to create these schools controlled school structure, content and teaching. An analysis of intersecting contexts requires that we also examine which systems (the national examination system in the case of Integrated Studies in Japan) or who (government or non-profit agents, men, the wealthy) has control over educational processes.

Often, local pedagogies can be subsumed by the power of national and international contexts or communities. Tabulawa (2003: 7), for example, argues that learner-centred pedagogy promoted by international agencies in Africa and other aid-receiving countries represents a 'process of Westernization disguised as quality and effective teaching. Learner-centred pedagogies reflect an ideological push away from authoritarian structures and traditional ways of thought', and towards an acceptance of liberal democratic ways of thinking and interacting. Liberal democratic thinking and behaviour are required for the neoliberal economic development promoted by international aid agencies. Tabulawa suggests that this is not a neutral shift, based in cognitive/educational terms and a need to respond to the specific needs of local communities, but a political process through which international organizations hope to influence countries on the periphery to accept ideologies that might neutralize national and local forces.

Others, however, argue that critical, dialogic approaches to teaching and learning provide opportunities for formerly colonized societies to achieve liberation. Shizha (2005: 77) suggests that Freirian approaches to critical thinking and dialogue, especially at the local level,

allow teachers, parents and students to challenge colonial ways of thinking and knowing:

> Teachers are liberated from being dominant sources of knowledge, while students are liberated from being passive recipients of 'knowledge'. Teaching and learning become participatory activities in which students go back to their communities to elicit cultural knowledge from elders, conduct research and take back to the community knowledge 'refined' by the school.

Shihza argues that what Tabulawa describes (negatively) as a Western pedagogical approach to promote liberal democracy is actually a (positive) form of Africanization of the school curriculum that reflects a movement away from Eurocentric methods of teaching and learning and towards a critical consciousness that incorporates multiple perspectives.

CONCLUSION

In this chapter I have suggested that we expand our notion of the communities of practice that shape the learning process to include the multiple local, national and global contexts within which learners experience the world. I argue for a broader idea of community, one that includes not only the specific people with whom we engage but also the more abstract communities in which we participate as members of local, national and global societies. These complex communities, or contexts, are, perhaps, represented in the individual behaviours and beliefs of those with whom we come into contact, and in that way are part of our immediate communities of practice. But they are also broader symbolic or invisible communities that shape our participation, our experiences, our ideas of what constitutes knowledge and our identities as learners.

Wenger (2009: 213) suggests that focusing on participation in communities of practice as a way of understanding learning has implications for the organizations involved in teaching and learning: 'For organizations, it means that learning is an issue of sustaining the interconnected communities of practice through which an organization knows what it knows and thus becomes effective and valuable as an organization'. The intersections of the contexts in which learning occurs can never be neutral, however. Power may be exerted by global forces and organizations that control actual funding or pathways to status; local practices may subvert national imperatives for change, as they did with Japan's Integrated Studies programme. Educators will always work in the interstices of contexts, balancing power issues and exploring what constitutes the best possible intersections for their students in a given set of historical, cultural and political, local, national and global contexts.

REFERENCES

Aikman, S. (1999) *Intercultural Education and Literacy: An Ethnographic Study of Indigenous Knowledge and Learning in the Peruvian Amazon*, Amsterdam: J. Benjamins.

Anderson-Levitt, K. (2003) *Local Meanings, Global Schooling*, New York: Palgrave Macmillan.

Bjork, C. (2009) 'Local implementation of Japan's Integrated Studies reform: A preliminary analysis of efforts to decentralise the curriculum', *Comparative Education*, 45(1): 23–44.

Carnoy, M. (2007) *Cuba's Academic Advantage*, Stanford, CA: Stanford University Press.

Cowen, M. and Shenton, R. (2003) *Doctrines of Development*, New York: Taylor and Francis.

Glassman, D. and Millogo, M. (2007) 'Mali, 1192–2003: The first experiment', in D. Glassman and M. Millogo (eds) *Community Schools in Africa: Reaching the Unreached*, New York: Springer.

Harber, C. (1997) 'The struggle itself was a school: Education and independence in Eritrea', in *Education, Democracy, and Political Development in Africa*, Brighton, UK: Sussex Academic Press.

Harber, C. (2002) 'Education, democracy and poverty reduction in Africa', *Comparative Education*, 38(3): 267–76.

Hirshon, S. (1983) *And Also Teach Them to Read*, Westport, CT: Lawrence Hill and Co.

Hornberger, N. (2003) *Continua of Biliteracy: An ecological framework for educational policy research and practice in multilingual settings*, Clevedon, England: Multilingual Matters.

Horsky, B. and Chew, P. (2004) 'Singapore: Schools in the service of society', in I. Rotberg (ed.) *Balancing Change and Tradition in Global Education Reform*, Lanham, MD: Scarecrow.

Kaplan, S. (2006) *The Pedagogical State: Education and the Politics of National Culture in Post-1980 Turkey*, Stanford, CA: Stanford University Press.

Kellner, D. (2005) 'The conflicts of globalization and restructuring of education', in M. Peters (ed.) *Education, Globalization and the State in the Age of Terrorism*, Boulder, CO: Paradigm Publishers.

Kirk, J. (2011) 'Education and fragile states', in K. Mundy and S. Dryden-Peterson (eds) *Educating Children in Conflict Zones*, New York: Teachers College Press.

Lave, J. and Wenger, E. (1991) *Situated Learning: Legitimate Peripheral Participation*, Cambridge: Cambridge University Press.

Levers, L. (2006) 'Ideology and change in Iranian education', in R. Griffin (ed.) *Education in the Muslim World*, Oxford, England: Symposium Books, pp. 149–89.

Moll, L. and Amanti, C. (eds) (2005) *Funds of Knowledge: Theorizing Practices in Households, Communities and Classrooms*, Mahwah, NJ: Lawrence Erlbaum.

Reimers, F. (2006) 'Citizenship, identity, and education: Examining the public purposes of schools in an age of globalization,' *Prospects*, 36(3): 275–94.

Samoff, J. (2013) 'Institutionalizing international influence', in Arnove, R., Torres, C. and Franz, S. (eds) *Comparative Education*, Lanham, MD: Rowman and Littlefield.

Semali, L. (1999) 'Community as classroom: Dilemmas of valuing African indigenous literacy in education', *International Review of Education*, 45(3/4): 305–19.

Shizha, E. (2005) 'Reclaiming our memories: The education dilemma in postcolonial African school curricula', in A. Abdi and A. Cleghorn (eds.) *Issues in African Education*. NY: Palgrave McMillan.

Street, B. (1999) 'The meanings of literacy', in D. Wagner, R. Venezky and B. Street (eds) *Literacy: An International Handbook*, Boulder, CO: Westview Press, pp. 34–42.

Swift-Morgan, J. (2006) 'What community participation in schooling means: Insights from Southern Ethiopia', *Harvard Educational Review*, 76(3): 339–68.

Tobin, J., Hsueh, Y. and Karawawa, M. (2009) *Preschool in Three Cultures Revisited*, Chicago: University of Chicago Press.

Tabulawa, R. (2003) 'International aid agencies, learner-centred pedagogy and political democratization: A critique', *Comparative Education*, 39(1): 7–26.

Wenger, E. (2009) 'A social theory of learning', in K. Illeris (ed.) *Contemporary Theories of Learning: Learning Theorists ... In Their Own Words*, Oxford: Routledge.

Wood, F. (2007) 'Community schools: The solution to local needs', in D. Glassman and M. Mollogo (eds) *Community Schools in Africa: Reaching the Unreached*, New York: Springer.

26

Learning in a Professional Learning Community: The Challenge Evolves

Vicki A. Vescio and Alyson Adams

INTRODUCTION

Within the context of schools in the United States, Professional Learning Communities (PLCs) have become commonplace. Defined by specific characteristics and structures, PLCs are theoretically touted as an avenue for teachers' professional development because they focus on collaboratively examining problems of practice to improve teaching and learning. Conceptualized in an era of increasing accountability in education, the underlying premise of PLCs is that collaboration will facilitate teacher learning and result in changing classroom practices that lead to improved student achievement (Riveros, 2012). Thus the ultimate goal of PLCs has been that they engage teachers in the type of professional development that will help to meet the increasing pressures associated with student success on state mandated, high stakes testing. These core assertions of PLCs have even led some school districts and states to require them as a regular form of teacher professional development.

In 2008 we published a literature review that examined empirical research on the impact of PLCs on teaching practice and student learning (Vescio et al., 2008). Back then we talked about a lack of research to support the idea that PLCs led to demonstrated changes in teachers' classroom practices. However, we also noted the potential promise of PLCs as demonstrated by findings in a limited number of empirical studies (Dunne et al., 2000; Englert and Tarrant, 1995; Hollins et al., 2004; Louis and Marks, 1998; Strahan, 2003). Since conducting that literature review over six years ago, the continued proliferation of PLCs has led us to wonder how the research on this pervasive form of professional development has also evolved in terms of its focus on teacher and student learning. It is our contention that we need to maintain a focus of critically examining PLCs to determine new paths for creating conditions that help to deepen the work of teacher learning in order to support student learning.

With an emphasis on the collective work of teachers, PLCs are squarely situated in socio-cultural theories of learning and as such connect well to the theme of this book. That is, PLCs are places where teachers interact within a particular context to develop and arrive at individual visions of teaching and learning. In this manner, the contextualized and collective work of the group creates the learning environment for each individual. Starting with the assumption that it is practically impossible to separate the collective from the individual, and vice versa, the focus of this chapter is on examining the literature to develop a better understanding of the learning that occurs in PLCs. Specifically, after laying the groundwork for the practice of PLCs within a US context, we will examine the theoretical underpinnings of PLCs that support teachers' collective learning along with the challenges of bringing this to fruition. After this, we will examine a selected group of studies to offer our thoughts on how the work in PLCs might benefit from further enhancing conditions that have the potential to deepen teacher learning.

Consistent with the conclusions in our review of literature published seven years ago, we still believe that PLCs offer strong hope for teacher learning. However, we also believe that for PLCs to be effective vehicles for teacher learning we must accept the challenge of looking critically at ways to examine and support their continued evolution beyond merely serving as a means for improvements on high stakes tests (Cochran-Smith and Lytle, 2009; Nelson et al., 2012).

PROFESSIONAL LEARNING COMMUNITIES IN PRACTICE

Prior to beginning a discussion of the theoretical underpinnings of learning in communities, it is important to briefly talk about key issues associated with the evolution of how PLCs have come to be defined and practised within the context of schools in the United States. In general, PLCs have become a fashionable trend in school improvement initiatives

(Schmoker, 2004). This has not only occurred in the United Sates but in other countries such as Australia, Canada and the United Kingdom (Riveros, 2012). One of the problems with this type of rising educational fad is that terminology loses meaning over time due to overuse and misapplication. In this case, the term *Professional Learning Community* has come to signify any group of educators who meet on a regular basis for any purpose. In our experience we have worked with schools where the teachers and administrators label their meetings as PLCs, yet do little more than discuss administrative issues, curriculum pacing, or student behaviour problems. This claim to the name of a PLC without adherence to essential principles has served to minimize the potential of PLCs to promote teacher learning beyond surface levels.

In addition to a global claim of using PLCs, various researchers, scholars and education professionals who work in ongoing professional development groups have chosen to alter what they are naming their group so they can clearly articulate the criteria that define their work as well as maintain the integrity of their collaborative efforts. Examples of this can be seen in the empirical literature and include such names as – Critical Friends Groups (Curry, 2008; Wood 2007); Professional Development Communities (Hadar and Brody, 2012); Learning Teams (Gallimore et al., 2009); collaborative action research groups (Goodnough, 2010); and collective, inquiry, or teacher groups (Nelson, 2008; Slavit et al., 2013). However, as this prevailing body of literature demonstrates, the learning that occurs in these groups is less dependent on what they are called and is more a function of the focus and process that the group collectively engages in.

For simplicity purposes, in this chapter, we will use the classic expression of PLC and define it in terms of groups that are founded on and utilize five key characteristics associated with the work of DuFour (2004) and Newmann et al. (1996). The first of these characteristics is that the members of a PLC develop a *shared set of norms and values* regarding their purpose and ways of collaborating that serve as a foundation for the work they engage in. A second essential characteristic of a PLC is that the work is consistently and continuously *focused on student learning*. This notion is underscored by Gallimore et al. (2009: 538) who posit that to increase student achievement, teachers in PLCs need to focus on 'shared problems long enough to develop solutions that improve student outcomes'. A steadfast focus on student learning needs to be concurrently accompanied by *reflective dialogue*, which is the third characteristic of PLCs. It is imperative that educators engage in ongoing conversations about teaching and learning in order to examine existing practices and move in the direction of change. The next characteristic of PLCs is an enduring *focus on collaboration*. This means that effective PLCs utilize group structures and facilitation strategies that support teachers collectively working on issues of classroom practice and student learning (Gallimore et al., 2009; Slavit et al., 2013). The final characteristic of PLCs is that its members make their *teaching practices public* to one another so that problems can be explored and successes can be used as vehicles for further learning. With these defining characteristics as a foundation, all of the ongoing professional development groups mentioned above that use newer terminology in their names would qualify as PLCs and, in fact, will help us to build a case for how PLCs need to evolve in new directions to support enhanced levels of teacher learning.

THEORIES AND ASSUMPTIONS ABOUT LEARNING WITHIN COMMUNITIES

As a vehicle for teacher collaboration, the concept of learning communities is not new and has a rich theoretical basis. Teacher collaboration emerged as one way to break the norm of teacher isolation, first popularized by Lortie (1975). Little (1982) and Rosenholtz (1989) conducted in-depth studies of effective schools and workplace conditions to define concepts such as collaboration and collegiality that continue to fit well with modern definitions of PLCs (e.g. discussion of teaching practice; making practice public through mutual observation; collaborative planning, designing and evaluating curriculum and instruction; and learning with and from each other). Barth (1991) noted the difference between congeniality framed by polite interactions and friendliness, and collegiality framed by honest, reflective conversation that pushes learning. This was an important shift in thinking because, up to this point, collaboration was viewed as informal, and as a more pervasive characteristic of schools rather than the more formal group structure that we currently define as PLCs.

As the concept of teacher collaboration began to take hold in schools, it was clear that this was not a panacea for all that ailed schools. Collaboration had the potential to break the norm of professional isolation in schools (Little, 1982; Lortie, 1975), but simply putting teachers together in a group did not mean they would learn together. With this in mind, McLaughlin and Talbert (2001) conducted research that examined 22 high schools in an effort to further define the concept of teacher communities. In this research, McLaughlin and Talbert differentiate between traditional communities with formal hierarchies based on expertise, with a focus on accountability and standardized testing, and learning communities focused on the development of expertise through shared knowledge and collaborative learning. This work was significant as it served to define characteristics that are important for PLCs to function as sites of teacher learning.

The intentional linking of the term 'learning' to the concept of community brought a natural connection to theories in cognition and learning. As a result, Lave and Wenger (1991) added strong theoretical clout to the concept of learning in defined communities with their notion of *Communities of Practice*: groups of like-minded professionals who share common concerns and problems and work collectively to find solutions by learning and doing together. Focused on the learning of professionals, Lave and Wenger talk about learning that begins on the fringes of a community through *legitimate peripheral participation* and moves to full participation in the community over time as expertise and knowledge are built. Furthermore, in opposition to the belief that learning is individual and independent of context or intention, Putnam and Borko (2000) lay out a perspective of learning that defines cognition as: *situated* (dependent on physical and social contexts, and linked to authentic activity within the context); *social* (involving interactions with others in one's environment); and *distributed* (stretched across individuals and tools). Riveros' (2012: 604) work supports that of Lave and Wenger (1991) in that he suggests professional knowledge can be explored through proposing 'an ontology of teaching practices'. He further posits that this ontology of teaching practices requires acknowledging the situated nature of teachers, claiming that 'this *situatedness* is not something that *happens* to teachers, but is a characteristic of their *being* as teachers, which suggests that the nature of teachers' knowledge cannot be detached from the discussion about their situated teaching practices' (Riveros, 2012: 604).

Effective collaboration, as opposed to simple teamwork, should involve a collective of people engaging in both a learning stance and an inquiry stance. Lieberman and Miller (2008) define learning as a stance characterized by an orientation towards surfacing problems of practice, and viewing those problems as opportunities for dialogue around teaching and learning. Similarly, Cochran-Smith and Lytle (2009) suggest that having an inquiry stance includes an orientation where teachers treat their classrooms as ongoing sites for examining practice and raising questions about improving teaching and learning. Cochran-Smith and Lytle (2009: 141) further propose that central to a conception of inquiry as stance are practitioner inquiry communities that 'work together to uncover, articulate, and

question their own assumptions about teaching, learning, and schooling'.

Since PLCs are often used as a vehicle for teacher professional learning, it is also important to situate them within recent theories and assumptions about authentic, ongoing professional learning. Webster-Wright (2009) trawled through the professional learning literature and made an important distinction between continuous professional learning (CPL) and the notion of more traditional professional development (PD). She defines PD as based on a deficit model of linear teacher learning, as if learning is done to achieve an end result or fill a gap in a teacher's development. Rather, she posits that professional learning should be on-going/continuous and based in authentic learning experiences such as CPL. We can subsequently apply this to PLCs to speculate that communities with a PD orientation will learn to fill gaps in the knowledge or skills of its members, whereas communities with a CPL orientation will approach learning in a more broad and inclusive manner.

THE CHALLENGE

The complexity of learning within communities as outlined above is not built on a neat, linear theoretical framework of individual learning, rather it involves a nested system of individuals within a group operating in a larger school, community and national narrative about teaching and learning. This multifaceted view of learning is situated within complexity theory (Opfer and Pedder, 2011) where nested subsystems (teacher, school and the learning activity) intersect and interact with varying intensities to result in learning that is unpredictable yet patterned and connected over time. With this complexity at the forefront of our thinking, we turn to a selected sample of empirical studies on PLCs to examine elements of collaborative work that are significant for their potential to deepen and transform teacher learning.

CURRENT LITERATURE ON THE WORK OF PLCs

In the past six years with the proliferation of PLCs for teachers' professional development and the accompanying pressures exerted by accountability, there has been a concurrent growth in research that examines student achievement when teachers participate in PLCs. Collectively, the results of this research demonstrate a positive connection between teachers' participation in PLCs and student achievement (Gallimore et al., 2009; Mokhtari et al., 2009; Williams, 2013). For example, Mokhtari et al. (2009: 334) report on an elementary school that demonstrated 'significant improvement in student reading performance across all grades' over a two-year period after establishing PLCs that were singularly focused on improving reading achievement. Likewise, Williams (2013: 34) recounts research on state mandated testing in Texas that demonstrated 'significant differences in elementary, middle, and high school achievement … in reading after 3 years of district-wide implementation of PLCs'. Finally, Gallimore et al. (2009) conducted research that demonstrated significant improvement in student achievement when teachers met in PLCs that were providing the time to consistently work towards collectively solving instructional problems.

Despite adding credibility to the work of PLCs through establishing improvements in student achievement, the research described above, except in the case of Gallimore et al. (2009) does not concurrently focus on teachers' substantive learning. Rather, it is mostly implied that if student achievement increases then teacher learning must simultaneously be occurring. However, the two do not necessarily create a direct connection and in our thinking this creates a paradox for the use of PLCs as avenues for teacher learning. We say this because a focus on student learning is a foundational premise that should characterize the work of teachers in a PLC. However, when the sole focus of collaborative work is to improve test scores, the work of teachers

in PLCs is reactionary to testing pressures without a parallel regard for teacher learning beyond the use of strategies that will support achievement.

In addition, using student achievement as the sole purpose of PLC work is founded in a philosophy that tightly connects teachers' practices to improved test scores in a manner that views learning as achievement and test scores as the end point. This type of ideology serves to restrict the learning of both students and teachers and does little to support their development towards the greater learning stance proposed by Lieberman and Miller (2008), or an inquiry stance proposed by Cochran-Smith and Lytle (2009). In other words, we contend that PLC work that is focused on achievement as an endpoint is not transformational in a way that will sustain teacher learning beyond what is necessary for students to pass tests. This notion is specifically supported by Cochran-Smith and Lytle (2009: 140) who argue that, PLCs which 'limit the focus and tasks … to what fits within a narrow accountability frame may actually contribute to the de-skilling of practitioners and may constrain participants from contributing to more encompassing educational transformation'. These authors go on to suggest that teachers in learning communities need to 'embrace a much wider, deeper, and more critical agenda than test scores or "what works". Rather, they [should] work together to uncover, articulate, and question their own assumptions about teaching, learning, and schooling' (Cochran-Smith and Lytle, 2009: 141).

In this section of the chapter, we shift our focus to examining several recently published studies to discuss how they can support a deeper understanding of teacher learning in PLCs. We started by making the decision to limit our search of the literature to studies that were mainly focused on teacher learning in collaborative groups because the entirety of this chapter is centred on teacher learning. In choosing this literature we employed criteria that included examining empirical studies published in peer-reviewed journals after the date of our initial review of the literature. This meant that we looked at publications between 2008 and 2013. Our second criterion was that a published study should examine the work of teachers in a PLC that spanned a minimum of one year. We used this criterion because we believe that examining PLCs over a more extended period of time is integral to understanding how to deepen the learning of teachers who participate in these groups. The final criterion was to include research that examined PLCs that exhibited the characteristics associated with the work of DuFour (2004) and Newmann et al. (1996) as we discussed earlier in this chapter. Although the literature represented here is not exhaustive, we have chosen to discuss these studies because we feel they make a substantial contribution to understanding how to create conditions that will help to deepen the work of teacher learning in PLCs.

LITERATURE THAT DEEPENS OUR UNDERSTANDING OF LEARNING IN A PLC

There is small group of research studies that have begun to examine the work of PLCs in a way that can add to our understanding of teacher learning and serve as a basis for moving the work of PLCs to a deeper level. This collection of literature was characterized by three prevailing themes. First, there are two studies, one by Gallimore et al. (2009) and the other by Curry (2008), which examine *organizational features* that provided a platform for teacher learning over an extended period of participation in PLCs. Second, research by Hadar and Brody (2012) explores how *group and individual processes* interact to support or inhibit the potential for teacher learning. Finally, research by Horn and Little (2010), Nelson (2008), Nelson, Slavit, and Deuel (2012), and Slavit et al. (2013) has taken inquiry into PLCs to a deeper level by *examining teachers' conversations* during their collaborative work. These lines of research are

significant for providing insights into what happens in PLCs, including the struggles and successes along the path to potentially serving as transformational for teacher learning and development.

ORGANIZATIONAL FEATURES OF PLCs

Gallimore et al. (2009) and Curry (2008) conducted long-term research on PLCs that supports and extends the key organizational features and structures that must be in place in order to provide opportunities for teacher learning. Specifically, Gallimore et al. (2009) conducted a six-year case study of a struggling Title I elementary school to investigate how to construct, sustain and support school-based settings that nurture continuous teacher inquiry as well as improve student achievement. Despite the pitfalls that were previously discussed related to focusing on student achievement rather than student learning, this study offers valuable information because of its emphasis on examining the potential conditions that lead to teacher learning. In their PLC work, the teachers in this study engaged in recursive cycles of collaborative inquiry that kept conversations focused on student learning. The results identify four operational elements that the authors claim as 'critical to teachers sustaining and benefiting from instructional inquiry' (Gallimore et al., 2009: 548). These features include working in job-alike teams, using trained peer facilitators, engaging in inquiry-focused protocols and maintaining stable settings for PLC work. Gallimore and his colleagues conclude that these features allowed teachers to focus on problems of practice long enough to come up with solutions as well as to make connections between their teaching and student learning.

Curry (2008: 739) conducted a three-year study of six Critical Friends Groups (CFGs) in one high school to investigate the inherent possibilities and limitations 'that might influence the potential of these groups to serve as engines for instructional improvement and/or schoolwide reform'. Calling CFGs 'a particular type of school-based professional community' (2008: 735), Curry found structural components of CFGs that simultaneously served to enable and constrain the work of teachers. The first of these elements included a diverse menu of activities that served to both increase appeal to teachers yet limit the cohesion of their overall efforts. The second element was a decentralized structure, which gave CFGs a greater level of freedom over the nature and direction of their PD work but constrained efforts across CFGs to foster school-wide reform. An interdisciplinary membership of the CFGs promoted cross-discipline discussions and potential solutions to problems of practice yet inhibited deep exploration of specific content areas. Finally, CFGs' reliance on protocols for their work 'ensured substantive, focused conversations about teaching, learning, and reform' (Curry, 2008: 769), however, they also limited extended discussion on emerging issues and reified patterns of conversation that prohibited depth of exploration. Curry concludes that CFGs, by the very nature of their design, serve to accomplish some positive outcomes, despite having an overall limited utility for teacher learning.

INDIVIDUAL AND GROUP PROCESSES OF LEARNING IN A PLC

The findings of the Gallimore et al. (2009) and Curry (2008) studies are significant because they examine PLC work over extended periods of time to help bolster the conditions that are necessary for PLCs to serve as sites for potential teacher learning. In contrast, research by Hadar and Brody (2012: 148) takes a different, yet meaningful, direction to ask how 'group and individual processes interact to enhance or impede professional development of teacher educators in a Professional Development Community (PDC)'? Although focused on PLCs in higher

education rather than in K-12 schools, this research is significant because of its efforts to look at both individual and group processes of learning within a collaborative context. The authors studied 12 participants who took part in one of three year-long programmes designed 'for teacher educators to infuse thinking into college-level teaching' (Hadar and Brody, 2012: 148). The most significant result of Hadar and Brody's work advances a paradigm of thought that superimposes a community model of professional development with a personal trajectory of learning model to provide explanatory power about the interaction between individual and group elements of professional development in a PLC.

More specifically, in analysing the development of community, Hadar and Brody (2012) posit four sequential stages that include *breaking isolation*, *talking about student learning*, *improvement of teaching* and *professional growth/development*. While ongoing groups such as PLCs may not reach the final stage of *professional growth/development*, they do go through this process in sequence. In contrast, Hadar and Brody also found that individuals progress and regress through stages that include *anticipation/curiosity*, *withdrawal*, *awareness* and *dispositional change*. What is key is that the authors found *talking about student learning* became the connector between the group stage of *breaking isolation* and the individual stage of moving from *withdrawal* to *awareness*. Also important was the idea that a focus on improvement of teaching was never obtained by those individuals, and in some cases, groups of individuals that did not move past the stage of *withdrawal*. Yet, it was a focus on the improvement of teaching that allowed some of the individual educators to move from *awareness* to *dispositional change*, which corresponded with *professional growth/development* at the group level. It was interesting to note that some individuals as well as groups of individuals stayed at the level of *withdrawal* for the entire year of their work in a PLC.

Although more complex than what we have described here, what is so significant about the work of Hadar and Brody (2012) is that it provides a way of thinking about the complicated interaction that occurs between individual and group processes in a PLC. Having an understanding of the interplay of these processes can help teachers, administrators, university faculty, or anyone else who supports teacher learning through using PLCs. Hadar and Brody's work also adds credence to the foundational notions of the potential of collaboration developed by Lortie (1975), as well as Lave and Wenger's (1991) ideas on communities of practice serving as key pathways to teacher learning. It will become important to conduct further research in this area as well as to extend this line of inquiry by explicitly using this model as an entry point to facilitate PLC work and conduct research that closely examines the results.

TEACHER TALK IN PLCs

The final prevailing theme found in the literature we analysed connects to examining PLCs at the level of the conversations that occur among participants. This line of study offers avenues to understand how teacher talk in PLCs can promote or constrain deeper levels of learning. It is a critical line of research because the prevailing paradigms of discussion developed by teachers in PLCs will influence the questions they take up, their approach to finding answers, and the possibilities for solutions they see to those questions. Ultimately, it is these dominant discourse patterns that will determine whether the PLC functions to produce findings in order to increase test-driven achievement data or to alter teaching in a way that transforms learning for both teachers and students.

Claiming that the nature of interactions in PLCs frame how groups establish, maintain and contribute to learning, Horn and Little (2010) investigated two high school level PLCs in a comparative case study that examined conversational routines as part of a two-year project. More specifically, Horn and Little were interested in how conversational moments focused on problems of practice provided collective opportunities to support teacher learning. The two PLCs were comprised of teachers working in different academic departments; one was an Algebra Group and the other was an Academic Literacy Group. In studying the groups' discourse patterns, Horn and Little found that both groups used what they called normalizing responses to problems of practice. These were basically responses that defined the problems teachers were having as typical or an expected part of teaching. The differences in the groups came in how the normalized responses functioned 'to turn the conversations *toward* the teaching or *away from* the teaching as an object of attention' (Horn and Little, 2010: 192). Essentially, the Algebra Group used normalizing responses to move their conversation towards their teaching in a way that problematized practice and produced a platform for the types of questions and prompts that fostered deeper teacher learning. In contrast, the Academic Literacy Group's normalized responses turned the conversation away from teaching and instead focused on diagnosing and solving immediate problems. Horn and Little contend that this type of conversational pattern did not lend support to deep teacher learning.

In a series of research reports from a five-year project with secondary science and mathematics teachers, Nelson, Slavit and Deuel studied PLCs that engaged in collaborative inquiry with an emphasis on teachers' conversations. Starting with Nelson (2009), progressing to Nelson, Slavit and Deuel (2012), and concluding with Slavit, Nelson and Deuel (2013), these researchers 'analyzed teacher talk at a group level in order to more fully capture the dialogic aspects of collaborative inquiry' (Nelson et al., 2012: 5). Their ongoing efforts resulted in the development of a two-dimensional framework that analyses and describes how teacher groups engaged with student learning data through varying dialogic and epistemological stances (Slavit et al., 2013).

In an early report from this project, Nelson (2008) focused on three in-depth case studies of the PLC work of secondary maths and science teachers. The goal was to examine the intersections of teachers' dialogic stance, the collective activities and understandings they came to, and the impact this had on their classroom practices. It became evident that each of the three groups approached and enacted their PLC work in different ways, and that those approaches and interactions impacted teacher learning and subsequent classroom practices to varying degrees. Nelson concluded that the nature of the dialogue in PLCs was critical for whether or not teachers developed an inquiry stance towards their own as well as their students' learning. She further concluded that PLC groups that were characterized by an ontological inquiry stance provided greater opportunities for teacher learning that was transformational in terms of changing classroom practices.

In subsequent literature published by Nelson et al. (2012) and Slavit et al. (2013), the authors explore multi-year case studies of seven teacher inquiry groups (PLCs) to examine dialogic interactions around student learning. Claiming that, 'teacher interactions around student-learning data are often fundamental in establishing and refining inquiry directions, dialogic tendencies and overall group perspectives about teaching and learning (Nelson et al., 2012: 3), the authors developed a two-dimensional conceptual framework designed to explain and characterize crucial influences on teachers' interactions and the resulting learning as typified by changes in classroom practices. Although a detailed discussion of the framework is beyond the scope of this chapter, a basic description is necessary to understand how the work of Slavit et al. (2013) can be used as a tool to support teacher learning in PLCs, as well as 'an analytic framework for investigating important aspects of collaborative work related to student-learning data' (Nelson et al., 2012: 3).

The first dimension of the framework is rooted in the epistemological stance exhibited by a group of educators as evidenced by their dialogic interactions related to student learning data. Closely connected to the distinctions they define between student understanding and achievement, Slavit et al. (2013) characterize teacher groups as having an epistemological stance that is either *improving* or *proving*. They further define an *improving* epistemological stance as one that 'seeks to surface limitations in classroom practice through an examination of [student learning] data' (Slavit et al., 2013: 9). In contrast, they define a *proving* epistemological stance as one that seeks to identify and verify strengths and weaknesses in their practice by measuring changes in student achievement' (ibid.: 9). While both stances include a focus on student learning, the difference lies in the purpose of data. An *improving* stance uses data to raise questions and surface limitations of current understanding, while a *proving* stance uses data to answer questions. The distinctions on this dimension of epistemological stance developed by Slavit, Nelson and Deuel (2013) closely correspond with the point we made earlier in this chapter about whether or not PLCs should be focused on the end point of student achievement or learning.

Slavit, Nelson and Deuel (2013: 10), named the second dimension of their framework, 'dialogic stance toward student-learning data', and it is closely connected with the research by Horn and Little (2010) in that it focuses on the ways that teachers talk with each other about student-learning data. Slavit et al. (2013) characterize this dimension with the dichotomous terms of *negotiation* and *non-negotiation*. The differences between these two ends lie in the nature of a PLC's collective dialogic interaction as it relates to the 'connectedness of conversational turns, purpose of questions, nature of statements, and level of certainty in the talk' (Slavit et al., 2013: 11). *Negotiation* is characterized by inquiry-based, exploratory and connected talk whereas *non-negotiation* is demonstrated by more superficial, disconnected teacher talk in PLCs. Ultimately, we believe this two-dimensional model developed by Slavit, Nelson and Deuel can serve as a model for future PLC work as well as a starting point for continued research efforts.

EVOLVING TOWARDS DEEPER LEARNING WITHIN PROFESSIONAL LEARNING COMMUNITIES

The overall lesson from examining this literature demonstrates the complexity of teacher learning through collaborative endeavours. In much of the research that examined test focused PLC efforts, teachers and administrators exhibited many of the characteristics espoused in the literature (DuFour, 2004; Newmann et al., 1996). However, just as the ability of teachers and administrators to engage in PLC work has evolved over time, so too should our understanding of how PLCs function to support teacher learning. Beginning to take steps to deconstruct the complexity of what happens in PLCs and the resulting potential for teacher learning needs to be an ongoing focus of research. The frameworks developed by Slavit et al. (2013) as well as Hadar and Brody (2012) provide insights for understanding how to frame the learning that occurs in PLCs. The challenge as we move forward is to both deepen the development of these frameworks and to explore ways that educators at all levels of participating in, facilitating or studying PLCs continue to evolve by exploring how these frameworks can inform their work.

The very nature of collaboration is undergirded by the fact that individuals within a community differ in so many ways. For example, as previously mentioned, individuals bring their assumptions about knowledge and learning to the collaboration in a way that uniquely influences the potential for the groups' collective endeavours. This leads to groups taking on their own character and engaging in their PLC work in ways that are subsequently meaningful to where and how

they enter the work. However, one question that we should continually be mindful of is, what is the goal of teachers' participation in a PLC? Is it to simply promote higher achievement as measured by test scores or should PLCs be sites of deeper teacher learning? We contend that the latter should be what educators strive for in their collaborative work, and agree with Lieberman and Miller (2008) as well as Cochran-Smith and Lytle (2009) when they suggest that deeper levels of work are necessary to fundamentally transform the stance teachers take towards learning. We continue to hope that PLCs can and will serve a critical role in transformative teacher learning as long as our understandings of how they function to accomplish that goal continue to evolve.

REFERENCES

Barth, R.S. (1991) *Improving Schools from Within*, San Francisco: Jossey-Bass.

Cochran-Smith, M. and Lytle, S. (2009) *Inquiry as Stance: Practitioner Research for the Next Generation*, New York: Teachers College Press.

Curry, M. (2008) 'Critical Friends Groups: The possibilities and limitations embedded in teacher professional communities aimed at instructional improvement and school reform', *Teacher's College Record*, 110(4): 733–74.

DuFour, R. (2004) 'What is a "Professional Learning Community"?' [electronic version]. *Educational Leadership*, 61(8): 6.

Dunne, F., Nave, B. and Lewis, A. (2000) 'Critical friends groups: Teachers helping teachers to improve student learning' [electronic version], *Phi Delta Kappan*, 28.

Englert, C.S. and Tarrant, K.L. (1995) 'Creating collaborative cultures for educational change', *Remedial and Special Education*, 16(6): 325–36, 353.

Gallimore, R., Ermeling, B.A., Saunders, W.M. and Goldenberg, C. (2009) 'Moving the learning of teaching closer to practice: Teacher education implications of school-based inquiry teams', *The Elementary School Journal*, 109(5): 537–53.

Goodnough, K. (2010) 'Teacher learning and collaborative action research: Generating a "knowledge-of-practice" in the context of science education', *Journal of Science Teacher Education*, 21(8): 917–35.

Hadar, L.L. and Brody, D.L. (2012) 'The interaction between group processes and personal professional trajectories in a professional development community for teacher educators', *Journal of Teacher Education*, 64(2): 145–61.

Hollins, E.R., McIntyre, L.R., DeBose, C., Hollins, K.S. and Towner, A. (2004) 'Promoting a self-sustaining learning community: Investigating an internal model for teacher development', *International Journal of Qualitative Studies in Education*, 17(2): 247–64.

Horn, I.S. and Little, J.W. (2010) 'Attending to problems of practice: Routines and resources for professional learning in teachers' workplace interactions', *American Educational Research Journal*, 47(1): 181–217.

Lave, J. and Wenger, E. (1991) *Situated Learning: Legitimate Peripheral Participation*, Cambridge: Cambridge University Press.

Lieberman, A. and Miller, L. (2008) *Teachers in Professional Communities*, New York: Teachers College Press.

Little, J.W. (1982) 'Norms of collegiality and experimentation: Workplace conditions of school success', *American Educational Research Journal*, 19(3): 325–40.

Lortie, D.C. (1975) *Schoolteacher*, Chicago: University of Chicago Press.

Louis, K.S. and Marks, H.M. (1998) 'Does professional community affect the classroom? Teachers' work and student experiences in restructuring schools', *American Journal of Education*, 106 (4): 532–75.

McLaughlin, M.W. and Talbert, J.E. (2001) *Professional Communities and the Work in High School Teaching*, Chicago: University of Chicago Press.

Mokhtari, K., Thoma, J. and Edwards, P. (2009) 'How one elementary school uses data to help raise students' reading achievement', *The Reading Teacher*, 63(4): 334–7.

Nelson, T.H. (2008) 'Teachers' collaborative inquiry and professional growth: Should we be optimistic?' *Science Education*, 93(3): 548–80.

Nelson, T.H., Slavit, D. and Deuel, A. (2012) 'Two dimensions of an inquiry stance toward student-learning data', *Teachers College Record*, 114(8): 1–41.

Newmann, F.M. and Associates (1996) *Authentic Achievement: Restructuring Schools for Intellectual Quality*, San Francisco: Jossey-Bass Publishers.

Opfer, V.D. and Pedder, D. (2011) 'Conceptualizing teacher professional learning', *Review of Educational Research*, 81(3): 376–407.

Putnam, R.T. and Borko, H. (2000) 'What do new views of knowledge and thinking have to say about research on teacher learning?', *Educational Researcher*, 29(1): 4–15.

Riveros, A. (2012) 'Beyond collaboration: Embodied teacher learning and the discourse of collaboration in education reform', *Studies in Philosophy and Education*, 31(6): 603–12.

Rosenholtz, S. (1989) *Teachers' Workplace: The Social Organization of Schools*, New York: Longmans.

Schmoker, M. (2004) 'Tipping point: From feckless reform to substantive instructional improvement', *Phi Delta Kappan*, 85(6): 424–32.

Slavit, D., Nelson, T.H. and Deuel, A. (2013) 'Teacher groups' conceptions and uses of student-learning data', *Journal of Teacher Education*, 64(1): 8–21.

Strahan, D. (2003) 'Promoting a collaborative professional culture in three elementary schools that have beaten the odds', *The Elementary School Journal*, 104(2): 127–46.

Vescio, V., Ross, D. and Adams, A. (2008) 'A review of research on the impact of professional learning communities on teaching practice and student learning', *Teaching and Teacher Education*, 24(1): 80–91.

Webster-Wright, A. (2009) 'Reframing professional development through understanding authentic professional learning', *Review of Educational Research*, 79: 702–39.

Williams, D.J. (2013) 'Urban education and professional learning communities', *Delta, Kappa, Gamma Bulletin*, 79(2): 31–9.

Wood, D. (2007) 'Teachers' learning communities: Catalyst for change or a new infrastructure for the status quo?', *Teachers College Record*, 109(3): 699–739.

The Learner

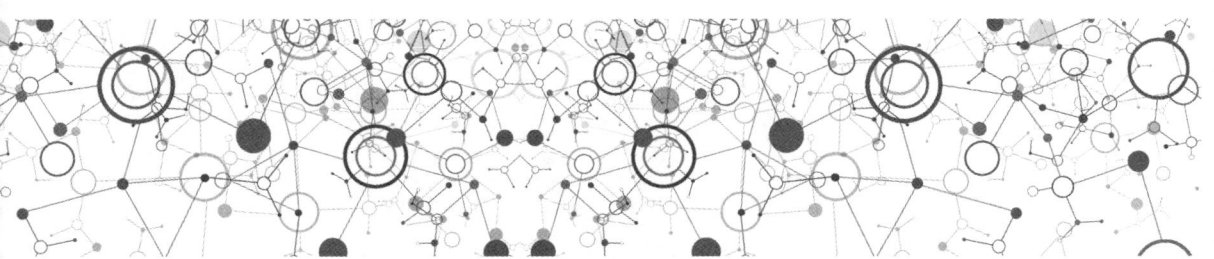

27

Introduction (Part IV)

Eleanore Hargreaves and David Scott

The chapters in Part IV of this book focus on how the learner orchestrates their internal processes of, and beliefs about, learning, as they engage in meta-cognition, meta-learning or critical reflection, making explicit links to their contextual tools, environments, histories and futures. They focus on the learner's relationships with teachers, peers and other learning sources. In these chapters, the various authors explore how the learner, in using meta-processes, asks not only questions about learning-*how*-to-learn, but also focuses on learning-*why*-to-learn.

Many of the chapters here are written from the perspective of a socio-cultural or situated-cognition theory of learning, which views the person and the environment as mutually constructed and mutually constructing. As a result they stress active, transformative and relational dimensions to learning, deeply embedded in the learner's complex contexts. In such constructivist theories, learning has an internalisation element, where what is formally external to the learner is interiorised by the learner; but it also has a performative element, where what is formally internal to the learner is exteriorised by the learner in or on the world. Whilst this whole book is about learning, Part IV foregrounds the internal struggle the learner has with themselves in learning and also in relation to the environment and others within it, past, present and future. Words from young learners themselves have therefore been included here.

An emphasis on the learner's contextualised experiences, feelings, beliefs and thoughts is relatively uncommon in policy directives or practitioner guidance where learning is more likely to be portrayed as linear and predictable, in keeping with the empiricist and behaviourist traditions. Learning in these traditions tends to be seen as a correct response to being taught content, rather than something which is complex and fluid and depends on the learner's contextualised experiences, feelings, beliefs and thoughts. Primary pupil Wayne expresses frustration with traditional approaches to learning (Hargreaves, 2012: 10):

Interviewer: You said every day for a year she's been telling you, 'Don't forget your full stops', something like that?
Wayne: Pretty much.
Interviewer: It feels like that, anyway? What happens to you when she says that? What do you think or feel?
Wayne: I always feel like (*sound of a plane plummeting*).
Interviewer: Oops. Yes.
Wayne: I always think, 'Maybe I can do it that way tomorrow,' and I always forget overnight.
Interviewer: You forget overnight?
Wayne: Yeah, my memory's gone a bit bad, but it's getting better. It's coming back.

Despite progress in research about learning which questions and indeed subverts these traditions (as illustrated in this handbook), for policymakers and practitioners the portrayal of learning as happening *to* the learner has immediate benefits: the teacher is seen to control learning in accordance with policy directives which reflect social norms and aspirations. Side-stepping the contextual complexity of learning, which relates to the experiences and contexts of the learner, is more popular for governments and makes day-to-day teaching appear more clear-cut for practitioners. Such empiricist theories of learning promote the idea that theorising and improving education is simply a matter of following the 'right' methods or procedures, and that this is an attractive and manageable task for policymakers and practitioners alike. As Mary Kalantzis and Bill Cope suggest in their chapter here:

> The moral economy of this single-minded content transmission speaks to unquestioning compliance in the face of epistemic authority, lack of critical autonomy on the part of the receivers of knowledge, and an absence of epistemic and social responsibility.

Such a content transmission approach suggests that through learning learners

themselves should replicate rather than help construct, that learning is purely adaptive rather than transformative and that learning should *conform to* behaviours, norms and strategies which constitute the social world and are external to the learner. This empiricist approach suggests that what is inside the mind of the learner changes and becomes synchronised with what is outside their mind: but that the outside itself remains the same. Primary pupil Deborah expresses this contradiction powerfully using the image of the learner as a postman who simply delivers letters (Hargreaves, 2013: 8):

Interviewer: Okay. So do you wish [the teacher] hadn't given you an example?
Deborah: If I ask for help, I need help, but most of the time I come up with stuff on my own.
Interviewer: Yes. So how does that make you feel when she does it for you?
Deborah: I'm not sure. Probably ... I'm not sure what it's called, but someone has the idea, and you just write it down for them, it's weird.
Interviewer: You end up feeling like a ... [Long pause]
Deborah: Postman.
Interviewer: Postman?
Deborah: Yeah, because they have to deliver letters.

It is no surprise, then, that behaviourist theories of learning continue to be drawn upon by the most politically powerful – often international and national policymakers – and simultaneously by the less powerful in societies – often teachers and students. Perhaps such a theory allows the most powerful to understate their own role in restricting the potentially emancipatory actions of the least powerful (cf. Hargreaves in this volume).

From the perspective of situated cognition or socio-cultural theories of learning, an explicit *acknowledgement of* learners' experiences and learners' views, itself challenges traditional power relationships, proposing more flexibility about who can give legitimacy to knowledge and how knowledge is construed. As noted in several chapters in this part of the book, the learner's original and innovative sense-making capacity can be embraced by teachers who encourage diversification from, and challenge to, the *status quo*. In this model, teaching is an ongoing process of *encouraging dialogue* about differences from, and changing assumptions within, a range of environments. The arrival of new media has the potential to enhance the development of diverse perspectives and identities further. As Joanna, a UK primary pupil recounts, pupils appreciate a challenge (cf. Hargreaves, 2015):

> Because if you're challenged you can, you know – it makes you a better learner. You don't want to be just doing things that you just like doing … You don't want to just be in your comfort zone … You want to be pushed, yeah.

Some authors in this Part of the book emphasise the *future* in their assessment of valuable learning outcomes from a socio-cultural perspective: for example, that meta-cognition, meta-learning and critical reflection, especially in dialogue with others, can help learners to cope in an unpredictable future world of work and family, making them better able to adapt to and direct a range of possible situations and to orchestrate their transactions within them. For example, Deborah Butler and Chris Watkins in their respective chapters illustrate conceptually as well as practically how learners can *step back from, view from above, take another perspective on*, or *look back over* their thinking and learning processes in order to take increased control of them and so maximise their impact in their future worlds. Karen Murphy, Carla Firetto and Valerie Long (in this volume) emphasise the need for diversity among views presented *to* learners to allow classrooms to support learners' growing capacity for making value judgements among a range of emerging choices.

Other authors here emphasise learners' relationships with figures and texts within the learner's *present and past* environments, which may nurture individual and social transformations, albeit not on every occasion. As Murphy, Firetto and Long note, the

historical emotional and social dimensions of each learner are key personally and socially to transformational learning, and this occurs in the present as much as the future (see also Carolyn Jackson in this volume). As Knud Illeris argues (in this volume), transformative learning can be defined as learning that involves change to the all-embracing historical identity of any learner and/or their situation. Tone Saevi in her chapter writes of the unpredictability of how a learner will develop, suggesting that learners have agency but need time and space to build up their own identities, drawing on the people and environments they relate to on a day-to-day basis. In this sense, learning can itself be described as continuing human *becoming* or actualisation, involving increased active engagement in dialogue with others, both now and in the future. The social media of the twenty-first century encourages this participatory engagement, in which the balance of cultural and epistemic agency is almost instantly transformed (cf. Kalantzis and Cope in this volume). A secondary-level student suggests improving pupils' engagement along similar lines (Burke and Grosvenor, 2003: 8):

> Instead of an authority structure [in classrooms] which destroys decision making and a sense of responsibility, and which outside the classroom can prove downright dangerous … children … feel empowered by the adults they come into daily contact with.

Adding a further dimension to the argument with which this introductory section began, Diane Reay reiterates in her chapter the pressing need to temper individualised notions of the learner with a focus on the influence of wider economic and cultural contexts which often embody not only irrationality and injustice but also unfathomable complexity and unpredictability. With these considerations in mind, the ensuing chapters aim to explore, problematise and also even *enable* learning that involves increased participatory engagement by all parts of society, in the pursuit of present and future beneficial transformations of identity and perspective.

REFERENCES

Burke, C. and Grosvenor, I. (2003) *The School I'd Like*, London: RoutledgeFalmer.

Hargreaves, E. (2012) 'Teachers' classroom feedback: still trying to get it right', *Pedagogies*, 7(1): 1–15.

Hargreaves, E. (2013) 'Inquiring into children's experiences of teacher feedback: reconceptualising Assessment for Learning', *Oxford Review of Education*, 39(2): 229–46.

Hargreaves, E. (2015) '"I think it helps you better when you're not scared": fear and learning in the primary classroom', *Pedagogy, Culture and Society* (in press).

28

Metacognition and Self-Regulation in Learning

Deborah L. Butler

INTRODUCTION

> The capacity to continuously learn and apply/integrate new knowledge and skills has never been more essential. Students should become self-directed, life-long learners, especially as they are preparing for jobs that do not yet exist, to use technologies that have not yet been invented, and to solve problems not yet even recognized as problems. (Dumont et al., 2012: 8)

This chapter describes what theory and research on 'metacognition' and 'self-regulation' can tell us about the nature of learning as it unfolds across the lifespan, in all sorts of activities, both within and outside of schools. To that end, across the chapter I trace the historical roots of metacognition and self-regulation as conceptual lenses for thinking about learning, surface insights generated from these two complementary perspectives, and develop an integrative framework that relates research on each. I close by identifying key issues requiring further investigation, and, correspondingly, important future directions.

However, before diving into this detailed analysis, it will be helpful to take a step back to consider the 'problem' these conceptual lenses were developed to solve. The historical roots of metacognition and self-regulation could certainly be traced back to key thinkers in education across the past century (e.g. James, Dewey, Vygotsky, or Piaget; cf. Fox and Riconscente, 2008). Their emergence can also be linked to the waning dominance of behavioural perspectives (through the 1950s), and, correspondingly, a renewed interest in cognition and mental experiences (see Bransford et al., 2000; Schunk and Zimmerman, 2006). But in this chapter my historical tracing starts with developments in the 1970s that motivated researchers to formulate metacognition and self-regulation as theories. What gaps in understandings were these conceptual lenses designed to inform? And, jumping ahead to 2015, why are these two perspectives continuing to garner such traction among researchers and educators across jurisdictions?

My interpretation is that, across the last forty years, researchers and educators have been attracted to these theories because of their potential to help in explaining what it takes for individuals to exercise agency and take deliberate control over their learning and performance (see Bandura, 1993; Bransford et al., 2000; Brown, 1978, 1980, 1987; Butler, 1998a; Flavell, 1976; Hacker et al., 2009a; Schunk, 2008). For example, starting in the 1970s, an interest in metacognition and self-regulation was inspired by the observation that, even when directly taught strategies for learning or problem-solving (e.g. for remembering, reading or writing), students often failed to use instructed strategies spontaneously or flexibly in new activities or environments (Flavell, 1976). Researchers wanted to understand *why*, even when students possessed the requisite knowledge for strategic learning or problem solving, they failed to mobilize that knowledge if not explicitly cued to do so. Both metacognition and self-regulation, as conceptual lenses for thinking about learning, were developed at least in part to explain observed gaps in students' strategic approaches to tasks (e.g. see Butler, 1998a; Efklides and Misailidi, 2010; Zimmerman, 2008).

Since that time, interest in fostering flexible, adaptive, deliberate and strategic approaches to learning has only intensified. On the one hand, research has clearly documented that learners' ability to take deliberate control over their performance predicts academic success (e.g. see Azevedo et al., 2005; Blair and Razza, 2007; Gettinger and Seibert, 2002; Pintrich and Schunk, 2002; Rimm-Kaufman et al., 2009). For example, for young learners, effective forms of self-regulation have been found to predict academic outcomes even more powerfully than do IQ or knowledge about reading and mathematics (e.g. Veenman and Spaans, 2005). On the other hand, it has also become increasingly clear that demands on learners in today's society extend far beyond just mastering content. Instead, as Dumont et al. (2012) describe in their summary of the OECD's report on *The Nature of Learning*, to thrive in the twenty-first century, individuals need to be lifelong learners with the capacity to self-direct learning and performance in a wide variety of situations. If they are to thrive in rapidly changing environments, they need to develop the capacity to seek, generate and mobilize knowledge and skills flexibly and adaptively across activities and environments.

What *is* lifelong or self-directed learning? What is required for students to take deliberate control over their own learning processes across contexts and over time? What are social and cultural influences on students' development of metacognition and self-regulation? Correspondingly, what can educators do to foster students' development of flexible, adaptive and strategic approaches to learning and problem solving? These are questions that can be informed by theory and research related to metacognition and self-regulation.

CONCEPTUALIZING METACOGNITION, SELF-REGULATION AND SELF-REGULATED LEARNING (SRL)

Efforts to clarify relationships among metacognition, self-regulation and self-regulated learning have spanned at least three decades (e.g. see Boekaerts, 1995; Brown, 1987; Corno, 1986; Dinsmore et al., 2008; Kaplan, 2008; Zimmerman 1995). Indeed, continuing this tradition, many researchers suggest that disentangling these perspectives should constitute an important future direction for theory development and empirical study (e.g. see Dinsmore et al., 2008; Efklides and Misailidi, 2010). In contrast, consistent with Kaplan's (2008) conclusion, in this chapter I make the case that searching for clear boundaries between these conceptual lenses is not likely to be fruitful. Instead, it might be more productive to think of the two overarching perspectives as providing complementary 'conceptual lenses' for viewing the same complex phenomenon.

Imagine, for example, that our challenge is to build from across research in these areas to advance understanding about deliberate, flexible, adaptive and/or strategic learning and problem solving as it unfolds in varying contexts. It follows that combining across perspectives is most likely to be productive. First, because both perspectives were inspired by a similar goal, it is to be expected that there will be overlaps in the dimensions of learning identified as important in each. Identifying these common dimensions affords opportunities to integrate research findings generated from complementary perspectives. At the same time, coordinating dimensions foregrounded uniquely by one or the other lens can help in uncovering the full

range of considerations that need to be taken into account if we are to understand and foster deliberate, strategic learning.

Thus, in this chapter my goal is to identify how taking up metacognition and self-regulation as conceptual lenses can enrich our understanding about deliberate, strategic learning. To that end, I start by tracing the historical origins first of metacognition, then of self-regulation and self-regulated learning (SRL). As I go, I tease out the dimensions of learning emphasized and elaborated from each perspective. Then, building from both commonalities and differences, I propose an integrative framework to characterize key qualities of individuals' deliberate, strategic learning as situated in the activities (see Figure 28.1).

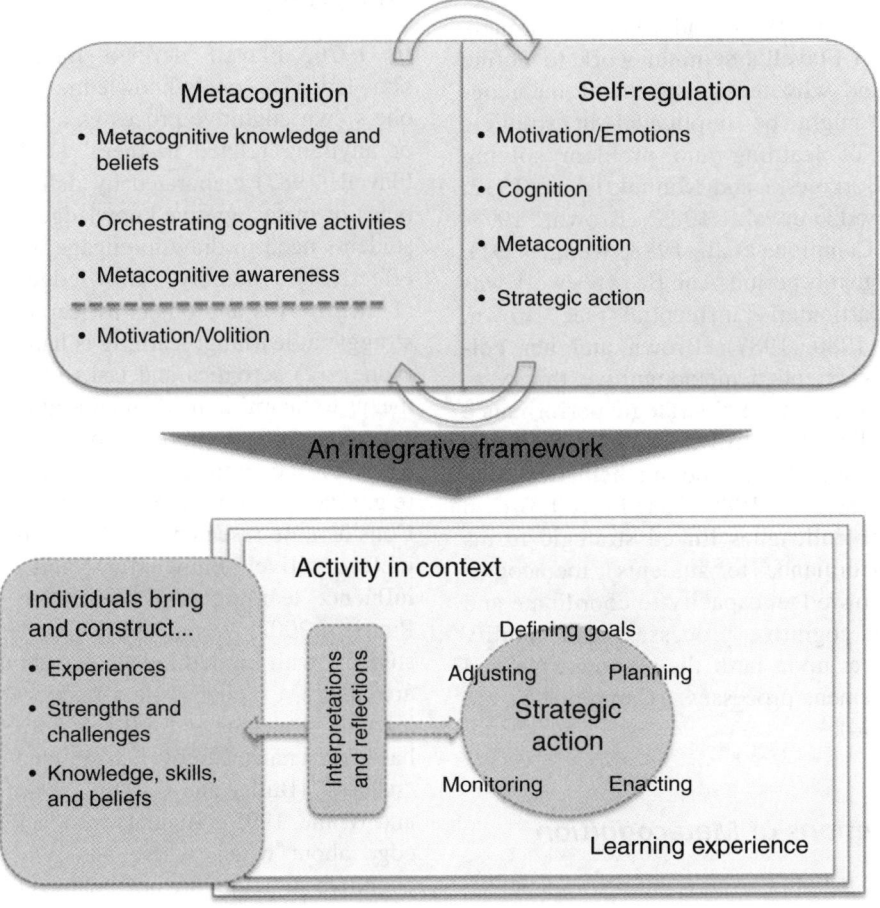

Figure 28.1   An integrative framework for investigating deliberate, strategic learning

METACOGNITION

It is widely agreed that metacognition, as a conceptual lens for understanding strategic learning and problem solving, originated in the work of John Flavell (1976, 1987). Flavell had observed that students who had been taught strategies for remembering information (e.g. rehearsing) were not spontaneously using those strategies to aid memory performance when not explicitly asked to do so. Flavell associated these 'production deficiencies' (i.e. failures to apply knowledge) with problems in metacognition. According to Flavell (1976), metacognition encompasses three important aspects of performance, namely *knowledge about*, *reflection on* and *regulation of* one's cognitive activities.

Across the 1970s and 1980s researchers built on Flavell's seminal work to define how and why these aspects of metacognition might be implicated in strategic forms of learning and problem solving (e.g. Borkowski and Muthukrishna, 1992; Borkowski et al., 1989; Brown, 1978, 1987; Campione et al., 1988; Wong, 1991). Through this period, Ann Brown's work was also particularly influential (see Brown, 1978, 1980, 1987). Brown and her colleagues extended metacognitive theory to account for students' strategic performance in reading (e.g. Brown, 1980; Palincsar and Brown, 1984) and mathematics (e.g. Campione et al., 1988). Like Flavell, Brown and her colleagues linked strategic forms of performance to students' metacognitive knowledge, capacity to coordinate and control cognitive processes, and 'ability to reflect upon both their knowledge and management processes' (Campione et al., 1988: 94).

Dimensions of Metacognition

Notable in both Flavell's and Brown's definitions is that, even in its earliest formulations, metacognition has been conceptualized as a multi-dimensional construct. Indeed, Butler described metacognitive theory as offering, not a unitary construct, but rather a 'coherent framework for relating the various metacognitive components that shape students' strategic approaches to tasks' (1998a: 279). As is represented in the top left corner of Figure 28.1, by that time metacognition was consistently associated with three related aspects, or dimensions, of learning, including students': (1) metacognitive knowledge and beliefs; (2) orchestration of cognitive activities; and (3) metacognitive awareness of knowledge and learning activities (Brown, 1987; Campione et al., 1988; Wong, 1991).

Metacognitive Knowledge and Beliefs

In 1976, Flavell defined metacognitive knowledge as 'one's knowledge concerning one's own cognitive processes and products or anything related to them' (1976: 232). Flavell (1987) elaborated by defining three types of metacognitive knowledge on which students need to draw to engage in learning effectively, namely knowledge about: (1) themselves and others as learners (e.g. I struggle at learning; learning is hard for everyone); (2) activities and tasks (e.g. what it means to 'learn' in mathematics in this classroom); and (3) cognitive processes productive for accomplishing academic work (e.g. strategies for learning in mathematics). Considerable research has documented how metacognitive knowledge and beliefs influence learning (e.g. see Butler, 1998a; Pintrich, 2002; Wong, 1991). For example, students with limited knowledge about tasks are likely to choose less-than-productive learning strategies and self-monitor progress based on a narrow or even misguided view of 'success' (Butler and Cartier, 2004b; Butler and Winne, 1995). Students who lack knowledge about when, where and why to use cognitive strategies are not well positioned to mobilize knowledge adaptively (Borkowski et al., 1989; Pintrich, 2002).

Orchestrating Cognitive Activities

Both Flavell (1976, 1987) and Brown (1978, 1980) emphasized that metacognitive performance requires individuals to orchestrate their cognitive processes in the service of achieving some kind of goal. Across the 1970s and 1980s, researchers labelled a variety of activity-orchestrating processes as 'metacognitive', including interpreting problems to discern what is required; allocating attention; planning and sequencing cognitive strategies; monitoring, checking or evaluating progress; testing and reality testing; and revising goals or strategies as needed (e.g. Brown, 1978, 1980; Butler, 1998a; Wong, 1991). Campione and Brown explained how these types of metacognitive processes serve as 'mediators of learning and transfer' (1990: 149). Through the 1970s and 1980s, a substantial body of research demonstrated the importance of metacognitive, activity-orchestrating processes in students' successful navigation of many different forms of academic work (e.g. see Borkowski, 1992; Brown et al., 1991; Butler, 1995; Graham and Harris, 1989; Swanson, 1990).

Metacognitive Awareness

Metacognition is associated with students taking deliberate control over their own cognitive activities (Brown, 1980). But to take deliberate control, learners need to be *aware* of their learning processes. Thus, over time, metacognition has also been described as encompassing individuals' conscious awareness of their knowledge and learning processes, reflections on learning and subjective learning experiences (Brown, 1987; Butler, 1998a; Campione et al., 1988; Flavell, 1976, 1987; Wong, 1991). Early researchers described how students' construction of knowledge, beliefs, and skills can emerge through reflections on learning experiences (e.g. see Butler, 1995, 1998b; Paris and Byrnes, 1989). More recently, Efklides and Misailidi also associated the emergence of

explicit, declarative knowledge with reflection, conscious analytic processes, and individuals' observations of themselves and others as 'agents capable of thoughtful and purposive action' (2010: 11).

That said, over time researchers have deliberated about the role of conscious and non-conscious processes in metacognition and learning (see Brown, 1987; Efklides and Misailidi, 2010). Imagine, for example, an individual engrossed in reading. Typically individuals only pause to reflect and 'take control' over their reading if they encounter a problem (e.g. they realize they missed an important point or that their attention has wandered). Awareness of comprehension breakdowns is metacognitive (i.e. reflecting 'metacomprehension'; see Brown, 1980; Kinnunen and Vauras, 2010). Further, consciously-mediated metacognitive processes are involved when individuals take a moment to identify a problem, reflect on possible solutions, and make adjustments accordingly. These activities exemplify metacognitive monitoring (i.e. judging progress) and control (i.e. making adjustments as needed) (Brown, 1987).

But what is it that brings comprehension problems to learners' conscious attention while they are engrossed in reading? Early on it was recognized that some metacognitive activity must take place outside of conscious awareness. In fact, Lyn Corno (1986) suggested that it is adaptive when, over time and through experiences, metacognitive processes become automated. Similarly, it is now recognized that metacognitive knowledge can build through more automated, non-conscious learning experiences (see Efklides and Misailidi, 2010).

Still, the hallmark of metacognition is students' ability to bring automatic processes to conscious awareness when more deliberate processing is called for (e.g. to identify and fix comprehension problems). For example, if we are to account for the strategic performance 'deficiencies' identified by Flavell and others through the 1970s and 1980s, we need to define what it takes for learners to *deliberately* mobilize knowledge in the face of unfamiliar problems, new situations or unanticipated challenges. It is in those cases that 'strategic' processing is required. As Butler identified, 'it is students' active and deliberative attempts to transfer strategy use across contexts or tasks that defines strategic processing, rather than the automatic implementation of well-learned routines' (1998a: 284).

Metacognition, Motivation and Volition

Because much early research that included attention to metacognition was problem-focused, in the sense that it was designed to account for challenges observed in students' strategic approaches to tasks, educators have elaborated descriptions of metacognition to include other culprits underlying less-than-strategic learning (see Figure 28.1). For example, by the early 1990s researchers had identified how different kinds of belief seemed to energize, or undermine, students' strategic approaches to tasks (Bandura, 1993; Borkowski and Muthukrisna, 1992; Schunk, 1994). These researchers started to describe 'metacognitive systems' as including cognitive, motivational, personal and situational dimensions (e.g. see Borkowski et al., 2000).

Over time, researchers have identified a range of motivationally charged beliefs that are strongly influential in how students take up learning tasks, including perceptions of self-efficacy, attributions, goal orientations, beliefs about intelligence and ability, perceptions of task value, and outcome expectancies (e.g. Dweck, 1999; 2010; Linnenbrink and Pintrich, 2003; Perry and Winne, 2004; Zimmerman, 1995, 2011). A common quality of many of these is that they reflect the extent to which students perceive themselves to be competent and in control over learning (e.g. see Schunk and Zimmerman, 2006).

For example, two types of motivational beliefs have often been incorporated into accounts of metacognition: attributions and self-efficacy (Borkowski, 1992; Schunk,

1994). Self-efficacy refers to students' beliefs in their capacity to achieve particular outcomes in a given situation (see Bandura, 1993). Attributions are the causal explanations students associate with successful or unsuccessful performance (see Borkowski, 1992). Both self-efficacy beliefs and attributional patterns shape how students take up strategies (or not) while working through learning activities. For example, research has shown that students who attribute success to factors within their control (e.g. effortful strategy use) are more likely to take up and persist in the use of strategies while learning.

Another significant elaboration to metacognitive frameworks came from Lyn Corno's rekindled attention to volition control processes (see Corno, 1993; Corno and Kanfer, 1993). Corno and Kanfer (1993) suggest that motivational beliefs and processes are pivotal when individuals are defining learning goals. Then, as a complement to motivation, volition control enables learners to see those goals through. Corno and Kanfer (1993) explain that, to sustain attention to goals, learners need to use strategies for: (1) metacognitive control (i.e. regulation of cognition); (2) motivation control (e.g. for sustaining commitment); (3) emotion control (e.g. for handling potentially intrusive emotions); and (4) environmental control (e.g. modifying environments and/or how they are engaging with others).

Reflections on Metacognition

It seems, then, that frameworks for thinking about metacognition have always been, and continue to be, multidimensional (see Figure 28.1). More recent research on metacognition has for the most part built on one or more of the core constructs associated with Flavell's original conceptualization. In so doing, it has contributed depth of understanding around many important issues. For example, over time, research has advanced understanding about interactions between metacognition and other learning dimensions (e.g. motivation, volition), how metacognition develops over time, metacognitive processes, qualities of metacognitive awareness, and how metacognition can be fostered in classrooms and technologically-supported learning environments (e.g. see Azevedo and Aleven, 2013; Bransford et al., 2000; Efklides and Misailidi, 2010; Hacker et al., 2009b).

SELF-REGULATION AND SELF-REGULATED LEARNING

Generally speaking, models of self-regulation describe how individuals take deliberate control of their thoughts and actions in order to achieve goals and respond to environmental demands (Zimmerman, 2008). Over close to 30 years, researchers have drawn on a model of self-regulation to investigate multiple aspects of performance. For example, early research on self-regulation was undertaken to help individuals in clinical settings take more deliberate control over 'challenging' behaviour (see Schunk and Zimmerman, 2006). Other research conducted from a developmental perspective has foregrounded processes associated with young children's development of emotional and behavioural regulation (e.g. Dinsmore et al., 2008; Spinrad et al., 2004). In this chapter, I narrow my attention to tracing applications of self-regulation applied to advance understanding about *learning* (e.g. see Schunk and Zimmerman, 1998).

What are the origins of self-regulation as a conceptual lens for thinking about learning? In his historical overview, Barry Zimmerman (2008) describes how budding attention to self-regulated learning (SRL) grew through the 1970s and 1980s to account for observed challenges in students' strategic approaches to tasks. The result is that conceptualizations of SRL have also built heavily on seminal work by researchers such as Flavell, Brown, Bandura, Pintrich, Corno, Schunk and others.

Zimmerman (2008) identified 1986 as a pivotal year in the development of SRL as a more unified perspective. In that year, a symposium was held at the annual meetings of the American Educational Research Association in order to 'integrate under a single rubric research on such processes as learning strategies, metacognitive monitoring, self-concept perceptions, volitional strategies, and self-control strategies' (Zimmerman, 2008: 167). Building from that symposium, Zimmerman developed his highly influential definition of SRL as reflecting 'the degree to which students are metacognitively, motivationally, and behaviorally active participants in their own learning process' (Zimmerman, 1989: 329). Two important points can be discerned from this definition and its origins. One is that, like metacognition, from the outset SRL provided more of a framework for relating important dimensions of learning than a unitary construct per se. As such, formulations of SRL tend to be multi-componential. Second, it is notable that Zimmerman's (1986) definition explicitly associated SRL with metacognition.

Over time, many different theoretical perspectives have been applied to the study of SRL (Zimmerman and Schunk, 2001). Striking is the variety of perspectives that have been adopted, including behavioural, cognitive-behavioural, constructivist, socio-cultural and socio-constructivist theories. Correspondingly, different frameworks for thinking about SRL have been put forward, each with its own particular emphases (e.g. see Boekaerts, 2011; Butler and Cartier, 2004a; Butler and Winne, 1995; Cartier and Butler, 2004; Corno, 1994; Paris et al., 2001; Pintrich, 2000; Winne and Hadwin, 1998; Zimmerman, 1989, 2001, 2008).

Given this remarkable variation, what unifies SRL as a coherent conceptual lens for thinking about learning? Across perspectives and over time, models of SRL tend to share several important qualities. First, these models are centrally concerned with describing how individuals develop the capacity to take deliberate control over their learning and performance. Indeed, the 'self' referred to in models of SRL reflects individuals' capacity to exercise agency as learners (Bandura, 1993; Zimmerman, 1986, 2008). Models of SRL typically describe individuals as active interpreters of the environments in which they find themselves (Bransford et al., 2000; Butler and Winne, 1995). Further, in contrast to perspectives on learning that position learners as passive recipients of environmental influences, models of SRL recognize learners as having the potential to both produce and respond to environments (Schunk, 2008; Schunk and Zimmerman, 2006).

A second common quality is that models of SRL incorporate social dimensions of learning. In other words, models of SRL are *not* typically applied to describe students learning independently by themselves without influence (Zimmerman, 2002). Instead, these models are designed to uncover how individuals develop capacities to exercise agency while engaged in socially rooted activities while working alone or with others. For example, many early conceptualizations of self-regulation built on Bandura's (1986, 1989) seminal work on the social foundations of thought and action (e.g. Zimmerman, 1989, 2000). These models have consistently represented reciprocal relationships among personal factors (e.g. cognitions), behaviour and environments. Drawing from Vygotsky's (1978) socio-cultural perspective, other researchers have investigated how self-regulation can be supported through social interaction (e.g. see Palincsar and Brown, 1984; Perry, 1998). Across the past decade, much progress has also been made in characterizing relationships between self- and social-forms of regulation (e.g. see Hadwin et al., 2011; Meyer and Turner, 2002; Volet et al., 2009a, 2009b).

Finally, contemporary research now consistently identifies SRL as a multi-componential, dynamic, recursive, situated activity (Butler, 2011). Consistent with this analysis, Dinsmore et al. (2008) characterize SRL as an integrative theory of learning that describes dynamic interconnections between cognition, motivation and context. Across perspectives and over time, models of SRL

have evolved to describe how individuals come to understand, reflect on, and self-direct their *motivation/emotions, cognition, metacognition* and *strategic action* during situated learning activities (see Figure 28.1).

DEVELOPING AN INTEGRATIVE FRAMEWORK

How, then, can we characterize the relative contributions of metacognition and SRL to conceptualizing deliberate, lifelong learning and problem-solving in the twenty-first century? As is hopefully apparent in my brief historical tracing (see Figure 28.1, above), both lenses offer multidimensional frameworks that relate important dimensions of learning. Ultimately both perspectives attend to knowledge, beliefs, awareness and processes implicated in the deliberate control of strategic, goal-directed action. So, how can we move forward in learning from these two complementary conceptual lenses?

MOVING FORWARD

One way forward might be to continue working hard on defining what is unique about each perspective (e.g. see Dinsmore et al., 2008). Unfortunately, given the many overlaps and convergences, defining clear boundaries between metacognition and SRL may be impossible (e.g. see Kaplan, 2008). Further, if it means that we lose sight of opportunities to synthesize research on similar issues from across perspectives, trying to carve out 'territory' unique to each might also be counter-productive. All that said, it is clear that we do need to develop a language for better coordinating descriptions of these two, continually developing perspectives. For example, unless connections are made more obvious, it might be puzzling when opening a handbook on *metacognition* to find that roughly half of the chapter titles focus on *self-regulation* (e.g. see Azevedo and Aleven, 2013).

One way forward might be for researchers to explicitly choose one or the other as a framework to work from as a conceptual tool. For example, in my own research to date, I have described myself as building from a socio-constructivist model of *self-regulation* to investigate deliberate, strategic forms of learning as situated in multiple layers of context (e.g. see Butler and Cartier, 2004a; Butler et al., 2011; Cartier and Butler, 2004). Within that framework, I include and relate dimensions of learning identified as influential across metacognitive and self-regulation lenses. To accomplish this, however, I am very careful about how I locate aspects of metacognition within the overall model. For example, I identify *metacognitive knowledge and beliefs* as something individuals bring to and build through learning experiences. Furthermore, I associate *metacognitive processes* with the cycles of strategic action central to self-regulation and link *metacognitive awareness* to individuals' reflection in and on learning before, during and after engaging in learning activities. Other researchers may prefer to use metacognitive theory as a superordinate framework for organizing multiple dimensions of learning. In so doing, it might be ideal if they were to carefully situate specific dimensions of learning included in multi-componential SRL models (i.e. emotions/motivation, cognition, metacognition, strategic action) within whatever conceptual framework they were applying.

Another choice might be to develop an integrative model, not to describe SRL or metacognition per se, but rather to afford investigating *deliberate, strategic learning* (see Figure 28.1, above). This way forward is consistent with Kaplan's (2008) recommendation. In his commentary on articles included in a special issue of *Educational Psychology Review* focused on relating metacognition, self-regulation and SRL, Kaplan concludes that a productive way forward might be to give up on efforts to distinguish them clearly, and instead move towards envisioning a multidimensional conceptual space for describing *self-regulated action*. Along those same lines, in this chapter I suggest a framework that could be fleshed out by integrating research on metacognition and self-regulation to characterize deliberate, strategic forms of learning as situated in context (see Figure 28.1, above). I confess that the framework I outline draws heavily on the socio-constructivist model of self-regulation on which I rely in my work (see Butler and Cartier, 2004a; Cartier and Butler, 2004). But, my point here is that modelling *deliberate, strategic learning* may help in identifying and coordinating the unique and converging contributions of research on metacognition and self-regulation. Further, creating a more 'purpose-driven' framework might help in uncovering issues that have yet to be addressed or need further explanation (see also Brydges and Butler, 2012).

AN INTEGRATIVE FRAMEWORK: POTENTIAL CONTRIBUTIONS

What are the key dimensions, and respective contributions, of the high-level, integrative framework represented in Figure 28.1? First, this particular depiction explicitly represents learning activity as socially situated. To that end, the nested set of rectangles at the figure's centre signify that learning activities unfold within overlapping and intersecting layers of context (e.g. a socially, culturally and historically positioned community, a school, a classroom). Being deliberately strategic requires that individuals know how to 'read' and negotiate expectations as constructed within and across these contextual layers, which may at times be conflicting (e.g. if values in families are not well aligned with expectations at school). At the same time, layers of context combine to create affordances and constraints that delimit individuals' opportunities to exercise agency, conceptualize learning and knowing, and construct knowledge, skills and beliefs (Bandura, 2006; Vygotsky, 1978).

Thus, a first contribution of this framework is that it explicitly depicts the social-environmental dimensions of learning that have been 'present', but not always foregrounded in discussions of metacognition and self-regulation. In so doing, this representation works against a common misconception that metacognition and self-regulation are theories focused narrowly on 'in the head' learning by individuals working by themselves without social influence (Zimmerman, 2002). It also suggests important questions we might take up when reviewing or generating research, such as: How do layers of context delimit opportunities for individuals to exercise agency? What qualities of learning environments foster the development of more deliberate approaches to learning? Or in what kinds of contexts and activities are individuals engaged in intentional learning?

Second, the box at the left side of the framework depicts how individuals bring to learning a variety of experiences, strengths and challenges, and knowledge skills and beliefs that shape, and are in turn shaped by, how they engage in activities. These include the wide range of metacognitive knowledge and motivational beliefs identified in this chapter as consequential in learning, as well as others not explicitly discussed here, such as prior content knowledge (see Bransford et al., 2000; Efklides and Misailidi, 2010), epistemological beliefs (see Schommer, 1990), particular kinds of learning strengths and challenges (e.g. in controlling attention) (see Butler and Schnellert, 2015), and cultural backgrounds and experiences (see Alton-Lee et al., 2001).

Contributions of this framework, from this angle, are that it: (1) creates a space for surfacing and coordinating attention to the range of experiences, strengths, challenges, knowledge, beliefs and skills that learners bring to contexts that might interact to influence how they engage in learning; (2) identifies one important source of differences in how individuals respond to and engage in particular learning activities and environments; and (3) emphasizes (in the two-way

arrow) how experiences, strengths, challenges, knowledge, skills and beliefs are not 'fixed' in individuals, but rather are continually and dynamically constructed, refined or transformed as individuals engage (and are supported to engage) in learning. We could advance understanding about important influences on students' engagement in deliberate, strategic learning if we were to synthesize and/or generate research in these areas.

Third, the framework presented in Figure 28.1 reflects how individuals' (metacognitive) learning experiences emerge as a function of individual–context interactions. This is depicted by locating 'interpretations and reflections' as mediating between what individuals bring to contexts and their engagement in strategic action. In this perspective features of contexts do not have a direct effect on learning. Instead, the effect of social and contextual features (e.g. explicit or implicit expectations; direct instruction about strategies; feedback) is mediated by learners' interpretations and reflections (Butler and Winne, 1995). For example, imagine a student enthusiastic about learning in science with a good deal of relevant background knowledge and skill. This student might perceive a project-based research activity in a science classroom to be interesting and exciting and so dive wholeheartedly into learning. In contrast, imagine another student with low confidence who is given what looks like a difficult project-based activity in an environment where assessments are comparative and public. A student in this 'position' is more likely to focus on protecting his or her well-being and reputation than on engaging in rich forms of learning (Boekaerts, 2011).

What are the potential contributions from this part of the model? First, the model describes how learning emerges from two-way, dynamic connections between individual and social processes. For example, it suggests how individuals' interpretations of contexts are coloured by their existing understandings and beliefs, but are also continually refined through social interactions embedded in learning activities. Second, the model recognizes how learning through action is constructed both consciously and non-consciously in both guided and more experiential forms of learning (Dumont et al., 2012). But it also accommodates findings suggesting that it is through reflecting in and on action (i.e. metacognitive awareness) that individuals can take more deliberate control over learning (see Butler, 2002; Butler and Schnellert, 2012; Efklides and Misailidi, 2010; Paris et al., 2001).

Finally, central in deliberate forms of learning are the strategic action cycles identified as pivotal from both metacognitive and self-regulation perspectives. Across lenses, it is recognized that students' deliberate, strategic performance relies on how they dynamically and iteratively engage in: interpreting activity demands and expectations, setting goals, planning, enacting strategies, monitoring progress and adjusting goals or strategies as needed (e.g. see Brown, 1987; Butler and Winne, 1995; Butler et al., 2011; Flavell, 1987; Winne and Hadwin, 1998; Zimmerman, 2008). Research questions inspired by this part of the model might include: 'What kinds of goals might learners set to guide learning and why?', 'Where, why and how might cycles of strategic action break down?' and 'How can environments be structured to foster learners' deliberate control over strategic action cycles?' Building on the seminal work on volition of Corno and her colleagues (Corno, 1986, 1993, 1994; Corno and Kanfer, 1993), research might also be conducted or synthesized to describe how individuals can learn to regulate all aspects of their performance in the service of learning (e.g. emotions, motivation, cognition, strategic action and environments; see also Butler et al., forthcoming).

CONCLUSION: FUTURE DIRECTIONS FOR RESEARCH ON METACOGNITION AND SELF-REGULATION

Research on metacognition and self-regulation has contributed substantially to understanding the nature of deliberate, strategic learning as situated in context. Indeed, lifelong learners are widely recognized as being both metacognitive and self-regulating (Bransford et al., 2000; Dumont et al., 2012; Zimmerman, 2008), and we have come a long way in addressing many of the questions suggested by the integrative framework as highlighted here. That said, to close out this chapter, I highlight just a few pressing challenges for research in this area.

Methodological Challenges

One of the most pressing challenges is to develop and refine robust methodological approaches for studying dynamic forms of deliberate, strategic learning as situated in context (Butler, 2011; Whitebread et al., 2009; Winne and Perry, 2000; Zimmerman, 2008). One important direction here is to construct and enact overall research designs with potential to trace learning dynamically as it unfolds in relation to contextual features and develops over time (Dinsmore et al., 2008). For example, Butler (2011) suggests the value of case study designs which allow for investigating complex phenomena as situated in context (Creswell, 2007; Yin, 2003). In a recent study, she and her colleagues (Butler et al., 2011) illustrated how a case study approach can be used to identify patterns that hold across cases while still preserving the meaning of action in context. But researchers are also constructing a range of dynamic, complex approaches to tracing the development of deliberate, strategic learning in the context of activities (e.g. see Zimmerman, 2008).

A second important methodological challenge is to identify robust approaches for 'measuring' or 'assessing' the multiple consciously-mediated and non-conscious dimensions implicated in deliberate, strategic learning. Fortunately, great strides are also being made in the development of strategies for 'seeing' metacognition and self-regulation in action (see Zimmerman,

2008). Examples include self-report tools, if used to capture students' beliefs, perceptions and reflections, rather than as indicators of actual behaviour (Butler, 2002, 2011), trace logs of self-regulating processes generated in computer-assisted environments (e.g. Winne and Perry, 2000; Winne et al., 2006), structured diary measures completed in tandem with learning (Schmitz and Wiese, 2006; Zimmerman, 2008), observational protocols (Perry, 1998; Whitebread et al., 2009), and 'micro-analytic' approaches (Cleary and Zimmerman, 2001).

Theoretical Directions

From a more theoretical perspective, numerous questions remain that need to be considered by researchers interested in understanding and advancing deliberate, strategic forms of learning (see Dinsmore et al., 2008; Efklides and Misailidi, 2010; Kaplan, 2008; Schunk, 2008; Zimmerman, 2008). Space limitations prohibit a comprehensive summary of possibilities. Instead, I highlight just three topics that deserve particular attention.

Exploring Agency

Models of self-regulation and metacognition position individuals as agents responsible for negotiating environments and driving their learning (Bandura, 1993; Hacker et al., 2009a). Therefore, it would be particularly useful to continue investigating the ways in which contexts afford, support and/or constrain individuals' capacity to exercise agency and associated implications (see Bandura, 1989, 2000; 2006; Butler et al., 2015; Perry, 2014; Schunk, 2008). It would be valuable to scrutinize opportunities for agency afforded within a particular classroom, school or jurisdiction. Also important is to critically assess whether and why some learners may have fewer opportunities to exercise agency than do peers. For example,

are students identified as having special education needs also supported to learn how to take deliberate control over their learning and performance (see Diaz-Greenberg et al., 2000; Perry, 2004)?

From an 'agency' perspective, we might also reflect on the origin of 'goals' strategic learners might pursue. Realistically, to survive in many environments (e.g. to pass courses in schools), individuals need to be able to interpret expectations as imagined by others (e.g. in current curricula) and then decide how to address them (by taking them up, ignoring them, or negotiating alternatives). Correspondingly, much research on metacognition and SRL has focused on how students learn to navigate the kinds of academic work set for them in classrooms (e.g. reading, writing, or maths tasks). Lifelong learners certainly need to build the capacity to interpret expectations and deliberately mobilize thoughts and actions to achieve them (Zimmerman, 2008).

But, as Dumont et al. (2012) signal, twenty-first-century learners may need to be as proficient in finding and defining problems as they are in solving them. Thus, they suggest that the development of lifelong, adaptive learners requires engaging students in a balance of guided action and experiential forms of learning. In these two approaches students take increasing responsibility, not only for self-regulating learning towards curricular goals, but also for defining goals and expectations. It also follows that goals pursued by 'self-regulating' learners do not have to be defined narrowly or instrumentally. Students can be engaged in imagining and pursuing goals that are exploratory, experiential or creative (Flum and Kaplan, 2006).

Conscious and Non-conscious Processes in Deliberate, Strategic Learning

Another intriguing direction for further study is to define the relative roles of conscious and non-conscious processes in *deliberate,* strategic learning (Efklides and Misailidi, 2010). Corno (1986) (and others) identified early on that some metacognitive processes become automated over time. Yet most models of metacognition and self-regulation also foreground the importance of individuals being able to take up deliberate, consciously-mediated processing when needed (e.g. when problems are encountered, in new situations). Thus, important questions remain; for example, about how conscious and non-conscious processes interact in adaptive forms of learning, whether and how individuals can learn to interweave them dynamically as needed, and whether and how both conscious and non-conscious processes might influence individuals' construction of 'metacognitive' knowledge, skills and beliefs.

A related question concerns how conscious and non-conscious processes might be implicated in the development of metacognition and self-regulation in young children (see Efklides and Misailidi, 2010). While it has long been recognized that young children engage in strategic action (e.g. Brown, 1987), early on it was assumed that young children's metacognition was limited until they developed the capacity to describe their experiences in words. But recent research is uncovering very young children's capacities for both metacognition and self-regulation (Lyons and Ghetti, 2010; Perry, 1998; Swalander and Folkesson, 2010; Whitebread et al., 2009). For example, infants as young as six months have been observed to turn away from an unpleasant object (i.e. a form of environmental regulation) (see Shaffer and Kipp, 2010). Similarly, research by David Whitebread and others (e.g. Whitebread et al., 2009) suggests that young children may possess and act on metacognitive knowledge, even when they are not explicitly aware of it or able to verbally express it (Efklides and Misailidi, 2010). Thus, the relative roles of consciously analytic and more implicit forms of learning in the development of metacognition and self-regulation definitely warrant further attention.

When and why accuracy might be expected

A final theoretical challenge highlighted here is to consider when and why we might expect metacognitive knowledge, beliefs or processes to be 'accurate' or well 'calibrated'. For example, if we ask students how 'confident' they are, either prospectively (i.e. before answering a test question) or retrospectively (i.e. that an answer given was correct), it is not uncommon to find mismatches between confidence and outcomes as assessed 'objectively' (e.g. test scores). But when and why should we expect subjective judgements or self-beliefs to reflect outcomes, especially as measured by tests? First, imagine what we are asking of students in terms of 'confidence' predictions. A test score on a given day likely emerges from a complex interaction between individual (e.g. knowledge, confidence, anxiety, test-taking strategies) and social factors (e.g. questions asked, scoring criteria). Can we expect pre-test confidence predictions to anticipate outcomes exactly, given this complexity? Second, it is interesting to imagine the relative roles of consciously mediated analytic processes and metacognitive experiences or 'feelings' (e.g. feelings of knowing) in situated self-perceptions (e.g. Efklides and Misailidi, 2010; Touroutoglou and Efklides, 2010).

A related question concerns the expected accuracy of 'self-assessment', especially in early learning. It could be argued that self-assessment should be more accurate than self-beliefs, since it should ideally emerge from a more objective, analytic judgement of progress in relation to goals. Nonetheless, self-assessment is often flawed, even for very capable learners such as physicians in medical practice (Eva and Regehr, 2011). When and why might we expect self-assessment to be 'accurate'? Eva and Regehr (2011) propose that situated self-assessments generated 'on-line' through monitoring in the midst of an activity may be more accurate than global judgements of one's learning needs made out of context. Brydges and Butler (2012) suggest that more accurate self-assessment can only be expected as individuals develop expertise in a particular area, because it is only then that they have developed the requisite understanding about goals and dimensions of practice on the basis of which they can anchor judgements of progress. In fact, becoming progressively more discerning in how one works through cycles of strategic action may be an integral process underlying the development of adaptive expertise.

In Closing

Of course there are many other important directions that researchers might take up in the on-going study of the roles of metacognition and self-regulation in learning. Research from both perspectives is thriving, and outstanding resources are available to readers who wish to probe deeper (see Azevedo and Aleven, 2013; Boekaerts et al., 2000; Dinsmore et al., 2008; Efklides and Misailidi, 2010; Kaplan, 2008; Hacker et al., 2009b; Perry, 2014; Zimmerman and Schunk, 2011). Here I close by returning to the purpose of this chapter. Hopefully the overview provided here helps in uncovering the great potential of these theoretical perspectives, particularly when taken up in tandem, to inform understanding about deliberate, strategic forms of learning.

REFERENCES

Alton-Lee, A., Diggins, C., Klenner, L., Vine, E. and Dalton, N. (2001) 'Teacher management of the learning environment during a social studies discussion in a new-entrant classroom in New Zealand', *The Elementary School Journal*, 10, 1: 549–66.

Azevedo, R. and Aleven, V. (eds) (2013) *International Handbook of Metacognition and Learning Technologies*, New York: Springer.

Azevedo, R., Cromley, J.G., Winters, F.I., Moos, D.C. and Greene, J.A. (2005) 'Adaptive human scaffolding facilitates adolescents' self-regulated learning with hypermedia', *Instructional Science*, 33: 381–412.

Bandura, A. (1986) *Social Foundations of Thought and Action: A Social Cognitive Theory*, Englewood Cliffs, NJ: Prentice-Hall.

Bandura, A. (1989) 'Human agency in social cognitive theory', *American Psychologist*, 44, 9: 1175–84.

Bandura, A. (1993) 'Perceived self-efficacy in cognitive development and functioning', *Educational Psychologist*, 28: 117–48.

Bandura, A. (2000) 'Exercise of human agency through collective efficacy', *Current Directions in Psychological Science*, 9, 3: 75–8.

Bandura, A. (2006) 'Toward a psychology of human agency', *Perspectives on Psychological Science*, 1, 2: 164–80.

Blair, C. and Razza, R.P. (2007) 'Relating effortful control, executive function, and false belief understanding to emerging math and literacy ability in kindergarten', *Child Development*, 78: 647–63.

Boekaerts, M. (1995) 'Self-regulated learning: Bridging the gap between metacognitive and metamotivational theories', *Educational Psychologist*, 30: 192–200.

Boekaerts, M. (2011) 'Emotions, emotion regulation, and self-regulation of learning', in B.J. Zimmerman and D.H. Schunk (eds), *Handbook of Self-Regulation of Learning and Performance*, New York: Routledge, pp. 408–25.

Boekaerts, M., Pintrich, P.R. and Zeidner, M. (eds) (2000) *Handbook of Self-Regulation*, San Diego: Academic Press.

Borkowski, J.G. (1992) 'Metacognitive theory: A framework for teaching literacy, writing and math skills', *Journal of Learning Disabilities*, 25: 254–7.

Borkowski, J.G. and Muthukrishna, N. (1992) 'Moving metacognition into the classroom: "Working models" and effective strategy teaching', in M. Pressley, K.R. Harris and J.T. Guthrie (eds), *Promoting Academic Competence and Literacy in School*, Toronto: Academic Press, pp. 477–501.

Borkowski, J.G., Chan, L.K.S. and Muthukrishna, N. (2000) 'A process-oriented model of metacognition: Links between motivation and executive functioning', *Issues in the Measurement of Metacognition*, Paper 2.

Available from: http://digitalcommons.unl. edu/burosmetacognition/2

Borkowski, J.G., Estrada, M.T., Milstead, M. and Hale, C.A. (1989) 'General problem-solving skills: Relations between metacognition and strategic processing', *Learning Disability Quarterly*, 12: 57–70.

Bransford, J.D., Brown, A.L. and Cocking, R.R. (2000) *How People Learn: Brain, Mind, Experience, and School*, Washington, DC: National Academy Press.

Brown, A.L. (1978) 'Knowing when, where and how to remember: A problem of metacognition', in R. Glaser (ed.), *Advances in Instructional Psychology*, Hillsdale, NJ: Erlbaum, pp. 77–165.

Brown, A.L. (1980) 'Metacognitive development and reading', in R.J. Spiro, B.C. Bruce and W.F. Brewer (eds), *Theoretical Issues in Reading Comprehension: Perspectives from Cognitive Psychology, Linguistics, Artificial Intelligence, and Education*, Hillsdale, NJ: Erlbaum, pp. 453–81.

Brown, A.L. (1987) 'Metacognition, executive control, self-regulation, and other more mysterious mechanisms', in F.E. Weinert and R.H. Kluwe (eds), *Metacognition, Motivation, and Understanding*, Hillsdale, NJ: Erlbaum, pp. 65–116.

Brown, A.L., Campione, J.C., Ferrara, R.A., Reeve, R.A. and Palincsar, A.S. (1991) 'Interactive learning and individual understanding: The case of reading and mathematics', in L.T. Landsmann (ed.), *Culture, Schooling, and Psychological Development: Human Development, Vol. 4*, Norwood, NJ: Ablex Publishing Co., pp. 136–170.

Brydges, R. and Butler, D.L. (2012) 'A reflective analysis of medical education research on self-regulation in learning and practice', *Medical Education*, 46: 71–79.

Butler, D.L. (1995) 'Promoting strategic learning by postsecondary students with learning disabilities', *Journal of Learning Disabilities*, 28: 170–90.

Butler, D.L. (1998a) 'Metacognition and learning disabilities', in B.Y.L. Wong (ed.), *Learning about Learning Disabilities* (2nd edn), Toronto: Academic Press. pp. 277–307.

Butler, D.L. (1998b) 'The Strategic Content Learning approach to promoting self-regulated learning: A summary of three studies', *Journal of Educational Psychology*, 90: 682–97.

Butler, D.L. (2002) 'Individualizing instruction in self-regulated learning', *Theory into Practice*, 41: 81–92.

Butler, D.L. (2011) 'Investigating self-regulated learning using in-depth case studies', in B.J. Zimmerman and D.H. Schunk (eds), *Handbook of Self-Regulation of Learning and Performance*, New York: Routledge, pp. 346–60.

Butler, D.L. and Cartier, S.C. (2004a) 'Learning in varying activities: An explanatory framework and a new evaluation tool founded on a model of self-regulated learning', paper presented at the Canadian Society for Studies in Education Annual Conference, Winnipeg, MB.

Butler, D.L. and Cartier, S.C. (2004b) 'Promoting students' active and productive interpretation of academic work: A key to successful teaching and learning', *Teachers College Record*, 106: 1729–58.

Butler, D.L. and Schnellert, L. (2012) 'Collaborative inquiry in teacher professional development', *Teaching and Teacher Education*, 28: 1206–20.

Butler, D.L. and Schnellert, L. (2015) 'Success for students with learning disabilities: What does self-regulation have to do with it?', in T. Cleary (ed.), *Self-regulated Learning Interventions with At-Risk Populations: Academic, Mental Health, and Contextual Considerations*, Washington: APA Press, pp. 89–111.

Butler, D.L. and Winne, P.H. (1995) 'Feedback and self-regulated learning: A theoretical synthesis', *Review of Educational Research*, 65: 245–81.

Butler, D.L., Cartier, S.C., Schnellert, L., Gagnon, F and Giammarino, M. (2011) 'Secondary students' self-regulated engagement in reading: Researching self-regulation as situated in context', *Psychological Test and Assessment Modeling*, 53, 1: 73–105.

Butler, D.L., Schnellert, L. and MacNeil, K. (2015) 'Collaborative inquiry and distributed agency in educational change: A case study of a multi-level community of inquiry', *Journal of Educational Change*, 16, 1: 1–26.

Butler, D.L., Schnellert, L. and Perry, N.E. (forthcoming) *Developing Self-Regulating Learners*, Don Mills, ON: Pearson.

Campione, J.C. and Brown, A.L. (1990) 'Guided learning and transfer: Implications for approaches to assessment', in N. Frederiksen, R. Glaser, A. Lesgold and M.G. Shafto (eds), *Diagnostic Monitoring of Skill and Knowledge Acquisition*, Hillsdale, NJ: Erlbaum, pp. 141–72.

Campione, J.C., Brown, A.L. and Connell, M.L. (1988) 'Metacognition: On the importance of understanding what you are doing', in R.J. Charles and E.A. Silver (eds.), *The Teaching and Assessing of Mathematical Problem Solving* (Vol. 3), Hillsdale, NJ: Erlbaum, pp. 93–114.

Cartier, S.C. and Butler, D.L. (2004) 'Elaboration and validation of the questionnaires and plan for analysis', paper presented at the Canadian Society for Studies in Education Annual Conference, Winnipeg, MB, May.

Cleary, T.J. and Zimmerman, B.J. (2001) 'Self-regulation differences during athletic practice by experts, non-experts, and novices', *Journal of Applied Sport Psychology*, 13: 61–82.

Corno, L. (1986) 'The metacognitive control components of self-regulated learning', *Contemporary Educational Psychology*, 11: 333–46.

Corno, L. (1993) 'The best-laid plans: Modern conceptions of volition and educational research', *Educational Researcher*, 22, 2: 14–22.

Corno, L. (1994) 'Student volition and education: Outcomes, influences, and practices', in D.H. Schunk and B.J. Zimmerman (eds), *Self-Regulation of Learning and Performance: Issues and Educational Applications*, Hillsdale, NJ: Erlbaum, pp. 229–51.

Corno, L. and Kanfer, R. (1993) 'Chapter 7: The role of volition in learning and performance', *Review of Research in Education*, 19: 301–41.

Creswell, J.W. (2007) *Qualitative Inquiry and Research Design: Choosing Among Five Approaches* (2nd edn), Thousand Oaks: Sage.

Diaz-Greenberg, R., Thousand, J., Cardelle-Elawar, M. and Nevin, A. (2000) 'What teachers need to know about the struggle for self-determination (conscientization) and self-regulation: Adults with disabilities speak about their education experiences', *Teaching and Teacher Education*, 16: 873–87.

Dinsmore, D.L., Alexander, P.A. and Loughlin, S.M. (2008) 'Focusing the conceptual lens on metacognition, self-regulation, and self-regulated learning', *Educational Psychology Review*, 20: 391–409.

Dumont, H., Istance, D. and Benavides, F. (eds) (2012) *The Nature of Learning: Using Research to Inspire Practice: Practitioner Guide from the Innovative Learning Environments Project*, OECD: Centre for Educational Research and Innovation.

Dweck, C.S. (1999) *Self-Theories: Their Role in Motivation, Personality, and Development*, Philadelphia: Taylor and Francis.

Dweck, C.S. (2010) 'Even geniuses work hard', *Educational Leadership*, 68, 1: 16–20.

Efklides, A. and Misailidi, P. (2010) 'Introduction: The present and future in metacognition', in A. Efklides and P. Misailidi (eds), *Trends and Prospects in Metacognition Research*, New York: Springer, pp. 1–20.

Eva, K.W. and Regehr, G. (2011) 'Exploring the divergence between self-assessment and self-monitoring', *Advances in Health Sciences Education*, 16: 311–29.

Flavell, J.H. (1976) 'Metacognitive aspects of problem solving', in L.B. Resnick (ed.), *The Nature of Intelligence*, Hillsdale, NJ: Erlbaum, pp. 231–5.

Flavell, J.H. (1987) 'Speculations about the nature and development of metacognition', in F.E. Weinert and R.H. Kluwe (eds), *Metacognition, Motivation, and Understanding*, Hillsdale, NJ: Erlbaum, pp. 21–64.

Flum, H. and Kaplan, A. (2006) 'Exploratory orientation as an educational goal', *Educational Psychologist*, 41: 99–110.

Fox, E. and Riconscente, M.M. (2008) 'Metacognition and self-regulation in James, Piaget, and Vygotsky', *Educational Psychology Review*, 20: 373–89.

Gettinger, M. and Seibert, J.K. (2002) 'Contributions of study skills to academic competence', *School Psychology Review*, 31: 350–65.

Graham, S. and Harris, K.R. (1989) 'Components analysis of cognitive strategy instruction: Effects on learning disabled students' compositions and self-efficacy', *Journal of Educational Psychology*, 81: 353–61.

Hacker, D.J., Dunlosky, J. and Graesser, A.C. (2009a) 'A growing sense of "agency"', in D.J. Hacker, J. Dunlosky and A.C. Graesser (eds), *Handbook of Metacognition in Education*, New York: Routledge.

Hacker, D.J., Dunlosky, J. and Graesser, A.C. (eds) (2009b) *Handbook of Metacognition in Education*, New York: Routledge.

Hadwin, A.F., Jarvela, S. and Miller, M. (2011) 'Self-regulated, co-regulated, and socially shared regulation of learning', in B.J. Zimmerman and D.H. Schunk (eds), *Handbook of Self-Regulation of Learning and Performance*, New York: Routledge, pp. 65–84.

Kaplan, A. (2008) 'Clarifying metacognition, self-regulation, and self-regulated learning: What's the purpose?', *Educational Psychology Review*, 20: 477–84.

Kinnunen, R. and Vauras, M. (2010) 'Tracking on-line metacognition: Monitoring and regulating comprehension in reading', in A. Efklides and P. Misailidi (eds), *Trends and Prospects in Metacognition Research*, New York: Springer, pp. 209–32.

Linnenbrink, E.A. and Pintrich, P.R. (2003) 'The role of self-efficacy beliefs in student engagement and learning in the classroom', *Reading and Writing Quarterly*, 19: 119–37.

Lyons, K.E. and Ghetti, S. (2010) 'Metacognitive development in early childhood: New questions and old assumptions', in A. Efklides and P. Misailidi (eds), *Trends and Prospects in Metacognition Research*, New York: Springer, pp. 259–78.

Meyer, D.K. and Turner, J.C. (2002) 'Using instructional discourse analysis to study the scaffolding of student self-regulation', *Educational Psychologist*, 37: 5–13.

Palincsar, A.S. and Brown, A.L. (1984) 'Reciprocal teaching of comprehension-fostering and comprehension monitoring activities', *Cognition and Instruction*, 1: 117–75.

Paris, S.G. and Byrnes, J.P. (1989) 'The constructivist approach to self-regulation and learning in the classroom', in B.J. Zimmerman and D.H. Schunk (eds), *Self-Regulated Learning and Academic Achievement: Theory, Research, and Practice*, New York: Springer-Verlag, pp. 169–200.

Paris, S.G., Byrnes, J.P. and Paris, A.H. (2001) 'Constructing theories, identities, and actions of self-regulated learners', in B.J. Zimmerman and D.H. Schunk (eds), *Self-Regulated Learning and Academic Achievement*, New York: Springer-Verlag, pp. 253–87.

Perry, N.E. (1998) 'Young children's self-regulated learning and contexts that support it', *Journal of Educational Psychology*, 90: 715–29.

Perry, N.E. (2004) 'Using self-regulated learning to accommodate differences amongst students in classrooms', *Exceptionality Education Canada*, 14(2 and 3): 65–87.

Perry, N. (2014) 'Classroom processes that support self-regulation in young children', Monograph, University of British Columbia.

Perry, N.E. and Winne, P.H. (2004) 'Motivational messages from home and school: How do they influence young children's engagement in learning?', in D. McInerney and S. Van Etten (eds), *Big Theories Revisited: Vol. IV: Research on Sociocultural Influences on Motivation and Learning*, Greenwich: Information Age, pp. 199–222.

Pintrich, P.R. (2000) 'The role of goal orientation in self-regulated learning', in M. Boekaerts, P.R. Pintrich, and M. Zeidner (eds), *Handbook of Self-Regulation*, San Diego: Academic Press, pp. 451–502.

Pintrich, P.R. (2002) 'The role of metacognitive knowledge in learning, teaching, and assessing', *Theory into Practice*, 41, 4: 219–25.

Pintrich, P.R. and Schunk, D.H. (2002) *Motivation in Education: Theory, Research, and Applications* (2nd edn), Upper Saddle River, NJ: Prentice Hall.

Rimm-Kaufman, S.E., Curby, T.W., Grimm, K.J., Nathanson, L. and Brock, L.L. (2009) 'The contribution of children's self-regulation and classroom quality to children's adaptive behaviors in the kindergarten classroom', *Developmental Psychology*, 45, 4: 958–72.

Schmitz, B. and Wiese, B.S. (2006) 'New perspectives for the evaluation of training sessions in self-regulated learning: Time-series analysis of diary data', *Contemporary Educational Psychology*, 31: 64–96.

Schommer, M. (1990) 'Effects of beliefs about the nature of knowledge on comprehension', *Journal of Educational Psychology*, 82: 498–504.

Schunk, D.H. (1994) 'Self-regulation of self-efficacy and attributions in academic settings', in D.H. Schunk and B.J. Zimmerman (eds), *Self-Regulation of Learning and Performance: Issues and Educational Applications*, Hillsdale, NJ: Erlbaum, pp. 75–99.

Schunk, D.H. (2008) 'Metacognition, self-regulation, and self-regulated learning:

Research recommendations', *Educational Psychology Review*, 20: 463–7.

Schunk, D.H. and Zimmerman, B.J. (1998) *Self-Regulated Learning: From Teaching to Self-Reflective Practice*, New York: The Guilford Press.

Schunk, D.H. and Zimmerman, B.J. (2006) 'Competence and control beliefs: Distinguising the means and ends', in P.A. Alexander and P.H. Winne (eds), *Handbook of Educational Psychology* (2nd edn), New York: Routledge, pp. 349–67.

Shaffer, D.R. and Kipp, K. (2010) *Developmental Psychology: Childhood and Adolescence* (8th edn), Belmont, CA: Wadsworth.

Spinrad, T., Stifter, C., Donelan-McCall, N. and Turner, L. (2004) 'Mothers' regulation strategies in response to toddlers' affect: Links to later emotion self-regulation', *Social Development*, 13, 1: 40–55.

Swalander, L. and Folkesson, A. (2010) 'Computer use in a primary school: A case-study of self-regulated learning', in A. Efklides and P. Misailidi (eds), *Trends and Prospects in Metacognition Research*, New York: Springer, pp. 395–426.

Swanson, H.L. (1990) 'Instruction derived from the strategy deficit model: Overview of principles and procedures', in T. Scruggs and B.Y.L. Wong (eds), *Intervention Research in Learning Disabilities*, New York: Springer-Verlag, pp. 34–65.

Touroutoglou, A. and Efklides, A. (2010) 'Cognitive interruption as an object of metacognitive monitoring: Feeling of difficulty and surprise', in A. Efklides and P. Misailidi (eds), *Trends and Prospects in Metacognition Research*, New York: Springer, pp. 171–208.

Veenman, M.V.J. and Spaans, M.A. (2005) 'Relation between intellectual and metacognitive skills: Age and task differences', *Learning and Individual Differences*, 15: 159–76.

Volet, S., Summers, M. and Thurman, J. (2009a) 'High level co-regulation in collaborative learning: How does it emerge and how is it sustained?', *Learning and Instruction*, 19: 128–43.

Volet, S., Vauras, M. and Salonen, P. (2009b) 'Self- and social regulation in learning contexts: An integrative perspective', *Educational Psychologist*, 44, 4: 215–22.

Vygotsky, L.S. (1978) *Mind in Society*, Cambridge, MA: Harvard University Press.

Whitebread, D., Coltman, P., Pasternak, D.P., Sangster, C., Grau, V., Bingham, S., Almeqdad, Q. and Demetriou, D. (2009) 'The development of two observational tools for assessing metacognition and self-regulated learning in young children', *Metacognition Learning*, 4: 63–85.

Winne, P.H. and Hadwin, A.F. (1998) 'Studying as self-regulated learning', in D. Hacker, J. Dunlosky and A. Graesser (eds), *Metacognition in Educational Theory and Practice*, Hillsdale, NJ: Erlbaum, pp. 279–306.

Winne, P.H. and Perry, N.E. (2000) 'Measuring self-regulated learning', in P. Pintrich, M. Boekarts and M. Zeidner (eds), *Handbook of Self-Regulation*, Orlando: Academic Press, pp. 531–66.

Winne, P.H., Nesbit, J.C., Kumar, V., Hadwin, A.F., Lajoie, S. and Azevedo, R. (2006) 'Supporting self-regulated learning with gStudy software: The learning kit project', *Technology, Instruction, Cognition and Learning*, 3: 105–13.

Wong, B.Y.L. (1991) 'The relevance of metacognition to learning disabilities', in B.Y.L. Wong (ed.), *Learning about Learning Disabilities*, New York: Academic Press, pp. 231–56.

Yin, R.K. (2003) *Case Study Research: Design and Methods* (3rd edn), Thousand Oaks: Sage.

Zimmerman, B.J. (1986) 'Development of self-regulated learning: Which are the key sub-processes?', *Contemporary Educational Psychology*, 11: 307–13.

Zimmerman, B.J. (1989) 'A social cognitive view of self-regulated academic learning', *Journal of Educational Psychology*, 81: 329–99.

Zimmerman, B.J. (1995) 'Self-regulation involves more than metacognition: A social-cognitive perspective', *Educational Psychologist*, 30: 217–21.

Zimmerman, B.J. (2000) 'Attaining self-regulation: A social cognitive perspective', in M. Boekaerts, P.R. Pintrich, and M. Zeidner (eds), *Handbook of Self-Regulation*, San Diego: Academic Press, pp. 13–39.

Zimmerman, B.J. (2001) 'Theories of self-regulated learning and academic achievement: An overview and analysis', in B.J. Zimmerman and D.H. Schunk (eds), *Self-Regulated Learning and Academic Achievement: Theoretical*

Perspectives (2nd edn), Mahwah, NJ: Erlbaum, pp. 1–38.

Zimmerman, B.J. (2002) 'Becoming a self-regulated learner: An overview', *Theory into Practice*, 41, 2: 64–70.

Zimmerman, B.J. (2008) 'Investigating self-regulation and motivation: Historical background, methodological developments, and future prospects', *American Educational Research Journal*, 45: 166–83.

Zimmerman, B.J. (2011) 'Motivational sources and outcomes of self-regulated learning and performance', in B.J. Zimmerman and D.H. Schunk (eds), *Handbook of Self-Regulation of Learning and Performance*, New York: Routledge, pp. 49–64.

Zimmerman, B.J. and Schunk, D.H. (eds) (2001) *Self-Regulated Learning and Academic Achievement: Theoretical Perspectives* (2nd edn), Hillsdale, NJ: Erlbaum.

Zimmerman, B.J. and Schunk, D.H. (eds) (2011) *Handbook of Self-Regulation of Learning and Performance*, New York: Routledge.

29

Pedagogy, Fear and Learning

Eleanore Hargreaves

INTRODUCTION

This chapter examines fear in the classroom, which is seen as a necessary side effect of authoritarian pedagogy, itself fuelled by historical purposes in education. It suggests that it is through the authoritarian pedagogy itself, based on fear, that purposes of schooling continue to focus on conformity rather than transformation. In reporting on some children's experiences of fear in the classroom, I am recognizing their untapped potential to transform their own schooling. At the same time I am making connections between their perceptions of how and why fear influences their learning within an authoritarian framework and investigating how the structures of authoritarian pedagogy seem to persist in a fear-inspiring manner. I use a broad conceptualization of fear, inspired by the pupils' ways of thinking about fear, to include anxiety, nervousness, worry, feeling pressured, dreading things, being uncomfortably tense and panicking.

I draw here as background on the perceptions of students about schooling in general,

recorded by Burke and Grosvenor (2003) in their study which explored the school that pupils would like best. I then discuss my own recent observations of and conversations with primary children specifically about fear in their classrooms. I have attempted to portray in this chapter how they believe fear manifests itself, what children say they fear in classrooms today and how they claim fear might affect them and their learning. I relate these findings to the four surveillance structures that persist even today in UK classrooms as backbones of authoritarian pedagogy, precisely *because* they limit the transformational nature of children's learning. I draw some conclusions about the circular nature of pedagogies and purposes for schooling.

PURPOSES FOR SCHOOLING

Bernstein (1995) distinguished between schools where framing is strong, impeding the learner from interpreting critically the rules and messages they are learning, and restraining them from contributing to their own development; and where framing is weak, allowing more scope for students to 'dissolve, fragment or otherwise disrupt the models of knowledge held' by the student and the teacher, which provides 'disjuncture in the minds of students, and the responsibility for replacement is devolved to the student' (Scott and Hargreaves, this volume, Chapter 37). Authoritarian pedagogies, where framing tends to be strong, function as though, during learning, change takes place in the mind of the learner who conforms to superior external social norms. Transformational pedagogies, where the framing is weaker, are underpinned by beliefs that the learner changes through learning, at the same time or consequently, facilitating the transformation of their social situation. One child in Burke and Grosvenor's (2003: 1) study suggested that schools should in this transformational way 'teach more about [how to deal with] the future and less about the past'.

Pinson (2004: 656) illustrated the distinction between strong, restrictive pedagogies and more transformation-facilitating ones, by claiming that in the USA the experience of schooling by certain racial groups was of prison-like constraint while other groups were selected to learn 'critical consciousness, individual liberation and participatory democracy' at more progressive schools:

> The spaces in schools in lower income areas with primarily African-American populations resemble prisons or military camps … accompanied by emphasis on policies such as standardization where the main aim of education is to discipline and conform the student population.

Harber (2004) claimed that education had always been divided along those lines, embodying a

> … conflict between education for control in order to produce citizens and workers who were conformist, passive and politically docile on the one hand and those who wanted to educate for critical consciousness, individual liberation and participatory democracy on the other. (cited in Jackson, 2010: 46)

The illustrations suggest that the task of public schooling for the masses is not only to develop new skills for the industrial sector but primarily to inculcate habits of conformity, discipline and morality that would counter the widespread problems of social disorder (Harber, this volume).

The political purpose for learning is therefore embedded in its pedagogy, albeit sometimes implicitly. However, to conceive of schooling as a process in which governments betray their citizens is inaccurate. Often, authoritarian pedagogies that inhibit critical transformation and thus promote the *status quo* are sustained without parents' or teachers' opposition. Indeed, Giroux (2000: 4, cited in Burke and Grosvenor, 2003: 60) has explained that reforms towards making schooling more critically tranformational have been rejected by the public as either 'irrelevant' or 'unprofessional'. In England, for example, parents tend to believe that when teachers use coercive methods at school, children benefit more than when teachers give students more freedom or choice (cf. Flink et al., 1990). Parents from poorer English backgrounds coerce their children to succeed in the current schooling system for fear of their children ending up in the poor social position where they found themselves; while parents from more privileged backgrounds coerce their offspring through the same schooling system they themselves enjoyed, for fear that they will *not* end up with the same social privileges that they themselves had (Jackson, 2010). Thus governments with tendencies towards authoritarian pedagogies in education tend to find support among both sets of parents in whose interests it is to sustain the status quo.

While teachers in some countries may take up the profession of teaching because they care in a pastoral way about children, the very boundaries of how they think about the purpose of their job can also be shaped by insistent – but often implicit – messages encrypted in policy. Initial resistance to coercive government initiatives can gradually be worn down by day-to-day habits, rules and fears in schools, as teachers learn to 'self-police' themselves as well as being policed by senior staff and educational authorities (Moore, 2005). This has happened in England since its National Curriculum and Assessment system was introduced in 1988. This National Curriculum has become like second nature for younger teachers, despite the fact that only thirty years ago no such national prescriptions existed and the very idea of all teachers teaching the same topics in the same order was almost unthinkable.

The English National Curriculum provides a useful example of one set of aims of a Conservative Government whose implicit assumptions about curriculum are indicative as much through what is not mentioned, as they are through the aims it states explicitly. It aims explicitly to introduce pupils to the essential knowledge they need to be educated citizens. It introduces pupils to the best that 'has been thought and said' (DfE, 2014) but it does not clarify who decides what is 'best' and what constitutes a person who is 'educated', suggesting an inclination towards sustaining the *status quo*. However, the previous Labour Government was equally wedded, according to Fielding (2007: 383), to the purposes of 'efficiency and effectiveness' within the 'hegemony of insistent instrumentalism' rather than trying to create 'an inclusive, creative community … in a democratic society'. Certainly the current explicit curriculum purposes in England do not include the aspirational features of transformational approaches such as inclusivity, creativity, community or democracy; rather they hope to nurture 'successful learners, confident individuals and responsible citizens … providing a foundation for lifelong learning' (Fielding, 2007: 383).

These purposes stress the *individual's* responsibility *to* society and their *consequent* need for success and confidence in learning – often indicated by high test scores – in order that the country thrive competitively. Its aims thus fit most closely into those focusing on producing citizens and workers who are conformist, passive and politically docile, controlled by fear of sanctions, rather than the more transformational aims of nurturing critical consciousness, individual liberation and participatory democracy, recognizing that learning is itself a social practice that has the potential to transform its social context and the practice of learning itself.

Although today these policies are encouraging a return to authoritarian – including explicitly coercive – approaches to education (Meadmore and Symes, 1997), over the course of the twentieth and the start of the twenty-first century, these have been challenged and sometimes replaced by more transformational approaches to schooling that emphasized the need to critique unjust structures and habits in order to transform communities into more just entities. Transformational approaches encourage, in contrast to authoritarian pedagogies, children's identity formation and transformation rather than adaptation to strict social norms, cultivating criticality towards society at large, including their own contexts. The controlling surveillance structures which underpin authoritarian pedagogy therefore stand in harsh conflict with these values of belief in human agency and transformation.

It is sobering to note how lucidly students in Burke and Grosvenor's (2003) study wrote about their 'ideal school' and the kind of transformational pedagogy they desired, in which the authoritarianism – autocracy even – of the teacher would be replaced by an interplay of critical ideas among teachers and students. One student suggested that '[s]chools would be part of the local and international community and would take part in solving some of its problems … it would mean pupils and teachers were not just working for some esoteric result' (Burke and Grosvenor, 2003: 63). Another pupil wrote:

Instead of an authority structure which destroys decision making and a sense of responsibility, and which outside the classroom can prove downright dangerous, priority is given to structuring relationships such that children can talk to adults, can lean on and trust adults, can ask things of adults, can in short feel empowered by the adults they come into daily contact with. (2003: 8)

SUSTAINING THE STATUS QUO CURRICULUM IN ORDER TO CONSTRAIN TRANSFORMATION

What makes transformation less likely, is that the selections of curriculum knowledge and assessment criteria that are imposed on pupils through the authoritarian system are culturally, historically and socially *produced*, selected by groups of people with specific social, cultural and economic interests, understandings and perspectives. In line with policies held in England in the 1930s which reinforced the idea of genetically superior individuals, these groups of people assume an entitlement based on their success to date within the *status quo*.

And yet their particular choices of curriculum and assessment have come to be seen by pupils, parents and teachers as *the* essential programme for schooling. This distortion is helped by the imposition on subjects of a notion of objectivity that acts to bind those within the system to a truth which is hard to resist. Bourdieu's (1971) argument is that any claim to the superiority of one curriculum selection or one assessment criterion over another comes about as the result of an 'investment' of value rather than of any *intrinsic* worth. It is the validation and imposition of a selected curriculum and assessment criteria to the advantage of some and to the disadvantage of many, that Bourdieu is partly referring to in his use of the term 'symbolic violence' (cited in Moore, 2005). The disadvantaged many might be expected to achieve much more impressively if assessed by different criteria in relation to different curriculum selections.

If schools do not aim towards transformation by encouraging a *critical reflection on* curricula and their assessment criteria with students, as Moore suggests (2005: 7), we risk simply transferring the site and mode of symbolic violence so that students end up committing it upon themselves. Thus the strong frames of the learning and teaching of these curricula and their assessments become policed not only by the hierarchical

observation of the normalizing external test, but by the student's own internalized, acceptance of what is right and wrong in their learning (Foucault, 1979). This self-policing may also be carried out by teachers upon themselves. In this sense, as Daniels (this volume) suggests, institutional structures need to be analysed as historical products which themselves are subject to dynamic transformation and change, when people act within and on them. But when such action is made conceptually difficult by the systems in place, such an analysis will be rare. Such an analysis is thwarted to a great extent by fear: pupils' and parents' fear, teachers' fear and ultimately, policy makers' fear (cf. Jackson, 2010). As one perceptive student in Burke and Grosvenor's (2003: 65) study claimed, '[Certain curriculum areas] may all be perceived as "dangerous", as they can incite people to think freely and originally, and possibly to challenge the schools' authority. A good system need not fear analysis and scrutiny'.

HISTORICAL PEDAGOGICAL CONTEXT

A band of efficient schoolmasters is kept at much less expense than a body of police or soldiery. (H.L. Bellairs, Victorian author of a report on the South Wales coalfield, cited in Harber, this volume)

This quotation underlines the job teachers do to carry out government's aspirations for order and control. In England, this is more the case since the Reform Act of 1988 when central government for the first time provided instructions not only about how schools were administered, but also about how teachers taught and pupils learnt. Lefstein (2002, 1631–2, based on Foucault, 1979) summarized four systemic surveillance structures which embodied the authoritarian pedagogic approach as a means of enabling teachers to police students' actions:

1 Distribution of pupils in particular, prescribed groupings, often to ensure pupils did not communicate with each other. One simple but easily imposed means for inhibiting critical thinking is silencing pupils' speech by keeping pupils apart.

2 Teachers' control of the activity, whereby the teacher dictated the content, pace and order of pupils' activities. This dictation might be more or less autocratic (Meighan and Harber, 2007), but when the teacher remains as the primary knower (Nassaji and Wells, 2000), the pedagogy continues to be authoritarian.
3 Hierarchical observation, whereby figures more powerful even than the teacher were near at hand to enforce obedience. In schools today, these figures might be the deputy head or head teacher, the local authority personnel or even government inspectors (Ofsted).
4 The normalizing judgement or examination, by which pupils were labelled as failing or otherwise. Current examples of how this judgement is conveyed include standardized tests, as well as ability grouping, class division by age-group, and the strong centralized control of curriculum.

Because teachers depended on these structures in order to control both pupils' behaviour and, indirectly, their thinking, teachers often resorted to threats of fearsome punishments when these structures were challenged (Jackson, 2010). To coerce pupils to adhere to the rules, threats of physical punishments which provoked considerable terror, were common in UK schools, even into the late twentieth century and they still continue today in some countries (as further illustrated by Harber, this volume). The assumptions underlying these punishments were that, among the masses of children in the public school system, children needed to be coerced to learn and that lack of learning was due to laziness.

Foucault (1979) accounted for the development of authoritarian pedagogic structures by describing how the major problem facing eighteenth-century social organizers, including organizers of schools, was how to manage multitudes of people in relatively limited spaces so that productive outcomes were maximized and threats to the organizers' control minimized (Lefstein, 2002: 1629). In this climate, the usefulness of outcomes was of prime concern, as it was in factories; therefore regard to the feelings, thoughts or indeed rights, power or freedom of the learners who participated in the processes was systematically dismissed. Against this background, authoritarian

schooling has developed in the UK and other countries with a minimal focus on how children's feelings – for example fear – might interrelate with their learning processes, and how these might actually affect the value of the outcomes. Today these outcomes are more akin to the outcomes sought after in corporations or companies, rather than factories. Good outcomes, and the children who produced these, are prioritized over weaker ones, emphasizing difference between more and less useful pupils. As one pupil commented so pertinently in Burke and Grosvenor's study, 'The children who do well in exams think they're better than the kids who can't read! Surely we can't go on thinking like that!' (2003: 62).

In addition, fear seems to have become accepted as part and parcel of strongly framed learning and teaching in authoritarian classrooms. And yet, as this volume suggests, an acceptance of either authoritarian pedagogy or children's fears within it, is most likely to be critically challenged and subsequently transformed when such critical challenge and transformation become the focus of classrooms themselves, in an atmosphere devoid of pupil–teacher fear or indeed teacher–head-teacher or head-teacher–school-authorities fear. The following sections explore, drawing on pupils' own words, some pupil–teacher fears that tend to impede the possibility of critical challenge and transformation in pupils' learning.

CHILDREN'S FEAR DURING LEARNING

It was Laila in Year 3 (aged 7–8 years) who advised: 'I think it helps you better when you're not scared' (all names are pseudonyms). Findings from four parallel data collection methods (observation, children's drawings, children's sentence writing, interviews) in a recent research project (for full details see Hargreaves, 2015, in press) suggested how the 60 pupils in two UK primary classes perceived that fear affected their transformational learning in negative ways: '[When I'm afraid] I lose my confidence and mess up my learning' was a common sentiment. The Year 6 pupils (aged 10–11 years) also mentioned that when one is feeling fear in class, 'You're too busy thinking about what has happened and there is not enough room in your head for learning'. Sapphire, a relatively tall girl in Year 6, described how fear led to her going 'blank' and feeling really small:

> Everything just goes blank … And you just, your mind is so, not really focused, but just so focused on everyone else … Sometimes I feel like everyone's like so much taller than me … and then the teacher's like really, really big.

Children in both year groups (Years 3 and 6) described how their learning slowed down, their handwriting deteriorated and they found it harder to concentrate when they were feeling fear. Far from being empowered by learning, in these cases they felt belittled and uncertain. As one Year 6 respondent wrote: 'I keep getting [a glass of] water and try to concentrate but my head spins'. A Year 3 child suggested that fear reduced her motivation to keep trying: 'It feels like you have hit a brick wall because you don't want to go any further'.

THE FOCUS OF CHILDREN'S FEARS

The fear of the 60 children in this study seemed to be directed towards the future negative consequences of stepping out of line from the classroom regime. These consequences might be punishments or cross and disappointed words from teachers; they might be embarrassing or hostile words or actions by other pupils; or they might be consequences brought about by the incompetence of the children themselves, as they perceived it, and in this sense related to a huge but vague sense of fearfulness about who they were in relation to expected norms.

Despite the case study school being a school where active, collaborative and self-directed learning with transformational aspirations was strongly encouraged, there were still specific school-wide sanctions in place

for certain 'mis'-behaviours, which appeared to frighten the children: such as the punishment system of yellow and red warning cards for bad behaviour. The red card led to being 'told off' by the head or deputy head teacher, of whom many children were frightened. Jem (Year 6) described the deputy head as 'like a tiger who might pounce at any time'. In addition, the offence was written in the 'home talk' books for parents to see, extending the sense of fear related to stepping out of line.

Other punishments that scared the pupils were being deliberately separated from their friends (Evlyn, Year 6), as teachers used the distribution of pupils to maintain order; getting the 'mean' look from the teacher (Andrew, Year 6) because she was the person pupils sought to please at all times; and being kept indoors, alone, at lunchtime. Peter (Year 6) was particularly worried about being kept in at lunchtime:

> I think the only times when I feel scared *and* tense is when I'm told in the first lesson 'You're staying in at lunch', so then I have like several other lessons to go through worrying about that, so I think that's a really bad thing … I just feel like collapsing.

Although they told me the teachers were good and patient, some children were scared that the teacher would be cross if they did not know what to do or got the wrong answer. Sapphire (Year 6) described how, especially when you did not know a teacher well, you were scared to answer a question in class, and asked yourself, 'Shall I answer? And if I get it wrong, what am I going to do?' Carl (Year 3) became especially scared if he perceived the teacher to be 'tired' and therefore less patient than usual. This was reminiscent of the child in Burke and Grosvenor's (2003) study who wrote: 'It really is important that teachers are happy because if they are not, they are not very nice to the rest of the class' (p. 87). This fear of the teacher's wrath led to the children in my own study not asking the teacher a question when they were unsure, clearly a detrimental act to learning. Some Year 3 children feared making any mistakes. Miss Thorn, the Year 3 class teacher, narrated how Mary (Year 3) struggled to hear any criticism:

> If I wrote a comment in her book, like: 'Please can you try and put in your capital letters and full stops', something like that, she would burst into tears, because she would take it really personally that she had failed.

In an even more extreme Year 3 case, the teacher kept correcting Carl's unruly handwriting, to the point where he was scared to come to school at all.

It became clear that children found it particularly scary when teachers shouted – so perhaps this was at the back of their minds whenever they did something that might be disapproved of. In this case, the 'symbolic violence' becomes practical psychological violence. Pupils described being very frightened by shouting: even Year 3 class teacher, Miss Thorn, could appear scary when she raised her voice. Mrs Wesley, the Year 6 class teacher, said she rarely shouted at Year 6 because she felt children learnt more when they were not afraid. However, the teacher in the next door classroom made them scared because the children could hear her shouting through their wall. Mr Omer, deputy head-teacher, was singled out as particularly scary. Nearly all the interviewed children advised teachers not to shout if they wanted best learning. It seemed common sense to them that shouting was unhelpful.

FEAR OF BEING LOST

There seemed to be a fear among the sample children of being 'lost', either physically, cognitively or emotionally. As Foucault put it, through the authoritarian pedagogic system which focuses on *difference*, the individual child can '… be described, judged, measured, compared with others, in his [sic] very individuality; and it is also the individual who has to be trained or corrected, classified, normalized, excluded, etc.' (1979: 191, cited in Scott, this volume, Chapter 37). Fear of being lost among the rules and

expectations was not surprising. The pupils knew that they were being judged for compliance at nearly all times.

Children felt scared when the people they were with were unfamiliar, whether adults or children. For example, children were afraid:

> 'When I learn with teachers I don't know'
>
> 'When you're on a table with no friends'
>
> '[When] there is an inspector or someone monitoring our lesson'.

But there was a less tangible but more intense sense of fear, related to not knowing how to behave appropriately. Year 3 children described a mortifying fear, when:

> 'I don't think I can do it and I don't believe in myself'
>
> 'I am rubbish at something and I don't feel confident'.

Harris (Year 3) described how Carl (Year 3) would go red in the face and become very still when he felt this kind of debilitating fear. Miss Thorn also told me about Carl:

> Every time he doesn't understand a concept immediately he cries, so you have to take him out … and it always needs one-to-one reassurance from an adult, always.

Andrew and Norbert (Year 6) recognized this sense of fear in other people whom they pitied:

Andrew: When the teacher says to someone, 'Stand up!' it's someone who's about to cry because they're not doing it right. I really want to just break the rules and help them …

Norbert: When that's you, it's worse, because nobody can help you. You feel like you're trapped in a bubble.

Adelaide (Year 3) painted a sorry picture of herself on an occasion when she did not know how to proceed:

Adelaide: I felt really, like, 'I wish this day didn't come'. And I'm really, like, I'm sad, I'm grumpy …

Harris: When she's stuck, she can get very, very, very grumpy.

It was striking that some children brought up the topic of silence in the classroom: silence as contributing to this sense of panicky uncertainty, silence which 'actually scares me' (Harris, Year 3). Both Clare and Jerry (Year 3) claimed they felt uncomfortable when it was silent, while Carl (Year 3) found it 'creepy': all of which stopped them from concentrating and certainly prevented them from having learning conversations.

FEAR OF HOSTILE WORDS OR ACTIONS BY OTHER PUPILS

Jem, in Year 6, showed an awareness of the increasing potential for older children in primary school to worry about being judged negatively by peers:

> If you're in Year 4, 5 and 6, maybe, you might get scared because you're really self-conscious kind of thing. Because you think everyone's looking at yourself ... I think I feel a bit more scared in front of the girls, because they always like giggle to each other and stuff ...

Andrew (Year 6) feared to *ask* questions in class, in case his peers considered him to be weak. Peter (Year 6) was afraid to *answer* questions in case he was seen to be 'geeky'. Mrs Wesley narrated how Jack (Year 6) had been so afraid to admit that he could be wrong, he had consistently failed to act on her written feedback comments. Fear of looking stupid or not being or saying the right thing was particularly acute for Mona too, Mrs Wesley suspected, because she was 'at the bottom end of the [top literacy] set'.

Even in Year 3, Harold calculated that it took him 'about three days' to recover from his embarrassment when he had not been following the lesson and said the wrong thing. He described how: 'Everyone started laughing and I got really embarrassed and red'. Geraldine [Year 3] said she found it particularly embarrassing reading with older pupils during 'paired reading':

> And we don't know what a word is, like a really hard one, because I've got a really hard book. I get

a little bit embarrassed, because I don't know what it is ... Because then [the older child might] think, 'She's a little bit dumb, isn't she?'

For some children, then, embarrassment about not knowing an answer or appearing stupid was so painful that they would avoid it whenever possible, even when this diminished their learning opportunities.

Given the fear potential of other children's judgements, I was interested to know how well peer assessment worked in the case study classrooms. The following Year 3 dialogue suggested that fear could impede potentially transformational learning through peer assessment:

> EH: Do you ever get anxious when [a peer's] assessing you?
> Anna: Yeah, it's hard.
> Saul: I feel a bit anxious, because I don't know what they're going to write. And if they write something ... that makes me anxious just in case they write something.
> EH: Something negative? Something bad? ... And what would happen if they did? ...
> Anna: Saul would probably go cuckoo (Laughter) ...
> Saul: I'd feel a bit angry with them, because it's not really a kind comment.
> Anna: I just wouldn't feel confident. I wouldn't be confident in writing a story again.

All the Year 3 children worried about what their peers would say about their work during peer assessment. Harris, Harold and Rory (Year 3) also worried about feeding back on someone else's work. Harris sometimes found it all correct with nothing 'wrong' to comment on. Harold did not understand the assessment prompts provided by the teacher. Rory could not read his partner's writing – nor could he relate the assessment prompts to his own writing – but he was afraid to ask.

CONCLUDING THOUGHTS: PEDAGOGY, FEAR AND LEARNING

The recent study reported here suggested that the primary-school children in the two case study classes experienced a range of fears which seemed to be related to the authoritarianism of the classroom. However, this authoritarianism was infrequently autocratic and tended towards the more democratic end of the spectrum described by Meighan and Harber (2007). Indeed, at times the children displayed behaviours and strategies characteristic of some transformational aspects of learning, as explicitly desired by their two teachers. However, the fact that they experienced frequent and sometimes intense fears was indisputable; hand in hand with the school's adherence to traditional authoritarian pedagogy (as well as the more transformational pedagogies). The children's comments suggested that the traditional structures of teacher authoritarianism might continue to interfere excessively with transformational aims. The crux of the matter appeared to be the coercion these structures continued to wield over the pupils. Surprising, even shocking, as this may seem, coercion continued to underpin nearly all classroom activities, despite the teachers' alternative aspirations. They might have been in a stage of transition. It was more likely, however, that the teachers, like many other educators, had come to accept authoritarian pedagogy, and the fear it generates, as normal. In accepting these aspects uncritically, the pupils' own capacity for critical reflection and change was constrained.

For example, being coerced at times to sit in silence and away from friends could be, the pupils claimed, frightening and detrimental to their learning. Being kept away from friends at lunch time as a punishment led to resentment as well as fear, and perhaps interfered with the child's developing identity and sense of community membership. In Year 6 especially, these aspects of learning needed particular focus in order to support a positive personal identity formation for this age group (Eckert et al., 1996). Pupils' capacity to make an informed critique of their own and others' situations and to take constructive action on the basis of this was clearly impeded by antisocial methods of control. The pupils' suggestion that the teacher should get to know

his/her pupils on an *individual and social level* would go some way to addressing fears related to the enforced distribution and separation of pupils.

The source of coercion – and fear – was that the teacher ultimately controlled the pace, order and nature of the pupils' school activities. Despite overtly encouraging critical self-reflection, peer dialogue and peer assessment, and providing a range of self-help resources, ultimately the teachers in this school called the tune. The children's choices in my study were limited by the teacher, which meant their sense of self and conceptions of what was possible were insufficiently developed. For this reason, fear of disappointing or failing the teacher diverted the children dramatically. The children's fear itself was an illustration of their lack of confidence with the unknown and the unpredictable, to which their teachers habitually impeded access.

What became evident in this study was the children's fear of their constant surveillance by the teacher and senior colleagues. Not only did the teacher give them the 'mean look' when they were not working hard, but the pupils seemed to sense that they should be concentrating and understanding correctly all the time. There was little freedom for taking it easy or for thinking about what to them were more important issues, such as playground relationships or the world outside. A slip in their attention risked causing a teacher to shout in a scary way. The children's suggestion may be useful that teachers should try not to shout but to talk quietly to pupils in private, and that they should walk around the classroom to find out how children are feeling rather than reprimanding their behaviour in an autocratic way. This would be one small step towards weakening the teaching frame of the authoritarian classroom.

The teachers' hierarchical observation is linked to the normalizing judgement. In its widest sense, this seemed to be experienced by pupils as a belief that they needed to become something better: that who they were and what they could do was always open to the teacher's criticism and the judgements of the wider system. The pupils in this sample also described their fears of classroom tests and Standard Assessment Tests, which compounded the power of the hierarchical observation. And this fear of not being 'normal' in an acceptable way led to some of the most destructive habits against transformational learning: not daring to answer a question, fearing to ask the teacher a question, fearing to admit being uncertain in front of the teacher and/or peers, fearing to be in the wrong 'ability set'; which were all related to their fear of the normalizing judgement. They described failing to take risks; failing to trust their own judgments; and being constrained by the judgements of their peers as well as teachers and senior teachers.

In conclusion, by examining the often unexamined world of pupils' feelings, the potentially negative impact of sustaining authoritarian pedagogy in the primary school was illustrated. While it was not pleasant for these pupils to feel fear, this is not the most important point: fear which drives learning forward because it has been chosen by the learner could transform in a positive direction. The danger of the fears described in this study was their tendency to stifle the children's desire precisely to take on risky, potentially scary learning. Their fears centred around not doing the right thing, and their constant worry about this tended to impede them from reaching out of their comfort zones and critically challenging the class, the school and the society around them. Jack (Year 6) saw the value in being pushed out of his comfort zone:

Because if you're challenged you can, you know – it makes you a better learner. You don't want to be just doing things that you just like doing … You don't want to just be in your comfort zone … You want to be pushed, yeah.

REFERENCES

Bernstein, B. (1995) 'Codes oppositional, reproductive and deficit: a case of red herrings', *The British Journal of Sociology*, 46, 1: 133–142.

Article Stable URL: http://www.jstor.org/stable/591627

Bourdieu, P. (1971) 'Intellectual field and creative project', in M. Young (ed.) *Knowledge and Control*, London: Collier-Macmillan, pp. 161–88.

Burke, C. and Grosvenor, I. (2003) *The School I'd Like*, London: RoutledgeFalmer.

Department for Education (DfE) (2014) Statutory guidance. National curriculum in England: framework for key stages 1 to 4. No 3. Updated 2 December 2014 https://www.gov.uk/government/publications/national-curriculum-in-england-framework-for-key-stages-1-to-4/the-national-curriculum-in-england-framework-for-key-stages-1-to-4

Eckert, P., Goldman, S. and Wenger, E. (1996) *The School as a Community of Engaged Learners*, Institute for Research on Learning Report no. 17.101. Menlo Park, CA: IRL.

Fielding, M. (2007) 'The human cost and intellectual poverty of high performance schooling: radical philosophy, John Macmurray and the remaking of person-centred education', *Journal of Education Policy*, 22, 4: 383–409. http://dx.doi.org/10.1080/02680930701390511

Flink, C., Boggiano, A. and Barrett, M. (1990) 'Controlling teaching strategies: undermining children's self-determination and performance', *Journal of Personality and Social Psychology*, 59, 5: 916–24. http://www.selfdeterminationtheory.org/SDT/documents/1990_FlinkBoggianoBarrett_JPSP.pdf

Foucault, M. (1979) *Discipline and Punish: The Birth of the Prison*, New York: Random House.

Giroux, H. (2000) *Stealing Innocence: Youth, Corporate Power and the Politics of Culture*, New York: Palgrave Macmillan.

Harber, C. (2004) *Schooling as Violence: How Schools Harm Pupils and Societies*, Abingdon: RoutledgeFalmer.

Hargreaves, E. (2015) '"I think it helps you better when you're not scared": fear and learning in the primary classroom', *Pedagogy, Culture and Society* (in press).

Jackson, C. (2010) 'Fear in education', *Educational Review*, 62, 1: 39–52.

Lefstein, A. (2002) 'Thinking power and pedagogy apart: coping with discipline in progressivist school reform', *Teachers College Record*, 104, 8: 1627–55.

Meadmore, D. and Symes, C. (1997) 'Of uniform appearance: a symbol of school discipline and governmentality', *Discourse: Studies in the Cultural Politics of Education*, 17, 2: 209–25. DOI: 10.1080/0159630960170206.

Meighan, R. and Harber, C. (2007) *A Sociology of Educating*. New York: Continuum.

Moore, A. (2005) 'Some advantages and disadvantages in modes of formative assessment: misrecognition, internalisation and the influence of the "backwash" effect', *Annual Conference: International Studies in Sociology of Education*.

Nassaji, H. and Wells, G. (2000) 'What's the use of "triadic dialogue"?: An investigation of teacher student interaction', *Applied Linguistics*, 21: 376–406.

Pinson, H. (2004) 'Conflict, violence and militarization in education', *British Journal of Sociology of Education*, 25, 5: 653–62. DOI: 10.1080/0142569042000277191

Williams, H. (2003) 'Cheaper then the police', *The Guardian*, July 23.

30

Meta-Learning in Classrooms

Chris Watkins

INTRODUCTION

I was talking with four 10-year-old students in a school in an underprivileged part of Sheffield about their experiences of learning in classrooms when one of them said that they 'distil' their lessons. After asking them for some explanation, I asked whether they could distil our conversation so far. 'Yes', they said, and, as they turned to discuss it in pairs, I heard one use the word, meta-learning. When the paired conversation ended I enquired: 'Did I hear you use the word meta-learning?'; 'Yes'; 'What's that? Metal-earning?'; 'Nothing to do with metal'; 'Knowing yourself as a learner – which is a good thing'.[1] That conversation and that 10-year-old represent what I hope to illuminate in this chapter.

THE CLASSROOM CONTEXT

Social psychology has demonstrated that human behaviour is closely linked to the context in which it occurs, so it is important to consider the context of the classroom and the way it can influence this topic. One of the most curious things about classrooms is how little they focus on learning. Since classrooms appeared on this planet 5,000 years ago they have been characterised by teacher-driven activity systems. The relationship is one where the teacher initiates, the pupils respond and the teacher evaluates: the most compressed example is still recognisable: 'Six sixes?'; 'Thirty-six'; 'Good girl'. This is known as the Initiation-Response-Evaluation cycle and research of the last fifty years continues to find it as the dominant pattern in current classrooms (Bellack et al., 1966; Cazden, 2001).

The effect of this is that learners' experiences as learners are hidden. After four decades of studies of classroom learning issues using hidden microphones and video cameras, Nuthall's final (2007) book was given the title *The Hidden Lives of Learners*. He had summarised this earlier as: '[w]ether a student learns or not reflects the students' understanding of classroom tasks, management of social relationships, and the extent to which the student shares the cultural understandings and background knowledge of the teacher and other students' (Nuthall, 1999: 213). Another curious thing about classrooms is how much they stay the same. Despite changes in rhetoric over decades and centuries, the dominant patterns return. Even across the varying national cultures of our world, patterns of classroom interaction are so similar that a video study found no one country was different on all the aspects observed (Hiebert, et al., 2003).

Some analysts of classroom and school culture point to a connection between these two curious elements. As Sarason puts it (2004: 43), '[y]our conception of the learning process not only has enormous implications for classroom learning contexts but also goes a long way to explaining why educational reforms, resting as they do on a superficial conception of learning, will continue to be disappointing'. These two features of classrooms need to be understood and talked about as part of any development of more learning-centred classrooms (see also Watkins, 2015).

CONCEPTIONS OF LEARNING AND META-LEARNING

The way in which learning is talked about (or not) is important and may reflect different underlying conceptions of learning. These in turn may have implications for the focus of this chapter. Conceptions will be considered in three areas: in the academic literature, in learners' minds, and in classrooms. Interactions and influences between the three will be noted.

Some academic conceptions of learning have no concept of meta-learning, for example, a behaviourist model does not pay attention to the learner's awareness at all so has no need of a concept of meta-learning. The term *metacognition* came to prominence after Flavell's (1976) introduction. He had been influenced by Piaget and constructivist views of learning, and at a similar time Sternberg (1977) had been reclaiming the notion of intelligence by emphasising meta-components. In Flavell's (1976: 232) terms, '[m]etacognition refers to one's knowledge concerning one's own cognitive processes and products or anything related to them'. He went on to suggest that: '[m]etacognition refers, among other things, to the active monitoring and consequent regulation and orchestration of these processes in relation to the cognitive objects or units on which they bear, usually in the service of some concrete goal or objective'. So it is a form of knowledge, and at this stage the connection between monitoring and regulation seems to be assumed, without clarifying what forms of monitoring lead to self-regulation.

Flavell also mentioned – in passing – meta-memory and meta-learning. Soon after this, Brown (1978) observed that the proliferation of *metas* in the literature might suggest that this was an epiphenomenon. She clarified that taking a perspective on one's own activity (knowledge, memory, learning) is crucial for developing conscious control in such activities as deliberate learning and problem-solving. That phrase *taking a perspective* is an important one in understanding meta processes, and relates to everyday phrases such as *step back*, *view from above*, *take another perspective*, *look back over*, all of which imply the possibility of viewing our activity from a stance other than being solely involved in it.

Soon, reviews of the metacognitive instructional literature showed 'a substantial effect' (Haller et al., 1988: 5) on reading. Importantly the title of that review was *Can Comprehension Be Taught?* Here already were signs that the dominant classroom view of learning was influencing the approach to research and development. Work on metacognition soon became confounded with work on study skills, but later meta-analyses demonstrated again that these might have again fallen prey to the dominant teaching model. It became clear that learners may possess learning strategies, but not employ them, or employ them ineffectively. So it is the process of selection and use that comes to the fore. This is where the metacognitive strategies of monitoring and reviewing are vital: indeed Hattie's review (Hattie et al., 1996) concluded that direct teaching of study skills to students without attention to reflective, metacognitive development may well be pointless.

Gradually researchers came to identify

[the] problem of [learners'] understanding: they had little insight into their own ability to learn intentionally: they lacked reflection. Children do not use a whole variety of learning strategies because they do not know much about the art of learning. ... Furthermore, they know little about monitoring their own activities; that is, they do not think to plan, orchestrate, oversee, or revise their own learning efforts. (Brown, 1997: 400)

Here the thinking relates directly to the developing understanding of the self-regulating learner. Indeed one of its main architects defined this area of direct inclusion of metacognition: '[i]n general, students can be described as self-regulated to the degree that they are metacognitively, motivationally, and behaviorally active participants in their own learning process' (Zimmerman, 1989: 329). More recently the skills have been called *self-managing*, *self-monitoring* and *self-modifying* (Costa, 2004: 6).

A range of studies have demonstrated a relation between metacognition, self-regulation and school performance, in one case showing that 'different areas of self-regulation could explain 34% of variance of school performance in the primary school, about 21% in the secondary school and nearly 14% in the university education' (Vukman and Licardo, 2010: 267). This is one of the largest effects from a single variable, yet it is a variable that is mostly hidden in the lives of classrooms, but it is having a significant effect. Those learners who learn self-regulation from other contexts of their lives are the ones who succeed in teacher-driven systems.

The first academic texts where the title used the term meta-learning were both research degrees completed by teachers – in Toronto (Maudsley, 1979) and London (Jones, 1983). Novak (1983) used the term, but Biggs (1985: 204) is most often cited as the origin, with his 'being aware of and taking control of one's own learning'. Again the connection between awareness and control seems to be assumed.

LEARNERS' CONCEPTIONS OF LEARNING

While the idea of metacognition was developing as a key element in a richer conceptual model of learning, some researchers began to focus on the view of learning held by children themselves. The pioneering work of Pramling (1983) showed that young children from 3 to 8 years showed a developmental progression in their view of learning, from learning to do, to know, and to understand. She went on to research classroom interventions with 5-year-olds and showed their conceptions were developed through *metacognitive dialogues* as a continuous feature in the classroom (since the focus was their learning experiences, these may have rightly been called *meta-learning dialogues*). 'This development did not occur as a consequence of training any general strategies, but as a consequence of changing perspective' (Pramling, 1988: 277).

Studies across a range of ages of learners often distinguish conceptions of learning: increasing one's knowledge; memorising and reproducing; applying; understanding; seeing something in a different way; or changing as a person, i.e. seeing oneself in a different way (Marton et al., 1993). Although researchers may identify such differences, learners themselves do not always experience the school experience which helps them do the same: by the age of 14 or 15 pupils have been reported to have no clear understanding of how they learn (Berry and Sahlberg, 1996).

A learner's conception of learning affects how s/he goes about learning: quantitative conceptions (the earlier ones in the list above) are related to superficial approaches rather than a focus on understanding. This distinction was also described as 'surface versus deep' views of learning, and shown to be significantly related to how learners operate in classrooms (Dart et al., 2000). More recently another conception of learning as duty has been added (Purdie and Hattie, 2002), with findings such as '[t]he conception that learning is a duty predicted lower achievement and the conception of learning as continuous predicted higher achievement' (Peterson et al., 2010: 167). There is little research on learners' conceptions of meta-learning, but, even at higher education level, attempts to develop richer conceptions of learning have had to face the challenge of those students who did not see any value in reflecting on learning, and those who saw learning as bound by fixed ability rather than learner agency (Connolly and Ward, 2011).

CLASSROOM CONCEPTIONS

In the classroom, conceptions of learning are dominated by teaching. This can be described as *Learning = Being Taught*, whereas richer conceptions of learning would be *Learning = Individual Sense-Making* and *Learning is Building Knowledge as part of doing things with Others* (L = BT, L = IS, L = BKO; Watkins, 2003: 10–16). In the academic literature these are instruction, construction and co-construction, and relate closely to research on teachers' conceptions of learning: transmission, transaction and transformation (Brody et al., 1991: 3).

The implications for learners are that children point to the teacher as being responsible for their learning. As one student put it: 'I learn because people tell me', and a headteacher suggested that: 'Learning is something you do to children' (Lodge, 2002: 27). Yet research has shown that some classrooms do develop a learning orientation, and that the key influence is the way the teacher talks about learning, as an active process that requires student involvement and discussion; that understanding, rather than memorisation and replication, is important; and that interaction is a key feature (Patrick et al., 2001). But the teacher's role in highlighting learning is necessary but not sufficient. It has been shown that if teachers highlight learning as a construction in their classes, some students become increasingly metacognitive and report evidence of revision of their learning processes. Others report little or no effect (Thomas and McRobbie, 2001). This result fits with many others which show that teacher-driven changes to classrooms can have divisive results, and requires us to think through what else is necessary for a real change in the culture of the classroom. How, with the teacher's leadership, can we develop a co-constructive change in classroom learning?

Part of the challenge in developing meta-learning in classrooms is that many of the embedded norms of schooling lead us to approach it in a teacher-centred way: *Let's teach them more about their learning*, or *Let's tell them how to be better learners*. The contradictions inside these statements can take a while to spot. But researchers had identified this thirty years ago: '[m]ost programs do not train students to take responsibility for and control over their own learning … consequently, generalization and transfer effects are limited. … When strategies are taught and used mechanically, the label Metacognition is inappropriate' (Baird and White, 1984: 8).

What about classroom conceptions of meta-learning? If a focus on learning in classrooms is rare, then a focus on meta-learning may be more so. At the time of writing, searching the internet for the phrase (i.e. including the inverted commas): 'meta-learning in classrooms' gave zero results. This review of conceptions raises two key questions for meta-learning to be successful in classrooms: *How do we come to know ourselves as learners?* and *How do we un-hide (i.e. dis-cover) the lives of learners in classrooms?*

CLASSROOM PRACTICES: TOWARDS A NARRATIVE APPROACH

In an earlier review (Watkins, 2001) it was suggested that teachers can promote learning about learning by using classroom activities which: make learning an object of attention;

make learning an object of conversation; make learning an object of reflection; and make learning an object of learning. Developing that suggestion in light of the last thirty years' research, I now propose that if meta-learning is to develop in classrooms, then two principles must apply. The first is that meta-learning will only help learners make the connection between monitoring and controlling their learning if the monitoring engages the agency of the learner. And the second is that meta-learning will only help people 'know themselves as learners' if the language used is owned by the learners themselves. These principles can be advanced through classroom practices of the following sorts: noticing, narrating and navigating.

Noticing

This is the first step: to stimulate and credit learners with the fact that they direct their attention and that this is a key building block. It can develop further into a focus on one's own activity: that key element of noticing what you are doing while you are doing it. We might underestimate young people's noticing: a teacher in a West London school put a sign up at the front of her classroom for 5/6-year-olds, saying, 'What have you noticed today?'. She reported back to the project group: 'I soon took that down!'; 'Why?'; 'Because they noticed so much and it took ages for them to tell me it all'. She then changed to having the pupils tell interested others in the class, and in so doing the practice contributed to a more shared classroom culture of noticing.

When the focus of the noticing is some aspect of our own functioning, we are 'going meta', 'What did you notice about your reading?' 'What did you notice about your conversation?' and so on. Here again the style of language may again be highlighted: at worst, responses like 'My reading was good' will show a surface (performance judgement) conception and little opening for development. The style of language used needs to promote learner agency and ownership if this is to be avoided.

Narrating

Bruner (1985) made an important distinction between two modes of thought: narrative and paradigmatic. A paradigmatic way of understanding involves the use of general theories, and formal systems based on categorisation. It shows in approaches such as 'learning styles'. The language of 'learning styles', despite its weak theoretical foundations, dubious measurement protocols and overblown claims (Coffield et al., 2004) can turn into a language of learn-er styles, which then repeats the school tendency of categorising learners, and no improvement in pedagogy occurs. Some practitioners have reported that starting their development using learning preferences did not generate the dialogue about learning that they were seeking (Martin and Roberts, 2007). The contrast is a narrative way of understanding, which is more particular, time-sensitive, and involves human action and intent. Bruner believed that the two are irreducible to each another.

Knowing yourself as a learner is not achieved by categorising yourself according to someone else's paradigm. It is achieved by remembering, telling and discussing stories of yourself as a learner. And it is crucial to note that the only form of language humans have for relating experience is narrative (Ricouer, 1984). Open-ended invitations of the form: 'Tell me about some learning you've enjoyed' will elicit a storied response with key players, actions and so on.

Another important aspect of a narrative approach is shown when numbers of people tell their stories: the conversation develops richly. This is partly because 'one story leads to another', and when the stories are the narrator's learning experiences, conflictual discussion is rare; respect for the authentic voice of the learner is common. It is also common that the conversation rises above the particular examples. As narrative therapists in other contexts have put it: 'sharing is caring but meta is better' (Christofas et al., 1985). And this process builds a shared culture; as Pramling Samuelsson (2004: 32) put it: '[l]anguage and narratives are constructions in groups that make individual memories into shared conceptual systems'.

Building a narrative with focus can be helped in a range of ways which promote extra perspective on one's learning experiences. Photographs of learning situations, children's own drawings of occasions they remember, and even video-recordings can be helpful in creating both focus and perspective. Researchers with children finding difficulty in reading video-taped the extra help sessions they received and then played them back to the children, finding '[w]hen given an opportunity to view and talk about what they had done in intervention sessions, children in the current study were able to demonstrate greater metacognitive awareness than they had during the lessons' (Juliebo et al., 1998: 31).

Appreciative Inquiry is an approach to change which is especially useful in developing against the grain of a dominant culture (Hammond, 2000). It starts with examining participants' best experiences in the area under review, and then goes on to identify how more such experiences could be helped to happen. Using such an approach for a small number of after-school sessions, Davies (2013: ii) found that 'the children experienced significant shifts in their understanding of learning and their perceptions of themselves as learners', even those who had been convinced by school and low grades that they were 'no good' at learning.

With a wider sample Carnell (2005) found that talking with young people about learning reveals the dominant discourses, but talking with them about their best experiences reveals richer conceptions. Such talk needs to be practised and developed as a key part of changing the culture. A framework that can help with appreciative narratives of learning is the storyboard. This is a single sheet of paper with a simple set of frames for the beginning, middle and end of the story, with space for drawing and writing. They can be focused on specific areas such as 'a time when I learned really well with others', phrased in a positive way, and when the young person has

illustrated the story, a prompt asks them to identify their contribution to the story going so well, for example, 'I can help myself learn well with others by ....'. An early example for me was a class teacher using a very open-ended title: 'My most impressive learning'. The range and depth of stories told, both in and out of school, was a very rich surprise to the teacher.

On another occasion I was asked to meet a class whose teacher described them as 'not taking responsibility'. I imagined that was a statement about the culture, so asked the pupils to complete a storyboard on 'a time when I took charge of my learning'. They extracted:

Things I do that help me to take charge of my learning

I gave myself time to stop and think

I experimented and checked my results

I got stuck, then I thought for a second, then I found an answer

I got stuck, then I used my imagination to take charge

I kept thinking 'I have to do it'

I told myself that I had to do it, so I did!!

I concentrated and believed in myself

I pulled myself together

I said to myself 'I can do it'

I said to myself 'I believe in myself'

I said to myself 'I believe I can do it' I gave myself hope

I believed in myself and doing what I want to do, not what I have to do

I watched others and kept on practising

I saw my friends and said 'they're human as well: if they can do it then I can do it'

I kept on trying until I got the hang of it

I didn't give up

I pushed myself and read it over and over and over again

I push and push and push myself to write

I used the two 'p' words – patience and perseverance

The teachers were surprised and impressed with the effective skills and self-talk which the pupils used, and which had previously been unknown to them. For the rest of that school year they built on learner responsibility, and the results improved.

Appreciative storyboards are a good start to the exchange of stories, and they also generate interested dialogue between participants. As such they are a good contribution to developing the culture, a concept which sometimes is talked about in disempowering ways, but those who have studied it define it in a grounded way 'the ensemble of stories we tell ourselves about ourselves' (Geertz, 1973: 448).

Navigating

One of the richest metaphors for talking about learning is that of journey. Of course 'learning journey' can be reduced to non-learning talk (such as the tests and targets in the government publication under that title (DfEE, 2000), which in 128 pages only uses the word *learn* twice, and these were both references to something that parents could do). More common usage of *journey* brings in plenty of other useful parallels for learning: destination, map, choice of route, navigating. Imagine a whole classroom wall with the class account of their developing journey. I have even seen children appropriate road signs and adapt them to create messages for learning.

Navigating a journey puts someone into a meta position, but it also puts them in the driving seat, another important metaphor for highlighting learner agency and the self-directed learner. The three phases of planning, monitoring and reviewing can be put in everyday accessible terms:

Before starting

Where do we want to get to?

Which way should we go?

Has someone got a map? Or shall we make up our own route?

Is there anything to remember from previous journeys?

Do we need to take any equipment?

On the road

How's it going?

Are we on track?

Do we need to change direction?

Shall we check back on the map?

Has anyone gone another way?

Cor look!

Journey's end:

Where did we get to?

Is this the place we planned? Maybe it's better!

Shall we take a photo/send a postcard?

Did anyone get here by another route?

How would we do it another time?

Where next?

The final stage of reviewing can sometimes be promoted by learning logs, a means of recording reflections over time. Here again, the format of a learning log can be too much teacher-defined, even using a tick-box format. This turns out to be less effective than a dialogic approach: 'The learning log did stimulate student reflection, but did not prompt the level of learning strategy awareness that emerged in the semi-structured interviews' (Stephens and Winterbottom, 2010: 72).

Rather than logs, we may have learning journals. After all, some teachers reminded me, when you're on a journey you take a journal. This stance on a reflective record helps us use more student-centred prompts, in the style of 'What would you like to remember about today's journey?' In a project with high school students, developing their explicit knowledge of learning included open-ended prompts for reflection in learning journals, and led to a better end-point: 'Those students who planned and monitored their work produced essays of higher quality' (Conner and Gunstone, 2004: 142).

As well as individual learning journals, a whole class may review the journey they have been making together. During one such review with a class of 8-year-olds the teacher was interested in the current state of the earlier distortions of learning, so she asked: 'What's the difference between learning and work, or is there none?'. One student replied: 'When you work, you work for someone else, and when you learn you learn for yourself and do different things'. Another continued 'I don't think there is a difference, because like when you're working as a teacher you can learn from your students'. The latter comment seemed a good indicator of a learning-centred classroom, when students know that their teachers are learning from them.

TEACHERS AS LEARNERS

There are many pressures on teachers to focus on teaching rather than learning, and these maintain the long-standing stereotype of teaching. But all teachers have experienced times when learning was really good in a classroom, and their analysis of their experiences fits with decades of research. So appreciative inquiry will be appropriate here to develop from their best experiences of active, collaborative, learner-driven classrooms (Watkins et al., 2007). This accords with research on the 'Learning How to Learn' project in the United Kingdom, which found that in the cases where classrooms became more learning-centred there was only one process which explained the development: enquiry by teachers (Pedder, 2006).

Professional development of teachers along these lines has been shown to be effective: 'involvement in a systematic exploration of the learning process, with teachers explicating their knowledge of learning, has a direct impact on the display of effective teaching behaviours and on teachers' personal explicit theory of learning' (Munro 1999: 151). And this capacity of teachers is deemed more important if we accept the idea of a fast-changing world, acknowledging '[t]he significance of meta-learning ability, which is found to be an essential component for the professional development of teachers in a changing context' (Pui-wah, 2008: 85).

In the early stages of development teachers too will show the dominant conceptions; in one study 'two groups have been distinguished: a group of teachers having a broad vision about learning to learn and a group of teachers with a narrow vision' (Waeytens et al., 2002: 305). But in another parallel with the process for children, Carnell (2001) found that staff involved in action research on their pedagogy overcame their initial hesitations, and their learning was developed through dialogue, which included a focus on their own learning and therefore became meta. She concluded that '[t]hrough meta-learning dialogue generated from action research, teachers create conditions to make their own and young people's learning more effective' (Carnell, 2001: 54).

The processes and outcomes are clear; the restraining forces seem strong (at first), making this area of theory and practice more of a challenge than it rightly should be. But in schools that take the journey to become learning-centred (as sampled briefly in the opening dialogue and see Reed and Lodge (2006)) the effects are inspiring.

NOTE

1 See https://www.youtube.com/watch?v=2rL33 mK8ksg

REFERENCES

Baird, J. R. and White, R. T. (1984) 'Improving learning through enhanced metacognition: a classroom study', paper presented at the Annual Meeting of the American Educational Research Association, New Orleans, LA.

Bellack, A., Kliebard, H. M., Hyman, R. T. and Smith, F. L. (1966) *The Language of the Classroom*, New York: Teachers College Press.

Berry, J. and Sahlberg, P. (1996) 'Investigating pupils' ideas of learning', *Learning and Instruction*, 6, 1: 19–36.

Biggs, J. B. (1985) 'The role of metalearning in study processes', *British Journal of Educational Psychology*, 55, 185–212.

Brody, C. M. and Hill, L. R. (1991) 'Cooperative learning and teacher beliefs about pedagogy', paper presented at the Annual Meeting of AERA.

Brown, A. L. (1978) 'Knowing when, where, and how to remember: a problem of meta-cognition', in R. Glaser (ed.), *Advances in Instructional Psychology* (Vol. 1, pp. 77–165), Hillsdale NJ: Lawrence Erlbaum.

Brown, A. L. (1997) 'Transforming schools into communities of thinking and learning about serious matters', *American Psychologist*, 52, 4: 399–413.

Bruner, J. S. (1985) 'Narrative and paradigmatic modes of thought', in E. Eisner (ed.), *Learning and Teaching the Ways of Knowing*, Chicago: University of Chicago Press.

Carnell, E. (2001) 'The value of meta-learning dialogue', *Professional Development Today*, 4, 2: 43–54.

Carnell, E. (2005) 'Understanding and enriching young people's learning: issues, complexities and challenges', *Improving Schools*, 8, 3: 269–84.

Cazden, C. B. (2001) *Classroom Discourse: The Language of Teaching and Learning* (2nd edition), London: Heinemann Educational.

Christofas, S., Goldsmith, A., Marx, P., Mason, B. and Peatfield, P. (1985) 'Working systemically with disadvantaged families and the professional network: sharing is caring but meta is better', in D. Campbell and R. Draper (eds), *Applications of Systemic Family Therapy: The Milan Approach* (pp. 163–172), London: Grune and Stratton.

Coffield, F., Moseley, D., Hall, E. and Ecclestone, K. (2004) *Should We be Using Learning Styles? What Research Has to Say to Practice*, London: Learning and Skills Research Centre.

Conner, L. and Gunstone, R. (2004) 'Conscious knowledge of learning: accessing learning strategies in a final year high school biology class', *International Journal of Science Education*, 26, 12: 1427–43.

Connolly, R. and Ward, S. (2011) *Enacting Metalearning*, York: Higher Education Academy, Palatine (Performing Arts Learning and Teaching Innovation Network).

Costa, A. L. (2004) 'Why we need self-directed learners', in A. L. Costa and B. Kallick (eds), *Assessment Strategies for Self-directed Learning* (pp. 1–17), Thousand Oaks, CA: Corwin Press.

Dart, B. C., Burnett, P. C., Purdie, N., Boulton-Lewis, G. M., Campbell, J. and Smith, D. (2000) 'Students' conceptions of learning, the classroom environment, and approaches to learning', *Journal of Educational Research*, 93, 262–70.

Davies, A. (2013) 'Appreciating learning: children using Appreciative Inquiry as an approach to helping them to understand their learning', unpublished MSocSci thesis, University of Waikato.

Department for Education and Employment (DfEE) (2000) *Learning Journey: A Parent's Guide to the Secondary School Curriculum*, London: DEE.

Flavell, J. H. (1976) 'Metacognitive aspects of problem-solving', in L. B. Resnick (ed.), *The Nature of Intelligence* (pp. 231–235), Hillsdale NJ: Lawrence Erlbaum.

Geertz, C. (1973) *The Interpretation of Cultures: Selected Essays*, New York: Basic Books.

Haller, E. P., Child, D. A. and Walberg, H. J. (1988) 'Can comprehension be taught? A quantitative synthesis of "metacognitive" studies', *Educational Researcher*, 17, 9: 5–8.

Hammond, S. (2000) *The Thin Book of Appreciative Inquiry*, Bend, OR: Thin Book Publishing.

Hattie, J., Biggs, J. and Purdie, N. (1996) 'Effects of learning skills interventions on student learning: a meta-analysis', *Review of Educational Research*, 66, 2: 99–136.

Hiebert, J., Gallimore, R., Garnier, H., Givvin, K. B., Hollingsworth, H., Jacobs, J., Chui, A. M.-Y., Wearne, D., Smith, M., Kersting, N., Manaster, A., Tseng, E., Etterbeek, W., Manaster, C., Gonzales, P. and Stigler, J. (2003) *Teaching Mathematics in Seven Countries: Results From the TIMSS 1999 Video Study*, Washington, DC: US Department of Education National Center for Education Statistics.

Jones, S. (1983) 'Learning and meta-learning with special reference to education for the elders', unpublished MPhil thesis, University of London Institute of Education.

Juliebo, M., Malicky, G. V. and Norman, C. (1998) 'Metacognition of young readers in an early intervention programme', *Journal of Research in Reading*, 21, 1: 24–35.

Lodge, C. (2002) '"Learning is something you do to children": discourses of learning and student empowerment', *Improving Schools*, 5, 1: 21–35.

Martin, S. and Roberts, A. (2007) 'Scaffolding conversations about learning: a work in progress', *Teacher Leadership*, 1, 2: 31–8.

Marton, F., Dall'Alba, G. and Beaty, E. (1993) 'Conceptions of learning', *International Journal of Educational Research*, 19, 3: 277–300.

Maudsley, D. B. (1979) 'A Theory of meta-learning and principles of facilitation: an organismic perspective', unpublished Ed.D. thesis, Ontario Institute for Studies in Education, Toronto.

Munro, J. (1999) 'Learning more about learning improves teacher effectiveness', *School Effectiveness and School Improvement*, 10, 2: 151–71.

Novak, J. D. (1983) 'Can metalearning and metaknowledge strategies to help students learn how to learn serve as a basis for overcoming misconceptions', in H. Helm and J. D. Novak (eds), *Proceedings of the International Seminar on Misconceptions in Science and Mathematics* (pp. 118–30), Ithaca NY: Cornell University.

Nuthall, G. (1999) 'Learning how to learn: the evolution of students' minds through the social processes and culture of the classroom', *International Journal of Educational Research*, 31, 3: 141–256.

Nuthall, G. (2007) *The Hidden Lives of Learners*, Wellington, NZ: NZCER.

Patrick, H., Anderman, L. H., Ryan, A. M., Edelin, K. C. and Midgley, C. (2001) 'Teachers' communication of goal orientations in four fifth-grade classrooms', *The Elementary School Journal*, 102, 1: 35–58.

Pedder, D. (2006) 'Organizational conditions that foster successful classroom promotion of Learning How to Learn', *Research Papers in Education*, 21, 2: 171–200.

Peterson, E. R., Brown, G. T. and Irving, S. E. (2010) 'Secondary school students' conceptions of learning and their relationship to achievement', *Learning and Individual Differences*, 20, 3: 167–76.

Pramling, I. (1983) *The Child's Conception of Learning*, Göteborg: Acta Universitatis Gothoburgensis.

Pramling, I. (1988) 'Developing children's thinking about their own learning', *British Journal of Educational Psychology*, 58, 3: 266–78.

Pramling Samuelsson, I. (2004) 'How do children tell us about their childhoods?', *Early Childhood Research and Practice*, 6, 1 (online).

Pui-wah, D. C. (2008) 'Meta-learning ability – a crucial component for the professional development of teachers in a changing context', *Teacher Development*, 12, 1: 85–95.

Purdie, N. M. and Hattie, J. (2002) 'Assessing students' conceptions of learning', *Australian Journal of Educational and Developmental Psychology*, 2: 17–32.

Reed, J. and Lodge, C. (2006) *Towards Learning-Focused School Improvement*, Research Matters series, No 28, London: INSI: Institute of Education.

Ricoeur, P. (1984) *Time and Narrative. Volume I* (trans. K. McLaughlin and D Pellauer), Chicago: University of Chicago Press.

Sarason, S. B. (2004) *And What do You Mean by Learning?* Portsmouth NH: Heinemann.

Stephens, K. and Winterbottom, M. (2010) 'Using a learning log to support students' learning in biology lessons', *Journal of Biological Education*, 44, 2: 72–80.

Sternberg, R. J. (1977) *Intelligence, Information Processing, and Analogical Reasoning: The Componential Analysis of Human Abilities*, Hillsdale, NJ: Lawrence Erlbaum.

Thomas, G. P. and McRobbie, C. J. (2001) 'Using a metaphor for learning to improve students' metacognition in the chemistry classroom', *Journal of Research in Science Teaching*, 38, 2: 222–59.

Vukman, K. B. and Licardo, M. (2010) 'How cognitive, metacognitive, motivational and emotional self-regulation influence school performance in adolescence and early adulthood', *Educational Studies*, 36, 3: 259–68.

Waeytens, K., Lens, W. and Vandenberghe, R. (2002) '"Learning to learn": teachers' conceptions of their supporting role', *Learning and Instruction*, 12, 3: 305–322.

Watkins, C. (2001) *Learning about Learning Enhances Performance*, London: Institute of Education School Improvement Network (Research Matters series No. 13).

Watkins, C. (2003) *Learning: A Sense-Maker's Guide*, London: Association of Teachers and Lecturers.

Watkins, C. (2015) 'Developing learning-centred classrooms and schools', in M. Myhill and R. Maclean (eds), *International Handbook on Life in Schools and Classrooms: Past, Present and Future Visions*, Amsterdam: Springer.

Watkins, C., Carnell, E. and Lodge, C. (2007) *Effective Learning in Classrooms*, London: Paul Chapman/Sage.

Zimmerman, B. J. (1989) 'A social cognitive view of self-regulated academic learning', *Journal of Educational Psychology*, 81, 3: 329–39.

31

Transformative Learning

Knud Illeris

TRANSFORMATIVE AND SIGNIFICANT LEARNING

The concept of *Transformative Learning* was launched in 1978 by Jack Mezirow, Professor of Adult Education at Teachers College, Columbia University, New York. He defined the term as learning which involves changes in meaning perspectives, frames of reference and habits of mind. The immediate background for this was an investigation of women's learning and liberation processes in community college re-entry programmes, inspired by Paulo Freire's work *Pedagogy of the Oppressed* (1970), about illiterate Brazilian rural workers, Jürgen Habermas's (1971 [1968]) theory of communicative action, and Roger Gould's (1978) psychiatric understanding of *Transformation, Growth and Change in Adult Life*.

It is worth noting that in 1951 the American humanistic psychologist, Carl Rogers (1969), had launched a similar concept of *significant learning*, which supplemented his notions of client-centred therapy and student-centred learning, and which he defined as learning involving change in the organization of the self. Rogers's approach never had the same impact as the later initiative by Mezirow, because social conditions only gradually made it appropriate and attractive to understanding learning in this way. But there are also some fundamental differences between the two approaches, and by comparing them, some important characteristics of Mezirow's thinking can be identified, which may have contributed to the latter's success.

There are two principal areas of difference between the two theorists. First, Rogers refers to the self, which is the psychological core of the person, as a whole, and includes cognitive, emotional and social dimensions, as well as the individual's understanding and experience of themselves; whereas Mezirow refers to individual meaning perspectives, which are principally cognitively-founded attitudes and understandings of the relationship between the person and their surroundings. Second, Rogers's understanding is part of a much broader psychological and theoretical conception of the person, while Mezirow's interest is focused more directly on specific learning processes. Mezirow's more focused approach has been part of the reason for the rapidly growing impact of Transformative Learning during the 1980s and 1990s as it has been reasonably easy to understand and follow for adult educators of all kinds, can be combined with many different types of learning content, and does not directly demand specific psychological qualifications to understand it.

The most comprehensive account of Mezirow's understanding of Transformative Learning is given in his book *Transformative Dimensions of Adult Learning* (Mezirow, 1991), and also in a series of edited books by Mezirow and Associates (1990, 2000; Mezirow, Taylor and Associates, 2009). Other important milestones in the development and practice of Transformative Learning have been the start of the very ambitious AEGIS (Adult Education Guided Intensive Study) doctoral programme at Teachers College in 1981, the introduction of regular conferences on Transformative Learning since 1998, the publication of the *Journal of Transformative Education* since 2003, and the first Transformative Learning conference in Europe, in Athens, 2012.

A CRITIQUE OF MEZIROW'S CONCEPTION

But, as the years have passed, there has emerged a growing dissatisfaction with Mezirow's conception and a desire to frame the concept in a more inclusive way. The most influential critique focuses on Mezirow's cognitive orientation and consequently his insufficient understanding of the emotional dimension of Transformative Learning. When people change their understandings and attitudes it usually involves much more than cognitive insight, and strong emotions are often important incentives. This

objection to Mezirow's original programme of understanding has been made by many theorists, most significantly by Patricia Cranton and John Dirkx, who are both important figures in Transformative Learning debates and advocate a Jungian approach (Cranton, 2005 [1994]; Dirkx, 2006, 2012). This has been explicitly recognized by Mezirow (2006, 2009); but he has not since then suggested any other formulation or definition.

Another important critique, originally made by Stephen Brookfield, who was for many years Mezirow's colleague at Teachers College, is that Transformative Learning cannot take place and be understood independently of social and political conditions (e.g. Brookfield, 1987, 2000). Later Edmund O'Sullivan and his collaborators went further in this direction by developing a cosmological approach to Transformative Learning, including issues of sustainability (O'Sullivan et al., 2002; O'Sullivan, 2012). With regards to the relations between Transformative Learning and other kinds of learning, Illeris (2004, 2007, 2014) made a similar point. Transformative Learning is better understood and practised inside and as a part of a comprehensive theoretical framework of learning.

The importance of this insight has latterly and indirectly been confirmed by a growing realization that all learning which in any way goes beyond the remit of traditional classroom teaching can be claimed to be transformative, and thus has come to mean more or less the same as 'good learning' (Newman, 2012, 2014). Another indication that the concept has been weakened is when the organizers of the 11th Transformative Learning Conference in San Francisco, 2012 systematically referred to Transformative Learning not as a specific kind of learning but as a movement, more or less in line with other popular movements such as mindfulness or survival programmes.

There seems to be an obvious risk that the concept of Transformative Learning may be losing its significance and thus its emancipatory power, which have been in the past the source of its importance and popularity. This was precisely what happened to the similar concept of *experiential learning*, which was developed in the 1980s with roots in the path-breaking works of David Kolb (1984) and David Boud et al. (1985), and rapidly gained a central position in the field of adult learning and education (e.g. Weil and McGill, 1989; Wildemeersch and Jansen, 1992). It reached its peak of popularity at the 1996 conference in Cape Town, then gradually declined in importance, and after the 2003 conference in Sydney more or less disappeared, because it became clear, as Kolb had already suggested in 1984, that all learning is in some way experiential.

THE NEED FOR A NEW DEFINITION

As a consequence, it is therefore important for Transformative Learning to reconfigure itself in new, more precise, and also fundamentally more demanding ways, so that it includes all the dimensions of learning and at the same time also includes a limitation or threshold to exclude trivial and insignificant applications of the concept. In 2000 Robert Kegan raised this problem by asking of Transformative Learning: 'What "Form" Transforms?' in a book chapter called a 'Constructive-Developmental Approach to Transformative Learning' (Kegan, 2000). However, Kegan did not propose a new definition, but rather a specific approach; his contribution was more about the 'how' than about the 'what' of Transformative Learning, and although his critique resulted in much discussion it did not lead to any fundamentally new framing of the concept.

But as the need for change and redirection gradually become more and more urgent, two more explicit and elaborated answers to Kegan's question were recently given. The first of these was provided by Mark Tennant, who is particularly well known for his book, *Psychology of Adult Learning*, which since 1988 has been published in three editions (Tennant, 2005 [1988]). In his later years Tennant has focused on the psychology of the self, mainly inspired by Michel Foucault and other French postmodern philosophers (Tennant, 2009 [1998]). In 2012 he published a book called, *The Learning Self: Understanding the Potential for Transformation* (Tennant, 2012), in which he proposed that Transformative Learning should be defined and understood as learning involving changes in the self; a formulation which certainly resembles Rogers's notion of significant learning, but is in no way related to it. However, Tennant's proposal is an improvement because the idea now includes both cognitive ideas and emotional patterns, and at the same time excludes what is subjectively trivial and insignificant.

The second answer to Kegan's question is provided by Illeris (2014), and given on the basis of a thorough examination of a broad range of terms and concepts, which might be relevant in this context. Illeris (2014) suggested that *identity* is the most appropriate term for what is transformed by Transformative Learning as it is a concept that is close to a notion of the core self, but also explicitly includes the individual's social attitudes and relationships. So Illeris (2014: 40) argued that Transformative Learning should be defined as 'all learning that implies change in the identity of the learner', both because it is comprehensive, and because it has become central in the last three decades to contemporary personality psychology, social psychology and sociology, and therefore has been closely analysed and positioned in relation to current developments in the organization and practice of late modern societies. This needs to be substantiated in the following way.

IDENTITY AS THE TARGET OF TRANSFORMATIVE LEARNING

There is an agreement that the modern understanding of the concept of identity was developed by the German-American psychoanalyst Erik Erikson, principally in his two books, *Childhood and Society* (1950) and *Identity, Youth and Crisis* (1968). Erikson constructed a model of eight life-stages, which he called *epigenic*, meaning that development passes through intervening, crisis-like transformations so that later stages are indirectly present in earlier stages and are subsequently passed on to the next stage. Central to this process is the crisis leading from youth into early adulthood, which, if it is successfully achieved, results in the development of a personal identity, or if it is not successfully achieved, leads to identity confusion.

Identity was understood by Erikson as a psycho-social mental phenomenon, covering both the persistent experience of being the same in all the different situations and phases of the life-course, and the totality of how the person relates to and wishes to be perceived by others. Thus, according to Erikson, identity is developed during the life stage of youth, at that time estimated to last some 4–5 years between the ages of 14 and 18, finally coming to fruition during the youth crisis at the age of about 18–20, and from then retained and further consolidated throughout adulthood. In this framework Erikson was in agreement with contemporary humanist psychologists such as Gordon Allport (1961) who wrote about 'the mature personality', and Carl Rogers (1961) who used the expression 'the fully functioning person'.

However, very soon, the stability of adult identity began to be questioned as leading psychotherapists reported rapidly growing changes among their clients from classic neurotic symptoms to a new and more diffuse kind of personality problem, termed 'narcissist disorder', which included experiences of emptiness, absurdity, meaninglessness, lack of self-perception, initiative and job-satisfaction, and a tendency to engage in routine behaviour (e.g. Kohut, 1971, 1977). This led to the narcissism debate in which the American historian Christopher Lasch identified a state of decay in cultural values (Lasch, 1979). In contrast, Thomas Ziehe, working in a German university, saw it as a reasonable reaction to contemporary phenomena such as the disintegration of the nuclear family, intensification of work, increasing compensatory consumption, and new possibilities for individual and social emancipation (Ziehe, 1975; Ziehe and Stubenrauch, 1982).

This amounted to radical new understandings of the concept, first in French postmodern philosophy (e.g. Foucault, 1982), then in German and British sociology (e.g. Giddens, 1990, 1991; Beck, 1992 [1986]), followed soon after by the breakthrough in American psychology of social constructionism (e.g. Gergen, 1991, 1994). In different ways, these new understandings led to a new kind of individualized relationship between the individual and society, having important consequences for the condition and importance of identity development.

The source of this was the general de-traditionalization in the late 1960s and it persisted with growing intensity through the 1970s. Existing traditions, norms, rules and ways of behaviour were gradually phased out and replaced by more free and casual modes, and, especially among young people, a revolt against social structures, which gradually led to an extensive individualization of social and societal structures. People could and should choose their own lives through personal choices of consumerism, life style, relationships, education, job, sexuality and general behaviour. At the formal level, society, legislation and administration also gradually treated people more and more as individuals with individual rights and duties, and all this made it increasingly necessary for everybody to develop a persona or identity which could guide and co-ordinate the rapidly growing number of individual choices, understandings, meaning perspectives, ways of living, behaviour patterns and the like that the individual was required to make and have. In this way a person's identity changed from a lifelong, well established, and, only in very urgent cases, changeable, centre of consciousness, into an organ for maintaining a *balance* between stability and flexibility, between 'ontological security' and 'existential anxiety', as Giddens expressed it (1991).

It is in line with this gradual and profound change in the individual's life condition that

Transformative Learning has today become a central issue; in contrast to Rogers' similar concept of significant learning, which was launched too early to fit with the prevailing zeitgeist. Transformative Learning can in this perspective be defined, described and understood precisely as the process by which we are able to change and develop our identity, not on a daily level, but stepwise through adult life. Whilst identity is the structural answer to the individual's handling of contemporary life conditions, Transformative Learning is the corresponding practical tool by which that identity is kept up-to-date. If we do not, more or less regularly, change important elements of our identity we cannot accommodate and cope with the ever-changing surroundings and life conditions we all experience. These changes are made through learning processes, which take on the character of transformations.

NEW DEVELOPMENTS IN TRANSFORMATIVE LEARNING

Having come to the conclusion that the concept of Transformative Learning today needs to be reframed, and that this should be related to identity-development as the central and co-ordinating process, combining meaning perspectives with a much wider range of psychological and social processes, and managing and controlling the relationship and interaction between the individual and her or his surroundings, it becomes possible to contemplate a range of new kinds of conditions, connections and fields in which Transformative Learning may be activated, and new kinds of ways in which it may be applied. Precisely because identity today is a part of all our thoughts, understandings, actions and relationships, changes in identity are also possible and relevant in very many different situations. In Illeris (2014) I have made a more comprehensive examination of the most important of these new possibilities. Here I summarize some of these ideas.

TRANSFORMATIVE LEARNING IN YOUTH

The first of these is that linking Transformative Learning to identity makes it possible to solve what has always been an open question: when can, and how does, Transformative Learning come to fruition? Transformative Learning has always, in theory as well as in practice, been related to adulthood. But where does it come from? It cannot only be a gift from heaven or a public right assigned at the age of majority. However, by connecting it to identity, the ability to engage in Transformative Learning is developed as part of identity development, which has been studied and discussed in psychology ever since the work of Erikson (1950, 1968).

Some basic identity elements are originally developed in early childhood, such as gender identity, family identity, and, later perhaps, religious and national identity, but in Erikson's worldview these are what he called identifications, because they are transferred from parents or others and in no way chosen by the child. Genuine identity development takes place during the period of youth, which today is no longer just a period of some 4–5 years between the ages of 14 and 19, but must be seen as starting at early puberty, at the age of 11–13, and lasting until a reasonably coherent and stable identity is achieved, usually in the middle or last half of the 20s.

However, in relation to Transformative Learning, it is important that transformations cannot take place before there is something to transform, i.e. before there are some well-established identity elements and at least also a kind of early identity pattern or structure. As described by Thomas Ziehe (and Stubenrauch, 1982) the identity process starts with trial-and-error activities, which he calls search movements. Youngsters experiment with more or less provocative ideas, standpoints or ways of behaving, in order to see what reactions they provoke, and in this way get an idea of whether they are worth going on with, or whether they should be changed or discarded, but all of this is not so much planned and controlled as it may seem. On the contrary, in school these search movements are often quite disturbing and derailing in relation to teaching and learning activities.

But gradually, through the early teenage years, experiences form the outlines of a pattern, which can be a foundation for an identity formation; and when this begins to have the character of a coherent structure, at least in certain areas, the possibility of transformations appears. So from about the age of 16–18 Transformative Learning may take place, first on a limited scale, and probably not in full until some time during the late 20s.

DIFFERENT KINDS OF TRANSFORMATIVE LEARNING

The recognition that identity is the target of Transformative Learning also made it possible to differentiate between different kinds of Transformative Learning, because development and transformation of identity may assume many forms in the light of the multitude of changes the individual and groups of individuals are subjected to. Clearly Mezirow identified the kinds of transformations he found most important and wanted them to be as emancipating and progressive as possible. In line with this, it is striking that all the cases and examples, which have been collected together and published in books such as *Transformative Learning in Practice* (Mezirow et al., 2009), are about progressive Transformative Learning in a very wide range of different contexts. But sometimes changes in identity have to be regressive rather than progressive, for example, when life conditions deteriorate, as in cases of unemployment, divorce or other crisis situations. In Illeris (2014) I give examples of different kinds of adult courses and education, which can be characterized as regressive Transformative Learning, and I suggest that this is possibly the most pressing challenge to Transformative Learning today and how to deal with it in practice.

In connection with this there will also be situations that can lead to what is logically the next step, which is to try to realize and practice what I have termed restorative Transformative Learning. This is achieved by turning regressive Transformative Learning practices into new, progressive and more realistic transformations. This is possible precisely because the learner is in a situation of change, and, if not too depressed by the regression, will be eager to try out other ways (an example of this can be found in Illeris (2014: 98)).

COLLECTIVE OR COMMUNAL TRANSFORMATIVE LEARNING

As identity as a mental construct also includes personal attitudes to relationships between the individual and other individuals or groups, and how one wishes to be experienced by others, Transformative Learning when defined in relation to identity can also be practised as a collective or communal activity and learning. This is in principle the case as soon as two or more individuals in a common process make more or less parallel transformations. These transformations will never be quite the same between two or more learners because learning as a mental process of acquisition is always individual and influenced by the results of subjectively relevant prior learning. But nevertheless, the learning situation and objective may be so alike in a group of people with similar backgrounds that they can identify enough to be able to work together, or take a course together, and on mainly equal terms. Seen from the point of view of learning, this is a very favourable situation because the participants then have the possibility both to help and support each other and also to create an atmosphere of security and goal-directedness, which may qualify the activities and strengthen the learning outcomes.

Transformative Learning activities, as practised by Freire and observed by Mezirow, have to a great extent profited by such collectivity.

But the very extensive individualization which has taken place since then has made such collective learning more difficult to establish in practice, and, if the differences between the participants are too big and the solidarity too weak, intended collective Transformative Learning activities may end up in conflicts and disagreement. This may harm the collectivity and result in a range of heterogeneous transformations.

TRANSFORMATIVE LEARNING, DEFENCE AND RESISTANCE

Learning research and learning theory have mainly been preoccupied with what happens when somebody learns something, and this is certainly the case in relation to Transformative Learning. But it is even as important to also consider what happens when people do not learn what they intend to learn or what they should or are supposed to learn, or when they only learn in insufficient or distorted ways. Nevertheless, this area of non-learning and mis-learning has only been taken up by very few researchers or peripherally in relation to other considerations. Apart from my own work (Illeris, 2007, 2014) I can only refer to Peter Jarvis (2012) and his references to David Hay (2007) and Ian Kinchin et al. (2008) for serious attempts of this kind. And these sources do not go very deeply into the psychological aspects of non-learners and non-learning.

However, to find the roots of non-learning, insufficient learning and distorted learning as mass phenomena, which they certainly are today, and not only occasional occurrences, it seems necessary to go back to the middle of the twentieth century, when a situation arose in which ordinary people in their daily lives began to cope with a bigger amount of information and impressions than they had capacity to take in as learning, and therefore had to develop what the French philosopher, Henri Lefebvre (1947), and later the German social psychologist, Thomas Leithäuser (1976,

2000) called 'everyday consciousness' as a psychological barrier or defence to avoid being overloaded.

Today this has become the situation for all of us all the time – just think of how the TV news constantly provides us with new information and impressions, or the many changes in our life conditions provoked by happenings and decisions all over the world, which influence our situation and understanding. This implies that we all have to develop a psychological defence system towards learning which reaches much further and may include all kinds of input; and unlimited openness to all the input we receive would inevitably lead to a mental breakdown. But this also leaves us with a very intrusive task of selection, what to take in and what not to take in, which we deal with in two different ways: a lot of information and impressions we simply reject (after half an hour of TV news, five minutes later we only have the ability to recall very limited parts of the content), and quite a lot of what we do take in we will distort so that it is in accordance with what we already know, think and mean, and therefore it will not result in learning. These are psychological processes with which we all have to deal today. Seen from the point of view of learning this means that we accidentally and unconsciously miss learning possibilities which could have been useful and desirable, and this inevitably also happens in educational situations (the immediate pedagogical answer being that important points and conclusions should be emphasized several times and from different perspectives).

The strongest of these defence mechanisms is no doubt identity defence; the closer an input is to the core of our identity, the more we are inclined to reject or distort it. And this sets the scene for very many possible situations of Transformative Learning, which is actually quite sensible because the essential challenge is to keep a subjectively defined balance between the stability and flexibility of our identities. So the conclusion in relation to Transformative Learning, understood as a change of identity elements, is that such learning has to do with balance; and therefore the task of a teacher, instructor, guide or coach is to lead the learner to relevant situations in which this balance is challenged in a clear and well substantiated way, leave decisions and consequences to the learner, and be ready with any mental or practical support if the learner takes up the challenge and tries to come through with some kind of Transformative Learning.

Finally, I will here mention that in addition to learning defence there are also situations in which it would be relevant to talk about learning resistance, the main difference being that defence is there in advance of the given learning situation, whereas resistance is directly provoked by the situation. This occurs when what could be learned is so unacceptable to the learner that she or he cannot or will not take it in, but on the contrary reacts by showing strong opposition, and it may be a difficult and uncomfortable situation for a teacher and other learners. But nevertheless it can be very important to try, eventually later and in a one-on-one conversation, to take up the situation and reaction with the learner, because there is so much mental energy invested in a reaction of this kind that allows Transformative Learning to be the outcome. For many years I started my courses on learning theory with university students by asking them to think of some event in their lives by which they had learned something which they regarded as really epoch-making for them, and far more than half of the answers always referred to situations of learning resistance.

TRANSFORMATIVE LEARNING AND COMPETENCE DEVELOPMENT

Today educational learning is usually formally targeted at the development of competencies. This term has taken over from earlier concepts like knowledge and skills or qualifications and is basically a more appropriate formulation, because competencies are about what a learner actually can do and manage in

practice. The transition to this term was strongly promoted by international educational agents, primarily the OECD, and there was a long process to reach an appropriate definition and specification of what should exactly be the content and understanding of the term. Finally the most authoritative formulation became as follows:

A competence is defined as the ability to successfully meet complex demands in a particular context of work and in everyday life through the mobilization of psychosocial requisites (including both cognitive and non-cognitive aspects). This represents a demand-oriented or functional approach to defining competencies. The primary focus is on the results the individual achieves through an action, choice, or way of behaving, with respect to the demands, for instance, related to a particular professional position, social role, or personal project. (Rychen and Salganik, 2003: 43)

This definition is at the same time very ambitious, very open and broad, and yet precise in some important parts, signified by the terms 'complex demands', 'psychosocial requisites' and 'cognitive and non-cognitive aspects'. It is certainly about the applications of the competencies in relation to the complex and ever-changing challenges of today's working and everyday life.

But it also operates at the supranational level, in this case mainly the European Union, where this ambitious understanding has been fundamentally betrayed in many ways, most powerfully by having the member states prepare lists of the competencies acquired in each of their publicly acknowledged school and educational programmes, in order that employers cross-nationally can judge the actual suitablility of applicants for specific jobs and tasks. These lists for each country include thousands of 'competencies', the great majority of which are certainly far from satisfying the definition above and with absolutely no guarantee that everyone who has been through the education or course in question actually commands each of them, but only that they have probably been through a process which should formally include some acquaintance with this or that competency.

However, if taking the quoted or some other of the many ambitious definitions seriously, it is in the present connection clear that competencies living up to these definitions must be complex in their scope, psychosocial in their practice, and cover both cognitive and non-cognitive dimensions; or, to express the essence of this more directly, must cover both relevant insight, skills and personal qualities, or both relevant professional qualifications and a sustainable personal identity.

So there is a close and mutual connection between competence and identity: a person cannot be competent in an area if the relationship to this area is not an integrated part of her or his identity, and that identity cannot include a commitment to a certain area or job or function without somehow being competent in relation to it. And obviously this implies that the acquisition and development of competencies to some extent must employ Transformative Learning.

It is precisely this connection which right from the start has made Mezirow's AEGIS doctoral programme so very significant and esteemed, because it intentionally includes challenges and demands which encourage and promote Transformative Learning. And this is also in addition to more general and humanistic arguments and interests concerning why the connection between Transformative Learning and identity development is so important to realize, maintain and understand.

REFERENCES

Allport, G.W. (1961) *Patterns and Growth of Personality*, New York: Holt, Rinehart and Winston.

Beck, U. (1992 [1986]) *Risk Society: Towards a New Modernity*, London: Sage.

Boud, D., Keogh, R. and Walker, D. (eds) (1985) *Reflection: Turning Experience into Learning*, London: Kogan Page.

Brookfield, S. (1987) *Developing Critical Thinkers: Challenging Adults to Explore Alternative Ways of Thinking and Acting*, Milton Keynes: Open University Press.

Brookfield, S. (2000) 'Transformative Learning as Ideology Critique', in J. Mezirow and Associates (eds) *Learning as Transformation: Critical Perspectives on a Theory in Progress*, San Francisco, CA: Jossey-Bass.

Cranton, P. (2005 [1994]) *Understanding and Promoting Transformative Learning*, San Francisco, CA: Jossey-Bass.

Dirkx, J. (2006) 'Engaging Emotions in Adult Learning: A Jungian Perspective on Emotion and Transformative Learning', in E.W. Taylor (ed.) *Teaching for Change*, New Directions in Adult and Continuing Education.

Dirkx, J. (2012) 'Nurturing Soul Work: A Jungian Approach to Transformative Learning', in E.W. Taylor and P. Cranton (eds) *The Handbook of Transformative Learning: Theory, Research, and Practice*, San Francisco, CA: Jossey-Bass.

Erikson, E.H. (1950) *Childhood and Society*, New York: Norton.

Erikson, E.H. (1968) *Identity, Youth, Crisis*, New York: Norton.

Foucault, M. (1982) 'Technologies of the Self', in L.H. Martin, H. Gutman and P.H. Hutton (eds) *Technologies of the Self: A Seminar with Michel Foucault*, Amhurst, MA: University of Massachusetts Press.

Freire, P. (1970) *Pedagogy of the Oppressed*, New York: Seabury.

Gergen, K.J. (1991) *The Saturated Self: Dilemmas of Identity in Contemporary Life*, New York: Basic Books.

Gergen, K.J. (1994) *Realities and Relationships*, Cambridge, MA: Harvard University Press.

Giddens, A. (1990) *The Consequences of Modernity*, Stanford, CA: Stanford University Press.

Giddens, A. (1991) *Modernity and Self-Identity*, Cambridge, UK: Polity Press.

Gould, R. (1978) *Transformation, Growth and Change in Adult Life*, New York: Simon and Schuster.

Habermas, J. (1971 [1968]) *Knowledge and Human Interests*, Boston, MA: Beacon Press.

Hay, D. (2007) 'Using Concept Mapping to Measure Deep, Surface and Non-learning Outcomes', *Studies in Higher Education*, 32(1): 39–57.

Illeris, K. (2004) 'Transformative Learning in the Perspective of a Comprehensive Learning Theory', *Journal of Transformative Education*, 2(2): 79–89.

Illeris, K. (2007) *How We Learn. Learning and Non-learning in School and Beyond*. London: Routledge.

Illeris, K. (2014) *Transformative Learning and Identity,* London: Routledge.

Jarvis, P. (2012) 'Non-Learning', in P. Jarvis and M. Watts (eds) *The Routledge International Handbook of Learning*, London: Routledge.

Kegan, R. (2000) 'What "Form" Transforms? A Constructive-Developmental Approach to Transformative Learning', in J. Mezirow and Associates (eds) *Learning as Transformation: Critical Perspectives on a Theory in Progress*, San Francisco, CA: Jossey-Bass.

Kinchin, I., Lygo-Baker, S. and Hay, D. (2008) 'Universities as Centres of Non-Learning', *Studies in Higher Education*, 33(1): 89–103.

Kohut, H. (1971) *The Analysis of the Self: A Systematic Approach to the Psychoanalytic Treatment of Narcissistic Personality Disorders*, New York: International Universities Press.

Kohut, H. (1977) *The Restoration of the Self*, New York: International Universities Press.

Kolb, D.A. (1984) *Experiential Learning: Experience as the Source of Learning and Development*, Englewood Cliffs, NJ: Prentice-Hall.

Lasch, C. (1979) *The Culture of Narcissism: American life in an age of dimishing expectations,* New York: Norton.

Lefebvre, H. (1947) *The Critique of Everyday Life*, London: Verso.

Leithäuser, T. (1976) *Formen des Alltagsbewusstseins*, Frankfurt A.M.: Campus [The Forms of Everyday Consciousness].

Leithäuser, T. (2000) 'Subjectivity, Lifeworld and Organization', in K. Illeris (ed.) *Adult Education in the Perspective of the Learners*, Copenhagen: Roskilde University Press.

Mezirow, J. (1978) *Education for Perspective Transformation: Women's Re-entry Programs in Community College*, New York: Teachers College, Columbia University.

Mezirow, J. (1991) *Transformative Dimensions of Adult Learning*. San Francisco, CA: Jossey-Bass.

Mezirow, J. (2006) 'An Overview on Transformative Learning', in P. Sutherland and J. Crowther (eds) *Lifelong Learning: concepts and contexts*, London: Routledge.

Mezirow, J. (2009): Transformative Learning Theory, in J. Mezirow, E.W. Taylor, and Associates (eds) (2009) *Transformative Learning in Practice: Insights from Community, Workplace and Higher Education*, San Francisco, CA: Jossey-Bass.

Mezirow, J. and Associates (eds) (1990) *Fostering Critical Reflection in Adulthood: A Guide to Transformative and Emancipatory Learning*, San Francisco, CA: Jossey-Bass.

Mezirow, J. and Associates (eds) (2000) *Learning as Transformation: Critical Perspectives on a Theory in Progress*, San Francisco, CA: Jossey-Bass.

Mezirow, J., Taylor, E. and Associates (eds) (2009) *Transformative Learning in Practice: Insights from Community, Workplace and Higher Education*, San Francisco, CA: Jossey-Bass.

Newman, M. (2012) 'Calling Transformative Learning into Question: Some Mutinous Thoughts', *Adult Education Quarterly*, 62(1): 399–411.

Newman, M. (2014) 'Transformative Learning: Mutinous Thoughts Revisited', *Adult Education Quarterly*, 64(4): 345–355.

O'Sullivan, E. (2012) 'Deep Transformation: Forging a Planetary Worldview', in E.W. Taylor and P. Cranton (eds) *The Handbook of Transformative Learning: Theory, Research, and Practice*, San Francisco, CA: Jossey-Bass.

O'Sullivan, E., Morrell, A. and O'Connor, M.A. (eds) (2002) *Expanding the Boundaries of Transformative Learning*, New York: Palgrave.

Rogers, C.R. (1951) *Client-Centered Therapy*, Boston, MA: Houghton-Mifflin.

Rogers, C.R. (1961) *On Becoming a Person*, Boston, MA: Houghton-Mifflin.

Rogers, C.R. (1969) *Freedom to Learn*, Columbus, OH: Charles E. Merrill.

Rychen, D.S. and Salganik, L.H. (eds) (2003) *Key Competencies for a Successful Life and Well-Functioning Society*, Cambridge, MA: Hogrefe and Huber.

Tennant, M. (2005 [1988]) *Psychology and Adult Learning*, London: Routledge.

Tennant, M. (2009 [1998]) 'Lifelong Learning as a Technology of the Self', in K. Illeris (ed.) *Contemporary Theories of Learning*, London: Routledge.

Tennant, M. (2012) *The Learning Self: Understanding the Potential for Transformation*, San Francisco, CA: Jossey-Bass.

Weil, S.W. and McGill, I. (eds) (1989) *Making Sense of Experiential Learning: Diversity in*

Theory and Practice, Buckingham: Open University Press.

Wildemeersch, D. and Jansen, T. (eds) (1992) *Adult Education, Experiential Learning and Social Change: The Postmodern Challenge*, Haag: VUGA.

Ziehe, T. (1975) *Pubertät und Narzissmus*, Frankfurt A.M.: Europäische Verlagsanstalt [Puberty and Narcissism].

Ziehe, T. and Stubenrauch, H. (1982) *Plädoyer für ungewöhnlisches Lernen*, Reinbek: Rowohlt [Pleading for Unusual Learning].

32

Learning and Pedagogic Relations

Tone Saevi

INTRODUCTION

In thinking about relationships in the context of education and learning we can easily come to the conclusion that it should be about the ways in which we as adults and teachers relate to children in order to help them to achieve better learning outcomes, or to optimize their learning opportunities, or as a means to influence their well-being, encourage their socialization and improve their mental health. The relationship between adult and child then would be about how well the adult controls and masters the child's educational achievements and is able to distinguish between normal and abnormal psychological-educational progress. Education as intimately linked to rational progress and achievement, and as the basis for a personal and social humanity, is the Western idea of teaching and learning originally formed in the Enlightenment. To the degree that the relation between adult and child is not taken for granted or ignored, it tends to turn into a means of detecting problems with and in the child (i.e. poor quality of skills or lack of motivation for learning, problems with social adaptation, misbehaviour, etc.) that need to be attended to, corrected or diagnosed.

In this way the educational discourse is being fed by principles from psychology such as learning and development, from sociology of how children are expected to take on roles and pre-designed systems, and from market-based ideologies, all of which presuppose that the individual fits into a certain regularity and social order. Children are being psychologically compared to and defined by the group and not understood as unique human beings, and are being judged by their fit with the status quo. Testing is often standardized and the results of the tests are then compared to a particular norm. Relational problems are frequently the basis for research on better learning methods or models, and on ways of distinguishing and identifying children's potential and limitations. Relations between adult and child, in this scenario, become one among many variables that are controlled and managed for children's learning to be successful. The relation between adult and child, teacher and student, then, is foregrounded to the extent that it promotes educationally desirable pre-chosen qualities, and is identified as an instrumental and rational tool for the adult or teacher. The child is the object of learning, care and adjustment, and is valued to the degree that he or she adapts to the norms and regulations set for education. Yet, is this what we really want for our children and young people? And is this what we consider education and learning to be?

There is another way of understanding the relation between adult and child in educational settings. In this chapter, I explore what learning in pedagogic relationships might indicate if education and learning are understood as responsible, risky, non-reciprocal acts, and the relationship between adult and child is seen as a personal existential relationship without an epistemological purpose as its first premise. And I will try to show how matters of life are not primarily about learning or mastering certain skills, but about helping the child to grow up in and to humanness, with and through the support of human and democratic, moral, ontological and existential intentions, incarnated in the pedagogical relationship.

In the first section, I articulate the problem, expressed as the difference between learning as a fixed outcome-oriented teacher discourse, and learning as a relational and existential endeavour without a specified end. In the following sections, I reflect on the conditions for changing our understanding of education and learning, by foregrounding some of the epistemological premises that structure today's educational practices, and contrast these with other possibilities. I present a set of experiential events depicting the pedagogical relationship, through which I hope to show that the premise for my understanding of the current state of education as well as of my theoretical sources comes from and via these examples.

THEORETICAL KNOWLEDGE OF PERFECT LEARNING

The internationalization of the Anglo-American interpretation of education and educational research in recent decades has offered new and revitalized discourses of the significance and meaning of education. The conceptual and social hegemony of the English language, combined with the Bologna process, has boosted the objective of building a *Europe of Knowledge* (Bologna Declaration, 1999: 1). Following in its wake, Europe has abandoned the broader understanding of education as Pädagogik, the moral and pedagogic interest in the life of the child and young person, and accepted a narrower understanding of education as schooling. Education has come to mean learning, which as the single focus of the knowledge society, increasingly has become a rationalized, measurable, politicized and simplified phenomenon, expressed in abstract language as lifelong learning, accountability and evidence, which has more to do with the economy, business and competition than with the lives of children and young people. The psychological and evidence-oriented notion of learning has become the fall-back device of the professional teacher, and the 'non-specialized' meanings of older educational terms are either being re-defined or replaced with terms or meanings that are specialized and instrumentally charged.

The word *education* originally referred to the process of nourishing and rearing a child, but has gradually come to refer to the systematic instruction, schooling or training given to the young (Oxford English Dictionary). The term *learning* orients to the action of receiving instruction or acquiring knowledge, indicating a psychological and teleological process that leads to the modification of behaviour or the acquisition of new abilities or responses, and the biological connotation of natural development by growth or maturation. The interest in children in today's educational monoculture refers principally to their ability to succeed and adapt to the current market.

As the majority of educational research today is grounded in the sciences of human behaviour and cognition they are also psychologically and utility validated. Phylogeny, the biological basis for learning and development, takes precedence over ontogeny, the history, life and reality of the human being (Friesen and Saevi, 2010). The objective of psychological research in education is efficient learning, the desired outcome of education, and education as socio-economic means (e.g. Hattie and Yates, 2014; Kirby and Lawson, 2011; Shell et al., 2010). Consequently, the interest is in methods and models made for effecting children's learning achievements. One device among others for proficient learning is the quality of the teacher–child relationship (e.g. Myers and Pianta, 2008; Pianta and Stuhlman, 2004; O'Connor et al., 2011). This relationship is systematically calculated through the teacher's psychological superiority, and educationally identified in epistemological outcomes. The prevalent use of the terms, education and learning, as psychologically and epistemologically loaded phenomena, can be contrasted with the German term Pädagogik, whose meaning is only partly covered by the English terms, education and learning. Pädagogik as academic discipline, in contrast to the unified field called 'educational research' or 'educational studies', refers to a number of different terms, all denoting aspects of the discipline of Pädagogik, such as Erziehungswissenschaft, Bildungswissenschaft, Pädagogik and Didaktik (Biesta, 2013a). None of these terms is directly translatable to education or learning, although they include both phenomena. In fact, Pädagogik contradicts the idea of teaching and learning as curriculum planning spelled out as educational psychology promoting learning outcomes (Biesta, 2006; Hopmann, 2007; Künzli, 1998; Westbury et al., 2000), and offers an existential, moral-laden and democratic alternative, with the pedagogic relation as its fulcrum (Saevi, 2011).

INTERPRETING EDUCATION AS RELATIONAL

Within the variety of views on the meaning, content and aim of Pädagogik, Oelkers (2001: 255) identifies three common characteristics of theories of education in the European tradition. The first is that all these theories focus on morality, the second is that they refer to the interaction between human beings, and the third is that education has to do with the necessary tension between authority and freedom expressed in the asymmetric relationship between adult and child. As a discipline with its own concepts and theories based on a moral-laden interest in the life of the child and young person, rather than as a theoretical study of the object of education (Biesta, 2011), education is understood as an existential endeavour implying attentiveness to relations and contexts. Education understood like this requires an anthropological and experiential onto-epistemological interest in the meaning of educational events. A first-hand concern for the adult is to be attentive to the existential meaning held within a particular educational situation and in particular to how that situation is experienced by the child. In interpreting education as experiential and profoundly relational, Pädagogik and phenomenology coincide in their shared focus on the concrete, situated, singular and irreplaceable human experience taking place in the complexity and paradoxes of our moral-relational life world. The purpose of pedagogic-phenomenological life world research is to keep the experiential qualities of education open rather than to efface, explain and resolve educational obstacles. The frame of the concrete contextual educational encounter between adult and child is personal, intentional and moral, and has the shape of a relation, which in the European tradition is called the pedagogical relationship (Langeveld, 1969, 1975; Saevi, 2013, 2014a; Spiecker, 1984; Spranger, 1958; van Manen, 1991, 2012).

Researchers, opposing the contemporary psychological-rational market-oriented educational trend, inquire into a range of aspects of education that together represent an alternative to mainstream research. Some research has taken an educative, democratic and moral focus as the basis of education, its aim and purpose (e.g. Biesta, 2006, 2010; Bingham and Sidorkin, 2004; Säfström, 2003, 2011). Others explore the meaning of professionalism and what a professional teacher actually is (e.g. Biesta, 2012; Lippitz and Levering, 2002; van Manen, 2012). Some attend to educational dilemmas in curriculum and didactic theory and practice about teaching and learning (e.g. Gundem and Hopmann, 1998; Hopmann, 2007; Künsli, 1998), while still others address the devalued position of the child, in particular the unsuccessful child in educational institutions (e.g. Løvlie, 2013; Säfström, 2011). Many publications address the dearth of pedagogical qualities within the narrow understanding of educational practice, and critique the tendency to see the pedagogical relation as an educational medium for outcome and efficiency (e.g. Levering, 2011; Sævi, 2013, 2014b; van Manen, 2012). The pedagogical relationship as an existentially charged relationship addressing the subjective and democratic aspects of education is the focus of the work of Mollenhauer (2014), Biesta (2004), Bingham and Sidorkin (2004) and Todd (2014). The *sui generis* qualities of the pedagogical relationship, the essential pivot required for education to be pedagogic, are emphasized by phenomenological researchers such as Langeveld (1969, 1975), Spiecker (1984), Saevi (2011, 2013, 2014a, 2014b) and van Manen (1991, 2012).

THE RELATIONAL EXPERIENCE

Instead of orienting towards epistemological aims, a phenomenological Pädagogik focuses on existential questions related to how to help children be and become democratic, autonomous and authoritative persons, who are able in their turn to give others the same possibility. Thus, the formulation of educational aims

of purpose and content presupposes an experiential validation for the educational moral expressed in these aims and thus weaves theory and practice together in the meaning of the human experience. This way of thinking actualizes normative questions such as: Why is this purpose a good purpose? Why should the child learn this and not something else? How do we know that these aims are good and right? Considerations about right and good in educational practice and research imply reflections about the relationship between adult and child, by highlighting an experiential interpretive understanding of right and wrong, good and bad, and of what these qualities mean in concrete encounters in classrooms and in other learning contexts. Hence, the most appropriate way of representing the pedagogic relationship in educational reflection is the use of concrete examples that allow the detailed meaning of relational situations to express itself in experiential practice and thus make education and learning recognizable, coherent and theoretically meaningful. Two ordinary situations depicting an adult–child relationship exemplify this.[1]

It is Monday morning in the City-park of Bergen. A father and his little son have just left the bus and are on their way through the park to kindergarten. The three-year-old walks a few meters ahead of his father, stops by the low fence separating the pathway from the lawn down to the lake, and stands for a few moments looking at the ducks swimming down there. The father also stops and looks at his son. After a few moments, he says 'Come now, let us continue'. The little boy starts walking again and his father is close behind.

Somewhere else in the City-park another little boy about the same age walks with his father on his way to kindergarten. The son lets go of his father's hand and runs toward the low fence to have a look at the ducks. 'Come back! You are supposed to walk with me' the father says immediately, grasps his son's hand and continues. (Saevi, 2013: 236–237)

These two examples instantly speak to our common-sense view of what pedagogy is, and at the same time reveal the attitudes and values of the parents' responses to similar actions. In the first situation, the father waits for his son, gently telling him after a while that they should continue. He seems attentive to the pedagogical quality of giving his son the space to explore on his own and to initiate their shared events. He appears to value his son's interest in what is around them and perhaps intuitively he does not intervene in the situation when the little boy wants to look at the ducks for a moment. The other father feels that it is important that his son walks with him and that they are not distracted by what is around them. Perhaps he wants the child to learn that one should not take unnecessary detours. While the first father lets his son try out the situation on his own, the second has a more determined and perhaps controlling approach. Who is right? That is hard to tell on a general basis. We might have preferences, but my point is not to decide pedagogical right from wrong. The point is that these two examples show that we think differently in and about situations where adults and children interact. There is always an alternative way of acting (and thus thinking) in and about the relation between child and adult, and the alternative is related to what the adult finds important in life and how his or her life directly plays out in the concrete relational encounter.

As adults, we live in relation to children and cannot opt out if we are actually together with them in homes, educational institutions and other settings. We cannot refrain from relating to children if we are with them, and, as Mollenhauer (2014) suggests, this is a seemingly unimportant, but nonetheless profound, basis for education. As adults, like the fathers above, we always have alternative ways of being and acting. We can be and act in different ways and with different intentions in our relationships with children. We might be attentive or distant, accepting or devaluing, open or reserved, lively or resigned, inviting or authoritarian. But we always *are* some way or another, and our being and acting means something to the child.

THE RELATION SPEAKS

Next to our parents or caregivers, the most common adult relationship of children and young persons is with teachers in kindergarten and school, and leisure-time leaders. In addressing the child or young person these encounters are more or less close, caring, reliable and constant, and by necessity they form a multifarious and paradoxical experience, life affecting and important for both, but crucial for the child and young person. Oda is a young girl who struggles with learning how to read and write. Often her learning deficiencies are obvious to herself as well as to the teacher and her classmates. Here, though, she tells about an incident in class that is significant for her.[2]

> When my answer is wrong, I know it immediately because Per [the teacher] looks at me with this particular humorous glance and says, after just a little pause: 'Yes ...?' Then I understand that he wants me to give the question a second thought. He just leans back comfortably and waits. That's why I like him so much. I feel relaxed and smart with him. (Saevi, 2005: 162)

The teacher looks at Oda, leans back and waits. What does he wait for? A new attempt from Oda to provide the right answer? That would be a very teacherly response to a student giving the wrong answer. Teachers frequently want students to learn new things, to be more knowledgeable, more critical and liberated in their perspectives. They want them to learn about the world, and in particular about what they and us (and the current society) find important. We as teachers constantly strive to make children and young people conscious and aware of issues that we consider relevant for their present and future lives. This endeavour, though primarily epistemological and focused on educating the other, is based on 'a rationale for delivering the "secrets" of a pre-disclosed, idealized understanding of [a rationality based] humanity' (Säfström, 2003: 21). Yet, a teacher always has a variety of alternative actions and motifs and we do not really know what this teacher in this particular situation actually is waiting for. His look might simply be an approving look that recognizes Oda for who she is; a student with a particular learning problem. He does not make a judgement about this, but tactfully passes over what should not in this particular situation be paid attention to (Saevi, 2005: 164). His look might open up to Oda a space unknown to herself as well as to her teacher; a space for potential freedom and transformation of self. The teacher trusts her without certainty, and acts without knowing the outcome of the situation, although he seems to believe that something will open up and be meaningful to Oda some time in the future. He has a perspective on her as well as his own life and creates an opening, a space for her, simply with a glance. The opening up of possibilities and keeping them open by being in a young person's life is how pedagogical relations speak and how children experience the meaning of the relationship.

BEING ATTENTIVE TO THE POSSIBLE

As long as there have been two generations of human beings, education in some form or another has taken place. The adult generation encounters the new generation with the intention of appealing to, opening up, and sharing insights with them about the world they both live in. Children are driven by their given human openness for development, Bildung and physical, mental and social maturation, and by their inherent capacity for curiosity, learnability and personal orientation. This potential is directed towards the world and represented by the adult in the culture (Mollenhauer, 2014), and the relation is the frame within which the child can address, and be addressed by, the world. The crisis that occurred in the culture when the 'learning self of the child' (Augustin, 1974: 8) '… was suppressed by the question of how the adult could teach the child that which should be learned' (Mollenhauer, 2014: 32), was caused by the introduction of a Western approach to teaching and learning. The autonomous realization of the child, by the child, was influenced by the adult in a double meaning of the term. The child orients to the adult world to realize his or her life project, and in turn the

adult influences the child in the direction of 'something', which is the imperative of the society and the intention of the culture.

Learning is theoretically and experientially connected to other educative phenomena like teaching, thinking, Bildung, development, motivation and change. There are different types of learning and obstacles to learning discussed in learning theories and experienced in classrooms. The particular perception of learning in pedagogical relationships is a phenomenological existential perspective, consciously aware of the diversity of human learning perspectives. However, coming from a Continental educational tradition where the focus is on learning as an integrated part of human life with others and the world, learning is subordinated to teaching, and both are included in the pedagogical relation. Likewise, in this tradition, teaching and learning are not determined causes of one another. Unlike in trade where nothing is sold if nobody has bought it, teaching without something learned is not automatically result-less teaching. Teaching might generate learning in due course when the child is ready, when the situation opens up or when suddenly something makes sense to the child. Teaching and learning are potential but not fixed transactions.

… AND BEING AWARE OF THE LIMITATIONS

Children's lives and life conditions could be different if we as adults aim and act differently because children can only realize their life projects within the frame provided by the adult in the culture. '[T]hey can only imagine this [their own growing up] in terms of the adult life that is already presented all around them' (Mollenhauer, 2014: 8). The generational relationality makes sense as an educative relation if we understand educational relationality as interwoven in the particular way of life presented and represented by the adult in the culture. The adult incorporates in the relation the presentation and representation of the meaning of the way of life in the culture in which they both live, and as such the pedagogical relation is an example of how life can be lived, situated and incarnated (Saevi, 2014b). The relation is a moral-practical unity that makes possible parenting and education; an existential opening for the adult's attentiveness and response to the experience of the child in the setting (Saevi, 2013: 238). The relation between adult and child, the pedagogical relationship, is an asymmetric relationship, which unlike adult relationships, is unequal per se.

The adult cannot ignore this asymmetry without simultaneously abolishing the relation as a pedagogic relationship. Skjervheim (1992: 29) argues that the difference between this asymmetry and what he calls a 'fundamental methodic asymmetry', is that the latter is a systematically maintained domination of the thoughts, virtues and self-understanding of one of the parties of the relation, whereas the former is not structured in this way, and this constitutes a critical and moral distinction in education. The reason is that the adult's acknowledgement of this asymmetry keeps open certain possibilities, involving as it does a self-questioning by the adult of their intentions and actions. Fundamental methodic asymmetry, on the other hand, reifies this asymmetry and excludes new interpretations of the relation from situation to situation. The pedagogical relation ceases to exist as pedagogic when the child takes over the responsibility for him or herself, others and the world. This further shows the decisive significance it has for the child that the relation with adults has the form of a pedagogical relationship based on factual asymmetry and attentiveness to the child's situation of existential reliance and exposure.

RESPONSIBILITY AND HESITATION

In the pedagogical relationship adults have alternative ways of acting and thinking. Understanding the situation and its possible meanings for the child is an existential act with moral implications that demands sensitivity and a certain pedagogical hesitation. This is vital because as an adult in educational situations one has responsibility for another human being. Children turn to adults and trust adults to help them. Children are vulnerable and lack the experience to protect themselves or to strike back if they are used or misused for the benefit of the adult. Children learn from the situations they are in with adults, and as an adult I ought to ask myself what they learn from being with me. The pedagogic relationship is concrete, moral, autonomous and meaningful in itself, and addresses the existence and co-existence of the child as well as the adult. The relationship is personal and situated and constitutes the frame for the pedagogical qualities of educational situations. One might say that the pedagogical relation is life itself, incarnated and incorporated in the adult and cultural condition. The pedagogical relation then is neither a tool for someone's interests or a medium for a more or less successful educational project. The pedagogical relation quite simply is a practical-moral educational togetherness. The relation is a responsible closeness with and to the child and his or her life by an adult that comes from the outside and thus encounters another that is different and thus existentially unknown. The adult first of all is responsible for who he or she is, acts and thinks in relation to the child.

This responsible responsibility embodies a certain hesitation for the other as other, and how one as an adult encounters the otherness of the child. The adult–child encounter is not a pedagogical encounter without this morally laden pedagogical hesitation that cares responsibly for the child by trying again and again to act justly towards the child without at any time having an end-point (Derrida, 1997; Levinas, 1998). Justice to the otherness of the child (or any other human being) can never be achieved by aiming at social or political equality through laws and regulations. Although we always attempt to strive for human equality as a democratic objective, this is not sufficient as an objective for humanness, because complete justice is never possible. The pedagogical demand is not to stop acting responsibly and justly with children and young people, and at the same time accept the existential complexity and paradoxical conditions under which we as human beings live.

THE RELATIONSHIP AS A FULCRUM FOR PEDAGOGIC PRACTICE

The relation between adult and child as the necessary 'fulcrum' for education (Saevi 2011) includes an understanding of education as multifaceted, complex, interpretive and paradoxical. Education cannot be reduced to one particular interpretation of what practice, theory and research should be, or to particular research evidence that is shown to have improved practice. Education and educational research cannot be detached from inter-human relations, direct or indirect, present or intended, to abstract verifiable matrices, or to general rationality or economic confirmation of what education is or should be. On the contrary, the educational intent orients to the other, the child or young person, and acts *as if* the other understands, learns and has potential (Langeveld, 1969; Mollenhauer, 2014).

Not knowing the outcome of education and still trusting that there will be some outcome, now or later, is an educational intent that is carried by the adult's responsible ability and willingness to dwell in a kind of moral-pedagogical hesitation on behalf of the uniqueness of the child. The unique indefinite child has a potential that is both undecided and undecidable, and fundamentally unknown to the teacher. As the pedagogical relation is an existential relationship between adult and child, the adult can only partly reflect on the relation and plan it in advance. The relation is understood and interpreted as a pedagogical event when it takes place as a concrete and situated relation in practice, or when we as adults reflect on it in retrospect as a relational episode, which points back to a concrete example from practice (e.g. Mollenhauer,

2014; Saevi, 2011; van Manen, 2012, 2014). In concrete practice with each other as adult and child, we live and see the dilemmas and rational contradictions that pedagogical relations inevitability must have if they are to be open to existential questions concerning how the child can learn and be taught about life, self and others.

Continental education practice, i.e. Pädagogik, traditionally has an interpretive and moral basis (Biesta, 2011; Saevi, 2011, 2014a), and understands human existence as *experienced* and *sensed* before it is rationally explained. Pedagogic practice is experienced before it can be talked of in a symbolic, abstract way. This means that it is not sufficient for education to have an epistemological and methodical language alone that is able to speak of rational, efficient and future-oriented matters. Children's lives and life worlds are here and now, and hold paradoxes, contradictions and complexities, only partly communicated, although recognizable and sensed by the child (and the adult) in pedagogical settings. The pedagogical relation is vital to children to allow them to speak of that which can only partly be spoken of, but still belongs to human (and childhood) life and existence. How can that which in life is paradoxical, sensed in ruptures, disjointed and at least partly unspeakable, still be relationally expressed to children, and why are these aspects of life so important that they must have priority over useful knowledge of rational, representative and socializing processes?

Let me return to what I initially indicated about the pedagogical relation as the fulcrum of existential pedagogical practice rather than the teacher's means for efficient learning or for the progress of other socially or politically desirable qualities in the child. The relation between adult and child is always an asymmetric encounter in which the radical openness and still indecisive nature of the child some way or another is expressed. To care responsibly for the child and young person's state of being as a child or young person, personal life and existence must have priority over all other potential purposes, aims or objectives in situations where these are in conflict. The language of education must be a language that can speak to the lived experience of the child *before* it challenges rationality and cognitive potential, as what is lived and experienced is more basic and must have existential priority over what is thought and said. This insight is supported by Merleau-Ponty (2002) and Levinas (1998: 3), in that the former shows how the *immediate sense of self and others in the world* is a premise for reflection and understanding *of* self and others, and the latter suggests that 'to understand our situation in reality is not to define it, but to be in an affective state. To understand being is to exist'. It is in pedagogic relationships and with unspecialized language that we can speak (if only partly and insufficiently) of life and all its inconsistencies, where adult and child dwell together and live for short or long periods of time, and interpret their different experiences in different ways in the situations they encounter. Research, as well as human and educational experience, admits that a pedagogical practice where the pedagogical relationship is the fulcrum seems to be the form of practice that best accounts for existential complexity and aporetic difference, characteristic of life and pedagogic life between older and newer generations. The existential language that is spoken *in* and *with* the pedagogical relation (although hesitant and in part), might speak of issues of life and learning that the epistemological language of schooling, skills, learning-outcomes and educational future prospects cannot speak of. An unspecialized language – democratic, existential, experiential and thus understandable for both child and adult – might put into words that which does not fit, is multi-interpretive, inconsistent and meaningless, but in and because of its rational ruptures, discontinuity and disturbances still somehow is part of life as it is lived and experienced by the persons in the situation and thus is experienced as true.

What is pedagogical, that which touches the lives of children and young persons' existence and life, can to a lesser degree be expressed in words than we tend to believe.

The lived life of adults and children – who they are in life in each of their unique ways – needs a language that is incorporated in the experience of life and incarnated in our relational existence (Saevi, 2014b). Education understood like this is first and foremost a question of *who* I am as an adult and *how* I intend and act in relation to this child or young person in this concrete situation. Who I am and how I act is prior to any epistemological demands of knowledge, learning and outcomes. The pedagogic relationship is the way to be together that opens the possibility for the adult to be close enough to see the unique child and young person and distinguish this singular person from all other persons in the world. And at the same time the pedagogic relationship demands sufficient distance between the adult and the child for the responsible and authoritative potential of the child to find space.

NOTES

1   The example is to be found in Saevi (2013). The idea behind the example is from Barritt et al. (1985).
2   The description is taken from a collection of interviews from 2001–2002 with learning disabled high school students in Norway that are described, translated and referenced in Saevi (2005) and presented in a number of later publications.

REFERENCES

Augustin, A. (1974) *St. Augustine's Confessions* (transl. R.J. O'Connell), Cambridge, MA: Belknap Press.

Barritt, L., Beekman, T., Bleeker, H. and Mulderij, K. (1985) *Researching Educational Practice*, Grand Forks, ND: Center for Teaching and Learning, University of North Dakota.

Biesta, G.J.J. (2004) '"Mind the Gap!" Communication and the Educational Relation', in C. Bingham and A. Sidorkin (eds), *No Education Without Relation*, New York: Peter Lang, pp. 11–22.

Biesta, G.J.J. (2006) *Beyond Learning: Democratic Education for a Human Future*, Boulder, CO: Paradigm Publishers.

Biesta, G.J.J. (2010) *Good Education in an Age of Measurement*, Boulder, CO: Paradigm Publishers.

Biesta, G.J.J. (2011), 'Disciplines and Theory in the Academic Study of Education: A Comparative Analysis of the Anglo-American and Continental Construction of the Field', *Pedagogy, Culture and Society*, 19, 2: 175–92.

Biesta, G.J.J. (2012) 'Giving Teaching Back to Education: Responding to the Disappearance of the Teacher', *Phenomenology and Practice*, 6, 2: 35–49.

Biesta, G.J.J. (2013a) 'Å snakke "pedagogikk" til "education". Internasjonalisering og problemet med konseptuell hegemoni i studiet av pedagogikk' [Speaking 'Pädagogik' to 'Education'. Internationalization and the problem of conceptual hegemony in the study of education], *Norsk Pedagogisk Tidsskrift*, 3, 97: 172–84.

Bingham, C. and Sidorkin, A. (2004) *No Education Without Relation*, New York: Peter Lang.

Bologna Declaration (1999) http://www.ehea.info

Derrida, J. (1997) 'The Villanova Roundtable: A Conversation with Jacques Derrida', in J. Caputo (ed.) *Deconstruction in a Nutshell: A Conversation with Jacques Derrida*, New York: Fordham University Press.

Friesen, N. and Saevi, T. (2010) 'Reviving Forgotten Connections in North-American Teacher Education: Klaus Mollenhauer and the Pedagogical Relation', *Journal of Curriculum Studies*, 42, 1: 123–47.

Gundem, B.B. and Hopmann, S. (1998) (eds) *Didaktik and/or Curriculum: An International Dialogue*, New York: Lang.

Hattie, J. and Yates, G.C.R. (2014) *Visible Learning and the Science of How We Learn*, New York: Routledge.

Hopmann, S. (2007) 'Restrained Teaching: The Common Core of Didaktik', *European Educational Research Journal*, 6, 2: 109–24.

Kirby, J.R. and Lawson, M.J. (2011) (eds) *Enhancing the Quality of Learning: Dispositions, Instruction, and Learning Processes*, Cambridge: Cambridge University Press.

Künzli, R. (1998) 'The Common Frame and the Place of Didaktik', in B.B. Gundem and S. Hopmann, *Didaktik and/or Curriculum: An International Dialogue*, New York: Lang, pp. 29–46.

Langeveld, M. (1969) *Einführung in die theoretische Pädagogik*, Stuttgart: Klett Verlag.

Langeveld, M. (1975) *Personal Help for Children Growing Up*, The W.B. Curry Lecture delivered at The University of Exeter on 8 November.

Levering, B. (2011) '"The Interest of the Child" Seen from the Child's Perspective': The Case of the Netherlands', *Ethics and Education*, 6, 2: 109–23.

Levinas, E. (1998) *Entre Nous: Thinking of the Other*, New York: Columbia University Press.

Lippitz, W. and Levering, B. (2001) 'And Now You Are Getting a Teacher With Such a Long Name …', *Teacher and Teacher Education*, 18, 2: 205–13.

Løvlie, L. (2013) 'Verktøyskolen'['The tool school'], *Norsk Pedagogisk Tidsskrift*, 3: 185–98.

Merleau-Ponty, M. (2002) *The Phenomenology of Perception*, New York: Routledge Classics.

Mollenhauer, K. (2014) *Forgotten Connections: On Culture and Upbringing*, New York: Routledge.

Myers, S. and Pianta, R.C. (2008) 'Developmental commentary: Individual and contextual influence on student–teacher relationships and children's early problem behaviours', *Journal of Clinical Child and Adolescent Psychology*, 37, 3: 600–8.

O'Connor, E.E., Dearing, E. and Collins, B.A. (2011) 'Teacher–child relationship and behavior problems trajectories in elementary school', *American Educational Research Journal*, 48, 1: 120–62.

Oelkers, J. (2001) *Einführung in die Theorie der Erziehung*, Weinheim: Beltz.

Pianta, R.C. and Stuhlman, M.W. (2004) 'Teacher–child relationships and children's success in the first year of school', *School Psychology Review*, 33, 3: 444–58.

Saevi, T. (2005) 'Seeing Disability Pedagogically: The Lived Experience of Disability in the Pedagogical Encounter', doctoral dissertation, University of Bergen, Bergen.

Saevi, T. (2011) 'Lived Relationality as Fulcrum for Pedagogical-Ethical Practice', *Studies in Philosophy and Education*, 30: 455–61.

Saevi, T. (2013) 'Ingen pedagogikk uten en "tom" relasjon: Et eksistensielt-fenomenologisk bidrag' [No education without an empty relation: An existential-phenomenological contribution], *Norsk Pedagogisk Tidsskrift*, 3, 97: 236–47.

Saevi, T. (2014a) 'Phenomenology in Educational Research', *Oxford Bibliographies in Education*, Luanna Meyer (ed.), New York: Oxford University Press.

Saevi, T. (2014b) 'Eksistensiell refleksjon og moralsk nøling: Pedagogikk som relasjon, fortolkning og språk' [Existential reflection and moral hesitation: Education as relation, interpretation and language], *Norsk Pedagogisk Tidsskrift*, 4, 98: 248–59.

Säfström, C.A. (2003) 'Teaching otherwise', *Studies in Philosophy and Education*, 22, 1: 19–29.

Säfström, C.A. (2011) 'Rethinking emancipation, rethinking education', *Studies in Philosophy and Education*, 30: 199–209.

Shell, D.F., Brooks, D.W., Trainin, G., Wilson, K.W., Kauffman, D.F. and Herr, L.M. (2010) *The Unified Learning Model: How Motivational, Cognitive, and Neurobiological Sciences Inform Best Teaching Practices*, Dordrecht: Springer Netherlands.

Skjervheim, H. (1992) *Filosofi og dømmekraft [Philosophy and Judgement]*, Oslo: Universitetsforlaget.

Spiecker, B. (1984) 'The Pedagogical Relationship', *The Oxford Review of Education*, 10, 2: 203–9.

Spranger, E. (1958) 'The Role of Love in Education', *Universitas: A German Review of the Art and Sciences Quarterly* [English Language Edition] 2, 3: 536–47.

Todd, S. (2014) 'Between body and spirit: The liminality of pedagogical relationships', *Journal of Philosophy of Education*, 48, 2: 231–45.

van Manen, M. (1991) *The Tact of Teaching*, Ontario: The Althouse Press.

van Manen, M. (2012) 'The Call of Pedagogy as the Call of Contact', *Phenomenology and Practice*, 6, 2: 8–34.

van Manen, M. (2014) *Phenomenology of Practice: Meaning-Giving Methods in Phenomenological Research and Writing*, Walnut Creek: West Coast Press.

Westbury, I., Hopmann, S. and Riquarts, K. (eds) (2000) *Teaching as a Reflective Practice: The German Didactic Tradition*, Mahwah, NJ: Erlbaum.

33

Affective Dimensions of Learning

Carolyn Jackson

INTRODUCTION

In the classroom there sits an emotional elephant that many try to ignore. (Newton, 2014: x)

Affect and emotion play key roles in education, indeed, Pekrun and Linnenbrink-Garcia (2014: ix) argue that '[e]motions have emerged as one of the most salient topics in current educational research'. At one level this is not surprising. Anyone who has experienced schooling will know that emotions – fear, embarrassment, hope, pride, shame, boredom, enjoyment, disappointment – abound in schools; even in adulthood, thinking back to schooldays tends to prompt strong emotions. Schools are undoubtedly emotional places. Indeed, as Hascher (2010: 13) reminds us, 'there is rarely any learning process without emotions'. Given that, it is perhaps surprising that the field of educational emotion research is a nascent one that has developed mainly over the last 10–15 years in what has been termed an 'affective turn' (Pekrun and Linnenbrink-Garcia, 2014). And the education

field has lagged behind others – for example, psychology, biology, sociology and anthropology – where the study of 'affective life' has a longer history (Greco and Stenner, 2008). Before the 1990s most educational researchers focused largely on the cognitive outcomes of schooling and neglected emotions (Hascher, 2010). Today the dominance of the standards discourse in education means that policy concerns are focused on attainment rather than experiences of schooling (Jackson et al., 2010). Yet affect influences the way students approach (or avoid) learning; levels of engagement; interactions with peers and teachers; performances on tests; interpretations of and reactions to feedback; the list could go on. Affect is a central yet neglected dimension of learning.

In this chapter I argue that educational researchers and teachers ought to pay more attention to the affective dimensions of learning and schooling. Furthermore, I suggest that researchers need to build upon but go beyond the limited work that has already been undertaken in this sphere, which is overwhelmingly dominated by quantitative, psychologically-informed research. In order to understand more fully affective practices in education, we need to consider the ways in which they are constructed and sustained at different levels (for example, individual, classroom, school and nation), how they intersect and the effects of them. I start by providing a brief overview of how affect and emotion are conceptualised in general, and then in educational research more specifically, and flag the difficulties of navigating a field in which there is a profusion of contested terms. In an attempt to illustrate some of the reasons to research affect, I then focus on fear and schooling before ending with a brief conclusion.

CONCEPTUALISING AFFECT AND EMOTION

Conceptualising and defining affect, emotion and other related terms are far from straightforward; conceptualisations vary between and within disciplines, as do the theoretical and methodological lenses through which they are examined (Linnenbrink, 2006). Some writers and researchers use the terms *affect* and *emotion* interchangeably, while others regard such use as deeply problematic (Greco and Stenner, 2008). When distinctions are made they are not always consistent and, as Greco and Stenner (2008: 11) point out, the 'theoretical resources' informing them differ; affect may be linked to psychoanalytic theory or Deleuzian philosophy, for example. Greco and Stenner's (2008: 12) position is that insisting on a terminological distinction is not inherently helpful, they argue that 'terminology serves first as a marker of difference for groups of intellectuals, keen to distinguish their own approach from that of specific others … however, shared terminology need not imply a shared theoretical position'.

In general, *emotion* is associated particularly with biological, psychological or neuroscientific research. As Wetherell (2012: 2)

suggests, 'affective scientists' from such disciplines:

> investigate emotional states and the distinctive perturbations they cause in the body and mind. Sometimes 'affect' includes every aspect of emotion and sometimes it refers just to physical disturbance and bodily activity (blushes, sobs, snarls, guffaws, levels of arousal and associated patterns of neural activity), as opposed to 'feelings' or more elaborated subjective experiences.

Wetherell (2014) conceptualises *emotions* as 'the conventional cultural packets or prototypes for affect, e.g. anger, joy, sadness, disgust, shame, surprise' that 'register evaluations of events, standpoints on what is happening, and investments'. *Affect*, she suggests, is a 'broader, more generic term. It includes reactions that may be difficult to categorize and which may not be organised into conventional categories'. She argues that both affect and emotion are usually action oriented, that is, they 'push us to do something' (Wetherell, 2014).

Perhaps unsurprisingly, in educational research, definitions and conceptualisations are also contested. For example, Pekrun and Linnenbrink-Garcia (2014: 2–3) note that in the broader educational literature affect is often used to denote a wide variety of non-cognitive constructs including emotion, but also to denote self-concept, beliefs and motivation. In contrast, in emotion research, affect refers to emotions and moods more specifically. Shuman and Scherer (2014: 16) note that 'the words affect and emotion are sometimes used synonymously with the feeling component; more commonly though, affect is seen as a larger category that includes, among others, emotions and moods, and emotion is viewed as multi-componential and includes, among others, a feeling component'. Other contested concepts also enter the fray, for example, mood. Some educational researchers regard mood and emotion as distinct, while others consider them to be on a continuum (Linnenbrink, 2006). While there is no consensus about this, generally emotions are seen to be specific and moods more diffuse and lacking a specific referent. Moods are also generally regarded as lasting longer than emotions (Shuman and Scherer, 2014), as Fiedler and Beier (2014: 37) explain:

> Emotions are bound to specific eliciting stimuli and characterized by situation-specific appraisal functions. For instance, embarrassment is an emotion elicited by failure experience or revelation of intimate secrets but does not fit a frustrating or provocative situation. As a consequence, emotions are bound to a specific stimulus context and therefore unlikely to carry over to many other stimulus contexts. Moods, in contrast, are unspecific, typically quite enduring affective states, with often indeterminate origins. When people are in an elated or melancholic mood state, the origin or eliciting experience is often unknown, and maybe attributed to a wrong cause.

In her overview of research about learning and emotion (which includes affect), Tina Hascher (2010: 14) argues that emotions are generally thought to include physiological, psychological and behavioural aspects. She suggests that commonly emotion is seen to have five components. First, the *affective* component is the subjective experience, for example, feeling nervous before an exam. Second, the *cognitive* component represents thoughts in relation to that emotion, for example, thinking about the causes and implications of failing an exam. Third, the *expressive* component involves the expression of emotion, for example, a look of fear or joy. Fourth, the *motivational* component relates to the impulses for action stimulated or inhibited by the emotion, for example, working hard on a task because it is enjoyable. Fifth is the *physiological* component, for example, increased heart beat and sweating caused by anxiety during an exam. Hascher (2010: 14) lists eight indicators commonly used to analyse the quality of an emotion:

1   Valence (pleasant = positive, unpleasant = negative, and ambivalent);
2   Arousal level (deactivating–activating);
3   Intensity (low–intense);
4   Duration (short–long);
5   Frequency (seldom–frequent)
6   Time dimension (retrospective such as relief, actual such as enjoyment, prospective such as hope);
7   Point of reference (self-related such as pride, oriented towards another person such as sympathy, referring to an activity such as boredom);
8   Context (during learning, in achievement situations, during instruction, in social interactions and so on).

Another distinction made is between traits and states. Trait-like affect is regarded as a general way of responding which varies between people but is relatively stable over time. State-like affect is less stable over time, as it reflects a response to changing environments (Linnenbrink, 2006).

Hascher's overview of research on learning and emotion presents a landscape that is overwhelmingly dominated by psychological research. It is this type of work that Wetherell (2012) argues is too narrow. Wetherell suggests that the basic emotion terms used in this sphere – for example, sadness, anger, fear, happiness – do not reflect the range of possible affective performances, scenes and events. She argues that affect could relate to much more general modes of influence, movement and change:

> We could talk, for instance, about 'being affected' by an event, even if it is not quite clear what the impact is. Affect in this sense need not be confined to humans or even animate life – the sun affects the moon, a magnet affects iron filings, and the movement of waves affects the shape of the coastline … Affect now means something like a force or an active relation. The term loses its moorings in studies of human emotion and expands to signify disturbance and influence in their most global senses. (Wetherell, 2012: 2)

Wetherell (2014) incites us to research such 'affective practices', yet how we do this is far from straightforward, and Wetherell offers very few pointers in this regard. To illustrate some of the reasons to consider affective practices I turn to focus on fear and anxiety in schooling, with a particular focus on fears around exams and tests. This is only one very small and focused aspect of what Wetherell (2014) is calling for, yet even this research is challenging in a host of ways.

FEAR, ANXIETY AND SCHOOLING

Even with what might be considered a 'single emotion' such as fear/anxiety, we face many of the issues that we encountered with bigger related concepts such as emotion, affect, mood, etc. Namely, variations in the way fear and anxiety are defined and conceptualised lead to differences in how they are understood and explored. For example, fear and anxiety are used interchangeably by some writers (for example, Bourke, 2005; Bauman, 2006; Gill, 2007) but not others (for example, Ahmed, 2004; Salecl, 2004). Rachman (1998: 25–6) attempts to draw the following, and perhaps most common, distinction between fear and anxiety:

> Anxiety is one of the most prominent and pervasive emotions. It is a feeling of uneasy suspense, the tense anticipation of a threatening but vague event. Fear and anxiety share some common features, but fears tend to have a specific, usually identifiable focus, and to be more intense and episodic.

In other words, as Ahmed (2004: 64) points out, in this model 'fear *has* an object' (original emphasis) whereas anxiety does not. By contrast, Bauman (2006: 2) argues that fear is most intense when it has no object:

> Fear is at its most fearsome when it is diffuse, scattered, unclear, unattached, unanchored, free floating, with no clear address or cause, when the menace we should be afraid of can be glimpsed everywhere but is nowhere to be seen. 'Fear' is the name we give to our *uncertainty*: to our *ignorance* of the threat and of what is to be done. (original emphasis)

So conceptualisations of fear vary considerably, and even many researchers who attempt to distinguish between fear and anxiety (e.g. Rachman, 1998) recognise that the distinction is blurred, and as a result the two terms are frequently used interchangeably. In this chapter I use the terms fear and anxiety interchangeably for two main reasons. First, although conceptually fear and anxiety may be regarded by some (but not all) as distinct, it is difficult to disentangle them empirically. Second, the frequency with which the two terms are used interchangeably in the literature makes attempting to separate them very difficult, and somewhat arbitrary.

RESEARCH ON FEAR/ANXIETY IN EDUCATION

In general, research suggests that fear and anxiety are pervasive in schools. Indeed, anxiety is the most frequently reported emotion in education. For example, in a series of interview and questionnaire studies with high school and university students, anxiety was the emotion reported most often, constituting 27% of all emotional episodes experienced in various academic situations such as attending class, studying, and taking tests and exams (Pekrun and Perry, 2014: 122). It is also the emotion that has been most researched in educational contexts. As with research on learning and affect in general, the vast majority of work on fear in education has been conducted by psychologists who usually attempt to measure fear levels using self-report measures and explore the bio-psychological effects on individuals and their performances (Gower, 2005; Putwain, 2007). Most attention has been afforded to test or examination anxiety; psychologists generally regard test anxiety as a multi-dimensional construct consisting of three facets: cognition (e.g. worry, test-irrelevant thoughts); affect (e.g. emotionality, physiological reactions); and behaviour (e.g. study avoidance) (Soysa and Weiss, 2014: 2). In general, findings suggest that test anxiety 'is associated with impaired test performance and knowledge acquisition in academic skill areas', also that students report more test anxiety in relation to high-stakes tests (Segool et al., 2013: 495), and pressure is inversely associated with attainment (Samdall et al., 2004). Thus, contrary to many common-sense beliefs that fear helps to motivate pupils, a pretty robust pattern in the literature is that high levels of examination-related anxiety generally have a debilitating effect on attainment (Zeidner, 2007) and can lead to disengagement.

Even though most attention has been afforded to test anxiety there is not an extensive literature, especially outside of the USA. Indeed, Putwain (2007) points out that in the UK test anxiety was largely ignored until relatively recently. Furthermore, despite the value of the work by psychologists this is limited in that it almost entirely uses quantitative approaches and focuses on individuals. Thus, it tends not to explore in-depth the experiences of students in terms of: the sources of their fears; how fears are reproduced and sustained; or the effects of fears. Nor does it address questions about the different scales of fear and how they intersect – for example, fears at the level of the individual, the school, the local community, the nation and beyond – nor about the politics of fear, for example, what fears are generated at particular times and by whom, and who benefit and who lose most (see Jackson, 2010).

While these are the types of questions that might typically be tackled by sociologists of education and those interested in the politics and philosophy of education, fear and anxiety in educational contexts have been neglected by such scholars and educational researchers in general (Zembylas, 2009; Jackson, 2013; Hargreaves, 2015). I am not suggesting that fear has received no attention by sociologists of education, it has *emerged* in numerous studies; but in most cases it is a by-product rather than a focus (e.g. Reay et al., 2007; Williams et al., 2008). The relatively small amount of sociologically-informed qualitative work that has focused on anxieties in education (e.g. Denscombe, 2000; Hargreaves, 2015; Jackson, 2006, 2010, 2013) inevitably raises more questions than it answers. Nevertheless, it begins to shed light on some of the complex ways that fears work and intersect, and highlights the need for more research in this sphere. It also emphasises the need for teachers to be more attuned to the effects of fears and other affective practices in educational settings, and the ways teachers influence them as well as the ways they are themselves influenced by them (see also Newton, 2014). There is space here to provide only a few illustrations. I draw these mainly from my own qualitative work, which I outline briefly.

My project, funded by the Economic and Social Research Council (ESRC), explored, among other issues, fears about failure in secondary schools (academic and social 'failure'). Data generated during this project include questionnaire data from approximately 800 pupils and interview data from 153 pupils in Year 9 (aged 13–14 years) and 30 teachers. Six secondary schools located in the north of England were involved: four co-educational (Beechwood, Elmwood, Firtrees, Oakfield), one girls' (Hollydale) and one boys' (Ashgrove). Based initially on data from Office for Standards in Education (Ofsted) reports, and supplemented by information from schools, schools were selected to ensure a mix of pupils in terms of social class and ethnicity, and a mix of schools in terms of overall examination results and gender of intake (single-sex and co-educational). For more details see Jackson (2006). Through this work I have begun to demonstrate how fears circulate and intersect in classroom contexts, and some of the factors that create, exacerbate and reduce them (Jackson, 2006, 2010, 2013; see also Hargreaves, 2015).

My research suggests that the vast majority of pupils – girls and boys – are anxious about academic 'failure' (amongst other things), and these fears are particularly pronounced around tests and exams, especially those that are used to rank schools publicly, for example, Standard Assessment Tasks (SATs).[1] Overall, 68% of interviewees reported being anxious about SATs. Many of these explained their anxieties in terms of fears about failing, and some conveyed them vividly:

CJ:	Were you worried about them [SATs] beforehand?
Jenny (Firtrees):	Yes I was scared to death! I thought oh no I'm not going to be able to do them, I'll get stuck half way through and I won't be able to answer any of the questions.
CJ:	Were you nervous about your SATS?

Steph (Hollydale):   I was, yes. Going in I was shaking because there was so much pressure almost like put on you before them. You almost like, you know people were willing you to do well and inside you were thinking I don't know if I can do it, but yes I was quite nervous.

As flagged earlier, educational psychologists have demonstrated that high levels of examination anxiety can have negative impacts on student performances for a variety of reasons. For some students fears of academic failure prompt a range of defensive strategies that are likely to lead to failure or disengagement from learning (Martin and Marsh, 2003). Such defensive strategies are prompted largely by the convergence of two sets of factors. First, in societies where academic credentials are heralded as key indicators of ability and worth, demonstrations of academic 'inability' are very problematic. Second, schools are places where ability is frequently tested and exposed. In such contexts there are two key ways to avoid being regarded as lacking ability and, therefore, worth. One is to avoid failure, which is not always possible as schooling operates as a competitive system in which not everyone can be a 'winner'. The second is to avoid the negative implications of failure (i.e. lack of ability). Defensive strategies are linked to the latter; they enable students to create generally false but plausible explanations to justify or excuse (potential or actual) poor academic performance (Covington, 1998). In general, such excuses allow individuals to blame factors other than lack of ability for academic 'failure', and so act to protect them from the damning implication that they lack ability and, therefore, worth. Defensive strategies are varied; one example is disruptive behaviour, as it blurs the relationship between 'failure' and lack of ability.

Where pupils exhibit disruptive behaviours failures may be attributed to being inattentive in class rather than to a lack of ability per se, and the behaviour may act to deflect attention away from poor academic performance and onto their behaviour instead (Khoo and Oakes, 2003). However, while defensive strategies may feel like friends in the short term, in the long term they are likely to increase the chances of failure. Thus, individuals' fears may prompt them to respond in ways that enhance the chances that their fears turn into reality. This is summed up neatly by McGregor and Elliot (2005: 229):

> it is not surprising that individuals high in fear of failure orient to and seek to avoid failure in achievement situations. Indeed, when possible, such individuals seek to select themselves out of achievement situations in the first place. Ironically, and poignantly, in so doing, those high in fear of failure keep themselves from the mistakes and failures that many achievement motivation theorists view as the grist for the mill of competence development … In essence, the avoidance of mistakes and failures stunts the growth and maturation of persons high in fear of failure, which, over time, merely leads to more mistakes and failures. As such, the avoidance of failure is likely to be a self-perpetuating process in that the very process of avoiding failure is likely to serve a role in maintaining and exacerbating the tendency to avoid failure.

So fear as a motivator is unlikely to be successful long term; yet many teachers do attempt to motivate through fear and, relatedly, embarrassment and shame. There were numerous examples of this in my research, and such tactics tended to exacerbate pupils' fears about academic failure. Teachers incited fears in a variety of ways, including emphasising the dire consequences of academic 'failure' for pupils' future careers and life chances, as well as spelling out the negative implications for the school if results were not 'up to standard'.

There is space here to illustrate and discuss only one example of the ways in which teachers attempted to motivate through fear or shame. As such, I have chosen to focus on a relatively common tactic, namely, making pupils' marks known to the whole class by, for example, reading them out. In all schools in my research there were instances of this practice, although it was more prevalent in some than others. It was a practice identified by pupils across the schools to be a significant pressure that provoked anxiety and potentially embarrassment. Clare at Firtrees, for example, suggested that the public reporting of scores made tests much more stressful for fear of being embarrassed publically.

Clare: It doesn't bother me doing tests, but it's just that she shouts them out – your score. If she just like gave them you then that would be alright. But your mind's like, when you're doing a test, that she's going to shout it out – the score that you've got – and then you just try and do your best to get a higher mark.

CJ: So why is it particularly important that she calls them out, is it about being so public, can you say a bit more about why it matters so much?

Clare: 'Cos if she shouts them out and you've got a low mark everyone looks at you and your friends are like 'are you alright, you've got a low mark but you'll be better next time' and you're a bit embarrassed.

Richard at Elmwood also disliked the public announcement of results. He, like Clare, was anxious not to appear 'stupid' and felt embarrassed if he got a low mark.

CJ: Some people have told me that teachers actually read out the results in some classes.

Richard: Yeah, I don't really like it 'cos if you get a rubbish score … some people laugh at you sometimes.

CJ: So do they [teachers] do that very often?

Richard: Yeah, they do it near enough all the time. Some teachers don't [read out the scores] 'cos they know some people get embarrassed and get upset when they read the answers out.

CJ: Why do you think teachers do that?

Richard: To see if, you know, that if you do get embarrassed, you know you have to try harder so that you won't get embarrassed.

There were even more remarkable examples in my research of the ways teachers would attempt to highlight and shame (relatively) low attainers. For example, Lawrence (Ashgrove) explained that in his top set maths class pupils are seated according to relative ability: 'clever ones' at the back of the class, 'not as clever' ones at the front.

Lawrence: There's a bit of rivalry in the classroom … 'cos part of the system is if you're not as clever then you sit at the front in the middle, which is better because it's easier to hear. Then the clever ones sit towards the back …

CJ: So it's quite an explicit way of ranking people in the class then?

Lawrence: Well, in my first lesson in maths I was sat right at the front after a bit, which I wasn't too worried about because it was the first time I'd been in set one. But it helped me because the very next test I was sat quite a bit further back and it wasn't, well it wasn't because of the extra pressure, it was more because I was at the front and I could see everything she was doing and I couldn't miss a word and you don't lose your attention as easily when you're sat towards the front. And I think that was the main aim of it rather than just to embarrass us.

The teacher's method of seating pupils according to ability is striking for its emphasis on making performance visible; it is difficult to imagine a more overt and visual way of ranking a class according to individual (grade) performance. Lawrence attempts to find positive aspects of this method of spatial organisation: 'less clever' ones can see and hear the teacher and are less likely to get distracted. However, underlying his response is also recognition that some students are explicitly positioned as bottom of the class, and that this is embarrassing (see Wilkins (2011) for a similar example). Such strategies strongly emphasise relative ability comparisons and promote classroom climates that emphasise performance (*demonstrating* competence) rather than learning (*developing* competence), and are likely to foster fears of academic failure, embarrassment and shame.

Richard's analysis of why teachers announce test results to the class is insightful; it is likely that these teachers do believe that such practices will motivate pupils, that they will shame them into working harder so that they are not bottom of the class. However, such tactics, as previously discussed, are likely to be counterproductive; for many students they prompt defensive behaviours that hinder rather than help learning. Teachers need, therefore, to understand affective practices and processes much more fully and to consider the ways in which their own practices impact their students (see also Newton, 2014). However, in saying this I am not adopting a simplistic 'blame the teacher' approach. Teachers themselves are also under pressure to perform, and for many fear plays a big part in their day-to-day lives. For example, teachers too are under considerable pressure to deliver good results and many fear the consequences of their pupils' 'failure' as much as the pupils themselves (see also Denscombe, 2000; Hall et al., 2004). This is understandable, as the consequences of 'failure' for teachers can be considerable:

> If we don't get 20% [A*–C grades at GCSE] the Government will close us. So that's what we've been told that by the Head. And so obviously all the departments are now thinking, you know, come August we're all going to be a nervous wreck, but nobody will sleep the night before the results come out. And if your results aren't at 20% how are you going to feel? You know, could you have done any more? … And yet I think, you know, we've done everything we possibly can to get it. So this is the government dangling this in front of us, saying, not looking at the children, not looking at the children that come in, because value added, we're well above. … No, this is the magic figure, 20%. So, whether we get it or not I don't know. … So we've been working on that really hard to do it this time. So all the staff are under the pressure of failing and if your department doesn't do well, there's like what happens next? (Ms Brian, Beechwood)

The naming and shaming that some teachers do in their classes is mirrored and reproduced at different scales: at the levels of the school,

the local community, the nation and beyond. For example, fears about the UK performing relatively poorly on the international education stage have led to a growing emphasis on standards, and to increasing pressures from the government for schools in the UK to be performing as well as, and ideally better than, their international competitors.

Thus, over the last two decades or so we have witnessed increasing pressure on schools to raise standards, coupled with the introduction of various mechanisms to monitor, publicise and, in many cases, 'shame' their performance. In England, the most notable of these mechanisms are: SATs; inspections by Ofsted; publication of school league tables; and the public 'naming and shaming' of 'failing' schools. While 'naming and shaming' of schools is no doubt driven by motives to improve schools' performances (much like the naming and shaming of pupils may be driven by teachers' motives to improve pupils' performances), fears of 'failing' and being shamed often prompt strategies at school level – for example teaching to the test – that are counterproductive to high-quality learning experiences for pupils.

So educational researchers need to explore not only how fear is created and exacerbated at the individual level, the classroom level and the school level, but how it is created nationally and internationally. As Shirlow and Pain (2003) argue, we need to consider different scales of fear and how they operate. We also need to ask questions about who constructs these fears – because they are socially constructed – and who benefits and who loses most as a result of them. In other words we should think more about the politics of fear in relation to education. It is beyond the scope of this chapter to discuss this, but for more discussion see Jackson (2010).

CONCLUSION

The prevalence and importance of affective dimensions of learning mean they deserve much more attention from educational researchers than they have received to date. Furthermore, we need to extend considerably the types of research conducted in this sphere in order to understand further the complex ways that affective practices work and intersect. Importantly, we need to consider affect at different levels, and engage with questions around the politics of affect in relation to education. However, this process will not be an easy one. Research in this sphere is complicated by several factors, including difficulties regarding conceptualisation and methods for research. There has not been space in this chapter to consider the methodological difficulties of researching affect, but there are many. However, despite the challenges it is time we stopped ignoring the emotional elephant in the classroom.

NOTE

1 SATs are assessments of pupils in England at ages 7 and 11 (and age 14 until 2008). At age 7 assessment is principally by teacher assessment (sometimes using informal tests); at age 11 assessment is by national tests and teacher assessment in English, maths and science. Attainment is indicated in terms of levels, and there are expected levels of attainment set by the Government's Department for Education.

REFERENCES

Ahmed, S. (2004) *The Cultural Politics of Emotion*, Edinburgh: Edinburgh University Press.

Bauman, Z. (2006) *Liquid Fear*, Cambridge: Polity Press.

Bourke, J. (2005) *Fear: A Cultural History*, London: Virago.

Covington, M.V. (1998) *The Will to Learn: A Guide for Motivating Young People*, Cambridge: Cambridge University Press.

Denscombe, M. (2000) 'Social conditions for stress: young people's experience of doing GCSEs', *British Educational Research Journal*, 26, 3: 259–74.

Fiedler, K. and Beier, S. (2014) 'Affect and cognitive processes in educational contexts', in R. Pekrun and L. Linnenbrink-Garcia (eds), *International Handbook of Emotions in Education*, London: Routledge, pp. 36–55.

Gill, T. (2007) *No Fear: Growing up in a Risk Averse Society*, London: Calouste Gulbenkian Foundation.

Gower, P.L. (ed.) (2005) *New Research on the Psychology of Fear*, New York: Nova Science Publishers.

Greco, M. and Stenner, P. (2008) 'Introduction: emotion and social science', in M. Greco and P. Stenner (eds), *Emotions: A Social Science Reader*, London: Routledge, pp. 1–21.

Hall, K., Collins, J., Benjamin, S., Nind, M. and Sheehy, K. (2004) 'SATurated models of pupildom: assessment and inclusion/exclusion', *British Educational Research Journal*, 30, 6: 801–17.

Hargreaves, E. (2015, forthcoming) '"I think it helps you better when you're not scared": fear and learning in the primary classroom'.

Hascher, T. (2010) 'Learning and emotion: perspectives for theory and research', *European Educational Research Journal*, 9, 1: 13–28.

Jackson, C. (2006) *Lads and Ladettes in School: Gender and a Fear of Failure*, Maidenhead: Open University Press.

Jackson, C. (2010) 'Fear in education', *Educational Review*, 62, 1: 39–52.

Jackson, C. (2013) 'Fear in and about education', in R. Brooks, M. McCormack and K. Bhopal (eds) *Contemporary Debates in the Sociology of Education*, Basingstoke: Palgrave Macmillan, pp. 185–201.

Jackson, C., Paechter, C. and Renold, E. (2010) 'Introduction', in C. Jackson, C. Paechter and E. Renold (eds) (2010) *Girls and Education 3–16: Continuing Concerns, New Agendas*. Maidenhead: Open University Press, pp. 1–18.

Khoo, A.C.E. and Oakes, P.J. (2003) 'School misbehaviour as a coping strategy for negative social comparison and academic failure', *Social Psychology of Education*, 6: 255–81.

Linnenbrink, E.A. (2006) 'Emotion research in education: theoretical and methodological perspectives on the integration of affect, motivation, and cognition', *Educational Psychology Review*, 18: 307–14.

Martin, A.J. and Marsh, H.W. (2003) 'Fear of failure: friend or foe?', *Australian Psychologist*, 38, 1: 31–8.

McGregor, H.A. and Elliot, A.J. (2005) 'The shame of failure: examining the link between fear of failure and shame', *Personality and Social Psychology Bulletin*, 31: 218–31.

Newton, D.P. (2014) *Thinking with Feeling: Fostering Productive Thought in the Classroom*, London: Routledge.

Pekrun, R. and Linnenbrink-Garcia, L. (eds) (2014) *International Handbook of Emotions in Education*, London: Routledge.

Pekrun, R. and Perry, R.P. (2014) 'Control-value theory of achievement emotions', in R. Pekrun and L. Linnenbrink-Garcia (eds) *International Handbook of Emotions in Education*, London: Routledge, pp. 120–41.

Putwain, D. (2007) 'Test anxiety in UK schoolchildren: prevalence and demographic patterns', *British Journal of Educational Psychology*, 77, 3: 579–93.

Reay, D., Hollingworth, S., Williams, K., Crozier, G., Jamieson, F., James, D. and Beedell P. (2007) '"A darker shade of pale?" Whiteness, the middle classes and multi-ethnic inner city Schooling', *Sociology*, 41, 6: 1041–60.

Rachman, S. (1998) *Anxiety*, Hove: Psychology Press Ltd.

Salecl, R. (2004) *On Anxiety*, London: Routledge.

Samdall, O., Dür, W. and Freeman, J. (2004) 'Life circumstances of young people: School', in C. Currie et al. (eds), (2004) *Young People's Health in Context: International Report from the HBSC 2001/02 Survey* (Health Policy for Children and Adolescents, No.4), WHO: Regional Office for Europe, Copenhagen.

Segool, N.K., Carlson, J.S., Goforth, A.N., Von der Embse, N. and Barterian, J.A. (2013) 'Heightened test anxiety among young children: elementary school students' anxious responses to high-stakes testing', *Psychology in Schools*, 50, 5: 489–99.

Shirlow, P. and Pain, R. (2003) 'The geographies and politics of fear', *Capital and Class*, 80: 15–26.

Shuman, V. and Scherer, K.R. (2014) 'Concepts and structures of emotions', in R. Pekrun and L. Linnenbrink-Garcia (eds), *International Handbook of Emotions in Education*, London: Routledge, pp. 13–35.

Soysa, C.K. and Weiss, A. (2014) 'Mediating perceived parenting styles–test anxiety relationships: academic procrastination and maladaptive perfectionism', *Learning and Individual Differences*, 34: 77–85.

Wetherell, M.S. (2012) *Affect and Emotion: A New Social Science Understanding*, London: SAGE.

Wetherell, M.S. (2014) 'The turn to affect', paper presented at Taking 'Turns': Material, Affective and Sensory 'Turns' in the Academy, University of Manchester, 3 July.

Wilkins, A. (2011): 'Push and pull in the classroom: competition, gender and the neoliberal subject', *Gender and Education*, 24, 7: 765–81.

Williams, K., Jamieson, F. and Hollingworth, S. (2008) 'He was a bit of a delicate thing': white middle-class boys, gender, school choice and parental anxiety, *Gender and Education*, 20, 4: 399–408.

Zeidner, M. (2007) 'Test anxiety in educational contexts', in P.A. Schutz and R. Pekrun (eds) *Emotion in Education*, Burlington, MA: Elsevier, pp. 165–84.

Zembylas, M. (2009) 'Global economies of fear: affect, politics and pedagogical implications', *Critical Studies in Education*, 50, 2: 187–99.

34

The Impact of Gender, Race and Class on Learning Dispositions in Schools

Diane Reay

INTRODUCTION

This chapter draws on a case study of an inner-city primary classroom in order to make the case for a sociologically informed view of learning. The importance of developing more sociologically informed understandings is made starkly apparent when you enter the term 'sociology of learning' into Google Scholar. Hundreds of entries on learning sociology come up but nothing on the sociology of learning. However, in contrast, when you enter 'psychology of learning' over a million entries appear, primarily on the psychology of learning. It is this imbalance, the centrality of psychological understandings of learning and the marginalization of sociologically informed views that characterize the field of learning theory. Yet, as Biesta et al. (2011: 88) state 'learning lives are always structured lives' in which social class, race and gender influence learning in deep and complex ways. The need to temper individualized notions of learning and the learner, and to focus on the influence of wider economic and cultural contexts, is particularly important in the age of 'concerted cultivation' (Lareau, 2004), where resources, social power and privilege have a considerable impact on the development of learning dispositions.

The twenty-first century is the era of Baby Einstein and accelerated learning for the middle and upper classes, in which the learning dispositions of their children are developed, nurtured, accelerated, even imposed, through cultural activities such as Baby Mozart and Baby Ballet (DeLoache et al., 2010). Vincent and Ball (2006) write about the work of the bourgeois family which through learning activities, private tuition, and visits to galleries and museums induct their children 'into the "caste" of those who understand'. It is from such parental work that learning dispositions of entitlement, curiosity and confidence flow. In contrast, access to a wide range of enriching learning activities from birth onwards is largely inaccessible to those with insufficient economic and cultural resources.

LINKING DISPOSITIONS WITH POSITIONS

In the next section I draw on my own empirical work on primary classrooms, using Bourdieu's concepts of field, habitus and capitals to provide an analytic lens for understanding how gender, race and class contribute to learning dispositions in the primary classroom. Space is too limited to provide a detailed account of Bourdieu's conceptual framework (although see Reay, 2004), but I will give a brief synopsis. Bourdieu sees habitus as a system of dispositions that potentially generate a wide repertoire of possible actions, simultaneously enabling the individual to draw on transformative and constraining courses of action (Bourdieu, 1990c: 87). However, the addendum in Bourdieu's work is always an emphasis on the constraints and demands that impose themselves on people.

Yet, despite this implicit tendency to behave in ways that are expected of 'people like us', for Bourdieu there are no explicit rules or principles that dictate behaviour. The practical logic which defines habitus is not one of the predictable regularity of modes of behaviour, but instead 'that of vagueness, of the more-or-less, which defines one's ordinary relation to the world' (Bourdieu, 1990b: 78). A further key quality of habitus is its ability to hold agency and structure in tension as embodied dispositions. Bourdieu (1996: 182) describes habitus as social position embodied in bodily dispositions. Thus it enables us to keep in view both the individual and the social nature of learning (Hodkinson et al., 2008). Habitus is a portfolio of dispositions to all aspects of life (Bloomer and Hodkinson, 2000: 589) in which learning dispositions are constitutive of the habitus, albeit only one part of the battery of dispositions that make up the habitus.

Bourdieu's related concept of field adds to the possibilities of his conceptual framework. It gives habitus a dynamic quality, and links the dispositions of habitus to positions within varying fields. Field for Bourdieu is the context in which practices take place. It is important to emphasize the relational aspects of habitus and field. As Bourdieu himself points out:

> The relation between habitus and field operates in two ways. On one side, it is a relation of conditioning: the field structures the habitus, which is the product of the embodiment of the immanent necessity of the field (or of a hierarchy of intersecting fields). On the other side, it is a relation of knowledge or cognitive construction: habitus contributes to constituting the field as a meaningful world, a world endowed with sense or with value, in which it is worth investing one's energy. (Bourdieu in Wacquant 1989: 44)

This dynamic relationship between habitus and field allows us to understand learning as always in process, influenced by context but simultaneously influencing and having an impact on that context. But also habitus as 'the product of the embodiment of the immanent necessity of field (or of a hierarchy of intersecting fields)' (Bourdieu in Wacquant, 1989) points to notions of learning in which some dispositions are foregrounded in certain contexts, while others become far more salient when that context changes. And the array of capitals, cultural, social, economic and symbolic, individuals have access to, make a difference to the choices and options available to them. We see this very powerfully in the data I draw on below where class, gender and ethnic resources mean that some students can move powerfully across a variety of different educational fields; their learner identities have a degree of fluidity, while other students are fixed within these same fields (Skeggs, 2004).

'SADDOS' AND 'GOOD GUYS': EMBODYING THE WRONG AND RIGHT LEARNING DISPOSITIONS

In my ESRC research project with Madeleine Arnot on consulting students about their teaching and learning we explored the complex relationships between class, race, gender, and learning dispositions (Arnot and Reay, 2006). One of the four case studies from that research project, which I draw on in this chapter, focused on social and learner dispositions in a primary classroom in a multi-ethnic, urban primary school. Information on both ethnicity and class position came from three sources: a brief questionnaire to parents which included questions on educational credentials and occupations (over three-quarters of the families completed these); knowledge obtained from the class teacher; and, in addition, we asked the children themselves. Using these sources of information meant we could clarify and substantiate information that may have proved more ambiguous had it come just from one source.

Our choice of focus group interviews as the main research method was decided from the outset of the project, although we also employed individual interviews with students, parents and teachers, as well as classroom observation. We wanted to find out whether students felt that they belonged as individuals, and as groups, within the school community. Focus group interviews were clearly an appropriate research method for attempting to access group as well as individual voices (Gibson, 2012). Past research experience of utilizing focus groups (Reay and Lucey, 2000) had convinced us that they were an effective research tool for eliciting commonalities and differences of opinion among children (James, 2007). In this project, they proved useful in revealing consensus among students, and providing a forum for contestation and for challenging opposing viewpoints about inclusion, and the range of learning dispositions in the classroom. Although focus groups were our main research tool, we also gathered a substantial amount of data through participant observation. In all, I spent at least one day a week in the classroom over a period of six months.

The data presented challenges the binary between individual and social views of learning that has been common in educational research, and points to the need for more sociologically inspired understandings of learning that recognize its classed, gendered and racialized nature (Chubbuck, 2010). Rather, we understand this relationship as the social and the individual compounding and conflating with each other, but at other times clashing and conflicting. The mainly working-class culture of the peer group shaped the relationship between the field of official school knowledge and those other fields for the development of positive learning dispositions. Being positioned centrally within the field of official school knowledge sometimes resulted in low status in other fields, such as those of the peer group culture, and its sub-fields of gender and social class. In particular, the two quiet, well behaved, middle-class girls were caught up in a difficult balancing act between 'doing girl' and managing successful learning (Skelton et al., 2010, 186). Despite being good learners, their disposition to learning, which was one of conscientiousness, conformity and relative passivity, translated into low status within the pupil peer group hierarchy (Read et al., 2011). Notwithstanding the status which came through their middle-class cultural capital within official discourses of teaching and learning, they were still often marginalized within the field of the working-class, male peer group culture where neither their middle class-cultural capital nor their femininity was valued:

Diane: Which children are doing best at learning?
Martin: Navid and Yussef
Diane: What about the girls?
Del: Melanie
Diane: Not any other girls?
Del: Stephanie and Nancy work hard but they aren't that good.

In this quotation the high achievement of Stephanie and Nancy, the other two members of the top set, is viewed as inconsequential due to a combination of their traditional femininity and diligent attitude to schoolwork (Reay, 2001; Skelton et al., 2010). Whenever children in the class gave examples of good learners, Stephanie and Nancy were always excluded from the litany:

Jason: Some people are quicker than others
Jordan: Like Navid and Melanie and Yussef.

Despite a recognition that Nancy is doing well academically, any praise is qualified by the criticism that she is 'trying too hard':

Del: They always say that girls are better than boys but I don't agree.
Martin: Except for Nancy, she's just perfect. Yuk (all the group giggle)
Marvin: She's a pain.
Del: She is always trying, trying, trying … (group giggle)

Clearly visible in the other children's judgement of Nancy and Stephanie is a disparagement of academic success when it is vested in traditional femininity (Barnes, 2011; Paechter, 2010). This collective opinion was impacting on Nancy's sense of herself as a learner. As she asserted:

I know I'm in the top group but I'm not seen as one of the clever children. I'm not really clever. I'm in the top group because I work hard.

Here we can see 'the internal–external dialectic of identification' (Jenkins, 2004: 24) through which Nancy's learner dispositions are being shaped.

But the working-class boys found it even more difficult to hold on to a sense of themselves as successful learners. These boys used the concept of intelligence to underscore the differences they perceived between learners. The classroom set children in ability groups for Mathematics and English, and the boys in the bottom groups, in particular, articulated a painful awareness of the readiness of schools to attribute successful learning to 'ability'. They catalogued a range of innate factors which combine to exclude themselves, for example: 'You've got to be clever': 'you have to be intelligent to be a good learner'; 'you have to be clever to get jobs, important jobs'; 'some kids are just stupid at maths, they're just no good at it'. The danger for these boys is the role that such intrinsic qualities play in shaping their learning dispositions and especially their levels of confidence. In the focus group interview these lower achieving, working-class boys described invidious evaluations of their own intelligence:

Jason: People say we're stupid.
Dean: Yeah, telling you you're stupid.
Jason: People undermine your confidence by putting you down.
Del: People putting you down makes you feel like you are thick and then you feel like you just don't want to try. Your feelings are hurt.

However, despite denigrating their own learning abilities, this group, like all of the others, expressed admiration and respect for Melanie, Yussef and Navid. When asked which children got the most positive attention from teachers all the groups cited these three. They had reached the peak of two hierarchies of esteem, those of official knowledge and learning, and the peer group. Impressively, Melanie had contrived to position herself centrally within the working-class, ethnically diverse peer group. As Marvin claimed, 'Mel is one of the good guys'. Unlike the other girls she had worked extremely hard at her centrality. This was apparent in her self-designation and performance as a tom-boy. It was also visible in her professed 'laid-back' approach to school work:

You can't just say 'Oh, I don't care about what was on TV last night, let me get on with my writing' because everyone would think you were a saddo.

Both Stephanie and Nancy's conformity and Melanie's bravado positioned them in very different spaces within the field of the classroom, and with very different degrees of agency. While Stephanie and Nancy's status within the peer group was damaged by their conventional femininity and ready compliance, Melanie possessed a cultural repertoire that allowed her to move across the different fields of peer group and mainstream schooling without losing status in either one. While there were times when, in common with the majority of girls in the class, she displayed dispositions of conformity and obedience, at other times she revealed a strong sense of confidence and self-assurance. As she told me in the individual interview:

> There are probably quite a few things I know that the teachers don't.

Despite occupying the same position in the field of the peer group culture as Navid and Yussef, her learning dispositions were subtly different. In the interview with the class teacher, Mrs Wilson commented:

> Some of the top group, especially Stephanie and Melanie often ask my opinion about their work. They ask what they need to do to improve it especially in literature.

> When asked if the boys make similar queries, she laughed and commented: 'It's a girl kind of thing'.

Yet, Navid and Yussef, the two working-class, ethnic minority, boys who shared the 'top pupil' position alongside Melanie were not uncomplicatedly acting out 'a boy kind of thing'. Both Navid and Yussef were complexly positioned in relation to the fields of home, school and the peer group. Navid and Yussef had both moved to the UK when they were babies, Navid from Iran and Yussef from Somalia. They were living on one of the most demonized council estates in the area, and both families were subsisting on state benefits. Despite being described as working class by school staff, and performing 'working-class lad' (Willis, 1977) very well, their class positioning was more complex and ambiguous. All four parents were university educated and, when I interviewed them, expressed far higher educational aspirations for their children than the majority of working-class parents living in the area. Despite their families' lack of economic capital, Navid and Yussef displayed a habitus of entitlement, characterized by dispositions of academic confidence and certainty, the heritage, I suggest, of their parents' cultural capital. They were both included in the school's gifted and talented programme. In contrast to the other working-class boys who had all failed to survive the designation of being 'gifted and talented', Navid and Yussef were both succeeding in the

group without having to face wider male peer group disapprobation. I would argue that their complex and contradictory positionings, together with that of Melanie, can only be understood if the fields of social class, official learning and the peer group are over-laid with further fields of gender and ethnicity, together with an analysis of the different capitals that are valued and esteemed in each of those fields. Only then can we untangle the dynamics of power and influence, and the range of learning dispositions in the class.

If we focus on the field of gender dynamics what becomes evident is Melanie's claim to high status femininity and her adroit performance of such femininity. In the quotation below Melanie both asserts her own position on the gender continuum and articulates the distinction between herself and Stephanie:

Melanie: If you're clever, but not too clever and if you're really cool you are popular. But if you are like really clever and geeky and always talk about science then you're unpopular. If you're a girlie like Stephanie you're unpopular and if you're an airhead then you're unpopular as well.

And:

Melanie: If we talked about work we'd be known as the saddos of the class. Talking about your work is really sad.
Carly: Stephanie loves talking about her work
Melanie: She's really sad.

Evident in the quotes are the ways in which those, like Melanie, with more of the cultural capital valued within the peer group, had the power to actively position Stephanie as a 'sad', 'geeky' learner and a despised unpopular 'girlie'.

In contrast, Melanie's distinction came through playing down her academic ability and stressing the difference between herself and girls who occupied more conventional femininities. Unlike Stephanie and Nancy, Melanie had developed habitus as 'an art of invention and reinvention' (Bourdieu, 1990a). Melanie can be seen to fit Renold and Ringrose's description (2012: 47) of 'a phallic girl'. She recognized and responded to prevailing gender hierarchies which situated being male with having more power and status, and displayed little interest in performing heteronormative femininities (Archer et al., 2012). Yet this was no easy task, especially as her social class operated as both an asset and a handicap. Middle-classness was a social marker that, at times, carried considerable risks in a classroom where 'poshness' was disparaged, and Melanie came from the most economically and culturally privileged family in the class. Her parents were both senior academics, and she talked about the extra work both parents set her. She was also the only child in the class to assert the superior knowledge of her parents over that of the school and its teachers. Her abundant cultural capital is evident in the quotation below:

> All the things our teachers tell us, I don't usually do. I do it in the way my Mum or Dad tells me because they're university lecturers so they know better.

However, at the same time she emphasized separating the two spheres, and that is clearly what she succeeded in doing in her own practice:

> When you go home people don't know and don't care if you're doing homework or if you've got a tutor as long as you don't boast about it. But like if you're really posh and you act posh in the classroom, showing off then all the other kids hate you.

What remains silent in Melanie's text but was revealed when I interviewed her parents is that Melanie had a tutor for both English and Maths. The children, including Melanie, talked disparagingly about posh children, but the category never included Melanie herself. Melanie persistently deployed her cultural capital; it was apparent in her learning dispositions of confidence, assertiveness and ability to challenge teachers' knowledge. Yet, she was also engaged in a strategic positioning that necessitated a partial masking of both her femininity and her middle-classness. Unlike Navid and Yussef, Melanie has had to disguise normative, middle-class, learning dispositions that accrue profits of social and cultural capital

in social fields other than the predominantly working-class primary school in which she was striving for dominance. We glimpse the ways in which learning dispositions are context-dependent, situated, uncertain, and, to an extent, volatile (Sadler, 2002).

In contrast to Navid and Yussef, Melanie had developed a high level of awareness and self-consciousness; a hyper-reflexivity in relation to her positioning in these myriad overlapping fields. As Pomerantz and Raby (2011) found in their study of 'smart girl identities' in Canadian schools, Melanie has had to develop her smartness as a multifaceted category that demanded far more than being 'good at school', she has learnt to be 'street-wise' as well as 'learning-wise'. Her habitus has had to evolve and adjust to the unfamiliar field of the predominantly working-class, pupil peer group. In this she has been extremely successful, developing new dispositions that accord with the field. Her hyper-reflexivity in the field has enabled her to acquire a socio-analysis of her positioning within schooling. Bourdieu argues that some individuals are able to develop strategic behaviour through 'socio-analysis' (Bourdieu, 1990a: 116), becoming reflexively aware of the workings of the field they find themselves in (Bourdieu, 2004).

While Navid and Yussef were Bourdieu's 'fish in water' (Bourdieu, 1990a: 108) within a peer group that was predominantly working class and male dominated, Melanie has engaged in a complex re-invention in order to be dominant within the field. Yet, there remain similarities. In addition to their evident high attainment, what Melanie, Yussef and Navid shared across differences of gender, ethnicity and social class positioning were key learning dispositions, namely a sense of entitlement, a self-assured relationship to knowledge, and the confidence to challenge (Lareau, 2004). All three displayed high visibility within both the classroom and the playground, alongside an investment in attention-seeking behaviour. Like the girls Renold and Ringrose (2012) write about, Melanie had managed to subvert symbolic boundaries so she could speak from positions which were perceived to be traditionally male domains. In contrast, Nancy and Stephanie were clever but not in a valued way. They had not learnt the ability to modulate learning dispositions that accrue disapprobation in the predominantly working-class peer group.

STRUGGLING TO HOLD ON TO POSITIVE LEARNING DISPOSITIONS AT THE BOTTOM OF THE CLASSROOM HIERARCHY

The repercussions for the white middle-class girls, Nancy and Stephanie, were less apparent than the consequences of the power dynamics in the classroom for two working-class, minority ethnic, boys. The two children who were the real 'saddos' in the class, were Ong who was Vietnamese and Ali who was Bangladeshi. These boys faded into the margins because, unlike the other working-class boys in the class, they were both quiet, well behaved and tried hard with their school work. Historical legacies, current economic conditions and the concern over boys' underachievement make it extremely difficult to construct a learner identity as an academically successful working-class boy (Stahl, 2013). While boys like Navid and Yussef presented a socially mobile, working-class identity that was more congruent with middle-class values, and were sufficiently rich in resources of hegemonic masculinity to negotiate the position of academically successful, working-class boy without incurring social costs (Ingram, 2011), Ali and Ong had little choice. Both were subjected to social marginality and invidious judgements on the basis that they were not important enough to matter:

Diane: So does anyone get left out?
Joseph: Ong and Ali.
Del: Yeah, Ong and Ali
Matty: Cos they're sad
Diane: Why are they sad?
Matty: Cos they don't say anything and no one wants to play with them.

And:

Stephanie: I think Ong gets left out a lot
Nancy: Yes, Ong and Ali
Stephanie: The other boys are a bit unkind to them cos they don't wear trendy clothes.
Nancy: It's not their fault. I don't think their families have got much money.
Stephanie: Ong's very quiet but he's nice though.
Nancy: They're a bit little and weak like …

Ong and Ali possessed habitus that embodied low economic, social and cultural capital, and very different types of masculinity to those valorized in the class. The consequences were classroom marginalization and denigration (see also Phoenix, 2004). Being diligent, well behaved and obedient in the classroom as a boy is often devalued and maligned because of its equation with femininity (Renold, 2001: 375). It is also likely, as Archer and Francis (2005) found in relation to the Chinese boys in their study, that their minority ethnic status as Vietnamese and Bangladeshi was also a factor. While Navid and Yussef managed to avoid connotations of femininity despite their high achievement by investing heavily in laddish behaviour (Francis, 2001), Ong and Ali were 'feminized' within the classroom context because of their learning dispositions of hard work, conformity and relative passivity (see also Archer and Francis, 2007); the very qualities that had also led to Nancy and Stephanie's social marginalization. The boundaries of possibility for Ong and Ali were policed by more powerful others, forcing them to construct narrow boundaries for themselves that limited the potential for positive social and learner identities. They came to see themselves as they were seen by others, as neither popular nor good learners. Listening to what the other children in the classroom said it became clear that learning for Ali and Ong was a fraught process despite their dispositions to work hard. It was also evident in what Ali and Ong themselves said:

Diane: How do you feel when you are learning in school, Ali?
Ali: I find it a bit hard. I get worried, but … it's … does anyone else get worried?

Ong: Yeah, I do
Diane: You get worried Ong?
Ong: Yeah, sometimes I nearly cry
Diane: You nearly cry?
Ong: Yeah, because your head gets all muddled up and your eyes get hot and sweating and all sweat comes out and people think you are crying.

They also had a sense of unfairness in relation to the classroom:

Ong: We aren't in the top sets.
Diane: So what sets are you in?
Ali: Like middle ones.
Ong: For maths not too bad sets but English the worst
Ali: That's not fair cos Yussef's in the top set and he just mucks around.

CONCLUSION

As Bloomer and Hodkinson (2000: 589) argue 'learning is a participatory act – a profoundly social and cultural phenomenon, not simply a cognitive process'. In this class we can see vividly a range of different learning dispositions and the extent to which they shift both across and within different groups of pupils, and, in particular, the complex dialectic between class, gender, ethnicity and perceived academic ability in which generalization on the basis of different categories fails to capture the messiness of the power dynamics and learning dispositions in play. We can also see clearly from the interactions in the class how researching classroom life provides a powerful lens on a range of learning dilemmas and how children and young people negotiate these. The children's learning experiences reveal regular conflicts and tensions across masculinities, femininities, academic performance, social class, ethnicity and peer group popularity. Access to, and possession of, various capitals can lead to positive or negative resolution of such conflicts and tensions in ways that enhance or diminish children's sense of themselves as positive and successful learners. Some children, for whom learning is a mobile

resource, have the power to shift in and out of different learner identities, while others are fixed in and through the representations of more powerful others. In all this movement and messiness Bourdieu's concepts of field, capitals and habitus can be productively deployed to show how learning dispositions are reproduced, defended, challenged and reconstituted, and the ways in which key social markers such as class, race and gender are affirmed and dismissed at different times and in different contexts within educational settings. It is in such seemingly mundane interactions within classrooms, and between students who identify and are identified according to a variety of social categories, that the active construction of successful and failing learners within school settings becomes apparent.

In this chapter I have drawn on Bourdieusian concepts to look at learning dispositions at the micro level. But, Bourdieu's work can also be deployed to explore macro dimensions of learning in schooling. In particular, his work with Passeron (Bourdieu and Passeron, 1977) on the reproduction of classed identities within the French educational system is a powerful analysis of how structural inequalities at the institutional, and wider economic level, impact on classed learning dispositions. What is important is for educational research and theory to engage with both the macro and the micro level of learning, to examine learning as an ongoing accomplishment within the spheres of the local, the nation-state and the global.

These children's narratives reveal some of the ways in which school micro-politics work to construct children as learners, and shape their learning dispositions. However, reverberations from state and government policy at the macro level, such as those on assessment and testing, also have powerful 'aftershocks' on children in classrooms, labelling and constructing some as 'good learners' but also resulting, for others, in a negative sense of themselves as learners.

So what lessons can we learn from the complex, and at times confusing, power dynamics in this primary classroom? I suggest that despite our post-structuralist times, sexism, racism and classism are rife, and although the ways in which they are played out in classrooms has changed dramatically since the days I was a primary school pupil in the late 1950s, they still have considerable power to damage children's sense of themselves as positive learners. What has remained the same is that too little of the learning in classrooms focuses on teaching children to be collaborative and cooperative, and to care for, and respect each other, regardless of difference. This is primarily a consequence of policies imposed from outside the classroom, resulting in an overriding preoccupation, particularly in working-class schools, in raising literacy and numeracy levels.

A second linked policy preoccupation, with testing, assessment and ranking encourages individualized competitive learning dispositions, and increasingly a sense of shame and failure in those positioned at the bottom of assessment hierarchies. This obsession with 'the basics' and testing marginalizes the broader curriculum, and more holistic, child-centred approaches to learning. It also instrumentalizes children as only valuable for what they achieve, undermining their sense of having intrinsic value. So what can we as educationalists do? As a sociologist of education I believe that, in the main, schools reflect the societies they are part of, rather than having the capacity to transform them. According to Ball (2010: 156), if we are to address persistent educational inequalities of social class, increasingly the school is the wrong place to look and the wrong place to reform. Instead, we need to focus on 'the economics of the family' in which upper- and middle-class families are able to use their economic and cultural advantages to ensure their children are always able to do better than less advantaged children. I would argue that the origins of racism and sexism, likewise, lie outside the school in families and wider society. We need a much fairer society economically, but also culturally, so that the United Kingdom becomes a society that views learning dispositions of confidence, entitlement, cooperation, curiosity, creativity and reflexivity as the right of all children. And, here, schools have an important role as places to ensure that right is realized.

REFERENCES

Archer, L. and Francis, B. (2005) '"They never go off the rails like other ethnic groups": Teachers' constructions of British Chinese pupils' gender identities and approaches to learning', *British Journal of Sociology of Education*, 26(2): 165–82.

Archer, L. and Francis, B. (2007) *Understanding Minority Ethnic Achievement: Race, Gender, Class and Success*, London: Routledge.

Archer, L., DeWitt, J., Osborne, J., Dillon, J., Willis, B. and Wong, B. (2012) '"Balancing acts": Elementary school girls' negotiations of femininity, achievement, and science', *Science Education*, 96(6): 967–89.

Arnot, M. and Reay, D. (2006) 'Power, pedagogic voices and pupil talk: The implications for pupil consultation as transformative practice', in R. Moore, M. Arnot, J. Beck and H. Daniels (eds), *Knowledge, Power and Social Change*, London: Routledge, pp. 75–93.

Ball, S.J. (2010) 'New class inequalities in education: Why education policy may be looking in the wrong place! Education policy, civil society and social class', *International Journal of Sociology and Social Policy*, 30(3/4): 155–66.

Barnes, C. (2011) 'A discourse of disparagement. Boys' talk about girls in school', *Young: Nordic Journal of Youth Research*, 19(1): 5–23.

Biesta, G., Field, J., Hodkinson, P., MacLeod, F. and Goodson, I. (2011) *Improving Learning Through the Lifecourse: Learning Lives*, London: Taylor and Francis.

Bloomer, M. and Hodkinson, P. (2000) 'Learning careers: Continuity and change in young people's dispositions to learning', *British Educational Research Journal*, 26(5): 583–97.

Bourdieu, P. (1990a) *The Logic of Practice*, Cambridge: Polity Press.

Bourdieu, P. (1990b) *In Other Words: Essays Towards a Reflexive Sociology*, Cambridge: Polity Press.

Bourdieu, P. (1990c) *Sociology in Question*, Cambridge: Polity Press.

Bourdieu, P. (1996) *The Rules of Art*, Cambridge: Polity Press.

Bourdieu, P. (2004) *Science of Science and Reflexivity*, Cambridge: Polity Press.

Bourdieu, P. and Passeron, J.C. (1977) *Reproduction in Education, Society and Culture*, London: Sage.

Chubbuck, S. (2010) 'Individual and structural orientations in socially just teaching: Conceptualization, implementation, and collaborative effort', *Journal of Teacher Education*, 61(3): 197–210.

DeLoache, J., Chiong, C., Sherman, K., Islam, N., Vanderborght, M., Troseth, G., Strouse, G. and O'Doherty, K. (2010) 'Do Babies learn from baby media?', *Psychological Science*, 21(11): 1570–4.

Francis, B. (2001) *Boys, Girls and Achievement: Addressing the Classroom Issues*, London: Routledge.

Gibson, J. (2012) 'Interviews and focus groups with children: Methods that match children's developing competencies', *Journal of Family Theory and Review*, 4: 148–59.

Hodkinson, P., Biesta, G. and James, D. (2008) 'Understanding learning culturally: Overcoming the dualism between social and individual views of learning', *Vocations and Learning*, 1(1): 27–47.

Ingram, N. (2011) 'Within school and beyond the gate: The complexities of being educationally successful and working class', *Sociology*, 45(2): 287–302.

James, A. (2007) 'Giving voice to children's voices: Practices and problems, pitfalls and potentials', *American Anthropologist*, 109: 261–72.

Jenkins, R. (2004) *Social Identity*, London: Routledge.

Lareau, A. (2004) *Unequal Childhoods: Class, Race and Family Life*, Berkeley CA: University of California Press.

Paechter, C. (2010) 'Tomboys and girly-girls: Embodied femininities in primary schools', *Discourse: Studies in the Cultural Politics of Education*, 31(2): 221–35.

Phoenix, A. (2004) 'Using informal pedagogy to oppress themselves and each other: Critical pedagogy, schooling and 11–14 year old London boys', *Nordisk Pedagogik*, 1: 19–38.

Pomerantz, S. and Raby, R. (2011) '"Oh, she's *so* smart": Girls' complex engagements with post/feminist narratives of academic success', *Gender and Education*, 23(5): 549–64.

Read, B., Francis, B. and Skelton, C. (2011) 'Gender, popularity and notions of in/authenticity amongst 12-year-old to 13-year-old school girls', *British Journal of Sociology of Education*, 32(2): 169–83.

Reay, D. (2001) 'Spice girls, "nice girls", "girlies" and tomboys: Gender discourses, girls' cultures and femininities in the primary classroom', *Gender and Education*, 13(2): 153–66.

Reay, D. (2004) '"It's all becoming a habitus": Beyond the habitual use of Pierre Bourdieu's concept of habitus in educational research', *Special Issue of British Journal of Sociology of Education on Pierre Bourdieu*, 25(4): 431–44.

Reay, D and Lucey, H (2000) 'I don't like it here but I don't want to be anywhere else': Children living on inner London council estates in *Antipode* 32 (4), 410–28

Renold, E. (2001) 'Learning the "hard" way: Boys, hegemonic masculinity and the negotiation of learner identities in the primary school', *British Journal of Sociology of Education*, 22(3): 369–84.

Renold, E. and Ringrose, J. (2012) 'Phallic girls? Girls' negotiation of phallogocentric power', in J. Landreau and N. Rodriguez (eds) *Queer Masculinities: A Critical Reader in Education*, Dordrecht: Springer, pp. 47–67.

Sadler, R. (2002) 'Learning dispositions: Can we really assess them?', *Assessment in Education*, 9(1): 45–51.

Skeggs, B. (2004) *Class, Self, Culture*, London: Routledge.

Skelton, C., Francis, B. and Read, B. (2010) '"Brains before beauty?" High achieving girls, school and gender identities', *Educational Studies*, 36(2): 185–94.

Stahl, G. (2013) 'Habitus disjunctures, reflexivity and white working-class boys' conceptions of status in learner and social identities', *Sociological Research Online*, 18(3): 2. http://www.socresonline.org.uk/18/3/2.html 10.5153/sro.2999

Vincent, C. and Ball, S. (2006) *Childcare, Choice and Class Practices: Middle-Class Parents and their Children*, London: Routledge.

Wacquant, L. (1989) 'Towards a reflexive sociology: A workshop with Pierre Bourdieu', *Sociological Theory*, 7: 26–63.

Willis, P. (1977) *Learning to Labour*, Farnborough: Saxon House.

35

Learning and New Media

Mary Kalantzis and Bill Cope

INTRODUCTION

'Learning' is the process of coming-to-know, be that the ontogenesis of knowing across the lifespan of an individual person, or the phylogenesis of social knowing. Learning is at times formal – a premeditated agenda in the institutions of education. At other times it is informal – an incidental aspect of lifeworld experience.

'Media' bridge the ontogenesis and phylogenesis of knowledge. To return to the etymology of the word, media are middle-objects, conditions or technologies that facilitate human communication, between one and one, one and many, or many or many. Media are agents of cultural 'between-ness'. They bridge spatial separations, so that people not in each other's immediate physical presence can connect. They bridge time, so ideas, information and cultural representations from another time (a minute ago or a century ago) can be re-heard and re-seen. Media, in other words, are material means for the production and distribution of meanings across space and time.

In this definition, media are as old as human drawing and writing. However, the forms of media have changed fundamentally across the long arc of human history. One such transformation, beginning half a millennium ago with the invention of print, was the mechanical reproducibility (Benjamin, [1936] 2008) of human communications. With it came a whole communicational infrastructure of typographic culture (Eisenstein, 1979) – books, libraries, newspapers, schools. The twentieth century saw a cascading series of transformations around photographic reproduction and its derivatives – cinema, television, photo-lithographic printing. In the twenty-first century, we now find ourselves in the midst of a new series of transformations, centred around the digitization of text, image, sound and data and the global interconnection of these digitized meanings through the medium of the internet. This latest phase in the development of media, we call 'new media'.

What make these 'new media' different? In the mass media of the twentieth century, journalists, television producers, radio announcers and authors were the producers of cultural and informational messages, a small creative elite in the 'culture industries' (Adorno, 2001), in the employ of a smaller controlling and owning elite. The consumers of their products were their readerships, audiences, patrons. Culture flowed from a few producers to many consumers. These media were driven by economies of scale – technologies of 'broadcast' to 'mass markets', shaping 'mass culture'. Their effect was to position the spoken-to-many in a particular relationship of knowledge and culture to the speaking-to-few.

These media relations were aligned with the epistemic relations of 'didactic pedagogy' (Kalantzis and Cope, 2012b). In the words of St Benedict, founder of the Western medieval monastic models of epistemic authority, that later became the modern university, and later still, the modern school, 'For it belongeth to the master to speak and to teach; it becometh the disciple to be silent and to listen'. The cognitive masters of the earlier modernity were the players in the 'culture industry' – and the teachers. Their disciples were readerships, viewers, listeners – and students. Authority 'belongs' to some, according to St Benedict. Quiescent epistemic acceptance 'becomes' the rest of us.

The new media and social media are by comparison 'participatory' (Haythornthwaite, 2009; Jenkins, 2006). The balance of cultural and epistemic agency is transformed. Tweets and smart phone images become the news because everyone can be a reporter. No need to send a camera crew to a news event. (They'll get there too late most of the time, anyway.) Someone will be there to take a picture, or make a video, or tweet an observation, and share it with the world. The mass media of an earlier era is also displaced in this act of 'upload' by the participatory media of the social web. Everyone is a reporter now. And it's not just the big news. It's the micro news of the meal I am having, the people I am with,

the thing-of-note I just saw or read on the web, and my opinions and my feelings of the moment. The old, hierarchical role divisions of cognitive and cultural labour are becoming blurred. Readers are simultaneously writers; viewers are simultaneously image makers. New reciprocities, new sociabilities emerge: to like in order to be liked; to follow in order to be followed; to friend in order to be friended – a discourse that is by turns, mutually affirmatory and narcissistically exhibitionist. In these new media everyone is a maker of meaning, culture and knowledge. The old divisions between creators and consumers are blurred. Creating and consuming cultural meanings are not even separate spaces, times, events. They are intertwined into each other in dialogical discourse.

Of course, the situation is not all good, only different and complicated. After all, these same new media that invite us to participate also watch our every move – cravenly in order to sell us stuff, or chillingly as they watch us with suspicion. They take our intellectual work and our lives and make money out of us. Divide today's Facebook or Twitter capitalization by the number of users and you'll be surprised what you're worth to them. You're doing the cultural and epistemic work. They're not paying you for the work you do, but your participatory fortune has become their monetary fortune.

So, new media have a different underlying cultural and epistemic logic from the broadcast or mass media of an earlier media. What are the possibilities for a corresponding 'new learning'? In this chapter we want to analyse the shape of an emerging 'new media' in order to create an account of a 'new learning' that uses these new media and that is appropriate to social conditions broadly created by these new media. The chapter draws upon and extends earlier writings of ours (Cope and Kalantzis, 2010, 2013), as well as our own research and development work creating and evaluating a new media/new learning environment, *Scholar*, with the support of a series of research and development grants from the Institute of Education Sciences[1] and the Bill and Melinda Gates Foundation.

The opening premise in our argument is that new learning does not necessarily follow from new media. To return to the schools of didactic pedagogy and the foundations of mass-institutionalized education from the mid-nineteenth century, for the first time in human history, schools served as a publicly enforced site of socialization and knowledge transmission. Among the main epistemic artefacts of modern schools were teacher talk and factually or deductively definitive textbook content. Student response was framed in terms of right and wrong answers, either to the question the teacher was asking in class, doing an assignment or responding to questions in a test. Several centuries later, much schooling is still a variant of this didactic paradigm.

Then new media arrives in the classroom. And nothing changes because we soon shape these technologies into the time-tested image of didactic pedagogy. We throw away the printed books, and replace them with e-books, but these still position learners as consumers of content created by experts for their consumption. We create the 'flipped classroom' (Bishop and Verleger, 2013). But all this means is that we record the traditional teacher lecture so the students can still impassively listen to it, albeit now at any time they find convenient. And we check that students have remembered what they have consumed with computer quizzes, albeit more often now because they can be embedded into the e-books and adaptively adjust the questions to the response of the student. Nevertheless, all they do is replicate the old memory game that was the summative, selected response test.

Moreover, after half a century of application in traditional educational sites, the overall beneficial effects of computer-mediated learning remain essentially unproven. In his examination of 76 meta-analyses of the effects of computer-assisted instruction, encompassing 4,498 studies and involving 4 million students, John Hattie concludes that 'there is no necessary relation between having computers, using computers and learning outcomes'. Nor are there changes over time in overall effect sizes, notwithstanding the increasing sophistication of computer technologies (Hattie, 2009: 220–1). Warschauer and Matuchniak (2010) similarly conclude that technology use in school has not been proven to improve student outcomes, though different kinds of pedagogical applications of technology do. More recently, in a review of technology integration in schools, Davies and West (2014) conclude that although 'students … use technology to gather, organize, analyze, and report information, … this has not dramatically improved student performance on standardized tests'.

Technologies do not in themselves change anything in education. However, we also want to suggest that new media offer a number of pedagogical openings, or affordances. Changing the medium does not necessarily change the message. In finely grained analysis, Hattie reveals that although computers do not themselves lead to improved learning outcomes, specific applications of computers can. In a disaggregated view of the meta-analyses, Hattie concludes that certain uses do produce gains for learners, for instance when the student is afforded a degree of control or self-regulation in learning, when a diversity of teaching strategies is used, when peer learning is optimized and when teachers are highly competent in technology use (Hattie, 2009: 222–7). These modulations in the research evidence also reflect the wide range of applications of computers, across the spectrum of instructional design, pedagogical approach, epistemological frame and assessment/feedback mode. So the key is to explore differential effects on learner performance according to the exploitation of specific affordances in new media.

In this chapter, we are going to explore seven new learning affordances opened up by new media: ubiquitous learning, active knowledge production, multimodal knowledge representations, recursive feedback, collaborative intelligence, metacognitive reflection and differentiated learning. None of these aspirations is new – many in fact, are in spirit as old as the progressive or authentic pedagogy of Rousseau, Montessori and Dewey. However, the new media facilitate an economy of effort that makes these ideals more pragmatically realizable than in the past. Not that the technology itself is intrinsically a catalyst for educational change. To reiterate, the very same technologies that offer these practical openings for educational transformation, can also be used to breathe new life into the most didactic of pedagogies, even intensifying the legacy processes of transmission of content, stimulus–response learning behaviour, modification, and rigid standardized testing. For this reason, we want to explore some of the ways in which new media can bring to practical realization new learning.

UBIQUITOUS LEARNING

Ubiquitous learning means learning any time, any place (Cope and Kalantzis, 2009). Older versions of the idea of formal learning out-of-school included homework, self-paced textbooks and 'distance education'. Ubiquitous learning is a riff on the idea of 'ubiquitous computing' (Twidale, 2009). Once science fiction, with the rise of laptop computers, tablets and smart phones, ubiquitous computing is an idea that arrived a long time ago in a very ordinary and pervasive way – in every store, every workplace, and almost every home, handbag or pocket. But only recently in schools, if yet. And when it does arrive there, it is often in ways that hardly do justice to the dynamic knowledge potentials of new media.

Internet-mediated computing, and particularly 'Web 2.0' (O'Reilly, 2005), 'cloud computing' (Reese, 2009) and 'semantic publishing' (Cope et al., 2011a) technologies

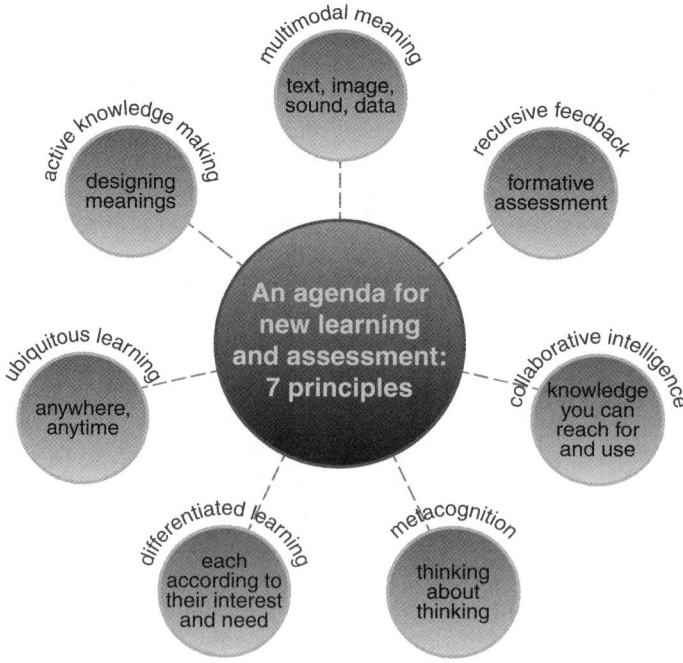

Figure 35.1   e-Learning ecologies: seven affordances

create possibilities for something that is more thoroughly transformative in education. The significantly new things that can be offered by ubiquitous learning environments range from student discovery of multimodal content originating from a variety of authentic sources, to intensive simultaneous interactions in which everyone in the learning community can be actively engaged, and far more responsive feedback and assessment systems.

Perhaps most significant, however, is that the traditional educational distinctions of time and space no longer matter. Before, the central point of all learning was necessarily confined to the four walls of the classroom, and the times delimited by the cells of the timetable. Ubiquitous learning means you can do all the stuff of traditional classrooms, and more, and anywhere, and anytime. Learners using ubiquitous computing technology are able to perform the same acts of knowledge-making and knowledge interaction – and new ones as well – inside the classroom as they can outside of the classroom.

Scale also disappears as a factor in learning – a class of three and a class of three thousand can be configured to work the same way, be that the video lecture, textbook and test routine of didactic pedagogy, or highly reflexive social relations of knowledge, including giving and receiving peer feedback, collaborative writing, and threaded discussions.

Does this spell the end of the traditional school? Not necessarily, because school is as good a place as anywhere to work in these technology-mediated ways. One thing will remain constant: society has devolved to schools the responsibility of keeping children in a relationship of duty-of-care during specific times in order to free parents up for work. However, its classrooms – more broadly conceived as learning ecologies – may alternatively have larger numbers of students than the historical norm, or fewer.

MULTIMODAL MEANING

The new media are multimodal. We can do all of text, still image, moving image and sound together now, on the one recording/transmitting device. In an earlier modernity, the book or the newspaper mainly consisted of typeset text. It was not until the application of the new technologies of photolithography in the mid-twentieth century that image and text could be easily brought together, which is why until then newspapers had no photos and books needed separate sections for 'plates' (Kalantzis and Cope, 2012a).

Digitization further inveigles text and image. Analogue film and television had very little writing, until digitization. Now news, business and sports channels stream written words over image over sound. The internet also brings it all together, where barely a page operates in a purely written-textual mode. It is not just that these modes are juxtaposed in digital media. They functionally depend on each other. They form a grammatical and structural unity: the comment that makes no sense without the image; the caption that points to criterial features in the image; the textual metadata that makes an image discoverable and links the preceding image to the next.

The grounding for this multimodality is practical, material, tangible, a product of industrial design even before reaching the consumer. Then once in the consumer's hands, meaning is a matter of manufacture. These modes are all made of the same material stuff, text and image of pixels, and one layer behind that, sound and manipulable data as well in common binary encodings. This is how we can manufacture all these meanings in the one recording and dissemination device. This device – a phone, a tablet, a laptop – becomes a cognitive prosthesis for the purposes of both representation (lending support to our thinking-for-ourselves) and communication (defying distance by connecting us through telepresent messaging-for-others).

Now that we have at hand the tools for fully multimodal knowledge representation, we can offer these to our learners. Our times require us to move beyond the handwriting book or the word processor. Instead, our learners should be working in the twenty-first-century world of web communications. This is a pedagogical imperative as well as a practical one, so students can represent their meanings independently and simultaneously in different modes – written, oral, visual, audio and dataset. Each mode complements the other – the diagram and the text, the oral and the written explanation, manipulable data and its synthetic summary. Each can say the same kinds of things as the other, and is also an irreducibly different mode of representation.

Much can be learned by moving backwards between modes, representing meaning in one mode then another – a cognitive process we have called 'synesthesia', extending by metaphor the meaning of a word whose origins lie in cognitive psychology (Kalantzis and Cope, 2012a: Chapter 7). Take the science experiment – the representation of its results can include words, diagrams, tables, dataset, and also a video demonstrating the experiment itself. Learning is deepened as students shift from one mode to another, making their meanings one way, then another complementary way.

ACTIVE KNOWLEDGE MAKING

The characteristic mode of acquisition of knowledge after the introduction of mass-institutionalized education in the nineteenth century involves the following configuration: a bureaucratic apparatus that prescribes content areas to be learned in the syllabus; textbooks that lay out the content; teacher recitation; teacher–student question and answer routines; filling out answers in workbooks; reading texts and answering comprehension questions; writing short texts to check what had been learned. The patterns of practice were predictable and straightforward.

This heritage classroom is, in essence, an epistemic architecture grounded in a communications technology. The communications technology is defined by the walls of the classroom, containing thirty or so children and where one teacher or one student can speak at a time. Here, teachers and textbooks present pithy concentrations of the world in the form of history, or grammar, mathematics, or whatever. These are essentially monologues, bodies of knowledge spoken in a singular, synoptic voice, whether the voice be that of the teacher or textbook author. Students read silently, write quietly, and avert their eyes from lateral 'copying' glances as they fill out their worksheets or respond to quizzes. These are almost solitary processes, even when other learners are so close at hand. The aim is that facts are to be committed to memory and theorems learned from which unequivocal answers can readily be deduced. These memories and the application of the theorems can be measured in tests that have right and wrong answers, at the end of a lesson, or week, or a chapter, or a course.

In this knowledge architecture, students are primarily configured as passive knowledge consumers. The knowledge that is transmitted to them takes the form of a univocal narrative. It is declarative knowledge. The moral economy of this single-minded content transmission speaks to unquestioning compliance in the face of epistemic authority, lack of critical autonomy on the part of the receivers of knowledge, and an absence of epistemic and social responsibility. This may have been appropriate, perhaps, for an earlier era of industrial discipline and mass conformity.

It also aligned with the cultural logic of broadcast or mass media. In this old, cognitive-epistemic regime, the ability of the spoken-to-many to speak back was very limited – a carefully vetted letter to the editor, the occasional person who managed to get through to a talk-show host, just one at a time. Discursively, this relation was modelled in response to the single student who answered the teacher's telling question on behalf of the whole class. For the vast majority of audiences (and students), these moments of participation were tokens, for rhetorical effect only. Media and discursive participation were at best vicarious.

The sensibilities, habits of mind and skills of heavily didactic pedagogy are not well aligned to the spirit and practical needs of our times, with its intensively participatory new media. Going forward into the future, workers, citizens and learners will not be well served by these kinds of knowledge architectures. New media not only afford us the opportunity to create environments of participatory learning in schools, where learners are knowledge producers at least as much as they are knowledge consumers. Indeed, the new media also suggest we should do this, so education remains apt to our times and aligns with the media sensibilities of new learners.

So, for instance, learners will examine multiple sources (discovering texts with different perspectives, conducting their own observations, indeed acting as researchers themselves). They will collaborate with peers in knowledge production, as co-authors, as peer reviewers, and as readers and discussants of finished works shared by and with other learners. They will create always-original knowledge syntheses based on unique life experiences and perspectives.

In these ways, it is possible to use new media to supplement the predominantly hierarchical knowledge flows of our recent past (expert to novice, authority to authorized, teacher to student) with relations of lateral knowledge co-creation. This fits nicely with wider contemporary shifts in the 'balance of agency' (Kalantzis and Cope, 2012b), where consumers are becoming 'prosumers' with their customizable products and interfaces; where reading (in so far as it is a kind of consumption) is intermingled with writing (in so far as it is a kind of production) in the new media; where amateurs are barely distinguishable from professionals in web knowledge spaces like Wikipedia; and

where the pleasure of the narrative in gaming is not simply vicarious as it is in television or cinema because now you are positioned as a character with shared responsibility for the story's ending.

RECURSIVE FEEDBACK

Old media were linear – the one-way flows of information and culture from television studio to viewer, from newspaper office to reader, from radio studio to listener, from movie lot to audience. New media are by comparison recursive. At the beginning of the computer age, Norbert Weiner attempted to capture the logic of self-adjusting systems, both mechanical and biological, with the concept of 'cybernetics' (Weiner, 1965 [1948]). The Greek *kybernetis*, or oarsman, adjusts his rudder one way then another, in order to maintain the course of the vessel. Whereas the communicative logic of the old media was linear (knowledge creator to passive knowledge consumer), new media is dialogical and recursive, to the point even where it is hard to distinguish creator and consumer. Feedback is pervasive. Web reputation and moderation systems add social filters to the feedback (Farmer and Glass, 2010). The 'quantified self' of ubiquitous devices provides continuous feedback on self in space and society, from walking directions, to exercise routines, to the social reach of a post.

Feedback systems in traditional schools were, like old media, linear, starting with the curriculum and ending with the test. (The step after that in the curriculum was something different.) In this regime, the summative test is separated from learning – an at-the-end managerial thing, a retrospective judgement which can do little in an immediate sense to further learning. It also conceives knowledge in a peculiar way, using as it does quite different devices from the ordinary processes of engaging with knowledge and learning themselves. Assessment becomes a strangely school-ish game in which students do things like discriminating atomized right responses from trick 'distractors', designed to look right but which are deceptively, deliberately not right. In recent decades, the obsession with testing for the purposes of institutional accountability has magnified everything that was problematic about these linear processes. New media technologies, however, mean that assessment does not have to be this way anymore (Cope et al., 2011b).

New media enables a renewed focus on formative assessment – assessment that is on-the-fly, and that makes in a detailed and constructive way a direct contribution to student learning (Black and Wiliam, 1998; Wiliam, 2011). In the era of social knowledge technologies, no learning environment should be without always-available feedback mechanisms – machine feedback and machine-mediated social feedback. Then, when it comes to summative assessment, all we need to do is present a retrospective view of student progress, using no more and no less than all the data collected in the formative assessment process. In fact, we might in the not-too-distant future be able to abandon summative assessment, and its perverse peculiarity as an artefact and its baleful institutional effects. And this because there is so much assessment going on, all the time – recursive feedback from so many perspectives, of everything the learner does in digitally mediated learning environments.

New media also facilitate a broader range of assessment modes. The machine itself can provide some feedback using natural language processing algorithms, and this feedback is computable. There is also the possibility of constant, machine-mediated human feedback, 'crowdsourced' (Surowiecki, 2004) from multiple perspectives – teacher, peers and self. Revealingly, we have shown in our research that the mean of two or more peers' assessments is remarkably close to the score of an expert rater (Cope et al., 2013). Teachers and learners are all assessing learning, and every one of their perspectives has distinctive value. In fact, as perspectives

vary, the feedback may be more extensive, more thought-provoking, more rapidly provided and thus more valuable, than the most assiduous of lone teacher-markers. We can also moderate the various ratings and calibrate results via processes of inter-rater reliability, and the result may also be a more reliable assessment. One effect of distributing assessment responsibilities in this way is to make assessment processes explicit and remove the trickery. This is also to democratize assessment, where teacher and students are all measuring learning against the same criteria, in the same ways. Mixed with and moderated against a variety of assessment modes, there remains value in survey-based assessment, particularly if it is used for formative purposes. Recent advances in survey psychometrics, including computer-adaptive testing and diagnostic testing, also offer new potentials for this assessment mode (Chang, 2012, 2014).

The overall result of combining this information is a phenomenon that has been termed 'big data' in education, accompanied by the emerging educational subfield of 'learning analytics'. Leaders in this emerging area speak clearly to what they consider to be a paradigm change. Bienkowski et al. (2012, p. ix) point out that 'educational data mining and learning analytics have the potential to make visible data that have heretofore gone unseen, unnoticed, and therefore unactionable'. West (2012, p. 1) directs our attention to ' "real-time" assessment [with its] … potential for improved research, evaluation, and accountability through data mining, data analytics, and web dashboards'. Behrens and DiCerbo (2013) argue that:

technology allows us to expand our thinking about evidence. Digital systems allow us to capture stream or trace data from students' interactions. This data has the potential to provide insight into the processes that students use to arrive at the final product (traditionally the only graded portion). … As the activities, and contexts of our activities, become increasingly digital, the need for separate assessment activities should be brought increasingly into question. (2013, p. 9)

Chung traces the consequences for education in these terms:

> Technology-based tasks can be instrumented to record fine-grained observations about what students do in the task as well as capture the context surrounding the behavior. Advances in how such data are conceptualized, in storing and accessing large amounts of data ('big data'), and in the availability of analysis techniques that provide the capability to discover patterns from big data are spurring innovative uses for assessment and instructional purposes. One significant implication of the higher resolving power of technology-based measurement is its use to improve learning via individualized instruction. (Chung, 2013, p. 3)

DiCerbo and Behrens (2014, p. 8) conclude:

> We believe the ability to capture data from everyday formal and informal learning activity should fundamentally change how we think about education. Technology now allows us to capture fine-grained data about what individuals do as they interact with their environments, producing an 'ocean' of data that, if used correctly, can give us a new view of how learners progress in acquiring knowledge, skills, and attributes.

Learning analytics is also expected to do a better job of determining evidence of deep learning than standardized assessments – where the extent of knowing has principally been measured in terms of long-term memory, or the capacity to determine correct answers (Knight et al., 2013). As Behrens and DiCerbo (2013; DiCerbo and Behrens, 2014) characterize the shift to big data, we move from an item paradigm for data collection with questions that have answers that can be correct and elicit information, to an activity paradigm with learning actions that have features, offer evidence of behavioural attributes, and provide multidimensional information. How, raising our evidentiary expectations, can educational data sciences come to conclusions about dimensions of learning as complex as mastery of disciplinary practices, complex epistemic performances, collaborative knowledge work and multimodal knowledge representations? The answer may lie in the shift to a richer data environment and more sophisticated analytical

tools, many of which can be pre-emptively designed into the learning environment itself, or 'evidence-centred design' (Mislevy et al., 2012; Rupp et al., 2012).

So what might we achieve with these modes of assessment that extensively use new media? One effect may be to reframe the assessment question from 'how did we do?' to 'how are we doing?' – 'we' being the learner, the class, the teacher. Assessment's primary reference point would not then be a managerial focus on results (framing our assessment question in the past perfect tense), but a formative focus on progress and improvement (framing our assessment question in the present continuous tense).

Moreover, as well as being able to measure individual work, we can measure social interactions and peers' contributions to others in the form of the feedback they have provided. In other words, we can assess learning interactions as well as learning artefacts. We can also build recursive feedback – feedback whose value is weighted by feedback on feedback, and ratings that are moderated by inter-rater reliability calculations. We can, in other words, calibrate crowdsourced assessment so it is increasingly reliable, and perhaps even more so than the expert marker assessment in isolation.

We could even take a more audacious step, in the direction of a 'no failure' educational paradigm, where you can keep taking on feedback until you are as good as good is supposed to be. This is by way of contrast with the distribution of students across a bell curve, where the few can succeed only because most are destined to be mediocre or fail. A culture of mutually supportive constructive feedback not only models the ideals of a knowledge economy where teamwork and networked collaborations are more valuable than ever; assistance helps the stronger as well as the weaker. It sets community standards, where the weaker see models in the works they review that are stronger and the completed works of peers published to a web portfolio. And, in feedback-on-feedback and the measurement of constructive interactions, peers are offered help credits rather than being rewarded with the beating-the-other-person credits of the normal distribution curve.

COLLABORATIVE INTELLIGENCE

Traditionally, schooling has been based on the idea of individual intelligence, where intelligence itself is narrowly conceived as personal memory and the mechanical skills of deduction. The human mind, however, is an intrinsically social thing (Gee, 2013 [1992]). Our cognitive capacities reside in the language we have inherited and the ways of seeing we have learned. Intelligence is our capacity to reach for always-available social memory and to apply available logics and computational tools. It is what we can do together in communities of practice. Today, through ubiquitous computing and the social web, externalized memory and computational tools are accessible that have historically unprecedented power. At the same time, work, public and community life is more manifestly energized by collaborations. In the new media, peer-to-peer collaborations, from Wikipedia to the video library that is YouTube, are the product of massive social collaborations. So much for the culture of closed book examinations or isolated, individualized student work. The new media have made these ideas and practices anachronistic.

As students increasingly do their school work in new media environments, instead of memory work we can focus our evidentiary work on the knowledge artefacts that learners create in digital media – a report on a science experiment, an information report on a phenomenon in the human or social world, a history essay, an artwork with exegesis, a video story, a business case study, a worked mathematical or statistical example, or executable computer code with user stories. These are some of the characteristic knowledge artefacts of our times.

In the era of new media, learners assemble their knowledge representations in the form of rich, multimodal sources – text, image, diagram, table, audio, video, hyperlink, infographic, and manipulable data with visualizations. These are manifestly the product of distributed cognition, where traces of the knowledge production process are as important as the products themselves – the sources used, peer feedback during the making, and collaboratively created works. These offer evidence of the quality of disciplinary practice, the fruits of collaboration, capacities to discover secondary knowledge sources, and create primary knowledge from observations and through manipulations. The artefact is identifiable, assessable, measurable. Its provenance is verifiable. Every step in the process of its construction can be traced. The tools of measurement of artefacts are also expanded – natural language processing, time-on-task, peer- and self-review, peer annotations, edit histories, navigation paths through sources. In these ways, the range of collectable data surrounding the knowledge work is hugely expanded.

Our evidentiary focus may now also change. We no longer need to seek elusive forms of evidence, for example the traditional constructs such as the 'theta' of latent cognitive traits in item response theory, or the 'g' of intelligence in IQ tests. In the era of digital we don't need to be so conjectural in our evidentiary argument. We don't need to look for anything latent when we have captured so much evidence in readily analysable form about the concrete product of knowledge work, as well as a record of all the steps undertaken in the creation of that product.

We also need to know more than individualized, 'mentalist' (Gergen and Dixon-Román, 2013) constructs can ever tell us. We need to know about the social sources of knowledge, manifest in quotations, paraphrases, remixes, links, citations, and other such references. These things don't need to be remembered now that we live in a world of always-accessible information; they only need to be aptly used. We also need to know about collaborative intelligence where the knowledge of a working group is greater than the sum of its individual members. We now have analysable records of social knowledge work, recognizing and crediting for instance the peer feedback that made a knowledge construct so much stronger, or tracking the differential contributions of participants in a jointly created work.

In these ways, artefacts and the processes of their making may offer sufficient evidence of knowledge actions, the doing that reflects the thinking, and practical results of that thinking in the form of knowledge representations. As we have so many tools to measure these artefacts and their processes of construction in the era of new media, we can safely leave the measurement at that. In these ways then, new media and its associated 'big data' learning analytics may shift the focus of our evidentiary work in education, to some degree at least, from cognitive constructs to what we might call the 'artefactual'. Where the cognitive can be no more than putative knowledge, the artefactual is a concretely represented knowledge and its antecedent knowledge processes.

METACOGNITION

Metacognition is a means to think more deeply, at a higher level of abstraction. It also produces efficiencies in thinking and learning. Conceptualization at higher levels of abstraction broadens the scope of application and transfer for ideas and understandings. There is a growing literature on the significance of metacognition in learning (Bereiter, 2002; Bransford et al., 2000).

Processes of metacognition align with the logic of new media. James Gee argues that computer games demand meta-level thinking about the semiotic domain – it is not enough to play the game; to play it well you have to develop an understanding of its design principles and underlying architecture (Gee, 2003). New media cannot be 'read', page after page;

they require an understanding of navigational schemes and information architectures.

Meanwhile, in education, didactic pedagogy operates within a flat epistemic world of single-layered, cognition: information that can be remembered, routines by means of which answers can be deduced, and correct applications of concepts. Metacognition adds a second layer of thinking, of the same order as the navigational architectures of new media. This layer consists of a meta-understanding of the nature of disciplinary practice. This layer is generative, supporting transfer of understanding across contexts, including contexts not yet encountered. It also supports mnemonic work, using devices to assist recall (tags, annotations, codings, bookmarks) that speak to general levels of meaning.

As an instance of media supported learning, we take the example of student peer reviews of written science arguments. In revising their arguments in the light of peer feedback, a learner may be asked to analyse whether a claim is adequately supported by evidence, and thus to consider the nature of the relationship of claims and evidence in science. This creates a dialectical play between first level cognition (thinking about climate change or hydraulic fracking, perhaps), and a second order of reflective thinking about the ways in which valid scientific claims must be supported by evidence (Cope et al., 2013). In this formative assessment process, students externalize and analyse their written representations of science against specific criteria, becoming more analytic in their science thinking (Driver et al., 2000). Munford and Zembal-Saul (2002) summarize the metacognitive benefits to students: opportunities to learn not only content but also about disciplinary theories and processes, including an understanding of the role of documentary knowledge representations and social interaction in the process of knowledge construction; engagement with discourse that renders learners' understanding and thinking visible, thus providing a valuable tool for reflection and assessment; and support for developing different ways of thinking and enhancing understandings of disciplinary ideas.

DIFFERENTIATED LEARNING

Mass media built mass audiences, to whom were transmitted mass culture. Culture moreover, was homogenized, assumed to be uniform and, to the extent that it was possible, made uniform by the mass production and distribution of newspapers, television, radio and best-selling books. The logic of mass production produced with it cultures of mass consumption. This was intrinsic to the economies of scale that characterized the systems of cultural production and distribution in the era of mass communications.

Today, there are no such economies of scale in the media. Every Facebook feed, every Twitter stream, is uniquely customized for and by the user to suit their interests, identity, and place in the world. Big contributors (famous people, companies, large movements) get equal billing with friends, colleagues and the smallest of minority interests. Diversity is everything. Divergence – of identity, taste, affiliation, stance, interest – is the norm. In the era of new media, our persons are becoming more different.

Heritage classroom communication architectures are like the old, mass media. They are oriented to one-size-fits-all transmission of identical content. The teacher speaks to the middle of the class, which means that what they are saying is not understandable for some students and boringly obvious for others. Progressing through the textbook, all students need to be on the same page at the same time. And when it comes to the test, there is just one set of right answers – 'standardization' is made a virtue. This arrangement is premised on a homogenizing knowledge focus and learning pace. Homogenization, however, is a premise that fails as often as it succeeds.

Few would disagree nowadays that differentiated learning is better. But it is harder work than homogenizing teaching. It is more of a logistical challenge for the teacher. It requires that you are a better teacher, with a broader repertoire of strategies, and superb classroom management skills.

New media make differentiated instruction more feasible. Learners can be doing the same thing at their own pace, or they can be doing different things according to their needs or interests. Such is the objective of adaptive, personalized or differentiated instruction which calibrates learning to individuals (Conati and Kardan, 2013; Shute and Zapata-Rivers, 2012; Walkington, 2013; Wolf, 2010).

This becomes all the more feasible once the teacher has an immediate view of where they are up to in a project status screen. Indeed they can click right into the student's work and see their most recent keystroke. Moreover, positioning the student as a knowledge producer affords more space for student voice, interest, experience and localized relevance. In general terms, the intellectual project might be the same, but the topics may vary. Or, where the aim is collaborative knowledge creation, every student might be working on one distinctive piece in a jigsaw puzzle of class knowledge that is later disclosed when it is published and shared with the class community. Instead of forcing homogeneity, such a classroom operationalizes the principle of productive diversity or the complementarity of differential knowledge and experiences. Students might go on to cite each others' works as knowledge sources, as distributed expertise. Such a learning ecology is one that harnesses learner identities, deepens their sense of engagement, and increases their motivation to devote time to task and engage with others in their knowledge community.

Then assessment becomes a somewhat different process than in the past, not measuring capacities to remember identical things or correctly deduce the same answers, but measuring higher order comparabilities and equivalences between knowledge artefacts which may in substance be different. In this assessment regime, you don't have to be the same to be equal. At this point, managing learner differences may become easier than one-size-fits-all teaching.

Computer-mediated learning environments are now available whose intrinsic mechanism and advertised virtue is divergence – variously named as adaptive or personalized learning (Conati and Kardan, 2013; Koedinger et al., 2013; McNamara et al., 2012; McNamara and Graesser, 2012; Wolf, 2010). In these learning environments, recursive, dynamic, recalibrating systems are the new norm. Such environments are unstandardized by design. The data they generate are dynamic because they are built to be self-adjusting systems. They are difference engines.

CONCLUSION

None of the seven ideas that we have outlined in this chapter is new to the theories or practices of education. In fact, each of them has its origins in pedaogical propositions that have frequently been made, in one form or another, since the first moments of modern, mass-institutionalized education.

The moment of new media is a moment of profound social transformation. 'Disruptive' is a word often applied to new information and communications technologies, to the point at times where the word is almost a cliché. However, we would not want to disrupt traditional schooling for disruption's sake. It is simply, pragmatically, to keep education relevant to our changing times. When we turn our attention to the new media, for every moment of mendaciousness on the part of the new media behemoths, we also see glimpses of new social possibility. As it is with new media, so it is with new learning. For every distressing moment where technologies reproduce the worst of didactic pedagogy, there are other moments where something powerfully generative is happening – liberating, even. The agenda now is not just to use new media in learning. It's to do powerfully reflexive pedagogies,

and in so doing to open out new social relations of knowledge and culture.

NOTE

1 US Department of Education Institute of Education Sciences: 'The Assess-as-You-Go Writing Assistant: A Student Work Environment that Brings Together Formative and Summative Assessment' (R305A090394); 'Assessing Complex Performance: A Postdoctoral Training Program Researching Students' Writing and Assessment in Digital Workspaces' (R305B110008); 'u-Learn. net: An Anywhere/Anytime Formative Assessment and Learning Feedback Environment' (ED-IES-10-C-0018); 'The Learning Element: A Lesson Planning and Curriculum Documentation Tool for Teachers' (ED-IES-IO-C-0021); and 'InfoWriter: A Student Feedback and Formative Assessment Environment for Writing Information and Explanatory Texts' (ED-IES-13-C-0039). Scholar is located at http://CGScholar.com

REFERENCES

Adorno, W. (2001) *The Culture Industry: Selected Essays on Mass Culture*, London: Routledge.

Behrens, J. and DiCerbo, K. (2013) 'Technological Implications for Assessment Ecosystems', in E. W. Gordon (ed.) *The Gordon Commission on the Future of Assessment in Education: Technical Report*, Princeton NJ: The Gordon Commission, pp. 101–22.

Benjamin, W. (2008) [1936] 'The Work of Art in the Age of its Technological Reproducibility', in M. W. Jennings, B. Doherty, and T. Y. Levin (eds) *The Work of Art in the Age of its Technological Reproducibility and Other Writings on Media*, Cambridge, MA: Harvard University Press.

Bereiter, C. (2002) *Education and Mind in the Knowledge Age*, Mahwah NJ: Lawrence Erlbaum.

Bienkowski, M., Feng, M. and Means, B. (2012) 'Enhancing Teaching and Learning Through Educational Data Mining and Learning Analytics: An Issue Brief', Office of Educational Technology, U.S. Department of Education, Washington DC.

Bishop, J. and Verleger, M. (2013) 'The Flipped Classroom: A Survey of the Research', American Society for Engineering Education, Atlanta GA.

Black, P. and Wiliam, D. (1998) 'Assessment and Classroom Learning', *Assessment in Education*, 5: 7–74.

Bransford, J., Brown, A. and Cocking, R. (2000) 'How People Learn: Brain, Mind, Experience and School', edited by N. R. C. Commission on Behavioral and Social Sciences and Education, Washington, DC: National Academy Press.

Chang, H. H. (2012) 'Making Computerized Adaptive Testing Diagnostic Tools for Schools', in R. W. Lissitz and H. Jiao (eds) *Computers and their Impact on State Assessment: Recent History and Predictions for the Future*, Information Age Publishing, pp. 195–226.

Chang, H. H. (2014) 'Psychometrics Behind Computerized Adaptive Testing', *Psychometrika*.

Chung, G. (2013) 'Toward the Relational Management of Educational Measurement Data', The Gordon Commission, Princeton NJ.

Conati, C. and Kardan, S. (2013) 'Student Modeling: Supporting Personalized Instruction, from Problem Solving to Exploratory Open-Ended Activities', *AI Magazine*, 34: 13–26.

Cope, B. and Kalantzis, M. (2009) 'Ubiquitous Learning: An Agenda for Educational Transformation', in B. Cope and M. Kalantzis (eds) *Ubiquitous Learning*, Champaign IL: University of Illinois Press.

Cope, B. and Kalantzis, M. (2010) 'New Media, New Learning', in D. R. Cole and D. L. Pullen (eds) *Multiliteracies in Motion: Current Theory and Practice*, London: Routledge, pp. 87–104.

Cope, B. and Kalantzis, M. (2013) 'Towards a New Learning: The "Scholar" Social Knowledge Workspace, in Theory and Practice', *e-Learning and Digital Media*, 10: 334–58.

Cope, B., Kalantzis, M., Abd-El-Khalick, F. and Bagley, E. (2013) 'Science in Writing: Learning Scientific Argument in Principle and Practice', *e-Learning and Digital Media*, 10: 420–41.

Cope, B., Kalantzis, M. and Magee, L. (2011a) *Towards a Semantic Web: Connecting Knowledge in Academic Research*, Cambridge UK: Woodhead Publishing.

Cope, B., Kalantzis, M., McCarthey, S., Vojak, C. and Kline, S. (2011b) 'Technology-Mediated Writing Assessments: Paradigms and Principles', *Computers and Composition*, 28: 79–96.

Davies, R. S. and West, R. (2014) 'Technology Integration in Schools', in J. M. Spector, M. D. Merrill, J. Elen, and M. J. Bishop (eds) *Handbook of Research on Educational Communications and Technology*, Springer, pp. 841–53.

DiCerbo, K. and Behrens, J. (2014) *Impacts of the Digital Ocean on Education*, London: Pearson.

Driver, R., Newton, P. and Osborne, J. (2000) 'Establishing the Norms of Scientific Argumentation in Classrooms', *Science Education*, 84: 287–312.

Eisenstein, E. (1979) *The Printing Press as an Agent of Change: Communications and Cultural Transformation in Early-Modern Europe*, Cambridge: Cambridge University Press.

Farmer, F. R. and Glass, B. (2010) *Web Reputation Systems*, Sebastapol CA: O'Reilly.

Gee, J. P. (2003) *What Video Games Have to Teach Us about Learning and Literacy*, New York: Palgrave Macmillan.

Gee, J. P. (2013) [1992] *The Social Mind: Language, Ideology, and Social Practice*, Champaign IL: Common Ground.

Gergen, K. J. and Dixon-Román, E. (2013) *Epistemology in Measurement: Paradigms and Practices*, The Gordon Commission, Princeton NJ.

Hattie, J. (2009) *Visible Learning: A Synthesis of Over 800 Meta-Analyses Relating to Achievement*, London: Routledge.

Haythornthwaite, C. (2009) 'Participatory Transformations', in B. Cope and M. Kalantzis (eds) *Ubiquitous Learning*, Champaign IL: University of Illinois Press.

Jenkins, H. (2006) *Confronting the Challenges of Participatory Culture: Media Education for the 21st Century*, John D. and Catherine T. MacArthur Foundation, Chicago.

Kalantzis, M. and Cope, B. (2012a) *Literacies*, Cambridge, UK: Cambridge University Press.

Kalantzis, M. and Cope, B. (2012b) *New Learning: Elements of a Science of Education*, Cambridge, UK: Cambridge University Press.

Knight, S., Buckingham Shum, S. and Littleton, K. (2013) 'Epistemology, Pedagogy, Assessment and Learning Analytics', in *Third Conference on Learning Analytics and Knowledge (LAK 2013)*, Leuven, Belgium: ACM, pp. 75–84.

Koedinger, K., Brunskill, E., Baker, R. and McLaughlin, E. (2013) 'New Potentials for Data-Driven Intelligent Tutoring System Development and Optimization', *AI Magazine*, 34: 27–41.

McNamara, D. and Graesser, A. (2012) 'Coh-Metrix: An Automated Tool for Theoretical and Applied Natural Language Processing', in P. M. McCarthy and C. Boonthum-Denecke (eds) *Applied Natural Language Processing: Identification, Investigation and Resolution*, Hershey PA: IGI Global, pp. 188–205.

McNamara, A., Graesser, C. and Danielle, S. (2012) 'Reading Instruction: Technology Based Supports for Classroom Instruction', in C. Dede and J. Richards (eds) *Digital Teaching Platforms: Customizing Classroom Learning for Each Student*, New York: Teachers College Press, pp. 71–87.

Mislevy, R., Behrens, J., Dicerbo, K. and Levy, R. (2012) 'Design and Discovery in Educational Assessment: Evidence-Centered Design, Psychometrics, and Educational Data Mining', *Journal of Educational Data Mining*, 4: 11–48.

Munford, D. and Zembal-Saul, C. (2002) 'Learning Science through Argumentation: Prospective Teacher's Experiences in an Innovative Science Course', *Annual Meeting of the National Association for Research in Science Teaching*, New Orleans, LA.

O'Reilly, T. (2005) 'What Is Web 2.0? Design Patterns and Business Models for the Next Generation of Software'. http://www.oreillynet.com/pub/a/oreilly/tim/news/2005/09/30/what-is-web-20.html

Reese, G. (2009) *Cloud Application Architectures: Building Applications and Infrastructure in the Cloud*, Sebastatpol, CA: O'Reilly.

Rupp, A., Nugent, R. and Nelson, B. (2012) 'Evidence-Centered Design for Diagnostic Assessment within Digital Learning Environments: Integrating Modern Psychometrics and Educational Data Mining', *Journal of Educational Data Mining*, 4: 1–10.

Shute, V. and Zapata-Rivera, D. (2012) 'Adaptive Educational Systems', in P. Durlach and A. Lesgold (eds) *Adaptive Technologies for Training and Education*, New York: Cambridge University Press.

Surowiecki, J. (2004) *The Wisdom of Crowds: Why the Many Are Smarter Than the Few and How Collective Wisdom Shapes Business, Economies, Societies and Nations*, New York: Doubleday.

Twidale, M. B. (2009) 'From Ubiquitous Computing to Ubiquitous Learning', in B. Cope and M. Kalantzis (eds) *Ubiquitous Learning*, Champaign IL: University of Illinois Press.

Walkington, C. (2013) 'Using Adaptive Learning Technologies to Personalize Instruction to Student Interests: The Impact of Relevant Contexts on Performance and Learning Outcomes', *Journal of Educational Psychology*, 105: 932–45.

Warschauer, M. and Matuchniak, T. (2010) 'New Technology and Digital Worlds: Analyzing Evidence of Equity in Access, Use, and Outcomes', *Review of Research in Education*, 34: 179–225.

Weiner, N. (1965) [1948] *Cybernetics, or the Control and Communication in the Animal and the Machine*, Cambridge, MA: MIT Press.

West, D. (2012) *Big Data for Education: Data Mining, Data Analytics, and Web Dashboards*, Washington DC: Brookings Institution.

Wiliam, D. (2011) *Embedded Formative Assessment*, Bloomington, IN: Solution Tree Press.

Wolf, M. A. (2010) 'Innovate to Educate: System [Re]Design for Personalized Learning, A Report From The 2010 Symposium', Software and Information Industry Association, Washington DC.

Zembal-Saul, C. (2005) 'Pre-service Teachers' Understanding of Teaching Elementary School Science as Argument', in *Annual Meeting of the National Association for Research in Science Teaching*. Dallas TX.

36

Harnessing the Power of Knowledge and Beliefs in Teaching and Learning: Interventions that Promote Change

P. Karen Murphy, Carla M. Firetto
and Valerie A. Long

INTRODUCTION

To break with the 'cotton wool' of habit, of mere routine, of automatism, is (as we shall see) to seek alternative ways of being, to look for openings. To find such openings is to discover new possibilities – often new ways of achieving … (Greene, 1988: 2)

Arguably, much of what takes place in classrooms is guided by the habits and routines of the teachers and students who inhabit them (James, 1890). As James suggested, habits of mind and action are routinized over time through repeated exposure and involvement. Certainly, the ways in which the teacher chooses and facilitates content-area learning, the expectations teachers and students set for their instruction and learning, and the nature of the discourse in the classroom all influence the 'cash value' of students' experiences during their time in school. Similarly, everything in and about the classroom, from the time allotted to each school subject to the classroom rules and physical organization of

the students, ensures fairly consistent and predictable routines – routines that, like cotton wool, swaddle us in comfort and complacency and offer little cause for change or alteration. Yet, as Greene so eloquently articulates, the bounty of throwing off the security of our cotton wool of habits is new possibilities and ways of being, and potentially, higher levels of achievement come to light.

Of course, just as cotton wool is common, practical and serves many purposes in daily life, some habits and routines productively advance pedagogy and learning. No doubt, it is better to provide instruction when the desks are organized such that the students can *see* the teacher. In other cases, the habits and routines of teachers and students simply maintain the status quo. That is, teaching and learning remain in stasis, resulting in relatively linear changes to students' academic development. In still other cases, the routines and habits of those that dwell in classrooms are non-productive and actually inhibit student learning. A classic example is a learning environment with relatively little classroom management such that students shout over the teacher, disrupt instruction, or even bully other students. Sometimes, however, the non-productive habits and routines are subtler and less apparent to the untrained professional (e.g. parent). For example, a teacher who consistently instructs students to re-read as the primary reading strategy is ostensibly arming students with a relatively ineffective strategy. Similarly, a classroom where the teacher holds the speaking floor for long periods of time, asks all of the questions, and maintains sole interpretive authority is one in which the students will be unprepared for independent learning, and their learning trajectory will likely be relatively level (Wilkinson et al., 2010).

The difficulty is not so much that habits and routines guide our classrooms, teaching and learning, but rather, that such routines and habits often go unnoticed and unevaluated. Like cotton wool wrapping, these habits are remarkably comfortable and familiar and, therefore, difficult to change. As James (1890) astutely points out, habits and routines go unevaluated and resist modification because they, in many ways, form the very essence of our cognitive architecture in the form of deeply entrenched neural pathways. That is, habits and routines are the outward manifestations of what we know and believe, which makes them extremely powerful in driving teachers' and students' thinking, as well as their actions. As such, the challenge is not just to alter the outward manifestation or the 'habit of action.' Indeed, the challenge is to harness the power of teachers' and students' knowledge and beliefs in order to drive their habits and routines to optimize teaching and learning.

Within the present chapter, our overarching goal is to explore ways to harness the power of teachers' and students' knowledge and beliefs so as to improve pedagogy and learning. To accomplish this goal, we have divided the chapter into several sections. First, we briefly provide conceptual definitions of the terms knowledge and beliefs. Second, we turn to the roles that knowledge and beliefs play in teachers and teaching as well as in learners and learning. Then, we overview a series of empirically tested interventions that have been shown to harness the power of knowledge and beliefs in teaching and learning. Finally, we share implications for research and practice.

DEFINING KNOWLEDGE AND BELIEFS

Philosophers, psychologists and educators have written extensively about the nature and definitions of knowledge and beliefs and their function in various aspects of life (e.g. Alexander et al., 1991; Scheffler, 1965). As might be expected, definitions and conceptualizations vary widely, and consequently, the operationalizations and empirical outcomes are often conflicting (Fives and Buehl, 2012; Muis, 2004; Vosniadou, 2013). Our goal herein is not to delineate or even articulate the many definitions of knowledge and beliefs, rather we encourage readers strictly interested in definitions to peruse the numerous articles (e.g. Alexander and Dochy, 1995; Southerland et al., 2001), chapters (Murphy and Mason, 2006) and books (Scheffler, 1965) on the topic.

Rather, we provide definitions of these terms as a way of establishing a common lexicon, as well as a conceptual undergirding regarding the relations between these two constructs. As mentioned previously, definitions of knowledge and beliefs vary within and across domains of study. For example, philosophers often intertwine the definitions of these terms with a conceptualization of their relations. Specifically, within the philosophical literature knowledge is often defined as justified, true belief (Ryle, 1949; Scheffler, 1965). The justification component then plays a central role in the extent to which it is appropriate for an individual to claim that they 'know' something. Beliefs, by comparison, simply refer to one's initial understanding of a phenomenon (Peirce, 1994; Scheffler, 1965). Psychologists (e.g. Nisbett and Ross, 1980; Rokeach, 1968) and educators (e.g. Alexander et al., 1991; Pintrich et al., 1993) are more apt to subsume beliefs as a type or component of knowledge. Indeed, in their classic article in which they explore knowledge terms, Alexander and colleagues suggest that knowledge essentially refers to everything known, including beliefs.

Although the definitions and conceptualizations of philosophers and psychologists are well intended, our own perspective is that there is much to be gained from the individuals about whom we are writing. Simply put, we believe that understanding how teachers and students define and conceptualize these terms is fundamentally important if we are to fully understand the best ways to harness the power of these constructs for teaching and learning. As such, our definitions of knowledge and beliefs draw heavily on the work of Alexander and colleagues who studied how teachers and students of varying educational levels conceptualized knowledge and beliefs (e.g. Alexander and Dochy, 1995; Alexander et al., 1998). The participants represented varied cultural backgrounds (e.g. Netherlands, Singapore or the United States) and their educational experiences were also diverse (i.e. seventh grade through Masters level students to professors of education). Necessarily, the cotton wool of their day-to-day existence also diverged. In spite of the educational and cultural differences, the respondents in these studies understood knowledge as factual, externally verified, or widely accepted, and beliefs were understood as ideas or thoughts that individuals perceived as true or wanted to be true. Unlike knowledge, beliefs also included subjective claims of which the truth or validity was unimportant. This is not to say, however, that the respondents failed to value their beliefs. On the contrary, the study participants perceived their beliefs as extremely important, and, as Peirce (1994) suggested, desired to maintain them in the face of contradictory evidence. These respondents also understood knowledge and beliefs as having shared overlap. That is, there are those things that I know but don't believe, there are

those things that I believe but know very little about, and there are also things that I both know something about and believe.

Based on the aforementioned research, we operate from the perspective of knowledge and beliefs as constructs that overlap and share at least partial variance. Knowledge refers to 'all that is accepted as true that can be externally verified and can be confirmed by others on repeated interactions with the object (i.e. factual)' (Murphy and Mason, 2006: 306). Belief, by comparison, refers 'to all that one accepts as or wants to be true. Beliefs do not require verification and often cannot be verified (e.g. opinions)' (Murphy and Mason, 2006: 306–307). As suggested by Rokeach (1968), individuals often ascribe importance to beliefs, which provides a will to act. Moreover, not surprisingly, individuals in the studies conducted by Alexander and colleagues (e.g. Alexander and Dochy, 1995; Alexander et al., 1998) suggested that they were willing to hold on to their beliefs despite conflicting evidence. Peirce (1994) offered a potential explanation for this intriguing but perplexing phenomenon. Peirce held that people find comfort in the known and are willing to maintain a perspective until the habit of action leads to consequences that outweigh the cost of maintaining their belief (Peirce, 1994). And so it is that we cling to the cotton wool of habits that surround and ensconce us, performing, sometimes, great feats to maintain that comfort until the vulnerability of its loss becomes apparent and profitable to us. What this means is that harnessing the power of teachers' and students' knowledge and beliefs will require not only that these individuals are aware of their knowledge and beliefs, but also that they come to the perspective that holding on to them is no longer advantageous.

TEACHER KNOWLEDGE AND BELIEFS

In order to harness the power of knowledge and beliefs in the classroom, we must first consider the effects of *teachers'* knowledge and beliefs on students' learning outcomes. In this section, we provide a description of the various facets of teachers' knowledge and beliefs. Then, we address the research on the effects of teachers' knowledge and beliefs on students' learning. We conclude with suggestions for how to harness the power of teachers' knowledge and beliefs so as to promote students' learning.

Facets of Teachers' Knowledge and Beliefs

In 1986, Shulman examined various teacher certification and licensure exams to understand more about expectations for teachers' knowledge. Shulman found that older exams (circa 1875) largely focused on teachers' content knowledge (i.e. knowledge of specific subject matter), while newer exams (circa 1980) placed a stronger emphasis on teachers' pedagogical knowledge (i.e. knowledge of various principles of teaching; Shulman, 1986). In response, Shulman (1986, 1987) argued for the consideration of additional constructs that make up a teachers' knowledge base, including pedagogical content knowledge (i.e. knowledge that blends both content and pedagogy). Shulman asserted that pedagogical content knowledge 'is the category most likely to distinguish the understanding of the content specialist from that of the pedagogue' (1987: 8).

Although Shulman's conceptions about the categories of teachers' knowledge were not without criticism (see Calderhead, 1996), they were very influential in shaping the extent literature (Borko and Putnam, 1996; Baumert et al., 2010), as well as contemporary teacher certification exams, particularly in the United States. However, the pendulum has swung back a bit on this testing trend. Many contemporary teacher certification and licensure exams now require teachers to demonstrate evidence of content knowledge, pedagogical knowledge, and pedagogical content knowledge (Voss et al., 2011). For example,

the Praxis II® tests that are currently required in many areas of the US for teacher certification include Subject Assessments, Principles of Learning and Teaching Tests, and Teaching Foundations Tests (Educational Testing Service, 2014). Clearly, these types of tests emphasize the forms and facets of knowledge that have been shown to influence student learning (e.g. Voss et al., 2011). Indeed, teachers must possess relevant knowledge of their content area or domain, knowledge of how to teach, and some understanding of the intersection of content and pedagogy.

Assessing teachers' knowledge as the only measure of teacher proficiency is problematic; ultimately, we must also consider teachers' beliefs (Woolfolk Hoy et al., 2006). In order to better understand the teacher characteristics that influence students' learning, we must more carefully understand the aspects of teachers that affect their instructional practices, including their beliefs. As is the case with the more general forms of knowledge and beliefs, there is variability regarding the conceptualization and operationalization of teacher beliefs despite attempts to address the messiness of the lexicon (Fives and Buehl, 2012; Pajares, 1992). Definitional issues notwithstanding, there is agreement that teachers' beliefs influence student learning. As Pajares (1992: 307) averred, 'the beliefs teachers hold influence their perceptions and judgments, which, in turn, affect their behavior in the classroom'. In their working framework, Fives and Buehl (2012) went even further to suggest that beliefs function as filters, frames and guides that influence teachers' instructional practices in their classrooms.

Effects of Teachers' Knowledge and Beliefs on Students' Learning

The question that remains is how and in what ways do teachers' knowledge and beliefs influence student learning. Early evidence studying the relations between teachers' content knowledge and students' learning resulted in somewhat mixed findings (presented by Byrne in 1983, as cited in Darling-Hammond, 2000; Ashton and Crocker, 1987). One explanation for the inconsistent findings suggested that while teachers' content knowledge was correlated to student achievement, the added benefit to students' achievement was reduced once teachers' knowledge reached a saturation point (Monk, 1994). Later criticism also suggested that the mixed findings may have been due to the way researchers measured teachers' content knowledge (i.e. the number of courses taken in that subject area; see Borko and Putnam, 1996). Instead, Borko and Putnam (1996) argue for the importance of strong content knowledge, as more knowledgeable teachers place a greater emphasis on 'conceptual, problem-solving, and inquiry aspects of their subjects' (p. 685), whereas 'less knowledgeable teachers tend to emphasize facts, rules, and procedures and stick closely to detailed lesson plans or the text, sometimes missing opportunities to focus on important ideas or connections among ideas' (p. 685).

In reviewing a series of qualitative studies on teachers' mathematical content knowledge, Baumert et al. (2010: 139) offered this clear and concise summary: 'a profound understanding of the subject matter taught is a necessary, but far from sufficient, precondition for providing insightful instruction'. Further, Baumert et al. suggested that pedagogical content knowledge is necessary 'over and above … [content knowledge] to stimulate insightful learning' (2010: 145). Literature reviews by Ashton and Crocker (1987) and Monk (1994) offer empirical support for this assertion.

Yet the research on the congruence of teachers' beliefs and their practices is inconclusive (Fives and Buehl, 2012). For example, Sosu and Gray (2012) found that teachers' beliefs about ability and the learning process affected their approach to teaching (i.e. either constructivist or direct transmission). However, Olafson and Schraw (2006) reported that the majority of the teachers in their study 'held beliefs that were incongruent with their practices' (p. 79) and, despite the fact that every teacher in the study rejected a traditional view of teaching, 'the majority of participants continued to report traditional practices' (pp. 79–80). Olafson and Schraw suggest that this may be due to the influence of external factors (e.g., time constraints, a school culture fixated on testing, etc.) or a discrepancy between beliefs and actions.

In one of the few mediation studies, Baumert et al. (2010) found that students' mathematics achievement was mediated by measures of instructional quality (i.e. cognitive activation, instructional alignment and individual learning support) for teachers' pedagogical content knowledge, but not teachers' content knowledge. A more recent study replicated similar patterns regarding pedagogical content knowledge, while also considering the effect of teachers' beliefs on mathematics achievement (Kunter et al., 2013).

Yet, for teachers' constructivist beliefs there was not a mediation effect of cognitive activation or learning support on mathematics achievement after accounting for other teacher variables (e.g. pedagogical content knowledge). Kunter et al. explain that this may be due to the positive correlation between pedagogical content knowledge and the constructivist beliefs held by teachers. Thus, future studies should account for the relationship between these teacher characteristics, as well as their unique influence on their instructional practices and consequently the learning outcomes of their students.

In this section, we have shown that aspects from both teachers' knowledge and beliefs influence teachers' instructional practices, and subsequently influence student learning, either directly or indirectly. As aptly articulated by Peterson, Carpenter and Fennema (1989: 568): '… teachers' pedagogical content knowledge and beliefs about student knowledge influence teachers' classroom practice, which in turn influences their students' learning and achievement'. Importantly, however, we feel strongly that more research is necessary in order to understand and situate the mixed findings and to possibly identify the specific facets and functions of teachers' knowledge and beliefs that influence students' learning outcomes (Hennessey et al., 2013).

LEARNER KNOWLEDGE AND BELIEFS

Although the extant literature pertaining to the mediating role of teachers' knowledge and beliefs on students' learning remains in its infancy, there is a rich body of empirical research in which learners' knowledge and beliefs have influenced subsequent learning (e.g. Murphy and Mason, 2006). Indeed, perhaps one of the single most replicated findings within the research emanating from educational psychology is that an individual's store of prior knowledge affects all subsequent learning in profound ways (e.g. Alexander et al., 1991; Murphy et al., 2012). Specifically, contemporary research has shown that, as in other aspects of life, the rich get richer. This phenomenon is so apparent in educational and psychological research that it has been termed the 'Matthew Effect' (Stanovich, 1986). Stanovich has proposed that a number of factors contribute to this finding, particularly in important content areas like reading. For example, students with deeper and richer repertoires of prior knowledge generally have more extensive vocabularies and varied declarative and conceptual understandings, as well as procedural and conditional awareness of how and when to make use of strategies when they face learning challenges. As an additional learning buoy, students with deeper and richer levels of prior knowledge also generally possess relatively higher levels of efficacy and motivation relative to their less knowledgeable peers (Bandura, 1997; Winne, 1996).

Likewise, over the last twenty years, educational and psychological researchers have come to understand that students' beliefs also play a powerful role in learning (e.g. Andiliou et al., 2012). As we alluded to in our definitions of these terms, however, the

role of beliefs in learning varies somewhat from that of knowledge. In essence, whereas prior knowledge plays a role in the extent to which an individual can adequately process and assimilate content and experiences into their existing cognitive structures, one could argue that the role of beliefs in learning is somewhat different, particularly at the early stages of content learning (Murphy, 2007). Indeed, as James (1890), Peirce (1994) and others (e.g. Greene, 1988) have suggested, beliefs can be understood as habits of action. As such, our beliefs influence the extent to which we will choose to process knowledge and experience, as well as the depth to which we will modify our existing understanding so as to assimilate or accommodate the object of knowledge or experience (Murphy and Mason, 2006). In many cases, students' beliefs function as habits of action such that they process information in ways that allow them to maintain prior understandings, a sort of my-side bias (James, 1890; Stanovich and West, 2007). Of course, there are also instances, as is highlighted in much of the conceptual change literature, in which students alter what they know and believe (e.g. Chinn and Brewer, 1993; Nersessian, 2013; Miyake, 2013). At times, this process of knowledge and belief change is gradual and incremental (Vosniadou, 1994; Vosniadou et al., 2001) and other times this process is thought to be more rapid and potentially radical (She, 2002, 2004).

The pressing question, of course, is what factors affect the extent to which students maintain or alter their existing understandings (Chinn et al., 2013; Sinatra and Mason, 2013). Empirical findings reveal that the content and materials to be learned (e.g. health, Kaufman et al., 2013; history, Carretero et al., 2013; or mathematics, Vamvakoussi et al., 2013), as well as the nature and characteristics of the learner (e.g. Sinatra and Mason, 2013) dynamically influence the extent to which individuals will alter their understandings as they interact with information and evidence. Our understanding of these dynamic interactions is somewhat restricted due to the nature of existing process models. In essence, many models of change severely limit the nature of change upon which they focus. For example, Pintrich et al. (1993) focused on the role of motivation whereas Dole and Sinatra (1998) focused on engagement of knowledge, and Petty and Cacioppo (1986) attended to modifications of beliefs. Fewer theoretical models, by comparison, have been created to capture the dynamic changes that occur as knowledge and beliefs interact during learning, particularly from text. One exception is the *Characteristics of the Learner and Argument Interaction Model* [CLAIM] (cf. Murphy (2007) for extended discussion), which depicts the learner interacting with text, as well as the anticipated outcomes of such interaction. Rooted in American pragmatist philosophy (e.g. Peirce, 1958; cf. Murphy, 2007), as well as the levels of processing (Craik and Lockhart, 1972; Lockhart and Craik, 1990) and dual processing models (Petty and Cacioppo, 1986) from psychology, Murphy's CLAIM depicts behaviour as being driven by one's beliefs. When acted upon, the beliefs are strengthened and become more entrenched, as long as the practical consequences of behaving in accordance with the habits are positive. If the practical consequences of acting on a belief are negative, then doubt ensues and the individual is forced to consider the viability of maintaining those beliefs.

CLAIM is also supported by findings from the cognitive and social psychology literature, which suggest that acquisition of understandings proceed along a continuum from sensory perception (i.e. Recognition Level) to levels associated with pattern discernment (i.e. Explanatory Power Level) and, finally, to semantic/associative stages of enrichment (i.e. Examined Understanding Level). As often depicted in levels of processing models, Murphy (2007) draws on the principle that individuals can acquire representations with very little cognitive effort (i.e. peripheral processing based on text cues or heuristic strategies), but that well-integrated, examined understandings are the

result of sustained cognitive processing in which individuals integrate the understanding within larger cognitive semantic and associative structures (i.e. elaboration, Petty and Cacioppo, 1986). Importantly, it is the integration of learner characteristics with text characteristics that predicts the alterations or modifications of learners' understandings. At the initial or Recognition Level, learners' knowledge and beliefs are generally shallow, partial, or disjointed, and when reading an easily comprehended, non-refutational text, the learner can readily process the message peripherally based on some textual cue (e.g. biased evidence, credibility of the source, or text length). This type of interaction will generally strengthen learners' prior understandings or allow for superficial acquisition of additional representations. As is the case with accretion, this type of growth does not imply additional depth of processing, but rather the maintenance or strengthening of the initial impression or the acquisition of a new representation (Carey, 1987). In essence, the learner becomes more deeply embedded in the cotton wool of their understandings. Of course, this type of superficial processing can easily lead learners to acquire inconsistent knowledge and beliefs (Bigozzi et al., 2002).

Much of this change is premised, however, on the nature of the text. As such, modifications of the structure and content of the text could potentially lead the same learners to deeper, more meaningful learning. Indeed, learners with low to moderate levels of knowledge and beliefs about a topic who read and process a refutational text from a source they view as credible are more likely to engage the text and process the arguments (Andiliou et al., 2012; Murphy and Alexander, 2004). The same could be said of learners with moderate to high levels of knowledge and beliefs on a given topic. What seems to differentiate these two groups of learners is that learners with low to moderate levels of knowledge and beliefs are likely to be swayed by emotive, text-based arguments, whereas the learners with relatively higher levels of knowledge and beliefs are more persuaded by rational, non-emotive arguments (Andiliou et al., 2012; Murphy, 2001). The process of engaging and processing the arguments in the text lead the learner to find consistency or inconsistency between the arguments and their own understandings. Perceived consistency leads to no substantive change, but the individual will likely gain the ability to explain their understandings in greater detail (e.g. explain the process of photosynthesis; Mikkilä-Erdman, 2001). Learners' stores of knowledge and beliefs become affectively charged and less fragmented through weak restructuring (Carey, 1987).

The situation is very different, however, if learners' knowledge and beliefs substantively vary from those presented in the text. In such cases the students will need to assess the practical consequences of maintaining their current understandings (Murphy, 2007). Learners will doubt their understandings if the consequences are substantive. In essence, these learners attempt to cognitively let go of the warmth of their cotton wool, and to explore alternative possibilities and potential perspectives. Necessarily, this type of processing is effortful and requires motivation (Pintrich et al., 1993; Sinatra and Mason, 2013). Learners with relatively higher motivation will exert additional cognitive effort in an attempt to deeply explore and modify their perspectives. Murphy has proposed that this type of processing will lead to a state of examined understanding in which learners can either justify their prior understandings or modify them in substantive ways so as to align with the new knowledge and beliefs (i.e. weak restructuring or radical restructuring; Carey, 1987).

In essence, when students continue to engage deeply with the understandings they acquired at the Explanatory Level, there is the possibility that they will encounter information, data, or even discourse, that is either inconsistent or puzzling in relation to their prior understandings (e.g. anomalous data; Chinn and Brewer, 1993). It is the discord that propels students towards Examined Understanding, and as individuals progress through this level, they struggle to make sense of their experiences given a particular contextual environment (Mason, 2001). By attempting to dynamically model both the nature of the content or text, and the influence of learner characteristics, Murphy's CLAIM provides initial mooring points for teachers as they strive to help their students leave the comfort of their cotton wool perspectives.

In the section that follows we highlight a number of interventions that have been shown to increase the likelihood that the aforementioned changes in students' understandings will occur in classroom settings. Prior to overviewing the empirical findings pertaining to interventions it is important to note that we understand the teacher–learner relationship in the same way that we understand the content–learner characteristic relations; that is, we understand these relations as multidimensional, dynamic and reciprocal. In essence, classroom interventions that rely on teachers likely influence the nature of the teacher's pedagogy, which in turn alters how the teacher interacts with students, which subsequently modifies how learners engage with content. These interactions and engagements alter learners' knowledge and belief acquisition and provide feedback to teachers regarding their pedagogy. Our sense is that these are the very types of dynamic interactions that allow teachers and students to harness the power of their knowledge and beliefs to enhance teaching and learning.

Interventions in Students' Knowledge and Beliefs

Despite the stubbornness of unquestioned and perhaps even unacknowledged beliefs, the constraining nature of prior knowledge, and the ease and security of maintaining the status quo with regard to both, several studies show that certain instructional methodologies and materials can effect changes in students' knowledge and beliefs. For the purposes of this chapter, we highlight a sample of these interventions. As noted, the definitions and distinctions between knowledge and beliefs overlap and blur and, thus, we discuss some interventions that sought to effect change in learners' knowledge or their beliefs about knowledge and knowing (i.e. epistemic change; Hofer and Pintrich, 1997). Muis and Duffy (2013) assert that researchers have found the constructs of epistemic change and conceptual change so closely linked that epistemic change models, for example Bendixen's (2002), are explicitly based on earlier conceptual change models like that of Pintrich et al.'s (1993).

The interventions can be grouped into approaches that focus on students' *thinking*, the nature of the *text*, or classroom *talk*. The first approach is to directly instruct students to be aware of their own *thinking*. These interventions target students' metacognitive awareness as they read and confront content that challenges their pre-existing knowledge and beliefs. A second approach manipulates the presentation of text in such a way that students are more likely to note that the content addressed in the text calls for deeper processing or requires some activity on their part to reconcile their knowledge or beliefs with the information presented in the text. These studies present students with a single refutational text or multiple conflicting texts and have investigated the effects of these structures on knowledge and beliefs. The last type of intervention focuses on talk and includes discussion approaches that promote changes in students' knowledge and beliefs through interpersonal, dialogic exchanges with peers.

Thinking Interventions: Focus on Metacognition

Muis (2004) reviewed 33 studies examining the impact of beliefs on mathematical learning and located only two studies that explicitly asked students to consider their beliefs. She concluded, however, that although beliefs can change through adaptations in the instructional environment, an individual's explicit awareness of her or his beliefs is a critical impetus for change and, furthermore, 'may be necessary for the perseverance of

more availing beliefs regardless of the instructional environment' (Muis, 2004: 362). The following intervention study examines this conclusion by asking students to acknowledge and consider their beliefs while they read text.

Maier and Richter (2014) employed a meta-cognitive strategy intervention to counteract the text-belief consistency effect, which holds that when texts are not consistent with prior knowledge, readers have difficulty recalling the inconsistent information. This is also known as my-side or confirmation bias (Nickerson, 1998; Stanovich and West, 2007). Readers were taught three strategies: (a) to be aware of prior beliefs and their influence on processing; (b) to monitor for both intra- and intertextual inconsistencies; and (c) to critically evaluate the claims of all arguments, both consistent and inconsistent with their beliefs. The readers in the metacognitive strategy group who also received positive feedback did not show evidence of the text-belief consistency effect after reading two texts (i.e. one belief-consistent and one belief-inconsistent text) on a controversial scientific issue. In short, the intervention completely eliminated the text-consistent bias effect, and these readers were able to build equally strong situation models for both texts.

Text Interventions: Focus on Structure or Content

A second pathway to change uses text structure or content to draw the reader's attention to prior knowledge and beliefs while engaging with ideas or concepts that may be inconsistent with their thinking. Refutational texts begin by acknowledging common misconceptions or naive conceptions held by many students and then explicitly challenge those ideas. An intervention developed by Kienhues, Bromme, and Stahl (2008) was aimed at influencing domain-specific beliefs through the use of such texts. Students were separated into two groups based on their epistemic perspective (i.e. naive or sophisticated) and then were split again so half of each group read a two-sided refutational text and the other a one-sided informational text. The naive group that read the refutational piece did, in fact, shift from a naive to a more sophisticated perspective. However, surprisingly, the sophisticated group reading the informational piece also shifted, yet they shifted to espouse a more naive epistemic perspective after reading the one-sided piece. The authors thus caution that for the more sophisticated readers, the 'exemplary principle' may mislead students into believing that the non-controversial presentation (i.e., the one-sided information text) indicated that science knowledge was simple, straightforward and certain. This explanation conforms with Kendeou, Muis and Fulton's (2011) findings which demonstrated that readers with sophisticated epistemic beliefs use significantly more strategies, especially conceptual change processes, when reading refutational text but not when reading non-refutational text.

A similar study looked at prior knowledge instead of beliefs. Kendeou and van den Broek (2007) found that readers with low prior knowledge read more slowly and engaged in more conceptual change strategies than high prior knowledge readers when reading a refutational text. In contrast, when reading non-refutation texts, learners with misconceptions read at the same speed and with similar processes as did high prior knowledge readers. In other words, participants with misconceptions about a topic were more strategic and engaged in conceptual change processes only when they read a text that addressed common misconceptions; they read a non-refutational text without employing these strategies. While some have concerns about the use of refutational texts in classrooms – they are generally authoritative (i.e. arguing for a 'right' view) and thus viewed by some as manipulative and anti-constructivist – they are undeniably instrumental for aiding learning and can also be used to help students think critically about the power of persuasive writing (Hynd, 2001).

Another method of configuring text presentation as a means of promoting change in beliefs or knowledge is to present students with multiple documents that portray different, conflicting perspectives on a single topic. Ferguson, Bråten, Strømsø and Anmarkrud (2013) compared an experimental group that read multiple conflicting documents with a control group that read the same number of documents on the same issue that were consistent with each other. They found that tenth-graders who read conflicting text changed their domain- and topic-specific beliefs; however, there were no such changes in the contrast group whose readings were consistent across texts. Additionally, the experimental group outperformed the control group on a measure of comprehension related to the topic. Therefore, text that is structured to confront the complexity of an issue and includes elements of conflict elicited changes in students' beliefs and fostered better comprehension while the non-controversial text did not effect such changes.

Talk Interventions: Focus on Discussion

A final intervention approach that is very promising is one that employs *talk* or discussion as a means of effecting changes in knowledge and beliefs. Walker, Wartenberg and Winner (2013) engaged second graders in philosophical discussions around children's storybooks and then measured changes in their argumentation skills and beliefs. They showed that 63% of the children in the intervention group shifted from an absolutist (i.e. there is one right answer) to a predominantly multiplist (i.e. there is more than one right answer) or evaluativist (i.e. there are different perspectives with varying merits) strategy, while only two children (11%) in the control group shifted their beliefs. Discussion-group students also made significant improvements in constructing their own arguments as well as opposing arguments.

Hatano and Inagaki (2003) found that the majority of fourth grade students who had misconceptions about the concept of conservation and then observed an experiment changed their pre-experiment predictions to align with the scientific law. However, before they viewed the experiment, the students were separated into two groups: one group engaged in a discussion with their peers and the second group did not partake in discussion. The majority of students who engaged in discussion, which included explaining their predictions and responding to challenges, were able to provide an explanation of the experiment result, whereas most control students could describe what they observed but were not able to offer an explanation for the result. In fact, more than 25% of the discussion students produced sophisticated explanations related to unobservable particles that contributed to overall weight while none of the control students offered such reasoning. Moreover, students who discussed their ideas before observing the experiment showed more progress in applying the principle of conservation to novel examples at post-test. Hatano and Inagaki (2003) believe that this dialogical and sociocultural approach is effective because students have to commit to their ideas by stating them aloud to peers, convince others of their view by making their thinking explicit, and consider different points of view. Similarly, Vosniadou (1994) suggested that learners who verbally share and defend their explanations become metaconceptually aware of their own beliefs and presuppositions, and this is a precondition of changing their mental representations.

Another dialogic intervention based on a social constructivist approach is Quality Talk, a discussion model that promotes high-level comprehension and epistemic cognition through small group, text-based discussion (e.g. Li et al., 2014; Murphy et al., 2014). This approach has been employed in both upper elementary grades and high-school level classes across different content areas and has been shown to increase reading comprehension and conceptual science knowledge. What makes Quality Talk unique is that it truly involves teachers as agents of change and assumes that the

knowledge and beliefs of teachers and students influence learning outcomes, as well as future instruction. Teachers receive initial and ongoing professional development, learn to code their own discussion videos, and play an interactive role in the intervention process by working closely with coaches and their students. The students, in turn, receive explicit instruction regarding their role in the discussion and are encouraged to offer their perspectives, to weigh evidence, and come to examined understanding as a result of participating in the discussion.

Grade 4 students participating in Quality Talk discussions and lessons engaged in significantly more exploratory talk about text with their peers over the course of the year (Murphy et al., 2014). Exploratory talk events are instances when students engage in the co-construction of knowledge, reason collectively, challenge each other's ideas and claims, and consider and respond to challenges or alternative propositions (Mercer and Littleton, 2007). Additionally, the students in Quality Talk discussion groups had significant fluency gains from fall to winter and faster rates of improvement compared to the national average (Murphy et al., 2014).

Dole (2000) contends that strong and enduring change in conceptual knowledge will only come through a learner's high engagement with text. This occurs when a learner engages deeply with the issues raised in the text and weighs ideas thoughtfully. Discussion is an ideal instructional model to promote this kind of high engagement and critical thinking. As Muis and Duffy (2013: 222) conclude: '... social interactions in a classroom are particularly key to fostering this change [in beliefs]'.

While there is clearly agreement among researchers that change is laborious and often slow, especially when referring to permanent or long-term changes requiring revision to prior knowledge or knowledge integration (Vosniadou and Tsoumakis, 2013), these studies demonstrate that knowledge and beliefs are potentially malleable. By explicitly teaching students metacognitive thinking strategies, presenting and organizing text presentations to invite students into a deeper consideration of their knowledge and beliefs, and giving students opportunities to engage in dialogue with peers where meaning is negotiated and positions are challenged, researchers were able to promote change in learners' knowledge and beliefs.

CONCLUSION

In sum, knowledge and beliefs influence the interaction between the teachers' and students' internal characteristics (e.g. cognitive and affective factors), the learning task (e.g. learning materials such as the text or learning activity), and the sociocultural context (e.g. the where and with whom of learning). In this chapter we have examined research and interventions that focused, usually separately, on these intersection points. Looking forward, we encourage researchers to continue to sort out and define these sometimes cloudy terms and further investigate the promising, yet preliminary, results of interventions based on metacognitive strategy instruction, text structure and content presentation, and classroom discussion.

Changing knowledge and beliefs is at the heart of both research and teaching. Nevertheless, there is a critical difference between the perspectives of researchers and the teachers who put research into practice. While researchers are often concerned with the important issue of etiology (e.g. examining the causes of resistance to conceptual change), teachers are not as occupied with this question, nor should they be. The teacher has a different role to play and limited time to accomplish an admittedly daunting task. Moreover, the teacher faces multiple learners each day, and these individuals compel them to action. While researchers are charged with asking *why*, the teacher has a pressing need to know *how* to change learners' knowledge and beliefs. It

is also important to consider that knowledge and beliefs are often value-laden and therefore bring an ethical as well as an affective/emotional dimension to any discussion of effecting change (Fives and Buehl, 2012). While this is a critical area of research and investigation, we contend that it is an essential aim of education that students, as well as teachers, are empowered to think critically, argue and weigh ideas, seek and evaluate evidence, and, ultimately, understand their capacity to make meaning.

We argue in this chapter that the knowledge and beliefs of teachers impact their interactions with students, thus influencing what students believe as well as how they think. Further, what students know and believe has profound implications on their future learning and a seemingly reverberating effect on teachers' pedagogy. In this way, one's knowledge and beliefs both limit and enable change and growth. They are the cotton wool of comfort, as well as the springboard to new possibilities. Moreover, well-thought-out, classroom-based, teacher facilitated interventions can create conditions that encourage teachers and students to become aware of, and possibly alter, their knowledge and beliefs. Understanding these pathways is the first step in harnessing the power of knowledge and beliefs, in order to better position learners to take advantage of the universe of information available to them in the twenty-first century, and the potential they have to analyse, shape and contribute to that knowledge. As we began this chapter with the sage words of Maxine Greene, so we return to her here with a passage that speaks to the potential of thinking, text, and talk to harness the power of knowledge and beliefs to promote learning:

> The challenge is to make the ground palpable and visible to our students, to make possible the interplay of multiple voices, of 'not quite commensurable visions.' It is to attend to the plurality of consciousnesses – and their recaltritrances and their resistances along with their affirmations … The principles and the contexts have to be chosen … by persons able to call, to say, to sing, and – using their imaginations, tapping their courage – to transform. (Greene, 1995: 198)

REFERENCES

Alexander, P. A. and Dochy, F. J. R. C. (1995) 'Conceptions of knowledge and beliefs: A comparison across varying cultural and educational communities', *American Educational Research Journal*, 32(2): 413–442. DOI:10.3102/00028312032002413.

Alexander, P. A., Murphy, P. K., Guan, J. and Murphy, P. A. (1998) 'How students and teachers in Singapore and the United States conceptualize knowledge and beliefs: Positioning learning within epistemological frameworks', *Learning and Instruction*, 8(2): 97–116. DOI:10.1016/S0959-4752(97)00004-2.

Alexander, P. A., Schallert, D. L. and Hare, V. C. (1991) 'Coming to terms: How researchers in learning and literacy talk about knowledge', *Review of Educational Research*, 61(3): 315–343.

Andiliou, A., Ramsay, C. M., Karen Murphy, P. and Fast, J. (2012) 'Weighing opposing positions: Examining the effects of intratextual persuasive messages on students' knowledge and beliefs', *Contemporary Educational Psychology*, 37(2): 113–127. DOI:10.1016/j.cedpsych.2011.10.001.

Ashton, P. and Crocker, L. (1987) 'Systematic study of planned variations: The essential focus of teacher education reform', *Journal of Teacher Education*, 38(3): 2–8. DOI:10.1177/002248718703800302.

Bandura, A. (1997) *Self-Efficacy: The Exercise of Control*, New York: W. H. Freeman.

Baumert, J., Kunter, M., Blum, W., Brunner, M., Voss, T., Jordan, A. and Tsai, Y.-M. (2010) 'Teachers' mathematical knowledge, cognitive activation in the classroom, and student progress', *American Educational Research Journal*, 47(1): 133–180, DOI:10.3102/0002831209345157.

Bendixen, L. D. (2002) 'A process model of epistemic belief change', in B. K. Hofer and P. R. Pintrich (eds), *Personal Epistemology: The Psychology of Beliefs about Knowledge and Knowing* (pp. 191–208), Mahwah, NJ: Lawrence Erlbaum Associates.

Bigozzi, L., Biggeri, A., Boschi, F., Conti, P. and Fiorentini, C. (2002) 'Children "scientists" know the reasons why and they are "poets" too: Non-randomized controlled trial to evaluate the effectiveness of a strategy aimed at

improving the learning of scientific concepts', *European Journal of Psychology of Education*, 17(4): 343–362.

Borko, H. and Putnam, R. T. (1996) 'Learning to teach', in D. C. Berliner and R. C. Calfee (eds), *Handbook of Educational Psychology* (pp. 673–708), New York: Simon and Schuster Macmillan.

Calderhead, J. (1996) 'Teachers: Beliefs and knowledge', in D. C. Berliner and R. C. Calfee (eds), *Handbook of Educational Psychology* (pp. 709–725), New York: Simon and Schuster Macmillan.

Carey, S. (1987) *Conceptual Change in Childhood*, Cambridge, MA: MIT Press.

Carretero, M., Castorina, J. A. and Levinas, L. (2013) 'Conceptual change and historical narratives about the nation: A theoretical and empirical approach', in S. Vosniadou (ed.), *International Handbook of Research on Conceptual Change* (2nd edn, pp. 269–287). New York: Routledge.

Chinn, C. A. and Brewer, W. F. (1993) 'The role of anomalous data in knowledge acquisition: A theoretical framework and implications for science instruction', *Review of Educational Research*, 63(1): 1–49. DOI:10.3102/00346543063001001.

Chinn, C. A., Duncan, R. G., Dianovsky, M. and Rinehart, R. (2013) 'Promoting conceptual change through inquiry', in S. Vosniadou (ed.), *International Handbook of Research on Conceptual Change* (2nd edn, pp. 539–559). New York: Routledge.

Craik, F. I. M. and Lockhart, R. S. (1972) 'Levels of processing: A framework for memory research', *Journal of Verbal Learning and Verbal Behavior*, 11(6): 671–684.

Darling-Hammond, L. (2000) 'Teacher quality and student achievement: A review of state policy evidence', *Education Policy Analysis Archives*, 8. DOI:10.14507/epaa.v8n1.2000.

Dole, J. A. (2000) 'Readers, texts, and conceptual change learning', *Reading and Writing Quarterly: Overcoming Learning Difficulties*, 16(2): 99–118.

Dole, J. A. and Sinatra, G. M. (1998) 'Reconceptualizing change in the cognitive construction of knowledge', *Educational Psychologist*, 33(2/3): 109–128.

Educational Testing Service (2014) *The Praxis Series*. Retrieved from https://www.ets.org/praxis

Ferguson, L. E., Bråten, I., Strømsø, H. I. and Anmarkrud, Ø. (2013) 'Epistemic beliefs and comprehension in the context of reading multiple documents: Examining the role of conflict', *International Journal of Educational Research*, 62: 100–114. DOI:10.1016/j.ijer.2013.07.001.

Fives, H. and Buehl, M. M. (2012) 'Spring cleaning for the "messy" construct of teachers' beliefs: What are they? Which have been examined? What can they tell us?', in K. R. Harris, S. Graham, T. Urdan, S. Graham, J. M. Royer, and M. Zeidner (eds), *APA Educational Psychology Handbook, Vol 2: Individual Differences and Cultural and Contextual Factors* (pp. 471–499), Washington, DC: American Psychological Association.

Fives, H. and Buehl, M. M. (in press) 'The functions of teachers' beliefs: Personal epistemology on the pinning block', in G. Schraw, J. Lunn, L. Olafson and M. VanderVeldt (eds), *Teachers' Personal Epistemologies: Evolving Models for Transforming Practice.*

Greene, M. (1988) *The Dialectic of Freedom*, New York: Teachers College Press.

Greene, M. (1995) *Releasing the Imagination: Essays on Education, the Arts, and Social Change*, San Francisco, CA: Jossey-Bass.

Hatano, G. and Inagaki, K. (2003) 'When is conceptual change intended? A cognitive-sociocultural view', in G. M. Sinatra and P. R. Pintrich (eds), *Intentional Conceptual Change* (pp. 407–427), Mahwah, NJ: Lawrence Erlbaum Associates, Inc.

Hennessey, M. N., Murphy, P. K. and Kulikowich, J. M. (2013) 'Investigating teachers' beliefs about the utility of epistemic practices: A pilot study of a new assessment', *Instructional Science*, 41(3): 499–519. DOI:10.1007/s11251-012-9241-6.

Hofer, B. K. and Pintrich, P. R. (1997) 'The development of epistemological theories: Beliefs about knowledge and knowing and their relation to learning', *Review of Educational Research*, 67(1): 88–140.

Hynd, C. R. (2001) 'Refutational texts and the change process', *International Journal of Educational Research*, 35: 699–714.

James, W. (1890) *The Principles of Psychology*, New York: Holt. Retrieved from http://archive.org/details/theprinciplesofp01jameuoft

Kaufman, D. R., Keselman, A. and Patel, V. L. (2013) 'Conceptual understanding in the domain of health', in S. Vosniadou (ed.), *International Handbook of Research on Conceptual Change* (2nd edn, pp. 240–252), New York: Routledge.

Kendeou, P. and van den Broek, P. (2007) 'The effects of prior knowledge and text structure on comprehension processes during reading of scientific texts', *Memory and Cognition*, 35(7): 1567–1577.

Kendeou, P., Muis, K. R. and Fulton, S. (2011) 'Reader and text factors in reading comprehension processes', *Journal of Research in Reading*, 34(4): 365–383. DOI:10.1111/j.1467-9817.2010.01436.x.

Kienhues, D., Bromme, R. and Stahl, E. (2008) 'Changing epistemological beliefs: The unexpected impact of a short-term intervention', *British Journal of Educational Psychology*, 78: 545–565.

Kunter, M., Klusmann, U., Baumert, J., Richter, D., Voss, T. and Hachfeld, A. (2013) 'Professional competence of teachers: Effects on instructional quality and student development', *Journal of Educational Psychology*, 105(3): 805–820. DOI:10.1037/a0032583

Li, M., Murphy, P. K. and Firetto, C. M. (2014) 'Examining the effects of text genre and structure on 4th- and 5th-grade students' high-level comprehension as evidenced in small-group discussions', *International Journal of Educational Psychology*, 3(3): 205–234.

Lockhart, R. S. and Craik, F. I. M. (1990) 'Levels of processing: A retrospective commentary on a framework for memory research', *Canadian Journal of Psychology*, 44(1): 87–112.

Maier, J. and Richter, T. (2014) 'Fostering multiple text comprehension: How metacognitive strategies and motivation moderate the text-belief consistency effect', *Metacognition and Learning*, 9(1): 51–74. DOI:10.1007/s11409-013-9111-x.

Mason, L. (2001) 'Responses to anomalous data on controversial topics and theory change', *Learning and Instruction*, 11(6): 453–483. DOI:10.1016/S0959-4752(00)00042-6

Mercer, N. and Littleton, K. (2007) *Dialogue and the Development of Children's Thinking: A Sociocultural Approach*, New York: Routledge.

Mikkilä-Erdmann, M. (2001) 'Improving conceptual change concerning photosynthesis through text design', *Learning and Instruction*, *11* (3), 241–257. doi:10.1016/S0959-4752(00)00041-4

Miyake, N. (2013) 'Conceptual change through collaboration', in S. Vosniadou (ed.), *International Handbook of Research on Conceptual Change* (2nd edn, pp. 466–483), New York: Routledge.

Monk, D. H. (1994) 'Subject area preparation of secondary mathematics and science teachers and student achievement', *Economics of Education Review*, 13(2): 125–145.

Muis, K. R. (2004) 'Personal epistemology and mathematics: A critical review and synthesis of research', *Review of Educational Research*, 74(3): 317–377.

Muis, K. R. and Duffy, M. C. (2013) 'Epistemic climate and epistemic change: Instruction designed to change students' beliefs and learning strategies and improve achievement', *Journal of Educational Psychology*, 105(1): 213–225.

Murphy, P. K. (2001) 'What makes a text persuasive? Comparing students' and experts' conceptions of persuasiveness', *International Journal of Educational Research*, 35(7/8): 675–698. DOI:10.1016/S0883-0355(02)00009-5.

Murphy, P. K. (2007) 'The eye of the beholder: The interplay of social and cognitive components in change', *Educational Psychologist*, 42(1): 41–53. DOI:10.1080/00461520709336917.

Murphy, P. K. and Alexander, P. A. (2004) 'Persuasion as a dynamic, multidimensional process: An investigation of individual and intraindividual differences', *American Educational Research Journal*, 41(2): 337–363. DOI:10.3102/00028312041002337.

Murphy, P. K. and Mason, L. (2006) 'Changing knowledge and beliefs', in P. A. Alexander and P. H. Winne (eds), *Handbook of Educational Psychology* (2nd edn, pp. 305–326). Mahwah, NJ: Lawrence Erlbaum Associates.

Murphy, P. K., Alexander, P. A. and Muis, K. R. (2012) 'Knowledge and knowing: The journey from philosophy and psychology to human learning', in K. R. Harris, S. Graham, T. Urdan, C. B. McCormick, G. M. Sinatra and J. Sweller (eds), *Theories, Constructs, and Critical Issues* (pp. 189–226). Washington, DC: American Psychological Association.

Murphy, P. K., Greene, J. and Firetto, C. M. (2014) *Quality Talk: Developing Students' Discourse to Promote Critical-Analytic Thinking, Epistemic Cognition, and High-Level Comprehension. Annual Performance Report for the Institute of Education Sciences (IES)*, University Park, PA: Authors.

Nersessian, N. J. (2013) 'Mental modeling in conceptual change', in S. Vosniadou (ed.), *International Handbook of Research on Conceptual Change* (2nd edn, pp. 395–411), New York: Routledge.

Nickerson, R. S. (1998) 'Confirmation bias: A ubiquitous phenomenon in many guises', *Review of General Psychology*, 2(2): 175–220.

Nisbett, R. E. and Ross, L. (1980) *Human Inference: Strategies and Shortcomings of Social Judgment*, Englewood Cliffs, NJ: Prentice Hall Press.

Olafson, L. and Schraw, G. (2006) 'Teachers' beliefs and practices within and across domains', *International Journal of Educational Research*, 45(1–2): 71–84. DOI:10.1016/j.ijer.2006.08.005.

Pajares, M. F. (1992) 'Teachers' beliefs and educational research: Cleaning up a messy construct', *Review of Educational Research*, 62(3): 307–332. DOI:10.3102/00346543062003307.

Peirce, C. S. (1958) 'The fixation of belief', in P. P. Wiener (ed.), *Charles S. Peirce: Selected Writings* (pp. 91–112). New York: Dover.

Peirce, C. S. (1994) *The Fixation of Belief: The Collected Papers of Charles Sanders Peirce, Electronic Edition*, 5. Retrieved from http://pm.nlx.com.ezaccess.libraries.psu.edu/xtf/view?docId=peirce/peirce.05.xml;chunk.id=div.peirce.cp5.19;toc.depth=1;toc.id=div.peirce.cp5.19;brand=default

Peterson, P. L., Carpenter, T. and Fennema, E. (1989) 'Teachers' knowledge of students' knowledge in mathematics problem solving: Correlational and case analyses', *Journal of Educational Psychology*, 81(4): 558–569.

Petty, R. E. and Cacioppo, J. T. (1986) 'The elaboration likelihood model of persuasion', in L. Berkowitz (ed.), *Advances in Experimental Social Psychology* (Vol. 19, pp. 123–205), New York: Academic Press. Retrieved from http://www.sciencedirect.com/science/article/pii/S0065260108602142

Pintrich, P. R., Marx, R. W. and Boyle, R. A. (1993) 'Beyond cold conceptual change: The role of motivational beliefs and classroom conceptual factors in the process of conceptual change', *Review of Educational Research*, 63(2): 167–199.

Rokeach, M. (1968) *Beliefs, Attitudes, and Values: A Theory of Organization and Change*, San Francisco, CA: Jossey-Bass.

Ryle, G. (1949) *The Concept of Mind*, New York: Hutchinson.

Scheffler, I. (1965) *Conditions of Knowledge: An Introduction to Epistemology and Education*, Chicago, IL: Scott Foresman.

She, H. C. (2002) 'Concepts of a higher hierarchical level require more dual situated learning events for conceptual change: A study of air pressure and buoyancy', *International Journal of Science Education*, 24(9): 981–996. DOI:10.1080/09500690110098895.

She, H. C. (2004) 'Fostering radical conceptual change through dual-situated learning model', *Journal of Research in Science Teaching*, 41(2): 142–164, DOI:10.1002/tea.10130.

Shulman, L. S. (1986) 'Those who understand: Knowledge growth in teaching', *Educational Researcher*, 15(2): 4–14.

Shulman, L. S. (1987) 'Knowledge and teaching: Foundations of the new reform', *Harvard Educational Review*, 57(1): 1–21.

Sinatra, G. M. and Mason, L. (2013) 'Beyond knowledge: Learner characteristics influencing conceptual change', in S. Vosniadou (ed.), *International Handbook of Research on Conceptual Change* (2nd edn, pp. 377–394), New York: Routledge.

Sosu, E. M. and Gray, D. S. (2012) 'Investigating change in epistemic beliefs: An evaluation of the impact of student teachers' beliefs on instructional preference and teaching competence', *International Journal of Educational Research*, 53: 80–92. DOI:10.1016/j.ijer.2012.02.002.

Southerland, S. A., Sinatra, G. M. and Matthews, M. R. (2001) 'Belief, knowledge, and science education', *Educational Psychology Review*, 13(4): 325–351. DOI:http://dx.doi.org/10.1023/A:1011913813847.

Stanovich, K. E. (1986) 'Matthew Effects in reading: Some consequences of individual differences in the acquisition of literacy', *Reading Research Quarterly*, 21(4): 360–407.

Stanovich, K. E. and West, R. F. (2007) 'Natural myside bias is independent of cognitive ability', *Thinking and Reasoning*, 13(3): 225–247.

Vamvakoussi, X., Vosniadou, S. and Van Dooren, W. (2013) 'The framework theory approach applied to mathematics learning', in S. Vosniadou (ed.), *International Handbook of Research on Conceptual Change* (2nd edn, pp. 305–321), New York: Routledge.

Vosniadou, S. (1994) 'Capturing and modeling the process of conceptual change', *Learning and Instruction*, 4(1): 45–69. DOI:10.1016/0959-4752(94)90018-3.

Vosniadou, S. (2013) 'Conceptual change in learning and instruction: The framework theory approach', in S. Vosniadou (ed.), *International Handbook of Research of Conceptual Change* (2nd edn, pp. 11–30), New York: Routledge.

Vosniadou, S. and Tsoumakis, P. (2013) 'Conceptual change', in J. Hattie and E. M. Anderman (eds), *International Guide to Student Achievement* (pp. 51–53), New York: Routledge.

Vosniadou, S., Ioannides, C., Dimitrakopoulou, A. and Papademetriou, E. (2001) 'Designing learning environments to promote conceptual change in science', *Learning and Instruction*, 11(4–5): 381–419. DOI:10.1016/S0959-4752(00)00038-4.

Voss, T., Kunter, M. and Baumert, J. (2011) 'Assessing teacher candidates' general pedagogical/psychological knowledge: Test construction and validation', *Journal of Educational Psychology*, 103(4): 952–969. DOI:10.1037/a0025125.

Walker, C. M., Wartenberg, T. E. and Winner, E. (2013) 'Engagement in philosophical dialogue facilitates children's reasoning about subjectivity', *Developmental Psychology*, 49(7): 1338–1347. DOI:10.1037/a0029870.

Wilkinson, I. A. G., Soter, A. and Murphy, P. K. (2010) 'Developing a model of Quality Talk about literary text', in M. G. McKeown and L. Kucan (eds), *Bringing Reading Research to Life* (pp. 142–169), New York: Guilford Press.

Winne, P. H. (1996) 'A metacognitive view of individual differences in self-regulated learning', *Learning and Individual Differences*, 8(4): 327–353. DOI:10.1016/S1041-6080(96)90022-9.

Woolfolk Hoy, A., Davis, H. and Pape, S. J. (2006) 'Teacher knowledge and beliefs', in P. A. Alexander and P. H. Winne (eds), *Handbook of Educational Psychology* (2nd edn, pp. 715–738), Mahwah, NJ: Lawrence Erlbaum Associates.

37

An End-Piece with Some Reflections on Learning

David Scott and Eleanore Hargreaves

EXAMINATION

Michel Foucault provides an example of the construction of a pedagogic formation in relation to the use and development of examinations. In *Discipline and Punish: The Birth of the Prison* (Foucault, 1979), Foucault surfaces the common-sense discourse that surrounds examinations by showing how they could be understood in a different way. Previously, the examination was thought of as a mechanism for combating nepotism, favouritism and arbitrariness, and for contributing to the more efficient workings of society. The examination was considered to be a reliable way for choosing the appropriate members of a population for the most important roles in society. As part of the procedure a whole apparatus or technology was constructed which was intended to legitimise it. This psycho-metric framework, though continually changing, has served as a means of support for significant educational programmes in the twenty-first century, i.e.

the establishment of the tripartite system in the United Kingdom after the Second World War, and has continued to underpin educational reforms since the passing of the Education Reform Act for England and Wales in 1988. Though purporting to be a scientific discourse, the theory itself is buttressed by a number of unexamined principles: a particular view of competence; a notion of hierarchy; a view of human nature and a correspondence idea of truth. Furthermore, the idea of the examination is firmly located within a discourse of progression: society is progressively becoming a better place because scientific understanding gives us a more accurate picture of how the world works.

In contrast, for Foucault (1979: 184) the examination:

> combines the techniques of an observing hierarchy and those of a normalizing judgement. It is a normalizing gaze, a surveillance that makes it possible to qualify, to classify and to punish. It establishes

over individuals a visibility through which one differentiates them and judges them.

The examination therefore allows society to construct individuals in certain ways and in the process organises itself. Knowledge of persons is thus created in particular ways which has the effect of binding individuals to each other, embedding those individuals in networks of power and sustaining mechanisms of surveillance which are all the more powerful because they work by allowing individuals to govern themselves. The examination introduced a whole new mechanism which both contributed to a new type of knowledge formation and constructed a new network of power, all the more persuasive once it had become established throughout society.

This mechanism works in three ways: firstly, by transforming 'the economy of visibility into the exercise of power' (Foucault, 1979: 187); secondly, by introducing 'individuality into the field of documentation' (p. 189); and thirdly, by making 'each individual a "case"' (p. 191). In the first instance, disciplinary power is exercised invisibly, and this contrasts with the way power networks in the past operated visibly, through the explicit exercise of force. This invisibility works by imposing on subjects a notion of objectivity that acts to bind examined persons to a truth about that examination, a truth which is hard to resist. The examined person understands him or herself in terms of criteria that underpin that process, not least that they are successful or unsuccessful. The examination therefore works by 'arranging objects' (Foucault, 1979: 187) or people in society. In the second instance, the examination allows the individual to be archived by being inscribed textually. Furthermore, it is possible to understand this process even when the rhetoric of what is being implemented is progressive and benign. Over the last twenty years in English schools, the proliferation and extension of assessment through such devices as key stage tests, records of achievement, examined course work, education

certificates and school reports *and* evaluation through such devices as school inspection, teacher appraisal, profiles and the like, means that teachers and students are increasingly subject to disciplinary regimes of individual measurement and assessment which have the further effect of determining them as cases. The third of Foucault's modalities then is when the individual becomes an object for a branch of knowledge:

> The case is no longer, as in casuistry or jurisprudence, a set of circumstances, defining an act and capable of modifying the application of a rule; it is the individual as he [sic.] may be described, judged, measured, compared with others, in his very individuality; and it is also the individual who has to be trained or corrected, classified, normalized, excluded, etc. (Foucault, 1979: 191)

One final point needs to be made about the examination, and this is that for the first time the individual can be scientifically and objectively categorized and characterized through a modality of power where difference becomes the most relevant factor.

Hierarchical normalization becomes the dominant way of organizing society. Foucault is suggesting here that the examination itself, a seemingly neutral device, acts to position the person being examined in a discourse of normality, so that for them to understand themselves in any other way is to understand themselves as abnormal and even as unnatural. This positioning works to close off the possibility for the examinee of seeing themselves in any other way.

INTELLIGENCE

Learners are constructed pedagogically. An example of this process is the application of the notion of intelligence, and in particular, the use of the idea of a fixed innate quality in human beings which can be measured and remains relatively stable throughout an individual's life. This has come to be known as an intelligence quotient and is measured by various forms of testing, e.g. the 11+ test. The 11+ had a significant influence on the formation of the tripartite system of formal education in the United Kingdom as it was used to classify children as appropriate for grammar schools (those who passed the 11+), technical schools (those who passed the 11+ but were considered to be better suited to receive a focused technical education), and secondary moderns (the vast majority, who failed the 11+ and in the early days of the tripartite system left school without any formal qualifications).

Central to the concept of the intelligence quotient is the tension between the relative emphasis given to genetically inherited characteristics and the influence of the environment. Many contemporary educationalists believe that children's early and continuing experiences at home and at school constitute the most significant influence on their intellectual achievement. However, early exponents of the argument that genetic inheritance determines intellectual potential saw intelligence, measured by tests, as the factor which could be isolated to produce a 'quotient' by which individuals could be classified. Regardless of environmental factors such as teaching and learning programmes or socio-economic variables, it was argued, some people were born with low levels of intelligence. Schooling could bring them to a certain level of achievement, but there would always be a genetically imposed ceiling on their capabilities. An extreme version of this belief was that intelligence, like certain physical characteristics, followed a normal curve of distribution, so that within any given population there were a set number of intelligent people and a set number of less intelligent people. It was further argued that those individuals who were most generously endowed were obviously more fitted to govern and take decisions on behalf of those who were less fortunate.

The use of IQ tests was widely accepted as a selective device among academics and the writers of government reports, including, for example, the Spens Report (1938) and the Norwood Report (1943), both of which influenced the writing of The United Kingdom Education Act of 1944. The 1944 Education Act incorporated the beliefs that intelligence testing could reliably predict who would succeed academically at a later point in time, and that children could and should be divided into categories based on the results and educated separately.

Soon after the 1944 Act was passed, the use of IQ tests to allocate places began to be discredited. One of the appeals of the policy was its supposed objectivity and reliability. If intelligence was innate and could be measured, then the tests would simply reflect this notionally 'pure' relationship, but this is not what happened. A number of other problems with this idealised concept became apparent. IQ tests should by definition be criterion referenced. If children had the intelligence, the theory went, then the tests would show it. All children who demonstrated their intelligence by achieving the designated mark ought to be awarded a place at a grammar school. In practice, Local Education Authorities set quotas for grammar school entrance. Furthermore, different Local Education Authorities set different quotas (Vernon, 1957). The quotas also discriminated against girls and the argument was frequently made that since girls developed earlier than boys in their intellectual abilities, fewer girls should be given places in grammar schools because this would unfairly discriminate against boys who would catch up later.

A second problem with IQ tests was that if intelligence, as measured by the tests, was innate, then coaching and practice ought not to improve pupils' test scores. However, it was reported that pupils' performances were indeed enhanced by preparation for the tests, demonstrating that a supposedly free-standing assessment was being connected to the curriculum in contradiction to the intentions which lay behind it (Yates and Pidgeon, 1957). More importantly, Yates and Pidgeon's findings threw into question the notion of an innate and immutable intelligence quotient. Finally, the deterministic beliefs underlying the system implied low academic expectations for pupils who failed the 11+. A low IQ score at 11 ought to be a reliable guide to the rest of their school careers. However, it quickly became apparent that some of those who failed were capable of achieving high-level academic success.

This complicated story illustrates one of the problems with a symbol-processing approach to the relationship between mind, society and reality, which we discussed in the introduction to this volume. What was considered to reside in the nature of reality, i.e. innate qualities of intelligence in human beings, was shown to have undeniably social or constructed dimensions to it. Powerful people had constructed a tool or apparatus for organising educational provision, and given it credibility by suggesting that it was natural and thus legitimate.

THE SITUATEDNESS OF THE LEARNER

Robin Usher (1997) suggests in relation to finding out about the world that knowledge, and hence learning, has a con-text, pre-text, sub-text and inter-text. Knowledge-construction is a textual practice. Learning may be understood in a similar way. The context comprises the situatedness of the learner in the act of learning so that they are immersed in structures or significations of gender, sexuality, ethnicity, class and such like. Furthermore, the learner is situated within various pre-texts or discourses about the way the world is structured so that the learning strategy is always underpinned by pre-organised meanings. The pre-text always has attached to it a sub-text, in that the learning strategy and the knowledge that is subsumed within it are distinctive ways of knowing the world. Finally, each learning setting makes reference to other forms of learning, other knowledge constructs and other historical meaning formations – the inter-text.

An example from a formal learning situation will illustrate this. If a child is taught history in a formal setting such as a school, then that child is situated in particular discourses surrounding gender, ethnicity, sexuality and class, both in the subject matter of their learning and in the way that they are expected to learn what is being presented to them, i.e. the pedagogic formation. For example, the teaching and learning strategy itself may be explicitly racist, again either through neglect, distortion or ideological bias. Indeed, the child learning history is subsumed within particular learning strategies that act to organise the way they can see the world and its history. These pre-organised meanings are underpinned by particular conceptions of knowledge, ideas about what is appropriate to learn in formal settings, and views about which aspects of the culture should be passed on from generation to generation and in what way. For example, history may be taught as a series of 'facts' about the world, and this teaching strategy is then reinforced by assessment strategies, which downplay the socially constructed nature of what happened in the past. Finally, the historical knowledge which is imparted and the way in which it is taught has a history, and refers to other ways of seeing the world.

However, within this general framework, learners have more control in some settings than in others. The teaching and learning strategy is constructed strongly or weakly (cf. Bernstein, 1985), where strong and weak are defined in terms of the capacity of the message system to restrict or allow different meanings, interpretations and actions. Each learning moment focuses on a particular aspect of knowledge, whether chosen by a teacher or not. This is made visible by the act of delivery. However, there are always invisible dimensions: what is not chosen and why it was not chosen are invisible.

The teaching device itself is weakly or strongly framed as well. If the teaching device is text-based, as in many forms of distance learning, it may allow the reader or learner the opportunity to interpret or read it in a number of different ways, or it limits these opportunities. On the other hand, oral commentary in the form of lectures, contributions to seminars, or contributions to tutorials by the teacher, operate in different ways. Again, this form of delivery is strongly or weakly framed. However, there are a number of differences when compared with text-based approaches. The spoken text is likely to be multi-faceted; that is, because of its greater informality and flexibility (it has not been subject to revision and redrafting) it is likely to incorporate a range of different modalities, i.e. at any one moment it may be more authoritative than at another moment. It is therefore likely to be more fragmented. Fragmentation allows the student a greater degree of choice because it surfaces for the attention of the student a range of possibilities that they can then make a choice about. The boundary between what is visible and invisible is also weakened.

The most common teaching device in formal settings involves student–teacher interchanges. Again, these may be strongly or weakly framed. If they are strongly framed, the teacher/student relationship may be such that the effect of the exchange is that the student is dispossessed of certain faulty, inadequate or insufficiently complex ideas, so that they now know or can do that which was originally intended by the deliverer. However, there is another possibility, which is that the teacher does not have in mind a particular model of what the student should be able to do after the programme of study, and indeed is prepared to modify their teaching strategy in the light of what emerges. It is therefore weakly framed. The purpose of the exchanges is to dissolve, fragment or otherwise disrupt the models of knowledge held by the student, and, at best, the teacher. This is liminality at work. Here, there is no attempt made to provide a replacement, since the purpose is to provide disjuncture in the minds of students, and the responsibility for replacement is devolved to the student.

Finally, there are the structural dimensions of the learning setting itself. These comprise in part particular spatial and temporal arrangements. Distance learning approaches are constructed in particular ways so that the learner is allowed some licence in when

and where they choose to study. Face-to-face teaching settings are constructed in terms of timetables, sequences of learning, particular relations between teachers and learners and organised places where the teaching takes place. All these various forms of structuring influence what is learnt, how it is learnt and how that knowledge is used in other settings and other environments. Situated-learning approaches acknowledge that these arrangements for learning are constructed by communities of people. They also suggest that learning is itself a social practice that has the potential to transform the practice itself. What this means is that learning, knowledge and its outcomes have to be understood historically and as being socially embedded. Regardless of whether this learning is informally or formally structured, how it takes place will allow the learner greater or lesser freedom to interpret the new rules they are learning and contribute to their development. Finally, learning in this instance is located in time and place, takes on a particular form that determines what is learnt and may or may not contribute to successful induction. Situated-learning approaches reject the view that our representations of reality are given in a prior sense or that the human mind is constructed in a particular way which determines what and how we learn, but instead argue that learning is embedded within arrangements made by particular societies. The source of learning is therefore particular social practices.

Liminality is the sense of ambiguity or disorientation that occurs during a learning episode, where participants no longer subscribe to a particular way of thinking or seeing the world, but have not yet fully adopted, or adapted to, a new way of structuring their identity, their time or their thinking. This book has been about this sense of liminality.

REFERENCES

Bernstein, B. (1985) 'On Pedagogic Discourse', *Handbook of Theory and Research in the*

Sociology of Education, New York: Greenwood Press.

Foucault, M. (1979) *Discipline and Punish: The Birth of the Prison*, New York: Vintage.

Norwood Report (1943) *Curriculum and Examinations in Secondary Schools*, London: Her Majesty's Stationary Office.

Spens Report (1938) *Secondary Education: Grammar and Technical High Schools*, London: Her Majesty's Stationary Office.

Usher, R. (1997) 'Telling a Story about Research and Research as Story-Telling: Post-Modern Approaches to Social Research', in G. McKenzie, J. Powell and R. Usher (eds) *Understanding Social Research: Perspectives on Methodology and Practice*, London: Falmer Press.

Vernon, P. (1957) *Secondary School Selection*, London: Methuen.

Yates, A. and Pidgeon, D. (1957) *Admission to Grammar School*, London: Newnes.

Author Index

Subject Index